A SOCIOLOGY OF EDUCATING

MEIGHAN, ROLAND
A SOCIOLOGY OF EDUCATING .

4036581 9 0010

A Sociology of Educating

THURBOOK TECHNICAL COLLEGE LIBRARY

Second Edition

ROLAND MEIGHAN

with contributions by
Len Barton and Stephen Walker

CASSELL

Cassell Educational Ltd: Artillery House,
                         Artillery Row,
                         London SW1P 1RT

ESSEX COUNTY LIBRARY

British Library Cataloguing in Publication Data

Meighan, Roland
   A sociology of educating. — 2nd ed.
   1. Educational sociology
   I. Title   II. Barton, Len   III. Walker,
   Stephen, *1944–*
   370.19   LC191
✓ ISBN: 0 304 31587 7

Typeset by Inforum Ltd, Portsmouth
Printed in Great Britain by Mackays of Chatham Ltd

Copyright © 1981 and 1986 Cassell Educational Ltd.
First published in 1981 and 1986 by Holt, Rinehart and Winston Ltd.
All rights reserved. This book is protected by copyright. No
part of it may be reproduced, stored in a retrieval system, or
transmitted in any form or by any means, electronic, mechanical,
photocopying or otherwise, without written permission from the
publisher.

Last digit is print no: 9 8 7 6 5 4 3 2

370.19

FZ74943

Contents

Acknowledgements

Many of the people who have contributed to this book cannot be adequately acknowledged. They include pupils, students, colleagues, friends and writers who have contributed ideas, comments or reactions that have become part of my consciousness or woven into my teaching and writing. Although I cannot name them, I recognize my considerable debt to them all.

Amongst those I can name are Len Barton, Christine Brown, Gerald Cortis, Lynn Davies, Clive Harber, Janet Meighan, Frank Reeves, Mike Roberts, Richard Szreter and Stephen Walker. Inadequacies in the work, however, remain the writers' sole responsibility.

The author and publisher would like to thank the following for permission to use material in this book:

British Journal of Educational Psychology
Department of Education & Science
Education Otherwise
Educational Review
Grant MacIntyre
Heinemann
Sophia and Frances Howard
Ivan Read
Journal of Curriculum Studies
New Science Publications
Open University Press
Oxford University Press
Penguin Books
Peter Davies Ltd
Punch
Routledge and Kegan Paul
Anthony Rudolf
Social Science Teacher
Times Educational Supplement

Preface to the First Edition

Many harsh things have been said about the writers of books. Samuel Johnson observed, 'Your manuscript is both good and original: but the part that is good is not original, and the part that is original is not good.' A gibe about bland writing comes from Charles Colton: 'Many books require no thought from those who read them, and for a very simple reason – they made no such demand upon those who wrote them.' But the most helpful advice I found came from Anthony Hope: 'Unless one is a genius, it is best to aim at being intelligible.'

This book is written with three audiences in mind. First, those who are beginning a career in education, such as students on initial teacher education courses. Second, experienced teachers on in-service courses with little or no sociological study in their previous courses. The third group that may find the material of interest is comprised of educationalists whose previous sociological study has been limited to the structural functionalist perspective.

The title of the book contains the verb 'educating' rather than the noun 'education', and this indicates that a particular perspective is employed for large sections of the book, namely the interactionist perspective. Since the perspectives are discussed at some length, it is sufficient to say that a key concept in the interactionist approach is that of the contradictions and ironies in social life. Key ideas in other approaches may be harmony in society and its organizations, or conflict in social structures.

This book is meant to be a progress report. Its intention is to stimulate sociologically informed thinking about educating rather than to provide any final conclusion or necessarily 'true' message. It is meant to be interpreted as constructive doubt and review, rather than the establishment of certainties.

The structure of the book is idiosyncratic and needs some explanation. Many sociology of education texts begin with an account of sociological concepts and theories and then use these to scrutinize education. Others develop a sociology of education which reflects on the theories and concepts of the parent discipline of sociology at the end. This book does neither. It begins with a light-hearted taste of sociology to give something of the flavour of this approach to thinking about society, and then gives three sociological accounts of topics unrelated except in their tendency to be provocative. These topics are assessment, the pupils' viewpoint and the teacher as a victim. I hope that this first part will establish some of the excitement and interest of sociology, as well as some of its relevance to an understanding of schooling.

The section on sociological theories and perspectives comes in the middle of the book, on the logic of a 'time out' in sports like basketball. It seems appropriate, after doing some sociological thinking, to reflect on the theoretical nature of the enterprise before undertaking some more investigation in the remainder of the book. (Len Barton and Stephen Walker have written this theoretical section at my invitation.) Users of the book are, of course, at liberty to ignore these ideas and use the material in any order they think fit.

Any selection of the concepts of a book is somewhat arbitrary. Those selected by the writer are: the hidden curriculum for Part Two, ideologies of education for Part Three, and educational life chances for Part Five. The final part, alternatives in education, uses the concepts of the previous parts to analyse various educational institutions. These are selected as the concepts that have emerged in the writer's teaching, reading and research as the most significant of those so far developed.

I have tried to write in an intelligible style and if I have been successful, there is the potential penalty of being interpreted as facile and simplistic, since, as research quoted in the book indicates, the same idea expressed in difficult and dense language gains higher applause as 'more academic' and 'superior in depth'. As Molière observed, 'That must be wonderful; I don't understand it at all'. However, I shall take the risk, and aim at communication rather than mystification.

ROLAND MEIGHAN

Preface to the Second Edition

Many people have made comments on the first edition, and I offer them my gratitude. Responses have ranged from pointing out that the comment in the first preface describing 'educating' as a verb is inaccurate, to the observation that some themes are missing, such as pastoral care. Suggestions for the second edition have been made in profusion, so that a book twice the size might result if all the ideas were incorporated.

A common response from lecturers using the book has been a plea to change as little as possible of the existing text; in recognition of the problems created when a course has been based on a text and a new edition arrives, I have respected this plea as far as possible. Although the final part, on 'alternatives', has been considerably redrafted, the structure and contents of the rest of the book are substantially the same, though additional chapters have been included. In Part One, the 'Familiarization' section is expanded to include a chapter entitled 'Parents as Educators?', whilst Part Two, 'The Hidden Curriculum', has a new chapter, 'Marking, Testing and Examining'. In Part Three, 'Ideologies of Education', there is a new chapter called 'A Case Study: Democratic Education'. Part Four, on sociological perspectives, has a new chapter, 'Doing Research in Schools and Classrooms', to replace the brief overview of sociological research in education that may people suggested was too limited to be of much use. Part Five remains somewhat similar to that in the first edition, but Part Six has been redrafted, partly to allow for recent developments and partly to take account of the publication of a separate book on this theme; that is, C. Harber, R. Meighan and B. Roberts (eds.) (1984) *Alternative Educational Futures* (Holt, Rinehart and Winston).

At the end of each chapter there is a new section entitled 'Signposts'. These are seen as signposts to further work developing out of the themes of the chapter concerned, to allow students to pursue ideas introduced briefly in the text. The routine of having a summary at the end of each chapter has been varied in response to comments from users of the first edition that sometimes it would be a useful exercise for students to write their own summary.

The nature of education in the UK and elsewhere has continued in a state of flux and change since the date of the first edition with educational cuts, massive unemployment, attempts to centralize control of the education system, a reassessment of the educational roles of parents, and so on. I have attempted to encompass as many of these issues as possible and also to increase the coverage of primary education.

The book maintains an interactionist perspective for the most part, and the nature of this approach is commented on throughout. Nevertheless, it has been said that the interactionist perspective remains elusive. I would prefer to say that it remains complex.

The following quotation gives some idea of the complexity of the interactionist approach of the book:

> For neither learning nor teaching is a process, nor can they ever be fully controlled. They are, if they can ever be defined, a continuous social interaction between individuals, who are themselves a product of interactions with the world around them. Even a relationship with an object, a problem, or a subject of study has a strong element of interaction. The objects, the problems or the subjects of study act on the learner, or an observer, no less than the living beings. *Whatever we do, the doing does something to us!* This is an inescapable, instantaneous relationship. Sentient beings are affected by this reciprocity always – even plants are now known to respond to animals and people.
>
> It is not even an interaction; that would be far too simple to even attempt to describe learning and teaching as such. It is an inter-reaction. For apart from interacting with the outside world, the individual interacts within himself as to how he interacted in the past, interacts now and hopes or fears to interact in the future.
>
> J. Wankowski, 1981

The book remains dedicated to constructive doubt. The writer sides with those who observe that they wish they were as certain of anything as others are about everything.

Postscript

I was rather taken aback when reading the proofs to note the sexist language of several quotations used in the text. I hope it is some measure of my own consciousness that I now notice them and am distressed by them. Any lapses into sexist language in the main text are also a cause of regret.

To Janet and James
In memory of Shirley

PART ONE

Familiarization

The opening section is rather unconventional, since it is based on the ideas of browsing in libraries, familiarization through wandering around a new place, tasting or taking an aperitif. A rigorous, structured opening has been discarded for something more eclectic and appetite-whetting. Chapter 1 attempts to review observations made about sociology and the sociological enterprise rather than develop a conceptual map or a systematic account of the discipline. The remaining chapters of Part One are connected in two ways. First, they are rather provocative ideas: assessment, the pupils' viewpoint, the teacher as victim, and the parent as educator. Second, they can be seen as examples of the interactionist concept of layers of meaning mentioned in the previous chapter. The interpretation of the phenomenon of schooling varies according to the situation of the viewer: there is no objective entity called 'school', only overlapping and varying accounts can be obtained. If, at the end of the section, the reader is not curious about the sociological contribution to the understanding of the processes of educating and is not intrigued by the possibilities of a sociological imagination, the writer has failed in his intentions.

Chapter 1

A Taste of Sociology

'Gossip: sociologists on a mean and petty scale.'
Woodrow Wilson

INTRODUCTION

People usually ask for the recipe after tasting the dish rather than before tasting it. Following this kind of logic, this introduction will avoid definitions and lists of concepts in favour of observations about sociology. This approach is not original. One of the most famous expositions in this style is that of Peter Berger in his book *Invitation to Sociology* (1966), so perhaps it is appropriate that a first quotation should come from this source:

> What interests us is the curiosity that grips any sociologist in front of a closed door behind which there are human voices. If he is a good sociologist, he will want to open that door, to understand these voices.

Of course, if this were the sum total of the sociological enterprise, then sociologists justifiably would be accused of being merely eavesdroppers or voyeurs, and indeed such accusations have been made. The point that sociology has as its outcome more than just the satisfaction of personal curiosity has been made many times, and the ancient nature of this kind of thinking is often stressed. There is a sense in which sociology is one of the oldest of the sciences:

> As soon as people began to reflect on the way in which their society was or should be organized and hold views on man and his destiny, the rise and fall of peoples and civilizations, they were thinking in sociological terms, although they called themselves philosophers, historians, thinkers, law-givers or seers.
>
> Abraham, 1966

THE STUDY OF THE SOCIAL LIFE CREATED BY PEOPLE

Reflecting on society has not always been regarded as necessarily desirable:

> To quote from a matchbox – sociology is the study of those who don't need it by those who do.
>
> Weightman, 1977

This joke suggests a suspicion of those who study others. In addition, the common confusion between psychology and sociology is present, and the joke could more accurately be applied to psychology in its study of people as individuals, rather than sociology, where the subject matter is, more centrally, the institutions, cultures and social systems created *by* people, and in turn, influencing people's behaviour.

Sociology is the source of fewer jokes than psychology, and this itself is an interesting feature for reflection. Psychologists seem to have been 'recognized' rather more than sociologists. One possible explanation lies in the success of psychology in establishing a claim to be special, and mysterious, rather like the impression many people have of physics:

> People do not expect to have special knowledge of a subject like physics . . . But because they are familiar with the objects the sociologist studies, they feel they already have a special knowledge of them and resent any sociological claim that they do not.
>
> McGee et al., 1977

GENERAL CERTIFICATE OF EDUCATION

ADVANCED LEVEL

SOCIOLOGY

Time: Two Hours

Only Six Questions To Be Attempted

1. *'Sociology is the study of people who do not need to be studied, by people who do.'*
'Somebody introduced the Black Death. Somebody introduced Income Tax. Somebody introduced sociology.'
'All the Golden Ages of man, all the Belles Epoques, were characterised by one thing: an absence of sociologists.'
Which of these hostile assessments do you find most wounding? Which of them comes nearest to the truth? How would you attempt to improve the public image of sociology, while covertly furthering its subversive aims?

2. Johnny is a married man with ten children in institutions and a wife who resides in a battered wives' home. He has now found happiness with a 'Common Law Wife' just out of school who is about to bear him another child. They live in a retarded caravan which has broken down in North Ham, where Johnny draws Social Security. He is unable to work because, 'That's the way I've always been, innit?' He is claiming a council flat at North Ham, but the Council is reluctant to advance him over the heads of 15,000 people who have been on the housing list for an average of twelve years.
Explain why we are all to blame for the dilemma in which Johnny finds himself. How would you set about fanning the country into a state of white-hot indignation on his behalf?

3. State which of the following you consider the ultimate in obscenity: (a) an unearned income of £50,000 a year; (b) *Oh Calcutta!*; (c) anyone over thirty enjoying sex; (d) the headmaster of a comprehensive school who dismisses his 'D' stream as 'a shower of dimmies'; (e) the Young Conservatives. Give reasons for your choice.

4. *'A democracy is that form of government which prevails in one form or another in the decay of a State.'* Though widely discredited at the time, this judgment by the Duke of Northumberland in 1909 is now recognised to be correct. Suggest ways in which the sociologist can contribute to the decay of the State and the enervation of the Constitution, while preserving lip-service to democracy.

5. Distinguish between:
   (a) a revolution and a revolutionary situation;
   (b) justice and social justice;
   (c) a committed person and a biased person.
Describe how a court of social justice would operate in a revolutionary situation.

6. As a 'mildly radical' sociologist, how would you set about undermining any *two* of the following:
   (a) The Bank of England;
   (b) Mr Hughie Green;
   (c) Civilisation as we know it;
   (d) The international Freemasonry conspiracy.

7. Len and Linda are living in London waiting and working for the Revolution. They pay a week's rent to a landlord and then sit tight, making no further payments, for seven months, which is the time it takes the landlord to get an eviction order. They then repeat the performance a few streets away.
Given the exploitative world we live in, do you regard this as an acceptable design for living? Can you think of any reason why the rest of us should not do the same?

8. Compose a short Pop song embodying
   either
   The jubilant cry of an unmarried father who has broken his bourgeois shackles;
   or
   The lament of a Sixth Former who sees for the first time his classroom as the nursery of a counter-revolutionary ideology.

9. 'It seems to be a law of Nature,' writes Townend, 'that the poor should be to a certain degree improvident, that there may be always some to fulfil the most servile, the most sordid and the most ignoble offices. The stock of human happiness is thereby much increased.' Do you accept this law of Nature? If not, how would you work to overturn it? Is it better to leave the ignoble offices to immigrants, as at present? As a sociologist, what other ignoble offices would you be prepared to fulfil?

10. What are the epistemological problems involved in the tying of academic sociology, and in particular structural-functional theory, to a 'conservative' ideological standpoint, with its temptation to treat man as *homo sociologicus?* And do you think that people with white stone balls on their gateposts deserve everything that is coming to them?

Figure 1.1   A spoof examination paper in sociology by E.S. Turner. From *Punch*, 2 October 1974. Reproduced by permission of *Punch*.

One sustained joke about sociology appeared in *Punch*, 2 October 1974, in the form of an 'examination paper'. (See Figure 1.1.) Some of the questions in the spoof examination paper can be said to raise important issues about sociology and sociologists. Thus the statement, 'Somebody introduced the Black Death. Somebody introduced Income Tax. Somebody introduced sociology' is stated in a more sympathetic form as the point of a discussion by Cuzzort and King (1976):

> Even if the people who have the official title of 'sociologist' were to cease offering their interpretations of social conduct to the world, the world would still demand that somebody tell it what is going on.

The introduction of sociology or its equivalent is seen by Cuzzort and King as inevitable and desirable, though whether they would say the same about the Black Death and Income Tax is another matter.

Another source of humour in the 'examination questions' is the questioning approach assumed in the jokes to be revolutionary:

> As a 'mildly radical' sociologist, how would you set about undermining any two of the following:
>
> (a) The Bank of England;
> (b) Mr Hughie Green;
> (c) Civilization as we know it;
> (d) The international Freemasonry conspiracy.

The nature of this questioning approach is the subject of considerable comment by writers on sociology:

> The power of sociology lies in its capacity to make connections between phenomena and events which people in society regard as unconnected.
>
> Gomm, 1978

> We are aiming at what we believe to be the fundamental rationale for sociology as a discipline – the exposure of prevailing practice to critical scrutiny and analysis.
>
> MacDonald et al., 1977

> Sociology can perhaps be best regarded as an attempt to 'name that which secretly keeps society going'.
>
> Whitty and Young, 1976

SOME SOCIOLOGICAL THEMES

The following poem combines a statement about the point of questioning institutions, cultures and social conduct, and a useful content list of themes covered in sociological writings. The exceptions are perhaps the themes of 'unconscious' and 'genes', which psychologists would claim as their particular province, 'climate', which is the concern of geographers, and 'deep linguistic structures', which are studied by psycholinguists. Additionally, a sociologist would study the phenomenon of 'belief in God' rather than a theological study based on the assumption of a God.

The Humanist's Sonnet
by Anthony Rudolf

I am determined by my class
I am determined by my sex
I am determined by my God
I am determined by my genes
I am determined by my unconscious
I am determined by my childhood
I am determined by my death
I am determined by my climate
I am determined by my homeland
I am determined by my work
I am determined by my newspaper
I am determined by my deep linguistic structures
I am determined by my etcetera
I am determined to be free

From the *New Humanist*. Reproduced with the permission of Anthony Rudolf.

This 'freedom' of the last line can easily be misinterpreted. The kind of freedom to which sociological inquiry contributes is a matter of continual debate among sociologists. Freedom is not seen as 'doing as one pleases'. Even choosing between alternatives is only a partial freedom.

> Freedom is first of all the chance to formulate the available choices, to argue over them – and then the opportunity to choose. That is why freedom cannot exist without an enlarged role of human reason in human affairs.
>
> Wright Mills, 1959

PERSONAL CONCERNS AND SOCIAL STRUCTURES

The issues raised in *The Humanist's Sonnet* include a further theme, the link between personal concerns and social structures. A key feature of the sociological imagination, C. Wright Mills argued, was an awareness of this interplay. People in a mass society have personal problems which are intertwined with the social structure, but many do not recognize the connections. Knowledgeable people do. They understand that what they think are personal troubles are very often also problems shared by others, and are incapable of solution by any one individual. Then only modifications of the structure of the groups in which they live, and sometimes the structure of the entire society, can be effective initiatives.

SOCIOLOGICAL QUESTIONS

Therefore sociological questions are couched in terms of the social world that people create:

> The sociologist's questions always remain essentially the same: 'What are people doing with each other here?' 'What are their relationships to each other?' 'How are those relationships organized in institutions?' 'What are the collective ideas that move men and institutions?'

Berger, © Peter Berger, 1966. Reprinted by permission of Penguin Books Ltd.

Another famous attempt to outline the kinds of questions of a sociological approach is that of C. Wright Mills. Classic social analysts, he suggests, have consistently asked three sorts of questions:

1. What is the structure of this particular society as a whole? What are its essential components, and how are they related to one another? How does it differ from other varieties of social order? Within it, what is the meaning of any particular feature for its continuance and for its change?
2. Where does this society stand in human history? What are the mechanics by which it is changing? What is its place within and its meaning for the development of humanity as a whole? How does any particular feature we are examining affect, and how is it affected by, the historical period in which it moves? And this period – what are its essential features? How does it differ from other periods? What are its characteristic ways of history-making?
3. What varieties of men and women now prevail in this society and in this period? And what varieties are coming to prevail? In what ways are they selected and formed, liberated and repressed, made sensitive and blunted? What kinds of 'human nature' are revealed in the conduct and character we observe in this society in this period? And what is the meaning for 'human nature' of each and every feature of the society we are examining?

Wright Mills, 1959

From *The Sociological Imagination*. Reprinted by permission of Oxford University Press.

SOCIOLOGY – FOR WHAT PURPOSES?

Sociologists are not agreed on the purposes of their study. Although there is general agreement that understanding social life is a key feature, the uses of sociology are disputed. One point of view is as follows:

The good spy reports what is there. Others decide what should be done as a result of his information. The sociologist is a spy in very much the same way. His job is to report as accurately as he can about a certain social terrain. Others, or he himself in a role other than that of sociologist, will have to decide what moves ought to be made in that terrain. We would stress strongly that saying this does *not* imply that the sociologist has no responsibility to ask about the goals of his employers or the use to which they will put his work. But this asking is not sociological asking. It is asking the same questions that any man ought to ask himself about his actions in society. Again, in the same way, biological knowledge can be employed to heal or to kill. This does not mean that the biologist is free of responsibility as to which use he serves. But when he asks himself about this responsibility, he is not asking a biological question.

Berger, 1966

According to this view, the findings of a particular sociological investigation can be used for quite contradictory purposes and by different groups of people. The spy's reports are also useful to the enemy, though for different reasons. The reports might, for example, give information about the enemy's lack of information.

Berger goes on to argue that there is nothing inherent in the sociological enterprise of trying to understand society that necessarily leads to this practice, or to any other. The findings of sociological inquiry may be used by social workers, salesmen, nurses, evangelists or politicians – in fact, by anyone whose activities involve the manipulation of people, for whatever purpose and with whatever outcome.

An alternative view is held by those who see prescriptions for changing cultures and institutions as a major concern. The idea is contained in the statement of Marx: 'The philosophers have only interpreted the world in various ways; the point, however, is to change it.'

THE IRONY OF HUMAN ACTION

Those who would urge caution about this commitment to change society do so on various grounds, one of which refers to the difficulty of ensuring that change goes as planned. One finding derived from interactionist sociology is that of the irony of human action:

> the outcome of ideas is commonly very different from what those who had the ideas in the first place planned or hoped. Such a consciousness of the ironic aspect of history is sobering, a strong antidote to all kinds of revolutionary utopianism.
>
> Berger, 1966

Another reason for urging caution is that discovering 'error' does not automatically guarantee a superior alternative, since the alternative actions possible are multitudinous:

> Some 'advanced thinkers' are of the opinion that any one who differs from the conventional opinion must be in the right. This is a delusion; if it were not, truth would be easier to come by than it is. There are infinite possibilities of error . . .
>
> Russell, 1950

Russell argued in his writings that the prior outcome of all critical and reflective thinking, not just sociological, was constructive doubt. (See Russell, 1926, *On Education*.) It follows that any social change should be subject to review and revision rather than implemented as the right answer.

SOCIOLOGY AS UNCOMMON SENSE

A view frequently encountered is that sociology is just common sense. Yet wherever sociology is studied it tends to have a disturbing effect, a disturbing of that very common sense in question. Even though the sociologist investigates and reflects on the familiar society, and even though the categories employed in the analysis are only refinements of the categories which other people use – power, class, status, or race – the findings are often unexpected and can contradict common sense.

Therefore one claim made by some sociologists is that their intention is to 'improve' on common sense and 'expose' some of the folk interpretations of social behaviour as false, distorted or incomplete. Berger (1966) employs an interesting range of images to convey this point. He uses phrases such as 'seeing through' and 'looking behind' very much as such phrases would be employed in common speech – 'seeing through his game', 'looking behind the scenes' – in other words, 'being up on all the tricks'.

The sociologist is seen as trying to penetrate the smoke-screen of the official versions of reality, those of the manager, the civil servant or the teacher, and to grasp the signals that come from the 'underworld', from the worker, the client or the pupil.

In setting about this kind of task, sociologists may find themselves in strange company, associating with the outsiders, the outcasts and the minorities, and on a broad range of missions. They may become involved in matters that others regard as sacred or distasteful. They will seek the company of judges or criminals, depending not on personal preferences but on the questions being asked. They will be interested in the human interaction that goes with warfare, with crime or with religion, and also in the relations between people in a classroom, or in a group of children playing in the street.

The outcomes of these missions are not guaranteed. The investigation may yield something fresh and unexpected. This may be something totally unfamiliar or it may be the familiar taking on a new meaning. Sociology may make us see in a new light the very world in which we have lived all our lives.

LAYERS OF MEANING

One reason why something fresh and unexpected is sometimes the outcome is related to the complexity of human social behaviour, with its various layers of meaning. An individual may sample only a few of these layers of meaning in the routines of everyday life; e.g. teachers are unlikely to gain a view of school from the point of view of the pupils unless they make a special effort to gain this information. A sociologist is more likely to collect such data. A chapter that follows (Chapter 3) gives an account of pupils' perspective and shows how the evidence demonstrates that holders of a traditional transmission view of education believe nonsense about pupils and that radical educationalists embrace a delusion regarding pupils' aspirations.

THE INVISIBLE SOCIAL WORLD

A large part of the introductory literature to sociology is taken up with questions of appropriate methods of study and the claim for the scientific nature of sociology. Sociology may be a network of propositions about the social life created by people just as physical science is a network of propositions about physical reality, but the difficulties of procedure are increased when the invisibility of the subject matter is recognized:

> It comes as a mild shock to most people to be told that the entire web of human social interrelations is founded on many invisible and indirect meanings which we bestow on various individuals. Not only have we never seen a family, we have never seen a student or a teacher. Nor have we ever seen a scientist, a saint, or a sinner. So it is with socially defined statuses. We can observe the people who occupy such statuses; but, until we are informed that they occupy a certain status and are expected to behave accordingly, we cannot respond in any appropriate manner . . . The social world is, then, largely an invisible world. This constitutes a major methodological problem for the sociologist. Sociology is supposed to be a science; and science, after all, is based on observation. What kind of

science is it that devotes itself to an examination of events which are, by their very nature, not directly observable?

Cuzzort and King, 1976

CONCLUSION

Sociology, then, is many things, some of them paradoxical.

It is a relatively new discipline, yet its quests and questions are among the most ancient forms of reflective thought.

If sociologists were not available, some form of substitute reflection on social behaviour would probably emerge: yet sociological thought and inquiry are also resisted and resented.

Everyone tends to feel familiar with the world of the sociologist: as members of the social world we should be the experts on it. Yet commonsense views are frequently disturbed by the inquiries of sociologists.

Sociology, in attempting to free us from the determining effect of social frameworks, may only make the strength of the structures more apparent and the sought-after freedom more elusive.

Sociology attempts dispassionate inquiry, yet cannot eradicate values from its investigations, the investigator or the subject of the investigation. The sociologists, like good detectives, suspect everything and everybody, *including themselves*.

Sociologists themselves are far from united on many issues related to their discipline, yet have some unity in their undertaking to meet argument with argument and to acknowledge the value of the constructive doubt, and in their willingness to live with the creative uncertainty of a constantly changing subject matter.

If this buffet, this smörgåsbord is to your taste, welcome to sociology!

Further Reading

Berger, P. (1966) *Invitation to Sociology*. Harmondsworth: Penguin. Well known as a lively, interesting and readable introduction to sociological thinking.
Berger, P. and Kellner, H. (1983) *Sociology Reinterpreted*. Harmondsworth: Penguin.
Brown, C. (1979) *Understanding Society*. London: John Murray Ltd. The opening chapter has a very intelligible introduction to sociological theory and the problems of social research.
Cuzzort, R. and King, E. (1976) *Humanity and Modern Social Thought*. Hinsdale, Illinois: Holt Dryden. The first chapter of this book is a well-written account of some of the basic problems of social thought, its premises, sources of error, and degrees of objectivity. The rest of the book gives a very useful account of the work of well known sociologists including Durkheim, Marx, Weber, Mead, Wright Mills, Becker, Goffman, Garfinkel and Berger.
Lee, D. and Newby H. (1983) *The Problem of Sociology*. London: Hutchinson. This book develops some of the themes of the chapter.
Wright Mills, C. (1959) *The Sociological Imagination*. Oxford: Oxford University Press. This is harder reading than the previous five. It is thorough and worth the effort of reading, but perhaps is best tackled after reading one or more of the above.

Discussion and Activities

1. Write down your definition of sociology. Compare it with the definitions written by fellow students, and check it against dictionaries, particularly sociological dictionary definitions. The working definition of this chapter is that *sociology can be seen as the systematic study of the social life (institutions, cultures and behaviour patterns) created by people and in turn influencing their behaviour in a continuous interaction.*
2. In C. Brown's *Understanding Society* there is an interesting activity: draw a picture or diagram which represents society to you. The first chapter of this book contains a discussion of common responses to this activity, including variations on circles, triangles, networks and stick figures.
3. Conduct an informal survey of opinions about sociology among your friends and relations. How many of these responses are misunderstandings of the kind mentioned in this chapter? Are there regular patterns in the responses? How can we cope with a diversity of interpretations?
4. Take some of the questions from the spoof examination paper (Figure 1.1) and discuss the ideas that are being parodied, misrepresented or accurately stated in each case.
5. Refer back to *The Humanist's Sonnet* by Anthony Rudolf. Prepare an account of how each influence has contributed to your own self concept.

Signposts

1. The limitations of sociology
This chapter has suggested some of the positive features of sociology but an awareness of limitations is worth some enquiry. A start can be made with Shipman, M. (1972) *The Limitations of Social Research*, Harlow: Longman. Further sources are Burgess, R.G. (ed.) (1984) *The Research Process in Educational Settings: Ten Case Studies*, Lewes: Falmer Press; and Burgess, R.G. (ed.) (1984) *Field Methods in the Study of Education*, Lewes: Falmer Press.

2. The ethics of sociology
If you join a group to study it, what happens if you are required to follow the members into illegal or immoral acts? This was a dilemma presented in Patrick, J. (1973) *A Glasgow Gang Observed* Eyre-Methuen. Further ethical issues are raised in Berger, P. (1977) *Facing Up To Modernity*, Harmondsworth; Penguin Books.

3. The looking-glass self
The looking-glass self is an idea attributed to Charles Horton Cooley (1902). Our reflection in a mirror gives us information about appearance and Cooley proposed that our reflection in other people's attitudes to us and our interpretations of how they see us, are used as key sources of information about our self-concept. George Herbert Mead (1934) took the idea further in noting a process he called 'taking the role of the other' whereby a kind of internal debate can take place as an individual rehearses possible courses of action and possible consequences. Mead stresses that in play, children develop this activity and develop their self concept at the same time. An excellent summary of this aspect of interactionism, symbolic interactionism, appears in chapter one of Hargreaves, D.H. (1972) *Interpersonal Relations and Education*, London: Routledge and Kegan Paul. (See also the quotation from Wankowski in the preface to the second edition of this book.) As an activity derived from this concept, you should be able to interview yourself about your experience of schooling or pretend to be a stranger trying to interpret puzzling aspects of schools such as bells or uniforms or compulsory religious assemblies.

Chapter 2

A Sociology of Assessment in Schools*

'assessment, far more than religion, has become the opiate of the people'
Patricia Broadfoot

INTRODUCTION

The purpose of this chapter is to show how a sociologist uses apparently simple questions to analyse behaviour. The behaviour chosen is that of assessment in schools, since this is a familiar activity to most readers. It is also an activity commonly regarded as a very important aspect of schooling, and a 'good' school is often defined as one where pupils achieve many examination passes in the General Certificate of Education (GCE).

Many concepts in the human sciences turn out to be ambiguous. It often helps to select from the competing ideas a working definition. Such a definition may be refined and clarified during subsequent analysis, but it establishes a starting point. The working definition adopted here will be a broad and general one, in the hope of opening up a wide range of issues. At the outset, assessment will be taken to mean *collecting information, on which to base judgements about learning experiences, in schools.*

In Chapter 1, it was stated that a key question asked by sociologists was 'what are people doing with each other here?'. To pursue this question in the case of assessment, we will ask four related questions:

1. Who assesses?
2. What is assessed?
3. How is assessment undertaken?
4. Why is assessment taking place?

WHO ASSESSES?

The participants in the assessment activity in schools appear to be teachers, pupils and examiners. In some instances the teacher doubles as the examiner. Parents, employers

---

* An earlier version of the material contained in this chapter appeared in the *Social Science Teacher*, Vol. 7, . No. 2, in 1977.

and administrators figure as consumers of assessment results rather than as participants in assessment. Several combinations of the participants are possible:

1. Pupils could assess pupils.
2. Pupils could assess teachers.
3. Pupils could assess examiners.
4. Teachers could assess pupils.
5. Teachers could assess teachers.
6. Teachers could assess examiners.
7. Examiners could assess pupils.
8. Examiners could assess teachers.
9. Examiners could assess examiners.

These interactions do all take place in schools within the definition of assessment which has been stated, but, based on observations and experiences of schools, the incidence and the significance accorded to them appear to vary considerably.

Pupils Assess Pupils

The highest *incidence* appears to be that of pupils assessing pupils. They are together for much longer periods of time both in and out of classrooms. Dreeben (1968) discusses the complexity of this activity, since the classroom is a public place where a pupil has to please at least two audiences that are present, teachers and fellow pupils, and possibly also 'absent' audiences of parents and examiners. This public assessment, Dreeben suggests, relates to at least three things:

1. learning;
2. institutional adjustment;
3. character.

Dreeben argues that, in the way schools are organized and operate at present, peers are more involved in the last two processes, and 'being smart', 'cissy', 'teacher pleaser' or 'cool' are examples of these assessments. Even 'private' consultations between one teacher and one pupil usually take place in the presence of an attentive set of pupil eavesdroppers. But the highest incidence of assessment is not accorded the highest significance (at least not formal significance), since at the end of the schooling experience the certificates and reports record other kinds of assessment, not pupils' assessments of each other. These assessments of each other do have some effects, however, and an example is the case of girls in general, whose 'failure' in school is now well documented. The peer group assessment of what is appropriate for a girl appears to be one of a number of powerful influences shaping a girl's self-concept and, in the vast majority of cases, steering her gently but inevitably away from a career into domesticity. (This subject is given fuller treatment in Chapter 25.)

Pupils Assess Teachers

Little formal notice is taken of this activity, high in incidence though it may be. Indeed, attempts to research this activity and to establish the validity and reliability of these assessments and possible uses of such feedback have been treated with hostility by some teachers, as will be shown in the next chapter. So, although pupils are often the most experienced assessors of teachers, little formal significance is attached to this.

Teachers Assess Pupils

The incidence of this activity is high and the assessment covers at least the three areas mentioned, i.e. learning, institutional adjustment and character. When a teacher makes the judgement of 'good pupil', it tends to cover all three. This activity is accorded more formal significance, since written reports, record cards and marking of work stem from it.

Examiners Assess Pupils

When we consider examiners assessing pupils, we have an activity of rather low incidence, since it takes place only at certain prescribed times, and only at certain stages in a pupil's school career. Yet it is accorded high significance. The examination results, grades and certificates are heavily stressed and considerable expenditure of money and resources is involved.

The simple question 'Who assesses?' therefore yields a puzzle for sociologists. Why are the assessments of most incidence given least significance and those of least incidence given highest significance? The mystery is deepened when you gain information that this external examiner activity is absent from equivalent schools in other countries like Sweden, where assessment is school-based and undertaken by the teachers. Indeed, this system replaced an external-examiner-based system some years ago.

There are, of course, comments to be made on other possible combinations, e.g. teachers assessing teachers (possibly a more frequent activity in team teaching situations) and examiners assessing teachers (this figuring in current discussions about teacher accountability, perhaps), but this is an exercise readers will be invited to undertake for themselves at the end of the chapter.

WHAT IS ASSESSED?

A lot of things happen in classrooms. People talk, people listen, people make decisions, people produce written material, people work in groups, people work on their own, people laugh (sometimes), people learn. Activity includes reading, writing, answering questions, drawing and reasoning. Among the learning outcomes are blocks of information, attitudes, thinking skills and manual skills. Mammoth taxonomies exist to indicate the vast quantity and diversity of classroom activity. Blooms' *Taxonomy of Educational Objectives*, which has three volumes, is one example.

From this wealth of happenings, some are habitually selected for assessment by the participants. The selection differs according to the point of view. For examiners, the written end-product of an examination is selected. For pupils, the characters of their teachers, in terms of good humour and patience and their instructional skills of explaining clearly and organizing effectively, are given emphasis (see Chapter 3). Teachers appear to select scholastic behaviour, institutional adjustment and personal character when assessing pupils, though their final judgement emphasizes written end-products, as in the case of the examiners.

The assessments of examiners and teachers tend to stress end-products rather than processes. Diagnosis, adjustment, reappraisal and adaptation appear to be accorded little respect in terms of assessment. One outcome of this, according to Holt (1969), is 'right answerism'. Pupils learn that the right answer means a great deal to teachers and examiners, whereas the way of obtaining it is seen as of less significance. Holt documents some of the strategies developed by pupils for gleaning the right answer and thereby pleasing the teacher.

In a now famous passage, Postman and Weingartner (1971) point out some probable consequences, usually unintended, of the kind of approach that stresses certain selected end-products. Students may learn that:

– Passive acceptance is a more desirable response to ideas than active criticism.
– Discovering knowledge is beyond the power of students and is, in any case, none of their business.
– Recall is the highest form of intellectual achievement, and the collection of unrelated 'facts' is the goal of education.
– The voice of authority is to be trusted and valued more than independent judgement.
– One's own ideas and those of one's classmates are inconsequential. Feelings are irrelevant in education.
– There is always a single, unambiguous Right Answer to a question.

One of the clients passes judgement:

> Half-educated children emerge from school clutching their exam certificates . . . They believe themselves to be 'educated'. To some extent they are, I suppose. But are they better equipped to understand and live with their fellow human beings? Moreover, has their education encouraged them to think creatively and originally? Isn't this what education should be about?
>
> Anthony, aged 18, in Blishen, 1969

There is one other possible subject of assessment; that is, the courses or learning experiences themselves. Although it is people and their performances that are usually assessed, there have been some attempts to assess courses rather than learners. One was the programmed learning movement of the 1960s, which resulted in carefully structured courses that were tested for their effectiveness in teaching. Courses that did not teach over 90 per cent of the 'target' learners were rejected as unsuitable. This was perhaps the most radical idea of the whole movement, because it shifted blame for failure to learn from the learner to the learning experience provided, in these cases a learning programme. The Open University has adopted a similar approach to its tuition services through its educational technology staff.

The simple question 'What is assessed?' thus yields another puzzle. Why is this particular selection of what will be assessed made? Who decides, and for what reasons? Some light may be thrown on these questions by considering how assessment is undertaken.

HOW IS ASSESSMENT UNDERTAKEN?

The definition of assessment given earlier implies five processes. These are:

1.   deciding what information to collect;
2.   deciding on a format or means of collecting it;
3.   collecting the information;
4.   recording it;
5.   using the information.

The second, third and fourth processes appear to be essentially *technical* problems in deciding which method is appropriate to achieve the ends specified in the first and last of the processes listed. Therefore the use of the information seems to be one of the critical questions in finding out how assessment takes place.

There are several possibilities. Firstly there is a *diagnostic* possibility. The information is gathered to tell the teacher what the next stage of learning should be. An assessment of this kind might show that the learner has gained sufficient understanding of one stage to proceed to the next. Alternatively, it might show that further work on the first stage is necessary. An example is that of reading schemes where performance on one book is used to decide whether the pupil transfers from, for example, level two, book 2A, to level three, book 3A, or has further practice at level two by going on to book 2B or 2C.

A variation of this is *diagnostic self-assessment*. Here the information tells the learners themselves what the next activity might be, e.g. a new activity or further work on the current learning. One firm produces a reading scheme, consisting of boxes of reading cards, in which pupils can assess their own performance. Another possibility is *criterion referencing*. Here criteria of performance are available to show whether a minimum standard has been reached and, if more than the minimum, what standard has been reached. Individuals are tested, either by themselves or by others, against the criteria rather than against other people. They are allowed many, sometimes unlimited, attempts. Practical examples of this process are the driving test, first-aid proficiency tests, physical and athletic tests and reading schemes.

If there is a group of related activities then a set of criteria can be stated and a personal profile of achievement levels recorded. In the driving test, for example, an examiner might record 'just competent on gear changes, very competent on hand signals, competent on steering, very competent on braking', etc.

Another possibility is *norm-referencing*, where the performance of one individual is compared with the performance of others to arrive at a rank order of candidates. The principle in play here appears to be that of rationing. Only a limited number of places are available, e.g. at a university, so those candidates with lower performance at a particular time are rejected. The selection of a football team is subject to a similar principle, since only 11 players are required. Assessments of this kind tend to be undertaken by others: self-assessment on a norm-referencing basis seems to be rare. 'Test your own IQ' is one of the few examples of norm-referenced self-assessment. The difference in practice between assessment systems based on criterion referencing and norm-referencing may be considerable. If the driving test, which tests a very compli-cated and sophisticated set of psychomotor skills, quick decision-making and informa-tion usage, were to be based on norm-referencing, the assumption would be made that there was only a limited 'pool of ability' to drive, so only a minority of the population could pass the test. However, the driving test is actually based on criterion referencing and so most of the population can, and do, become qualified drivers.

On the other hand, if criterion referencing were used in our schools instead of a norm-referenced system of examinations, where a set percentage of candidates must fail, the result would be something like the Open University system, in which it is assumed from the start that most of the learners can achieve at least a pass, if the courses are well designed and second and third chances are available for the small minority with learning difficulties. As a result, the ultimate pass rate of candidates who complete Open University courses is high, often 80 per cent or more. For individuals the importance of this change is sometimes dramatic, and it is almost commonplace now for individual Open University students, previously written off by the norm-referenced school system as complete failures, to achieve honours degrees in the criterion-referenced system. The individuals concerned frequently report that they do not regard themselves as exceptional. An Open University graduate writes:

> I know that I was no more intelligent than the rest of the kids at my school. Only unlike the others, I met a man who helped me obtain a desire for education.
>   My case does not show how intelligence wins through. My case shows how, year after year, we allow the intellectual abilities of thousands upon thousands of children from the working class to go to waste.
>
> Simkin, in *Sesame*, April 1976

Although there are examples of all these kinds of assessment in schools, the most highly valued ones appear to be those with certificates as an end product – GCE 'O' level, GCE 'A' level, CSE etc. – and these are, in most cases, norm-referenced, since only a specified percentage are allowed to pass or to receive a particular grade.

There is another puzzle for sociologists here. Of all the types of assessment available to schools, why is this one stressed so heavily?

The *technical* questions of whether to use examinations, essays, multiple-choice tests, objective tests, oral assessment, reports, profiles, or other formats are interesting, and most debate in schools and education literature appears to be on these issues. Consequently many books are available advising teachers on the technicalities of assessment. There are questions here that have been investigated by sociologists. They include questions such as 'Why do so many techniques use written assessments?', 'What are the hidden unintended effects of each of these techniques?' and 'Where there is a discrepancy between the actual reliability of a technique and its believed reliability, why does the belief tend to persist despite the evidence?'.

WHY ASSESSMENT?

Earlier we noted that what is assessed with most significance in schools tends to be end-products rather than processes of learning, learners rather than courses, teachers or examiners, and written material rather than other activities. Moreover, this assessment is norm-referenced rather than criterion referenced, or diagnostic and performed by others rather than self-assessed. This suggested the idea of rationing, so what might be being rationed?

First, since the certificates accorded so much significance are used to get jobs, occupations are rationed by this kind of assessment. Why schools are used in this way is not immediately clear, as more than one writer has noted. Holly (1973) has described the schools as being used to do the employers' sorting task for them instead of educating pupils. It does not always happen like this in other countries, and the case of Sweden, where the whole norm-referenced external examination system is simply absent from schools, has already been mentioned.

Second, occupations are given different social ranks, some being seen as 'superior', 'upper class', 'white-collar' or 'professional'. So perhaps along with occupational placement goes social placement into a social class and a linked set of life chances. In Swedish society social placement appears to be more muted and the distinctions between social classes less marked, with life chances less differentiated. The theme of social class difference is developed in a later chapter.

Third, not all the reasons are likely to lie outside the school, and listening to talk in staff-rooms suggests another possibility: examination classes are said to be easier both to control and to teach, for the pupils can constantly be reminded of the consequences of failing the examination and thereby are 'motivated' and brought under control. Husen (1974) describes this view of education in the following way: 'Pupils undertake to learn mainly to avoid the disagreeable consequences if they do not: low marks, non-promotion, censure, punishment, etc.'. Husen argues for an alternative criterion reference approach which he sees as preferable to this.

However, the case can be overstated and contradictions overlooked because there are other ideas talked about in schools, e.g. diagnostic reasons for assessment, personal development based on personal profiles, and the autonomy that derives from self-assessment, but if we stay close to Berger's question, 'What are these people doing with each other here?', the picture is closer to Husen's description. There have been some changes in emphasis in the assessment of some pupils with the development of the CSE in recent years. Here, teachers, who in Hipkin's (1975) view are better qualified to assess their pupils' abilities and potential and should therefore be given the central responsibility for assessment, rather than examiners, are more closely involved in the task of assessment in 'Mode III' assessments, where the school has a large say in both syllabus and assessment. However, this change has been limited in the main to the CSE and is not a marked feature of the higher status GCE. Moreover, one researcher has found that this approach is currently in reverse and that the activity of examination boards is reducing these teacher-based and school-based Mode III opportunities (Whitty, 1978).

To go further into the question of 'Why assessment?' will require the more systematic use of concepts. The one I have chosen to use is ideologies of education.

IDEOLOGIES OF EDUCATION AND ASSESSMENT

'Ideology' may be defined in various ways. The meaning intended here is that of a broad but interlinked set of ideas and beliefs about the world which are held by a group of people and which those people demonstrate both in behaviour and conversation to various audiences. These systems of belief are seen by the groups holding them to be descriptions of 'the way things really are', and they are the means by which sense is made of the world. 'Ideologies of education' refer to the broad set of ideas and beliefs, held by a group of people, about the formal arrangements for education, specifically schooling and often, by implication and extension, also about the informal aspects of education.

An analysis of competing ideologies can be attempted by comparing them on a series of key component features which will be called 'theories', bearing in mind that this is an ambiguous word that has both common and technical uses. In general, any ideology of education will contain various theories, including:

1. A theory of knowledge.
2. A theory of learning and the learner's role.
3. A theory of teaching and the teacher's role.
4. A theory of resources appropriate for learning.
5. A theory of organization of learning situations.
6. A theory of aims, objectives and outcomes.
7. A theory of assessment to discover whether learning has been successful.

The use of the concept of ideology here is to enable the puzzle about assessment outlined earlier to be explored further by showing how the selections of who assesses, what is assessed and how assessment takes place form part of one of several competing patterns of ideas and beliefs about education.

A wide variety of ideologies of education has been described in educational literature. They include: transmission and interpretation (Barnes and Shemilt, 1974); authoritarian and democratic (Lippitt and White, 1958); open and closed (Kohl, 1970); meaning making and meaning receiving (Postman and Weingartner, 1971); autonomous study (Husen, 1974); and the ubiquitous 'traditional' and 'progressive'.

A comparison of three of these ideologies on four of the features given above (i.e. theory of knowledge, theory of learning, theory of teaching and theory of assessment) will show how the ideas about assessment vary with the ideology of education concerned. Table 2.1 makes such a comparison.

The central point that emerges from Table 2.1 is that there appears to be no neutral view of assessment: all the alternatives can be said to be political because they make assumptions about what counts as good education and bad education, and each has consequences for what happens to the learners after assessment is over. Under one system they may go into a lower-paid occupation, believing that they had their chance and were not 'up to standard' and that is that. Or they may go to such a job believing that second and third chances are available and that they may well achieve more later. Or, under another system, they may go to such a job believing that they are capable of learning and re-learning whenever an opportunity arrives.

Table 2.1 *Comparison of ideologies of education*

Transmission ideology	Interpretation ideology	Autonomous ideology
Knowledge is believed to exist in the form of public disciplines, known as subjects, developed in the past and currently being extended.	Knowledge is believed to exist in the knowers' consciousness and in their ability to organize thought and action. Subjects are one of several available resources.	Knowledge is believed to exist in the present and future, since existing subject knowledge is seen as limited in coping with modern complex problems.
The learners' performance is valued in so far as they measure up to the standards and criteria of the subjects.	The learners' activity to interpret their reality is valued, so that criteria arise from both learner and teacher.	The learners' performances in learning techniques of learning and developing new knowledge and understanding are valued.
The teacher's task is perceived as correcting the learner's performance according to the subject criteria known by the teacher.	The teacher's task is perceived as the setting up of a dialogue in which the learners can reshape their knowledge through interaction both with others and with subjects seen as resources.	The teacher's task is perceived as organizing learning experiences so that the learners gradually learn how to make all the decisions about learning for themselves.
Assessment will be of the end product in some examination, probably written, supervised by teacher or examiner, and where entry to the subject is rationed for some reason, norm-referencing will be the system adopted.	Assessment will take place throughout the course as a means of monitoring the reshaping of knowledge, phase by phase. It will tend to be criterion referenced wherever possible to achieve this result.	Assessment will gradually pass from the control of the teacher to the learners as they learn how to assess effectively their own learning. It will tend to be criterion referenced throughout.

CONCLUSION

All sociological analyses tend to be incomplete and this attempt is no exception. The approach adopted has been an interactionist one and the four questions chosen ask about the interactions of the participants with each other, with their school institution and their society, and with the network of alternative ideas about education and assessment. An important question is what is missing from this kind of analysis?

One missing idea is that of a historical discussion. Norm-referenced assessment was seen as a better way of allocating scarce occupations and life chances than patronage, and merit was seen as a fairer rationing idea than favouritism. Out of this view grew ideas such as equality of opportunity and the wastage of talent. A structural conflict approach such as the Marxist sociological perspective would usually give a prominent place to a historical discussion in the analysis. The differences between the various sociological perspectives are the subject of later chapters.

SUMMARY

1. Some kinds of assessment occur very frequently in British schools. Examples are pupils assessing each other and pupils assessing teachers.
2. Some kinds of assessment are rare events in British schools. Examples are examiners assessing pupils and examiners assessing teachers.
3. The rarest assessments, those with low incidence, are given the highest formal significance or valuation, whereas the most frequent assessments, those with high

incidence, are usually given least formal significance.

4. Of the wealth of happenings in classrooms, certain things are selected for formal assessment. These tend to be written work taken as the end product of the learning process.

5. For pupils the characters of their teachers are given most emphasis.

6. The consequences of stressing written end products for formal assessment may be right answerism, the development of strategies to find approved answers without necessarily developing thinking strategies, and other outcomes such as the belief that recall is the highest form of intellectual activity.

7. The assessment of courses and learning experiences tends to be overlooked in favour of assessing the learners' performance. Blame for poor performance tends to be attached to the learners rather than to the learning experiences.

8. Formal assessment in British schools is usually norm-referenced, specifying that only a fixed proportion of candidates can be successful, and the alternatives of diagnostic assessment and criterion referenced assessment, where most candidates are expected to succeed eventually, are largely overlooked.

9. Assessment of a norm-referencing kind may have more to do with allocating occupations, social class positions and life chances than with anything else.

10. Within schools, norm-referenced assessment systems may be seen as one means of motivation and one method of control.

11. The choice of an assessment system may relate to other ideas and beliefs about education that form a coherent pattern described as an ideology of education.

12. Competing ideologies of education exist, each making assumptions about what counts as good or bad education and each having consequences for the learners' fates: this suggests that there can be no *neutral* view of assessment or education. Each competing ideology of education is political because of its assumptions and its consequences.

13. The interactionist approach adopted in this chapter has strengths and weaknesses. One weakness is the tendency to overlook the historical dimension.

Further Reading

Blishen, E. (1969) *The School That I'd Like*. Harmondsworth: Penguin. The pupils' viewpoint is the subject of Chapter 7, 'This Almighty God'.

Broadfoot, P. (1979) *Assessment, Schools and Society*. London: Methuen. Few books appear to approach assessment from a sociological perspective, but this is one exception. Another follows, below.

Broadfoot, P. (ed.) (1984) *Selection, Certification and Control*. Lewes: Falmer Press.

Dore, R.P. (1976) *The Diploma Disease*. London: Allen and Unwin. This book develops the proposition that schooling is increasingly dominated by the business of qualification at the expense of the business of education.

Hartog, P.J. and Rhodes, E.C. (1935) *An Examination of Examinations*. London: Macmillan. A classic study of examinations.

Hextall, I. (1976) 'Marking Work' In *Explorations in the Politics of School Knowledge* (eds.) Whitty, G. and Young, M.F.D. Driffield: Nafferton Books. This is a paper analysing the implications of the daily task of marking.

Hipkin, J. (1975) 'Time to Abolish Exams?' *Where*, **109**. This article presents the case for school-based assessment.

Lauwerys, J.A. and Scanlon, D.G. (eds.) (1969) *World Yearbook of Education: Examinations*. London: Evans. Another excellent study of examinations.

Discussion and Activities

1. Write comments on the combinations of participants in assessment not developed in the chapter, e.g. teachers assessing teachers, teachers assessing examiners, examiners assessing teachers.
2. Discuss whether the quotation given at the head of this chapter is justifiable.
3. Discuss the questions about technical aspects of assessment given at the end of the section 'How Is Assessment Undertaken?'.
4. Conduct an informal survey of beliefs about assessment among your friends and relations.

    (a) Do they believe that 'O' level and CSE grading systems are consistent? Compare with the findings of A. Wilmott and D. Nuttall in a Schools Council investigation 1975: they found that the life chances of large numbers of candidates are based on a statistically unreliable examination system. Their findings indicate that:

    > when it comes to an individual candidate every grade on a five-point scale should be read plus or minus one. That is, a real distinction can be drawn between two candidates with grades separated by two points, but if you are comparing a grade one with a grade two, or a two with a three, the difference quite likely depends on the luck of the draw.

    A quarter of 'O' level and CSE candidates are given the wrong grades as indicated above, and the chances of substantially improving exam consistency are remote.

    (b) Do they believe that script markers are reasonably consistent? Compare with:

    > All the experimental data has shown that for a particular performance expressed in terms of an exam script, assessment by different examiners produces marks with considerable variability such that in the determination of these marks, the part played by the examiner can be greater than that of the performance of the examinee.
    > Pieron, 1969

    > . . . the standards set by examinations whether those of a basic pass or an ABC . . . grading system are in the last analysis wholly subjective. They are based on what candidates, in the opinion of the examiners (or chief examiner) *should* attain; no internal consistency or other form of reliability is published. The exam boards do not consider it part of their duties to inform teachers and pupils of the reliability and validity of their products.
    > Lewis, 1978

    (c) Do they believe that the standards in one subject at 'A' level are similar to those in another subject? Compare with:

    > Recent research by Alison Kelly of Edinburgh University has produced evidence that there were wide variations in the standards expected by different disciplines at the Higher Grade Exams of the Scottish Certificate of Education. Research in Britain suggests that such variability is not affected by national boundaries.
    > 'Tough Exams', *New Society*, 13 April 1976

    (d) Do they believe that the standards of different examination boards are similar? Compare with the findings that candidates can improve results by changing boards, in J.F. Scott, *Comparability of Grade Standards in Mathematics at GCE A level* (Schools Council/Evans/Methuen, 1975).

    (e) Check out the features of the new GCSE examination. Are any of the difficulties indicated above resolved by this scheme?

Signposts

1. Assessment in primary schools
Much of the writing concentrates on secondary schooling and beyond. Work on primary school assessment can be found in Black, H. and Broadfoot, P. (1982) *Keeping Track of Teaching*, London: Routledge and Kegan Paul, in Richards C. (ed.) (1982) *New Directions in Primary Education*, Lewes: Falmer Press, and in Galton, M. and Simon, B. (eds.) (1980) *Progress and Performance in the Primary School*, London: Routledge and Kegan Paul.

2. The assessment of teachers
There is a link here with the chapter on teachers as victims and a starting point is Grace, G. (1985) 'Judging Teachers: the social and political contexts of teacher evaluation.' *British Journal of Sociology of Education*, **6**, 1.

Chapter 3

Pupils as Clients?*

'I don't think any teacher can understand the problems pupils have; they do not stop and listen long enough or try to understand. If they did, the relationship between pupil and teacher would improve.'

15-year-old pupil, Birmingham, 1977

INTRODUCTION: SOCIOLOGICAL PERSPECTIVES

Some of the issues raised in this chapter require some awareness of the different perspectives within sociology. These are described in more detail in Part Four, and the account given here is only a brief introduction. One feature that complicates this issue is that there is no universally agreed categorization of the perspectives and the reader will encounter categorizations which are different from the one that follows.

Here, three broad groupings of the sociological perspectives – macro, micro and interactionist – will be proposed.

Macro Perspectives

There are several of these, but they all have a common feature: they start with a view of societies, cultures and institutions as having set patterns of rules and behaviours, with the result that individuals are seen as being forced, persuaded, manipulated, or socialized into some degree of compliance with these patterns.

Two major sub-types of macro perspective are frequently described: structural functionalist and structural conflict.

Structural functionalist
This approach is based on an assumption that society is a structure or framework of parts which are closely linked together. Each of these parts, e.g. the economy, the family, education, performs a function in keeping society going. For the most part this structure is seen as relatively harmonious, because there is seen to be general agreement or consensus about the usefulness of the whole pattern.

Structural conflict
This approach disputes that all groups are relatively well served by the structural

---

* An earlier version of this chapter appeared in *Educational Review*, Vol. 29, No. 2.

arrangements, and the idea of a conflict of interests is stressed. Some groups are seen as having advantageous positions over others and they will strive to keep this situation as it is, while other groups are seen as trying to obtain an alternative structure, with a redistribution of advantages and scarce items. One kind of conflict approach, known as Marxist, is derived from the ideas of Karl Marx.

Micro Perspectives

There is a variety of micro perspectives and a confusion of labels, including some lengthy ones like 'ethnomethodology' and 'phenomenology'. Other labels used are 'interpretivist', 'symbolic interactionism' and, confusingly, since it will be treated here as a separate category, 'interactionist'. At this stage these labels, and the variations they signify, need not detain us: they will be explained in Part Four.

What these micro perspectives have in common is a view that, instead of individuals being forced by the patterns of society or pulled by the strings of society like puppets, individuals create society every day by their social actions. Change occurs when individuals cease one set of social actions and start another. Social order is seen as an active production by members of society, and meaning is seen as being negotiated by social actors rather than being imposed upon them.

Interactionist Perspectives

There are several interactionist perspectives, some inclined towards a micro view, some towards a macro view. What they tend to have in common is a view of society as a loose network of related parts in a constant state of flux. This network can be sometimes harmonious, sometimes conflict-laden, sometimes rigidly structured, sometimes more open and flexible, and sometimes can contain some or all of these features in a contradictory state of affairs.

Interactionist perspectives tend to have a Janus view. Janus was a Roman god, the guardian of gates and doorways, who had two faces looking in different directions. Interactionist perspectives tend to look two ways, both at the patterns of society stressed by the macro sociologists, and at the work and negotiations that individuals accomplish in keeping society going, as stressed in the micro perspectives.

THE STRUCTURAL FUNCTIONALIST VIEW OF PUPILS

A structural functionalist view of education tends to stress the activity of schools in training and selecting children so that they fit into some necessary slot in a relatively harmonious society. This view implies that children need to be manipulated in some way for that society's convenience or for some other reason. The images used by people who take this view stress this. The teacher is said to be like a potter moulding clay, or like a gardener cultivating plants, or a builder building a house on sound foundations. In each case pupils are seen as things been processed, and often as having no rights. (Stone and Taylor, 1976, researched legal cases involving pupils' rights. One example was that pupils who were pacifists could still be compelled to join the cadet force of the school: the right of conscientious objection allowable to adults could be overruled by the head teacher.)

This is often the official view. In 1976 the Prime Minister, James Callaghan, made a speech about education, and the Secretary of State for Education, Shirley Williams, followed this by starting a series of public debates about education. The people to be involved included teachers, employers and trade unions. Pupils were not mentioned at first. Later a proposal to invite pupil representatives was negatively received by teacher representatives. This is consistent with a functionalist view: why should you consult the clay about what kind of pot it is to be made into?

It might seem that any attempts to establish the pupils' point of view and to take it into account are bound to be using perspectives other than the functionalist. Some head teachers I consulted appeared to think like this (Meighan, 1977a). Here are some of their reactions to a research project on consulting pupils about teaching:

> It is dangerous to involve children in this kind of comment on their teachers.
> Discipline would be adversely affected by this kind of exercise.
> It is bad for classroom relationships.
> Children are not competent to judge these matters.

These reactions occurred despite the fact that the teachers had been provided with a written briefing that summarized several previous researches, both in the UK and in the USA, in which the findings contradicted all the above statements. (This is not particularly unusual. People operating with particular views of teaching might often behave like this when first given information that is contrary to their beliefs. We are all, from time to time, liable to prefer 'not to let the evidence confuse the issues involved'.)

However, it does not follow that consulting pupils automatically suggests a non-functionalist perspective, because there are several approaches to manipulating pupils. One is based on confrontation, where teachers order pupils to behave in certain ways and rely on fear and punishment to get their way. But other functionalist approaches are based on persuasion, coaxing and more subtle forms of control. Consulting pupils and using some of their responses can become a means of coaxing them into niches of society rather than ordering them into them. Nevertheless, many attempts to establish the pupils' point of view do use other perspectives, e.g. structural conflict and interactionist.

WHICH PERSPECTIVE IS IN USE?

This is often a difficult question to answer because the perspectives in sociology overlap a great deal and researchers often use more than one perspective in the course of their research. There are often clues to the perspective being used in studies of the pupils' point of view, in the concepts used, the methods of inquiry, and the kind of questions asked. Studies using a conflict perspective may often use the concept of alienation in schooling. Studies using a functionalist perspective would be likely to ask a question such as, 'What are the best teachers you have had like?' rather than 'If you designed the ideal school, what would it be like?'. The first question limits the pupils to the status quo, whereas the second question is more radical, in allowing the pupils to consider alternatives, whether or not they have experienced them. Micro-sociological studies would be likely to gain data from spontaneous discussion, conversation with pupils and 'uncensored' or anonymous written material that was not going to be used to grade pupils or be marked by teachers. (See Woods, 1976.)

AN INTERACTIONIST APPROACH

An interactionist approach would tend to explore the network of perceptions in play. This might result in studying several of the 'layers of meaning' referred to in Chapter 1, or in concentration on one layer of meaning, in this case that of the pupils. The questions involved might include the following:

1. How do pupils interpret the experience of schooling? Are they critical? Is there a division of opinion? How do the 'successful' react? How do the 'unsuccessful' react? Do boys and girls react in the same way? How do 'deschooled' pupils educated at home react?
2. How reliable and valid are pupils as judges of their school experiences? Do they judge some aspects of schooling accurately and other aspects inaccurately? Is consultation welcomed by pupils?
3. What do pupils see as ideal in schooling? What is a 'good' teacher, as they see it? How do they define a 'bad' teacher?
4. How much are the pupils aware of any aspects of the 'hidden' curriculum?
5. The pupils' view of school includes their view of fellow pupils, and this raises even more questions, e.g. how do peer groups operate in schools? What is the influence of such groups? Is there a youth culture opposing a school culture?

STUDIES AVAILABLE

There is only a limited number of studies of the pupils' point of view of schooling in Britain available. Therefore a first conclusion is that this is a neglected issue in educational research.

In some studies the viewpoint of pupils has been one aspect of a larger study. In his analysis of a boys' secondary school, Hargreaves (1967) obtained information from the pupils about how they interpreted some of the features of school life, especially streaming by ability.

In contrast, the study by Blishen (1969) concentrates entirely on the pupils' view of schooling by providing selections from essays, written mostly by secondary school children, on the theme of 'The School That I'd Like'.

The educational weekly, *The Times Educational Supplement* (1969), carried a two-part study entitled 'Child's Eye View of Teacher', which contained a summary of primary school children's comments on their teachers.

The following year there appeared a study of early school leavers' views of teachers and schools by Maizels (1970), and three years later a pair of studies reporting the views of primary and secondary school children in turn was produced by Blishen (1973a, b).

A comparative viewpoint was available in two educational paperbacks. One by Holt (1969) reported his observations of how pupils reacted to schooling in the USA, while the other was written by eight Italian boys protesting about their experience of schooling in Italy (School of Barbiana, 1970). Another writer in the USA, Jackson (1971), was writing about a 'hidden' curriculum of influences in school that affected pupils considerably but was hardly recognized by teachers.

However, since 1973, there has been a growing number of researchers interested in the pupils' view of schooling, and one collection of articles is entitled *The Learners' Viewpoint* (Meighan, 1978b).

The influence of growing youth unemployment is reflected in subsequent studies by Gow and McPherson (1980) and by White and Brockington (1983). Further collections are edited by Hughes (1984) and by Hammersley and Woods (1984).

HOW DO PUPILS INTERPRET THE EXPERIENCE OF SCHOOLING?

The studies so far suggest some tentative conclusions. First, primary school pupils do appear to be more satisfied with their experiences than secondary school pupils. Second, where dissatisfaction is expressed, it is just as likely to come from 'successful' as 'unsuccessful' pupils.

Primary School

In response to a request to seven- to eleven-year-old school children for written portraits of teachers came 1200 replies, which were analysed by Makins (1969), She noted how children had watched their teachers with obsessive concern, noting manner-isms, subtle changes in mood, and detailed variations in behaviour; they remark on teachers who talk to lonely, left-out children during playground duty and those who are angry with children because they are angry themselves. She concludes that, on the whole, these pupils love their primary schools: 'It is a sad fate to go home. I would like to stay for more education with the great 5'10" Mr Henshaw.'

The really popular teachers managed without many sanctions and did not shout at pupils very often. They let children talk, they explain clearly, they encourage, they are interested. Makins comments that the essays contained evidence that what children learn matters much less to them than how they are taught. Teachers who are good at something – music, art, photography, sport (it does not appear to matter what it is) – are appreciated, and so are student teachers who come prepared with new projects.

> On the evidence of our critics, hundreds of teachers are managing to make school so interesting that there is no time or reason for the old tricks and giggles and avoidance routines – and to establish a relationship with children makes the rituals of classroom warfare unthinkable.

Other studies, e.g. Blishen (1972a, b), support these findings.

Secondary School

The contrast with pupils' reports of their secondary schools is marked. For example, a study by Maizels (1970) concentrated on a sample of how 330 'unsuccessful' pupils who had recently left school at the earliest possible date, or were just about to leave, rated teachers in their secondary school. Schools and teachers were negatively rated for the most part. On the judgements given, Maizels concludes, few of the schools would get a 'pass' mark. Only a minority of pupils felt that their teachers had encouraged them, listened to what they had to say, praised them when they did well, had been pleasant, kind or sincere, or had kept their promises. Only 34 per cent of boys and girls had felt that their teachers had treated them like human beings.

The responses of some of the 'successful' pupils were obtained in an essay competition describing 'The School That I'd Like'. (Only children reasonably fluent in terms of literary skills and whose parents or teachers read the *Observer*, the newspaper which organized the competition, were likely to be included in such a sample.) Blishen (1969) comments that the essays amounted to an enormous, remarkably good-humoured, earnest, frequently passionate and, at best, highly intelligent plea for a new order in our schools, to replace what was currently seen as dreary and boring.

What the pupils mean by dreary and boring is diagnosed in some detail: 'Everything learnt is second-hand if it comes from the teachers and very often out-of-date and misleading if it comes from books.' 'Far better to replace constipated ways of teaching with more active lessons . . . '. The assessment of their experience of schooling was wide ranging and took in, among other things, the dullness of building design and dreary, unimaginative furniture, examinations and their distorting effect on learning, the role of the prefect as peer group policeman, the limiting effect of timetables, bells, the triviality of many school rules, and the idea of compulsory worship and religious education as attempted indoctrination. Blishen comments that the image of the prison returned to him again and again as he read the essays. A further study of secondary school children was undertaken by Blishen in 1973.

'Deschooled' Pupils

Some parents exercise their legal right to educate their children at home. (The organization that supports such cases is Education Otherwise, and it is studied in a later chapter.) The views of such children are of particular interest, since they often have an alternative experience with which to make comparison. Here are two examples:

> The school I'd like is what I have: my mother teaches my brother and me at home. We study maths, English, science, history, geography, French and scripture.
>
> This system has many advantages. The most important is that we can learn at our own speed: thus I have recently started A-level maths but am still struggling with O English, while my brother, who is three and a half years younger, is advanced in English but only average at arithmetic. Another advantage is that we have much more free time than other children; we don't waste time travelling to and fro and, as we have individual work, the education officer agreed to shorten lesson times for us. I spend a lot of my leisure time reading, bird watching, stamp and coin collecting, doing jigsaws, carpentry, painting, listening to radio, watching TV, swimming, playing chess, draughts, tennis and table

tennis. Another advantage is that we are not hedged in by a lot of silly rules and regulations. We are also free from bullying big boys and from pressure to start bad habits like smoking and drug taking. We dress in comfortable, sensible clothes and do not have to wear some ridiculous uniform, nor do we have to play compulsory games. Again, we have home cooking all the time.

When my mother started, a lot of people told her she was foolish because we would never learn to mix. I don't think this is true because, although I've always liked some time by myself, my brother likes and has lots of friends with whom he goes to play and who come and play with him . . . It was also said that we would grow up selfish: I hope we're not. About once a fortnight we have a stall in our front garden to aid Oxfam and have collected £4 2s 3d so far this year. We also do a few odd jobs around the house. People also said Mother would find it too much. I know we get her down at times, but she survives and looks, so people say, much younger than she is . . .

The only disadvantage of the system to my mind is the difficulty of doing much advanced practical work in science because of the amount of apparatus required.

I think it would solve a lot of problems if more people followed our system . . .

Frank (aged 12)
From Blishen, 1969.

Copyright © Penguin Books and contributors. Reprinted by permission of Penguin Books Ltd.

Why I like to be taught at home

I like to be taught at home because I get more attention. For in a class there may be 40 or more children with only one person to teach them. Also if there are a lot of people in a class, each child can get only a fraction of the teacher's attention. Of course, not every pupil in a class behaves as he or she should and the teacher has to sort out fights and squabbles and make rules as to how to behave.

All this wastes time that you could be learning in. But when you are at home, there is no-one to fight with (except your Mum), no-one to queue with to get your books marked and find out what your next bit of work is. I have found, especially in maths, that some people are stuck with their sums and cannot get on without help from the teacher. It has taken me ten minutes standing waiting for my turn.

Another thing is that it is more peaceful and quiet at home because even when everyone is silent there is still a sound which you are only aware of if you have heard real silence.

Sophia Howard (aged 10)

From *Education Otherwise Newsletter*, No. 8, December 1978. Reprinted by permission of Sophia and Frances Howard.

HOW USEFUL ARE THE JUDGEMENTS OF PUPILS ABOUT SCHOOLING?

Beliefs about the usefulness of pupils' judgement of schooling are plentiful, whereas evidence is not. Investigations into the characteristics of pupil perceptions of schooling have taken place in the USA. The most systematic attempts appear to be those of Veldman and Peck (1963). The conclusion they reached was that pupil perception of teaching performance was reliable enough and valid enough in most aspects of classroom technique to be worth considering as useful feedback to teachers about their performance. The general conclusion from the limited research available is that this holds good for samples of British children (Meighan, 1974a, 1977a) although there appear to be a few technical aspects of performance, e.g. the effective use of questions and of teaching aids, where the perceptions of pupils are less reliable. 'Usefulness', however, can be interpreted in other ways. Are the perceptions useful as feedback so that performance is improved?

The impression of students who took part in research on pupils' perceptions was that it did make a difference and that they did modify or attempt to modify their classroom technique because of things that children had drawn to their attention.

Another aspect of usefulness is whether the act of consultation affects relationships. Some head teachers feared that it would lead to a deterioration, but the students reported otherwise. Several reported that they were less tense with the children concerned afterwards and, in one case, a 'difficult' group simply ceased to be difficult. Obstruction gave way to co-operation, to the surprise of both student and supervising teacher. The pupils appeared to regard someone who consulted them and took their opinions seriously as being on their side. Werthman (1963) reports some similar responses in his studies of delinquents in schools.

WHAT DO PUPILS SEE AS IDEAL?

There appears to be a high degree of consensus among pupils of all ages about the ideal teacher. The list of qualities children wish to see in their teachers is extensive:

> They should be understanding, the children say, and patient; should encourage and praise wherever possible; should listen to their pupils and give their pupils a chance to speak; should be willing to have points made against them, be humble, kind, capable of informality, and simply pleasant; should share more activities with their children than they commonly do, and should not expect all children to be always docile. They should have conscience about the captive nature of their audience; should attempt to establish links with parents; should be punctual for lessons, enthusiastic within reason; should not desert a school lightly; should recognize the importance to a child of being allowed to take the initiative in school work; and, above all, should be warm and personal.

Blishen, 1969

Copyright © Penguin Books and contributors. Reprinted by permission of Penguin Books Ltd.

Blishen goes on to say how the children saw clearly that these 'new' teachers could not operate easily in the present context of secondary schooling and that widespread changes in the organization of schools might be necessary.

The bad teacher, as defined by pupils, uses fear as a means of dominance, is extremely moody, miserable, indifferent and lazy. The study by Maizels (1970) shows a similar picture. The unfavourable references to teachers in her study were over-strictness, having favourites, being sarcastic, being moody, and over-emphasis on time-keeping. Only a few teachers were remembered as kind, sincere, keeping their promises, reliable, pleasant, full of ideas, efficient and encouraging.

The bad teacher, in the essays written on the theme of 'The School That I'd Like' (Blishen, 1969), is found guilty of remoteness, lack of sympathy and attachment to trivial rules, and fails to admit ignorance or uncertainty. Such teachers made schools unhappy places, and denied children the kind of relationship with teachers they were seeking and expressing in their view of the ideal teacher.

Teachers are a central focus in children's comments about schools, but the context in which teachers operate is also of concern. Blishen (1969) reports how children commented on various other aspects of secondary schooling. The overwhelming majority wanted mixed schools and comprehensive schools. The buildings came in for considerable negative comment: children were tired of square rooms, unimaginative decoration, desks and the lack of common rooms for pupils. Examinations were seen as a significant cause of 'constipated' teaching and distance in teachers, and alternative forms of assessment were desired. Prefects, homework, bells and religious education all received considerable scorn and alternatives for some of these were suggested. For example, religious assembly and instruction were interpreted as a form of indoctrination that represented a failure to look at a wide range of religions, philosophies and moralities. (It was six years later that a private member's bill was drafted to propose a remedy for precisely this failure! – British Humanist Association, 1975.)

The comments of the children were surprisingly sober and considered, Blishen comments, and intelligent alternatives to the status quo were presented in most cases.

DO PUPILS RECOGNIZE THE 'HIDDEN' CURRICULUM?

'The hidden curriculum' is a term used to refer to those aspects of learning in schools that are unofficial, or unintentional, or undeclared consequences of the way teaching and learning are organized and performed in schools. A later chapter looks at this concept in detail.

Jackson (1971) uses the term to describe the unofficial three R's – Rules, Routines and Regulations – that pupils must learn in order to survive comfortably and effectively in schools. Other aspects include the messages learnt from school buildings, the influence of teachers' expectations, the kind of knowledge implied by teaching techniques, the effects of different usages of language and the sex roles projected by an institution. The idea of a hidden curriculum is closely linked with the notion of labelling processes and self-fulfilling prophecies, and one consequence may be the alienation of many pupils from learning.

The responses of the children in the various studies are often reminiscent of Goffman's theory of total institutions (see Goffman, 1961), in which he analyses in detail the coercive, non-negotiable and non-consultative nature of many contemporary institutions, including armies, asylums, monasteries, hospitals and prisons.

Goffman also talks about depersonalization, and this idea is also seen by a high school pupil in the USA:

> School is like roulette or something. You can't just ask: Well, what's the point of it? The point of it is to do it, to get through and get into college. But you have to figure the system or you can't win, because the odds are all on the house's side. I guess it's a little like the real world in that way. The main thing is not to take it personal, to understand that it's just a system and it treats you like the same way it treats everybody else, like an engine or a machine or something mechanical. Our names get fed into it – we get fed into it – when we're five years old, and if we catch on and watch our step, it spits us out when we're 17 or 18, ready for college.
>
> Cited in Silberman, 1971

The effect of 'trading for grades' gradually replacing all other educational activity is described by Becker (1968), and also by the boys in the School of Barbiana:

Day in and day out they study for marks, for reports and diplomas. Languages, sciences, history – everything becomes purely pass marks. Behind those sheets of paper there is only a desire for personal gain. The diploma means money . . . you have to be a social climber at the age of twelve.

Letter to a teacher, 1970

The process of labelling and the consequence of alienation, for some pupils at least, are indicated in the above comments from pupils. Some pupils are able to recognize some aspects of the hidden curriculum. The material quoted earlier from pupils being educated at home shows an awareness of several other aspects, including 'denial, delay and interruption', key ideas in Jackson's analysis of the hidden curriculum, as outlined in Chapter 6.

CONCLUSION

Nice Strict and Nasty Strict

Your strictness is not strict (if you see what I mean). A nice strict.

Fourth year pupil

The research I conducted on pupils' views of teaching performance yielded these two categories of 'nice strict' and 'nasty strict', and they accord with the descriptions of good and bad teachers given earlier. These findings disappoint at least two audiences in education: the traditional transmission educationalists and the radical educationalists.

The traditional transmission educationalists tend to believe that pupils should not be consulted, are not competent to make judgements about schooling, and will abuse any attempts by teachers to gain their views, leading to poorer discipline, and they generally accept the spirit of 'you do not consult the clay about what kind of pot it wants to be'. The findings that pupils make sound judgements, and that relationships do not deteriorate but often improve, do not match these beliefs.

The radical educationalists tend to believe that there is a pool of untapped radical desires in the consciousness of pupils, desires for democratic relationships and autonomous situations:

Many of the pupils of the future will not accept, as many of us did and still do, the dictatorial methods of teachers who regard the classrooms as their own little despotic kingdoms.

Kohl, 1970

The findings that most pupils ask for a more kindly authoritarian situation, the 'nice strict' regime, rather than for participation, autonomy and a democratic set of relationships do not match these beliefs either.

In short, the research supports the proposition that the transmission view, as given above, is just plain wrong, and that the radical view, as given above, is a delusion. However, the study by Blishen (1969) holds a little hope for the latter view, since pupils in his sample, mostly the articulate and the highest achievers, did ask for a more participative and consultative relationship, and did ask for rather more than just 'nice strict'.

The View from the Girls

One serious limitation of the studies to date is the habit of putting boys and girls together and reporting the pupils' view of schooling. However, the evidence that school may, to some extent, present a different experience for girls has emerged. Schooling appears to be significantly sex-typed, a theme explored in Chapter 25. Other differences, like social class, skin colour and geographical region, may be other important factors as yet largely unexplored.

The Neglect of the Pupils' Viewpoint

The reasons for the neglect of the pupils' view may be related to the low power and status of both child and pupil roles, as Calvert (1975) suggests. The existing definitions of the situation appear to consider teaching as more important than learning, and the teacher's activity as more central than the pupils', despite the official rhetoric of educational writing and debate that makes claims for the pupils' welfare as the central focus. Calvert argues that this became clear after considering the politics of education. Every other group involved in education – teachers, administrators, planners, parents, employers – can obtain a better hearing for its point of view, through pressure groups or other channels, than can pupils. Moves to establish pupil pressure groups and children's rights are very recent, and often result in highly emotional, if not hysterical, responses from senior educationalists.

Apart from the low status of both child and pupil roles, the writings about education are produced largely for an audience of teachers, who have the problems of teachers as their major preoccupation. The studies of the pupils' experiences themselves are mostly directed at the teachers and their problems. Few books are written about schooling for pupils, the *Little Red Schoolbook* being one exception.

This emphasis on the teachers' views is reinforced by the apparent contradiction that the teacher needs the pupil more than the pupil needs the teacher. The teacher's position is an occupational one that requires some degree of commitment, since livelihoods are at stake. The pupil has no choice, and is not paid to pursue the role allotted, and many pupils remain uncommitted and indifferent, obtaining self-esteem in peer group and other activities. Successful performance of role can therefore be more important to a teacher than to a pupil.

For these reasons the role of pupil tends to be defined by the teacher, and the pupil's viewpoint neglected:

> Because the teacher thus defined the pupil role, he tends to see himself as the more decisive participant in the performance, and thinks of the pupil's role as more receptive than his own. Things are done by the teacher to or for the pupil, just as things are done by the doctor to or for his patient; and the pupil, like the patient, is expected to conform to the expectation thus set up for him.
>
> Calvert, 1975

In this situation, sociological studies of the pupils' view of schooling that are undertaken from perspectives other than the structural functionalist are likely to be disturbing and to yield the insights that radically question what was assumed about a familiar scene, thus producing the 'uncommon sense' referred to in the opening chapter.

SUMMARY

Although research on the point of view of the pupils is limited, there emerges a considerable degree of consensus in the general findings:

1. Primary school children tend to enjoy school, whereas secondary school children tend to be less happy with their school experiences.
2. Both 'successful' and 'unsuccessful' pupils in secondary schools record dissatisfaction. It is not just a reaction of the 'failures'.
3. The dissatisfaction appears to be marked, and not a minor feature. Only the minority of secondary schools appear to achieve even a pass mark in the eyes of the pupils.
4. The views of the pupils are not merely negative. They are sympathetic to the difficulties of teachers. They are able to offer a wide range of constructive, and mostly feasible, alternatives.
5. The perceptions of pupils show high degrees of reliability and validity.
6. The pupils' views about preferred teachers show a high degree of consensus, as do their views of 'bad' teachers.
7. Pupils are able to recognize some aspects of the hidden curriculum and some of the labelling processes, and record their feelings of alienation that result.
8. A structural functional view tends to dominate educational thinking, so investigations of the pupils' view are often seen as radical even when they are not.
9. The pupil's layer of meaning is rarely known to teachers in any systematic way, so findings are often disturbing and represent 'uncommon sense'.
10. The pupils' preference for 'nice strict' over 'nasty strict' disappoints the beliefs of both transmission educationalists and radical educationalists.
11. The experience of schooling of girls may well differ from that of boys, therefore making generalizations about the pupils' view open to question.

Further Reading

Blishen, E. (1969) *The School That I'd Like*. Harmondsworth: Penguin. One of the most readable accounts of the pupils' point of view.
Blishen, E. (1973) 'Pupils' Views of Primary Teachers. *Where?*, 84.
Blishen, E. (1973) 'Pupils' Views of Secondary Teachers'. *Where?*, 86.
Educational Review, **30**, 2. This special edition of *Educational Review* is entitled 'The Learners' Viewpoint', and it was published in 1978.
Gow, L. and McPherson, A. (1980) *Tell Them from Me*. Aberdeen: Aberdeen University Press.
Hammersley, M. and Woods, P. (eds.) (1984) *Life in School*. Milton Keynes: Open University Press.
Hughes, J. (ed.) (1984) *The Best Years: Reflections of School Leavers in the 1980s*. Aberdeen: Aberdeen University Press.
Stone, J. and Taylor, F. (1976) 'The Sad Tale of Pupils' Rights', *Where?*, 122.

Tucker, N. (1979) 'Pupils' Views of Teachers'. *Where?* 152 and *Where?* 155.
White, R. and Brockington, D. (1983) *Tales Out of School*. London: Routledge and Kegan Paul.

Discussion and Activities

1. One straightforward activity is a replication of the study by Blishen. Either write your own account or ask some pupils to write their account of the school that they would like. The findings in *The School That I'd Like* could be used as cue material in any preliminary discussion if you think this is appropriate. Northamptonshire LEA organized a consultation with pupils over the curriculum. For an account, see Makins, V. (1984) 'Giving the Customers a Say' in *Times Educational Supplement*, 23 November 1984.
2. An activity that might appeal to some readers is to research your own teaching style by getting a class to write answers to questions about classroom performance. Here are the questions used in previous research. (They could be extended or modified as thought fit.)

    (A) Preparation:
        (1) Do you think that my lessons are well prepared?
        (2) Do the lessons have enough interest for you?
        (3) Do you feel that I have organized everything well before the lessons start?
        (4) Do the lessons seem to have a pattern? (Or are they confusing?)
    (B) Presentation:
        (5) Do I speak clearly and use my voice well?
        (6) Are my explanations and instructions clear?
        (7) Do I use questions well?
        (8) Do I use teaching aids well?
    (C) Attitudes:
        (9) Do I treat you fairly?
        (10) Am I good humoured enough?
        (11) Am I too harsh or too soft with anyone?
        (12) Do I seem to be sympathetic with you?
    (D) Class management:
        (13) Am I strict enough or too strict with the class?
        (14) Is my organization of activities during the lesson sound?
        (15) Are the start and end of lessons effective?
        (16) Do I manage the time available well?

    An account of the research appears in the *British Journal of Teacher Education*, Vol. 3, No. 2.
    Note. Student teachers should make sure that their supervisors give clearance to this activity.
3. Client is an analogy. To what extent would other analogies help describe the situation of pupils? Suggestions: prisoners, partners, apprentices, slaves, conscripts, parishioners. One interesting reference might be Easthope, G. (1980) 'Curricula Are Social Processes' in Barton, L. et al. (eds.) *Schooling, Ideology and the Curriculum*, Lewes: Falmer Press.

Signposts

1. Gender
The experience of girls and their perspective may differ in some respects from that of boys. Some starting points are: Davies, L. (1984) *Pupil Power: Gender and Deviance in School*, Lewes: Falmer Press; Stanworth, M. (1983) *Gender and Schooling*, London: Hutchinson; and Weiner, G. (ed.), (1985) *Just a Bunch of Girls*, Milton Keynes: Open University Press.

2. Pupil culture
The idea that peer interaction is a crucial feature of the pupils' perspective is developed in McPherson, J. (1983) *The Feral Classroom*, London: Routledge and Kegan Paul, and in Hammersley, M. and Woods, P. (1984) *Life in School: The Sociology of Pupil Culture*, Milton Keynes: Open University Press.

3. Employment and unemployment
How pupil viewpoints are influenced is the subject of Willis, P. (1977) *Learning to Labour*, Farnborough: Saxon House; and Hughes (ed.) (1984) and Gow and McPherson (1980).

Chapter 4

Teachers as Victims?

'It is difficult to get a man to understand something when his salary depends on his not understanding it.'

Upton Sinclair

INTRODUCTION

Description and analysis in human affairs often proceed by the use of analogies, sociologists use a variety of these in their work. Each analogy presents possibilities of clarification as well as problems of distortion. The analogy of teacher as victim stresses the possibility of constraint, of limited choices, of imposed conditions of work. The distortions produced by the idea of victim include the possible conclusions that teachers are helpless victims, that constraints do not change, and that limited choices are equivalent to no choices. An analysis taking the idea of teacher as victim takes up most of this chapter, and these distortions need to be borne in mind.

ANALOGIES OF THE TEACHERS' SITUATION

Role

A common analogy in sociological writings about teachers is that of role. In common with many sociological analogies, it is derived from drama. Some analyses of this kind proceed by listing alternative roles and describing the content of each. Two basic sets of roles are often proposed, one concerned with the activities of instruction and evaluation and the other concerned with maintaining control and generally creating the conditions for learning to take place (see Hoyle, 1969). These two main roles may be broken down into sub-roles, and Hoyle gives a list of examples that include:

1. Representative of society: inculcates moral precepts.
2. Judge: gives marks and ratings.
3. Resource: possesses knowledge and skills.
4. Helper: provides guidance on pupils' difficulties.
5. Referee: settles disputes among pupils.
6. Detective: discovers rule breakers.

7.   Object of identification: possesses traits which pupils may imitate.
8.   Ego-supporter: helps pupils to develop confidence in themselves.

Another use of role theory stresses the process of performing a role with the flexibility of conduct that is required, and the complexity of managing impressions in public. (See D.H. Hargreaves, 1972.) This approach is often referred to as dramaturgical, and the writings of Goffman provide many examples. In this analogy, social life is seen as an elaborate form of drama requiring that people project a convincing image of themselves to their audiences. Therefore a key idea here is that of the presentation of self, which is indeed the title of one of Goffman's books. But this analogy, too, has limitations. The teacher lacks a well-developed script and has an unchanging audience, whereas actors in theatres commonly have both a full script and a succession of new audiences:

> Unlike the actor on the stage, however, the teacher has not been given an exciting script written by a great dramatist. He has not been given the benefit of make-up and costumery, and he has the additional handicap of having to appear before young people day after day after day in a setting which does not have the aesthetic enhancements that most good theatres possess.
>
> E. King, 1973

Cultural Worker

An analogy from the world of work is that of cultural worker. The worker is envisaged as someone who works to the designs of others: the bricklayer follows the architect's plan, the car assembler works to the specification of the designers, and the navvy moves earth according to the maps produced by others. The cultural workers, whether they be teachers, journalists, artists or civil servants, are seen as people who reproduce culture in the form of language, values, attitudes, images, rules and information. They are seen as perpetuators rather than innovators, and their task is to reproduce the cultural apparatus to the design of others. C. Wright Mills argues that the cultural apparatus is composed of all the organizations in which artistic, intellectual or scientific work goes on and therefore involves a complex set of institutions including schools, theatres, newspapers, studios, laboratories, museums and magazines.

> Inside this apparatus, standing between men and events, the images, meanings, slogans that define the worlds in which men live are organized and compared, maintained and revised, lost and cherished, hidden, debunked, celebrated. Taken as a whole, the cultural apparatus is the lens of mankind through which men see; the medium by which they interpret and report what they see.
>
> Wright Mills, 1959

Wright Mills sees a strong likelihood that cultural workers will be in co-operation with the ruling group not least because of the prestige that this ensures. Association with authority lends increased importance to the work.

This analogy of cultural worker has limitations when applied to teachers. Not least of these is over-generalization. Some teachers innovate, some marginally, some more radically: some change does occur from within schools. The autonomy of teachers may be overstated, but it can also be understated, and an analogy interpreting teaching as solely technical, as the activity of a cultural worker and nothing more, runs this risk.

A further limitation is that the analogy of cultural worker may distract attention from the contradictions of the teaching task; e.g. teachers are expected both to preserve the cultural status quo *and* to produce innovators who will develop new technologies, new industries, new sources of wealth and other fresh cultural ideas.

Other Analogies

The analogies of teacher as victim, the role of the teacher and teacher as cultural worker do not exhaust the possibilities. Other analogies that occur in sociological and educational writings from time to time include the teacher as a control agent, acting as a kind of police officer or prison officer. Other analogies may stress the manipulative task of teaching, seeing teachers as technicians of an educational production line, or potters moulding human material, or gardeners tending young human stock. An alternative occupational comparison is that of a profession.

These analogies have several drawbacks, including the tendency to over-simplify by selecting one aspect of the complex task of teaching and thus being incapable of describing the diversity of actions and outcomes. They also share some of the limitations of the other analogies mentioned earlier, e.g. a strong tendency to overlook the contradictory nature of teaching actions.

A more complex analogy that has been used recently is that of scripts. Scripts appear both in music, as musical scores, and in drama, as play scripts, but a more modern version is that of the television script. The analogy of scripts may prove to be useful in the case of teaching if it extends the idea of role. Roles are seen as linked in a script which defines the setting, the action, varying audiences both in the studio and outside in their homes. The script also has a history behind it, exists alongside alternative scripts, and is subject to various kinds of scrutiny as regards its suitability. The teacher may be seen as appearing in a variety of roles, including producer, actor-producer, producer-manager, or director. At the end of this chapter you will be invited to use this analogy as a descriptive and analytical idea.

SOCIOLOGICAL QUESTIONS ABOUT TEACHERS

The questions asked in a sociological approach were discussed in a previous chapter. If we insert 'teachers' into one of the sets of questions given, it reads as follows. 'What varieties of teachers now prevail in this society and in this period?' 'And what varieties of teachers are coming to prevail?' 'In what ways are teachers selected and formed, liberated and repressed, made sensitive and blunted?'

One way of assembling some ideas and evidence about this set of questions is to adopt a biographical approach, to follow the experience of a teacher taking up an appointment at a school. The experiences of a student teacher starting a teaching practice would provide many similar features. Since few teachers are involved in designing and setting up a new school, the situation encountered is that of an assorted kit of items chosen and designed by others. The quality of the thinking behind this package is outside the control of the incoming teacher, and it may be resistant to change:

each social situation in which we find ourselves is not only defined by our contemporaries but predefined by our predecessors. Since one cannot possibly talk back to one's ancestors, their ill-conceived constructions are commonly more difficult to get rid of than those built in our own lifetime.

Berger. 1963

The situation facing the person in a new appointment can be described in various ways. It is a ready-made set of recipes; it is an existing perspective; it is a cultural world presented to the stranger; it is a kit of ideas issued to the new recruit. Whichever analogy is used, there is a complex of features involved. What follows is a catalogue of features, each briefly illustrated. A fuller treatment of each of these features will be given in later chapters. The analogy in use here is that of the teacher as victim.

THE TEACHER AS VICTIM

School Buildings

Kohl reports how teachers in his seminars drew or wrote about school. The drawings were dominated by boxes represening rooms, papers, books, tables and buildings. Memories of school were predominantly rectangular.

It is no accident that spatial memories are strong. The placement of objects in space is not arbitrary and rooms represent in physical form the spirit and souls of places and institutions. A teacher's room tells us something about who he is and a great deal about what he is doing.

Kohl, 1970

The spaces provided by architects tend to be permanent and may well outlast the beliefs about education that underpinned the design instruction. To an incoming teacher, the arrangement of rooms, corridors, furniture, display areas and specialized facilities, e.g. a library or a hall, is of interest in at least three ways:

1. It suggests possibilities and opportunities for teaching and learning.
2. It places constraints on what can happen for whatever spatial layout is met; some teaching and learning possibilities are eliminated or made very difficult.
3. It implies an ideology of education, i.e. a pattern of assumptions about knowledge, teaching, learning, relationships, organization, assessment and resources. One such pattern might be that school knowledge is best regarded as different subjects, that teaching is essentially instructing, that learning is essentially absorbing the information and ideas of the teacher, that relationships are authoritarian, that organization is into groups of about 30 learners called a class, that assessment is the judging of written end-products and that appropriate resources are books, written by teacher-commentators, called textbooks. A building designed with these assumptions in mind presents problems to an incoming teacher who does not accept one of these propositions and severe difficulties to one who rejects the whole set. One interesting account of how a teacher dealt with his 'open' ideology of education in a 'closed' building and situation is H. Kohl's *The Open Classroom* but, for the most part, teachers can be seen as victims of the building design.

Figure 4.1 (a) The traditional layout of a public school headmaster's study. (b) Full frontal confrontation, the most common arrangement. (c) Ideal for the authoritarian; the visitor is left isolated in space. (d) The less authoritarian favour this arrangement; an open door is desirable. (e) A 'modern' headmaster may favour the informality of soft chairs around a coffee table. This first appeared in *New Society*, London, 24 October 1974, the weekly review of the social sciences.

The Head Teacher

Head teachers may be regarded as victims too: they also receive a building, usually handed on from predecessors. They also receive, without much power of negotiation, many of the other features listed later, e.g. the external examination system. In C. Wright Mills's analogy, the head teachers are the *foremen* cultural workers, controlling those in their charge to some extent, but in turn controlled by others. However, in exercising their control over the particular schools in their charge, they have power to vary the regimes in various ways, e.g. by keeping power, or by delegating, or by democratizing.

Some strong clues may be present in the head teacher's room layout, although these are, of course, only clues, and not conclusive evidence. In a democratized regime the head teacher may not even have a room, if the decision of the school senate was that no room was necessary for this purpose. A decision of this kind was made by the Countesthorpe Community College in 1970, although later the decision was revised.

Research by K. Evans (1974a) suggests that varying patterns of head teachers' room arrangement may be found representing degrees of authoritarianism. In Figure 4.1(e) the most 'modern' head teachers, in the words of Evans, 'relegate their bureaucratic function to the wall'. The head teacher rotates towards the centre of the room in a swivel chair, and can arrange more democratic or consultative groupings around a coffee table if desired. But the layouts of most head teachers' rooms are of the other four kinds. The language of the arrangement and the objects in the room are authoritarian rather than consultative or democratic. Evans comments that these various layouts bear little relation to the practicalities of sources of light and heat, but are related to the way head teachers wish to present themselves and manage relationships. Teachers have little control over the head teachers' choices of regime and therefore can be victims of a particular head teacher's ideology of education.

The Timetable

Sooner or later the new teacher will be given a timetable. In a primary school this could be flexible. Certain fixed periods of time in a week might be labelled as assemblies, physical education, games or music, and the rest would be at the discretion of the teacher, provided that certain activities, such as reading, writing and mathematics, appeared regularly.

In a secondary school the 'cultural worker' interpretation is more clearly made, since decisions about which groups meet with a given teacher in which places, for how long, and how often are usually presented to the staff and are open to only minimal negotiation.

The Organization

Underpinning the timetable there are many organization decisions also presented to a new teacher for largely unquestioning acceptance. The actual size of classes will depend upon decisions about how many senior staff need to be free for administrative tasks. The composition of classes will depend on whether the organization is a 'streaming by achievement' system, a mixed achievement grouping system, grouping for subjects by sex, or some mixture of these. Age grouping by years is a common feature of such plans.

Other organizational decisions to be accepted may include rules, punishments, dress, break times, house systems and midday meal arrangements.

The Curriculum

The decisions about the content of the curriculum vary in scope, and several levels of decision can be described. The new teacher will be presented with a range of these decisions and those at the most general level are usually the least negotiable. Thus a teacher may feel that compulsory religious education is a dubious idea, but since it is required by law, no negotiation is possible.

Second, within the school, decisions will have been taken about whether the curriculum should differ for boys and for girls. The incoming teacher may feel that boys should be as versed in domestic science as girls or, conversely, that they should not. Whichever way the decision has gone, it will be presented for acceptance by the new staff member.

At another level of decision making, the curriculum may exclude some subjects. The incoming teacher might be a social science graduate, but find that the social sciences are absent from the curriculum, and that the post offered is in English, History, or some other subject.

Within each area of the curriculum, decisions are likely to have been made about the syllabus, and about the appropriate external examination where this applies. This provides a useful example of the effect of the thinking of predecessors, since cohorts of children will already have experienced some years of the prescribed syllabus, making any changes difficult to implement and usually taking several years to phase in.

Therefore, in the area of the curriculum alone, the teacher may be presented with a wide range of ready-made practices to accept, with the expectation that they will be perpetuated. The analogy of the incoming teacher as a victim of circumstances therefore begins to gain plausibility.

Assessment

In a previous chapter the wide range of possibilities in assessment was outlined and the frequent selection of certain kinds of assessment of a limited nature was indicated. The incoming teacher to a primary school may not believe in giving marks of a norm-referencing kind, where pupils are compared with one another in performance, but may prefer to mark pupils against their own personal performance on a 1–3 system, where 1 means worse than the pupil's last work, 2 is as good as the last effort, and 3 is an improvement on the previous performance. Yet the end-of-session report may insist on class positions because that is the assessment system operating throughout the school.

The system of assessing reading progress against a set reading scheme may be preferred to a teaching and assessment programme based on children's conversations and the writing of their own reading books and materials.

In a secondary school, an incoming teacher may not believe in the norm-referenced system of automatically failing a set percentage of pupils, but nevertheless may be required to prepare the classes for an external examination based on just such a 'rationing of success' assumption.

Resources Available

The incoming teacher may find that the school has a fully operational resources centre with well-developed retrieval, storage and indexing facilities for multi-media resources, a reprographic system and an equipment store with booking facilities. However, the teacher concerned may not believe in such a 'luxury' approach, preferring a 'no-nonsense, textbook-based system'. Alternatively, a teacher trained to use a resources centre may encounter a school with stockrooms filled only with textbooks.

In a less extreme situation, it may be that the range of resources is more limited than a particular teacher might wish: the carefully accumulated overhead-projector transparencies may prove useless if the school has no suitable equipment. Or the reading scheme used by the school may be just the one the teacher has come to regard as a hindrance. Or, if the school has modern maths textbooks, whereas the teacher trusts only traditional maths, the resources presented create problems. The possibilities of a mismatch between the kit of resources awaiting teachers and their personal preferences are considerable. In all cases the teacher has to accept, for some time at least, the resources based on decisions made by others and become, in some cases, an unwilling victim of circumstances.

Teaching Methods

The resources available imply a pedagogy: these teaching methods may also present problems of a mismatch between the school's existing recipes and the incoming teacher's beliefs and preferences. Thus a teacher who believes in having a class of children working from a standard textbook may be alarmed to find that the stock cupboard contains sets of five or six textbooks of varying kinds because the previous teacher believed in a group work system where pupils compared several textbooks in a research-based pedagogy. The writer had such an experience when this approach was so foreign to the views of the incoming teacher that he concluded that the pupils had stolen from the full sets available until only a small number of each remained.

Teachers who are used to an interpretation theory of teaching, which stresses dialogue with pupils, discussion and research-based written work, may encounter a school that has a transmission view, which stresses listening to the teacher and taking dictated notes. The pupils may quickly tell the teacher what they have learnt – that 'real' work is not discussion or research, but taking down notes from an 'expert' teacher.

Expectations of the Clients

The analogy of client presents problems in the case of teaching. Teachers appear to have multiple clients, including parents, employers and the pupils themselves. In addition, there are other sets of expectations to be considered: the head teacher's, those of colleagues, and those of inspectors from the Local Education Authority and the Department of Education and Science. (A student on teaching practice also has the tutor to consider.) The initial allocation of clients is not within a teacher's control. Like priests and prostitutes, they have little say in whom they serve.

As was indicated previously (Chapter 3), the expectations of pupils show a high degree of consensus: the 'nice strict' teacher is preferred to the 'nasty strict' teacher. In the cases of parents and of employers, there appears to be less consistency. For example, it is commonly asserted that the basic requirements of employers as regards Maths and English are not being met, yet studies of employers' wishes show only limited agreement on these basic requirements (see Fitzgerald, 1976).

Whatever the particular features of these varying expectations of parents, pupils and employers, as well as the other people involved, they confront the incoming teacher, and the expectation is usually that they be accepted and accommodated.

Aims, Objectives and Outcomes

Since the objectives of education have been listed in impressive taxonomies, their quantity is known to be considerable: Bloom's *Taxonomy of Educational Objectives* fills three books. It is no surprise, therefore, to find that schools vary in the priority they place on their aims, objectives and outcomes. The aims may include:

1. Preparation for society as it is currently.
2. Preparation to perpetuate the way it is currently organized.
3. Preparation to change society through research and innovation.
4. Preparation to adapt to changes that occur in an uncertain future.
5. Preparation for personal development.
6. Preparation for the needs of the economy as a worker.
7. Preparation for life as a consumer.
8. Preparation for leisure.

Incoming teachers may find that the particular selection and the priorities already established in the school are not the same as their own preferences. The action required is likely to be the same as with the other parts of the 'kit' presented to the newcomer, i.e. accept and adjust.

CONCLUSION

This analysis based on the analogy of the teacher as victim may be used to stress an important sociological finding: that individual items in a network of influences may seem trivial if taken alone; it is the *cumulative effect* of such a network of influences that is significant.

The incoming teacher may have to accept a timetable: this seems to be trivial. And also the head teacher's theory of education may have to be accommodated: still relatively trivial perhaps. But the newcomer also has to accept the particular organizational decisions, the building and furniture, the curriculum of the school, the assessment system adopted, the particular resources available, the approved pedagogy established in the school, the particular expectations of the clients and others, and the selection of aims, objectives and outcomes (with their established order of priorities).

Thus the analogy of victim does not seem too far-fetched when the cumulative effect of all these features is totalled.

However, this chapter began with a caution about the use of analogies: the limitations of the idea of teacher as victim need to be considered in order to establish its usefulness. Furthermore, the contradictions that occur in such a complex network of influences may provide scope for either variation or change (see Grace, 1978).

SUMMARY

1. Description and analysis in sociology often proceed by the use of analogies.
2. Analogies can clarify, but can also distort.
3. Many analogies in sociology are derived from drama: one example is that of the teacher as role player.
4. An analogy from the world of work is that of the teacher as a cultural worker who perpetuates the cultural apparatus to the designs of others, rather than innovating.
5. Teaching is seen as analogous to other occupations – police officer, technician and professional.
6. The analogy of teacher as victim gains plausibility if we list the kit of ideas given to a new teacher. This kit is made up of a given set of buildings, a head teacher who has a particular ideology of education, a timetable, an organizational style, a curriculum, an assessment system, a set of resources, an expected teaching method, the expectations of various clients, and a set of aims, objectives and outcomes.
7. The cumulative effect of a network of influences may be considerable, whereas individual items within a network may appear to be trivial when considered singly. This constitutes an important contribution of sociology to the understanding of social situations.

Further Reading

Barton, L. and Walker, S. (eds.) (1981) *Schools, Teachers and Teaching*. Lewes: Falmer Press.

Etzioni, A. (1969) *Th Semi-Professions and their Organization*. West Drayton: Collier Macmillan. An analysis of teaching as a semi-profession.

Hammersley, M. (1977) *The Social Location of Teacher Perspectives*, Milton Keynes: Open University Press. An analysis of teaching as a profession. Section 4 is particularly relevant.

Hanson, D. and Herrington, M. (1976) *From College to Classroom*. London: Routledge and Kegan Paul. Contains an interesting account of a new teacher being the victim of the head teacher's ideology of education (pp. 44–52).

Hoyle, E. (1969) *The Role of the Teacher*. London: Routledge and Kegan Paul. The analogy of teacher as role player is the subject of this book.

King, E. (1973) 'The Presentation of Self in the Classroom', *Educational Review*, **25**, 3. The ideas of Goffman on the role of the teacher are the subject of this article.

Kohl, H. (1970) *The Open Classroom*. London: Methuen. An account of one teacher who refuses to be a helpless victim.

Toogood, P. (1984) *The Head's Tale*. Telford: Dialogue Publications. A head teacher resigns rather than be a victim of LEA policy.

Discussion and Activities

1. The analogy of scripts was introduced in this chapter. Give an account of teacher behaviour using this idea. Are teachers both actors and scriptwriters?
2. Describe your teaching practice in terms of the teacher as victim, or interview someone who has just experienced a final teaching practice.
3. Is the analogy of victim more applicable to secondary school teachers than the primary school situation?

Signposts

1. Conflict theory
From a conflict theory point of view, professions can be seen as interest groups protecting their members' privileges, rather than as groups operating a service-to-others ethic. A source on this approach is Johnson, T.J. (1972) *Professions and Power*, London: Macmillan. See also Lawn, M. (ed.) (1985) *The Politics of Teacher Unionism*, Beckenham: Croom Helm.

2. Bureaucratic settings
The traditional image of a professional is that of a person working alone to an ethical code of the occupation. What are the consequences of having professionals working in large bureaucratic organizations with rule systems and hierarchies with chains of command? A starting point is Ozga, J. and Lawn, M. (1981) *Teachers, Professionalism and Class: A Study of Organized Teachers*, Lewes: Falmer Press.

3. Influence systems
What influences teachers most? And what has least effect? One study is Taylor, P.H.T. et al. (1974) *Purpose, Power and Constraint in the Primary School Curriculum*, London: Macmillan.

4. Change
What changes in the activity of teachers can be expected? Several writers have addressed this issue, e.g. Wragg, T. (1984) 'Education for the Twenty-First Century' in Harber, C. et al. (eds.) *Alternative Educational Futures*, London: Holt, Rinehart and Winston.

Chapter 5

Parents as Educators?

'All I ask of parents is that they should bring it to school clean and well-dressed . . . I shall do the rest.'

Primary school headteacher

INTRODUCTION

The concept of layers of meaning links the chapters of this first section. It draws to our attention the notion that there is no one agreed or true picture of a complex institution like a school. From the pupils' perspective, school looks different from either that of the teachers' or the parents' viewpoints. Moreover, each layer of meaning is segmented, e.g. teachers vary in their ideologies of education, parents vary in their social-class identities and pupils vary in their interpretations of the experience of schooling. Each layer of meaning turns out to be a rather loose identity that accrues to the participants initially by force of circumstance – that of being a five-year-old child in the UK rather than any other European country, or that of being appointed to the staff of a particular school at a particular era, or that of a parent living in a particular catchment area under a given political administration.

'SUCCESSFUL' PARENTS

The report of the Plowden Committee (1967), *Children and Their Primary Schools*, confirmed the findings of research studies undertaken in the previous 20 years or so that there was a statistically significant association between parental interest and encouragement of their children at school and educational performance in academic tasks. Whether performance was better where parents encourage or whether parents encourage where performance is notable, was not clear. (Statistical associations are, after all, only clues: there is a high correlation between bed and death since so many people die there. From this it does not follow that bed is so dangerous that it should be avoided.) The committee gave the interpretation that it was very likely a matter of continuous interaction rather than a one way causal effect.

The nature of such parental interest is not necessarily kindly. Musgrove (1966), summarizing research on the 'good' home as regards academic success, proposed that it was small, had ambitious parents, the father was at least a skilled manual worker and, in the case of a working-class home, the mother would have middle-class origins. (The problems associated with such a general social-class dichotomy are taken up in a later chapter.) The father could be ineffectual or even feckless but one parent has to be demanding as regards school attainment. Musgrove concludes:

> Relationships in the home are emotionally bleak. The family is unstable and has moved often; the mother goes out to work. The children grow up to be rather withdrawn and solitary, conscientious and given to self-blame. They are 'good grammar school material'.

In the view of Musgrove this does not present too attractive a picture: ruthless, demanding relationships lacking in warmth, and a view that happiness is almost an irrelevance lead him to observe that

> Neither humanity nor common sense seem to pay the highest dividends in the education system and social order which we have devised.

The American writer Eldridge Cleaver proposes that either you are part of the problem or you are part of the solution. Parents, homes and families are often presented to teachers in training as part of the problem, and this view tends to be confirmed by the behaviour and attitudes of experienced teachers. The process involved is identified in a study by Sharp and Green (1975). Much of the information about parents and homes is gained second-hand and then filtered through the concept of a 'good parent'.

'GOOD' AND 'BAD' PARENTS

In the study of primary schooling by Sharp and Green, four key dimensions of the 'good parent' role, as defined by the school, were identified.

1. The good parent needs to be knowledgeable about the way the school operates and its ideology of education.
2. There must be a strong interest in the education of their children and a motivation for them to succeed.
3. The parent has to be capable of cueing into the teachers' interpretation schemes, in particular the teachers' definition of 'the good parent'.
4. The parent has to be good at impression management and must be both willing and able to play up to the teachers' view of the 'good parent'.

The more any of these dimensions is missing, Sharp and Green proposed, the more likely it is that the relationship with the school will become negative and the label of 'bad parent' become affixed.

In the case of the first dimension of knowledgeability, the gathering of reliable information is not always an easy task. Visits to school-organized meetings, gleaning impressions from children, clues from the work brought home, talking with other parents – these were some of the methods available. Parents can occupy various stages of confusion about the school as a result; the more confused a parent, the less likely it was that dialogues with school staff would proceed smoothly and unambiguously. The variation amongst teachers regarding ideologies of education outlined in the previous chapter increases the difficulty of the task.

As regards the second dimension, there were differences amongst the parents as to their view of education. Almost all those in the Sharp and Green study registered interest but of different kinds. All appeared to regard reading, writing and numeracy as important, some supported a broader conception of education that valued an extended curriculum of creative and artistic activities, provided the three R's were dealt with, and a minority had the personal happiness of their children as the top priority above instrumental concerns. Because of these variations, some parents would connect with the teachers' view in play in a particular school more than others. Parents' interest relates to their particular view of education and how well they think the school actually works for and achieves this. Interest is developed in interaction between homes and schools, not a fixed trait possessed or not possessed at the outset. The allegiances of various groups of parents are there to be won or lost.

Reading the teachers' view of a 'good parent' was the crucial part of the third dimension of the task before the parents. Sharp and Green concluded that this required a stance of deference to the teachers' claim of superior knowledge, expertise and competence, trust in the teachers' judgement, and support for the teachers' definition of the situation. Parents vary in their effectiveness in this activity. Some are unsuccessful in the initial collecting of information about the school and misinterpretation results. Others may read the ideology of education of teachers and reject it, and so refuse to give the required deference. They fail in the fourth dimension of playing up to the teachers' definition of the 'good parent'. Through impression management the 'good parent' convinces the teachers that he or she is in unison with them. The 'good parent' does not actually have to be knowledgeable about the school or really interested in the education provided, or genuinely defer to the teachers. They only have to convince the teachers by their role playing skills that this is the case. Functional hypocrisy is sufficient and *necessary* since if the parents actually did no more than really leave everything to the activity of the teachers, then their children would be at risk. Not that the impression management is one-sided however, since teachers are involved in elaborate pretensions that all is well with the school in parents' evenings and school reports.

The successful parents in terms of having their children successful at school, avoid the label of interferers whilst actually interfering persistently. They pretend to meet the definition of 'good parent' by not interfering, by not teaching their children at home, by not helping them to read, write and develop numeracy, whilst they actually do all these things and also teach their children to act discreetly at school by not letting on.

There are illustrations of the irony of human action here. If the parents did follow the teachers' definition of 'good parent', their children are less likely to succeed. A further irony is that the school staff think they, by their teaching, make the difference in developing children well or otherwise, whereas Sharp and Green argue the crucial factor is the activity or lack of it on the part of the parents – how good they are as behind-the-scenes educators. There is more irony yet:

> Additional irony – those parents who are most in favour at the school are usually those who, amongst other things, appear by their actions in consistently teaching their children to read etc., most critical of it.
>
> Sharp and Green, 1975

One of the features that connects here is that of social class. If we ignore for the moment the problems of oversimplification implicit in the division into middle class (white-collar occupations) and working class (blue-collar occupations), we can take up a point that Sharp and Green make that middle-class parents are more likely to have the impression-management skills since they are in the repertoire of so many white-collar occupations, ranging from lawyers, who have to pretend that they believe a client to be guiltless, to a bank clerk, who has to fake pleasantness to obnoxious customers.

Part of the explanation for this state of affairs is political. In the schooling system in the UK, parents have been relatively low in terms of power. Even those happy with a school did not set the terms of the bargain but accepted them and manipulated them to their advantage. And if the parents are to some extent victims of the schools, pupils can be victims of both, being required to please teachers and please parents within a complex network of impression management which:

> may depend as much on mutual deception and misunderstanding as on a genuine communality of meaning.
>
> Sharp and Green, 1975

ALTERNATIVE VIEWS OF THE 'GOOD PARENT'

Alternative views of the role of good parent exist. One teacher in a reading workshop project that involved parents as educational helpers comments on the progress of a particular child:

> He's come on in leaps and bounds. He's very confident. I'm surprised at how he's come on – I couldn't have done it without his mum – it's a reading workshop success.
>
> Weinburger, 1983

The definition of 'good parent' can vary with country. The Home School Movement, as a voluntary organization, occupies a modest place in the Swedish schooling system, but its goals are widely accepted: that the care of children is everybody's business; that homes, schools and society should work together to create a safe and enriching environment for growing up; that all people concerned strengthen their sense of community and find common interest in their local school and the immediate environment. Parents are encouraged, in the words of their brochure, to do the following:

- Care about the everyday work in the class; visit the class, take part in the child's work and the teaching materials, talk about school with them, read books and watch TV together.
- Contact the teachers and other personnel in the school when you feel it's necessary. Attend private conferences and class meetings.
- Get in on preparations for and the execution of activities such as field trips, project work and encampments, etc.
- Take care of the class if the teacher must be away temporarily during the school day.
- Volunteer to come to class, when it's appropriate, and tell about your job or something else that interests you.
- Get to know your own child's friends and their parents, meet them in your free time, at home or outdoors, children and adults together.
- Help out if your child's friends or their parents are having difficulties just now.
- Have the students present when class meetings are planned and held.
- Whenever you're in class think of things which can be improved upon or what ways we parents and students could help.
- Volunteer yourself as a leader for children's and teenagers' free time activities.
- Try to get your colleagues at work to be interested in the schools.

That several of these ideas would usually get a defensive reaction from most school teachers in the UK is perhaps some measure of the differences in the dominant educational vision between the two countries.

PARENTS' CURRENT ACTIVITY AS TEACHERS

The title of this chapter implies that parents may increasingly come to be seen as having a teaching role, but this proposition disguises the characteristics of the current situation and obscures the range of existing parental activity. This existing activity is of several kinds.

Pre-school Activity

The education of children for the first five years of their lives is largely in the hands of parents. Pre-school educators have tended to develop a policy of working in partnership with parents rather than being in *in loco parentis*. Pre-school education of this kind, including pre-school enrichment projects and play group schemes, does not assume that parents are automatically competent teachers, but that given support, advice and guidance, they frequently become so.

One project that indicates the possibilities has been developed in Sandwell in the West Midlands. The Child Psychology Service, directed by T.A. Kelly, established a parental involvement in primary education project to help parents to increase their skills in helping the development of their young children. Sixteen schools were involved with a staff of four specially trained teachers whose task was to visit the homes of parents. These parents had older children in school who had been identified by a testing programme as failing to realize their potential and who also had younger siblings presumed to be equally at risk. The visits occurred weekly over a long period of time, up to five years in some cases, and attempted to establish relationships of mutual trust, to take equipment and toys and to provide advice, guidance and discussion about the pre-school education of the young children concerned. The results have proved encouraging in that most of the children involved have produced higher test results than the 'contact' child when admitted to school. There have also been reported improvements in the learning attitudes and achievement of most of the 'contact' children as well (Stevens, 1984).

Families that had previously been overwhelmed with difficulties have discovered new resources within themselves to improve, to maintain their improvement and finally to cope independently. The relationship built up over time with the mothers, and also fathers (since unemployment is high in the area), through the weekly visit is seen as a crucial factor:

> These mothers, many of whom have given up in most areas of their lives, who constantly underachieve because they have no self-respect or motivation, now find themselves in a situation where:
>
> (a) Someone offers them a way to achieve.
> (b) Offers them motivation.

(c) Offers them example – friendship, support, but never interference.
(d) Offers them praise when they succeed and further encouragement when they fail.
(e) Offers them consistency and an element of order and routine in which to operate (one weekly visit – same time – same day, etc.). Shows them that somebody cares very much what happens to them and their family.
(f) Is often able to liaise on their behalf with other professional agencies with whom previous contact might have been inhibited or inadequate.
(g) On a more material level, is in a situation to help with distribution of appropriate clothing and furniture – prams, cots, etc., between the network of families visited who all require certain material equipment at different stages of their child's development and then find it convenient to pass on or swop.

Stevens, 1984

Similar findings are recorded in a larger project based in Coventry and based on the Community Education Development Centre (Widlake and Macleod, 1984). Encouraging parents, mostly from working-class backgrounds, to help with reading, language activities and other support raised standards as the testing programme clearly demonstrated.

Projects Involving Parents as Teachers

It is an interesting question as to why only a few educators seem to regard parents as a resource. A common factor in conversations I have had with such educators is that they are both parents and teachers and have observed many limitations in what schools were achieving with their own children. They therefore devised strategies to remedy these limitations. It is then but a short step to advising other parents who are friends but not teachers, and an even shorter step to seeing scope in the idea generally.

Sociological research findings related to social class play a part here. Studies of the superior formal school achievements of the middle classes have indicated that the home support given to children varies in *technique* rather than in motive (Jones, 1966). In both the middle classes as a whole and the working classes as a whole, the range of motives is rather similar. The majority desire that their children succeed at school, whilst another group is ambiguous in outlook and a small number rather opposed to school. The middle-class parents, some of whom are teachers anyway, are able to turn their desire into reality by appropriate techniques and in displaying the confidence to carry off the surreptitious teaching of reading, writing and arithmetic referred to earlier, as well as exploiting holidays, weekends and television viewing as sources of general knowledge and discussion. One of the achievements of the play-group movement has been to pass on techniques to parents who previously lacked them.

In the USA the work of Dorothy Rich has been notable in using parents as teachers (Cookson, 1979). Her experience fits the profile outlined above. Her home learning methods evolved as she brought up her own daughters, and she introduced them into her teaching training activities at Trinity College, Washington. Out of this experience she developed the Home and School Institute. For some fifteen years now she has run workshops and courses, producing written advice notes on specific techniques or 'recipes' that give parents clear straightforward instructions for using domestic items (e.g. refuse), and experiences, such as visits to the supermarket, to help children acquire and develop skills in reading, writing and arithmetic as well as other learning habits.

Many middle-class parents recognized these 'recipes' as things they were already doing but could improve. They were welcomed by many working-class parents as being the missing techniques they were in need of. To try to cope with the anticipated and actual hostility of many teachers, the 'recipes' concentrated on items and experiences more likely to be found associated with homes than with schools so as to maintain a demarcation line: parents were to be seen as complementing rather than rivalling the school.

Some schools in the USA have adopted the Rich 'recipes' in a variety of ways (Cookson, 1979). One use is in remedial teaching. Thus at Damascus Elementary School in Maryland, parents with children having learning difficulties were persuaded to work with the recipes at home four nights a week for a year. The wary parents found that the results paid off, since nine out of thirteen children avoided the repetition of the first-grade year that had been envisaged for them.

The remedial aspects have also been the subject of a project in Birmingham in Britain. Glynn (1980) introduced a remedial reading tutoring programme to the parents of four 10-year-old boys with reading problems. Marked improvements in the boys' reading skills as well as in the parents' skills of helping were recorded over as short a period as three months. Glynn had developed his ideas in New Zealand schools and the project results in the UK confirm the successes he had recorded in Auckland. Work by Hewison and Tizard (1980) in the UK has shown similar results.

The idea of involving parents in children's reading has been increasingly welcomed in the case of UK primary schools. The Haringey Project based on an inner-city area in London was monitored by Tizard, Schofield and Hewison (1982). Hewison concludes that the project:

> demonstrated that most parents are willing as well as able to help their children with reading

and that as a result the children concerned benefited compared with children lacking such help (see also Griffiths and Hamilton, 1985).

The Belfield Project, Rochdale, shows similar results (Wilby, 1981). The Fox Hill Reading Workshop, Sheffield, is the subject of another report (Weinburger, 1983), and apart from confirming the findings of the other projects, it demonstrated how both teachers and parents learnt from the experience. A parent commented that 'I understand better what a teacher has to cope with having to teach children', and a teacher approving of the work of the parents states, 'They could have done all this before, but we didn't know'. In all the projects the reading standards are shown to improve.

In the case of children defined as having special educational needs, the Portage Scheme, first set up in Wisconsin USA in 1969, set out to teach parents to teach their children at home with the aid of a home-visiting teacher. The Portage Scheme has been adopted at Winchester and South Glamorgan in Britain, and the conclusion is that this approach has helped parents to be effective in teaching their handicapped children using an agreed system and to record the progress made:

> The Portage model recognises that children gain most from education when parents are closely involved in the teaching. Until now professionals trying to help severely handicap-

ped children have often looked for service improvements outside the home, e.g. smaller classes, purpose-built centres, increasingly complicated teaching aids and teaching methods, etc. Perhaps the most valuable resource of all has been left at home preparing tea for a returning child!

Cameron, 1984

Another project that ignored the demarcation line between home and school was the Parkway Programme, Philadelphia, where, amongst various radical aspects, only half the teaching was undertaken by teaching staff. The other teaching was performed by members of the community, many of them parents, who were recruited to match the declared interests of the students. Thus student requests to study psychology might lead to the recruitment of a local psychologist willing to take the class. This procedure of drawing course teachers from non-teacher trained members of the community is commonplace in Further Education and Evening Institutes but rare in schools.

One project with nearly a hundred years' experience of parents as educators is the World-Wide Education Service (WES) of the Parents' National Education Union, which was founded in the 1880s by Charlotte Mason. WES has concentrated on helping expatriate families in about a hundred countries to educate their children as an alternative to sending them to boarding school, but it also makes its service available to parents educating their children at home in the UK. The WES system provides guidance and training for the parents as an integral part of the course. One former WES pupil became chair-person of the Birmingham Education Committee and ultimately MP for Handsworth, Birmingham (see Boulter, 1984).

Education Otherwise

The role of the parents as educators becomes total where they decide to take up their option in law to educate 'otherwise than at school'. The organization Education Otherwise was set up in 1977 as a mutual aid venture by the small minority of parents who had decided to undertake home-based education.

The equivalent organization in the USA, Growing Without Schooling, was set up at about the same time. The motives of *some* of these parents were based on genuinely held and articulated principles and their reaction to what they saw as some harmful effects to mass schooling as documented in the writings of the so-called 'deschoolers', and more recently, in Hemming's work (1980). However, the majority appear to be simply desperate because their children are so unhappy at school, or are achieving little, or are both unhappy and achieving little (Meighan, 1984). The members of the non-achieving group often express a desire for links with local schools in some cooperative partnership or Flexischooling arrangement. Although this has happened in parts of the USA, few cases of British schools agreeing to this are known to the writer. Polarization is forced on such parents by LEAs who insist on *either* school *or* home education, but allow no cooperative partnerships. The nearest arrangement to a cooperative partnership that has been established so far appears to be that of super-vision by the Home Tuition section of an LEA.

Parents who survive the various inquisitions of the school, the LEA inspectors and the School Psychological Service, usually find the outcome is worth it. The success that can be achieved under a home-based scheme so startled one journalist that he wrote a book about one family's experiences (Deakin, 1973). My own research into Midland families has led me to the firm conclusion that the extreme suspicion, over-zealous attention and often naked hostility of some LEA officials is unwarranted, disreputable and a misuse of public money. One Midland LEA used large sums of public money to pay a barrister in a magistrates court hearing that resulted in an absolute discharge for the family.

PARENTS IN A CHANGING SOCIETY

There are a number of recent changes in the social context that have implications for education in general, and the potential development of parents as teachers in particular, not least because of the learning resources located in increasing numbers of homes. The credibility of parents as educators has increased as a variety of educational initiatives and projects have demonstrated positive outcomes to adopting various degrees of parental partnership.

Communication and Information Systems

It is no longer necessary to speculate about information systems since the television companies have already established CEEFAX and ORACLE and these forms of teletext are already in use in many homes and a familiar sight in the windows of TV rental shops. If the take-up of these services is as rapid as in the cases of radio, television and then colour television, over 90 per cent of homes will have them in the next five years or so. The GPO system, PRESTEL, is also available. Personal computers are now being purchased for home use. The likely picture that emerges is that of most homes gradually being equipped as sophisticated information retrieval centres, whilst schools, under financial pressures caused by cuts in government expenditure, go short of textbooks.

Knowledge Explosion

It is estimated that knowledge is expanding at the rate of a doubling in quantity every ten years. Some of this new knowledge renders existing knowledge as inadequate or inaccurate or out of date, or all three. Schools depend on teachers who are now taking up to four years to train, and on books that take two or three years to produce and then need a sales run of several years to be commercially viable. Therefore the basic sources of information used in schools easily become inadequate. Homes are less susceptible to such obsolescence since they have regular access to television and, increasingly, access to the information retrieval systems listed above.

Television

Pupils can quickly become aware of the gap between school knowledge and contemporary knowledge by viewing the lastest TV documentary and news programmes. Schools are ill-equipped to cope, for few have more than limited TV and video facilities and some have none. In this situation, TV viewed at home becomes an alternative source of culture, information and education. In providing more up-to-date information, the home can become a competitive rather than a complementary source of culture.

Work, the Economy and Schooling

The collapse of work as a dominant activity in modern industrial societies is widely forecast. With UK current unemployment figures of over three million, the forecasters are proving themselves correct in predicting the trend. Jenkins and Sherman (1979) demonstrate how the trend towards large-scale unemployment was evident before the advent of the micro-processor technology, which is having the effect of escalating the trend rather than actually causing it. They conclude that education for leisure is a top priority in this situation.

The reaction of educationalists has been ostrich-like. The current fashion is to cling to myths about school as 'preparation for work', meaning specifically manufacturing industry. Currently less than seven million people work in manufacturing industry out of an adult population of some 41 million. This figure is expected to reduce by about half to three and a half million in the next decade as trends leading to the 'collapse' of work continue. There are already 15 million 'non-working' adults comprising the retired, the unemployed, and housepersons, mostly female. The remaining 26 million work mainly in central and local government, the professions, retail industry, transport, entertainment and leisure industries. In reviewing the fallacies of the 'schools should serve the needs of industry' movement, Flude and Parrott (1979) comment:

> When Donald Schon wrote about institutions as 'memorials to past problems', and their 'dynamic conservatism' by which they struggle to retain their shape even when their original function has disappeared, he might have had British secondary schools in mind.

The priority of function for schools, Jenkins and Sherman argue, is not to serve the needs of the minority sector of manufacturing industry as it shrinks by half, but in education for choice in leisure activities. The home already has this topic as a main concern, for the use of evenings, weekends and holidays is high on its agenda. And because of increased unemployment, parents are more frequently at home with time to devote to children's learning.

Learning Theories

Hemming (1980) claims that the theories of modern psychology about brain functioning and learning have been largely ignored. The work of Piaget, Bruner and others is set aside in favour of older but fallacious ideas:

it is an extraordinary fact that the dominant influences operating in secondary education have no scientific basis whatever. They arise from dubitable philosophical ideas that had their origin in the distant past – the Greek view that the craftsman was inherently inferior to the thinker; Lockes' presentation of the mind as a clean slate, as a *tabula rasa*; Descartes' over-evaluation of the intellect, and his division of the human being into mind (exalted) and body (debased); puritan ideas about the special value of making the young do what they don't like doing

Hemming, 1980

A similar point is made by Husen (1974) when he argues that the key assumptions about learning that underpin schooling are all dubious. These assumptions are (1) that people will only learn to avoid disagreeable consequences, (2) what pupils can achieve is rationed by the possession of 'ability' and (3) that formal textbook tasks indicate the best kinds of 'ability'. Until these false principles are abandoned, Husen and Hemming see schools as continuing to limit the development of young people.

A similar conclusion was central to the group of writers rather misleadingly known as the 'deschoolers' who, on the whole, were in favour of regenerated schooling rather than doing away with it altogether. The consequences of contemporary schooling, based on fallacious principles were that:

the students who endure it come out as passive, acquiescent, dogmatic, intolerant, authoritarian, inflexible, conservative personalities who desperately need to resist change in an effort to keep their illusion of certainty intact.

Postman and Weingartner, 1971

The potential for homes to reverse this equation is clear in the responses of parents in Education Otherwise where they report the liberating effects of developing home-based education (see Meighan, 1984).

Educational Developments

There have been one or two recent educational developments that have involved homes in a systematic way as a learning resource and base. The first example is that of the Open University. Here learning at home is a key idea. The resources of the home, its television and radio, are taken into the network of learning experiences, and the postal service used as a major means of communication. The learning experiences are to some extent open to other members of the family to share, if so desired.

Deriving partly from the ten years of experience of the Open University is another idea, Flexistudy. This approach has been adopted by many Colleges of Further Education. As one prospectus states: 'Flexistudy enables students to study at home in their own time and at their own pace.' The students come to college from time to time to meet tutors and to use any college resources that they need.

Parents and Ideologies of Education

The existence of a series of competing ideologies of education with competing defini-tions of learning, teaching resources, knowledge, assessment, language usage, location, aims and organization, has been the subject of recent research (see Part Three). The notion that there is one view of education, a politically neutral view, is shown to be mistaken. Therefore the development of parents as teachers could follow several lines. It could be developed to serve any of the competing ideologies of education outlined in the research mentioned above. The example given earlier of parents used as remedial instructors at home, shows how incorporation into the existing authoritarian system and its aims can take place. One example of parents operating with an alternative ideology of education, is that of those parents in Education Otherwise who establish an autonomous education approach with its stress on self-education, personal confidence, problem solving, flexibility and adaptation (Meighan, 1984). Another is that of the democratic approach involving parents as equal partners, as found in the Danish Little Schools and proposed by the Campaign for State-Assisted Alternative Schools (see Diamond, 1984).

CONSEQUENCES FOR TEACHERS

As parents become defined more and more as part of the solution rather than as part of the problem, one outcome is a changed role for teachers who become more like their higher-status cousins – university teachers – in using a range of skills for tutorial, instructional, consultancy and research purposes. The model of teaching involved extends beyond the dominant idea of instruction, while the concept of 'good parent' becomes one of being an active rather than a passive supporter of teachers. The central concept of school becomes that of a learning centre (requiring similar kinds of adjustments already made in Colleges of Further Education to the idea of Flexistudy). The concept of flexischooling is the subject of a chapter in the final section of this book.

Part of the task of teaching can become that of 'training' parents by providing advice and guidance and monitoring their activities. The experience of pre-school educators and play-group organizers argues that this cannot be left to chance. A study in Oxfordshire concluded that teachers seemed to believe that parents could just pick up the aims and techniques as they went along. Smith (1980) found that this was not true: the parents needed some guidance and knew that they needed it. The practice of Dorothy Rich in the USA has proved successful partly because it is so explicit and does provide training sessions. On the other hand, some families in Education Otherwise have had impressive results by avoiding the official wisdom and pioneering new approaches, e.g. some families have developed a non-sexist education – a problem that still baffles most schools in the UK (see Chapter 25).

CONCLUSION

The educational role of a parent can be seen to be open to definition and redefinition as the identity is created and recreated in interactions amongst teachers, schools, politicians and social forces, such as a changing technology. Rival views exist in the UK, but the definition operating in the school studies by Sharp and Green (1975) is widespread as surveys of teachers' and parents' attitudes have shown. According to this definition, parents are expected to avoid either being interfering, by questioning school critically or admitting to direct teaching at home, or neglectful by not providing required clothing and skills of neatness and tidiness. The 'good' parent defers to the school and the professional claim of its teachers but becomes a victim if this is more than impression management.

The Taylor Report (1977) on the government of schools saw parents in a different light and sought to increase the power of parents to the point of power-sharing, for parents were seen as equal partners with teachers in terms of decision-making and responsibility.

The government Green Paper on parents (1984) takes a different view: parents are to be given more power still by having an overall majority on school governing bodies. Three views of power are contained in these alternative views. Parents are, in turn, under orders or equal partners or in charge. There are other views too for those parents who educate their children at home rather than send them to school, undertaking the autonomous education already available to them in law. Another view is represented by the members of CSAS (Campaign for State-Assisted Alternative Schools) since they ask for a more active and embracing partnership than that of being on the governing body in their vision of democratically run schools (see Diamond, 1984).

The review of parents and their relationship to the process of educating and the system of formal education renders all the common views problematic. How much do the experts really know? Do parents need training in existing techniques or scope to develop new approaches? Is an effective relationship with teachers that of participants, partners or paymasters? A later section of this book concentrates on the concept of ideologies of education and you will be able to look again at the material on parents and reconsider it in the light of the authoritarian, autonomous and democratic groupings of educational visions.

Further Reading

Craft, M., Raynor, J. and Cohen, L. (1980) *Linking Home and School*, London: Harper and Row.
Cyster, R., Clift, P.S. and Battle, S. (1983) *Parental Involvement in Primary Schools*, Windsor: NFER-Nelson.
Harber, C., Meighan, R. and Roberts, B. (1984) *Alternative Educational Futures*, London: Holt, Rinehart and Winston.
Holt, J. (1981) *Teach Your Own*, Brightlingsea: Lighthouse Books.
Sharp, R. and Green, A. (1973) *Education and Social Control*, London: Routledge and Kegan Paul.
Taylor Committee Report (1977) *A New Partnership for Our Schools*, London: HMSO.

Discussion and Activities

1. Compile a summary of the main points of the chapter and compare with the attempts of others if applicable.
2. Does the analogy of victim contribute to our understanding of a parent's situation in educational contexts?
3. In view of the quotation from Musgrove about the nature of homes that produce academic success, is the price too high?

4. Do projects that centre on mothers carry a hidden curriculum in that pupils have a model of a female more firmly slotted into the traditional patriarchal system. Is this liberation or confirmation?
5. If the educational standards of parents have increased steadily over the last 100 years, does this mean that the success of the education system will ensure its own redundancy?

Signposts

Language development
The role of parents in language development raises a variety of issues. One is social class, for one study concludes that when their parents were encouraged to help, children from less privileged backgrounds were not 'doomed to fail' but did as well as and frequently better than their middle-class peers; see Widlake, P. and Macleod, F. (1984), *Raising Standards*, Coventry: Community Education Development Centre. Another issue is that of the efficacy of the parental activity of story-telling; see Wade, B. (1984) *Story at Home and School*, Birmingham: Educational Review Publications.

Other studies have concluded that parents, irrespective of social class, are usually very skilled at responding to children's interests, expanding their language facilities and feeding-in relevant ideas and information, whereas teachers of young children are less skilled because of their anxiety to instruct (see Tizard, B. and Hughes, M. (1984) *Young Children Learning*, London: Fontana).

PART TWO

The Hidden Curriculum

This part attempts to show the range of the concept of hidden curriculum. The chapters that follow contain analyses that derive from the observation and interpretation of everyday events in classrooms, as well as propositions about the functions of the education system for a society and its economy. Therefore the material ranges from the micro-sociological to the macro-sociological: the former shows how the participants create patterns in their social behaviour and achieve outcomes in their day-to-day activities, while the latter stresses the patterns of the social structure, the economy and other institutions, and shows how this framework has a powerful influence on the processes of educating.

Chapter 6

The Hidden Curriculum: An Overview

'Education is what remains when we have forgotten all that we have been taught.'
George Halifax

INTRODUCTION

As a working definition, the hidden curriculum can be defined as all the other things that are learnt during schooling in addition to the official curriculum. Both limitations and advantages of this broad definition should emerge during the discussion in this and subsequent chapters. Some of the wide range of concerns generated by the apparently simple idea of the hidden curriculum are shown by this extract:

> The hidden curriculum is what is taught by school, not by any teacher. However enlightened the staff, however progressive the curriculum, however community-oriented the school, something is coming across to the pupils which need never be spoken in the English lesson or prayed about in assembly. They are picking up an approach in living, and an attitude in learning.
>
> The Canadian connoisseur of communication techniques, Marshall McLuhan, would say, I told you so: the medium is the message. The medium is the atmosphere of the school, the furnishing, the routing, the relationships, the priorities. And the message? Well, to limit our answer to the learning process itself, the message is that education is:
>
> Schooling;
> Grading and competition;
> Being measured;
> Mastering a curriculum;
> Getting a certificate;
> Being taught;
> Being taught by a teacher;
> Being taught by a professional teacher;
> Treating knowledge as a commodity;
> Getting specialized knowledge.
>
> Such lessons penetrate deeper than the level of consciousness. They inevitably go with schooling.
>
> Head, 1974

© David Head and contributors, 1974. Reprinted by permission of Penguin Books Ltd.

In a now famous passage, Postman and Weingartner (1971) point out some probable consequences, in terms of attitudes absorbed, of the hidden curriculum; students may well learn that:

Passive acceptance is a more desirable response to ideas than active criticism.

Discovering knowledge is beyond the power of students and is, in any case, none of their business.

Recall is the highest form of intellectual achievement, and the collection of unrelated 'facts' is the goal of education.

The voice of authority is to be trusted and valued more than independent judgement.

One's own ideas and those of one's classmates are inconsequential. Feelings are irrelevant in education.

There is always a single, unambiguous Right Answer to a question.

English is not history and history is not science and science is not art and art is not music, and art and music are minor subjects and English, history and science major subjects, and a subject is something you take and, when you have taken it; you have 'had' it and if you 'had' it, you are immune and need not take it again.

One could also add to this other possible 'learnings', including:

Competition is more important than co-operation.

Helping others is less important than getting on oneself.

Writing and reading are more important than talking and thinking.

Men are more important than women.

AMBIGUOUS IDEAS AND THEIR VALUE

The notion of a hidden curriculum is highly ambiguous. Some of the competing meanings will be discussed in the following pages, but it is perhaps useful to outline the problems and possibilities of ambiguous ideas. de Bono (1972) categorizes such ideas as 'porridge words', that can be stirred around to stimulate further ideas and further connections because of the lack of precision. Precise words exclude a great deal more than porridge words. Since one aspect of sociology mentioned in Chapter 1 was the capacity to make connections between phenomena and events which people commonly regard as unconnected, these words are of particular use to sociologists. One danger lies in slipping and sliding the meaning without warning, so that attempted analysis is replaced by spurious association. An example was given earlier in the assertion that sociology is the study of people who do not need studying by those who do. The ambiguous word here is people, because it can mean individuals or groups. Psychologists tend to study individual behaviour, whereas sociologists tend to study group behaviours, and this is why the writer got the joke wrong: it is more accurately a joke about psychologists.

DEFINITIONS OF CURRICULUM

The ambiguities spring from both words, curriculum and hidden. There have been many attempts to define curriculum including:

an elaborate device for filling the time available

F. Musgrove

a rough and ready bargain between what some people are prepared to teach and others are prepared to learn

D. Riesman

a mechanism for separating the children into good learners and poor ones

J. Henry

a social construction in which the selection and organization of knowledge into the timetable of the school is the result of a choice from possible alternatives.

M. MacDonald

a course of study

Oxford Dictionary

These attempted definitions stress various features. Some stress the planned aspect, some hint at the possibility of spontaneity. Others stress the short-term immediacy of 'filling time', others the long-term features of a course of study. One singles out the imposed nature of a curriculum, another the negotiation and bargaining aspects. One feature that the definitions appear to have in common is the idea of a sequence of events and experiences and the accumulation of ideas and information.

It is possible to distinguish other definitions:

1. Ones which stress the official timetable: the curriculum is seen as the planned instructional activities of the school.
2. Others that stress intention: the curriculum is everything organized by teachers, including lessons, clubs and out-of-school activities.
3. Others which stress anything connected with school that results in learning, whether intended or not.

The notion of a hidden curriculum is given most scope in the last case, but there are also hidden curriculum aspects of the first two. The hidden aspects of the official curriculum are rather overlooked in the working definition given earlier, and this is also a limitation of some of the existing studies of the hidden curriculum.

THE NOTION OF 'HIDDEN'

The ambiguities in the idea of 'hidden' are considerable. The reason for a learning to be hidden presents one problem. Is it hidden intentionally to manipulate and persuade? Is it hidden because nobody notices or recognizes it? Is it hidden because it has been forgotten or neglected? Is it hidden because the originator has left?

The outcomes of 'hidden' may be more significant than the reasons, and the analysis to follow will dwell on consequences. However, it is useful to bear in mind the variety of reasons lest the idea of a deliberate plot be assumed when none exists. The irony of human action was discussed in Chapter 1: the outcomes of ideas may turn out to be rather different from those originally intended. The case of corporal punishment in UK schools may be cited. When mass schooling was developed most major institutions, homes, factories, prisons, the army and navy used corporal punishment: schools merely fell into line. Today, when all the other institutions have, one by one, abandoned the practice, UK schools are left out on their own.

A CLASSIC STUDY ILLUSTRATING THE HIDDEN CURRICULUM

A well-known study in group behaviour is that of Lippitt and White (1958), on authoritarian and democratic regimes. Four small groups of ten-year-old boys were observed closely as they experienced three different regimes for craft-making activities such as mask-making. In the regime described as authoritarian, the adult leader determined all policies, techniques, activities and working companions, while using personal criticism of task performance and remaining aloof from the group. In the regime described as democratic, the adult leader encouraged discussion and used consultation about decisions while allowing a choice of both tasks and companions. (The use of the word 'democratic' to describe this kind of regime is perhaps misleading, and 'parental' or 'consultative' might have described more accurately what was an alternative kind of authoritarianism. This point is argued in Chapter 16.) In the third regime, laissez-faire, the boys were left more or less to their own devices, and this was effectively a non-leadership situation.

The same boys behaved quite differently under these different regimes, even though the task of craftwork remained constant. For example, they were aggressive or passive in the authoritarian situation and friendly and co-operative in the democratic situation. Some of the contrasts in regime and consequential behaviour are given in Table 6.1.

Table 6.1 Lippit and White experiment on group regimes

	Authoritarian	Democratic
Policy	Leader determined	Group consultations
Task method	Leader decisions	Choice from alternatives
Companions	Leader chosen	Chosen by members
Leader	Aloof and withdrawn	Involved and approachable
Structure of groups	Atomized	Sub-grouped
	Resultant behaviour	
Attitudes to work	Aggression or apathy	Interested
Attitudes to members	Competitive/scapegoating	Co-operative/friendly
Attitudes to leader	Submissive	Friendly
Leader leaves room	Work ceases	Work continues
Group morale	Unity low; tense	Unity high; relaxed
Task standards	High	Moderate
Response to problems	Disintegration into blame	Organized attack on problems

The central ideas of a hidden curriculum are well illustrated in Lippitt and White's study. The official 'curriculum' consisted of the tasks of craftwork. All the other learnings are unintended, or incidental or otherwise 'hidden' in some sense or other. Yet these learnings are considerable in range and significance, and the list given above does not exhaust the features observed in this experiment.

THE CLASSROOM AS A HAUNTED PLACE

The analogy of haunting is fraught with difficulties since it is a concept derived from superstition, with very low probabilities of factual existence. The more systematic and scrupulous studies of ghosts have placed them rather firmly in the area of illusion, suggestion and delusion, and only a small minority of cases investigated so far have failed to yield a natural, though often bizarre, set of circumstances. However, having acknowledged this, the analogy has some value in illustrating the hidden curriculum.

Many teachers have been heard to comment that when the classroom door closes, what happens next is within their control and direction: they claim autonomy. In considering this claim the notion of the classroom as a haunted place has its uses.

Ghosts of the Architects

The classroom may be said to be haunted by the architects who designed it and their advisers. Attempts to reshape the classroom have to fight the ideas of the originators. The result is often a confusion of ideas rather than a reversal of the ideas embedded in the walls and fabric of the building.

Ghosts of the Book Writers

Second, the classroom may be said to be haunted by the book writers, resource designers and materials producers. Their inaccuracies, distortions and biases are embedded in their writing and designing, and may pass unrecognized and unchallenged. They become absorbed along with the accurate material present. Reading schemes for primary schools provide an interesting example. Here, analyses have shown that, along with the carefully graded reading books designed to build up learner reading skills gradually, are often messages of nationalism, racism, sexism and social class bias. A study by Lobban (1975) showed that the world of the reading scheme was more sex biased than the real world. The world depicted was that of males who were active, dominant and involved in work and careers, whereas females were shown almost entirely in domestic roles. Since many children have working mothers this was a distortion of the world as it was, let alone a limited vision of what the world could be, and in the view of those seeking equal life chances for women, should be.

A second example is sex education books for secondary schools, which were surveyed by Hoffman (1975). She concluded that most of these books passed on the prejudices of the writers, often based on erroneous information, rather than informing pupils dispassionately about sexual behaviour. One error concerned the notion of the low female sex drive:

> The message is clear: male sexuality is genital, easily stimulated and urgent; female sexuality, where present, is diffuse, easily sublimated and will probably go away of its own accord.

Hoffman questions the insight into one's own or one's partner's sexual response that this gives. A probable consequence is that it would make girls fear their boyfriends and boys despair of their girlfriends. It would encourage boys to worry about their virility if their sex drive was not urgent and make girls ashamed if theirs was.

The 'ill-conceived constructions of our ancestors' are well represented in these books. Writers' prejudices, often based on Victorian beliefs about sex, come out in sweeping generalizations about all men requiring exciting sexual encounters and all women wanting love and marriage. One male writer speaks confidently about what females think and feel:

> Sex is less important to girls than their public image . . . Girls in fact seldom talk about sex as sex, and even when they do, they don't talk about it as boys do.
>
> Pomeroy, 1969

Hoffman goes on to comment on what she sees as the consequences of this kind of sex education, and suggests that in an overpopulated world, the first responsibility of the sex educator is to prevent unwanted births. When there are about a quarter of a million unwanted pregnancies in Britain each year and there are about 3000 people who catch VD for the first time each week, it is a plausible proposition that sex educators are failing in their task. Hoffman sees the emancipation of women and the right and ability of girls to act outside or at least in addition to the domestic sphere as doing nothing but good if they reduce the statistics of unwanted pregnancy and VD. In Hoffman's view, the realities of the modern world are that people are marrying younger, living longer and being forced by economic circumstances to have smaller families. It therefore becomes difficult to argue that marriage and a family are a full-time career. Her conclusion about most sex education books is that, apart from the hidden and often false messages they carry:

> they abrogate their main responsibility of reducing the abuses of human sexuality: unwanted pregnancies, abortions and VD, in favour of moralizing about chastity before or within marriage and promulgating their sexist views of society. They do not reflect life as it is, but generalize from extreme cases.
>
> Hoffman, 1975

Ghosts of Our Ancestors' Language and Thinking

Other ghosts inevitably haunting the classroom are the ancestors who developed our language. Since language is a major, if not the major, means of communication employed by teachers and pupils, any unrecognized limitations, distortions and biases will be absorbed. Some of the constructions were established by groups long since dead and, as was suggested in Chapter 1, the fallacious thinking of our ancestors is often more difficult to get rid of than contemporary errors. Language is the subject of a later chapter, so one or two examples will suffice here. The Engligh language has a marked tendency to use dichotomies, e.g. black/white, good/bad, strong/weak, and a consequence is the frequent oversimplification of complex phenomena (see de Bono, 1971). This limitation extends into sociology, and teaching is commonly analysed as if there were only two opposed types, e.g. open/closed, traditional/progressive, authoritarian/democratic. In the later section on ideologies it will be argued that there is a multiplicity of types of teaching.

Other commentators have noted the prevalence of rural imagery in an industrial society and, to a lesser extent, military imagery (Seabrook, 1971). In the latter case, describing a conflict at the outset as a battle or a fight, rather than as a problem to be solved or a conflict of interests needing to be negotiated, may have consequences for the subsequent sequence of events. One of the comments often made by visitors from countries where industrial relations are rather less fraught than those in Britain is that if at the outset you define the situation as a battle, it becomes seen by all concerned as a battle.

The analogy of ghosts could be pursued further or replaced by one from electronics, the idea of invisible force fields operating and invisible transmission through radio waves. Despite its disadvantages, one strength of this kind of analogy is that it helps to locate causes more accurately. Rather than assuming the malevolence or sinister nature of educators, these analogies suggest the possibilities of unwitting and unintended actions of those concerned and suggest a theory of a complex of causes. They are also optimistic analogies: ghosts can be laid, and force fields neutralized.

ATTEMPTS TO ANALYSE THE HIDDEN CURRICULUM

Jackson (1968) uses the term 'the hidden curriculum' to describe the unofficial three R's of Rules, Routines and Regulations that must be learnt by pupils in order to survive comfortably in most classrooms. Pupils must also learn to cope with the delay, denial and interruptions that accompany learning experiences in schools. Delay occurs when pupils wait in assembly, wait in corridors, wait for their turn on the apparatus, wait for the lesson to start, wait for the teacher to become available or wait to be invited to answer a question. It is quite startling to add up this delay: some children spend the majority of their time coping with delay, and most spend almost half their time in this way.

Denial occurs when pupils are forbidden to talk among themselves, cannot ask questions, cannot pursue a chosen activity, or cannot have a turn on apparatus because time has run out.

Interruption occurs when the bell rings in the middle of an activity, the nurse arrives to check hair, the equipment is needed elsewhere, or the teacher is called away during a discussion. Jackson (1971) concludes:

> for most students some of the time, and for some of the students most of the time, the classroom comes close to resembling a cage from which there is no escape.

Faced with rules, routines and regulations and the consequent delay, denial and interruption, pupils have to devise strategies for survival. Some of these strategies, Jackson argues, avoid or reduce confrontation with teachers but a price is paid in that effective learning of the official curriculum is reduced. These strategies include 'resignation' or ceasing to hope that school makes sense, and 'masquerade', or faking involvement. A more positive strategy is 'patience', and some children are already well trained in this before they come to school, whereas others start handicapped in this respect.

Holt (1969) describes another set of strategies children devise to reduce the fear and anxiety of classroom life: 'right answerism'. This is a collection of strategies to obtain the right answer or an approved response. These strategies have short-term survival value but, in replacing the activity of thinking out answers, in the long term reduce learning. These strategies include reading teachers' facial clues, noting the regularity of answer patterns and the prevalence of 'Yes' answers, noting that freak questions are signalled by a change of voice, giving faint and mumbled answers that maximize chances of misinterpretation for the right answer, and raising hands when many others are raised in the knowledge that the chances of being called on are small, and that this eventuality can be covered by a confused 'Oh, I forget'.

For Snyder (1971) the hidden curriculum is seen as associated most closely with the assessment system. A study by Becker (1968) of medical students demonstrated how 'trading for grades' rivalled and eventually replaced 'learning to think independently and critically':

> The realities of the situation lead him to define his classes as places in which he can get the grades he wants by performing as the teacher wants him to . . . they engage in two simultaneous enterprises. They search for cues that, properly interpreted, will yield an understanding of what the teacher will demand in return for a given grade. At the same time, they attempt to do the things they have decided are important to get the grade they want.
>
> Becker, 1968

Snyder sees the hidden curriculum as involving the selective negligence of the non-assessable or non-examinable aspects of the official curriculum. Students learn to translate the complex ideas of mathematics, physics, history, etc. into a set of discrete tasks defined by the rules of the grading system, all of which usually have very little to do with effective learning.

Snyder notes the ironical remark of one of the deschooling writers:

> Some true educational experiences are bound to occur in schools. They occur, however, despite, and not because of school.
>
> Reimer, 1971

Holly (1973) developed an analysis of the curriculum of British schools as alienated and alienating for those subjected to it. He analyses four aspects of schooling: matters of organization, the content of learning, teaching methodology and general values which are promoted. Using these headings, a useful analysis of the hidden curriculum is developed, although the term itself is absent. He concludes that the curriculum is defined as a course to be run, an activity to be completed as smoothly and efficiently as possible without reference to what the race means.

> it is the finishing tape that matters, the mark, the examination pass, the entry to a career or further education. This is essentially instrumental thinking. It is also essentially alienated, separating the meaning of the activity from the activity itself.

Vallance (1974), discussing education in the USA, stresses the hidden curriculum as a social-control device. She defines the hidden curriculum in terms of the non-academic consequences of schooling that occur systematically but are not made explicit in the official rationales for educational institutions. The social control function used to be made explicit, she argues, in that the 'civilizing of the working class' through education was publicly discussed. It became 'hidden' when schools were seen to be achieving such social control, and attention could drift to welfare of individuals. The increasing diversity of the demands of industry helped expand the official curriculum, thus assisting the 'hiding' process.

> Social control was not abandoned as an aim: it simply shifted its visibility as the goals of education came to be rephrased in terms of individual development within the social context.
>
> Vallance, 1974

Bowles and Gintis (1976) develop a correspondence theory of the hidden curriculum. The proposition is that attitudes engendered by most schools correspond to those of the social relations of work in a capitalist economy and constitute an attitudinal preparation for life in a class-divided society.

> Schools foster legitimate inequality through the ostensibly meritocratic manner by which they reward and promote students, and allocate them to distinct positions in the occupational hierarchy. They create and reinforce patterns of social class, racial and sexual identification among students, and allocate them to distinct positions in the occupational hierarchy of authority and status in the production process. Schools foster types of personal development compatible with the relationships of dominance and subordinacy in the economic sphere, and finally, schools create surpluses of skilled labor sufficiently extensive to render effective the prime weapon of the employer in disciplining labor – the power to hire and fire.
>
> . . . the educational system operates in this matter not so much through the conscious intentions of teachers and administrators in their day-to-day activities, but through a close correspondence between the social relationships which govern personal interaction in the work place and the social relationships of the educational system. Specifically, the relationships of authority and control between administrators and teachers, teachers and students, students and students, and students and their work replicate the hierarchical division of labor which dominates the work place. Power is organized along vertical lines of authority from administration to faculty to student body; students have a degree of control over their curriculum comparable to that of the worker over the content of his job.
>
> Bowles and Gintis, 1976

The *differential* effects of the hidden curriculum on different groups of pupils is the subject of an analysis by Hargreaves. For pupils identified as working class, the result is a destruction of their dignity. An important hidden curriculum message, Hargreaves argues, is that there is something wrong with being, and certainly with ending up as, working class.

> The majority of working class pupils must bear the scars of damaged dignity that goes with the inevitable stigma of being 'failures'; they know very well that they are 'written off'.
>
> Hargreaves, 1978a

An important ingredient is the learning of boredom:

> We learn reading and boredom, writing and boredom, arithmetic and boredom, and so on according to the curriculum, till in the end it is quite certain you can put us to the most boring job there is and we'll endure it.
>
> Common, 1951

Another ingredient to be learnt is that the few succeed at the expense of the many who fail. The destruction of dignity is implicit in this, for being inferior, unable and powerless, Hargreaves argues, is the opposite of having dignity, since this requires feelings of warmth, creativeness, critical capacities and powers of personal and social change.

This selection of studies is not exhaustive. Other writers, including Illich (1971), Dreeben (1968), Dale (1977), Henry (1963) and Lister (1974) have written on the theme of the hidden curriculum, and may be usefully consulted in further reading. An interesting collection of articles is contained in a reader edited by Whitty and Young (1976).

CONCLUSION

This chapter has attempted to show the range of the notion of a hidden curriculum. The various analyses outlined range from the observation and interpretation of everyday commonplace events in classrooms to the function of the education system for society and its economy. In other words, some of the analyses have been micro-sociological, stressing how the participants create patterns and consequences in their day-to-day constructions and reconstructions within schools, and others have been macro-sociological, stressing the patterns of society and its economy that form a framework for educational activity and powerfully influence the system of schooling.

Others have adopted an interactionist perspective, looking for a network of influences and allowing for contradictions within the network. Interactionist approaches are summed up in the following passage:

> In this perspective human action is not seen as fully determined by social, cultural, or psychological forces, and these forces are seen to be mediated in their impact by processes of social interaction. The outcome of any interpretive or interactional process is never entirely predictable, as it emerges from and is conditional upon the interplay of interpretations and actions.
>
> Woods, 1977a

Most of the writings about the curriculum miss out the notion of a hidden curriculum and concentrate on the official curriculum. Many students find such writings alienating and unconvincing because they tend to represent an incomplete analysis as complete, and separate the activity of the curriculum from the pattern of schooling as a whole. A series of six paperbacks on the curriculum, published by Open Books, illustrates the point. The most generous allocation of space to a discussion of the hidden curriculum is three pages in one of the books. The others do not mention it at all. One writer notes that it is a very powerful and significant feature, and then does not mention it again. Particular aspects, like the sexual divisions of the curriculum, are hardly noticed by any of the writers, and the pupils' interpretation and experience of schooling is conspicuous by its absence.

The problems of definition remain. It is not clear whether the hidden curriculum is a concept with a recognizable content or a theme of hiddenness which turns out to be a linking feature of other concepts, and indeed it may prove useful to make use of it in both ways. Several limitations of the definition given at the outset may now be seen, in particular that defining the hidden curriculum as the form or framework of schooling as against the content of the official curriculum is too limiting in that it obscures the hidden aspects of the official curriculum and ignores the self-defeating processes such as an assessment system encouraging selective neglect of parts of the official curriculum in the trading for grades.

The reactions to the idea of the hidden curriculum are worth noting. As noted above, many curriculum theorists ignore it or do not recognize it. Another reaction is to dismiss schooling and argue for a deschooled society.

An alternative reaction is pessimism and fatalism. Macro-sociological perspectives tend to contribute to this by stressing the enduring and powerful forces of a whole society socializing its members into compliance. Another reaction is management and administration. It is felt that, by careful administration, some of the most negative aspects of the hidden curriculum can be managed with less conflict.

A further response is reschooling. The view here is that different organizational patterns can be found in order to eliminate the hidden curriculum of contemporary mass schooling.

This differential response illustrates one of the points made in the opening chapter. The findings of sociological analysis may often lend themselves to widely differing, if not contradictory, policies. The good spy reports what is there. Others use the reports.

The remaining chapters of Part Two contain analyses of the hidden curriculum of selected aspects of schooling.

SUMMARY

1. The hidden curriculum is an ambiguous idea, but one capable of making connections between phenomena and events which often go unrecognized.
2. The definition of 'curriculum' in use is often the broadest possible – anything that results in learning. However, the narrowest definition – the planned instructional activities – still yields a hidden curriculum.
3. The definition of 'hidden' often implies motives. These can range from deliberate manipulation, to non-recognition, to persistence beyond the original needs, to the irony of unintended consequences.
4. The Lippitt and White experiment illustrates the wide range of learnings beyond the instructional task of the official curriculum.
5. Teachers who claim that they control what happens when the classroom door closes may not have recognized the 'ghosts' of the architects' design, the influence of the book writers and the legacy of our ancestors' thinking enshrined in language.
6. The rules, routines and regulations of schooling, leading to various pupil responses and strategies like 'resignation' and 'masquerade', is one aspect of the hidden curriculum analysed by Jackson.
7. The strategy of 'right answerism' employed by pupils is described by Holt.
8. The assessment system has its own hidden messages and 'trading for grades as more significant than learning to think' is one of these.
9. One consequence of the hidden curriculum can be alienation.
10. The social control aspects of the hidden curriculum have been analysed in terms of 'correspondence theory', where the attitudes inculcated by school are seen as corresponding to those required to maintain a capitalist economy and a class-divided society. An important ingredient is seen as the learning of boredom and its toleration.
11. Reactions to the idea of a hidden curriculum can range from dismissal, to pessimism, to fatalism, to reschooling, to deschooling.

Further Reading

Bowles, S. and Gintis, H. (1976) *Schooling in Capitalist America*, London: Routledge and Kegan

Paul. A Marxist interpretation of the hidden curriculum. Further work appears in the next reference.

Giroux, H.A. (1981) *Ideology, Culture and the Process of Schooling*, Lewes: Falmer Press.

Head, D. (1974) (ed.) *Free Way to Learning*, Harmondsworth: Penguin. The first chapter of this book has a clearly written account of the hidden curriculum.

Jackson, P. (1971) 'The Student's World'. In Silberman, M., *The Experience of Schooling*, Eastbourne: Holt, Rinehart and Winston. One of the micro aspects of the hidden curriculum is the subject of Jackson's exposition of Rules, Routines and Regulations and their consequences.

Whitty, G. and Young, M.F.D. (1976) *Explorations in the Politics of School Knowledge*. Driffield: Nafferton. This collection of papers contains some interesting material on various aspects of the hidden curriculum. Chapters 7 and 13 deal with an aspect not mentioned in the chapter you have just read – the mass media.

Whyld, J. (1983) (ed.) *Sexism in the Secondary School*. London: Harper and Row. Explores the hidden curriculum in respect of sexist messages (see also chapter 25, 'Gender').

Discussion and Activities

1. Is a hidden curriculum an inevitable part of any arrangement for educating?
2. The definition of 'hidden curriculum' given at the start of the chapter was said to be faulty. Attempt a revised definition.
3. Try to distinguish between the hidden curriculum of classroom practices, of schools, and of education systems, giving suitable examples.
4. Are there other 'ghosts' that haunt classrooms apart from the three mentioned? (Later chapters may contain ideas.)
5. What use can be made of the 'hidden curriculum' concept with a view to changing schools? The 'confidence-building curriculum' notion of Hemming (1980) is one starting point.

Signposts

1. Criticism of the 'hidden curriculum' concept

The concept of hidden curriculum has been the subject of critical comment. Two articles that attack the whole idea are Cornbleth, C. (1984), 'Beyond Hidden Curriculum?' *Journal of Curriculum Studies*, **16**, 1, 29–36; and Dreeben, R. (1976) 'The Unwritten Curriculum and Its Relation to Values, *Journal of Curriculum Studies*, **8**, 2, 111–124.

2. A hidden curriculum in Further Education

The hidden curriculum of Further Education has been a focus in the UK because of the establishment of Youth Training Schemes as a substitute for employment and as a response to youth unemployment.

Starting points: Gleeson, D. (ed.) (1983) *Youth Training and the Search for Work*, London: Routledge and Kegan Paul; Fiddy, R. (ed.) (1983) *In Place of Work: Policy and Provision for the Young Unemployed*, Lewes: Falmer Press; Barton, L. and Walker, S. (eds.) (1986) *Youth Unemployment and Schooling*. Milton Keynes: Open University Press.

Chapter 7

Space Talks: The Hidden Curriculum of Educational Buildings

'The thing which in the subway is called congestion is highly esteemed in the night spots as intimacy.'

Simeon Strunsky

INTRODUCTION: MESSAGES FROM SPACE?

Since many of the analyses used in sociology are derived from the theatre, it is perhaps surprising how little attention is given to analysing the set in which the dramas of education take place. If we turn to those who do give attention to physical space, i.e. planners, architects, industrial designers, we find that their work is guided largely by tradition and accumulated experience: by common-sense recipes rather than systematic, reflective studies. A few educational writers have given attention to the spaces provided for schooling, and the ideas of one teacher trying to achieve changes in his classroom make a useful starting point:

> The placement of objects in space is not arbitrary and rooms represent in physical form the spirit and souls of places and institutions. A teacher's room tells us something about who he is and a great deal about what he is doing.
>
> Kohl, 1970

In attempting to work out an alternative to the 'closed' teaching he saw around him, where classrooms were based on compulsion rather than participation, and imposing decisions rather than enabling choice-making, Kohl found himself questioning the spatial arrangements provided for him:

> Why does a classroom have to have a front, a back and two sides? The notion that there is a 'front of the class' and the authoritarian mode of delivering knowledge received from above, to students who are below – both go together.
>
> Kohl, 1970

In Chapter 4 reference was made to the layout of head teachers' rooms. There are interesting parallels between the range of layouts of heads' rooms and commerical offices. In his study of offices, Joiner (1971) observes that these are taken seriously in an organization like the civil service:

> The way we interact with one another, and the way organizations are run, influence the use of architectural space and our feelings about it. The civil service recognizes this by adhering to strict rules about size of room, and the amount and quality of furnishings, which an employee in each grade may use.
>
> Joiner, 1971

Two sorts of social information are in play, Joiner argues – information about the occupant, and information about how the occupant would like others to behave when in his or her office.

A RESEARCH ACTIVITY: THE SCHOOL BUILDING IN GENERAL

In the opening chapter, reference was made to the idea of layers of meaning and the view that an individual may sample only a few of these in the routines of everyday life. The school building provides an interesting example of layers of meaning.

The school building presents a different experience to each group of people involved. To an educational administrator it is a building of a certain size, for a defined set of pupils, and having a detailed schedule of furnishings. To a pupil it is a place where a large part of one's life is spent, other children are encountered, and teachers experienced. To teachers the school building is primarily a selection of rooms, perhaps inadequately equipped and serviced. To parents it may be predominantly the assembly hall where their child is performing or singing on a platform along with other children. To caretakers and cleaners it is often a place of problems of how to keep things clean, of pipes that burst, of floors to polish, windows to repair and fittings to maintain.

The research activity that follows will concentrate on the teachers' layer of meaning.

Background Propositions

The buildings available for schooling are of interest in at least three ways:

1. They suggest possibilities and opportunities for schooling.
2. They place constraints on what can be done.
3. They imply psychological, philosophical, sociological and pedagogical ideas about schooling that are often taken for granted, but are open to question.

Aim

The aim of this exercise is to analyse the various features of the building from the teachers' point of view, and to relate these to teaching possibilities, teaching constraints and the underlying theoretical assumptions about teaching and learning.

Procedure

1. Obtain a plan of a school or make a plan using paces as a measure or by sketching from memory.
2. Fill in the schedules below *or* design a preferred schedule suitable for the purpose.

   (a) General allocation of school spaces. Work out the percentage of school space given over to:

(1) general-purpose teaching spaces, e.g. classrooms;

(2) specialized teaching spaces, e.g. science rooms;

(3) multi-purpose teaching spaces, e.g. halls;

(4) circulation space, e.g. corridors;

(5) administration space, e.g. offices;

(6) other spaces, both teaching and non-teaching, e.g. staffroom, dining, caretaker.

(b) Write your comments, e.g. what assumptions are made here about how children learn, what they should learn, relationships between teachers and children, how the school is to be organized, sizes of groups appropriate for learning, structure of the staff, who has most space allocated, who has least, the key tasks of the institution.

(c) How does the building differ from a factory?

(d) What assumptions underlie the design of a factory?

(e) How do these differ from assumptions underlying the design of the school you are analysing?

(f) How are they similar to those of the factory?

(g) Comment on the teaching possibilities of the building.

(h) Comment on the limitations set by the building.

(i) How does the building differ from the houses and flats of the pupils?

(j) Any other observations.

Discussion

Clearly, findings will vary from building type to building type: a study of primary schools will not yield identical results to a study of secondary schools, nor open-plan buildings to 'egg-crate' plan buildings. However, some common propositions that emerge are:

1. A group size of 30 to 40 under the surveillance of one adult is often believed to be the most suitable for the learning process.

2. The process of education is seen as both orderly and apparently uncomfortable for the learners. The buildings tend to have the clinical austerity of places in which one is confined for purposes other than pleasure.

3. There is an asymmetrical relationship in the allocation of space and facilities: teachers have larger desks, padded chairs, lockable cupboards, and access to more of the school territory, whereas pupils have inferior claims on the building's resources. It is a teachers' building rather than a pupils' building: it is 'their' building rather than 'our' building.

4. The design on which classrooms are based is not unlike a factory, in that the children pass through 'stages of production or process', according to certain criteria like age and sex, in regular-sized compartments, in regular-sized groups, and at regular-sized desks or tables.

5. A 'production manager' (head teacher) is allocated extra space and facilities to supervise the production activities of the 'foremen and forewomen' (teachers).

6. The buildings tend to prevent or restrict individual learning and small-group learning.
7. The buildings tend to obstruct co-operative and democratic relationships.
8. The buildings provide some facilities not available in homes, such as libraries and physical-education equipment.
9. The buildings tend to introduce some ideas not present in houses and flats, like separate toilets for the sexes, learning regularly in large groups, and large areas of space with access forbidden to children.

There are many other possible observations. One analysis (Hardy, 1977) stresses how the inadequacies of design may force teachers into an authoritarian role to compensate:

One basic determinant of the relationship between teachers and pupils lies in the belief that where both see a system that is fair and sensible, there is less likely to be misunderstanding; but would a couple of 11 stone 16-year-olds, rocking gently on a new upholstered bench seat, see this if persistently a teacher on social area supervision during the lunch hour tells them to sit still?

Is the teacher being reasonable? What about the teacher who tells off a pupil for kicking the lavatory door open at the bottom with his foot? Unreasonable? Perhaps, but a metal kick-plate has already been provided for just such a purpose.

Surely the member of staff on outside break duty is being totally unreasonable in the eyes of the child when he insists that the two first-year pupils playing tick and dodging from each other's clutches around a pillar with an attached drainpipe should go elsewhere. Is it fair on a group of pupils that they should be excluded from their social area by a deputy head, who is tired of asking them not to lean on an internal wall with their heels against the bottom of it, while chatting about the success of the local soccer team, or who is going out with whom?

In these instances, most adults and children would feel the teachers are behaving unreasonably. It is just such petty attitudes of teachers that prevent many pupils from enjoying school.

The teachers' actions cannot be excused on the grounds that any of these instances amount to vandalism. Yet the effect is to continuously and imperceptibly erode relationships between the staff and the pupils. And without cause?

A closer investigation would show that the metal legs supporting the upholstered bench seat were fixed on to chipboard by ½ in. screws. Above the kick-plate on the lavatory door was a ventilation grill made of thin moulded plastic.

The problem with the pillar and its drainpipe was that they were attached by a thin plastic fastener. In dodging round the pillar from one side to the other with their hands on the pipe for support the fastener breaks, the pipe swings free, and water gushes everywhere when it rains.

The problem for the deputy head was that he knew that the interior wall was merely plaster-board concealed by hessian, and that anyone leaning against the wall talking can place their heel on the base of the wall, and either through tapping or continual pressure, a hole would soon appear which would progressively grow in size.

The quality of these fixtures is poor, and certainly not able to stand for long the fair wear and tear of young adolescents behaving in a not unreasonable manner . . .

In all of the instances described above, the teachers have been forced into an authoritarian and custodial role to offset the inadequacies of design. Architects have a constructive part to play, therefore, in helping pupils and teachers to establish better relationships.

Hardy, 1977

Open-plan schools provide interesting contrasts in a number of features of space and design, because the classrooms lost their 'front' and 'back', leaving teachers to move everywhere. Desks and tables were so arranged that pupils had eye contact with each other and they were likely to share more experiences and communicate with each other more frequently. The learning environment was likely to be more relaxed. In some schools corridors were turned into work areas and book reference places. Washing and toilet facilities were planned in direct association with learning spaces. (See Pearson, 1971.)

Older schools provided their own particular problems of spatial layout for the users to solve. Gould (1976) comments that in an Edwardian school building where he once worked several classrooms were connected so that the entrance to the first was through a cloakroom, the second was entered from the first, and the third from the second. The middle classroom acted as a passageway and the teacher in this room had to accept that other staff and pupils would come through at various times, some scheduled, some unscheduled.

The spaces outside the school building may be indicative of assumptions about relationships. Evans (1974b) notes that it was Simmel who first drew attention to the significance that a border-line has for a group. It defines who is included and who is excluded. In her study of infants schools, Evans notes that only one still displayed a notice saying that parents should not enter the school, but the same effect was achieved in other ways. Some head teachers wrote to parents asking them to say goodbye at the gate, and others did this verbally. In one school the parents toed a white line painted on the playground: beyond this they were not expected to pass.

Some of the territory within the school can be a source of dispute. Evans found that head teachers had mixed experiences with caretakers. One third of the head teachers were full of praise for their caretakers, but another third reported constant difficulties. One head teacher commented that her biggest problems in running the school were with the caretaker, who neglected the floors and carpets, and let the toilets become smelly. For even the smallest jobs he insisted on sending for an expert.

Relations between school and kitchen were sometimes good and sometimes bad. In one school the head teacher reported that the kitchen staff would wait until assembly started, and then start up a clatter of plates. Requests to stop were ignored. One woman appeared to get a great kick out of clanging metal containers. The head tried changing the time of assembly, but it made no difference. Then the time for the kitchen staff's tea-break was found out, so assembly was fixed for that time. The tea-break time was changed in response. In the end the head teacher flung open the door and yelled. 'Do we have to have this bloody row?'. Hardly the thing for the middle of infants' assembly, but it appeared to have some effect. The kitchen is technically out of the head teacher's jurisdiction, and is the territory of the school meals supervisor.

A RESEARCH ACTIVITY ON CLASSROOMS

In the classrooms of Downers Grove school, Chicago, for children of junior-school age, 'caves' have replaced desks. Each child has an octagonal plywood cave which is situated in a three-tiered honeycomb from floor to ceiling. The idea is analysed in a report by Bealing (1972):

> An article in this week's issue of *Educational Research* (Volume 14, No.3), 'The organiza-
> tion of junior-school classrooms', casts doubt on the revolution said to have taken place in

the organization of the classrooms of Britain's primary schools in recent years. 'Despite the relatively informal classroom layout adopted by the vast majority of teachers, there was so much evidence of tight teacher control over such matters as where children sit and move that it seems highly doubtful that there is much opportunity for children to choose or organize their own activities in most classrooms.' Practical necessity, rather than pedagogical theory, probably accounts for this, says the author of the article, Deanne Bealing.

Practical necessities do have a way of exerting their influence, so is it that to change the organization and behaviour in classrooms one needs to change the structure itself in a rather more adventurous manner than has yet been tried?

All the children of Downers Grove school in Chicago would answer yes – for they inhabit classrooms unique in this respect. There are no desks – instead, each child has an octagonal plywood 'cave' which is piled with others in a three-tiered honeycomb from floor to ceiling. The idea is to give every child his own area where he can stash his books, clothes, string and whatnot and read or draw whenever he feels that he wants to.

The project is the brainchild of the school head, Avery Coonley, who conceived the idea for the caves with educationist Larry Busch. The children climb into their hideouts by means of carpeted hand- and footholds on the lower caves, and each space contains a seat, working surface, a light and storage space. The seat and storage space can be folded flush with the walls in order to give more room.

The caves are – almost literally – the children's castles: they are assigned at the beginning of the year and from then on outsiders can enter by invitation only. The teaching day at Downers Grove is structured at present so that an hour and a half is set aside specifically to be spent in the caves, but children are allowed to spend as much time as they want there.

Schoolwork, as a result of this project, says Coonley, has become more original even over the few short months it's been in operation. The children stick with their various academic activities longer now and, because they can't look over each other's shoulders, there is more originality in their work. Often, just the opportunity to get away from the rest of the class is rewarding: fidgets often withdraw and only come back once they are more settled.

The children themselves (up to age 11 or thereabouts) like the cave arrangement: being able to get away from others, and somewhere to leave things lying about, are the main attractions. In fact, several want more privacy – the doorway closed up, for instance, and locks.

But the biggest changes have occurred in the children who are from larger families and who don't have rooms of their own at home. The caves are cheap to make, says Coonley, so they could be an effective help in inner-city schools.

(This first appeared in *New Society*, 29 June 1972, London, the weekly review of the social sciences.)

The point of introducing this data on caves in classrooms is as an alerting device: classrooms can be quite different from those with which we are familiar.

Background Propositions

The spaces available specifically for teaching are of interest in at least three ways:

1. They suggest possibilities and opportunities for teaching.
2. They place constraints on what can be done.
3. They imply psychological, philosophical, sociological and pedagogical ideas that are often taken for granted, but are open to question.

Aim

The aim of this exercise is to analyse the various features of teaching spaces and to relate these to teaching possibilities, teaching constraints and the underlying theoretical assumptions.

Procedure

1.   Make a sketch-plan of a room or space known to you, including its furniture. This can be based on an actual visit or drawn from memory.
2.   Make notes on the following features:

(a) The shape of the room/space.
(b) The arrangement of desks/tables.
(c) The arrangement of chairs.
(d) The position of the teachers' desk.
(e) The windows.
(f) The display boards (e.g. position, number).
(g) The storage units (e.g. position, access).
(h) Any other furniture and fittings.
(i) Has the room space a 'front' and 'back'?
(j) Access points (number, off a corridor?).
(k) Write your comments, e.g. what assumptions are made about how children learn and what they should learn, the relationship between teacher and pupils, how the school is to be organized.
(l) How does this room differ from a public house, a theatre, a church or a youth club?
(m) What assumptions underlie the design of a public bar, a theatre, a church or a youth club?
(n) How do these differ from the assumptions underlying the design of the room you are analysing?
(o) Comment on the teaching possibilities of the room/space.
(p) Comment on the limitations set by the room/space.

Discussion

As in the case of the school building as a whole, there will be variations in the findings from classroom to classroom and space to space. Some propositions that emerge are:

1.   In most classrooms the placement of tables, desks and chairs gives the room a front and a back. The teacher's territory is usually well marked by a larger desk, the position of the blackboard, a space to the doorway, the position of a waste-basket, or some combination of these. This teacher territory often may occupy as much as a third of the space available.
2.   Many classrooms, particularly in secondary schools, are rather Spartan in appear-

ance and in furnishings. The transitory nature of the pupils' stay is signalled in the lack of displays of work and other 'involvements' with the room, e.g. the occupants did not choose the decor or decorate the room themselves.

3. The arrangement of seating indicates an expected channel of communication. In most cases this is seen as mostly teacher-centred or entirely teacher-centred. Teachers have the power to vary this and some do, particularly in infant schools.

4. Classrooms tend to signal social distance and teaching styles which are authoritarian, i.e. the learners are dependent on the teacher throughout. The layout often suggests a confrontation. An analogy is that of battle: in battle, territories are clearly established, sorties into each other's territory are regarded with suspicion, and in battle there is victory, defeat or truce.

5. Primary schools show some differences from secondary schools. The teacher's territory is often well marked. In a study of infant schools:

> Of the 145 classrooms visited, there were only six which did not sport a teacher's desk or table. The most favoured position for this was still the traditional centre front, at right angles to the main access door. In 42 cases, the teacher was actually seated at her desk for the whole or part of the time the observer was in the room
>
> Evans, 1974b

On the other hand:

> No classroom displayed that arrangement of furniture upon the rectangular grid pattern still found at secondary level.
>
> Evans, 1974b

Evans concludes that, in her studies of infants' classrooms:

> elements of tradition and continuity are stronger in English infants schools than is sometmes assumed . . . Many teachers were at pains to describe themselves as 'old fashioned'.
>
> Evans, 1974b

6. Comparisons with a modern public house are interesting. As in schools, large numbers of people are catered for over long periods of time. The standards of decor and comfort are usually higher in the public house and informal grouping and activity are encouraged by the layout.

7. A youth club often has some of the features of comfort and decor absent from schools, as well as having involvement of the members in providing and choosing furniture and in undertaking decoration.

8. A theatre often has the territorial features of many classrooms, unless it is a theatre in the round. The performance is highly resourced, both professionally and technically, and the clients experience high levels of comfort and consideration.

9. The limitations set by classrooms can be overstated: theatre designers use a similar area to achieve remarkable variations. The Chicago experiment with 'caves' presents only one possible variation.

CONCLUSION

Space as a Silent Language

The hidden nature of space and its unrecognized influence on us are discussed by Hall (1959), who sees it as a silent language:

> Territoriality is established so rapidly that even the second lesson in a series of lectures is sufficient to find a significant proportion of most audiences back in the same seats. What's more, if one has been sitting in a particular seat and someone else occupies it, one can notice a fleeting irritation. There is the remnant of an old urge to throw out the interloper.
>
> Hall, 1959

Environmental Competence

There are many practical implications of studies of space in schooling. One is contained in the idea of environmental competence. This is defined as:

> (a) a person's ability to be aware of the surrounding environment and its impact on him; and (b) his ability to use or change his settings to help him achieve his goals without inappropriately destroying the setting or reducing his sense of effectiveness or that of the people around him.
>
> Steele, 1973

On this definition, it can be argued that the behaviour of many teachers shows limited environmental competence. A common arrangement of furniture in a secondary-school classroom is where the desks are set in rows facing the 'front' of the room defined by the teacher's desk and other features like a blackboard. The teachers can usually see all or most of the pupils and from their point of view the classroom is ordered and tidy. The pupils can see only their neighbours and the teacher. The message of the arrangement is to look ahead. Unless the room is raked, what they actually see is a cluttered space of people's shoulders, heads and bits of the teacher.

The learning message is 'sit and listen': a lecture or instructional approach is implied. This style is appropriate some of the time, but if a teacher desires general discussion or group discussion the furniture arrangements are opposed to it. The teacher may be attempting to exchange and explore ideas in a physical arrangement that inhibits this. In this situation many teachers accuse the pupils of being unresponsive, when in fact the teachers have not maximized the chances of getting responses. Discussion is also facilitated by comfortable furniture and pleasant wall and floor coverings, as evidenced in most modern public houses.

There are more mundane examples of environmental competence. Many student teachers have had to be warned about the territorial claims senior staff have on parts of the staffroom and on particular chairs, and those who have not been given such warnings may find that their image with the staff quickly becomes an unfavourable one.

Gould questions the placement of lockers and argues that crime can be created by the architecture:

> What is the effect of placing children's lockers in remote cloakrooms or public passage-

ways? They become not the personal space nor even the territory belonging to a particular group but anonymous areas which in time become fair game to any pilferer because he will probably be unseen and therefore uncaught.

Gould, 1976

The issue of environmental competence in classrooms was illustrated in a study of three primary-school classrooms in the USA by Zifferblatt (1975). The three teachers had similar views on teaching but their classroom performance varied with spatial usage. His conclusion was that, regardless of a teacher's intentions, the pupils' behaviour is also influenced by the architecture. If a teacher wants to work individually, the arrangement of the classroom needs to 'tell' the pupils to sit by themselves with minimal social accessibility and distraction. To ask a child to behave in a certain way and fail to back up that request with the appropriate room arrangement, Zifferblatt argues, is to do only half the job, and to create unnecessary confusion for the pupils.

The Historical Dimension

One dimension of the descriptions and explanations for spatial layout largely over-looked in this chapter is the historical dimension. One of the continuities in educational activity lies in the relative permanence of buildings, which may well outlast the theories of education on which their design was based. Later users may find that their different teaching ideas are effectively reduced or outlawed by the inherited architecture. (See M. Seaborne and R. Lowe, 1977, for a useful treatment from the historical point of view.)

However, the furniture is less permanent and provides more scope for modification. School furniture before 1944 tended to consist of items like the heavy cast-iron-frame desks, usually constructed in pairs. Light tubular furniture, stackable or mobile, increases the options open to teachers. Walls designed to have things pinned on them rather than painted brick designed purely to keep the roof up are another aspect of increased choice for teachers (Dale, 1972a).

The Pupils' Perspective

For the most part, the analysis so far has centred on the teachers' layer of meaning and the teachers' viewpoint, as have most of the limited researches available. To devote a little space to the pupils' viewpoint would seem to be appropriate. Blishen (1969) sums up the comments of pupils about their buildings in this passage:

> They cry out for colour, and are very conscious of the drab uniformity of many of the walls within which they sit. They would like to have some say in the ephemeral decoration of their schools. They long for attractive grounds, and especially for trees. 'We do notice' says one girl; and one is reminded of the statement that sometimes the best of teachers makes, that the school building doesn't matter. The roots of such a statement are obvious enough; a great many of our school buildings aren't even remotely enjoyable, and a teacher aware of this may feel a very real need to point out that a school can be a good one despite this seediness of its setting. And indeed it can: and if one had to make a choice, one would choose bad buildings and good teachers rather than bad teachers and a palace. Yet it is clear

to me, especially since I have always taught in buildings of a fairly monstrous character, that buildings do matter; that the fabric of a school does speak to the children, and that it says, 'I express the community's notion of what you are worth, of the environment you deserve.' An ugly, inconvenient, wholly unpleasing school building makes a daily statement to the children; and children *do* notice.

Blishen, 1969

Copyright © Penguin Books and contributors. Reprinted by permission of Penguin Books Ltd.

Theory and Practice

There is some light shed on the matters of theory and practice in the studies of educational spaces. The notion that 'theory' is opposed to practice is dubious in the light of evidence about space and behaviour. The theory underpinning the use of space may be implicit or explicit, recognized or unrecognized. A particular theory may be applied, misapplied, or avoided. But one of the assumptions of this chapter is that all practices have an underpinning theory and that alternative practices and theories can be discovered. Teachers who do not recognize these competing theories are vulnerable to having decisions made for them, rather than exercising the choices that are open to them.

It would be misleading to see space as determining. In the studies of classrooms (Evans, 1974b), head teachers' rooms (Evans, 1974a) and commercial offices (Joiner, 1971) the variety of uses of the same space and furniture is stressed.

People, it seems, whatever the architect had in mind, can impose quite a lot of themselves on their surroundings.

Joiner, 1971

But as Mead (1934) points out, the changes individuals make in the social orders in which they are implicated usually involve changes in themselves and in their self-concepts.

SUMMARY

1. Relatively little attention has been given to analysing the influence of the spaces provided in schools on educating.
2. Teachers' rooms may indicate a great deal about them and their views of education.
3. The experience of using a school building is one illustration of layers of meaning: it varies considerably with the groups of people involved.
4. A research exercise on the school building may yield a series of taken-for-granted assumptions about schooling.
5. Inadequacies of design may force teachers into a more authoritarian role to compensate.
6. A research exercise on classrooms may yield further taken-for-granted assumptions.
7. Many teachers show limited environmental competence: room arrangements often fail to back up the teachers' intentions.

8. Buildings may outlast the theories of education on which their design was based, and create problems for later users who have different ideas.
9. Pupils have considerable awareness of the buildings, and many would like some say and involvement in improving them.
10. Spatial influences are important rather than determining, but their importance is often underestimated.

Further Reading

Bennett, S.N. et al. (1980) *Open Plan Schools: Teaching, Curriculum, Design*. Windsor: NFER-Nelson.

Cosin, B., Dale, R., Esland, G. and Swift, D. (eds.) (1971) *School and Society*. London: Routledge and Kegan Paul. Two articles in this reader are especially worth consulting: Chapter 11, by E. Goffman, and Chapter 13, by D.J. Bennett and J.D. Bennett.

Dale, R. (1972) *The Context of the Classroom*. Milton Keynes: Open University Press. A very readable analysis of spatial aspects of schooling.

Seaborne, M. and Lowe, R. (1977) *The English School: Its Architecture and Organization 1870–1970*. London: Routledge and Kegan Paul. An investigation of the historical aspects of school buildings.

Discussion and Activities

1. Using the two research activities in the chapter for ideas, devise your own list of questions for research into specialized spaces in a school, e.g. a secondary-school science laboratory.
2. Teachers are sometimes thought to be akin to actors in having to give performances. Does this comparison break down in the case of environmental competence, with actors taking this much more seriously than teachers?

Signposts

1. Education without specialized buildings
The Open University, correspondence colleges and the radio schools of the Australian outback all operate without the normal spatial features of special educational building. A state school in the USA operates this way too; see Farrington, P., Pritchard, G. and Raynor, J. 'The Parkway Programme' in Raynor, J. and Harden, J. (eds.) (1973) *Readings in Urban Education Vol. 2: Equality and City Schools*. Milton Keynes: Open University Press.

2. Open-plan classrooms in primary schools
About 10 per cent of primary schools in England and Wales are open plan. One study is Bennett, S.N. et al. (1980) *Open-Plan Schools: Teaching, Curriculum, Design*, Windsor: NFER-Nelson. Primary schools are the focus of two articles: Cooper, I. (1982) 'The Maintenance of Order and Use of Space in Primary School Buildings' *British Journal of Sociology of Education* **3**, 3; and Cooper, I. (1981) 'The Politics of Education and Architectural Design: The Instructive Example of British Primary Education' *British Educational Research Journal*, **7**, 2.

Chapter 8

Timetables

'Work expands so as to fill the time available for its completion.'
Parkinson's Law

INTRODUCTION: THE ALLOCATION OF TIME

In situations where it is believed that there is not enough time to do everything, systems of allocating time to chosen activities have to be established. Breaking up time into small segments is common to most situations and occurs in other activities also, as this passage suggests:

> Everyone, even the backward mental hospital patient, makes use of various devices to break up the days, weeks, months, and years of his life into smaller units. Such division of large masses into smaller blocks occurs not only in relation to time. We divide books into chapters, chapters into sections, sections into subsections and paragraphs.
>
> Roth. 1963

These examples are probably different aspects of the same psychological phenomenon, Roth suggests.

Schools face a time allocation problem. There are competing claims about what should be learnt in schools and the number of subjects to be included in the curriculum is seen as being greater than the time available, so time is defined as a scarce item that needs to be rationed in some way.

The way in which time is allocated in schools can contribute some insights into what goes on there and the hidden assumptions involved, as with the spaces and the architecture.

The timetable becomes part of the consciousness of the pupils, and it is generally taken for granted. It is one of the features of the culture of the school that is taken for granted, seemingly obvious, and unquestioned:

> One reader . . . told us: 'Throughout my childhood and also in my first few years of teaching, I lived as if I were in Genesis: "He made the universe in six days, and the week into 35 periods." ' Indeed, the first thing a pupil in secondary school does on starting a new school year is to take down his timetable.
>
> Dale, 1972b

Within a very short time of entering a school, a pupil begins to take for granted that the school day is broken down into blocks of time called periods. Playtime is at a set time, and so is lunch time, the start of the afternoon and the end of the school day. This system was created by previous members of the school and has some theoretical base, but this is not explained to the pupil; and it becomes accepted as the 'natural', if not inevitable, way of doing things.

SOCIOLOGICAL QUESTIONS

A sociological approach tries to resist this 'taken-for-grantedness' and instead asks questions about the particular kinds of timetables in use, the assumptions underpinning these, and the implications and consequences for the learning of all who are involved. A number of general questions may be asked:

1. Who timetables?
2. What is timetabled?
3. How is the timetabling undertaken?
4. Why timetabling and what are its consequences?

A RESEARCH ACTIVITY: THE SCHOOL TIMETABLE

Background Propositions

The allocation of time in school is deliberate and codified in a timetable. The principles that underlie this allocation are of interest, since they may:

1. have implications for what is learnt;
2. imply psychological, philosophical, sociological and pedagogical ideas that may be taken for granted, but are still open to question.

Aim

The aim of this exercise is to begin the process of questioning and analysing the underlying assumptions of school timetables.

Procedure

Obtain a copy of a school timetable, or consider a timetable you have experienced, or obtain access to a timetable board. (A class timetable will yield some results if the school timetable is inaccessible.) It should be possible to deduce most answers from the timetable itself: any questions to school staff must obviously be handled with politeness and tact.

1. Who designed the timetable?
2. Who was consulted?

3.   Who, in the school community, was not consulted?
4.   When was it devised?

What assumptions are being made here?

5.   How are groups formed: Allocated? Chosen? Age? Sex? Attainment?
6.   Do all groups study the same subjects?
7.   If not, when do differences begin?

What assumptions are being made here?

 8.   Which three subjects/activities are most frequently timetabled?
 9.   Which three subjects/activities are least frequently timetabled?
10.   Which subjects/activities are absent from the timetable?
11.   Does the frequency of subject/activity timetabling vary with groups?

What assumptions are being made here?

12.   How long are the periods allocated?
13.   What subjects/activities are given double periods?
14.   Are the timetables of boys and girls the same?
15.   If they differ, give details.

What assumptions are being made here?

16.   How does the school timetable compare with:
      (a) An evening institute programme; or
      (b) A youth club programme (either one night a week or full time); or
      (c) A technical college timetable?
17.   Why was the timetable devised in this particular way?

DISCUSSION

One general difference in timetables that can be seen is between those of infants, junior and secondary schools. The secondary-school timetable tends to be made up of a wide variety of subjects and the task of fitting all these in with appropriate classes and teachers is complicated – so complicated that some schools use a computer for the purpose. In the infants schools there are usually broadly defined activities like language work, number work and creative activities based on art and crafts. Junior and middle school occupies an interim position where the inclusion of subjects like history, science and music means that a finer division of time is required than in an infants school.

Who Timetables and When?

The general question 'Who timetables?' raises some interesting issues. A hierarchy of some kind usually emerges. The pupils are rarely consulted. Usually only some of the teachers are involved, and these tend to be senior teachers. Caretakers and cleaners are usually expected to arrange their activities to fit in with the timetable. 'Outside' clients like parents are not usually consulted.

The answer to the question 'When was the timetable devised?' is usually that this takes place before the pupils arrive in school and, in the case of a new intake, before the children have been met. There is an assumption here that the needs, achievements and wishes of pupils can be predicted. The variations between schools, however, suggest that different schools may make different predictions about these needs and achievements. For example, one school may predict that pupils have no need of social science studies and so this subject never appears in their timetables. Another school may predict that social science is appropriate only for sixth formers. Yet another may have social science from the age of eleven onwards, while some primary schools introduce such studies from age eight onwards.

Some schools have challenged the assumption that a school timetable should be imposed in an authoritarian way upon learners, and have developed timetables based on negotiation:

> We talked . . . and about his timetable. On the basis of chats with his teachers at the other school, chats with me, and what he had heard from specialists here he chose the following subjects to study (in addition to what he would be studying in team time which would include maths, English, social studies and a variety of other things): art, visual communication, music, control technology, chemistry, PE and games. He had changed his mind about German after talking it over with his parents. He was especially excited by the idea of control technology because of the construction involved, music because of the possibility of using the organ and synthesizer, and visual communication because of a conversation with the person who was going to teach it who had talked about the possibilities of photography. Later he dropped PE and games and said he would play five-a-side 'during team time if he felt the urge'. He also added typing at my suggestion. . . .
>
> At the start of term I'd suggested to Phil that he kept a journal. This is how he described his school life after two weeks.
>
> 'I have been at this school now for two weeks and now I have settled in and doing subjects I like to do and enjoy. Once you get to know the other students they are friendly towards you. When you get down to hard work, time seems to pass a lot quicker, but the first week we were just working out timetables and going to different classes to see what the different subjects were like and so time seemed to drift slowly by! I like it at this school, you learn things at your own pace and not like at my last school where for example in maths you go through different subjects in that category like an express train so you don't gather much knowledge.'
>
> J. Watts, 1977

What is Timetabled?

Timetables indicate the dual nature of what is being processed in schools, knowledge and people.

People

Pupils are formed into groups and these groups tend to be allocated rather than chosen. Allocation takes place on the multiple criteria of age, sex and achievement. The first groupings experienced by pupils tend to be on the basis of age. Some infants schools developed a family grouping system where children of various ages worked with one teacher, but the most common system is to allocate children into 1st years, 2nd years, 3rd years, etc. Age grouping is less rigid in other educational institutions, e.g. technical colleges, the Open University and evening institutes.

The next experience of grouping may be by sex. Certain activities tend to be designated as boys' activities and others as girls' activities. Games provide an example: football for boys and netball for girls. Later, domestic science for girls and metalwork for boys are much more formally sex-typed aspects of the timetable. A few schools have adopted the alternative of non-sex-typed timetables, where all subjects are studied by both boys and girls. (In some countries, e.g. Sweden, a common timetable for both sexes is required by law.)

Grouping by achievement is encountered by most pupils sooner or later. An early experience may be grouping within classes into 'top' tables and 'bottom' tables. Later experiences may be streaming, when a whole class is grouped on the basis of similar achievement, and setting, where achievement in one subject or activity is the basis for grouping pupils together.

Teachers are allocated to the timetable on the basis of subject identification in most secondary schools, and on the basis of class teaching of a wide range of activities in primary schools. Middle schools and some secondary and primary schools have a mixed classification of subject and general teaching, and teachers do some of both.

Knowledge

The knowledge to be processed is allocated to periods of time by being divided up into subjects. These subjects are more loosely organized in some schools than in others: in infants schools it is often broadly based in terms of number work, language activities, creative activities, etc., while in secondary schools the division of knowledge into a range of subjects is usually more rigid.

Some subjects and activities are allocated more time than others. Frequently English and maths, or their equivalent, head the list and physical education, including games, is often third. Subjects that tend to be allocated least time are religious education and music.

Some subjects, such as ethics, philosophy, logic, sociology, anthropology, politics and psychology, are missing from the timetables of most schools. These omissions raise some interesting questions. For example, since logic, rather than mathematics, underpins most of the subjects on the timetable, there is a case for its being the basic tool subject. The courses in 'thinking' produced by Edward de Bono have been adopted on these grounds in some schools.

The assumptions made about knowledge make an interesting list of propositions:

1. Knowledge is best compartmentalized into subjects.
2. Some knowledge deserves more timetable space than other knowledge, and knowledge is thus stratified.
3. Some knowledge is legally compulsory, e.g. religious education.

4. Some knowledge is examinable and some is not; e.g. physical education is not usually examined.
5. Different children should have different packages of knowledge, rather than there being a common curriculum.
6. Some knowledge is suitable for boys and some for girls.
7. Some knowledge, e.g. economics, sociology, is seen as worthy of timetable space by some schools and not by others.
8. The most suitable knowledge for schools is past-orientated and based on an ancient system of subject classification, rather than present-orientated and based on integrated themes like censorship, terrorism and environmental pollution, which cross the ancient subject boundaries.
9. Future-orientated knowledge systems stressing the skills of learning to create new knowledge and cope with constant changes in information are given little space in most timetables.
10. Some knowledge within the subject traditions is best excluded from the timetable, e.g. logic, philosophy and psychology.

How is Timetabling Undertaken?

The division of time into periods, days and weeks has consequences for the type of learning that can take place. All subjects or activities have to be taught and learnt in a similar way, in regularized blocks of time. Some concession to variations in learning may appear in the form of double periods, but this illustrates the point that, if double periods are needed, why not a half day, a whole day, several days or a week?

This division of time has implications for teaching methods. It tends to place a premium on third- and fourth-hand experiences. In history this may mean reading what a teacher other than your own has to say about manor houses rather than visiting the one a few kilometres away. It may mean seeing a short film about canals instead of travelling along one in a barge. It may mean copying pictures of locks and lock gates rather than sketching from the original. It may mean reading a play over a series of lessons instead of attending a performance at a local theatre. When outings of the above type are organized, they are special events rather than the basic mode of learning.

The timetable tends to be imposed: it is a set menu rather than a choice-based menu. The contrast here is with an evening-institute timetable, which indicates a range of classes from which students can choose. A technical-college timetable is based on the same principle: students enrol for courses rather than have an imposed allocation of subjects. A youth-club timetable is negotiated even further, and is fashioned from the wishes and needs of the members.

Where choices are introduced, often in the third year of secondary schooling, they have been shown to be very limited and rather distorted (Weston, Taylor and Hurman, 1978).

Why Timetabling and with What Consequences?

At the beginning of the chapter we saw that breaking up time into small segments is a common activity. The timetable represents a school's attempt to cope with competing claims about what should be learnt in schools and by whom. A particular view of knowledge and a particular view of teaching and learning are implied in these arrangements. Therefore pupils involved in a timetable learn considerably more than where to go for a lesson at a certain time. They are being exposed to a series of hidden messages about what counts as knowledge, which knowledge is thought to be appropriate for them, and which knowledge is not made available to them.

There may also be more hidden messages related to fatalistic or humanistic views of time. On humanistic time tracks activities are governed by personal decision. On fatalistic time tracks activities are matters of obligation, outside the actors' control, leading to conformity and coercion rather than to individual expression:

> Persons on fatalistic time tracks find themselves suffering the inconveniences of time. Activities in which they are involved seem like slavery. Terms like 'rat race', commonly applied to obligatory activities in bureaucratic settings, apprehend the subjective sense of fatalism sensed in some occupations. While all individuals may experience events or activities fatalistically sometimes, certain segments of society are more likely to perceive their very existence in fatalistic terms.
>
> Lyman and Scott, 1970

One view is that these time tracks are related to social class. In this view the time perspective associated with white-collar workers tends to be future-orientated, impersonal, planned, and built on the notion of deferred gratification, whereas the time perspective of blue-collar workers tends to be present-orientated, personal, spontaneous, and implying immediate gratification. Schools and teachers tend to adopt the first view of time. Pupils used to the second view of time may quickly be seen as 'lazy, careless, impulsive, uninvolved'. A school's promise to pupils is that it will all be worth it in the long run:

> The pupils are promised that the value of subjects whose relevance is totally mysterious to them will some day be recognized, and with gratitude. Such encouragements and promises, it is argued, work very much better with the middle-class child, whose cultural background supports the deferment of gratification, than with the working-class child, whose time-perspective leads him to want his cake now.
>
> Dale, 1972b

From the teachers' point of view, a secondary-school timetable tends to mean facing a large number of groups for rather short periods of time. The relationships with pupils become fragmented and rather impersonal because of lack of continuity of contact. These short periods of contact tend to stress group rather than individual relationships.

From the pupils' point of view, the timetable may be seen as a limitation on their learning:

> I hope that all the schools of tomorrow will primarily have much more freedom and variety than those of today. By freedom I mean much more time to work individually on subjects or aspects of subjects the pupils find interesting; and by variety I mean more flexibility in the weekly programme of lessons.
>
> Gillian, 14
> (From Blishen, 1969)

Timetables tend to imply a dogmatic theory of the sequencing of knowledge. Lewis (1972) argues that it is probably correct to assume that no sequence is inviolable and a teacher who thinks otherwise is almost certainly a dogmatic person. There are usually several ways of sequencing educational material that are effective, even in a seemingly constrained field like mathematics. The dispute between traditional and modern maths is partly a difference of sequencing. Lewis goes on to suggest that there are bad ways of sequencing which need to be identified. A conceptual map of the knowledge area in question helps to identify good and bad sequences:

> When maps of this kind are produced, it usually becomes clear that, with a little ingenuity, courses could be arranged in a variety of different orders. It remains true, however, that some orders are better than others.
>
> Lewis, 1972

THE SOCIOLOGY OF TIME, AND TIME IN SCHOOLS

So far the analysis has concentrated on school timetables, but there are other timetables in operation. The school timetable yields a class timetable, and a pupil's individual timetable may be derived from that. There are also year timetables and career timetables. The external, imposed and seemingly inevitable aspects of time in the school timetable are open to subjective interpretations by the participants.

A class timetable may carry the indicators of maths, religious knowledge and history: the subjective interpretation may be a boring period of hard work with the autocratic Mr Smith, an insulting attempt at indoctrination by Holy Joe Jones, worthy only of maximum playing-up, and a regular lecture by the history lady that allows you to write up your science homework. An 'individual' timetable may repeat these subjective interpretations with other indicators like 'this is the lesson to skip' or 'truancy this afternoon will not be noted'. The ambiguity of experience is illustrated here: experiences on the timetable have to be interpreted as pleasurable, useful or tedious, and some autonomy for teachers and taught is suggested here.

The year timetable introduces other features. It is shorter than a calendar year and has within it paradoxes such as the compulsion to attend the school building for part of the calendar year, and the exclusion, on the threat of trespass, at other times in the year.

A career timetable is built out of the year timetables. Although the years are of similar length, some are marked off as special. Years of transfer from one school to another, examination years and school leaving years are examples. Some school career timetables are longer than others, for various reasons. Early starts are the experience of some because of accidents of birth dates or because of the 'optional' nursery-school experience. The sixth form experience is for some but not for others. 'Schooldays' can mean anything from 11 to 16 years in school. Life chances are involved here, since length of school career is strongly correlated with job prospects and standards of living.

Time in school links with time outside school, and the social class links have already been mentioned. The school career timetable provides another example of this link in the concept of 'planners' and 'drifters': usually pupils who are 'pushed' by parents who tend to plan adopt the 'rational, future-orientated' time perspective of the school, whereas drifters do not. Planners know what goals exist in the school and how to reach them, when important turning points have arrived, and what the consequences of the choices will be. Drifters are less certain of the goals and their order of importance, and where each of the possible choices will lead:

> Perhaps the difference between the two can best be summarized by a pair of similes. To the drifter the school career is like a pinball machine and he has little control over how he progresses from one end to the other. To the planner, on the other hand, the school career is like a road map with alternative but clearly marked routes to various valued destinations.
>
> Dale, 1972b

CONCLUSION

Many of the messages learnt from the spatial layout of schools and classrooms, as outlined in the previous chapter, are reinforced by the messages learnt from the timetables. To parody Kohl's comments about classrooms, a timetable is not an arbitrary arrangement of time: it represents in outline form the timetable designers' beliefs and assumptions about knowledge, about learning, about teaching and about the outcomes of schooling. This selection of beliefs, often made by ancestors long gone, is only one of several alternative sets of belief about these matters.

SUMMARY

1. The activity of breaking time into small segments is common to many situations.
2. In school there are competing claims about what should be learnt and so time has to be rationed as a scarce item.
3. Timetables are some of the most taken-for-granted aspects of school culture and the hidden assumptions are rarely investigated.
4. A given timetable is only one of several possible ways of organizing, and the one chosen will reflect features of an ideology of education.
5. Some of the features of the implicit ideology of education are revealed by asking questions about who timetables, when timetabling takes place and what is time-tabled.
6. From a timetable, pupils learn a great deal more than where to go at a certain time. They may also learn some messages of the hidden curriculum, e.g. which knowledge is seen as male knowledge and which is seen as female.
7. The hidden assumption of deferred gratification may be a more familiar message to one social class grouping than to another and consequent adjustment to it less of a problem.
8. The subjective interpretations of timetables by pupils and staff illustrate the ambiguity of many human experiences: the interpretations of like, dislike, useful, and useless have to be learned.
9. Many of the hidden messages of the spatial arrangements of schools are reinforced by the timetable arrangements.

Further Reading

Ball, S., Hull, R., Skelton, M., and Tudor, R. (1984) 'The Tyranny of Devil's Mill: Time and Task at School' in Delamont, S. (ed.) (1984) *Readings in Interaction in the Classroom*. London: Methuen.

Dale, R. (1972) *The Use of Time in the School*. Milton Keynes: Open University Press.

Roth, J. (1971) 'The Study of Career Timetables', in Cosin, B. et al, *School and Society*. London: Routledge and Kegan Paul. A useful summary of ideas.

Watts, J. (1977) *The Countesthorpe Experience*. London: George Allen & Unwin. This book contains some accounts of negotiated timetables.

Discussion and Activities

1. Obtain copies of some of the following: an evening institute prospectus; an infants school timetable; an Open University student's personal timetable; any other educational time-table. Compare them using some of the analysis of this chapter.
2. Discuss how you would organize your time if you decided to educate yourself or your children at home. Analyse your timetable using any appropriate questions from the research exercise in this chapter.

Signposts

1. Timetables and options for third-year pupils in British secondary schools
Many pupils in the third year of British secondary schools enter a process of sorting their timetables for the next two years at school. One study is Hurman, A. (1979) *A Charter for Choice*, Windsor: NFER-Nelson.

2. Transfer to secondary schooling
A new style of timetabling is encountered by those pupils who leave middle school for secondary school. See Measor, L. and Woods, P. (1984) *Changing Schools*, Milton Keynes: Open University Press. The same experience faces those who transfer from primary to secondary school, and a source here is Derricott, R. (ed.) (1984) *Curriculum Continuity: Primary to Secondary*, Windsor: NFER-Nelson.

Chapter 9

The Official Curriculum

'The wish to preserve the past rather than the hope of creating the future dominates the minds of those who control the teaching of the young'

Bertrand Russell

INTRODUCTION

This chapter concentrates on the hidden aspects of the official curriculum. Many of the writings on the hidden curriculum contrast it with the official curriculum, and the hidden aspects of the content of schooling, of school knowledge itself, can all too easily be missed in such an analysis. It is the 'ghosts of the school-book writers' referred to earlier and the ghosts of curriculum designers that are looked for in what follows.

The two examples looked at in Chapter 6 are worth considering again briefly to establish the approach. The world of the reading schemes in use in primary schools contains messages along with the carefully graded exercises to build up learner reading skills in gradual stages. These messages reflect the views of the writers about their world. One message is sexism: dominant males involved with careers and work are contrasted with passive females in domestic roles, and paralleled with similar roles for the children. Boys are involved in adventures, while girls help mothers with housework. Lobban (1975) concludes that this is even more sexist than the real world, and abdicates entirely any chance of helping boys and girls to think about possible future alternatives.

The other example given was sex education books, in which the writers pass on their views about chastity, marriage and sex rather than informing pupils dispassionately about human sexuality and the alternative views about it. In these accounts Hoffman (1975) shows that erroneous information is passed off as fact and that Victorian beliefs about sex are dominant and expressed as the one right way of interpretation.

KNOWLEDGE IN SCHOOL IS NOT NEUTRAL

The proposition argued throughout this chapter is that the common-sense view that knowledge in school is neutral is mistaken. This is not a new idea: in 1916 Russell was writing about school subjects in this vein:

> It is in history and religion and other controversial subjects that the actual instruction is positively harmful. These subjects touch the interests by which schools are maintained; and the interests maintain the schools in order that certain views on these subjects may be

instilled. History, in every country, is so taught as to magnify that country: children learn to believe that their own country has always been in the right and almost always victorious, that it has produced almost all the great men, and that it is in all respects superior to all other countries. Since these beliefs are flattering, they are easily absorbed, and hardly ever dislodged from instinct by later knowledge.

SOCIOLOGICAL QUESTIONS ABOUT SCHOOL SUBJECTS

The use of the word 'subject' here is not meant to exclude the content of infants and primary school curricula: 'reading', 'number' and 'creative activities' may be interpreted as broader, more loosely organized school subjects, and the subjects of secondary schools as narrower and more constrained versions of subjects.

Adopting a similar approach to that used earlier in an analysis of assessment, what follows will be an attempt to develop answers to the following questions:

1. Which subjects are selected, and which versions of subjects?
2. Whose subjects are these and who selects this knowledge?
3. Why subjects and what kind of knowledge is this?
4. How are subjects implemented and what kinds of presentation are adopted?

SCHOOL SUBJECTS

History

In the famous satire, *1066 And All That*, the outcome of much school history is portrayed as oversimplification:

> War with Zulus. Cause: the Zulus. Zulus exterminated. Peace with Zulus.

One aspect of this oversimplification is the charge that school history teaching promotes nationalism and ethnocentric attitudes:

> Every State wishes to promote national pride, and is conscious that this cannot be done by unbiased history. The defenceless children are taught by distortions and suppressions and suggestions. The false ideas as to the history of the world which are taught in the various countries are of a kind which encourages strife and serves to keep alive a bigoted nationalism. If good relations between States were desired, one of the first steps ought to be to submit all teaching of history to an international commission, which should produce neutral textbooks free from the patriotic bias which is now demanded everywhere.

Even though these comments were written by Russell in 1916, there appears to be only one case of their being taken seriously. The Scandinavian countries have a procedure for submitting their history books for scrutiny so that inaccurate or biased comments about each other can be identified. They can then be drawn to the attention of pupils, or the books can be rewritten or juxtaposed with alternative versions. In support of Russell's point, a recent survey of history books in use in junior schools in Britain came to the following conclusions about the teaching of the history of South Africa. Nash found that the bias of these books was evident in their selectivity. Only four of the books mentioned the existence of black slavery, and then only in passing:

> There were thousands upon thousands of slaves in South Africa during the seventeenth, eighteenth and nineteenth centuries, but children taught from these texts would never know. Even where proper mention is made, it is usually in emotionally neutral terms, as if making slaves of people were a quite acceptable and normal way of treating them. For example: 'To help them in their work they used slaves, who were Negroes brought from other parts of Africa and poor people from Asia.'
>
> Nash, 1972

Nash comments that this is written in the same tone in which we might say that people use knives and forks to eat with, so that no reader would guess that the scars of over 200 years of slavery remain, and that they still have a powerful influence on South Africa. In Nash's view, the most significant evasion of the texts is that there is no mention of white supremacy. The total control by the white population of government, military, judiciary, police, industry and the mass media is not indicated by the books he studied. The books avoid the word apartheid: only one text contains it, even though all these books were published or revised after 1948, when the apartheid policy was implemented.

When surveying the textbooks Nash had before him the following five questions:

1. Is a history of South Africa given or only a history of European settlement?
2. Is the history of black slavery discussed?
3. Is white supremacy admitted?
4. Are derogatory terms used when discussing black or coloured South Africans?
5. Is apartheid or segregation admitted?

The results are shown in Table 9.1.

Table 9.1 *Summary of bias in 14 primary-school textbooks in their accounts of South Africa*

	No	Yes
History begins before European settlement	12	2
Gives account of slavery	10	4
Discusses apartheid	12	2
Admits white supremacy	13*	1
Uses derogatory terms when discussing native Africans	4	10

* In four of these cases a bright child might infer from the context that the whites are in control, but there is no clear statement.

It might be said that South Africa is a particularly sensitive example and that perhaps the treatment of other countries is less slanted. Nash disagrees. Here are his findings about the history of India in the same books:

> The history of India, for example, provides a parallel case. This is essentially the story of the East India Company (presented as a respectable body of merchants engaged in legitimate trade) and its wars with the French and the Indians. A great deal is made of native atrocities (always exemplified by the black hole of Calcutta) and of Robert Clive. In the following passage note how, in typical schoolmasterly language, Clive 'punishes' the 'cruel' native ruler:
>
> 'You will remember Suraj Dowlah, a cruel native ruler of Bengal. He attacked the East India Company's fort near Calcutta, but he was punished by Bob Clive, who defeated his enemy at Plassey and then conquered Bengal.'
>
> And, of course, British rule – just as it was in South Africa – is unreservedly maintained to have been beneficial to the development of India: 'During the first half of Queen

Victoria's reign Britain had done much to help the millions of peasants who were ignorant and poor. Steamers now traded with all their ports; the first railroad was being laid between Calcutta and Bombay; and the telegraph enabled important messages to travel swiftly. Also, many cruel customs had been abolished, and plans had been made to feed sufferers in times of famine and to educate native children.'

One hardly has to be an expert on colonial history to appreciate that most of this is nonsense. The motives for expansion into India, even more than in Africa, were economic. The Indian subcontinent was virtually stripped of its wealth during the 200 years of British imperialism. Its thriving textile industry was ruined for the benefit of Lancashire and, by the end of the nineteenth century, returns from India provided more than two-fifths of Britain's balance of payments surplus. This surely benefited the Indians less than ourselves.

Nash, 1972

(This first appeared in *New Society*, London, the weekly review of the social sciences.)

Another hidden message of history teaching is sexism, according to various analyses of the content of textbooks and syllabuses. Millstein concludes from a survey of USA school books that history, as purveyed by such textbooks, was quite clearly *His*-story and not *Her*-story (Millstein, 1972). An interesting example of how such a bias can influence a writer is given in the two illustrations in Figure 9.1.

Figure 9.1 The medieval illustration shows women rabbit hunting. In '*A Portrait of Britain in the Middle Ages 1066–1485*' men have taken over in R.S. Sherriff's otherwise similar illustration. From the *Times Educational Supplement*, 29 November 1974.

The conclusion of Davies (1974) about sex bias in history teaching is that:

the hidden curriculum in history teaching is heavily biased towards sexual inequality. I am not complaining that most societies of the past were sexually unequal; that, fact or fiction, is beyond my desire or capacity to change. It is our present study of those societies that is sexist, and it bears a heavy responsibility for forming the belief that it is somehow abnormal to be female . . . the sexually prejudiced areas of our society are largely formed and reinforced by the way we teach and learn about the past.

Music

The content of school music has been subjected to analysis by Shepherd et al. (1977) and provides some very clear examples of selection in content. The consequence, they argue, is the alienation of pupils from music teaching: pupils in school are usually very interested in music, but they are usually not very interested in school music. The problem is rooted more in teachers' definitions of music than in the supposed lack of ability of pupils. The content of school music is usually defined so that:

> university students as much as kids in school music lessons get a hidden curriculum of themes like the following: that whilst popular music is socially significant and conditioned, 'serious' music is not, but reflects simply the creative purpose of the composer; that 'serious' music equals art, whilst popular music cannot be considered as 'proper' music at all; that 'serious' music is exempt from the commercial pressures which bedevil popular music; that analysis of music presupposes analysis of musical notation and that musical analysis can objectively elucidate the meaning of music and act as a guide to relative musical value.
>
> Vulliamy, 1978

All these assumptions, Vulliamy argues, can be shown to be dubious. First, the view that there is an objective yardstick by which you can measure classical music against jazz or rock music fails to recognize that the musical languages are quite different: the first uses a notated tradition, while the second two use improvisation in an aural tradition. It follows that there can be criteria for good and bad classical music and criteria for good and bad jazz, but not criteria to compare the two. The commercial pressures on popular music led to the pop musicians themselves identifying good 'pop' as against commercial 'pop', although the term 'popular' is a misleading oversimplification:

> it must be emphasized that the term 'pop' music is a thoroughly misleading one, in that it covers many different types of music, some of which are popular and some of which are not, some of which are found on LP records (which since 1968 have outsold singles in absolute terms) and some on singles records. Various types of so-called 'pop' music (soul, Tamla Motown, teenybopper pop, rock, folk, reggae, 'progressive' music, to name but a few) not only have very different musical origins and qualities but also appeal to widely different social groups.
>
> Vulliamy, 1978

Vulliamy states that the view that all 'pop' music is commercial is a vast oversimplification. Although the prime consideration of some musicians is money, others set out to create what they regard as serious artistic music. However, serious jazz or rock musicians who want to create music which, due to its experimental nature, is unlikely to be commercial, rarely get help from the grant-aiding bodies. They also miss out on media exposure: the BBC policy appears to be to exclude serious jazz and rock from the radio. Radio 1, which is said to be the popular music provision, promotes commercial singles, and the two categories of music shown to be most popular with schoolchildren, namely progressive rock, and reggae and soul, are largely absent.

Vulliamy concludes that there has been an almost total neglect of jazz, rock and other forms of music in schools in both the USA and the UK. Academic music is totally dominated by so-called 'serious' music in the notated European tradition, and neither 'O' level nor 'A' level syllabuses consider the various forms of Afro-American music with their non-notational traditions. The conclusion is that pupils' musical knowledge and concerns are invalidly rejected: school music is 'their' music, not 'our' music, and the reasons for this tell us more about the misconceptions of the musical establishments in universities and elsewhere than about the nature of music.

Domestic Science

The subject of domestic science raises other issues. First, it illustrates the idea of the stratification of knowledge, i.e. that some subjects are deemed to be more important than and superior to others. For the purposes of university entrance, an 'A' level in domestic science is usually counted as an 'O' level only. In studies of the sixth form curriculum, it consistently comes at the bottom of the list of acceptable subjects, whether viewed by university tutors, employers, teachers or pupils. Yet as those who have experienced domestic science courses have consistently reported, the courses are demanding in both written and practical examinations.

Domestic science is a required study in some European countries, and required equally for boys and girls. In Britain, however, it is defined in practice as a girls' subject. The actual questions used in examinations signal this clearly:

> You and your husband are going to spend a weekend with your parents. Launder a selection of your own and your husband's clothes: these should include a variety of fabrics and finishes. Name these fabrics with labels, when displaying your finished work. Prepare a meatless evening meal for the two of you, using up leftover cooked vegetables and stale bread.
>
> Metropolitan CSE paper, 1974

Defined as a girls' subject, domestic science becomes a potential carrier for sexist assumptions about society. In a survey of textbooks available for teaching the subject, Wynn (1977) discerns these messages to girls and to the few boys who study domestic science. She concludes that any girl doubtful of the positive virtues of household tasks would be under attack. It would be suggested that her marriage would break down. She would be warned that her man would turn to drink if the home were not organized to his satisfaction. So any man who drinks to excess is in a position to blame his wife's failings.

> There have been some concessions made to the present interests of girls. One of these has been the development of courses in 'good grooming', which includes hygiene, appearance, make-up etc. These courses, whilst seen by some as an antidote to the 'future housewife' orientation of home economics, actually serve similar interests. Such courses help girls to think of themselves as ornamental creatures whose main aim in life should be to catch a suitable husband
>
> Wynn, 1977

Wynn sees a theme which is missing from most domestic science courses: that of possible alternatives, especially those that would increase the chances of dual-career families. For Wynn the characteristics of domestic science teaching in schools are sexist in that they mark out an almost exclusive domestic role for women. Employment is seen as a temporary activity that fills in awkward bits of time for women, rather than as a serious alternative to domesticity. Wynn concludes:

> Women's tasks in the home are envisaged as inevitable as is the continuation of the family in its present form. Thus the stage is set for women to be used as cheap labour and to be exploited. The cultural pressures on women to conform to sex stereotypes start in infancy, and are reinforced in home economics.

Religious Education

Religious education has a unique place in the curriculum of schools in Britain since, here alone among the countries in Europe, it is compulsory by law. The only other compulsion of this kind is also religious – the daily act of worship in schools.

The hidden curriculum of RE teaching is perhaps indicated in the title of a document published in 1975 by the British Humanist Association arguing for the reform of the 1944 Education Act's provisions regarding the subject in schools. It was entitled 'Objective, Fair and Balanced', the assumption being that RE teaching was unbalanced, unfair and failed to be objective. One of the key objections of this document was that RE was often taught as if there were no alternative to Christianity, whether it be other religions or non-religious belief systems like Humanism, Existentialism or Marxism. Some advice to schoolteachers coping with young children's questions about religion will perhaps illustrate the point:

> Who made God? The simple answer to this is 'Nobody; God has always been there'. If He had been made by somebody else, we should then want to know who had made that person, and so we could go back until we got to someone who had started it all – and that Someone is God. If we reflect a little, we soon discover that all things begin with God. For instance, the table in the kitchen is made from wood, the wood came from a tree, but God put the tree there and made it grow. The child's woollen jersey came from a sheep – and who made the sheep and gave it life? – God.
> So we can go on, tracing all things back to God, who is the beginning of everything.
>
> Hunt, 1974

Objections to this advice as failing to be objective are made on two grounds:
1. The logical form of the question is not pursued: the next question, using such a logical sequence, must be 'and who started or created God?'. It is just as logical to argue that the universe has always been there as it is to argue that God has always been there.
2. By omitting any qualification like 'the answer that believers or Christians give is . . .', the hidden message is that everyone agrees that this is the answer: alternative answers, by implication, simply do not exist, or are not recognized.

Interestingly, Hunt goes on to say, with unconscious irony in the light of the objections claiming that this approach is dishonest:

> It is very important to give an honest and truthful answer to a child's questions.

The teaching of RE is difficult to analyse because there are many competing versions of the subject in existence at the same time. Stopes-Roe (1976) has listed three major versions which can be described as:

1. Religious instruction, where the intention is to convert children to Christianity.
2. Religious education, where the intention is to convert children to religious thinking and sympathies, without necessarily specifying which religion.
3. Life stances education, where the intention is to teach dispassionately about belief systems, whether supernatural or secular.

The outcome of much religious education in schools has been seen as the advocacy of belief rather than thought:

> The prevention of free inquiry is unavoidable so long as the purpose of education is to produce belief rather than thought, to compel the young to hold positive opinions on doubtful matters rather than to let them see the doubtfulness and be encouraged to independence of mind. Education ought to foster the wish for truth, not the conviction that some particular creed is the truth.
>
> Russell, 1916

In contrast, the advice offered to teachers in 1974 by Hunt stressed belief rather than thought:

> We know that there is a heaven because Jesus told us so . . .

> The fact that we don't know all the answers can be one way of pointing out how great and wonderful God is – the only Being who does know everything. There is nothing wrong in thus instilling a sense of awe into a child, and little children will happily accept that there is One who is above (in the right sense) us all, and to whom we can safely leave these big puzzles, because He loves us all so much.

An alternative view from the advocates of religious education is less dogmatic. As Owen Cole (1978) writes:

> if we are helping the pupil in his search for meaning we must not predetermine the limits and say that his solution will be religious. He should, therefore, be given some understanding of how people can work out their place in existence without reference to religion. Humanism provides such a coherent alternative view of life.

Political Education

In the UK, political education has tended to be neglected as part of the official taught curriculum. This is not the case in other states, as Harber (1984) has noted. However, the hidden curriculum of the rest of school life is highly political, as was seen in the overview chapter of this section of the book. Harber (1984) quotes a cartoon that summarizes the findings well. A head teacher explains to an inspector, 'we concentrate on the 3Rs here: rightwing views, reactionary ideas and respect for authority'. Harber's analysis concludes:

> The general thrust of schooling in terms of day to day messages and assumptions favours centre-right political values rather than centre-left ones.

It follows that the list of attitudes at the start of Chapter 6 and derived from Postman and Weingartner (1971) is, according to one point of view, the required outcome of education and is therefore good education.

The political education that does occur in the official curriculum has parallels with the case of religious education in having various forms related to different ideologies of the subject.

1. The British Constitution form – where the intention is to encourage children to adopt the British version of Westminster style representative democracy and therefore to perpetuate the status quo.

2. The democratic studies form – where the intention is to convert children to a generalized sympathy for democratic ideas without specifying a particular form of democracy.
3. The political enquiry form – where the intention is to explore critically all political belief systems, and encourage political thinking and political skills rather than specific political beliefs.

The Curriculum Review Unit's Initial Training Panel has outlined five rather than three possible positions on political education. These are conservative, liberal, a political, reformist and radical (Porter et al., 1983). However, Harber (1984) proposes that two positions occur more frequently in debates about the UK curriculum than any others. He describes these as the conservative and the liberal-reformist, the first limiting political education to the British Constitution approach, the second favouring the democratic studies form with the added idea of increasing the potential for democratic participation in economic, educational and political influence groups (such as pressure and interest groups). Harber (1984) argues that 'Conservative resistance to newer approaches in political education are not about a threat from the left but about a threat to their own hegemony'.

Russell, writing in 1916, saw the conservative approach as an infringement of the rights of children and tantamount to lying to pupils:

> Education is, as a rule, the strongest force on the side of what exists and against fundamental change: threatened institutions, while they are still powerful, possess themselves of the educational machine, and instil a respect for their own excellence into the malleable minds of the young. Reformers retort by trying to oust their opponents from their positions of vantage. The children themselves are not considered by either party; they are merely so much material, to be recruited into one army or the other. If the children themselves were considered, education would not aim at making them belong to this party or that, but at enabling them to choose intelligently between the parties; it would aim at making them able to think, not at making them think what their teachers think. Education as a political weapon could not exist if we respected the rights of children. If we respected the rights of children, we should educate them so as to give them the knowledge and the mental habits required for forming independent opinions; but education as a political institution endeavours to form habits and to circumscribe knowledge in such a way as to make one set of opinions inevitable.

Russell's analysis is lost on those who respond to any attempt to reform political education with the comment that it is left-wing indoctrination. Such responses can cover an undeclared desire for a status quo of right-wing indoctrination, as Harber (1984) noted.

Science

One view of science teaching in schools is that it serves as a sociological case study of the irony of human action. Science education was seen by its pioneers as radical, as leading to thought rather than belief, as undermining dogmatic forms of knowledge. Young (1976) argues that it has become almost the opposite, has developed as an alternative dogma, has become, in Russell's terms, 'a grave of intelligence'.

Young sees school science as carrying a series of hidden messages. The first, exemplified clearly in the specialized room of the laboratory, is that science is removed from everyday life:

> School science separates science from pupils' everyday lives, and in particular their non-school knowledge of the natural world. It is learnt primarily as a *laboratory* activity, in a room full of special rules, many of which have no *real* necessity except in terms of the social organization of the school.

In contrast, the Open University foundation course in Science operates without a laboratory, and undergraduate students do their experiments at home in the kitchen or garage, using a home experiment kit and improvised apparatus.

A second message, Young argues, is that if it is relevant science or applied science it is inferior. A rather startling example is the polarization of science and domestic science: the chemistry, physics and biology of kitchen, household, cooking, cleaning and house maintenance are so low in status that an 'A' level in its study counts as an 'O' level in one of the 'pure' sciences. Further examples are the separation of applied sciences like metalwork and woodwork, which then require a special project technology to try to upgrade these technological subjects in the knowledge hierarchy.

A third message stressed by Hine (1975) is that science, as presented in school, is dehumanized. He argues that there is no attempt to present Newton in the round, i.e. Newton as a person, his place in history, his non-scientific concerns. The work is extracted and presented out of human context as an explanation of so-called non-human events. This dehumanization makes the material completely different from that in other subjects.

> It is possible that a more complete study of Newton, including his preoccupation with magic, his relationship to his contemporaries, his particular use of the scientific method, to give only a few possibilities, could complement the study of Shakespeare, for instance. A study of Newton could show the fallibility of science, instead of emphasizing its dogmatic elements.
>
> Hine, 1975

The methods of teaching science in school are also held to carry hidden messages. In a study of how teachers use language in schools, Barnes, Britten and Rosen (1969) conclude about both arts teachers and later science teachers in their sample:

> teachers were teaching as though their tasks were more concerned with information than thought. If so, this is the version of the subjects that the children were learning.

This effect is reinforced by something like an obsession with technical terms:

> The act of giving a technical name seems for many teachers to have taken on a value of its own in separation from its utility.

Barnes finds that, whether they intend it or not, by their use of language, science teachers were portraying their subjects as ready-reckoner systems of true answers, rather than principles of thinking through problems and constantly reviewing answers always held as probabilities, rather than certainties. In addition, they were also signalling to pupils that their role as learners was passive: it was to reproduce information or reasoning, rather than to think for themselves.

None of these hidden messages is inevitable. An account by Hoskyns (1976) describes how he set about reducing both the message of laboratories as alien places and the message of the separation of pupils' everyday science and school science:

> I opened the labs in the lunch hour and after school and pursued a policy of reacting to whatever the students suggested with a 'yes' rather than a 'no'. I introduced a number of routines and activities which I dropped if students rejected them and kept if they were enthusiastic. The atmosphere in the lab was not right, so I fitted a hi-fi amplifier and speakers into the lab with a radio and turntable; some pupils actually found it easier to work with Radio 1 in the background, while others started to bring their own records. We started a record loan club. As I got to know the students (especially in the evenings when they came up to work in the Youth Centre) I decided to build on the success of the music and make available other facilities which could be loosely allied to physics. We introduced a loan service for equipment at the weekend. We designed and built radio-controlled cars and introduced photography with a permanent dark-room. We built a discotheque and used it in the school hall and local clubs. We encouraged those with an interest in electronics to build and test circuits out of *Practical Electronics* and similar magazines. We got some guitar amplifiers and cabinet speakers and let groups of two or three students use a room to practise with microphones and tape recorders in the Youth Centre in the evenings. I discovered that the computer terminal was free of charge after 6.30 p.m., so that students could run programmes up until 9.30 p.m. I got four people from Imperial College to help with the cars, the computing and the electronics in the evening. A number of third-year undergraduates came during the day and in the holidays to study the experiments in the Nuffield Course, to help students doing them and also to improve that section of the course for the following year. They responded particularly to the informality of the lab and the music and the confident way in which our pupils could talk about the difficulties they were having with the Physics.
>
> These sorts of facilities, which have developed over a number of years, are based upon an initial attempt to create the right atmosphere for mutual confidence between pupils and teachers. It is not particular innovations (music, model cars, etc.) that are important as any kind of magic formula. What is important is the continual effort to create a rich rather than a dessicated environment – one in which the activities and initiatives of the pupils and teachers are stimulated rather than stunted, and one above all in which pupils have time to explore and familiarize themselves with equipment, ask questions and regain the confidence their earlier experience of schooling has so often removed.

In his account, Hoskyns notes how important it was to involve pupils in course planning to maintain pupil interest and concerns. Each holiday or the end of a term was a period of intense discussion about what was to be done in the next term or half term, and this ensured that pupils' needs were central to the work that followed.

This approach also changed the use of resources. These became shelved until called on, rather than being fed in automatically to a pre-set plan. Such a course needed careful attention to structure, Hoskyns found, and, as a teacher, he could do too much or too little, for understanding came to be seen as a process that was full of contradictions. A student had to be free to pursue understanding in a way that was best for him, yet the information had to be available as he wanted it.

Hoskyns found that the creative skills were given a chance to develop in the writing up of the work. To the question, 'What shall I write?', he learnt to reply 'Just anything you have done', instead of prescribing a rigid format. He found that his reply 'just anything you have done' stimulated a clear, often beautiful piece of work.

Most science teaching in schools is not like this, Young (1976) suggests in his analysis of secondary-school teaching. He argues that it tends to produce three broad groupings of people ready to fit into niches in society. These are the pure scientists, whose relations with the natural world are of a rather abstracted nature; the applied scientists, whose identity is essentially pragmatic – given something to be done, it is done, but ends are given, not selected; and third, Young proposes, there is the large group, the mass of people whose schooling teaches them that science is a specialized activity over which they neither have nor could have control.

Other Subjects

Most of the subjects in the school curriculum have been held to carry hidden messages, and a few are worth mentioning briefly.

Social science

Like science, social science was thought to be radical in its content and therefore to lead pupils to question and think rather than accept and believe. In practice, Reeves (1976) argues, the content:

> has passed through a complex filtration process, analogous to the processes of a sewage works. By the time it reaches the student, through the filter beds of various committees, examination board, schools council, publishing houses, headmaster, head of department and teacher, it is likely to have been cleansed of its most interesting radical pollutants.

The result, Reeves argues, is that pupils learn the hidden message that the parts of society fit together to form a relatively smooth-running machine of splendid complexity, with opportunities for small cogs to become larger cogs provided they accept the modest starting positions awaiting the majority and believe in the virtue of the dominant group members.

Art

Art has been interpreted consistently as sculpture and painting, and the popular arts that many people practise, such as photography and gardening, either have been excluded or have been given supplementary status. The answer to the question 'Whose art?' often turns out to be 'their' art, high culture, upper-class art, and there are many similarities between art and music, examined earlier.

Languages

The case of languages raises an interesting issue. The attempts at future-looking, international co-operation- and communication-building languages like Esperanto are excluded from schools and universities. Examination boards refuse to recognize them. Latin, Greek and other ancient languages are 'suitable'; European languages are encouraged, but in a form that stresses written rather than spoken skills; Russian and Chinese are reserved for a minority-interest group. These selections make plausible the charge that schools celebrate the past rather than prepare pupils for the future.

Mathematics

Maths dominates the curriculum as a 'true' subject of certain facts and reliable information, though many mathematicians would hold to a relativity view of their discipline and see school maths as 'imitation maths' of inferior quality (Sawyer, 1943). It dominates because it is held to be essential to so many other subjects. Yet logic, which is essential to an understanding of even more subjects, is excluded. School mathematics encourages belief and linear thinking, as Sawyer (1943) suggests, while logic encourages question, analysis and lateral thinking. One attempt to rectify this situation is that of de Bono and his CORT materials, designed to help pupils to learn to think logically.

THE SOCIOLOGY OF KNOWLEDGE

The sociology of knowledge is concerned with the existential conditions of knowledge and therefore with the study of the relationships between thought and society. Among the basic premises are that ideas are produced and received in a socio-historical setting and that knowledge is permitted or limited by social structures. Micro-perspectives in sociology stress that individuals are not entirely passive in this but are engaged in an active process of constructing their own knowledge and their own reality.

Putting this more simply, the proposition is that the knowledge needed at a particular time is produced in a society and restrictions are made on any knowledge produced that is not interpreted as desirable. For example, the technological knowledge to effect moon landings was produced in two societies when the political and military needs were established.

This kind of analysis can proceed only with a particular view of knowledge. It requires that the idea of 'best' knowledge or 'true objective' knowledge be suspended. Instead, knowledge is defined as what the participants believe or think is knowledge. It embraces the members' expectations, attitudes, myths, information and misinformation.

A SOCIOLOGY OF SCHOOL KNOWLEDGE

A number of questions are raised by a sociological approach to knowledge and schooling. They include:

1. What knowledge is available in classrooms?
2. If there are different stocks of knowledge, where do they come from?
3. What are the characteristics of school knowledge?
4. What happens if two stocks of knowledge are in competition?
5. Is some knowledge rejected or avoided?
6. Do the institutional features restrict knowledge?
7. How is knowledge assessed and with what consequences?
8. What alternative theories of knowledge are available?

THEORIES OF SCHOOL KNOWLEDGE

Content

School knowledge may be interpreted as predominantly past-orientated, present-orientated or future-orientated. Past-orientated approaches will rely heavily on existing subject divisions on the grounds that the knowledge gathered in the past is comprehensive and reliable, and the allocation into subject areas soundly based.

Present-orientated knowledge approaches stress integration of some kind on the grounds that current 'problems' like terrorism, pollution, computer technology and mass-media communication are both cross-disciplinary and in need of new kinds of knowledge to cope with them.

Future-orientated knowledge approaches stress that the rate of change in technology and society, and the rate of production of new knowledge, imply that learners need to acquire skills of learning, relearning and developing new knowledge. Generally, education needs to cope with the 'knowledge explosion', where, it is argued, the amount of knowledge is estimated to be doubling every ten years.

It follows that a past-orientated view would favour Latin as part of the curriculum, a present-orientated view contemporary French and German, and a future-orientated view Esperanto as an international language with political implications for the 'problem' of nationalism.

Structure: Stratification of School Knowledge

Some knowledge in schools is granted high status and some low status. One division is between examined knowledge and non-examined knowledge. A case that illustrates this is that of the social sciences in the school curriculum. Cannon (1964) shows how social studies remained of low status until some of the individual social sciences became established as examination subjects at 'A' and 'O' level. Psychology, economics and sociology now attract large numbers of candidates, especially at 'A' level examinations.

The examination subjects themselves are ranked, though the perception of these rankings may vary. Among parents, perception varies with social class. Miles (1969) shows that the correlation between subjects at 'O' level and social class of parents supports the interpretation that parents in higher social/economic groups favour non-practical subjects like Latin, whereas the reverse applies in the case of parents in lower social/economic groups. Using IQ as an indicator, Miles argues that an undue number of higher social/economic background candidates are missing from the practical subjects and vice versa.

The interpretations by university admission personnel are available from a study of the sixth form curriculum (Reid, 1972). This shows that science subjects have wide acceptability, although internally ranked in the order of maths, physics, chemistry and biology, whereas arts and social science subjects have less acceptability. Thus a stratification of subjects is found on attempting entrance to a university: some subjects have greater market value than others. The rankings are given in Table 9.2.

Table 9.2 *Acceptability of 'A' level subject passes to a sample of university departments (n = 84)*

Mathematics (Pure)	0.92	German	0.63
Mathematics (Pure w. Stat.)	0.83	Economics	0.62
Mathematics (Pure w. Mech.)	0.82	Greek	0.62
Physics	0.81	Geology	0.61
Mathematics (SMP)	0.78	Biology (Nuffield)	0.60
Mathematics (Further)	0.78	Latin	0.60
Physical Science	0.71	British Government	0.49
Chemistry	0.70	General Studies	0.49
Further Mathematics (SMP)	0.69	Engineering Science	0.46
History	0.67	Scripture Knowledge	0.46
Biology	0.66	Music	0.44
Geography	0.66	Art	0.37
French	0.65	Elements of Eng. Design	0.27
English Literature	0.64	Geometry and Eng. Drawing	0.27
Chemistry (Nuffield)	0.64	Housecraft	0.15
Spanish	0.64		

Another aspect of stratification is that of subjects as opposed to integrated fields of study. Young (1971) argues that the modifications in the curriculum have been of two kinds. There are those that maintain the view of subjects as the most suitable way of organizing knowledge and therefore introduce new subjects or rewrite a syllabus for an existing subject. Second, there are those that propose an alternative view of knowledge, e.g. as integrated fields of study; innovations are then restricted to low-status pupils, thus confirming their official 'failure':

> by creating new courses in 'low status' knowledge areas, and restricting their availability to those who have already 'failed' in terms of academic definitions of knowledge, these failures are seen as individual failures, either of motivation, ability or circumstances, and not failures of the academic system itself. These courses, which explicitly deny pupils access to the kinds of knowledge which are associated with rewards, prestige and power in our society, are thus given a kind of legitimacy, which masks the fact that educational success in terms of them would still be defined as 'failure'.

Young also has suggested the main criteria for the established subjects with high status:

> These are literacy, or an emphasis on written as opposed to oral presentation; individualism (or avoidance of group work or co-operativeness) . . . which focuses on how academic work is assessed and is a characteristic of both the 'process' of knowing and the way the 'product' is presented; abstractness of the knowledge and its structuring and compartmentalizing independently of the knowledge of the learner; . . . finally and linked to the former is what I have called the unrelatedness of academic curricula, which refers to the extent to which they are 'at odds' with daily life and common experience . . .

The consequences of this stratification of knowledge are that teachers became stratified, pupils became stratified, school organizational systems stratify and the school 'product – pupils at the end of their school career – is stratified.

Subjects as Social Systems

The analogy of subjects as social systems includes the following propositions. Subjects tend to have:

1. Initiation procedures. Newcomers are required to prove their acceptability by undergoing examinations at various levels: 'O' level, 'A' level, university degree. This establishes their commitment to the 'tribe' of chemists, geographers, sociologists or whatever.
2. Specialist languages. Many of the terms used in subjects have everyday-speech equivalents, but a technical language is developed and subject members are required to use this to maintain credibility.
3. Boundary maintenance procedures. Considerable effort goes into marking off laymen from initiated members and also into defining how the subject differs from other subjects. 'Popularizers' are usually regarded with antagonism, because they appear to dispel some of the mystery of the subject.
4. Research conventions. The conventions of research-paper production and subject conferences encourage researches to stay within a discipline. Cross-disciplinary and interdisciplinary efforts are less likely to be acceptable. Also, the finance of research is organized by subject committees.

The operation of subjects as social systems has at least three possible consequences:

1. Teachers' activities are constrained and the way they perceive school activities and possibilities is limited:

> Just as most secondary teachers take their pupils as they find them, so they take for granted what it is they are supposed to be teaching. What they are teaching, if vague ideals like 'cultivation' and 'liberal knowledge' are set aside, is a body of subject matter related to their college or university specialism. Sometimes this knowledge is seen as simply utilitarian and directly vocational, sometimes as a training of the mind or even as an opportunity for self-awareness.
>
> Holly, 1973

Holly argues that subject specialists are recruited to teach predefined areas of knowledge in a way that is not really open to discussion. It is therefore a rationalization, not a rationale, for a true rationale is possible only where the decisions have not already been made. In most secondary schools all the real curricular decisions have been made, he suggests.

2. A rational debate about change is unlikely and the development of a present or future view of knowledge to replace the past orientation of subjects is made difficult:

> On the whole, the most well-established secondary school subjects are those which were developed at universities during the nineteenth century, the time when the secondary curriculum was last basically reformed from the classical tradition of the Renaissance – hence English, history, geography, arithmetic of the stocks-and-shares variety, Euclidian geometry, algebra, Newtonian physics, inorganic chemistry, 'governess' French, muscular-Christian games, classificatory biology, plus a residue of Latin.
>
> Holly, 1973

This is still the curriculum of the majority of secondary schools. To say that this curriculum in the last quarter of the twentieth century is at all rationally derived would be to fly in the face of reason, Holly concludes. Demonstrably it is the result of a historical process.

3. The stocks of knowledge brought to school by pupils are rejected. The knowledge

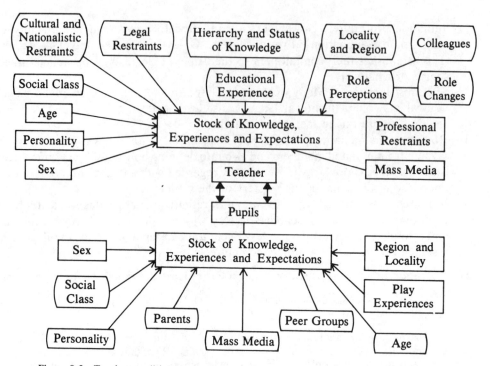

Figure 9.2   Teacher-pupil interaction as a confrontation of different stocks of knowledge.

and its sources available in classrooms can be represented diagrammatically, as shown in Figure 9.2.

The result of such a situation is that one definition of knowledge, a subject definition, is usually imposed, or an attempt is made to impose it, on the pupils. The case of music illustrated this well. The pupils' knowledge of music is rejected in an attempt to replace it with a subject-defined and, as Vulliamy argues, fallacious version of music. The outcome is that large numbers of pupils are alienated from school music and are prevented from having a sympathetic experience of classical among other musical forms, thus adopting an alternative fallacious view of music limited to Afro-American forms.

CONCLUSION

The case studies and the review of ideas from the sociology of knowledge should enable us to make some propositions in answer to the questions posed at the outset, which were:

1.   Which subjects are selected, and which versions of subjects?
2.   Whose subjects are these and who selects this knowledge?
3.   Why subjects and what kind of knowledge is this?
4.   How are subjects implemented and what kinds of presentation are adopted?

The following are some of the possibilities that were explored in this chapter:

1. The subjects selected tend to be those developed at universities during the nineteenth century. A few new subjects, e.g. sociology, have been partially adopted provided that they were presented as 'subjects'. The versions of subjects include history with strong nationalistic and sexist perspectives, music and art with a 'high culture' selection, domestic science with a sexist outlook, a non-radical version of science and social science, both stressing acceptance and right-answer systems, a parochial and non-internationalist version of languages, and a version of religion that excludes the outlook of many groups and individuals in Britain today.

2. Given the original date of many of these subjects, they often turn out to be the subjects of our ancestors: sex education has a Victorian morality and purpose; domestic science, the preservation of male dominance; RE, the prevention of a dispassionate look at alternatives to Christianity; and music and art, the subjects previously enjoyed by a wealthy minority group. The selection of this knowledge is maintained by the operation of subjects as social systems, thus tending to limit the outlook of teachers, to restrict change, and to perpetuate a past orientation of school knowledge.

3. Subjects tend to persist for historical and social rather than for rational or educational reasons. Present- and future-based systems of knowledge are available outside more than they are inside schools, in the mass media, in industry and in government information services, in order to deal with modern problems like pollution, terrorism, the knowledge explosion, computerization and energy provision. School knowledge tends to remain past-orientated, to encourage belief and acceptance rather than thought and adaptation, to be a filtered and selected kind of knowledge. It is mostly non-integrated, fragmented and specialized.

4. Subjects are implemented by subject teachers' perceiving their task as some kind of imposition requiring the rejection of much pupil knowledge. The social systems of subjects stratify teachers as well as pupils and schools, and limit perceptions of alternative ways of presenting knowledge.

Earlier in the book the limitation of analogies was mentioned; the hidden-curriculum concept stresses selected features. The above summary is not meant to be a complete statement of what subjects achieve.

As a note of caution, the official curriculum teaches more than its hidden curriculum aspects, so pupils may be receiving complex and contradictory messages. A remaining question, therefore, is which set of messages is the most effective, or do they cancel each other out? One answer is that of Postman and Weingartner, given in Chapter 6. However, it is not the only one.

SUMMARY

1. The central proposition of this chapter is that the common sense view that school knowledge is neutral is mistaken.

2. The case of history indicates how bias can enter a school subject through over-simplification and selectivity. These biases may be systematic in promoting sexism, or an ethnocentric view of the world, or some other set of beliefs.

3. School music can be shown to teach a dubious view of musical styles based on the fallacy of objective standards across musical languages.
4. The characteristics of domestic science, as taught in most schools, can be shown to be sexist.
5. The only compulsory subject, religious education, is a potential, and in many cases an actual, source of indoctrination, and this is recognized by religious as well as non-religious critics. Political education raises similar issues.
6. The teaching of science frequently results in a view of the subject as more concerned with information than thought, as well as producing an alienated response from the majority of learners.
7. Other school subjects like art, languages and mathematics can be shown to lack the neutrality commonly seen as associated with them. Conversely, the supposed radicalism of social science in schools can be shown to be almost non-existent.
8. School knowledge can tend to be past-orientated, present-orientated or future-orientated. The first appears to be more common than the last.
9. School knowledge is stratified into high and low status subjects, and consequences of this include the eventual stratification of both teachers and pupils.
10. School subjects take on some of the characteristics of social systems and are therefore capable of perpetuating themselves beyond their time of usefulness, leaving us tied to the inadequate formulations of our ancestors.
11. The stock of knowledge brought to school by pupils is frequently rejected in favour of the teacher's stock of subject knowledge.

Further Reading

Goodson, I. (1983) *School Subjects and Curriculum Change*. Beckenham: Croom Helm.
Hammersley, M. and Hargreaves, A. (eds.) (1983) *Curriculum Practice: Some Sociological Case Studies*. Lewes: Falmer Press.
Whitty, G. (1977) *School Knowledge and Social Control*, Milton Keynes: Open University, Press, has three case studies of music, domestic science and physics in section 4 and a fourth – social studies – in section 7.
Whitty, G. and Young, M.F.D. (1976) *Explorations in the Politics of School Knowledge*. Driffield: Nafferton Books. A collection of sociological writings on the school curriculum.
Young, M.F.D. (1971) *Knowledge and Control*. West Drayton: Collier Macmillan. A well-known collection of papers on the sociology of school knowledge.

Discussion and Activities

1. Take a subject that is not discussed in the chapter, e.g. English, geography, woodwork, physical education, and consider any hidden messages contained in their presentation in school.
2. Reading schemes are analysed by Lobban in terms of their sexist messages. Look at them in terms of their ethnic messages, their view of social class and their view of nationalism.
3. The compulsory act of worship has been seen as the source of varying degrees of attempted indoctrination. Discuss this aspect of the official curriculum. Useful sources are J. Hull's *School Worship: an Obituary* (SCM, 1975) and *Objective, Fair and Balanced* (BHA, 1979). The first gives a Chrisitan viewpoint, the second a Humanist viewpoint.

Signposts

1. Microcomputers
The arrival of microcomputers in schools could make Russell's verdict quoted at the head of this chapter questionable. A start can be made with Chandler, D. (1984) *Young Learners and the Microcomputer*, Milton Keynes: Open University Press. A source on primary schools is Garland, R. (1982) *Microcomputers and Children in the Primary School*, Lewes: Falmer Press.

2. Political education
The issue of political education in schools has received attention in the UK recently. One collection of ideas is Harber, C. and Meighan, R. (1984) *Political Education in 1984* Special Edition of *Educational Review*, **36**, 2. In Stradling, R. (ed.) (1983) *Political Education in West Germany and Britain*, London: Hansard Society, there appears a checklist of twenty strategies for teachers to make sure pupils remain uncritically attached to the status quo. Sample strategies are:

- Do not allow the School Council to develop to an extent where really important issues can be raised. The democratic decision-making in the School Council is only a simulation. Safe agendas are best managed by the Deputy Head (pastoral) who understands the complexities of pupils' thinking. Free votes are usually safe however on subjects such as coffee-machines, fund raising, and prefect duties.
  N.B. If a School Council does vote the wrong way on an important issue the following statement from the Head is always a winner. 'In considering your proposal I have had to take account of the quality of the argument. Unfortunately other factors which you failed to consider have had to be borne in mind and I find myself having to overrule your proposition.'
- Label political education teachers who use a variety of learning strategies as 'progressive'. Any movement away from 'chalk-and-talk' is likely to cause you difficulties with *your* classes. Flexibility is anathema to the dedicated teacher who cannot afford to waste time preparing interesting or stimulating lesson material aimed at the ability levels of the pupils. Remember, disinterested pupils do not deserve time to be spent on them.
- Never feel guilty about showing favouritism to nice, clean, quiet, well turned-out pupils. This favouritism is good political education for the 'thickees' and 'louts' in a society where we know preference is always given to those who grease quietly against those who complain noisily, or try to change the rules of the system.
- Never allow pupils to participate in making decisions about planning after-school activities, trips abroad, or about the distribution of funds they have raised. Participation is time-consuming and never leads to the outcome you want anyway.
- Real-life experience of the pupils to be ignored, since it confuses the formal learning they must acquire. In any case, text-book political theory is to be preferred because it remains non-active, and requires no real learning experience.

An interesting exercise would be to rewrite the twenty strategies to promote the opposite aim of encouraging political awareness.

Chapter 10

Organization

'Institutions are to be judged by the good or harm they do to individuals.'
Bertrand Russell

INTRODUCTION

Three terms that are found in sociological writings to describe the patterned activity of a place like a school are 'social system', 'organization' and 'institution'. These terms have various meanings and can be used to mean very similar things, or, with other definitions, to stress different aspects of patterning.

The concern of this chapter is not to discuss these concepts but rather to focus on organizational or institutional style to see whether there are hidden messages in the form of organization adopted for mass schooling.

One approach to organizational theory has been to look for the aims of the organization. Using this approach the question becomes one of whether or not schools are 'successful' in achieving their aims. One successful institution is an army. It sets out to turn men and women into killers, given certain stimuli like the 'enemy', 'patriotism' or 'survival', and has a long record of success in achieving this. Among unsuccessful institutions are perhaps large prisons like Pentonville, which set out to reform inmates, make the public safer, and deter criminals. From the sociological studies available, such institutions tend to have a reverse effect, in that they confirm criminality, 'educate' inmates into more sophisticated criminal methods (thus making them more dangerous to the public) and provide marks of status, since inmates are considered 'experienced' criminals in criminal circles (see T. and P. Morris, 1963). A partially successful institution is a hospital, which has high rates of success with some ailments and low rates with others.

The analysis of schools, then, becomes a question of locating them alongside armies, prisons or hospitals in terms of success in achieving aims. Different writers have come to contrary conclusions here, because the aims of schools are not agreed; an agenda of aims is given a different order of priority by different people (see Chapter 4 for a list of aims). To the parents of a sixth former who achieves university entrance a school is successful, while to other parents the success of this small minority is seen as being achieved at the expense of the rejection of the majority. We saw in Chapter 5 how parents had various agendas of aims and in Chapter 4 how teachers varied in their priorities.

ORGANIZATIONAL STYLES

The question investigated here is not related to a particular set of aims but rather what alternative organizational styles can be identified and what consequences do these have for the behaviour of the people involved.

Etzioni's Classification

Etzioni suggests a ninefold typology summarizing different kinds of compliance based on three kinds of power and three kinds of involvement of members. The three kinds of power are:

1. Coercive, based on punishment.
2. Remunerative, based on positive incentives.
3. Normative, based on agreed rules.

People go along with these kinds of power in three ways:

1. Alienative: grudging compliance.
2. Calculative: calculating involvement.
3. Moral: morally identified with the regime.

The most common patterns from the nine possible combinations are where the type of compliance is apparently matched by the type of power, i.e. alienative – coercive; calculating – remunerative; and morally involved – normative.

Etzioni's classification provides some interesting ideas, but has been criticized for a number of hidden assumptions as well as for the failure of this typology to take into account some examples of educational organization, such as the Hitler Youth or Spartan education.

> this very neat set of types harbours a whole series of psychological assumptions which are an integral part of the democratic ideology but which may be empirically incorrect. There seems, for example, to be as much valid educational evidence in support of a relationship between coercive power and moral involvement . . . as there is evidence supporting an association between coercive power and alienative involvement.
>
> Swift, 1969

Weber's Classification

Weber distinguishes between charismatic, traditional and bureaucratic forms of authority. Charismatic authority rests on the personal magnetism and public-performance skills of an individual to persuade followers to become disciples. The organizational style that results can often be arbitrary and loose:

> Because charismatic power rests, ultimately, on the unique impressions of the individual, it has an arbitrary and eccentric quality about it which makes it a potential source of

disruption to more rational forms of power utilizations. The charismatic leader, as Weber nicely put it, is not congenial to the idea of routine. To the contrary, because that person's power is lodged within personal qualities, he or she exists as a threat to routine and to the established order.

Cuzzort and King, 1976

Charismatic organizational styles usually give way to a more routinized form, which may be traditional or bureaucratic, to introduce stability and perpetuation. Traditional forms may find new leaders by searching for a new charismatic power in appointed persons, e.g. priests, or by hereditary systems, as in monarchies, or by selection or election.

Bureaucratic forms establish leadership by promotion. Bureaucracy, as Weber analysed it, in its ideal type was a detailed rule system for organizing large-scale administrative tasks rationally, to minimize personal idiosyncrasies of individuals, including charismatics. A useful summary of the key features is contained in Swift (1969):

> Fundamentally, a bureaucracy is a rational arrangement of 'offices' providing certain means for administration and control of the office-holders' actions. Officials enter the bureaucracy expecting security, specialization, salary and seniority based upon achievement and examinations. The rights, duties and qualifications of the official will be carefully defined so that he is replaceable with a minimum of upheaval to the smooth running of the organization. Offices will be hierarchically arranged so as to facilitate demarcation of responsibility and promotion according to ability.

Swift sees that among the intended consequences of all these arrangements are two that social commentators tend to fear – impersonality and uniformity. For goals to be achieved, the actions of each office-holder have to be predictable according to the rights and duties of the positions, and personal idiosyncrasies minimized.

There have been several attempts to elaborate and develop Weber's concept of bureaucracy. In the case of schools, one view is that an alternative mode of organization the professional, exists alongside some of the features of bureaucracy. The professional is believed to have appropriate skills, qualifications and attitudes related to a particular occupation which has its own professional code, ethic and organization, licensing practitioners to serve in or out of various kinds of organization. Bidwell's (1965) attempt to incorporate these two forms in relation to American schools leads to the listing of four major organizational features on which schools may be composed. These were the grouping of pupils into age cohorts, the contractual hiring of teaching staff as licensed professionals, the mixed organizational system of bureaucracy and professionalism, and the dual responsibility of educationalists to a clientele and to a public.

Another contribution has been the distinction between 'tall' and 'flat' organizational styles. Tall organizations have many levels of authority, and these are arranged in a tight hierarchy so that the shape of the authority structure is that of a pyramid. Flat organizations have few levels of authority and operate on the basis of teams making collective decisions, allowing for more professional and democratic forms of activity (see Cooper, 1965).

Goffman's Classification

Goffman's work on organizational style has produced the concept of a total institution. This describes the characteristics of a place of residence and work where the inmates are cut off from outside society for considerable periods of time. Prisons, mental hospitals, armies, monasteries and residential schools are examples. Although Goffman's work is related to such 'closed' organizations, the characteristics he describes provide one means of describing and comparing the organizational styles of other organizations, in this case schools. These characteristics include the following:

1. All aspects of life are conducted in the same place and under the same single authority.
2. Each phase of activity is carried on in the immediate company of a batch of others, all treated alike and required to do the same things together.
3. The day's activities are tightly scheduled, with one activity leading to another at a prearranged time.
4. The sequence of activities is imposed by a system of explicit formal rulings and a body of officials whose task is surveillance.
5. The various activities are brought together in a single rational plan designed to fulfil the official aims of the institution.
6. There is a basic split between a large managed group, the inmates, and a small supervisory group.
7. Each group tends to conceive of the other in terms of narrow, hostile stereotypes.
8. Staff tend to feel superior and righteous: inmates to feel inferior, blameworthy and guilty.
9. Social mobility between the two groups is severely restricted: social distance is great and formally prescribed.
10. The passage of information about staff plans for inmates is restricted, and inmates are excluded from decisions about their fate.
11. Incentives for work have little significance outside the institution.
12. Groups have only official points of contact.
13. There is a barrier between inmates and the outside world.
14. Inmates are dispossessed of basic rights.
15. High-ranking inmates have more authority than low-ranking supervisors.
16. Inmates are expected to internalize the norms of the staff.

This list raises a key sociological issue: that the effect of a pattern like this is cumulative. Taken individually, each of these features could be interpreted as trivial, but the cumulative effect of a set of features operating together can be powerful. Goffman says that institutions like this are the forcing houses for changing people and each is a natural experiment on what can be attempted on the self. Thus armies convert people into killers by using a total-institution pattern for their organizational style.

There is also a qualitative aspect to be taken into account; how coercive is each of the above features? Is negotiation possible? Can some kind of truce be called? The existence of a particular feature may vary in its effect according to who decided that that feature was desirable. An example is the existence of a school uniform. The effect is qualitatively different if a head teacher imposes a uniform, than if pupils and staff are consulted and a majority agree that it is a good idea.

The application of this list of characteristics to schools can indicate an index of how far a particular school is taking on the features of a total institution and how it compares with other schools in that respect. Some of the variations to be found may be as follows:

1. 'The same place – the school building – is a constant, but the freedom and frequency of visits, expeditions, field work and other uses of the 'outside' is a variable. 'The same single authority' varies according to the decision-making procedures, for in some schools the head teacher delegates and involves staff, sometimes parents, and occasionally pupils, while in others the head teacher retains all powers of decision-making.

2. Grouping systems vary from set 'batches', e.g. class or stream groupings, to other systems like setting, family grouping or individualized systems.

3. The timetable, as looked at in a previous chapter, shows variations in rigidity and flexibility. In secondary schools tight scheduling is very common.

4. There are variations in the amount of explicit rulings and surveillance needed.

5. The timetable embodies the 'single rational plan', but there are qualitative differences of when it was produced and how widely consultation was conducted.

6. The split between teachers and pupils varies with schools: in many, relationships are rather distant, in some they are closer, and in a few they are almost equal.

7. The hostility between the two groups is well documented in some cases. One teachers' union leader believes that 'the swish of the cane may be one of the essential sounds in education' (Casey, 1974). In others co-operation, sympathy and mutual concern are in evidence.

8. The variations in feelings of superiority and inferiority tend to parallel the incidence of hostility between the groups.

9. Pupils are rarely called on to help in teaching and mobility is restricted to some pupils becoming teachers through teacher-training establishments.

10. The secrecy of records about pupils and staff is still an emotive issue in education. Pupils usually learn about decisions on their fate after the event has taken place.

11. Ticks, stars, house points and grades have no value outside schools, although the minority who achieve certificates have a marketable commodity in terms of job applications, etc.

12. Most interaction takes place in classrooms; the amount taking place elsewhere varies from none to a substantial minority of time.

13. The 'symbolic barrier' is the white line on the playground or the printed notice commanding visitors to 'report' to a particular place to state their business. An interesting contrast is with another public building, the public library, which has open access, and a few schools operate rather like this.

14. The basic rights Goffman discusses include rights of dressing in clothes of one's own choice, of being able to use the toilet facilities whenever desired, of eating with some choices about times and foods, of being addressed by chosen names, and of being protected from body searches or physical assault, including physical punishments. Schools clearly vary in how much they infringe these 'rights'.

15. It is harder to find examples of high-ranking inmates, like tobacco barons in

prisons; the nearest equivalent would appear to be prefect systems, where old-established prefects may appear to be more powerful than new young teachers on the staff.

16.   Few schools appear to operate on the assumption that teachers can learn from the pupils, even when the pupils have considerable knowledge, e.g. about forms of music other than the classical.

One analysis of secondary schooling that contains many of the features of Goffman's total institution is that of James (1968):

> If for a moment we forget our preconceptions about secondary schooling and imagine ourselves able to start afresh, can we really be content with the way in which our young people's days are spent? Would we allow them, if we had the choice, to spend this time in squads (group is too rich a word) being addressed or grilled by adults, one adult after another, and in a totally incoherent order? . . . Would we not like them to learn to work co-operatively rather than in a moral climate so competitive that sharing is denigrated as 'cheating' and actually punished? Would we really wish them to find much of their satisfaction in having some others to be better than? . . . Who rescues the children at the bottom of the heap, the bottom children in the bottom stream? Sometimes a kindly, occasionally a superbly imaginative remedial teacher; certainly, never their peers in higher streams.
>
> Again, how do we explain a youth-time arbitrarily divided into spasms of 30, 40 or 45 minutes, punctuated by the clanging of bells, and often followed by a massive flocking in and out of corridors? How do we reconcile this planned incoherence with our knowledge of the different rhythms of learning different individuals have, of their different ways of thinking and learning? . . . Are we allowing millions of people in schools, children and adults, to spend their time disagreeably when it is quite unnecessary that they should do so?

In this passage, James also indicates some of the hidden curriculum of an organizational style with a high index on 'total' features. She includes:

1.   Competition rather than sharing.
2.   Superiority rather than equality of consideration.
3.   Incoherent learning rather than coherent.
4.   Learning being unpleasant rather than joyful.
5.   Learning consisting mostly of listening in groups.
6.   Fragmented knowledge.

Reynolds and Delinquent Schools

A study of school organizational styles in South Wales by Reynolds (1976) serves to emphasize the consequences of variations in some of the features Goffman described. Differences between nine schools in a Welsh valley were located in terms of rates of attendance, academic attainment and delinquency. Influences outside the school were found to be comparable for all the schools, suggesting that it was school differences that would yield possible explanations. The more 'successful' schools, with higher rates of attendance, higher academic attainment and lower levels of delinquency, tended to:

1.   be smaller in size;

2.   be lower in staff turnover;
3.   have smaller classes;
4.   have older buildings.

Reynolds investigated organizational features, and gives these particular stress in his analysis. Differences in organizational style were that the more 'successful' schools:

1.   were more likely to have prefect systems;
2.   enforced school uniform rules with less rigour, especially for fourth- and fifth-year pupils;
3.   enforced rules against three key behaviours, i.e. smoking, chewing gum and outside school behaviour, in a less obsessive and relentless manner; in Reynolds' terms, they opt for 'low rather than high control', over senior pupils in particular;
4.   used lower levels of physical punishment; the 'unsuccessful' schools use higher rates of coercion and produce lower commitment to the school on the part of the pupils as a result.

Reynolds describes the 'successful' schools in the sample:

> The successful school, on the other hand, does not fight battles over chewing gum, smoking and out-of-school behaviour that it knows it cannot win, and does not even attempt to enforce the wearing of school uniform when that enforcement becomes problematic. It does not use high rates of physical punishment and is not harshly authoritarian in its mode of control.

Reynolds summarizes the 'unsuccessful' schools as follows:

> The conflict between pupils and teachers is continually fuelled by the attempt of the staff to exercise control in areas of the pupils' lives where they expect autonomy, such as in their behaviour outside the school, and in some aspects of their behaviour inside it. In the schools like this one that have no truce, there are many pupils who wish for one.

Reynolds observes that where there is this sort of conflict in a school, there will invariably be vandalism within it, truanting from it, and delinquency outside it. The attempt of the teachers to exercise control over the pupils in areas of their life where they feel they should have some autonomy is likely to set in motion a circular process of deviancy amplification. The pupils will see the teachers as using illegitimate authority, and they are then less likely to be responsive in other areas of school life. Teachers will tend to respond by increased coercion, leading to a reaction in an increasingly alienated pupil body, of defiance to the 'oppressors'.

This research raises important issues for educational policies, Reynolds concludes, for his research supports the proposition that the organizational style of a school is an important influence upon its pupils' levels of vandalism, truancy, delinquency and educational failure. The common response has been to appoint more educational psychologists, advisers and social workers, and more recently to create 'disruptive pupil' units. These 'helping' professions 'help', or, Reynolds argues, 'force' the child to adjust to the school, whether the reality of the school is worth adjusting to or not.

> Instead of continually merely treating the deviant and delinquent children, we should perhaps begin to look and see if the reason for their rebellion lies squarely in the nature, process and operation of some of the schools that we offer them. If the reason does lie

there, then perhaps we ought to seek changes in some of our delinquents' schools.

Reynolds, 1976

CONCLUSION

One theme that emerges from these various approaches to the study of the organizational styles of schools is that some are capable of transmitting a marked authoritarian message. The message is that you are to do as you are told without question. Woods (1977b) sees this as contrasting with messages transmitted in families and other institutions in society, for with the reduction of the working week, greater affluence, mass production, the mass media, and increased mobility, patterns of leisure and behaviour have changed:

> Today, children have more freedom and independence, more discussion and contact with their parents, more money and material things, more outings and holidays, more lenient discipline, and fewer rules to obey and duties to perform, all of which increase the social distance between total institutions and the rest of society . . . Schools have been developing totalizing tendencies in a society which has not stood still, which, indeed, has been moving in the opposite direction.

Woods also sees this organizational style as opposed to some educationalists' views:

> Modern educationist thought, of course, explicitly rejects many of the features of total institutions which have long taken hold in schools. The split between inmates and staff, for example, regarded as inevitable by Waller in terms of 'social distance', . . . is deplored in the Plowden Report, which denounces the division into 'them and us' in many schools, and recommends more 'kindness, humanity and personal contact, and less authoritarianism' . . . One of the main changes, sought also by the Newsom Committee, was 'a change of heart in teachers'.

Finally, some psychological studies link in here: a study by Biber and Minuchin (1971) in the USA demonstrated how self-concepts of children varied with school regimes. The work of Milgram (1974) on the tendency of people brought up in authoritarian regimes to go along with orders even when those orders are malevolent indicated that behaviour similar to that of officials in Nazi Germany could be replicated in citizens of New York and other cities of the USA. In an authoritarian situation, people could be induced to hurt each other with electric-shock machines because the authority said it was necessary. The estimates of experts and others were that about 1 per cent of the population would do this, whereas incidences ranging from 33 per cent to over 50 per cent were actually recorded.

SUMMARY

1. One approach to organizational theory is to locate the aims of an organization and then judge whether it is successful in achieving them.
2. This approach yields different conclusions in the case of schools, since the aims of schools are in dispute: the agenda of aims is given different orders of priority by different people.
3. Etzioni's classification yields three common kinds of institution with contrasting

patterns of control and response from the membership.

4. Weber's three types of authority, charismatic, traditional and bureaucratic, have stimulated further work on organizational style. These include analyses identifying the tensions and contradictions between the concepts of bureaucracy and of professional.

5. Goffman's theory of total institutions has been used to describe some of the characteristics of schools. An index of how far a particular school is exhibiting the characteristics of a total institution can be the outcome of this kind of analysis.

6. The hidden curriculum of organizational style can include messages like: competition is preferred to sharing; incoherent learning, rather than coherent, is experienced; and learning is unpleasant.

7. The research of Reynolds supports the proposition that the organizational style of a school can influence levels of vandalism, truancy, delinquency and educational failure.

8. The marked authoritarian message of many schools can be seen as contrasting with the less authoritarian messages of other institutions in UK society.

Further Reading

Goffman, E. (1961) *Asylums*. Harmondsworth: Penguin. The idea of total institutions is analysed in this book, especially in section I, pages 15–115.

Handy, C. (1984) *Taken for Granted? Understanding Schools as Organisation*. York: Longman. An industrial management consultant analyses the organization and management of schools.

King, R. (1983) *The Sociology of School Organisation*. London: Methuen.

Milgram, S. (1974) *Obedience to Authority*. London: Tavistock. Obedience to authority in general, and obedience to malevolent authority in particular, is the subject of this book.

Barton, L. and Meighan, R. (eds.) (1979) *Schools, Pupils and Deviance*. Driffield: Nafferton Books. This collection of papers addresses the question of how far the organizational style of schools can create deviance in pupils.

Reynolds, D. (1976) 'The Delinquent School', in Hammersley, M. et al., *The Process of Schooling*. London: Routledge and Kegan Paul. A study of the influence of organizational style on schooling.

Rutter, M., Maughan, B., Mortimor, P. and Ouston, J. (1979) *Fifteen Thousand Hours*. London: Open Books. Another study of the influence of organizational style on schooling.

Discussion and Activities

1. A Marxist view that schools correspond to the values of the other institutions of a capitalist society was given in Chapter 6. Contrast this with the interactionist view, given in this chapter, that schools are out of step with the other institutions in society.

2. Take the list of Goffman's characteristics of a total institution and analyse an educational institution known to you. Compare your results with the discussion at the end of the section on Goffman's classification.

3. Do the messages of organizational style tend to reinforce the hidden curriculum messages of spatial layout and timetabling? Specify any messages they have in common.

Signposts

1. Disruptive units
Investigate the growth of disruptive units in school and the theories underpinning them. These references will help: *Behavioural Units* (booklet available from DES, Elizabeth House, York Road, London SE1 7PH), Chapter I of *Schools, Pupils and Deviance*, quoted in 'Further Reading', *Where?*, 158 (May 1980), 'Survey of Disruptive Units' and 'Disruptive Units – Labelling a New Generation'; and Lloyd-Smith, M., (ed.) (1984) *Disrupted Schooling: The Growth of the Special Unit*, London: John Murray.

2. Open schooling
Some schools and writers have tried to establish the organizational patterns of non-authoritarian schooling. Some examples are: Watts, J. (1980) *Towards an Open School*, London: Longman; Toogood, P. (1984) *The Head's Tale*, Telford: Dialogue Publications; A.S. Neill (1968) *Summerhill*, Harmondsworth: Pelican; Moon, B. (ed.) (1983) *Comprehensive Schools: Challenge and Change*, Windsor: NFER-Nelson; Fletcher, C., Caron, M., Williams, W. (1985) *Schools on Trial*, Milton Keynes: Open University Press.

Chapter 11

Teacher Expectations

'I am not an underachiever. My teacher is an over-expecter.'
Child's response to a school report

INTRODUCTION

If the hidden curriculum is broadly defined as everything else that is learnt in addition to the official curriculum, the research on the expectations pupils either read or absorb from their teachers' behaviour is worth careful scrutiny. The central proposition in studies of teacher expectations is that pupils tend to perform as well or as badly as their teachers expect. The teacher's prediction of a pupil's or group of pupils' behaviour is held to be communicated to them, frequently in unintended ways, thus influencing the actual behaviour that follows. A brief account of four of the studies follows and is intended to be an alerting device, to signal the thinking of this type of research.

FOUR STUDIES IN TEACHER EXPECTATION

Garwood and McDavid (1975)

This study established that teachers had stereotypes related to first names. Boys named David were viewed as good, strong, wise, active, serious, complex, sociable, excitable and masculine. The same teachers viewed the name Harold as signifying weak, bad, foolish, passive, humorous, simple, unsociable and calm. Names rated as desirable included Craig, Gregory, James, Jeffrey, John, Jonathan, Patrick, Richard and Thomas. Names rated by teachers as undesirable included Bernard, Curtis, Darrell, Donald, Gerald, Horace, Jerome, Maurice, Roderick and Samuel.

The evidence of a further study by Garwood (1976), seeking to relate teachers' ratings of first names to pupil self-concept and school achievement, supported the hypothesis that male pupils with first names that teachers considered desirable score higher on measures of self-concept and achievement than do those with first names that teachers rate as undesirable. The same effect had been shown in experiments where teachers graded work which was linked in authorship to desirable and undesirable names (Harari and McDavid, 1973). The authors saw this as evidence of teacher expectancy at work. A study in England noted similar results (Erwin and Caley, 1984).

Palardy (1969)

The subject of a second study was expectation and sex typing. Palardy (1969) compared five teachers of infants in the USA who believed that boys were almost as good as girls at learning to read, with five teachers who thought that boys were only about half as good as girls. At the outset the boys and girls had similar scores on pre-reading tests, and were from similar home backgrounds. After a period of time spent with their teachers the performance of the children varied according to the teacher they had. The boys taught by the teacher who believed that they were almost as good as the girls had progressed as well as the girls in their reading. The boys taught by the teacher who believed that girls were superior had not progressed as well as the girls in their class, and their performance was clearly below that of the boys working with the first teacher. The author concluded that a self-fulfilling prophecy was in evidence, so that the beliefs of the teachers were influencing the actual outcome in terms of reading performance.

Harvey and Slatin (1976)

A study by Harvey and Slatin (1976) used photographs of pupils to investigate expectations. The teachers, 96 in the sample, were shown 18 photographs of children from different social-class groups, evenly divided between the sexes, and evenly divided white and black. The teachers were invited to rate the children in the photographs on estimated school adjustment, aspirations, homework attitudes, parental involvement, and general school performance.

The lower-class children were rated in markedly less favourable terms, especially when they were black. The more experienced teachers were firmer in their categorizations than the less experienced, expecting the black children, in general whom they saw as lower class, to be failures. When asked how they arrived at their conclusions, teachers said that they based their ratings on similarities of the children in the photographs to those they had taught in the past, and on facial expressions.

Charkin et al. (1975)

If the studies are correct in concluding that pupils read teacher expectations and may be influenced by them, the problem of how these messages are passed on remains. A study by Charkin et al. (1975) investigated the possibility of non-verbal communication being one medium. A group of undergraduates comprising 24 men and 24 women taught a short lesson on house safety to a ten-year-old boy. A third of the sample were told that the boy had a high motivation to work and an IQ of 130. Another third were given no information, and the remaining third were told that the boy did badly at school and had an IQ of 84. An analysis of the videotaped lessons that followed showed that the non-verbal behaviour of the teachers varied. Those in the 'high expectancy' group leaned forward more than the other two groups, looked pupils in the eye longer, nodded their heads up and down more, and smiled more. The researchers concluded that these gestures provided easily recognizable indicators of approval which could be read by pupils, though not necessarily consciously.

FALSE EXPECTATIONS

Forming impressions of others serves an important function in everyday life, and categorizing others is necessary, or else remembering all the vast amounts of detailed information about all the people we meet would prove an impossible task. However, if these impressions are inaccurate or false they may end up hindering rather than helping. In the four studies quoted, teachers were prepared to make inferences about pupils (whom they had not even met in some cases) on the basis of their first names, their sex, their appearance, and information about their supposed ability. The effect of teacher expectation can start with false diagnosis:

> It is because most people are prepared to make inferences on the basis of the most slender evidence that so many of our initial inferences about other people are misleading and sometimes completely false . . . An elderly teacher once boxed the ears of a student teacher on his first day of teaching practice for running along a corridor. He had inferred from the student's age that he must be a sixth form pupil.
>
> Hargreaves, 1972

THE SEQUENCING OF TEACHER EXPECTATION

The build-up of expectations and the consequent actions and reactions make for a complicated story. It is possible to discern a number of stages:

1. Predictions based on a teacher's interpretive schemes or ideologies of education before meeting pupils for the first time.
2. The initial meetings.
3. Subsequent pattern of interaction.
4. Retrospective assessment and reflection, leading to reinforcement or modification of interpretive schemes.

The various studies of teacher expectation tend to try to illuminate one or other of these stages: studies following through all the stages are difficult to mount and therefore are rather rare.

This sequence, seen here for convenience as having four stages, will be followed in the analysis that follows, in an attempt to locate a number of the studies on teacher expectation. However, it is as well to remember that these stages are not always present in teacher–learner situations: sometimes learners are not actually met by their teachers and, in the absence of such meetings, inferences are made on even more limited evidence. A study of the behaviour of tutors in the Open University illustrates the point.

A study of the effects of penmanship and physical attractiveness on essay marking by Open University tutors was undertaken by Bull and Stevens (1976). The essay always had the same content but it was given to markers in variable handwritings or typed, and with different photographs, ranging from unattractive to attractive, attached. The judgements about good and bad handwriting and physical attractiveness were made by observers. The researchers found considerable variation in the marking that resulted. For 'style', the essay in typed form believed to have been written by an unattractive female received highest marks. The same essay in poor handwriting from an unattractive female received lowest marks. For 'talent', the essay in good handwriting from an attractive female was highly rated, but in the same handwriting from an unattractive female it was rated lowest of all. When markers believed the writer to be male, fewer differences related to handwriting and physical attractiveness were found. Half the markers were male. The results were complex, but evidence of the effect of expectation upon marking and grading was present in the data, the researchers concluded.

Predictions Based on Teachers' Interpretive Schemes

A later chapter looks more analytically at the interpretive schemes of teachers, under the heading of ideologies of education. Here the purpose is to review some studies that show some of the features related to teacher expectations and consequent pupil behaviour.

A study by Nash (1973), using a repertory grid technique, revealed a number of constructs employed by primary and secondary school teachers in Scotland. The repertory grid method is derived from Kelly (1955). Nash presented each teacher with three cards, each bearing the name of a child in the class, and asked how one differed in some significant way from the others. If the teacher comments on one being quiet and another noisy, the assumption is that this is part of that teacher's perceptual scheme. When no further differences emerge from this technique, the teacher's repertoire of personal constructs is assumed to be exhausted. A particular teacher's constructs may turn out to be:

bright	—	dull
quiet	—	noisy
mature	—	immature
well behaved	—	badly behaved
independent	—	gang member
able to work alone	—	unable to work alone
vivacious	—	subdued
good humoured	—	ill tempered
likeable	—	not likeable

Nash then compared the performance and behaviour of the pupils with the teachers' evaluations of them and concluded that the way the pupils were perceived by their teachers had a great influence upon their attainment. This was a greater influence than that of the pupils' social class, as indicated by parental occupation.

Nash also followed the progress of some of the pupils into secondary schools and concluded that their behaviour varied with different teachers according to the teachers' perceptions. Where pupils were perceived favourably they did well and said they liked being with that teacher. Where they did not do well, they were in the situation of not being favourably perceived by the teacher, and reported that they did not like being with that teacher. The profile of a particular child's performance thus varied according to their teachers' perceptions of them more than according to other features, like social class.

The work of Nash is in many respects a replication of the work of Becker (1952), working in Chicago schools, where he demonstrated similar results. Both pointed out that their researches did not remove social class as a source of influences on pupils, and indeed concluded that the teachers' perceptions of working-class children, perceived as less able, meant that these children could have no favourable evaluations from any teachers during their school experience. Nash quotes the work of Goodacre (1968) in support of his conclusions, since she showed that the perceptions of teachers about home background were least accurate in areas of low social class.

Part of a teacher's interpretive scheme may be expectations about gender. The study by Palardy (1969) quoted earlier gives one indication of the possibilities in primary schools: the outcome was that the teacher's expectation was met in that if boys were expected to do worse than girls at learning to read they did, and if they were expected to do as well as girls, they did. In a study by Davies and Meighan (1975) of sex typing in secondary schools teachers of both sexes, in a forced-choice question, showed a marked preference to teach boys rather than girls. Davies estimates that, on the basis of expectations theory, this preference is likely to be communicated to girls, and may help explain the deterioration of academic performance of girls in general during the secondary phase of schooling.

A study of how teachers plan their teaching (Taylor, 1970) throws some light on the interpretive schemes of teachers. The strongest influences reported by teachers were within schools, so the views of colleagues, particularly the head teacher, counted for much more in decision-making than outside influences like advisers, inspectors, teaching associations, parents, books or educational journals. The expectations of teachers, this study would suggest, are most heavily influenced by parochial features: studies of attempts to change curriculum practices by 'outsider'-based projects have frequently found this to their cost (e.g. Shipman, 1977). Thus if the local influence system stresses orderly classrooms and low noise levels, outside influences advocating alternative practices creating more noise and re-ordered classrooms have little chance of becoming established in the teachers' interpretive schemes.

Initial Meetings

Teachers take their expectations, based on their interpretive schemes, into the initial meetings with a new group of pupils. There are only a few studies that have followed what happens next. The experiments by Lippitt and White (1958) quoted earlier indicated that the behaviour of pupils soon took up a distinct pattern according to whether the regime of the teacher was 'authoritarian' or 'democratic'. The expectations of the teacher were read within a few minutes and the pattern became habitual within a few meetings.

Older pupils may be more deliberating in their evaluation of their teachers. Werthman (1963), in a study of secondary-age pupils defined as delinquent gang members, showed how the pupils make decisions about whether to accept or reject the authority of a teacher on various criteria related to how the teacher treats them, and how fairly marking of work is done. The initial meetings are key occasions, when the interpretive scheme of the teacher is 'researched' extensively by these pupils. Werthman reports how the marking characteristics of the teachers were established:

> As soon as the grade is handed down, gang members behave like good social scientists. They draw a sample, ask it questions, and compare the results with those predicted under alternative hypotheses. The unit of analysis is a set of relevant grades. The one received by a particular student is only a single member. No interpretation of a grade can be made before the others are looked at.

When their 'research' is complete, the delinquent gang members have their evidence about whether the teacher is fair, and is for them or against them. If the verdict is 'for them,' they give co-operation, if 'against them' they obstruct.

In a study by Lacey (1970), he isolates two mechanisms at work in initial meetings with pupils in the grammar school he studied. These were differentiation and polarization. *Differentiation* referred mainly to the activity of the teachers in ranking and categorizing pupils in their meetings with new classes, whereas *polarization* referred mainly to the activity within the pupil body as a reaction to differentiation, resulting in the emergence of pro-school and anti-school subcultures. The first few days established the bases for the later hardened and habitual patterns:

> As soon as the highly selected first-year population meets at the Grammar School and is allocated to the four first-year classes, a complex process of interaction begins. It takes place through a variety of encounters. Boys talk and listen to each other; talk and listen to teachers; listen to conversations; notice details of accent, gestures, clothing; watch others at work and at play in various situations and in innumerable different permutations.

The effect of differentiation and polarization was to reverse the self-concepts of a proportion of the pupils on intake, since the new arrivals at the grammar school consisted of eleven-year-olds accustomed to playing what might be termed the 'best pupil' role, and having a correspondingly positive self-image. Lacey reports that after six months in the second year the 'bottom' stream was already becoming polarized. This reversal of the performance and self-image of these pupils had taken only 18 months, and Lacey concluded that the interpretive schemes of the teachers, represented in particular in streaming practices, were a significant factor, and these operated swiftly: the die was cast in the initial meetings.

Subsequent Patterns of Interaction

There are many studies that concentrate on subsequent events when an expectation is in operation. Most of these have been in intellectual activities, so one that concentrates on the motor skills of swimming is interesting, if only for its novelty. Burnham and Hartsough (1968) administered a fake test supposed to predict psychological readiness to swim. The instructors, armed with this false information, gave their courses of instruction. Children designated as 'ready' tended to pass more of the tests than the average for their group.

Perhaps the most famous, as well as the most scrutinized and criticized, study is that of Rosenthal and Jacobson (1968) in the USA. Rosenthal noted that rats became brighter when expected to by their researcher, and wondered whether it was possible that children also become brighter when their teacher expects them to. He and Jacobson, of the south San Francisco unified school district, set out to see if this was so. Every child in an elementary school was given an intelligence test, a test described as one that would predict 'intellectual blooming'.

The school was in a lower socioeconomic area on the West Coast. There were three classrooms for each grade – one for children of above-average ability, one for children of average ability, and one for children of below-average ability. About 20 per cent of the children in each class were chosen at random to form the experimental group. The teachers were given the names of this group and told that these children had high scores on the test for intellectual blooming, and would show remarkable gains in intellectual development during the next eight months. In reality, the only difference between these children and the rest was in the minds of their teachers.

> At the end of the school year, all the children were again given the same IQ test. In the school as a whole, the children who had been designated as 'bloomers' showed only a slightly greater gain in verbal IQ (two points) than their classmates. However, in total IQ, the experimental group gained four points more on the average than their counterparts did, and in reasoning IQ the average gain was seven points more.

Various reviews of the work of Rosenthal and Jacobson have cast doubt upon the statistics (Snow, 1969), the technical design (Thorndike, 1968) and the failure of replication attempts (Claiborn, 1969). As a pioneer study, it has stimulated considerable research, and by 1973 Rosenthal was able to report that 242 studies had been completed, and that 84 had demonstrated that teachers' expectations do affect learners' performances. The other studies gave some clues that learners could resist expectation effects or be stimulated into 'confounding' behaviour to prove the teacher wrong, so that the expectation chain of events had several possible outcomes: self-fulfilling prophecy effects were not inevitable.

The expectations of lecturers and students regarding assessment and the effect on subsequent interaction was a central theme of a study by Becker (1968). Lecturers operated on a rhetoric of educational activity, e.g. learn the information and ideas of the course, or learn to see the world differently through a discipline, whereas students learned that what really counted for them, as well as in the final analysis the lecturers, was the grading of work.

> The realities of the situation lead him to define his classes as places in which he can get the grades he wants by performing as the teacher wants him to.
>
> Becker, 1968

The students therefore indulged in a complicated activity of 'trading for grades', of reading the lecturer for grading clues, preferences and idiosyncrasies, and this activity gradually squeezed out or eventually dominated all other kinds of learning. 'Trading for grades' largely extinguished education.

This is not unlike the conclusion of Holt (1969) regarding children in schools; he sees his pupils concentrating on obtaining the right answer by the use of a complex series of strategies of reading the teacher's face, voice, gestures and responses which may gradually exclude thinking through the logics of problems, especially since wrong answers obtained this way are usually heavily penalized. Strategies for deducing the right answer largely extinguish thinking, he concludes.

The work of Good and Brophy (1972) has concentrated on the differential expectations of teachers of different members of the same class. Teachers of primary-school children named pupils in their classes who fell into each of four groups – attachment, concern, indifference and rejection. The attachment-group members initiated contact with teacher about work more often than the others and conformed to classroom rules, therefore receiving few chastisements. In return they received praise and more reading turns, and were asked more questions requiring conceptual thought. The concern group, though initiating contact with teachers, were prone to guessing and were less accurate in their work, thereby having more opportunities to ask questions, and teachers initiated more private conversations with members of this group. Teachers tended to praise them more often for success and criticize them less often for failure.

The indifference-group members were passive and initiated few contacts with teachers. Although teachers asked them as many questions as other children, they made less individual contact with them and did not call on them to run errands or do special tasks. The rejection group sought out the teacher frequently and, particularly through calling out, received most disciplinary responses. They were active in class, but were given fewer reading turns and received less response from teachers for their work efforts.

These patterns were dependent on the teacher's expectations, and Good and Brophy (1970) indicated in another study how teachers behaved differently with a sample of high achievers than they did with a sample of low achievers. The former were consistently favoured, in demands for good performance, lower rates of criticism for wrong answers, help in rephrasing or repeating questions asked, and in the giving of praise for correct answers. When the teachers were informed about these patterns they changed their behaviour so that pupils were treated more equally, and the behaviour of the low group changed in respect to an improvement in behaviour and achievement.

Retrospective Assessment and Reflection

The initial meetings and subsequent interaction yield experiences which appear to reinforce or modify interpretive schemes of teachers, as well as those of pupils. However, only a few studies have monitored this feature. One such study is that of Fuchs (1968), of 14 newly qualified teachers in New York. She describes the process of the modification of their interpretive schemes by the influence of the 'parochial' features outlined in Taylor's study (previously mentioned).

First, the new teacher of class 1–5 in a slum school begins her career with a warm, friendly attitude toward her students. Early in the new teacher's career, however, a more experienced teacher exposes this new teacher to the widely held belief that the inferior backgrounds and the deficits in homes, e.g. lack of newspapers and parental care, prevent educational achievement. That the teachers and the school as an institution could contribute to the failure of the children is not considered.

Early in her career this new teacher is aware of her deficiencies. As yet, she has not unconsciously accepted the belief that the failure of children stems from gaps in their backgrounds.

By the end of the term, the eventual failure of most of class 1–5 has been virtually assured, for the teacher has come to rationalize this failure in terms of pupil inadequacy. Fuchs sees the good intention of the teacher defeated as her interpretive scheme is modified by in-school theories of pupil failure. The teacher has internalized the attitude that deficits of the children themselves explain their failure in school:

> The teacher of class 1–5 has been socialized by the school to accept its structure and values. Despite her sincerity and warmth and obvious concern for the children, this teacher is not likely to change the forecast of failure for most of these children – because she has come to accept the very structural and attitudinal factors that make failure nearly certain.

Fuchs notes that this teacher came to her job with very positive attitudes, but that her good impulses were not enough. This young teacher was socialized by the attitudes of those around her, and by the availability of a suitable rationale to explain her and the school's failure to fulfil their ideal roles:

> she came to accept traditional slum-school attitudes towards the children – and traditional attitudes towards school organization as the way things have to be. This teacher is a pleasant, flexible, co-operative young woman to have on one's staff. But she has learned to behave and think in a way that perpetuates a process by which disadvantaged children continue to be disadvantaged.

The study by Harvey and Slatin outlined at the beginning of this chapter showed that the judgements of teachers based on photographs of children were more firmly stereotyped in the case of experienced teachers. The interpretive schemes of inexperienced teachers were less stereotyped and judgements less dogmatic.

The account by Hoskyns (1976) of his experiments in physics teaching was outlined in Chapter 9 and provides an interesting case study of a reverse process. Here the interpretive scheme of the teacher was revised on the basis of a series of experiments in teaching methods.

CONCLUSION

A great deal of observational material reported in over a hundred different articles published in the last ten years has lent support to the proposition that teacher expectations can have a self-fulfilling prophecy effect. There are, however, many remaining areas of doubt. First, it is not clear how frequently this effect occurs. Second, it is not clear whether it affects some aspects of interaction, e.g. grading, more than others, e.g. praising and blaming. Third, it is not clear how significant teacher expectations are: they may be a minor rather than a major feature.

The studies have often proved to be difficult to replicate. The wide publicity given to the Rosenthal and Jacobson experiments may have made it more difficult to convince teachers about false information. In addition, the long chain of circumstances of a self-fulfilling prophecy means that breakdown can occur at various points, making replication problematic. This chain has been clearly spelt out by Barber and Silver (1968):

1. The student experimenter attended to the expectancy communication from the principal investigator.
2. The experimenter comprehended the expectancy communication.
3. The experimenter retained the communication.
4. The experimenter (intemtionally or unintentionally) attempted to transmit the expectancy to the subject.
5. The subject (consciously or unconsciously) attended to the expectancy communication from the experimenter.
6. The subject (consciously or unconsciously) comprehended the experimenters' expectancy.
7. The subject (consciously or unconsciously) retained the experimenter's expectancy.
8. The subject (wittingly or unwittingly) acted upon (gave responses in harmony with) the experimenter's expectancy.

As Nash (1976) comments:

> When one researcher, repeating another's work, fails to get the same result, it may be that the chain has failed at some point. And, since any replication involves a different set of people, this is hardly to be wondered at. This built-in problem of replication must be held in mind throughout.

However, as regards the hidden curriculum of schooling, the area of teacher expectation is potentially a considerable source of hidden messages, though precisely what weight is to be attached to it awaits the findings of more research.

SUMMARY

1. The central proposition in studies of teacher expectations is that pupils tend to perform as well or as badly as their teachers expect.
2. Some support for this proposition is given by studies of teacher ratings of pupils by first names, a study of variable reading performance according to teacher beliefs about boys' and girls' reading achievements, a study of teacher ratings of pupils by photographs, and a study of the non-verbal behaviour of student teachers in micro-teaching.
3. It is when the first impressions that a teacher forms are false or inaccurate that problems arise.
4. It is possible to discern four stages in the build-up of expectations:

   1. Predictions based on interpretive schemes.

    2. First meetings.
    3. Subsequent patterns of interaction.
    4. Retrospective assessment leading to reinforcement of interpretive schemes or their modification.

5. Teachers' interpretive schemes can be investigated using a repertory grid technique.

6. Studies by Nash and Becker suggest that teacher expectations can be a more powerful influence than social class features.

7. Part of a teacher's interpretive scheme may be expectations related to beliefs about gender.

8. The strongest influences on teachers' interpretive schemes appear to be parochial rather than outside-school influences.

9. In initial meetings, the interpretive scheme of the teacher may be researched intently by the pupils, who may modify their behaviour accordingly.

10. Initial meetings may show two mechanisms at work – differentiation and polarization. In some circumstances, pupils' self-concepts can be reversed in the process.

11. The studies of Rosenthal and Jacobson were an attempt to demonstrate how a self-fulfilling prophecy derived from teacher expectations can develop.

12. Becker's notion of 'trading for grades' and Holt's notion of 'right answerism' are other illustrations of the consequences of teacher expectancy.

13. A study by Fuchs indicates how the interpretive schemes of a new teacher can become modified by the theories of experienced teachers, to the disadvantage of the children she teaches.

14. There are considerable areas of doubt regarding teacher expectancy: its frequency and its significance are open to varying interpretations. Replication of studies has proved to be difficult due to the long chain of circumstances involved.

Further Reading

Connell, R.W. (1985) *Teacher's Work*. London: George Allen and Unwin.
Good, T.L., and Brophy, J.E., (1984) *Looking in Classrooms* (3rd edn.) London: Harper and Row. An account of techniques to increase teacher awareness.
Holt, J. (1969) *How Children Fail*. Harmondsworth: Penguin. An account of a teacher observing some of the mechanisms of expectancy at work in his own classroom.
Nash, R. (1976) *Teacher Expectations and Pupil Learning*. London: Routledge and Kegan Paul. A review of the material on teacher expectations.
Pidgeon, D. (1970) *Expectation and Pupil Performance*. Windsor: NFER. A review of the material on teacher expectations.
Rosenthal, R. and Jacobson, L. (1968) *Pygmalion in the Classroom*. Eastbourne: Holt, Rinehart and Winston. An interesting case study despite the various criticisms levelled at it.
Woods, P. (1983) *Sociology and the School*. London: Routledge and Kegan Paul.

Discussion and Activities

1. Some of the studies reported in the chapter could be replicated in the form of an exercise, e.g.

Harvey and Slatin's study based on photographs or Taylor's study of how teachers plan their courses. Start by reading the original study in full.

2. Do delinquent gang members or other 'troublesome' groups in the UK research their teachers as the USA teenagers reported in Werthman's study do? P. Willis, *Learning to Labour*, Saxon House, 1977 is one source of material if you have no direct friendly access to such a group.

3. Read the study by E. Fuchs, 'How Teachers Learn to Help Children Fail' in N. Keddie's *Tinker, Tailor . . . The Myth of Cultural Deprivation* (Penguin, 1973) and then interview some student teachers after a teaching practice, or teachers during their first year, to test for any evidence of the same re-socializing effects.

4. Discuss the proposition that the road to becoming an oppressive, bullying teacher is paved with good intentions. (See Chapter 4 for material.)

Signposts

Improving teacher awareness
This is the subject of Good, T.L. and Brophy, J.E. (1984), who set out to both survey recent research on expectations and to demonstrate how teachers can implement the findings to develop their teaching techniques. See also books by John Holt (1969, 1971 and 1973).

Chapter 12

The Hidden Curriculum of Language

STEPHEN WALKER AND ROLAND MEIGHAN

'It ain't what you say but the way that you say it'
From a song by 'Trummy' Young and Oliver

INTRODUCTION

The previous chapters of this book have been concerned with the exploration of a simple, though not unimportant, observation. This is that our understanding of life in schools will be incomplete unless we include in our analysis consideration of the *hidden* as well as the *overt* messages embedded both in the settings in which teachers and pupils operate and in the practices in which they engage. Of all the factors which contribute to the working of the process of educating, it is arguable that the way in which language is used in schools and classrooms can be regarded as the element of most obvious, and perhaps most crucial, significance.

First, it is significant because of the close relationship that exists, in our culture, between educational activities and language. The strength of this relationship is nicely pointed by Stubbs (1976), in his observation that:

> For us teaching and learning typically comprise linguistic activities such as: lecturing, explaining, discussing, telling, questioning, answering, listening, repeating, paraphrasing and summarizing.

It should, therefore, come as no surprise to us when observers of classroom interaction like Flanders (1970) report that two-thirds of the time spent in most lessons in 'traditional' classrooms is made up of talk and, furthermore, that, typically, two-thirds of this talk is done by the teacher. If one adds to this the time spent in the classroom on two other linguistic activities, reading and writing, it becomes clear that classrooms are language-saturated environments. Interestingly, however, the language used in school environments is often highly stylized, in terms of both its content and its structure. Consider, for example, the following three fragments of talk. One is taken from a cross-examination in a court, one from an exchange between a teacher and a pupil and one from a conversation which formed part of a radio 'phone-in' programme.

(1)

    A: I like tuh ask you something.

B: Shoot.
A: Y'know I 'ad my licen' suspendid fuh six mumts.
B: Uh huh.
A: Y'know for a reaz'n which, I rathuh not mensh'n tuh you, in othuh words – a serious reaz'n, en I like tuh know if I w'd talk to my senator, or – somebuddy, could they help me get it back.

(2)
A: You had had bronchitis, had you not?
B: Yes.
A: You have mentioned . . . about wearing a coat?
B: Yes.
A: It was not really a coat at all, was it?
B: Well, it is sort of a coat-dress, and I bought it with trousers, as a trouser suit.

(3)
A: No. No, it is not a pickpocket on the move. Mister Atkins?
B: Is it about a bird – that flies around?
A: About a – ?
B: A bird that flies a –
A: A bird that flies around. No. John?

Now, even though these fragments have been separated from their context and contain no obvious references which would reveal the sources from which they have been taken, we can easily distinguish between the speech of the casual conversationalist, that of the lawyer and that of the teacher, and thus identify which fragment belongs to which setting. We recognize, in the way the teacher uses a certain style, a familiar pattern of communication which we associate with the speech modes and language patterns of teachers in general. What is the precise nature of these 'styles' of communication? What purposes do they serve and what consequences might they have? Who determines the acceptability or non-acceptability of certain patterns of usage and on what criteria are these decisions made? Most importantly, what messages might be hidden in the *manner* in which communications are organized in social settings like classrooms, as well as in the *content* of what is said, written or read? These kinds of concerns provide a focus for what follows.

Before examining these questions, however, let us consider briefly a second reason for proposing that language usage has significance for the educational experiences of both pupils and their teachers. Language serves different, although not unrelated, functions; it allows communication, thought, social interaction and control. Thus, on the one hand, language is a device for the transmission of ideas, perceptions and concepts between individuals and, on the other, it is a means by which individuals order and direct both their personal social experiences and conceptualizations and their relations with other people. But these functions do not operate independently. Individuals come to recognize the ways in which others communicate – the linguistic rules they seem to obey, the styles to which they appear to conform, and the particular symbols they employ to describe the world and to order their knowledge of it. In learning how to use these practices for their own purposes, they internalize certain representations created by other people which can be used in the formulation of their own understandings and interpretations of the world. To this extent, the language environment in which school pupils are immersed will influence not only how they communicate with other people in school but also how they conceptualize and think about the messages to which they are exposed. In short, it will have an effect on their learning. As Douglas Barnes (1976) argues:

> we cannot consider language in the classroom only in terms of communication, but must consider how children themselves use language in learning. The major means by which children in our schools formulate knowledge and relate it to their own purposes and view of the world are speech and writing.
> . . . Not only is talking and writing a major means by which people learn, but what they learn can often hardly be distinguished from the ability to communicate it. Learning to communicate is at the heart of education.

But what kind of talking and writing is done in school? We need to have some idea of how this question has been answered and of suggestions about the specific messages transmitted through such communication practices before we can consider how these might be related to how learning itself is defined and accomplished.

SCHOOL LANGUAGE

Pre-school Experience

In some senses communication in schools and classrooms is no different from that regularly used in settings outside this environment – not surprisingly, as individuals communicating in any walk of life work with the same language base. Teachers and pupils bring with them into school a stock of meanings of words, understandings of linguistic rule systems and knowledge of language etiquette which they *share* because it is drawn from a linguistic heritage common to the culture in which they are located and which exerts a pressure upon them to conform to certain conventions affecting everyone. Such conformity is necessary because without it, although language could serve as a means by which individuals made subjective representations of the world to themselves, it could not act as a basis for the transmission of such ideas and perceptions from one individual to another. Indeed, as Berger and Luckmann (1967) argue:

> As a sign system, language has the quality of objectivity. I encounter language as a facticity external to myself and it is coercive in its effects on me. Language forces me into its patterns, I cannot use the rules of German syntax when I speak English; I cannot use words invented by my three-year-old son if I want to communicate outside the family; I must take into account prevailing standards of proper speech for various occasions, even if I would prefer my private 'improper' ones. Language provides me with a ready-made possibility for the ongoing objectification of my unfolding experience.

What is significant about this observations is that, in acquiring a language under these constraints, an individual is not simply learning a neutral sign and symbol system for personal and idiosyncratic use, but is also taking on ideas, meanings, conceptualizations, theories, attitudes and judgements which were deposited in the language system when they were first produced. In a very real sense language represents a huge repository of interpretations and knowledge by which the ideas and recognitions of our ancestors are preserved and handed on to succeeding generations. Thus, in learning a language we are exposed not only to predetermined definitions of the world, but also to predetermined explanations of it. Again, as Berger and Luckmann observe:

> With language, and by means of it, various motivational and interpretative schemes are internalized as institutionally defined – wanting to act like a brave little boy, for instance, and assuming little boys to be naturally divided into the brave and the cowardly. These schemes provide the child with institutionalized programmes for everyday life, some immediately applicable to him, others anticipating conduct socially defined for later biographical stages . . . Finally, there is internalization of at least the rudiments of the legitimating apparatus; the child learns 'why' the programmes are what they are.

Thus, before the child even reaches school, he or she will have been exposed to predetermined language patterns and the descriptive, prescriptive and evaluative messages hidden within them. This exposure has relevance for the process of educating in different ways.

First, it might be argued that the early language experience of school pupils encourages the employment of explanations and views that are taken for granted and seemingly self-evident, as opposed to encouraging them to use language boldly to create understandings, to question their experience. In Seabrook's discussion of the obsolescence and essential conservatism of much of the imagery which is used in modern English, especially in what he calls 'the language of suburbia', we can find illustrations of how this happens.

Seabrook (1971) claims that the English language abounds with words, phrases and maxims which not only are relics of another age but which seem peculiarly inappropriate to contemporary life. He notes the pervasiveness of imagery based on rural and military analogies which refer to experience no longer central to social life and which have little relevance in modern circumstances:

> They have become figurative and allusive designations of something quite different. Not many people set hand to plough, separate the wheat from the chaff, make a killing, make a last-ditch stand, sail near the wind, pay the piper or find a hard nut to crack. These expressions have been extended to cover a wide range of human situations, which they indicate only obliquely. Their homely reverberations often conceal, rather than illuminate, the context in which they are used.

The images mask, distort or hide what life is really like, giving it an appearance of homeliness, familiarity and simplicity. Indeed, of even greater concern to Seabrook is the possibility that popular usages of either redundant imagery or even more up-to-date set phrases and clichés serve not only to narrow our chance of engaging with conflicting ideas and sceptical interpretations by making attempts to explore more unfamiliar forms of expression more difficult and more threatening, but also to weaken our sense of responsibility for the reliability and the validity of the descriptions and judgements contained in our application of these formulations. He argues that:

> the familiar phrases do not only give us the consoling illusion that we understand, and can cope with, the world we live in and all its contingencies. Often there is also an implicit moral judgement. People shouldn't play fast and loose, blow hot and cold, be unable to see beyond noses, make mountains out of molehills, have bees in their bonnet, fish in troubled waters, build castles in the air, kick over the traces. These phrases, which present themselves so readily, diminish the ability to assess situations objectively, because of their ready-made judgement.

The child's pre-school language experience has relevance for later educational contact in another way. In learning *a* language the individual is also exposed to the often hidden message of what constitutes *'proper'* usage. Whether the environment in which language acquisition takes place is one in which a dialect variation of a language is the norm, or one in which a standard version of a language is the accepted mode, in their initial encounters children are presented with a situation which, albeit for the time being, represents the particular mode used as *the* form of expression. However, in accepting allegiance to a particular form of speech and expression, children are made vulnerable to fairly persistent social attitudes to different modes of language usage as they come into contact with other speech communities. These arise from the fact that in learning language we also learn ideas about what constitutes appropriate usage in different contexts and, on the basis of this, we also come to recognize that judgements of other users are made according to beliefs about what constitutes appropriateness; we learn how to use *our* understanding of language and appropriateness as a basis for ordering our impressions of others, as demonstrated in the way *they* organize communications. As Stubbs (1976) has noted:

> British people are very sensitive to the *social* implications of dialect and accent and the characteristic speech of our large cities, especially Birmingham, East London, Liverpool, Newcastle and Glasgow, is often regarded as 'slovenly' and 'ugly'. Giles (1971) carried out experiments in which people listened to standard and regional dialects. In fact, they heard the same speaker using different language varieties, but they did not know this! Speakers of standard English were *perceived as* more ambitious, more intelligent, more self-confident and more reliable.

Stubbs comments that, unreasonable as such linguistic stereotyping might appear to be, we need to be aware of the extent to which it is used in social interaction as a basis for evaluating individuals' intelligence and personal worth.

The importance of such stereotyping becomes critical if we consider how it might work in school. When we look at patterns of communication in classrooms later in this chapter, the proposition emerges that, at the very least, teachers sometimes show more concern with the *form* of their pupils' communications than with the content.

Perhaps the most significant message about schooling transmitted in the process of language acquisition concerns the assumptions to which children are exposed which refer to an education world they have yet to experience. In learning a language a child internalizes not only words and concepts which refer to objects, but also some which describe social categories and social roles. Thus the pupil entering school already has ideas about what terms like 'school', 'learning' and 'classroom' mean and about expectations which surround the general role categories 'boy' and 'girl', 'teacher' and 'pupil'. This should not be taken as a claim that the activities and understandings of the child in school are massively predefined or culturally determined. The specifics of classroom life will be created, negotiated and developed *in the course of interaction* in school, but this interaction takes place against a background of previously acquired expectations and understandings. We have only to observe groups of four-year-olds 'playing school' to notice that such children already have ideas about what activities in this setting are like and mean. What is important is that such ideas have been transmitted through a filter of values contained in other people's subjective interpretations of that setting; in taking on the perceptions of others the child is almost inevitably involved in taking on some of the judgements and evaluations carried in these perceptions.

Much of the discussion in this section has been to do with the way in which language might be seen as the vehicle by which general social messages relevant to the processes of educating are transmitted. But, in the distinctive way language is used in schools we can identify other types of subtle communication, and it is with these that the next sections will be concerned.

School Experience: General Patterns of Language Usage

As wat noted earlier, language practices in schools have characteristics which distinguish them from those used in other social settings. While we might not agree that communication in schools conforms to a type which Waller (1932) termed 'the didactic voice', dry, unemotional, impersonal and repetitive, there do seem to be certain regular patterns concerning writing and talking the persistence of which is curious. What patterns can we distinguish?

In the work of Basil Bernstein we find some suggestion of how we might attempt a description of some key elements of these patterns. Bernstein's writing (1973, 1977), concerned with his sociolinguistic theory and the relationship between language and education, is complex and often highly abstract. However, because it represents one of the few sustained attempts to explore language in education and because Bernstein's theory, in its development, has influenced the thinking of many educational practitioners and policy-makers, it is worth making a brief detour from the main discussion of this chapter to consider certain features of this work. Bernstein began his work in the late 1950s with the aim of devising a conceptual framework upon which the relatively poor educational attainment of working-class pupils (early leaving, poor test performances and low rates of 'academic' success), as against that of their middle-class peers, could be explored, in attempting this he has concentrated upon:

> how the class system acts upon the deep structure of communication in the process of socialization.
>
> Bernstein, 1973

This framework is based upon the postulate that the social relations of particular social groups (i.e. their work relationships or place in the scheme of how the social division of labour is managed, the nature of the belief system which holds their particular group together, the way in which family life is organized) will generate a *system* of communication specific to that group and their conditions of life. This system, once established, sensitizes or orientates both those using and those acquiring language to distinct 'orders' of meanings, relationships and relevances. Bernstein argues that these systems are distinguishable and can be placed on a continuum, moving from what he calls the restricted code, at one end, to the elaborated code at the other (RC/EC). Different orders of meaning, or the 'dominant principles' humans use to organize their thought about the definition of and the relations between objects and people, are distinguishable according to the criteria of *universalistic* characteristics (EC) – in which meaning is independent of the context in which it is being made, does not depend upon shared and taken-for-granted assumptions, is generally available and is therefore *explicit* – and *particularistic* characteristics (RC), in which the circumstances or context in which meaning is being made are essential for understanding; this renders such meaning useful only at a local level, it being *implicit*. The extent to which the major socializing agency, the family, favours one meaning system or another depends, in the main, upon the class position of the family and upon the role system dominant in the life of that family. By role system Bernstein means:

> how families determine the allocation of decision-making on the extent and kind of interaction between members of the family.

These role systems are themselves, in part, a reflection of the family's place in the wider social system. Bernstein distinguishes between *positional* families (in which decisions about interaction are made by reference to the formal position or the commonly held notions about roles in the family – father, mother, daughter, son – and hence involve role ascription) and *person-orientated* families (in which decisions rest upon individuals' unique attributes, and hence involve role achievement). The link between the family role system and communication codes is that, for Bernstein, the principles of management and control used to sustain one role system or another focus upon different orders of meaning. Or, in his own words:

> inasmuch as a role system is personal rather than positional, then it is a relatively more unstable system. It is continuously in the process of assimilating and accommodating the verbally realized but different intentions, qualification and motives of its members. Tensions will arise which are a function of the characteristic of the role system. Special forms of arbitration, reconciliation and explanation will develop. These tensions *only in the last resort* will be managed in terms of the relative power which inheres in the respective statuses. Social control will be based upon linguistically elaborated meanings rather than upon power.
>
> Bernstein, 1973

Now, the crucial element of Bernstein's theory is that the particular orientation of specific meaning systems (communication codes) and the particular forms of social control inherent in a specific role system (family types) are *realized* or actualized in distinctive speech forms (linguistic codes or speech variants) which are either elaborated or restricted. Because working-class families are, as a consequence of the social relations of their cultural position, more likely to develop a positional role system, members of these families are more likely to make significant use of a speech variant which requires little linguistic elaboration, i.e. is based upon the restricted code. The individual child acquires language in four crucial contexts – the regulative, the instructional, the interpersonal and the imaginative – and the words, structures and discourse possibilities to which the child is made sensitive are both transmitted and regulated by the communication code used by the family of socialization to order their understanding of the world. For most working-class children this code will be the restricted code.

The link between language usage and educational process, as framed by Bernstein, can now be considered. Because he believes that schools, almost by definition, 'are predicated upon an elaborated code and its system of social relationships', those children who, through primary socialization, have not been orientated or sensitized to such a code, and thus have not learned when meaning needs to be made explicit, will experience feelings of cultural discontinuity between life at school and life at home. This, Bernstein argues, is because:

> the school is necessarily concerned with the transmission and development of universalistic orders of meaning. The school is concerned with making explicit and elaborating through language, principles and operations, as these apply to objects (science subjects) and persons (art subjects).

Thus, most middle-class children can always be expected to perform more successfully in the present school system because the code around which the system is organized is that which is typical for middle-class family life, or, again in Bernstein's own words:

> The sequencing rules of educational transmissions, the pacing of this transmission (the rate of expected acquisition), its future relevance and its immediate irrelevance are, to say the least, based upon performance rules which the middle-class child embryonically possesses. Class regulates the elaborated codes of education and the family.
>
> Bernstein, 1977

As the above exposition of Bernstein's sociolinguistic theory has been, necessarily, over-compressed, two further points must be emphasized. First, it is important to recognize that *codes* are defined as underlying or generative principles. As Stubbs (1976) observes, 'people do not speak codes, just as they do not speak grammar: both grammar and codes are abstract, underlying systems'.

Second, and related to the last point, Bernstein insists that in suggesting that some children 'do less well' in school because they are made sensitive to a particular linguistic variant he is saying nothing about the child's linguistic or intellectual potential. Rather the theory focuses upon the kind of rules that the child or adult user will determine as appropriate to certain speech and cognitive contexts.

If Bernstein's account has validity, what implications might it have in terms of the hidden messages carried in school language? Perhaps the following:

1. That certain ways of thinking demand certain ways of communicating and talking – complex, explicit, elaborate and abstract. The message for some children is that the modes of communication most prevalent in their out-of-school experience are inappropriate in this domain. They must, therefore, decide whether to accept or reject a context which effectively devalues elements of the world from which they originate.
2. That learning and educational concerns are significantly to do with abstract principles and operations. The message for some children is that the affairs of everyday life, as expressed in the language of their culture, are distinctly separate from the world of learning.
3. That the apparently superior/inferior educational performances of their peers that pupils observe are explicable by reference to characteristics they bring to school rather than to aspects of how schools and classrooms are defined and managed. The message for some pupils is that their lack of achievement in school is not because the school is making an inadequate adjustment to their needs but because they are different from what is celebrated in school as the 'normal' pupil.
4. That the world is describable in concepts which are organized in a hierarchical structure. The message for all pupils is that modes of communication, like most

other social phenomena, can be perceived and evaluated in a ranked order. Ways of speaking are subtly represented to them in a framework based upon notions of better/worse, richer/poorer, high-status/low-status, most-acceptable/least-acceptable, rather than as being simply different.

However, it is important to emphasize that Bernstein's work has received a great deal of criticism. Lawton (1968) has criticized the constraining nature of the conditions of experimentation upon which Bernstein formulated some of his assertions; Rosen (1972a) has called into question Bernstein's definition of class and his characterizations of the life experiences of the various social groups he identifies; Trudgill (1974) and Labov (1969) regarded Bernstein's work as involving serious misunderstandings of the relationship between language and thought, explicitness and logic, and have suggested that we should regard elaborated and restricted speech variants as differences of style rather than of substance. For our purposes, however, the central critical concern must be with the explanatory power of Bernstein's theory with relation to the links between language usage and educational processes. Are patterns of communication in school based on an elaborated code? In his critique of Bernstein's 'idealized' portrayal of school language, Edwards (1976) suggests that this is not necessarily so, and comes to some rather different conclusions about the message the pupil receives when he or she experiences this communication form. He suggests that if we consider the typical characteristics of 'traditional' or 'hierarchically organized' schools, where, it can be argued, it is often the case that:

> meanings are too often 'given as part of a natural order which cannot be questioned . . . (and) that the boundary between teacher and learner is often too clear, the latter having too little discretion; and that the individual child is so submerged in the pupil role that meanings relate not to him but to the category in which he is fitted . . .

then we are left with an impression of a context which, according to Bernstein's own theoretical analysis, would be more likely to be predicated upon a restricted code than on the elaborated version.

Perhaps, then, we are not at present in a position from which we can talk about the 'underlying principles' which shape school language in general, but we can certainly scrutinize some of the actual communication practices found in schools, even if a comprehensive theory which explains why they are as they are is elusive.

The Written Language of Schooling

One distinctive feature of communication in schools and classrooms is that it involves fairly extensive deployment of the written word. Apart from talking, textbooks, worksheets and printed resource packages are by far the most popular and common devices used by teachers to stimulate pupils and introduce material for learning; and requiring pupils to write something about the things to which they have been introduced – short descriptions, essays, test answers or notes – is the main strategy by which children in schools are encouraged to record and demonstrate their knowledge and understanding. An almost unavoidable impression created in the classroom is that the literary mode is the best mode of communication for organizing learning and thinking about new ideas and experiences. But there is more to it than this. Other impressions are also created in the forms these writings take and the purposes for which they are used.

Consider first the language of textbooks. As was suggested in Chapters 6 and 9, a good deal of the *content* of the books used in schools carries covert judgements about what is often presented as 'objective' information. But in the *form* of the language regularly employed in some textbooks for school pupils there are also implied evaluations. Compare the following extracts quoted by Wilkinson (1975). The first is taken from a 14-year-old girl's notes on a text, the second from the text upon which she was working:

> There are two forms of energy. One is Kinetic energy when something is moving. When a man pedals a bicycle down a hill it is Kinetic energy. A body possesses potential energy if we force it to change shape. When we wind up a clock we force the spring to change shape.

> There are two forms of mechanical energy. A body has Kinetic Energy when it is moving; the more massive the body and the faster it moves, the more energy it has. A body possesses Potential Energy if a force has been applied to it to change its position or shape. A bicycle at the top of a hill and the wound-up spring of a clock have potential energy. Potential energy is stored energy.

How does the second extract differ from the first? It contains more technical terms; it is more impersonal; it is highly condensed and compressed; it is formal and somewhat colourless in tone; it is assertive in tenor; it is highly abstract, the information given being de-contextualized, separated from an everyday world which would give it purpose and relevance. Indeed, in some ways it seems to have different points of reference from those to which the girl's own formulation is addressed. For example, the terms 'energy' and 'force' appear to refer to general common-sense understandings in the pupil's version, and are associated with the activities of people, while in the textbook they have special reference, associated with objects and abstract ideas. (And, we might observe, this difference of reference seems to have interfered with the process by which the girl comes to terms with the information being presented.) The point here is that, in the course of giving information which is considered necessary to the development of a child's scientific understanding, the world from which such information is being drawn and to which it is applicable is presented, by virtue of the language used, as foreign and strange, set apart from the one which the learner inhabits. Might there not be two messages here, the one contingent upon the other? Not only is the language used to describe the concept dry, unfamiliar and out of touch with a living world, but so also, by implication, are the ideas which the language is expressing. Might an unintended consequence of using language which is different from that which we use to understand and organize our personal experiences and everyday lives be that it signals to the pupil that such is the character of the very knowledge and concepts we are trying to impart that the concerns of schooling are similarly dry and alien? Furthermore, might such usage not also convey the impression that what counts as learning, being able to move around in this curious educational domain with some familiarity, depends more upon an ability to articulate ideas and thoughts in abstract, remote and impersonal formulations than on being able to apply the ideas acquired to practical situations and everyday encounters? Harold Rosen (1972b), in his discussion of this formal and conventionalized language found in many of the texts used in classrooms, describes vividly some of the possible impressions its usage has for the reader:

> Language like this looks at children across a chasm. The worst way to bridge this chasm is to encourage children to take over whole chunks of it as a kind of jargon (examinations have been the great excuse). For fluent children, such as moderately successful grammar school pupils, this process is fatally easy. Probably few of us who have grown up in the system are free from some taint of this schooling. Instead of the new formulations representing hard-won victories of intellectual struggle or even partial victories, there are not even half-hearted skirmishes. Instead there is empty verbalism, sanctioned utterance and approved dogma; behind them is a void or a chaos. The personal view is made to seem irrelevant; it is outlawed . . .
>
> For other pupils, however, the gap between their own language and the textbook is so great that the textbook is mere noise. Their own language has not organized their thinking in such a way that they can be cognitively responsive in even a minimal sense. The textbook is alien both in its conventions and its strategies. The subject never comes through; it is another way of life. Though this is not a matter of language alone, language plays a big part. The willing bright pupil has sufficient language achievement behind him to enable him to mime the textbook though his hold may be precarious and over-dependent on verbatim memory. At least the morale will be high when he is confronted with new verbal experience. He has done it before; he will do it again. At the other extreme is the pupil who receives nothing but scrambled messages. He has failed to decode them in the past; he will fail again.

All this is not to claim that pupils should never be introduced to technical language, high-level conceptualization and the specialist linguistic conventions used to manage complex thought and interpretation. Rather it is to suggest that unless we are sure that, first, we make such introduction in a way which permits the pupils to handle initial encounters with these forms by using their own existing language competences and skills and, second, that we are not using these conventions to give the material status rather than to clarify meaning, then the message for many pupils is likely to be that the concerns of schooling have little to do with the concerns of life.

One dimension of this 'unreality' and the impact it has it caught by Jennifer, aged 15, when she writes:

> People who write in textbooks do not make mistakes – and the best way to learn is by your own mistakes.

In Claxton, 1978

However, the language of textbooks is not the only area relating to pupils' experience of the written word in which they might be exposed to some complex messages. In the writing that they themselves do we can identify the impact of other hidden communications. To help make such an identification we can ask three, not unrelated, questions. What do pupils write about? What form does their writing take? Why do they write?

Pupils' Writing

It is difficult to generalize about 'what' pupils in school write about, as this will vary from school to school and according to the demands of different teachers. Certainly pupils seem to do a lot of writing. For example, Nancy Martin (1971), in her study of the total writing done in one week by three classes of seven-year-olds, nine-year-olds and eleven-year-olds, reports that, for the seven-year-olds:

> The average amount written by each member of the class was 20 full pages, excluding pictures, and this covered about 15 different items . . . Within the average of different pieces of written work each child had made four or five diary entries and had written one or two generally long stories; he had also done two or more pieces of work headed 'Mathematics' and two or three brief reports of scientific experiments.

It is worth noting that quite often what children are asked to write about represents a subject division between areas of knowledge carried in the minds of the teacher. The observation made in Chapter 9, that school knowledge is 'mostly non-integrated, fragmented and specialized', is thus reinforced through this exercise. Equally significant is that, in many classrooms, writing represents the area in which a pupil makes his or her most major *individual* and *active* contribution to the communication process. Although much time is devoted to talk in schools, the individual's contribution to any period of talk is usually small, in that he or she is only one of many who share this period, and so writing about what they have been taught has become one of the principal methods by which pupils are given the opportunity to produce some kind of individualized response. The nature of this response can vary in type. James Britton (1971) has suggested that we can differeniate between different types of language usage (spoken and written) according to the nature of the 'typical functions' their production is designed to serve, and he proposes that these differences can be conceptualized according to the following continuum: *transactional – expressive – poetic*. What distinguishes these categories is the relationship between what is being expressed and the purpose of making that expression. Language can be used to 'get things done', in which case we are directly concerned with the consequences our usages have, the end in view, and we work with *transactional* language. Alternatively, language can be used to reflect on and evaluate reality, in which case we are concerned with the validity of our reflections rather than with any instrumental purpose, and we work with *poetic* language. In the former instance we assume the role of participant, and in the latter the role of spectator. The way in which Britton contrasts the extremes of his systems is shown in Table 12.1.

Table 12.1 *Contrast of the extremes of Britton's system*

Transactional (participant role)	Poetic (spectator role)
The utterance is an immediate means to an end outside itself.	The utterance is an immediate end in itself, and not a means, i.e. it is a verbal artifact, a construct.
The form it takes, the way it is organized, is dictated primarily by the desire to achieve that end efficiently.	The arrangement *is* the construct, i.e. the way items are formally disposed is an inseparable part of the meaning of the utterance.
Attention to the forms of the language is incidental to understanding, and will often be minimal.	Attention to the forms of the language is an essential part of a listener's (reader's) response.
The speaker (writer) is concerned in his utterance to enmesh with his listener's relevant knowledge, experience, interests; and the listener is at liberty to contextualize selectively what he finds relevant.	The speaker (writer) is concerned to create relations internal to the utterance, and achieve a unity, a construct that is discrete from actuality.

It is tempting to speculate that, although we can make few generalizations to describe what children write about in schools, as they progress through them they are increasingly required to produce writing from the point of view of the participant, that is, transactional writing, writing to report on the matters to which they have been introduced in lessons, to recount them or to record them. Necessarily this means that the practice of using language to stand apart from actuality and to contemplate it, the spectator role, is neglected – meanings and interpretations are taken up and *used* rather than explored and evaluated. Hence, implicit in much of the writing that pupils do, which is aimed at 'enmeshing' with the teacher's knowledge and interests, is, perhaps, a message that the affairs of school are to do with acceptance and conformity rather than with questioning and creating. We cannot, of course, be sure of this. Yet if we examine differences between how pupils write and how they talk about the same thing in school we can find some clues to what they appear to think is required of them in 'school writing'. Compare, for example, the differences between one nine-year-old girl's written and spoken accounts of a holiday episode:

> *The leaning tower pisa.*
> We went to piza. We all had an ice-cream. It was a very hot day I had a chocolate one. then we went to the tower I was the first one to the top. Piza is a very small town.

> It was a few months ag ago/ about half a year/ I think it was/ we went we went I think/ it was in italy/ and we/ we went to a big tower and it/ one of the seven wonders of the world and it was crooked it went like that/ and there were 200 steps and we had to go all the way up and/ I was the first one up and we/ I I almost got blown off the side when the bells went/we had it was about you had to put earplugs in mm but we didn't have any/ cause we didn't know they were going to go/ then then we had to go down again/ and then/ just across/ across the road there was another place when mm/ i think it was a/ it was round with a/ long round roof on/ and and/ somebody came in it made such an echo/ it was very very loud/ he was talking softly and when/ when he went in it made a very loud echo/ and then after that we went out again and we went down to the graveyard/ I dont know if we were allowed in but we did go in/ and mm/ there was a few graves and/ I wish Id seen some bones but I didnt/ I looked in every single grave that hadnt a grave top on/ but I didnt find any
>
> In Wilkinson, 1975

It could be that some of the differences we can observe in the two pieces above can be explained by saying that the girl found writing more difficult and demanding. But does this entirely explain the formality of the written version, the lack of interconnection, the absence of the spontaneity and attempted development of ideas demonstrated in the spoken version, that impersonality? Could it be that she has learned and is acting upon a message about writing in school – that accuracy and correctness of form are higher goals to strive for than is struggling to express personal feeling and emotions. Harold Rosen (1972b) reports that when a 16-year-old boy wrote in his geography book:

> An erratic is quite an exciting result of glaciation as a large rock not geologically the same as it surroundings may be found perched incredibly precariously on smaller stones. This is an erratic.

his teacher ringed the word 'exciting' and wrote by it 'No need to get excited. "Spectacular" a better word to use here'. Rosen comments:

> Every need to get excited, one would have thought; excitement about erratics cannot be so abundant that teachers can afford to dampen it.

More seriously, it can be argued that when teachers make this kind of insistence, which places conventions above subjective responses, they are not merely 'correcting' the pupils' writing but communicating to them expectations about what counts as acceptable education, knowledge and expression and about the status of these forms compared with more personal responses to the world. From instances of this kind we can also develop a more general realization about communication practices in schools, a realization which gets to the core of the idea of the hidden curriculum of language. When teachers set up and either insist upon or encourage their pupils' conformity to certain *styles* of communication in school, they are not just making use of a form of language to allow the mutual exchange of ideas and information. They are also making statements about their tacit understanding of *what* is being dealt with in this exchange, of *how* such exchanges are most appropriately managed, of *why* such exchanges are being promoted in that particular setting, and of the position particular individuals occupy in relation to one another in the exchange process and to the material that is being moved around. They are making a covert but influential statement of how they define the situation in the classroom – of what they regard as educational knowledge, as learning, as the purpose of education and as the roles of the teacher and the pupil.

An analysis made by Barnes and Shemilt (1974) of the responses of teachers in 11 secondary schools to questions about their reasons for setting written work and about how they evaluate it provides an illustration of what possible statements about how they define the situation teachers might make in this particular area of classroom communication. They found that, in their replies to questions, teachers described attitudes to written work in ways which could be categorized into two groups. The groups were distinguishable in terms of their justifications of why they set written work, what they were looking for in the work and how they used this work as part of their general teaching schemes. The first group indicated a feeling that written work was designed to enable the pupil to record and acquire knowledge presented, that work could be judged against some fair objective of correctness and thus production of something which conformed to the strictures of a predefined exercise, and that such products could be used to assess the pupil's response in terms of how close this came to what the teacher expected or understood the exercise to be about, and could thus be marked or handed back for correction. The second group indicated that written work was mainly aimed at providing a means by which pupils could extend their understanding and develop their personal feeling about and awareness of the material under consideration, that it could be judged in terms of what the pupil saw as the purpose of the work and of how it related to each particular pupil's individual circumstances, and that the responses the pupils made could be used either as the basis of a dialogue between teacher and pupil, in which the teacher would reply to the pupils' writing, or they could be used by the teacher to formulate how future work should be organized, or they could be displayed publicly and given a wider audience. Barnes and Shemilt regard the first group of teachers as conforming to a stereotype they call the *transmission* teacher, and the second as conforming to a type they label *interpretation* teachers. They suggest these differ in their attitudes to written work as follows:

1. 'The Transmission teacher . . . is primarily aware of writing as a means of measuring the pupil's performance against his own expectations and criteria. When

he sets written work his attention is focused upon the kind of writing he wants . . . He assumes that it is his business to define the task for the pupils, and to provide them with information about their success in measuring up to his standards. He values writing as a record to which his pupils can later look back, but assumes that they will address it to a general disembodied reader rather than to themselves or to him.'

2. 'The Interpretation teacher sees writing as a means by which the writer can take an active part in his own learning; as pupils write they can – under certain circumstances – reshape their view of the world, and extend their ability to think rationally about it . . . He tries to ensure that his pupils see the written work as relevant to their own purposes and sees writing as contributing to a dialogue in which he plays a crucial part.'

We can, I think, get some general impression of how writing might differ according to the type of teacher for whom it is being done, by comparing Stubbs's (1976) constructed examples of alternative ways pupils might write about a chemistry lesson, one personal, the other 'stylistically conventional'.

> Few things can be more beautiful than to watch crystals grow before your eyes in various shapes and hues. Yesterday, my friend and I dropped some warm, strong copper sulphate solution onto a microscope slide, and watched with delight as the liquid cooled and the tiny crystals took shape.

> Two or three drops of warm, concentrated copper sulphate solution were placed on a microscope slide. As the solution cooled, crystals were deposited. Solutions were selected so that varieties of crystal form and colours were investigated.

However, the important suggestion that Barnes and Shemilt (1974) make is that the communication system set up by teachers in classrooms is a reflection of their beliefs and assumptions about the business of educating – underlying ideologies of what constitutes learning and teaching. They hypothesize that these ideological differences can be summarized as in Table 12.2.

What is important for the present discussion is that, although few teachers make open and explicit statements about their views of knowledge, learning or the roles of individuals in the classroom, in the kind of writing they ask their pupils to do, in their communications about how it should be done, in the situations they create to promote writing and in the way they react to it, they cannot avoid making implicit indications of their views on all of these things. Pupils faced with writing tasks which require them to conform to a particular linguistic mode and to demonstrate their knowledge of the details of predefined material, and which are being done to be presented for assessment, are likely to build up very different ideas about what they are doing in school from those of pupils who are asked to write as part of a collaborative enterprise in which they are exploring reality with the teacher and other pupils.

The hidden curriculum of language

Table 12.2 *Ideological differences between the 'transmission' teacher and the 'interpretation' teacher*

The transmission teacher	The interpretation teacher
Believes knowledge to exist in the form of public disciplines which include content and criteria of performance.	Believes knowledge to exist in the knower's ability to organize thought and action.
Values learners' performances in so far as they conform to the criteria of the discipline.	Values the learners' commitment to interpreting reality, so that criteria arise as much from the learner as from the teacher.
Perceives the teacher's task to be the evaluation and correction of the learner's performance, according to criteria of which he is the guardian.	Perceives the teacher's task to be the setting up of a dialogue in which the learner can reshape his knowledge through interaction with others.
Perceives the learner as an uninformed acolyte for whom access to knowledge will be difficult, since he must qualify himself through tests of appropriate performance.	Perceives the learner as already possessing systematic and relevant knowledge and the means of reshaping that knowledge.

Classroom Talk

In more recent work, Barnes (1976; Barnes and Todd, 1977) has suggested that similar messages are conveyed in the way in which talking is organized in classrooms, an aspect of communication in school we have so far neglected in this chapter. As research in this area is fairly prolific, it is not possible to include all the details of such work. However, some of the more general observations that have emerged are as follows.

The teacher talks most
It has been found that most of the talk in classrooms is done by the teacher. Even in those classrooms where we find pupils talking to each other, be this officially sanctioned or privately established conversations, control of the main discourse system is maintained by, or quickly reverts back to, the teacher. As Edwards and Furlong (1978) observe:

> Verbal encounters are still the main means of transmitting knowledge, and they are encounters of a very distinctive kind. For older children especially, the main characteristics of classroom talk are not only that there is much of it, but that so much of what is said is both public and highly centralized.
>
> In traditional classrooms, the communicative rights of teachers and pupils are very unequal indeed. To adapt Flander's comment . . . teachers usually tell pupils when to talk, what to talk about, when to stop talking and how well they talked.

Restricted communication
When pupils do talk their communications are remarkably restricted. Bellack et al. (1966), for example, have suggested that the language interaction in classrooms can be broken down into four basic moves or categories which relate to the recognizable functions of language being used and to how instances of talk are structurally related. These are *structuring* moves (utterances working to create and direct the setting for talk

and activity in a lesson), *soliciting* moves (designed to elicit some kind of response), *responding* moves (which are directly tied to structuring moves) and *reacting* moves (talk designed to clarify, expand or evaluate a prior move without being directly elicited by the prior move). In classrooms teachers seem to use the soliciting moves most, while the pupils' contribution to the 'language game' is restricted mainly to making responding moves. Using a more sophisticated analytical system, which is based upon describing how each item of talk in a stretch of discourse or speech interaction is related, Sinclair and Couthard (1974) have confirmed this picture of the organization of talk in classrooms. They suggest that the structure of *discourse* in classrooms (i.e., those times when the pupil is asked to take a role in the talk, as opposed to when the teacher is conducting a monologue) quite regularly follows a three-move exchange pattern of:

Initiation → Response → Feedback

Or, to illustrate this sequence more concretely:

Question → Answer → Evaluation

More significantly, they observe that when this pattern is operating, it is the teacher who initiates and gives feedback, and the pupils who respond. Deviations from this course are noticeably rare. A great deal of teacher–pupil talk in classrooms, they suggest, follows the kind of pattern illustrated below:

Teacher:	Those letters have special names. Do you know what it is?	
	What is one name that we give to these letters?	(Initiation)
Pupil:	Vowels	(Response)
Teacher:	They're vowels, aren't they?	(Feedback)
Teacher:	Do you think you could say that sentence without having the vowels in it?	(Initiation)

Coulthard, 1977

Even when exchanges are enlarged, through one participant or other extending their turns at talking, the basic pattern of initiation – response – feedback remains the underlying principle of the exchange. Two points are worth noting. First, the pupil's part in the dialogue is structurally contingent upon the teacher's, hence control of the content or direction of talk is difficult for them to achieve. (Also, they have less opportunity to speak, the teacher having the option of taking two turns to every one of the pupil's turns.) Second, even though the pupils are being constrained or invited to take part in a dialogue, it is a subordinate role they are being given; in the structure their chances of initiating talk or introducing topics, of making statements, of asking questions and, crucially, of making evaluations and judgements, are significantly low.

An important consequence of teachers regularly taking control of who talks to whom about what in the classroom dialogue is that it can influence the development of pupil identities. In distributing speakership rights, the teacher might be tempted to give preference to those pupils who display a perspective of the classroom situation which conforms to that of the teacher. Or, as feminist writers have observed, the communication system in the classroom can operate in a way which re-enforces stereotypical gender roles and relations. Michelle Stanworth (1983), for example, in her study of the patterns of talk in a co-educational humanities lesson in a college of further education, notes that not only is it common for boys to be selected to talk much more frequently than girls but also that boys are invited to give views and build arguments whereas girls are invited to make passive responses.

'Recitation' and questioning

It has been found that a high proportion of teachers' talk consists of either 'recitation' or, particularly when they wish to bring the pupils into a dialogue, asking questions. To explore these two practices, Barnes (1976) analysed recordings he had collected in the course of following some first-year secondary-school pupils through their lessons for a day. He noted two important regularities in 'recitation':

1. As with the language of textbooks, teachers in their talk make extensive use of terminology which is special to the subject they are teaching. Very often they are well aware of this and 'present' the specific meanings to the class. However, even when they do this, Barnes suggests, 'the act of giving a technical name seems for many teachers to have taken on a value of its own in separation from its utility', and he argues that, although the use of subject terminology is seen by many teachers as an efficient way of expressing difficult concepts, it also serves a cultural function of preserving and signalling aspects of the teacher's role as being 'superior' to that of the pupil.

2. Teachers also make use of a language which, though not special to a subject, is strictly peculiar to school, 'the language of secondary education'. It is less likely to be explained to pupils, as it is part of the teacher's taken-for-granted perception of what is appropriate in school; indeed, it is sometimes used to explain subject–specialist terminology. For example, consider the abstract formulations this teacher uses to explain the concept 'city states':

> Teacher: They were called 'city states' because they were *complete in themselves* . . . They were governed by themselves . . . *ruled by themselves* . . . *they supported themselves* . . . These states were complete in themselves because the terrain between cities was so difficult that it was hard for them *to communicate* . . . Now because these people lived like this in their own cities *they tended to be* intensely patriotic towards their own city . . . Now, what's 'patriotic' mean?
>
> Barnes, 1976 (our emphasis)

Barnes makes other important observations about the practice of questioning, albeit on a rather 'impressionistic' basis. He argues that we can distinguish at least four broad types of questions: factual ('what' questions), reasoning ('how' questions), open (questions which permit a wide range of answers) and social (questions used to direct the course of a lesson rather than to work on the content). The teachers whose lessons he analysed asked mostly factual questions, some reasoning and few open ones, perhaps thus indicating to pupils, as Edwards (1976) suggests, the extent to which what is being considered in the lesson 'is to be received ready-made, whether it can be challenged and whether their own experience has anything relevant to contribute'.

Although a great deal of work on how talk is managed in classrooms is yet to be done, from the above we can suggest some of the messages to which pupils might be exposed which are hidden in the *way* talk is organized:

1. That school knowledge is something fairly fixed and closed and that it is quite different from, and of a higher order than, the knowledge they already possess.
2. That their role in the classroom is very subordinate to that of the teacher; they are required to be passive and to listen to those who are in authority over them by virtue of their possession of this 'superior' form of knowledge.
3. That learning involves 'answering' and not 'questioning', and that they will be judged to have successfully mastered something when their understanding approximates that of the teacher.

CONCLUSION

In this chapter the concern has been to explore how the *form* of language might carry hidden messages to the pupil as he or she prepares for or experiences schooling. There is one further point to be made. We may not like the contents of some of these messages. Yet, although teachers may have limited power over space, organization, subject and school knowledge, timetables and other carriers of the hidden curriculum, in the way they use language there is considerable power under their direct control. Perhaps they need be much less of a helpless victim in this aspect of schooling than in many others.

SUMMARY

1. Classrooms can be seen as language-saturated places and educating can be seen as revolving around activities like lecturing, explaining, discussing, telling, questioning, answering, reading, writing and listening.
2. Messages may be contained in both the manner in which language is used in classrooms and in the content of the communications.
3. Language serves at least three functions simultaneously in school: communication, thought and social interaction and control.
4. For communication between people to take place there must be some agreed set of ideas, and this linguistic repository of interpretations and symbols was largely the work of our ancestors.
5. The world of our ancestors was rural and military, and many of the images embedded within our language refer to experiences no longer central to life in a complex, industrial society, and our thinking is constrained and distorted as a consequence.
6. In learning language we also learn ideas about forms of expression and the social evaluations of dialect and accent.
7. Bernstein proposes that the social relations and life styles of particular social groups generate variable systems of communication, and that these can be placed on a continuum ranging from a restricted code through to an elaborated code.
8. The extent to which a particular family will favour one meaning and communication system to another is related to its social class position and its family role system.
9. Most pupils from the middle class are likely to perform more successfully in the

present school system because the code around which it is organized is the same one that is more frequently found in extensive use in middle-class family life, namely the elaborated code.

10. Most pupils from the working classes are likely to find that the modes of communication most prevalent outside school are often inappropriate in school, with the result that their school experience is one of conflict and potential alienation.

11. The theory of Bernstein has been subjected to a range of criticisms since it was first developed in the 1960s and 1970s. Much of this criticism has questioned the reliability of the description he offers of how language is actually used.

12. The written word is extensively used in schools in textbooks and other teacher-initiated material, as well as in pupils' work.

13. This written language tends to be formal and conventionalized, and a potential source of alienation from learning, for this transactional form of language contrasts with expressive and poetic forms, which encourage exploration and meaning-making.

14. The use of spoken language in classrooms shows some similar characteristics.

15. The use of language in classrooms varies according to ideologies of education: transmission and intepretation teachers have different theories of communication, and these are related to their theories of knowledge, learning, teaching, assessing, etc.

Further Reading

Barnes, D. (1976) *From Communication to Curriculum*, Harmondsworth: Penguin. An important book which looks at how patterns of communication in classrooms reflect different ideologies of learning and educating.

Barnes, D., Britton, J. and Rosen, H. (1969) *Language, the Learner and the School*. Harmondsworth; Penguin. This book, too, considers in greater depth some of the propositions in this chapter.

Edwards, A.D. (1976) *Language in Culture and Class*. London: Heinemann. Contains more detailed and critical reviews of issues concerning the relationship between patterns of communication and the processes of educating.

Postman, N. and Weingartner, C. (1969) *Teaching as a Subversive Activity*. Harmondsworth: Penguin, Chapters 2, 6 and 7 are lively and provocative sections on language and educating.

Stubbs, M. (1976) *Language, Schools and Classrooms*. London: Methuen. Another book containing critical reviews of issues concerning the relationship between patterns of communication and the processes of educating.

Discussion and Activities

1. Flanders found that two-thirds of the time spent in traditional classrooms is made up of talk, and two-thirds of this talk is done by the teacher. Observe any classrooms available to you to see if this conclusion still holds. Attempt to identify some of the main ways in which ideologies of educating are displayed in the organization of talk in this setting.

2. Bernstein proposes a relationship between social relations, life styles and language patterns. Does an examination of newspapers such as *The Guardian*, *The Times*, the *Daily Express*, the *Sun* and the *Mirror* provide support for this view?

3. Analyse any piece of writing produced by a pupil in school and attempt to determine the audience and purpose the writer seemed to have in mind and the distinctive characteristics of the style used.
4. Since television is beamed across social classes, does it operate as an ameliorating influence on language variations?

Signposts

Pre-school and early childhood education

It is interesting to explore how the patterns of verbal interaction a child experiences in the home, before he or she ever attends a school, prepare the child for life in classrooms. Several writers have suggested that a hidden curriculum operates in these situations just as much as in the classroom and that in pre-school conversations the child is already learning important things about learning, the role of the learner and the role of the teacher. For a general overview of patterns of discourse development through interaction, readers should consult Wells, G. and Nicholls, J. (1985) (eds.) *Language and Learning: An Interactional Perspective*, Lewes: Falmer Press. And two very good studies of the influence of early language experience upon how the child responds to interaction in the classroom are: Tizard, B. and Hughes, M. (1984) *Young Children Learning: Talking and Thinking at Home and at School*, London, Fontana; and Willes, M.J. (1983) *Children into Pupils*, London, Routledge and Kegan Paul.

Chapter 13

Marking, Testing and Examining

'In examinations the foolish ask questions that the wise cannot answer'
Oscar Wilde

INTRODUCTION

As noted earlier in the book, many concepts in the human sciences turn out to be ambiguous, so that it is useful to adopt a working definition. Such a definition may be refined and clarified during subsequent analysis, but at least an agreed starting point is established. Assessment was earlier taken to mean *collecting information on which to base judgements about learning experiences, in schools* (see Chapter 2).

Outside school, assessment is a regular feature of social life. We continually collect information about people, places and products, on the dress, behaviour and values of other people, on television, news, consumer goods and sport, and pass judgement on them.

In school, assessment is also rife at the informal level of observing and judging amongst the participants and interested outsiders too. However, the formal assessment system of marks, grades, tests and certificates will be the central focus of this chapter because it appears to carry many of the long-term significant messages about schooling. The messages carried by the assessment activity in schools turns out to be a complex set of ideas that becomes learnt by pupils in a process analogous to learning a board game like Monopoly where the rules are learnt as you play, without any encouragement to question the assumptions, the information, the evidence or to ask whether there are any better games to play. School assessment, unlike Monopoly (which you can reject as unworthy if you so judge), is compulsory.

Different pupils may learn different things from the network of ideas relating to assessment. One study by Miller and Parlett (1983) located a feature of the behaviour of learners that was described as cue consciousness. Learners were seen to fall into three groups: the cue-conscious, the cue-seekers and the cue-deaf. The cue-conscious recognized that they needed to work out certain things in order to do well under assessment. These included working out which pieces of work really counted and which were exercises, which method of presentation would get highest marks, what hints were available about examination topics, and what would please the staff marking particular work. None of this was declared – it was all part of the hidden curriculum.

The cue-conscious group were alert and took up any information that came their way. The cue-seekers were much more active. They quizzed members of staff, sought out information about external examiners, checked the research interests of staff and deliberately set out to create a good impression. The cue-deaf remained largely oblivious that this was an important feature of assessment: they had failed to become aware of this aspect of the hidden curriculum.

THE CONTEXTS

The messages about assessment are learnt in different contexts. Few homes utilize ticks, stars and grades to signal their assessment of children: parents use the currency of smiles, frowns, approving or disapproving remarks, praise or criticism and maybe the physical repertoire from kisses to smacks too. The significance of ticks, stars, and marks comes to the attention of children elsewhere.

Primary Schools

The Oracle research into the characteristics of primary schools produced information about their assessment activity (Galton and Simon, 1980). First of all there was a wide variety in the practices used so children would have to learn the particular form in use in their school. If they moved house, a new school could present a quite different set of features to be coped with. Some schools had checklists to note topics covered in English, maths and other areas of learning. Some noted grades. Others use standardized tests of reading, NFER tests or Richmond tests. Record cards containing personal information about pupils and parents occur in some. Parents may receive regular written reports from school but not in all cases. Day-to-day records tend to be idiosyncratic with some teachers keeping notebooks, others keeping them in their heads. The variety of format is deceptive; the outcome tended to be similar: a cumulative verdict on how the school personnel interpreted the achievement of each pupil in a similar range of curriculum areas with heavy stress on English and maths. On the basis of such research, those commentators who have alleged that British primary schools have neglected English and maths have to search hard to find many examples.

One case study of the assessment procedures of a primary school is reported in the work of Black and Broadfoot (1982). These procedures appear to be haphazard and confusing but are interpreted by the writers as part of a carefully orchestrated programme that leads to a centralized system of judging pupils not only in terms of formal learning but also in terms of the staff view of preferred personal and social development.

Secondary Schools

The reflections of one teacher on the activity of marking work in a secondary school contain an account of some of the messages relayed to children (Hextall, 1976).

Hextall argues that marking teaches children that teachers have power to place them in streams, bands, examination or non-examination groups. Teachers learn to play God:

> as well as marking the work of pupils who will become doctors, lawyers, teachers and accountants, and so on, we are also dealing with those who will enter occupations with high unemployment risks, with low rates of pay, with severe risks of industrial disablement and disease.

Hextall demonstrates that a myth develops about the objective nature of marking: the experts' evaluation is objective as part of a world without doubt. It is perhaps salutory at this point to recall the schoolteacher's verdict on Albert Einstein: 'Einstein, you will never amount to anything'.

There are more messages yet, Hextall points out. The pupils learn that to get good marks they must reproduce the known. The past is to be celebrated. If they do this they will produce a commodity that a teacher can price. Another related analogy here is that of the banking theory of education outlined by Freire (1972), where he sees education as having become a process whereby the teacher makes deposits into the accounts of the learners for receipt and storage until they need to be drawn on to buy certificates or grades.

Further and Higher Education

The work of Miller and Parlett (1983) on cue-consciousness was mentioned earlier as one of the findings of their study on students in Higher Education.

A study from the USA illustrates a related phenomenon, trading for grades. The study by Becker (1968) took as its subject medical students. Becker found that two activities were rivals for the students' attention. One was 'learning to think independently and critically' and the other was 'trading for grades'. The experience of the students led them to abandon the former in favour of the latter. Over time they gave more and more time to searching for cues to get the best grades from the lecturers and less attention to developing independent thought.

THE MESSAGES

A complex web of ideas exists about assessment in education, and the messages learnt relate to various aspects of the learning process. These aspects include what counts as learning, what counts as knowledge, the definition of a 'good teacher' and 'good schools', the self-concept of the students, the role of learners and authority, and the structure of society. The first four are dealt with here.

Learning

Husen (1974) notes that 'Pupils undertake to learn mainly to avoid the disagreeable consequences if they do not: low marks, non-promotion, censure, punishment, etc.' It is then a short step to the attitude that learning is a temporary nuisance that school imposes but that most adults are free from.

Learning becomes equated with work and is interpreted as dull even if it is not always unpleasant. This view confronts pupils educated at home who later return to school or college, who frequently report that they find their fellow students' alienated attitude to learning difficult to reconcile with their own enthusiasm and excitement. (The case study of democratic learning in Chapter 18 demonstrates that students in an institutional setting can also, under certain circumstances, report 'Intellectual exploration became an exciting and satisfying end in its own right, rather than a means to a boring and worthless end, e.g. exams, assessment'.)

A greater variety of things go on in classrooms than sometimes meets the eye. People talk, listen, make decisions, produce written material, work in groups, work on their own, sometimes laugh and sometimes cry, and the activities undertaken include reading, writing, answering questions, drawing and reasoning. The resultant learning includes attitudes, thinking skills, manual skills and information. Bloom's *Taxonomy of Educational Objectives* runs to three volumes in an attempt to catalogue classroom activity.

From this wealth of happenings, a selection takes place for the tasks of assessment. Examiners and teachers tend to stress end-products rather than learning processes so that diagnosis, adjustment, reappraisal and adaptation are accorded little respect in terms of marks. One outcome Holt (1969) demonstrates is 'right answerism'. Pupils absorb the idea that learning means finding the right answer whereas the way of obtaining it is seen as of much less significance and, moreover, that doubt and reservation are not welcome. Holt's remarkable journal records some of the strategies developed by his pupils for gleaning the right answer from him in order to please teacher.

Another feature common in the experience of teachers in secondary schools and further education settings is that students claim that debate and discussion is not 'real learning' – dictation of the right answer is real learning. Then by written recall of these right answers students can demonstrate that they are worthy of a certificate saying that they are good learners.

Knowledge

Students in the USA learn, Postman and Weingartner (1971) propose, that 'English is not history and history is not science and science is not art and art is not music and art and music are minor subjects and English, history and science major subjects, and a subject is something you take and, when you have taken it, you have "had" it and if you have "had" it, you are immune and need not take it again'.

There are several messages here. One is that knowledge is fragmented not integrated or networked. This way of classifying knowledge is through the concept of a subject using a scheme devised years ago by our ancestors and is thus past orientated (see Chapter 9). These subjects are stratified in respect of importance and significance as was seen in Chapter 8.

Having knowledge is equated with having memorized a great deal of information. In the UK this idea is celebrated in a popular television programme entitled Mastermind. It is an ironic title, for competitors are not required to demonstrate any powers of thought other than memory and Mastermemory, or to get rid of the sexism of the vocabulary, Supermemory, might be a more apt title.

These features led some writers to note that a commodity theory of knowledge was implied. Freire (1972), as noted earlier, called this the banking concept and he suggests that knowledge is seen as deposits to be placed into the students whose action is expected to be that of receiving and accumulating until the size of the deposit is asked for as a statement of the account in an examination.

One of the clients is not impressed by this approach to knowledge, as we noted earlier (see Chapter 2):

> Half-educated children emerge from school clutching their exam certificates . . . They believe themselves to be 'educated'. To some extent they are, I suppose. But are they better equipped to understand and live with their fellow human beings? Moreover, has their education encouraged them to think creatively and originally? Isn't this what education should be about?
>
> Anthony, aged 18, in Blishen (1969)

Teachers

When secondary-school pupils respond to discussion by judging that it is not 'real learning', they demonstrate a learning from the hidden curriculum: good teachers are instructors. They are not in agreement with Lao-tse (ca. 600 BC) and the view that 'of a good leader, when his task is finished, his goal achieved, they say "we did this ourselves" '. In contrast a good teacher, students have absorbed, does it to you, they instruct.

These good teachers are seen as subject experts. They have large deposits of information about one classified area of knowledge and can transfer these deposits to the learners, to use Freire's analogy.

Following through this ideology of education, such teachers need to be authoritarian. Independence of the experts would be an illogical thing to expect, so autonomy and democracy as approaches to learning become rejected (see Part Three).

The efficiency of such subject instructors lends itself to checks from outside and possibly payment by results, and is therefore not a professional task analogous to medicine or law. A semi-profession or qualifying association is the most that can be accorded such a limited activity, Etzioni (1969) concludes.

Schools

Pupils in UK schools absorb a view about 'good' schools. Their parents see 'good' primary schools as those that concentrate on reading, writing, and numeracy as we saw in Chapter 4. In secondary schools the preoccupation with public examinations is paramount. Broadfoot (1979) notes a contradiction here:

> It is indeed no accident that England and Wales are characterised by one of the highest degrees of school autonomy and at the same time, one of the greatest preoccupations with

public examinations of any country. As a result, 'good' schools tend to be identified as those with a good record of public examination passes

However, pupils in Steiner schools in the UK or those in schools in Sweden have to learn different messages since in neither case are public examinations in use. Some pupils are not impressed by the definition of good schools related to examination results, as the quotation from Anthony given earlier demonstrates (see Blishen, 1969).

Underpinning the notion of good schools is a well-established myth absorbed uncritically by most pupils, parents and teachers: it is that assessment by public examination is objective and accurate, whereas assessment by teachers and pupils is subjective and inaccurate. Broadfoot (1979) notes some of the features of the myth:

> The fact that the assessments are at best only a rough estimate of particular kinds of ability, despite the statistical finesse of the processing of the results and the large body of research directed towards improving their accuracy, has been extensively documented in a large number of research studies since the seminal work of Hartog and Rhodes in 1935. The vagaries of pupil performance and especially of exam stress, of differences between markers and the difficulty of questions, are only some of the more significant causes of inaccuracy which would seem to be largely unavoidable. It may well be partly for this reason that such certificate results are a very weak guide to the likely quality of future job or higher education performance. Indeed, Powell (1973) has documented a whole series of other influences on attainment in higher education of which the most obvious are motivation and effort, but which also include quite subtle dimensions excluded from certification assessment, such as introversion and extraversion and confidence.

The choice between public examinations and school-based assessment is not a choice between objectivity and subjectivity at all but a choice between two different kinds of inaccuracy, a choice of the lesser of two evils. Perhaps the difference between the Swedish education system and that of the UK is that in the former the issue has been faced and a choice of school-based assessment as the lesser evil has been made, whereas in the UK, since the myth of objectivity is still widely believed, the issue has not yet been faced and no real choice actually made. (An exercise on the myths of public examinations appeared at the end of Chapter 2.)

CONCLUSION

If the process of learning the hidden curriculum is analogous to the process of learning the board-game Monopoly, the messages learnt are not too dissimilar either. What is *not* learnt can be as revealing as what is learnt. Pupils do *not* learn:

1. that co-operation is a good idea – instead they learn that monopolizing the prizes is the desired goal;
2. that a critical stance is worthwhile – instead they learn fatalism or acceptance or nihilism;
3. that a consumer stance is sound – instead they learn to blame themselves for any failure rather than the learning experiences provided;
4. that helping fellow learners is desirable – instead they learn to keep ideas, information and sources to themselves.

What is learnt is both an ideology of education and an ideology of society in a complex and intertwined double set of messages, as Broadfoot (1979) comments:

> That education should be concerned to teach many things likely to be of little use in later life; that it should be conducted in hierarchical and bureaucratic institutions in which the pupil is relatively powerless; that it should foster competitiveness at a personal, institutional and even national level; that pupils should have almost no say in what they are taught and above all that allocation to differential social positions should take place largely on the basis of demonstrably inaccurate assessment mechanisms, may all be attributed to the prevailing hegemony which prevents genuinely alternative conceptions of education, even if conceived, from entering into any serious arena of debate.

Further Reading

Broadfoot, P. (ed.) (1984) *Selection, Certification and Control: Social Issues in Educational Assessment*. Lewes: Falmer Press. This reader takes up many of the issues raised in this chapter.

Black, H. and Broadfoot, P. (1982) *Keeping Track of Teaching*. London: Routledge and Kegan Paul. Various methods of assessment and their implications are documented.

Hextall, I. (1976) 'Marking Work' in Whitty, G. and Young M.F.D. (eds.) Explorations in the Politics of School Knowledge. Driffield: Nafferton Books. An analysis of the assumptions underpinning the everyday teacher's task of marking.

Miller, C.M.L. and Parlett, M. (1983) *Up to the Mark*. London: Society for Research into Higher Education. The strategies of learners in Higher Education are identified in this study.

(See also reading references at the end of Chapter 2.)

Discussion and Activities

1. Three 'messages' were not developed in this chapter: the self-concepts of learners, the structure of society and the concept of authority. Attempt a brief analysis of each. Material in Chapter 2 and in the Hidden Curriculum chapters should prove helpful.
2. Make a summary of the main points of this chapter.
3. What has been your personal experience of being marked, tested and assessed, and what do you think about it?
4. Discuss the following account of verbosity and marking:

   > Two Chicago English professors have found that a good way to improve your grade on a term paper is to use what they call 'verbose, bombastic' language.

   > Professors John Williams and Rosemary Hake say they took a well-written paper and changed the language a bit. They kept the ideas and concepts the same, but wrote two different versions – one in simplified, straightforward language and another in verbose language, loaded with pedantic terms.

   > They then submitted the two papers to nine high school teachers; they were surprised to find that all nine gave the verbose papers nearly perfect scores but downgraded the straightforward essays as too simple and shallow.

   > The professors then submitted the same two papers to 90 more teachers and came up with similar results. Three out of four high school teachers and two out of three college professors gave higher marks to pompous writing.

   > Reason to wonder what these same college professors mean, when they tell us, as they do all the time, that today's students 'can't write'.

   > Reprinted with John Holt's kind permission from 'Growing Without Schooling' No. 2 (729 Boylston Street, Boston, Massachusetts 02116)

Signposts

1. Wrong Verdicts

Einstein refused to accept the school's verdict on him as noted in the chapter. Can you locate other examples? Clients of the Open University known to you may be one source and also correspondence colleges. Dickenson, P. (ed.) 1982 *Could Do Better: School Reports and Memories of the Famous*, London: Arrow Books, is another source.

2. Grading Teachers

The idea of grading teachers and perhaps paying those who gain higher marks is proposed in both the UK and USA. A critical response to this idea appears in Rosenholtz, S.J. (1985) 'Political Myths about Education Reform: Lessons from Research on Teaching', *Phi Delta Kappan*, **66**, 5.

PART THREE

Ideologies of Education

The word 'ideology' has had a chequered career, as Chapter 14 will show. Currently it can be used for the purposes of preaching and prescribing a one right way, as an insult in locating opposing or different beliefs as lunatic or misguided, or as a means of comparing sets of ideas. The last use is the one that is advocated here.

For some, the very word 'ideology' is negative or tainted, and replacing the word with a synonym like 'philosophies of education' or 'alternative visions of education' may be advisable.

Chapter 14

The Concept of Ideology

'Every dogma must have its day.'
Carolyn Wells

INTRODUCTION

Ideology is a highly ambiguous concept, and it is necessary to have some discussion of the competing uses at the outset.

The Science of Ideas

An early usage of ideology was as a philosophical concept to distinguish a science of ideas from an ancient metaphysics. The use of ideology in this sense is now rare.

Revolutionary Thinking

Another usage of ideology as a concept, traced to Napoleon Bonaparte (R. Williams, 1977), was that of revolutionary thinking, this revolutionary thinking being interpreted as an undesirable set of ideas. Ideology thus threatened 'sound and sensible' thinking about a vision for a society. From this developed the notion of ideology as fanatical or impractical theories about society, and it was largely a term of abuse.

False Consciousness

One use of ideology by Marx and Engels in *The German Ideology* (1845–47) is related to the earlier view of undesirable sets of ideas. Ideology is intepreted as abstract thought about human society which was false:

> Ideology is a process accomplished by the so-called thinker consciously indeed, but with a false consciousness. The real motives impelling him remain unknown to him, otherwise it would not be an ideological process at all. Hence he imagines false or apparent motives.
> Engels, Letter to Mehring, 1893

The true consciousness is sometimes referred to as 'science', setting up a distinction between Marxism, as science, and other social thought, as ideology. This notion of ideology as illusion has become a common view:

> Meanwhile, in popular argument, ideology is still mainly used in the sense given by Napoleon. Sensible people rely on *experience*, or have a *philosophy*; silly people rely on ideology. In this sense, ideology, now as in Napoleon, is mainly a term of abuse
>
> J. Williams, 1977

Elsewhere Marx uses ideology in a more neutral sense where he refers to the legal, political, religious, aesthetic or philosophic as ideological forms in which men become conscious of conflict arising from conditions and changes in economic production. Ideology is not seen as false consciousness here. (See Marx, *Contribution to the Critique of Political Philosophy*, 1859.)

Competing Belief Systems

This second use of ideology by Marx is close to a more sociological use of the concept, where it refers to a group philosophy. Ideology is defined as a broad interlocked set of ideas and beliefs about the world held by a group of people that they demonstrate in both behaviour and conversation to various audiences. These systems of belief are usually seen as 'the way things really are' by the groups holding them, and they become the taken-for-granted way of making sense of the world.

It is this last use, of ideology as competing belief systems, that is used in the analyses of ideologies of education that follow, since this makes the concept capable of being used as an analytical tool to demonstrate alternative patterns of ideas that coexist and compete for acceptance.

INDIVIDUALS AND IDEOLOGY

A psychological view of ideology begins with the attitudes and opinions of individuals, and sees these as structured in a hierarchical manner. One attempt is that of Eysenck (1957) (Figure 14.1).

Specific opinions uttered on one occasion, such as 'what a naughty child that was in the supermarket', may give rise to habitual opinions uttered on several occasions, e.g. 'children should be seen and not heard'. A large number of habitual opinions about one central issue, e.g. the place and behaviour of children in society, is defined as an attitude. When groups of attitudes are related, this is referred to as an ideology.

This raises a difficult issue, that of the relationship between an individual's consciousness and the social world. The psychological analysis above tends to a psychological reductionist approach: the ideology is constructed out of the opinions of individuals. An alternative possibility is that the individuals' attitudes and opinions are fashioned out of the ideologies available in an inherited language, inherited institutions and the situations that present themselves over which individuals have limited control – a cultural formation approach. It is not necessary to decide for or against either of these

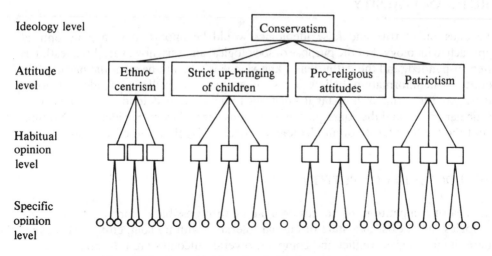

Figure 14.1 Eysenck's hierarchy of attitudes and opinions.

positions if they are both seen as partial explanations: both can be seen as having some credibility, as well as there being an interaction between the two sets of influences.

For the purpose of some sociological analysis it is useful to operate on the distinction that individuals have beliefs and opinions, whereas organized groups of people have ideologies. These ideologies are not just the sum total of the relevant opinions and beliefs of those concerned, unless they shared identical opinions, and we assumed you can add up opinions like coins:

> But if you 'add' one opinion to another, you get not only two opinions, but an argument, a debate, a belief and one of its presuppositions, a qualified agreement, an exemplification of a general idea in a particular situation, and so on. Since relations between ideas can assume different forms, and since ideas must be understood in terms of their relations to other ideas, we must be prepared to find an ideology containing more than all the relevant opinions and beliefs of those who adhere to it.
>
> Cosin, 1972

AVAILABILITY AND NON-AVAILABILITY

Systems of belief may have several states of existence. They may exist in theory only, since they have not yet been adopted or recognized, except perhaps in science fiction writing or futuristic novels. Ideologies may exist but be non-available because the sponsoring group lacks the means of transmitting the beliefs widely or chooses to remain small and exclusive. It has been argued by Allen (1975) that the term 'ideology' is best reserved for those systems of belief that are available, in that the sponsoring group has a means of transmitting the ideas widely and takes the necessary action to achieve this. For the purpose of the analysis to follow, 'ideology' will be taken to be any system of beliefs, whether available or not, whether theoretical or in practice, to allow the discussion to be as wide-ranging as possible.

TRUTH AND FALSITY

The question of true and false ideologies would be important in a philosophical approach to ideology. For the purpose of sociological analysis, however, this question is often suspended, and the definition of knowledge is taken to be what the participants define as true information, beliefs, ideas and attitudes. This allows any ideology to be investigated in terms of how far it functions to advance or defend the interests of a particular group, and the consequences of actions derived from that ideology. Nothing about the truth or falsity of an ideology is indicated by this kind of analysis.

IDEOLOGIES IN COMPETITION

The idea of competition introduces an analogy with possible distorting effects; e.g., ideologies can coexist in a state of mutual tolerance with no competition. However, where the ideologies conflict and compete, several outcomes are possible.

Domination

One ideology may achieve a position of dominance over the others. One way that this may be done is through cultural domination. Gramsci calls this cultural hegemony, where a dominant culture represents itself as the natural, obvious or mainstream culture and attempts to contain all others within it. Such a dominant culture becomes the basis of a dominant ideology.

Incorporation

One ideology may absorb, take over or combine with another in a variety of ways and, if this is successful, it is referred to as incorporation. One example is the proposition of the incorporation of radical educational ideas about equality in educational provision into the traditional educational ideology, by the offer of equality of opportunity in the form of an apparent equal start in the race to become unequal. This preserves the traditional idea of an élite but appears to shift the means of recruitment from aristocratic inheritance and patronage to merit. The incorporation is completed by ensuring that the competition is of such a nature that those who enter the élite under the merit system are similar to those who would have entered under the inheritance/patronage system.

Legitimation

To become dominant, one ideology has to achieve acceptance of its beliefs. One form of this is direct repression through armies, police, secret police and prisons. Esland (1977) makes the point that:

Of course, in many societies where the dominant group is insecure legitimation occurs through the methods of overt repression. Armies, secret police, machineries of summary imprisonment, torture and execution have been, and continue to be, used by rulers and their socially-powerful supporters to enforce their view of social order. Whether we talk about the Inquisition during the sixteenth century, or Stalinist Russia in the 1930s, or the student uprisings of 1968, we have to take account of the 'legalized' use of force which is always available to the controlling groups in a society.

Esland comments that, in contemporary Britain, it is important to remember that, just by being there, they are secondary reinforcement if the first line of legitimation gives way. There are also numerous techniques of counter-intelligence and monitoring dissent, so that an attack on the social order is likely to be anticipated.

A softer form of legitimation is in the use of major institutions such as education, mass media, religion, law and the economy to put over a 'consensus', 'common-sense' or 'sensible person's' point of view as against the 'lunatic fringe' view, which turns out to be almost any view inconvenient to the group with the dominant ideology. Control of the mass media and education may be one way of preventing an alternative ideology from becoming available; e.g. the British television companies and the schools combine to give special privileges to one form of the Christian viewpoint and to deny similar access by either other religions or non-religious life stances.

CONCLUSION: THE MULTIPLICITY OF IDEOLOGIES

The concept of ideology is ambiguous not only because of competing definitions but also because it is used to describe sets of ideas operating at various levels in society and in various contexts. A ruling class, or a middle class or a working class all may be said to have an ideology. Banks, retail organizations and trade unions may also be said to have them. So may the professions, education, the mass media and the nation. Pressure groups of various kinds, whether for car owners, pedestrians, for motorways or against motorways, may be said to have ideologies. It helps to try to specify the level or context of the ideologies in question, and when this shifts. This is not always easy. In the analysis that follows, ideologies of education operate at various levels, having several layers of meaning – nationally in the Education Acts, regionally in local education authority policies, locally in a particular school and internally between rival groups in a school. Furthermore, ideologies of education are linked with other ideologies – ideologies of politics, of the economy, of social classes. Failure to grapple with this has created considerable confusion in educational writing in the past.

SUMMARY

1. Ideology is an ambiguous concept: its meanings range from fanatical visions of society, to the false visions of others, to sets of belief that can be compared and analysed.
2. The approach employed in this book is the last – ideology as competing belief systems.

3. For the purposes of sociological analysis, it is useful to see individuals as having beliefs and opinions, and organized groups of people as having ideologies.
4. Ideologies may be theoretical, in not yet having been adopted, or non-available, because a sponsoring group lacks the means or the desire to transmit its belief system widely, or available, if it has both the means and policy of promulgation.
5. Issues of truth or falsity are seen here as philosophical rather than sociological concerns.
6. Where ideologies exist in a state of competition there are several possible outcomes, including domination by one, incorporation and legitimation.
7. Another aspect of ambiguity is that ideology can be used to describe sets of beliefs operating at various levels and in various contexts with several layers of meaning.

Further Reading

Althusser, L. (1971) 'Ideology and the State.' In Althusser, L. *Lenin and Philosophy and Other Essays*. London: New Left Books. A Marxist approach is given in this book, where a distinction is drawn between the role of ideology in repressive state apparatuses like the police and its role in ideological state apparatuses like the education system.
Cosin, B. (1972) *Ideology*. Milton Keynes: Open University Press. A discussion of the concept of ideology.
Williams, R. (1961) *The Long Revolution*. Harmondsworth: Penguin. A general analysis of ideologies and society.

Discussion and Activities

1. An informal survey of friends, relations and colleagues might establish which of the definitions of ideology given in this chapter is the one most commonly in use.
2. What distortions might arise by adopting a psychological reductionist version of ideology that sees it as being constructed out of the opinions and beliefs of individuals?

Signposts

To what extent is the compulsory act of worship in schools an attempt at 'cultural domination' and 'legitimation of a dominant group ideology'? A useful starter is Hull, J. (1975) *School Worship: An Obituary*. London: SCM.

Chapter 15

Ideologies of Education

'Do not do unto others as you would they should do unto you; their tastes may not be the same.'

George Bernard Shaw

INTRODUCTION

An ideology of education may be defined as the set of ideas and beliefs held by a group of people about the formal arrangements for education, specifically schooling, and often, by extension or by implication, also about informal aspects of education, e.g. learning at home.

DICHOTOMOUS APPROACHES

There have been a number of attempts to describe alternative ideologies of education. Some of these have been theoretical, while others have been based on empirical studies. A common approach has been to contrast two polarized types, a dichotomous approach:

teacher-centred	*v.*	child-centred (Plowden Report, 1967)
open teaching	*v.*	closed teaching (Kohl, 1970)
meaning receiving	*v.*	meaning making (Postman and Weingartner, 1971)
authoritarian	*v.*	democratic (Lippitt and White, 1958)
traditional	*v.*	progressive (Bennett, 1976)
transmission	*v.*	interpretation (Barnes and Shemilt, 1974)
open schools	*v.*	closed schools (Bernstein, 1967)
dependent study	*v.*	autonomous study (Husen, 1974)

As an example of this approach, look back at the conclusions of the empirically based study of Barnes and Shemilt (1974), referred to in Chapter 12. Their study concerned the way in which teachers use language in classrooms. Two contrasting patterns of language usage emerge; these were described as transmission and intepretation. These patterns were associated with two different ideologies of education, each having four elements (see Table 12.2).

The limitations of approaches based on dichotomies emerge if an attempt is made to link the ones listed above. There is some similarity in the ideas of teacher-centred, closed, meaning receiving, authoritarian, traditional, transmission, closed schools and dependent study, although there is considerable variety of emphasis. But the other partners of the pairs have little in common other than being contrasted with a similar alternative. Child-centred, open teaching, meaning making, democratic, progressive, interpretation, open schools and autonomous study vary considerably, and can be seen as alternatives to each other.

This becomes clear if we consider just one aspect, the activity of the learner. In the child-centred approach, the learners choose from a range of activities provided by the teacher, whereas in open teaching the learners make decisions about how learning is best undertaken. In meaning making, the activity of learners is similar. In the misleadingly named democratic system, learners respond to a pleasant authoritarian teacher who allows learners some privileges in a contrived, pleasant working atmosphere. Progressive teaching is seen as something similar. In interpretation teaching a negotiation takes place and a dialogue emerges at the initiative of the teacher. The learners in open schools are also involved in negotiations and dialogues. In autonomous study, the learners gradually take on all the decision-making about what to learn and how to learn until they are able to control all aspects of learning themselves.

The activity of teachers also varies. In some cases they make all the decisions but implement them in a pleasant, 'nice strict' fashion; in others they negotiate; in others they facilitate the decisions of the learners; in others they initiate a dialogue; in others they gradually hand over decision-making to the learners in a systematic way.

The conclusions are that these pairs of ideologies are operating at different conceptual levels and that there is a selection of contrasting pairs from a wider range of alternatives. The latter point is clear from the analysis above. The former point is clear if we note that some of these pairs are describing classroom teaching ideologies, others ideologies of the whole education system and others ideologies of whole schools.

ATTEMPTS TO IDENTIFY MORE THAN TWO IDEOLOGIES OF EDUCATION

A number of attempts go beyond dichotomies. One well-known attempt is that of Raynor (1972). He outlines four ideologies of education: aristocratic, bourgeois, democratic and proletarian. He defines as aristocratic the view which sees education as a means of preparing a young person for his social role as a gentleman and as a leader, so education is seen as a means of confirming a person in the social status into which he was born.

The bourgeois is that view of education which sees the examination system as the principal means of selecting the individuals who are to fill the élite roles in society, so success in education is seen as the means by which a person achieves the right to hold prestige positions in work and public life.

The democratic view of education is concerned with the problem of distributing education to everyone as a fundamental right, regardless of his social background and without concern for the social position he will eventually fill. The child's full development is the centre of the educational process.

Finally, proletarian is that view of education (initially held by the aristocratic sections in society, but later having a wider acceptance) which sees its purpose as fitting the mass of young people for the kind of work and life-style of the subordinate groups in society. It holds that the education offered should be utilitarian, practical and relevant. Here, too, education is seen as a means of confirming a person in his social status.

Another attempt is that of Cosin (1972). He distinguishes between élitist/ conservative, rationalizing/technocratic, romantic/individualist, and egalitarian/ democratic, and sums up the key differences between them as follows. Elitism is concerned with the maintenance of the established standards of cultural excellence through traditional methods of selection. Technocratic/rationalizing has as its central concern the vocational relevance of education. Romanticism is concerned with the development of all an individual's innate abilities. Egalitarianism concentrates on the principle that all have an equal right to be educated.

Davis (1969) also distinguishes between four ideologies of education: conservative, revisionist, romantic and democratic. They are defined as follows:

> Educational ideologies fall into four categories: conservative, revisionist, romantic and democratic. The first, obviously, is concerned to maintain something like the status quo though conservative positions range from crude dogmatism (which characterizes many of the essays in the Black Paper) to carefully formulated versions of élite culture (T.S. Eliot, F.R. Leavis and G.H. Bantock). The revisionist arguments are couched in economic language or in a psuedo-sociological concern with the 'wastage' created by the educational system. Its emphasis is on improving the system's efficiency in terms of the job requirements of the market. Not surprisingly, successive governments – Labour and Tory – have found this the most attractive stance to adopt, and most of the official reports have incorporated its logic. The romantic attitude (which might also be called the psychological) owes much to a concern with individual development and derives from the work of Froebel, Montessori, Freud, Pestalozzi and Piaget. It was central to the establishment of the private 'progressive' schools and has had considerable influence on some forms of curriculum revision and on the primary schools. Its official monument is the Plowden Report. Finally, the democratic socialist tradition, stemming from socialist and liberal thinkers of the nineteenth century, seeks equal opportunity for all (recognizing the difficulties presented by class and patterns of socialization), and the progressive elimination of the élitist values inherent in established education. In its most recent articulate form (Raymond Williams' *The Long Revolution*), the democratic socialist approach called for a 'public education designed to express the values of an educated democracy and a common culture'.
> This first appeared in *New Society*, London, the weekly review of the social sciences.

Bennett and Jordan (1975) attempted to go beyond the traditional/progressive dichotomy in an empirical study based on primary-school teacher self-reported teaching strategies. They established 12 types of teaching style among these teachers, based on six areas – classroom management and organization, teacher control and sanctions, curriculum content and planning, instructional strategies, and motivational techniques and assessment procedure. Most teachers could not be firmly identified as traditional or progressive (taken as equivalent to informal/discovery based teaching style) but had a mixed strategy. The 12 types identified were as follows.

> *Type 1*. These teachers favour integration of subject matter and, unlike most other groups, allow pupil choice of work whether undertaken individually or in groups. Most teachers in

this cluster allow pupil choice of seating; less than half curb movement and talk. Assessment in all its forms, tests, grading, and homework appears to be discouraged while intrinsic motivation is favoured.

Type 2. These teachers also prefer integration of subject matter. Teacher control appears to be low, but there is less pupil choice of work. However, most of these teachers allow pupils choice of seating, and only one-third curb movement and talk. Few test or grade work.

Type 3. This group favours class teaching and group work. Integration of subject matter is preferred and pupils are taken out of school. These teachers appear to be strict; most of them curb movement and talk and smack children who step out of line. The amount of testing is average, but grading and homework are below average.

Type 4. These teachers prefer separate subject teaching, but a high proportion allow pupil choice of work both in groups and individual work. None seats pupils by ability. They test and grade more than average.

Type 5. A mixture of separate subject and integrated subject teaching is characteristic of this group. The main teaching mode is pupils working in groups of their own choice on tasks set by the teacher. Teacher talk is lower than average. Control is high with regard to movement, but not to talk. Most give tests every week and many give homework regularly. Stars are rarely used as rewards. Pupils are taken out of school regularly.

Type 6. These teachers prefer to teach subjects separately, with emphasis on groups working on teacher-specified tasks. The amount of individual work is small. These teachers appear to be fairly low on control, and are below average on assessment and the use of extrinsic motivation.

Type 7. This group teaches separate subjects, using class teaching together with individual work. Teacher control appears to be tight; few allow movement or choice of seating, and offenders are smacked. Assessment is, however, not used much.

Type 8. This group of teachers has very similar characteristics to those in type 3, but they prefer to organize the work on an individual rather than on a group basis. Freedom of movement is restricted and most of the teachers expect pupils to be quiet.

Type 9. These teachers favour separate subject teaching, with pupils mainly working on tasks set by the teacher. Teacher control appears to be high; most curb movement and talk, and seat by ability. Pupil choice is minimal. Regular spelling tests are given, but few mark work or use stars.

Type 10. The teaching mode favoured by this group is teacher talk to whole class within separate subjects. Pupils work in groups, determined by the teacher on tasks set by her. Most teachers in this cluster curb movement and talk, and over two-thirds of them smack for disruptive behaviour. There is regular testing and most of them give stars for good work.

Type 11. All members of this group stress separate subject teaching by way of class teaching and individual work. Pupil choice of work is minimal, although most teachers allow choice of seating. Movement and talk are curbed, with smacking used as punishment.

Type 12. This is an extreme group in a number of respects. None favours an integrated approach. Subjects are taught separately by class teaching and individual work. None of the teachers allows pupils choice of seating and every teacher curbs movement and talk. These teachers are above average on the use of all assessment procedures and extrinsic motivation predominates.

The types have been placed, for the sake of clarity, in increasing order of 'formality'. This procedure may suggest that the cluster can be represented by points along a continuum of 'progressive-traditional', but this would be an over-simplification. The extreme types could be adequately described in these terms, but the remaining types all contain elements of both 'progressive' and 'traditional' practices.

These approaches have several features in common. They all attempt to go beyond dichotomous models to more complex versions, but the problems associated with the former remain:

1. They appear to be selecting from a wider range of alternatives, since the attempts do not match up well.
2. They are operating at different conceptual levels: some at the level of classrooms, some at the level of comparing educational systems across states and nations.

A Network of Ideologies

It is tempting to try to solve the second problem, i.e. operation at different conceptual levels, by categorizing into levels of operation. This would allow a comparison of ideologies of whole education systems, competing ideologies within a national system, ideologies within schools, and ideologies of classroom practice. However, level is an analogy with the built-in assumption of a hierarchy of power or influence of significance, and it therefore prejudges the relationships between these levels. One attempt to avoid this has been the distinction between ideologies of legitimation and ideologies of implementation. The first addresses the question of why, the second the problem of how. Legitimation refers to the goals, values and ends an education system should foster, whereas implementation refers to organizational alternatives, methods of attempting to achieve the legitimated goals and, in general, the means. A limitation of this approach is that most ideologies of education contain ideas about both ends and means.

A further possibility is to regard the ideologies as networked. The ideologies of education systems and of classrooms have some links, though they are not seen as tightly and completely linked. The ideologies of education in the classroom may have some links with other parts of the network, but also have logics of their own at the same time, according some autonomy of action. An example from RE teaching shows the possibilities of this pattern. RE teaching is compulsory by law, so secondary schools have appointed staff for the subject and allocated time on the timetable for an agreed syllabus to be taught. Many teachers, however, find this unteachable, either for their own personal reasons or because of the reaction of pupils, or both, and so they spend the time teaching and learning about issues like morals and decision-making in personal relationships, often without a specifically religious interpretation. The national ideology here has consequences for the school ideology but does not determine it.

Thus the notion of a network of ideologies allows contradictions to emerge which might be hidden in a view of levels, or a view of legitimation distinct from implementation.

ANALYTICAL MODELS BASED ON CRITERIA

An alternative approach to describing ideologies of education is to establish criteria of the major features of such ideologies and then to plot all the combinations that are possible. Some will exist in practice and others may not.

One attempt to identify national ideologies of education in this way is that of Smith (1973), and another is that of Hopper (1971). Smith's attempt is as follows:

Some Major Elements in a Provisional Model of Education Systems

I   Assumptions

(i)   An education system in an industrial society participates centrally in a complex series of distribution processes which include: the distribution of each generation among positions within the social structure, in particular to positions within the occupation structure; and the distribution among future role occupants within the occupational and other structures of 'knowledge', skills and perceptions.

(ii) Processes of selection (the distribution of students among educational routes leading to 'qualifications') and transmission (the distribution to students, within educational routes, of educational 'knowledge', training in technical and social skills, and ways of perceiving and thinking about the world) occur within an education system and represent its mode of participating in the wider societal processes of distribution.

(iii) The way in which the education system participates in these wider societal distribution processes varies according to: the character of the 'external linkages' of the education system with hierarchically ordered social strata and the occupational structure; the character of the structure of power relations through which constraints are imposed upon processes of educational selection and the transmission of educational knowledge; the character of the ideological forms which express valued objectives and procedures with respect to the education system.

II   Structural aspects

The above assumptions direct attention to four structural aspects of an education system:

(i)   The structural relationship between the education system and social stratification, that is the relationship between distribution processes occurring within the education system and distribution processes occurring between the education system, social strata and the occupational structure.

(ii) The structure of administrative control, that is the power relationships among agencies exercising continuing and direct control over the organization of selection and transmission.

(iii) Ideologies of implementation, which specify the appropriate criteria of student selection, character of educational knowledge and mode of transmission, and ideologies of legitimization, which justify the possession of power by controlling agencies and the objectives that should be furthered by the use of this power.

(iv) The organization of selection and transmission, that is, the administrative practices actually put into effect with respect to student selection, the character of educational knowledge and the mode of transmission.

This model can be used to compare features of different education systems in different countries and rival ideologies at the national level within one nation.

A model that concentrates on the ideologies within and among schools is that of Hammersley (1977). He develops five criteria – teacher's role, pupil action, view of knowledge, view of learning and teaching techniques – and breaks each of these down into subdivisions:

1. Definition of the teacher's role:
   (a) authoritative role <–> no distinct role
   (b) curriculum <–> method
   (c) narrow <–> wide
   (d) high degree of teacher control <–> low control
   (e) universalistic <–> particularistic
   (f) product <–> process
2. Conceptualization of pupil action:
   (a) licensed child <–> apprentice adult <–> adult
   (b) individualistic <–> deterministic vocabulary of motives
   (c) pessimistic <–> optimistic theory of human nature
3. Conceptualization of knowledge:
   (a) distinct curriculum <–> no distinct curriculum
   (b) knowledge objective and universally valid <–> knowledge personal and/or
       tied
   (c) hierarchical structure <–> no hierarchy
   (d) discipline-bound <–> general
4. Conceptualization of learning:
   (a) collective <–> individual
   (b) reproduction <–> production
   (c) extrinsic <–> intrinsic motivation
   (d) biological <–> cultural learning path
   (e) diagnosis <–> pupil intuition
   (f) learning by hearing about <–> learning by doing
5. Preferred or predominant techniques:
   (a) formal <–> informal organization
   (b) supervision and intervention <–> participation and non-intervention
   (c) imperative mode plus positional appeals <–> personal appeals
   (d) class tests <–> assessment compared to past performance <–> no formal
       assessment
   (e) grouping <–> no grouping
   (f) grouping by age and ability <–> random, friendship or pupil-choice grouping

An attempt which includes features from the approaches of both Smith and Hammersley, to give a model that might serve to analyse particular classrooms, schools or systems, is that of Meighan (1978a), mentioned briefly in Chapter 2. Here an ideology of education is taken to have various component 'theories'. 'Theory' here is used in its colloquial sense of a view about something rather than in its scientific sense. These components are as follows (the order is not significant):

1. A theory of knowledge, its content and structure.
2. A theory of learning and the learner's role.
3. A theory of teaching and the teacher's role.
4. A theory of resources appropriate for learning.
5. A theory of organization of learning situations.
6. A theory of assessment that learning has taken place.
7. A theory of aims, objectives and outcomes.

A later research study on children educated at home suggested an additional feature – a theory of the location of learning. There may be other candidates for inclusion in this list, e.g. a theory of language and its usage, and the components given above should not be regarded as exhausting the possibilities.

Each of these component theories can be analysed in detail by being broken down into subdivisions. The following discussion gives some examples of such subdivisions.

Theory of Knowledge: Its Content and Structure

Knowledge may be interpreted as predominantly past-orientated, present-orientated or future-orientated. Past-orientated approaches will rely heavily on existing subject divisions, on the grounds that the knowledge gathered in the past is comprehensive and reliable. Present-orientated knowledge approaches will stress integration, on the grounds that current problems like terrorism, pollution, computer technology and mass media are both cross-disciplinary and in need of new knowledge to cope with them. Future-orientated knowledge approaches will stress the rate of change and the rate of production of new knowledge and the consequent need for learners to acquire skills of learning, relearning and developing and adjusting to this 'knowledge explosion'. It follows that a past-orientated view would favour Latin, and a future-orientated view Esperanto as an attempted international language.

School knowledge may be interpreted as distinct from pupils' everyday knowledge. The teaching task, consequently, will vary, from replacing the false or inadequate knowledge, to establishing a dialogue, to grounding learning in the existing knowledge of the learners.

School knowledge may be seen as hierarchically structured, in terms of perceived difficulty and status of subjects, or of equal availability and similar status, or may not be seen as subjects at all. In the first case high-status subjects, e.g. mathematics, may be contrasted with low-status ones, e.g. domestic science, so GCE 'A' level in the latter will be interpreted as equivalent to only an 'O' level for the purposes of university entrance. This also illustrates a contrast between the view that knowledge is sex-typed, with some more appropriate to females and others to males, and the view that all knowledge is equally suitable for both sexes.

The view of knowledge which holds that only a limited number of subjects or studies are appropriate for schools may be contrasted with the view that a wide range should be included, with few exceptions, and with the view that there should be no exceptions. In the case of foreign languages, the first view might imply that one stipulated foreign language should be offered, the second view that a range of western European languages should be available, and the third that any language, including attempts at international languages like Esperanto, should be available. (Currently, few schools teach Esperanto, and they cannot get it established as an examination subject. In 1984, however, London University began its first course in the language as part of a degree course in linguistics.)

A Theory of Learning and the Learner's Role

One view of learning is that it is predominantly a collective activity best organized in groups, another that it is predominantly an individual activity. The contrast between a conventional university, with students attending lectures and seminars, and the Open University, with students at home studying from units and broadcasts, shows how the difference in emphasis leads to different organizational solutions.

A view of learning as competitive against others may be contrasted with a view that it is competitive against criteria of achievement. A further view is that it is a co-operative venture.

In one view learners learn to avoid disagreeable consequences like low marks, censure, non-promotion and punishment; in another view they learn to increase desired personal competence; and in another, intellectual curiosity is a feature of human consciousness unless it is discouraged.

In one view learning is related to ability manifested in the successful performance of the increasingly complex tasks provided in schools. In an alternative view, learning is related to the skill with which the learning situation has been devised: you do not kick the piano for playing the wrong notes, the argument runs.

Learning is best undertaken by listening; alternatively by seeing; alternatively by doing.

The learners' role is to receive without question decisions made by the teachers, or to engage in consultations and negotiations of the teachers' initiatives, or to make decisions for themselves.

The learners' role is to reproduce what the teacher knows, or to produce a personal synthesis from the resources available, or to produce new insights and knowledge. Learners are trainees, or scholars, or explorers.

A Theory of Teaching and the Teacher's Role

The expertise claimed for the teacher's role can be of various kinds. It can be based on the knowledge to be acquired where teachers are single-subject teachers or multiple-subject class teachers. Alternatively, the claim can be based on methods of achieving learning in learners, an educational technology or learning systems expertise. A third possibility is that of facilitator and consultant, where the teacher responds to the initiatives of the learners for instruction, advice on learning systems, or whatever counselling is appropriate. In this case the teacher is acting almost in loco parentis.

The teaching role is closely linked to the claim for expertise. Teachers may be predominantly instructors, learning-systems designers and administrators, or learning counsellors.

Teaching may stress product or process. If the stress is on product, then the task is to get learners to give correct answers. Where the stress is on process the task is to achieve thinking, e.g. thinking historically, thinking scientifically or thinking critically. The latter is not entirely specifiable or simple to assess, and requires some notion of 'constructive doubt' rather than the comfort of certainty.

Teaching may imply coercion, negotiation or control by democratic principles, with pupils' responses tending to compliance, bargaining and participant decision-making. The various forms of authoritarian teaching, where learners remain dependent on teachers, and non-authoritarian teaching, where learners either have or eventually gain independence, are discussed in detail in the next chapter.

A Theory of Resources Appropriate for Learning

Resources may be first-hand, second-hand, or third-hand experiences. First-hand experiences are research studies, simulations, or making one's own text or reading books. Second-hand experiences are accounts of first-hand experiences given in books, in films or by visiting speakers. Third-hand experiences are contained in items like textbooks, which give summaries of what people other than the writer experienced. Schools differ in the emphasis they place on these kinds of resources.

Resources may be books, multi-media materials or first-hand experiences. In the first case the prime resources for learning will be a school library, a class library and subject book storerooms. In the second, the outcome may often be a multi-media school resources centre. In the third case the whole environment of the learners, both in and out of school, is defined as the prime resource.

Resources may be available to learners with varying degrees of access. Access may be very limited, with resources available only through a teacher, or resources, e.g. domestic-science facilities, may be limited to one sex, or a resources centre may be open to teachers and sixth formers only. Alternatively, access may be licensed to insiders only: community schools operate on a different assumption – that both insiders and outsiders may have access to some resources. Open access to resources is another possibility.

A Theory of Organization of Learning Situations

The general organization of a school may be seen as one individual's responsibility – the head teacher's – or as a senior staff concern, or as a whole staff concern, or as the concern of the whole staff and senior pupils, or as the concern of the whole learning community, including service personnel such as caretakers and cleaners.

Grouping of learners may be organized on the basis of age, sex, achievement, or some combination of these, or none of these.

Timetables may be decided long before the arrival of the learners, thus predicting their activities, or as a result of learners' options, or negotiated with learners as a first activity of a new school year.

Teachers may be organized as subject teachers, as class teachers teaching a range of topics, or as a team of teachers working with a large group.

Other details of school organization may be expressed in various ways.

Resources
There may or may not be a resources centre, with various kinds of access.

Records
There may be open record systems or secret record systems, with reporting systems of various kinds.

Rewards and punishments
These may range from individual incentives to team incentives, from physical punishment to loss of privileges to restitutionary activities, decided in authoritarian or non-authoritarian ways.

School uniforms
These may be present, absent or voluntary, styles imposed or negotiated, decisions imposed or arrived at democratically.

House systems
These, or other sub-groupings of a school, may exist for various purposes, pastoral, sporting, or social.

Extra-curricular activities
These may range from school choirs, orchestras, plays, clubs and societies to none at all, as in many European countries, where schooling is limited to classroom learning.

A Theory of Assessment that Learning Has Taken Place

The views of who is best able to assess learning range from the external examiners of an examination board, to the teachers of the learners, to the learners themselves.

The notions of what should be assessed vary: the courses, for their efficiency in achieving learning; the teachers, for their results; and the pupils, for their achievement in learning.

The purposes of assessment may be diagnostic, to direct further learning, or for selection of some kind.

The method employed may vary from criterion-referencing, performance against known criteria, to norm-referencing, to produce an agreed proportion of successes and failures.

The assessment may focus on the processes of learning, adapting, revising and thinking, or on an end product of written right answers.

Assessment may refer to written performances, non-written performances, institutional adjustment or personal character.

The form of assessment may vary, from references to reports, to profiles, to certificates, to self-report profiles.

A Theory of Aims, Objectives and Outcomes

It is in the theories of outcomes and objectives that ideologies of legitimation link with ideologies of implementation, since the legitimation refers to the goals and ends of education, whereas the other theories of learning, assessment, organization, etc. refer more to the means of implementing such aims. (A list of aims, showing their variety, was given in Chapter 3.)

The society for which education prepares pupils may be envisaged in various ways. It may be seen as a society of rigid inequality where pupils are allocated to the roles of rulers and ruled according to birth or limited patronage and sponsorship. It may be envisaged as a state of fluid inequality, with mobility for some based on merit or some other principle of selection. Some visions stress some version of equality. Others stress a pluralistic society, with conflicts of interests resolved in a social democracy. Another alternative is an individualistic society with a high dispersal of, or access to, political power. The ideologies outlined by Raynor, Cosin and Davies, indicated earlier in this chapter, give names to these visions: aristocratic, élitist, egalitarian, democratic and romantic.

A well known attempt to classify theories of outcomes is that of Williams (1961), which is summarized conveniently by Young (1971) as shown in Table 15.1.

Table 15.1   *Williams' classification of theories of outcomes*

Ideology	Social position	Educational policies
Liberal/conservative	Aristocracy/gentry	Non-vocational – 'the educated man'; an emphasis on character
Bourgeois	Merchant and professional classes	Higher vocational and professional courses; education as access to desired positions
Democratic	Radical reformers	Expansionist – 'education for all'
Populist/proletariat	Working classes/ subordinate groups	Student relevance, choice participation

A Theory of the Location of Learning

Learning may best be undertaken in a special building, e.g. a school, college or university, or in a locality operating from an organizational base, as with 'anywhere', 'everywhere', 'street' schools, e.g. the Philadelphia Parkway Project, or using home as a base, as in the case of the Open University and the Education Otherwise families educating children at home.

CONCLUSION

These are examples of how the theories can be analysed further by proposing subdivisions, and do not exhaust the possibilities. Future work no doubt will extend the list. But enough has been achieved here, it is claimed, to demonstrate that, although the concept of ideologies of education is highly ambiguous, it is capable of being used as an analytical tool.

The attempts confined to dichotomies, it has been suggested, have severe limitations: first because they select two from a range of possible alternatives (frequently a different pairing each time), and second, because these attempts operate at various conceptual levels, ranging from national systems to individual schools, without always specifying the level in question.

Attempts to establish more complex typologies of four or more ideologies of education have pointed the way to a more systematic attempt based on criteria of comparison.

The attempt to establish an analytical model based on criteria has centred on the establishment of various component theories that make up an ideology of education. These theories can be looked at in detail by outlining subdivisions within these theories. A previous attempt along these lines (Hammersley, 1977) suggested that these subdivisons were dichotomous, but the attempt discussed here has demonstrated that frequently three or more alternatives can be discerned.

SUMMARY

1. An ideology of education may be defined as the set of ideas and beliefs held by a group of people about the formal arrangements for education, particularly schooling.
2. A common approach to describing alternative ideologies has been the dichotomous, which contrasts two patterns of assumptions.
3. Dichotomous approaches tend to understate the complexity of the activities of teachers and learners.
4. Attempts to locate more than two ideologies get nearer to the complexities of schooling, but still appear to be selecting from a much wider range of alternatives.
5. Analytical attempts based on criteria allow a wide range of actual and potential patterns to be identified.
6. The version used here proposes that any given ideology of education can be compared with others on the basis of a series of component theories about knowledge, learning, teaching resources, organization, assessment and aims.
7. Although the concept of ideology is ambiguous, it is capable of being used as an analytical tool to compare various patterns of educational beliefs and practices.

Further Reading

Bennett, N. (1976) *Teaching Styles and Pupil Progress*. London: Open Books. A complex attempt to describe ideologies of education.

Freire, P. (1972) *Pedagogy of the Oppressed*. Harmondsworth: Penguin. Uses a dichotomous approach.

Kohl, H. (1970) *The Open Classroom*. London: Methuen. Another interesting book which uses a dichotomous approach.

Postman, N. and Weingartner, C. (1971) *Teaching as a Subversive Activity*. Harmondsworth: Penguin. Also uses a dichotomous approach.

Raynor, J. (1972) *The Curriculum in England*. Milton Keynes: The Open University Press. A more complex attempt.

Taylor, L.C. (1971) *Resources for Learning*. Harmondsworth: Penguin. A particular component of an ideology is the focus of the whole book.

Toogood, P. (1984) *The Head's Tale*, Telford: Dialogue Publications. One head teacher's attempt to establish a variant ideology of education.

Watts, J. (1980) *Towards an Open School*, London: Longman. Another head teacher's experiences and reflections.

Discussion and Activities

1. Take the list of dichotomous approaches given at the start of the chapter and compare as many as you can, using the component theories approach.
2. Using the material in Chapter 12, produce an account of a further component – a theory of language and its usage.
3. Is the components approach, which aims to identify a variety of ideologies of education, itself ideological?

Signposts

Parents

A further component theory of an ideology of education may be that of a theory of parents and the parents' role. The material and reading suggestions of Chapter 5 should provide a starting point.

Chapter 16

Authoritarian and Non-authoritarian Ideologies of Education

'The golden rule is that there are no golden rules.'
George Bernard Shaw

INTRODUCTION

The model proposed in Chapter 15 has component 'theories' which make up an ideology of education. A specific ideology is seen as containing a view, stated or implicit, on most, if not all, of these theories. However, previous attempts to identify ideologies have given priority to one or other of these component theories and usually are given a label that indicates this.

The first example we will look at is that of R. Williams (1961). In devising his fourfold typology of Liberal/Conservative, bourgeois, democratic and populist/proletarian, Williams has implicit theories of knowledge, learning, teaching and the other component theories given earlier, but locates his classification, both by name and content, in the component of aims, objectives and outcomes.

By contrast, the attempt by Kohl (1970) to juxtapose open and closed classrooms gives priority to the components of teaching and the teacher's role and learning and the learner's role. The classification of Bernstein (1967) also uses the terms 'open' and 'closed', but gives stress to the components of organization of learning situations and of aims and objectives.

The classification of Barnes and Shemilt (1974) concentrates on the components of teaching language usage in particular, and the teacher's role, and develops from this an explicit account of the components of knowledge, its content and structure.

It follows that one advantage of the proposed model is that it enables the existing attempts to be located and compared, and goes some way towards reducing the confusion created by these rival attempts. Table 16.1 shows the picture that emerges as a first attempt at such a comparison.

Table 16.1   *Comparison of component theories*

	TK	TL	TT	TR	TA	TO	TAO	TLL
Williams (Liberal/Conservative, bourgeois, democratic, populist/proletarian)							X	
Kohl (open and closed classroom)		X	X					
Bernstein (open and closed schools)						X	X	
Barnes and Shemilt (transmission and interpretation)	X		X					
Postman and Weingartner (meaning-making, meaning-receiving)		X						
Lippitt and White (authoritarian democratic)		X	X				X	
Raynor (aristocratic, bourgeois, democratic, proletarian)							X	

X   = priority or stress given to this component or components
TK   = theory of knowledge, its content and structure
TL   = theory of learning and the learner's role
TT   = theory of teaching and the teacher's role
TR   = theory of resources appropriate for learning
TA   = theory of assessment of learning situation
TO   = theory of organization of learning situation
TAO = theory of aims, objectives and outcomes
TLL = theory of the location of learning

There are attempts that stress a theory of resources. Taylor (1971) juxtaposes learning based on resources with learning based on formal teaching and proposes a changed role for learners in the process. An attempt that gives priority to a theory of assessment is the proposal for an integrated social sciences advanced level GCE which links a school-based assessment system, similar to the Swedish system, to a theory of learning through student decision-making, first-hand experiences, and a network theory of knowledge. Both the Open University and Education Otherwise are examples where priority is given to the home as a learning location.

Another advantage of the approach based on component theories is that it enables ideologies of education that appear to be similar to be shown to vary in key details: they may share several component theories in common but vary crucially in one or two others. Sometimes it is possible to show that ideologies that are said to be contrasting in type are actually very close, because they have more in common in a range of component theories than is recognized. An example of this is the Lippitt and White pair of ideologies of education, authoritarian and democratic. It will be argued that the term democratic is highly inappropriate, because it turns out to be a variant form of authoritarian.

AUTHORITARIAN AND DEMOCRATIC IDEOLOGIES OF EDUCATION

Alternative Authoritarian Forms

If 'authoritarian' is taken to mean a discipline system with a dependence relationship in which one person is dominant and another or others dependent, it is possible to suggest several forms. One is the *autocratic* form. Here order is imposed through fear, which may be either physical or psychological. The images related to this form are those of a dictator, commanding officer or ringmaster. It is this form that is most frequently meant by the term 'authoritarian' and it is the form predominantly investigated in the Lippitt and White (1958) experiments.

Next there is a *parental* form. Here order is obtained through deference. The related images are those of a father, a mother, a priest or a village policeman. The paternal variant may be seen in many secondary schools, while the maternal variant occurs in many primary schools.

Third, there is the *charismatic* form. Here order is obtained through personal magnetism, public performance skills or emotional persuasion. The related images are those of a leader with his disciples, entertainer or pied piper.

Fourth, there is the *organizational* form. Here order is obtained through detailed organization, indicating a clear structure, giving full instructions and deciding ends and means in a systematic way. The related images are those of an architect, production planner or quantity surveyor.

Fifth, there is the *expertise* form. Here order is obtained through the possession of information demonstrated to be useful or believed to be necessary by the non-expert. Related images are a doctor or a scientist.

Sixth, there is the *consultative* form. Here order is obtained through the use of feedback from the learners so that they feel that the teacher has taken account of their ideas and responses. The related images are those of a market researcher or a diagnostician.

In all these cases the dependence relationship tends to persist unless the dominant person decides otherwise, though reactions from the submissive persons can occur. However, the degree of dependence appears to vary with each type. With the autocratic it may be 100 per cent, whereas with the other forms it may often be less than this.

The concept of authoritarian order thus breaks down into the types shown in Figure 16.1. (There are echoes here of the classical analysis by Max Weber of three types of authority – traditional, charismatic and bureaucratic.)

The various forms of authoritarian order shown in Figure 16.1 can be seen in classrooms in a single manifestation, where a teacher relies almost exclusively on one

Figure 16.1 Authoritarian order.

type to establish and maintain order. They are also seen in combination, where teachers use a variety of forms according to the situation, their moods or the stage of their relationship with the class (the 'start autocratic and ease up later to become consultative, parental, or charismatic' principle frequently advocated in the phrase 'start tough and ease up later').

Alternative Democratic Forms

The concept of democratic order also suffers from a similar lack of clarification, and again there is often a failure to distinguish between several types. If 'democratic' is taken to mean that a discipline system has an independence element in the relationship, with the possibility of all the persons in it having some agreed level of participation in decision-making, there are various possible forms.

One is the *agreed rules* form. Here order is obtained by appealing to rules agreed at some previous date. The teacher administers the rules, but these are open to appeals or changes. The related images are those of referee or judge.

Second, there is the *representative* form. Here the class elects spokesmen, either formally or by an identification process, and these spokesmen can influence the decisions made.

Third, there is the *committee* form. Here several representatives are elected or nominated to meet to make decisions. This is often in connection with a particular project, but it has a potential wider application.

Fourth, there is the *forum* type. Here all members of a class are involved in open discussion about decisions.

(In all these cases the amount of real independence in the relationship can be manipulated by the teacher, and sometimes eradicated, so that it becomes pseudo-democratic.)

The concept of democratic order thus breaks down into the forms shown in Figure 16.2.

MISUSE OF THE TERM 'DEMOCRATIC'

A summary of the Lippitt and White analysis of authoritarian and democratic regimes is given in Chapter 6. From this analysis it is clear that Lippitt and White's 'democratic' is a

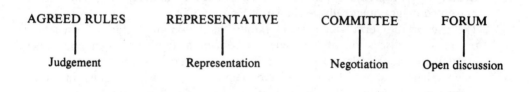

Figure 16.2   Democratic order.

misnomer. The independence relationship basic to the classification 'democratic' is missing, and the characteristics match none of the democratic forms briefly outlined. It is, however, close to the notion of parental authoritarian previously described. The conclusion is that, far from the Lippitt and White regimes being a contrasting pair, they are similar and represent two variants of the authoritarian group of regimes: autocracy and parentalism.

INADEQUACIES IN THE AUTHORITARIAN–DEMOCRATIC CONTINUUM VIEW

The above attempt to develop the concepts of authoritarian and democratic ideologies of education seems inadequate on at least four counts:

1.   The placing of each type on a continuum obscures the possibility that each may have its own continuum that can bridge into democratic forms. Thus the

AUTHORITARIAN ⟵————————————⟶ DEMOCRATIC

Autocratic

├——————⟶   (little potential for bridging
                                    into democratic forms)

Parental

├————————⟶

Charismatic

├————————⟶

Expertise

├——————————⟶

Organizational

├———————————⟶

Consultative

├———————————————⟶ (considerable potential for bridging
                                         into democratic forms)

Figure 16.3   The potential of the various forms of authoritarian regime for bridging into democratic forms.

organizational regime can remain exremely authoritarian, or can operate to transfer learners gradually into more independent systems of learning. This may be presented diagrammatically as shown in Figure 16.3.

2.   The use of the term 'democratic' rather than 'non-authoritarian' effectively prevents the discussion of ideologies of education involving an independence element for individuals rather than groups of learners. Such individually based independence systems of learning have been called by various names, including individualized study and independent learning. The term used here will be autonomous study, the term adopted by the Council of Europe Committee for General and Technical Education in 1975.

3.   The analysis is based predominantly on one component feature of ideologies of education, the theory of teaching and the teacher's role. The other features are not clearly indicated.

4.   The possibility of there being ideologies lying between the authoritarian and democratic regimes which could operate as bridges in either direction, i.e. towards more or less independence for learners, is overlooked. One such possibility is a *consultative* ideology of education, where negotiations take place at the initiative of the teacher at first, but later may become more democratic.

AUTHORITARIAN AND NON-AUTHORITARIAN

One limitation of the term 'democratic' has already been suggested: it obscures the possibility of other alternatives to authoritarian ideologies of education. One candidate for consideration is autonomous study, with its stress on individual learning rather than group learning, and this is the subject of the next chapter.

This suggests that there are at least three groups of ideologies of education: authoritarian, democratic and autonomous study. There can be overlaps, interactions and combinations among these, but they can also be identified as having distinct characteristics. 'Non-authoritarian' allows for alternatives other than democratic to be considered.

A second advantage of these terms is that they have reference to several of the component theories of ideologies of education, whereas some terms apply to only one, as was demonstrated earlier; it is possible to talk of authoritarian teaching, learning, knowledge, aims, objectives and outcomes, organization, resources and assessment. The term 'non-authoritarian' also applies to these various components. This is not, of course, returning to simple dichotomies, since these terms categorize groups of ideologies of education, and not simple alternatives.

BRIDGING

A consideration of autonomous study raises another issue regarding ideologies of education which leads to confusion. Autonomous study can be interpreted as:

1.   a method of teaching and learning within an ideology of education, e.g. transmission; or

2. an ideology of education in its own right; or .
3. an option available to learners operating in a democratic ideology of education.

In the first case we have a teacher-based system which uses, as one of a repertoire of techniques, autonomous study methods, whereas in the second case the notion of autonomous study dominates the theories of aims, learning, resources etc. This dual interpretation raises some practical possibilities of moving gradually from the situation where autonomous study is one item in the repertoire of one ideology of education to the situation where it is dominant, in other words the possibility of bridging from one ideology of education to another, if a teacher so desires. The necessity for developing such bridging techniques is signalled in a discussion by Goodson (1975) of the failure of one attempt, at Countesthorpe College, to move from a 'teachers' curriculum approach to an 'integration and individualization' approach. Here, it would appear, bridging strategies had not been clearly thought out, so the enterprise failed. Where bridging is taking place, a *hybrid* ideology of education may emerge which has some features of say, the authoritarian group and some features of one of the other groups. Bridging and hybrid ideologies of education appear to be significant for the understanding of the processes of curriculum change.

CONCLUSION

This chapter has tried to show how the approach using component theories that make up an ideology of education can be used to clarify some of the confusions that exist in this field:

1. Existing attempts to describe ideologies of education can be compared to show how they tend to give priority to one or other of the component theories. The labels used indicate this: compare 'bourgeois', stressing aims, 'transmission', stressing teaching and knowledge, and 'open', stressing teaching and/or organization.
2. Attempts at typologies claiming to be contrasting can sometimes be shown to be similar, e.g. Lippitt and White's authoritarian and democratic turn out to be autocratic authoritarian and parental authoritarian.
3. Another alternative can be identified, e.g. the autonomous study group of ideologies.
4. The possibility of developing bridging techniques to allow movement from one ideology to another emerges.

SUMMARY

1. Previous attempts to identify ideologies of education have tended to focus explicitly on one of the components and contain implicit theories of the other components.
2. One advantage of the component-theories approach is that previous attempts can be compared to reduce some of the confusion created by their different emphases.
3. Another advantage is that two apparently similar ideologies of education can be

shown to vary in one or two component theories.

4. Authoritarian ideologies of education have a common view of the learner's relationship to the teacher: it is one of dependence.
5. Various forms of dependence give rise to different types of authoritarian approaches, including autocratic, parental, charismatic, organizational, expert and consultative.
6. Democratic ideologies of education have a common view of independence in the teacher–learner relationship.
7. Various forms and degrees of independence give rise to different types of democratic approaches, including agreed rules, representative, committee and forum.
8. The component-theories approach allows confusions, like that of the Lippitt and White misuse of the term 'democratic', to be located.
9. The view that authoritarian–democratic is a simple continuum is open to a series of doubts.
10. The adoption of the term 'non-authoritarian' allows for other types of ideology of education to be discerned, e.g. the individual learning approaches of the autonomous education group.
11. The notion of bridging from one ideology to another emerges as a possible practical consequence of the component-theories approach to ideologies of education.
12. The identification of hybrid forms of ideologies of education may further the understanding of the processes of curriculum change.

Further Reading

Fletcher, C., Caron, M., and Williams, W. (1985) *Schools on Trial*. Milton Keynes: Open University Press. An account of four schools that developed non-authoritarian approaches.
Hammersley, M. (1977) *Teacher Perspectives*. Milton Keynes: Open University Press. Contains an account of four ideologies of education located using a checklist of features of educational practice that can be compared with the component-theories approach.
Husen, T. (1974) *The Learning Society*. London: Methuen. There are few attempts to describe the practice of non-authoritarian ideologies of education, but this and the following reference are two.
Freire, P. (1972) *Pedagogy of the Oppressed*. Harmondsworth: Penguin.
Moon, B. (1983) *Comprehensive Schools: Challenge and Change*. Windsor: NFER-Nelson. Accounts of six schools that developed non-authoritarian ideas.
White, P. (1983) *Beyond Domination*. London: Routledge and Kegan Paul. A philosophical approach to the issues of this chapter.

Discussion and Activities

1. Using the component theories approach, analyse the ideology of education of a school known to you.
2. Analyse the ideology of education of *The Countesthorpe Experience*, by J. Watts (1977) or *Pedagogy of the Oppressed*, by P. Freire (1972).
3. Since the term 'progressive' has been used to describe various forms of authoritarian and

non-authoritarian ideologies of education, is it redundant as a term in educaticnal discussion?
4. Take Table 16.1, which compares various attempts to locate ideologies of education, and develop it, e.g. by filling in the implicit theories of each component of the attempts listed.
5. Is the Open University an example of a hybrid ideology of education?

Signposts

1. Deschooling
The deschooling writers, writing in 1971, concluded that most children left school after ten years of schooling with little to show for it. Using a range of metaphors, e.g. prisons, hospitals, museums, the proposition was that schools made most young people hostile to the idea of education. An analysis of the ideas of these writers using the component theories approach is an interesting research activity. References: Freire, P. (1972) *Pedagogy of the Oppressed*, Harmondsworth: Penguin; Goodman, P. (1971) *Compulsory Miseducation*, Harmondsworth: Penguin; Hold, J. (1969) *How Children Fail*, Harmondsworth: Penguin (the ideas of John Holt about how children learn to fail in schools, based on observations of his own teaching); Illich, I. (1971) *Deschooling Society*, Harmondsworth: Penguin; Kozel, J. (1968) *Death at an Early Age*, Harmondsworth: Penguin; Lister, I. (ed.) (1974) *Deschooling*, Cambridge: Cambridge University Press (an attempt to assemble the ideas about deschooling in one volume); Reimer, E. (1971) *School is Dead*, Harmondsworth: Penguin.

2. Management of schools
The notion of organization and management of schools has developed in recent years, particularly on in-service courses for aspiring head teachers. What ideologies of education underpin such courses? See Handy, C. (1984) *Taken for Granted? Understanding Schools as Organizations*, York: Longman; and Hughes, M.G., Ribbins, P. and Thomas, H. (eds.) (1985) *Managing Education*, London: Holt, Rinehart and Winston.

3. Multicultural education
The term multicultural is highly ambiguous and covers a variety of contradictory ideologies of education. Some sources are Willey, R. (1984) *Race, Equality and Schools*, London: Methuen; Barton, L. and Walker, S. (eds.) (1983) *Race, Class and Education*, Beckenham: Croom Helm; and Cherrington, D. (ed.) (1985) *Ethnic Minorities in Education*, special edition of *Educational Review*.

Chapter 17

A Case Study in an Ideology of Education: Autonomous Study*

ROLAND MEIGHAN AND MICHAEL ROBERTS

'The object of teaching a child is to enable him to get along without a teacher.'
                                                          Elbert Hubbard

INTRODUCTION

It was personal experience of the limitations of the formal class lesson as a device for teaching adolescents of varying attainments that led both writers to experiment with pedagogical alternatives and to consider the notions of individualized learning, learning from resources, and autonomous pupil learning.

In one case this took the form of an indexed work-card system in geography teaching and, later, individual study folders in social studies. The individual study folders were of various kinds – stimulus, linear structured, multiple-staged, networked, learning choices and research folders – allowing pupils to move from highly structured work to more open-ended, autonomous work. (For a fuller account see Meighan, 1975.)

In the other, Michael Roberts devised a complete business studies course, the basis of which was a collection of linear and multi-stage folders with access to further multi-media resources. The course was designed to allow students choice of topic sequence. It contained built-in student self-assessment, which took the form of multiple-choice and sentence-completion tests and comprehension exercises, and more formal means of teacher assessment, such as essays, were also employed.

These initiatives were based on a hypothesis similar to the following:

> Individualized instruction, properly implemented and executed, holds its own in traditional measures of academic achievement and promises more in the development of personal characteristics; such as self-direction, self-respect and responsibility.
>   Talbert and Frase, 1969

The success of these two experiments led the writers to consider further possibilities. The incidental gain of self-direction, self-respect and responsibility might, after all, be a major outcome, and there emerged the possibility of seeing individualized work as more than just an extension of the repertoire of techniques available for the traditional

---

* This chapter first appeared, in a different form, in the *Journal of Curriculum Studies*, **11**, 1, 1979.

task of knowledge transmission. The new hypothesis seemed to be:

> What we have is a teaching-based system which provides some opportunities for independent learning: an alternative would be an independent learning system which provides opportunities for teaching.
>
> Taylor, 1971

The experience of the writers also illuminated a crucial practical problem. Given the status quo of transmission teaching, how could a teacher move to a situation of autonomous study? The individualized approaches held out promise as both the means and the end. They could act as bridging techniques by starting with highly structured, individualized work to lead to more and more pupil-directed opportunities over time, and ultimately to autonomous study. Or, to put it another way, the approaches developed by the writers appeared to have potential for shifting from one educational ideology, transmission, to an alternative, autonomous study.

PROBLEMS OF TERMINOLOGY

Even in the brief discussion so far a number of related terms have been used. They include 'individualized learning', 'learning from resources', 'autonomous pupil learning', 'individualized instruction', 'independent learning' and 'autonomous study'. Other terms used elsewhere include 'personalized instruction', programmed self-instruction', 'programmed learning' and 'self-instruction'.

The term 'autonomous study' is adopted here, since it is the term adopted by the Council of Europe Committee for General and Technical Education in 1975. Until then, the expression 'independent study', a term used in the USA, had been used, but the view was taken that this had connotations of non-direction and unstructured exploration which could be seen as threatening the assumptions of existing school organization. 'Autonomous study' was thought to avoid this problem, since it did not define in advance whether the study was closed or open-ended, structured or unstructured (see Marbeau, 1976).

What the term 'autonomous study' did signify was that pupils were afforded a greater degree of responsibility in their learning. The emergence of this as an essential objective of European education systems is traced by Marbeau (1976). He notes that the Berne conference of European Ministers of Education in 1973 acknowledged the need for a diversity of learning and teaching methods to achieve a more individualized education and promote independent study by pupils. The same conclusion emerges from a study of the objectives implicit and explicit in reports submitted by member states of the Council of Europe in preparation for the Klemskerke symposium in Belgium in 1976.

THE EMERGENCE OF THE AUTONOMOUS STUDY CONCEPT

In the view of Marbeau (1976) there are three main reasons why European school systems are paying attention to the idea of autonomous study. They are:

1. Changes in the social and economic environment of pupils.

2. Changes in information techniques.
3. Changes in theories of learning.

The first reason refers to the rapidity of social and technological change, requiring that members of modern societies face the necessity for constant adaptation. Husen (1974) argues that:

> people will have to learn new job skills many times in a lifetime . . . urban life will make even more strenuous demands on the intelligence and adaptability of city inhabitants: when, in fact, only the man who has never stopped learning will be able to cope.

All this implies emphasis on self-education and self-teaching, and the ability to do this will depend to a large extent on learning approaches gained during school years.

The second refers to changes in information techniques. The information provided by cinema, radio, television, newspapers, magazines and computer storage and retrieval systems has developed into an information source so rivalling the traditional school as to be described as the parallel school and to be seen by some deschoolers as the basis of a preferable educational experience. Marbeau argues that the school now finds itself in a situation where young people need the technical knowledge, critical attitudes and learning techniques to help them sift this welter of information throughout their lives.

The third reason, Marbeau suggests, is the development of recent theories of learning, especially those of Bruner (1966), which lay stress on the idea of pupils making meanings rather than passively receiving them, and of learning methods of learning and thinking rather than how to recall set bodies of information. Piaget (1964) is also concerned with the means by which learners actively construct and arrange their knowledge as their interpretational schemes develop. Particularly significant from the point of view of autonomous study is Bruner's stress on individual differences, and the consequences of this recognition for schooling:

> if a curriculum is to be effective in the classroom it must contain different ways of activating children, different ways of presenting sequences, different opportunities for some children to 'skip' parts while others work their way through different ways of putting things. A curriculum in short, must contain many tracks leading to the same general goal.
>
> Bruner, 1966

A fourth reason that has emerged since 1976 is the growth of youth unemployment throughout Europe, which has been particularly severe in the UK.

AUTONOMOUS STUDY AS AN IDEOLOGY OF EDUCATION

It was noted earlier that autonomous study can be regarded as a method that can serve various educational ideologies. First, it can be seen as serving a transmission ideology, as part of the repertoire of techniques available to a teacher for instructing pupils and helping them to pass their subject-based examinations. Second, it can serve an interpretation ideology by helping pupils in preparing projects studying particular themes and mounting investigations to further the dialogue between teacher and taught about the interpretation and reinterpretation of their world. Third, autonomous study can also serve an open, democratic ideology by being available as a technique when a learner or learning group chooses to call on it. Viewed thus, autonomous study is seen as a means to some other end. It is because of this flexibility as a means that it has potential as a bridging technique for changing from one ideology to another.

However, autonomous study can also be seen as an end in itself, and it therefore becomes, in this case, an alternative educational ideology. This ideology has theories of knowledge, learning, teaching and assessment that can be identified.

Theory of Knowledge: Its Content and Structure

In an autonomous study ideology, knowledge is seen as having a flexible structure, an expanding network, since it is believed to be fluctuating and growing quite rapidly. Traditional subjects are viewed with less reverence than in a transmission ideology, since they are seen as bodies of information with severe limitations for solving those contemporary 'problems' that cut across several disciplines, e.g. the problems of mass communication, pollution, terrorism and alienation. The view of knowledge is future-orientated, predicting that the methods of learning with a lighter loading of information will be more useful to pupils as they grow up than a heavy loading of existing information with a minor loading of methods of learning.

Existing subject bodies of knowledge are dethroned. They become useful, though limited, resources alongside other available knowledge resources, rather than the key resource.

Theory of Learning and the Learner's Role

To learn in a transmission ideology is to be passive and receive a content decided by someone else; it is 'meaning-receiving'. In the interpretation ideology, the learner is more active, in entering a dialogue with the teacher to interpret and reinterpret the world, using resources especially in traditional subjects, but the end is still tending to come to terms with a content selected by someone else. In the autonomous study ideology, the learner 'makes meanings' by mastering methods of learning to explore past, present and future problems of existence. The learners eventually arrive at a point where they are capable of making all the decisions about study, appropriate content, appropriate methods and appropriate assessments. The motivation for learning is intrinsic, rather than the extrinsic assumptions of pupils' undertaking to learn in order to avoid disagreeable consequences if they do not, e.g. low marks, non-promotion, punishment, censure. The learners are encouraged instead to strive to create new knowledge and fresh understandings. Their role is dynamic, not static.

Theory of Teaching and the Teacher's Role

The teacher's task in an autonomous study ideology is arranging learning activities so that pupils gradually learn to make more and more decisions about learning for themselves. In the study-folder system used by one of the writers, the first folders were highly structured, allowing a few decisions by the learner, the later ones allowing for more and more decisions by the learner, to the final step of a 'how to make your own folder' folder, where pupils learned to execute the whole process from topic selection, through information assembly, to assessment of the end-product. The teacher moves from being an organizer of learning experiences to a learning consultant during this process. This can be seen as a much more creative and dynamic role than that of the instructor in the transmission ideology and, arguably, a more professional role if it requires more skills and more complex techniques. But, as both writers found, it requires a change in self-concept, since identity and security no longer rest in being a subject expert. One result is a release from instruction and formal class teaching to give much more individual consultation and to have sustained personal contact with many of the pupils on a one-to-one basis during lesson time. Hunt (1976) summarizes the position as follows:

> When instruction is designed on an individual-needs basis, the teacher emphasis is likely to change from that of the 'fountain of knowledge' to one of an on-going learning counsellor. That is, professional responsibilities are likely to lie in his abilities for:
>
> (i) Identifying relevant student characteristics for a given task.
> (ii) Marshalling the instructional resources to facilitate maximum individual learning.
> (iii) In concert with the individual, selecting goals and determining performance standards.
>
> To date, we are a long way short of the realization of this utopia. It may take time to come; but the knowledge is already here. What is needed is a more careful examination of the individual qualities which affect learning, and the nature of the goals which society and the individual wish to acquire.

Theory of Resources Appropriate for Learning

An ideology of education wedded to subjects will concentrate on those resources that encapsulate the material, i.e. books, and teachers, seen as initiated subject 'experts'. The autonomous study ideology, being future- and present-orientated, implies that any resource that enables learning to learn to take place is potentially acceptable, whether it be books, discussions, television, photoplays, investigation, sociodrama, computers or trails. A particular situation may restrict this choice, for a school with no access to closed-circuit television cannot use this resource for pupils to make programmes. But in theory there is no restriction.

The relationship of learner to resources is direct, whereas access to resources is usually seen as monitored by a teacher in a transmission ideology, where the appropriate resources are selected and defined by someone other than the learner.

A Theory of Assessment

In the autonomous study ideology the teacher's role as assessor is a temporary one, since the learners are seen as engaged in a process of learning to assess their own learning appropriately. Ideas like self-assessment and groups assessing their members' learning, as well as external types of assessment, e.g. objective tests, standardized tests, teachers' judgements, are given credence. This is in contrast to the transmission ideology, where assessment is seen as initiation or verification of a candidate's suitability or performance by an initiated teacher or examiner. Assessment, in this view, is done *by* someone *to* someone else, and self-assessment is not seen as appropriate (see Chapter 2).

A Theory of the Organization of Learning Situations

In the transmission and interpretation ideologies the teachers organize the learning situation, in the former without consultation with pupils, in the latter often with some consultation. In the early stages of an autonomous study ideology, this teacher-based organization is similar, but the eventual outcome is that of adults directing their own learning for a whole lifetime, so the process of organizing the learning context itself is implicit in the theory. Since thousands of Open University students do this already by organizing their learning context (though, not, in this case, the content) at home, this is not a novel idea. The theories of 'education permanente' (where members of a society continue learning throughout their lifetime, in an organized way) are implied here (see Husen, 1974).

The organization of resources for learning by learners, rather than teacher organization of pupils in classes to receive the same instruction, raises other issues. Mixed ability 'teaching' now becomes feasible, since in a classroom the learners increasingly diversify and pursue different contents and different methods, while the teacher has time to conduct individual consultations to help and advise.

A Theory of Aims and Outcomes

Aims of education have been expressed in hundreds of statements. The general aim of an autonomous ideology can be expressed as follows:

> At the end of it all, the educator will insensibly stop being an educator, and find that he is talking to an equal, to an educated man like himself.
>
> Hare, 1964

This is in contrast with the outcomes of the transmission ideology, as shown in the research of Wankowski (1973), which included an analysis of sixth-form tuition experienced by undergraduates at Birmingham University. The author comments:

> it became apparent, during interviews, that many students were not adquately prepared for the more independent study techniques essential to University education.
>
> Wankowski, 1973

He suggests that sixth-form pedagogy, far from producing independent learners, trains students to depend on others, especially teachers. In the teaching of science subjects, Wankowski found predominant the 'one-way' method of communication in which the teacher, having organized his body of scientific knowledge, systematically presents it to his students with the directive 'this is what you need to learn'. In the teaching of humanities there was less direction, communication between teachers and students being more reciprocal, with the attitude 'let's see what we can learn from this' being adopted by the teacher. In the former, student participation in discussion and question-framing was minimal. The extent of teacher direction of student note-taking was considerable; indeed, Wankowski estimates that at least one teacher in five regularly dictated notes to students. Such evidence suggests that traditional sixth-formers are often in the hands of transmission teachers who direct and control the content, style and pace of student learning without regard to the possibilities of their students becoming independent learners.

Wankowski's research, which suggests a lack of emphasis upon the development of independent learning in sixth forms, points to the existence of a serious pedagogical gap in the transition from school to university which may contribute to learning difficulties and even failure for some undergraduates. Clearly a university education demands the ability to learn independently: students must, for example, be able to organize a large amount of material into some sort of priority for exploration and learning, and prepare exercises, papers and essays with little or no direction or supervision.

Wankowski argues that sixth-form pedagogy, by 'spoonfeeding' the student, creates a protective structure around him which may create a false illusion of himself as a competent and autonomous learner, and masks or accommodates anxiety and learning weakness. The illusion is created largely by the sixth-form environment, in which objectives in terms of 'A'-level performance are precise, there is copious and instant reinforcement of the 'body of knowledge' by feedback from a pedagogy in which the teacher systematically plans, directs and tests the students' acquisition of the 'body of knowledge', and in which the teacher is omnipresent for support, guidance and advice. Instead of being able to learn independently, the student learns to depend on his teachers. It is not surprising, therefore, that some students experience problems when exposed to the different learning requirements of university education. Wankowski prescribes a greater emphasis in the sixth form upon learning how to learn as a preparation for university pedagogy:

> the preparation should be active and exercised over a long period of time if it is to be effectively integrated by the pupil.
>
> Wankowski, 1973

It is reasonable to suggest that such preparation, to be effective, should commence long before students reach the sixth form. It might arise naturally from a lower-school curriculum based more on learning from resources than from teachers. To confront students in the sixth form with an entirely different set of pedagogical expectations which entail a large degree of independent learning is perhaps to make unacceptable demands upon them.

THE GENERAL STUDIES PROJECT (GSP) AND AUTONOMOUS STUDY: AN INVESTIGATION

The case for an empirical investigation of independent student learning as an example of autonomous study at sixth-form level in general studies is considered fully by Roberts (1977), the object of inquiry being the utilization of the resource packages produced by the Schools Council General Studies Project, which offered the means by which autonomous study might occur.

'Individualization of study' in the sense of giving students choice of topic for study and method of learning was a fundamental GSP precept. The Trials Officer perceived the resources as:

> making individual work a practical possibility by freeing both teacher and pupil from reliance on textbook and blackboard and class size units of instruction.
>
> Smale, 1974

GSP resource materials were structured in such a way that 'guided individual learning' by students could occur. Student instructions to work through source documents and other resource materials were contained in the study guide booklets which, the project claimed, 'could be used by the teacher as an alternative voice in the classroom' (Smale, 1974). 'Reference units' with additional details of source material were supplied to be used for further depth research by students on their own. It was hoped that teachers would emulate the GSP idea by producing their own materials and study guides, and by modifying those provided. The project suggested that 40 per cent of timetabled time for general studies be used for independent student work on GSP materials.

The expectation by the project that its resources would be used for student-centred activities, within which autonomous study was emphasized, was thus quite explicit in GSP dissemination literature.

METHOD OF INVESTIGATION

A pilot study of local GSP users indicated that the resources were not being employed for autonomous study and the objective of the main study, which was conducted in six institutions in the Birmingham area, was to investigate reasons for non-adoption. The principal research instrument was the semi-structured interview of the head of general studies. This was employed to allow depth probing of teacher perceptions and the pursuit of leads not envisaged in the interview schedule. A questionnaire to all general studies teachers in the six institutions surveyed was used as a supplementary instrument to yield quantifiable confirmation of the trends suggested in the interviews.

THE INTERVIEWS

Obstacles Perceived by Teachers

The interviews revealed the predominant use of GSP materials for 'class teaching', teacher-directed discussion being the norm. Restricted use of the materials for autonomous study is partly explicable by teachers' responses to the question, 'Why not let students work on their own from the study guides, or produce your own guides?'.

Teachers challenged the technical feasibility of GSP materials for autonomous study, claiming that content was 'loaded academically' and therefore was unsuitable for non-selective sixth-formers, and that its style and approach would not maintain

Table 17.1   *Obstacles percieved by teachers to the implementation of autonomous study using GSP resource materials*

Implicit source of obstacle	Nature of obstacle as perceived by teacher	Example of teacher response
Materials	Content of study guides	Concepts, language too difficult
	Structuring of study guides	Instructions lack sufficient detail
School	Limited time for student research	No sixth-form private study periods allowed
	Insufficient time for teacher to organize GSP materials for independent learning	Head of general studies has other duties
	Lack of resources in school	Library facilities inadequate
Students	Students could not work independently	Students have never been trained to work independently
	Students would not work independently	Students are motivated only by an exam in general studies
Teachers	Autonomous study precludes pursuit of other objectives	Discussion with groups ruled out
	Autonomous study incompatible with teacher's style	Teacher likes to take active role
	Autonomous study implies loss of control over student learning	Students would reach too narrow conclusions

sufficient student interest or involvement for independent learning. One teacher, who had never actually used the materials in their existing form for autonomous study, believed them to be inadequately structured for that purpose, since guide instructions lacked detail and material required simplification.

Of various institutional barriers, shortage of time was a frequently perceived obstacle. This may be partly attributable to the low status of general studies in some of the schools. Thus one teacher was reluctant to encourage independent student research in general studies because he feared it would be conducted at the expense of more important 'A'-level work. Where general studies received low priority in timetabling and staffing, teachers felt they lacked incentive, preparation time, and length of experience which they deemed essential for experimentation with autonomous study.

Several teachers believed that only their 'most able' students were capable of conducting their own research or beneficially choosing their own topics for study: the majority required close teacher direction and control. Students' inability to learn independently was attributed variously to literacy problems and previous lack of heuristic training, with assertions like: 'they prefer to be told what to do rather than choose for themselves. It's less demanding for them'. Teachers also doubted their students' motivation to work independently. Intrinsic interest in general studies was often deficient, they claimed, and students would not work independently without instrumental motivation such as an external examination.

An underlying message was transmitted in the interviews that autonomous study was not valued significantly by the teachers. While some gave explicit justifications for this in personal terms (see Table 17.1), interview probes elicited a degree of teacher anxiety about autonomous study, associated with an implied loss of teacher control over the learning situation. This anxiety was expressed in the following way by one teacher:

> Perhaps it stems from a sense of insecurity – you feel you would like to know exactly what the kids are taking in – a feeling that they are becoming conversant with information that you are already aware of. Whereas – perhaps branching out too much one could be in a situation where you are not in control of the learning situation. I want a clear idea of what the actual material is that they are going to be involved with and how they are going to tackle it.

Pressed to reveal what he perceived might happen in the absence of his control of the learning situation, he replied:

> Students can take too finite an approach to answering the problem set – their conclusions are too limited. Whereas – if you are going over a complex topic with them, various sides of the argument can be brought out.

One way of interpreting this comment is that this teacher's anxiety appears to stem both from a fear that his students may come to possess knowledge with which he is unfamiliar and from alarm at the prospect that they might not reach the kind of conclusions he wants them to reach.

From the evidence collected it seems that teachers deny both the suitability of GSP materials for independent learning and the feasibility of autonomous study per se, with the latter receiving the greatest weight of objection. Hoyle and Bell (1972) suggest that when an innovation is rejected teachers may attribute this to external factors when the more fundamental reason lies in the teachers' own attitudes. In the present context it is possible that, where teachers express reservations about autonomous study and ascribe as obstacles the unsuitability of GSP materials and their students' inability or unwillingness to work independently, it is in fact their own anxieties and perceptions which are the obstacles. Thus, as in the example described above, it may be that the teachers' own fear of losing control over their students' learning is the real barrier to their adoption of autonomous study. This view gains some support from the fact that few of the teachers interviewed had actually attempted to put the materials to the latter use, and some of their objections may therefore be considered as being largely hypothetical.

Teacher Understanding of Autonomous Study

Teacher ignorance or misunderstanding of autonomous study was suggested by responses to those interview questions in which teachers evinced failure to appreciate certain implications and possibilities of student learning from resources: indeed, two teachers commented that interview probes were making them aware of it for the first time.

In their views on the use of autonomous study as a technique for mixed-achievement groups, teachers' responses ranged from astonishment at the novelty of the idea to puzzled scepticism – 'it is theory rather than practice'. One teacher's insistence that all her students must cover the same knowledge content appeared to blind her to the possibility of pupils' working on different aspects of a study guide, each suited to the achievement level according to the teacher's judgement.

Three of the teachers interviewed accepted that individual tuition was hypothetically desirable and even necessary for autonomous study, yet rejected it as impractical because of lack of time; and one commented: 'it's disruptive since when you are dealing with one person you cannot deal with the rest of the class'. They had missed the implication that, with students occupied in independent work during lesson time, the teacher would be released to give tuition to individuals.

All department heads interviewed expressed reluctance to persuading colleagues to adopt the GSP approach:

> that doesn't leave any freedom for individual teachers to do their own course, and one approach, however good, is not suitable for everybody all the time.

The implicit inconsistency in such assertions about teacher individuality and choice is significant: only one teacher interviewed permitted his students any choice of topic for study, and none allowed choice of learning technique. Direction was the common, and apparently unquestioned, method. The transmission ideology of education was suggested by these teacher responses.

The interviews raised doubts about the effectiveness with which GSP philosophy had been disseminated, and this may partly account for teachers' misunderstandings. With one exception, all those interviewed claimed to have read the GSP unit 'Teaching and Learning', which expounds GSP philosophy and contains various references to independent learning. Only one teacher had further contact with the project, through attendance at a dissemination day conference in Birmingham. There had been no GSP information or guidance from any LEA representative; indeed, an inspector had visited one teacher seeking information himself.

One explanation of teacher attitudes may be in the fact that only two of the teachers had attempted even limited experimentation with GSP resources for autonomous study. If it is only through experience born from experiment that teachers become aware of the implications and possibilities, then the responses reported here are not altogether surprising.

THE QUESTIONNAIRE

Of 50 general studies teachers responding to the questionnaire, only six reported frequent use of GSP materials. Among different GSP resources available, study guides

Table 17.2   *Teaching approach using GSP materials*

	Teacher responses	
	n	%
(a) Allow students to work on their own, following study guides	5	14
(b) Work through materials with students, largely following the approach suggested in teaching notes and study guides	6	17
(c) Work through materials with students, largely following my own approach	10	29
(d) Use source documents as teaching aids to illustrate points etc.	14	40
	35	100

and source documents were used with twice the frequency of teaching notes or reference units, and three institutions reported little or no use of the latter. No teacher reported using secondary source material from the GSP resource bank.

Table 17.2 suggests that most respondents directed students to a varying extent – responses (b) to (d) – the most frequent use of GSP materials being as 'class teaching aids'. Only one teacher appears to have used the materials significantly for autonomous study or even discerned a connection between them. He alone perceived GSP materials as advantageous, in the following terms: 'it gives opportunity for students to pursue independent studies and to follow up their own interests'. The main value of the GSP perceived by other respondents confirms the pattern of use reported earlier, e.g. 'good starting point for discussion', and 'useful as back-up material after teaching'.

Questionnaire responses also suggest that GSP philosophy had not effectively permeated to the teachers. Eight respondents reported having read 'Teaching and Learning', but only one knew of the GSP 'Trials Report'. Apart from the teacher interviewed who had attended a GSP conference, and one other who had participated in a workshop, no further contact with the GSP was reported. Accordingly, it seems that few teachers knew that the GSP was advocating independent student work.

RESULTS OF THE INVESTIGATION

Limited Use of GSP Resources for Autonomous Study

Despite the provision of resources and explicit GSP recommendations, autonomous study was not significantly employed, there being only limited experimentation with topic choice and structuring, and little or no independent student research from GSP secondary resources. Teachers absorbed the resources into their existing pedagogical styles, which permitted close supervision and direction of student learning. The transmission ideology of education is in evidence here.

Suitability of GSP Resources for Autonomous Study

Doubts were expressed about the suitability of GSP resources for autonomous study, especially by teachers of non-selective groups who believed material content to be beyond the intellectual capabilities of their students. Resources were also criticized for being inadequately structured for independent learning. Since, however, these objections were largely conjectural, little weight can be attributed to them.

Teacher Rejection of the Feasibility of Autonomous Study

Teachers perceived a number of obstacles to autonomous study which emanated from their particular school or college situation, their students' capabilities and motivation, and their own attitudes and beliefs. These rationalizations appear to reflect their own anxieties about their capabilities.

Teacher Misunderstanding of Autonomous Study from Resources

There was some misunderstanding and ignorance of the implications and possibilities of independent learning with respect to the roles of both teacher and student. Imperfect understanding might be attributed to inexperience of the situation and unfamiliarity with the GSP philosophy pertaining to autonomous study.

GSP Dissemination Failure

GSP pedagogical suggestions advocating autonomous study were not effectively transmitted to the study teachers through literature, conferences, workshops, or in any other way. It may be that autonomous study was not employed because the possibility of using the resources in this way had simply not occurred to the teachers. The efficacy of the GSP diffusion programme might offer a fruitful area for further research.

CONCLUSION

In the schools studied the transmission ideology of education, with its particular theories of knowledge, learning, relationships, assessment, etc., appears to be dominant. The GSP, which has been described as the Schools Council project with the most potential for radical alternatives within it (Holly, 1973), was possibly ahead of its time, since neither the possibility of autonomous study as a strategy within transmission ideology nor the possibility of it as an end in itself appears to have been exploited. The criticisms of Wankowski (1973) about the consequences of this for the study techniques of sixth-formers entering university will, it would seem, hold for some time yet.

From the point of view of those who consider the transmission ideology of education to be inadequate as the dominant ideology for a modern industrial society, these results are disturbing. It appears that schools are not coping with the three aspects of such societies discussed earlier, i.e. rapidity of social and technological change, changes in information techniques, and changes in the theories of learning. Marbeau (1976) claims that educational trends in the UK are less favourable than those in other European countries in this respect, but considerably more evidence would be needed to establish this.

The use of autonomous study as a strategy within a transmission ideology has been developed by the Open University, albeit with a different clientele, but the practicalities of such an approach have been coped with in this case. From the research described above, it can be concluded that lack of understanding of, and sympathy for, autonomous study approaches appears to be a significant factor, for even when the General Studies Project provided the practical means, the opportunity was still disregarded.

SUMMARY

1. Individualized learning can be seen as one extension of the repertoire of techniques available for the traditional task of knowledge transmission.
2. Alternatively, it can be seen as autonomous education: an independent learning system aiming at self-direction and self-responsibility that provides opportunities for other forms of learning, e.g. by submitting to teaching when recognized as useful.
3. Individualized approaches can be seen as both a means and an end, by being used as a bridging technique to lead to autonomous learning.
4. Autonomous study emerged as a concern in European school systems because of changes in the social and economic environment of pupils, changes in information techniques, and changes in theory of learning.
5. Autonomous study, as a distinct ideology of education, has specific theories of knowledge, learning, teaching, resources, assessment, organization of learning situations, and aims.
6. The study of one attempt to facilitate the development of autonomous learning, namely the General Studies Project, suggests that the concept of autonomy is foreign to teachers schooled in a transmission ideology of education.
7. If the transmission ideology of education is seen as inadequate for the needs of a modern industrial society, schools are not coping with the aspects of social and economic change, or changes in information techniques, or changes in theories of learning.

Further Reading

Bruner, J. (1965) *The Process of Education*. Harmondsworth: Penguin. Discusses changes in learning theory.
Flude, R. and Parrott, A. (1979) *Education and the Challenge of Change*. Milton Keynes: Open University Press. The idea of recurrent education is taken up in this book.
Husen, T. (1985) *The Learning Society Revisited*. Oxford: Pergamon Press. A useful book to follow up some of the ideas in this chapter.
Jenkins, C. and Sherman, B. (1979) *The Collapse of Work*. Discusses changes in economic circumstances leading to a need for autonomous education.
Marbeau, V. (1976) 'Autonomous Study by Pupils'. In *Education and Culture*, 21. A debate on autonomous study in a European setting.
Skager, R. (1984) *Organising Schools to Encourage Self-Direction in Learners*. Oxford: Pergamon Press. Four case studies of schools are given in this book.

Discussion and Activities

1. What is the relationship between autonomous study and democratic education?
2. Discuss the significance of developments like CEEFAX, and PRESTEL for autonomous education.
3. Interview any Open University students you know, to establish how far autonomy has been developed as a strategy for achieving transmission within the Open University system of learning. Questions may be devised from the case-study material in this chapter.

Signposts

Study Skills
The idea that study skills are automatically absorbed by learners has been questioned recently as evidence emerged that achievement could be related as much to strategies of learners as to anything else. Study skills are of particular importance in autonomous forms of education since the learners learn independently. See Tabberer, R. and Allman, J. (1983) *Introducting Study Skills*, Windsor: NFER–Nelson; Skager, R. (1984) *Organising Schools to Encourage Self-Direction in Learners*, Oxford: Pergamon; Marshall, L.A. and Rowland, F. (1983) *A Guide to Learning Independently*, Milton Keynes: Open University Press; Gibbs, G. (1981) *Teaching Students to Learn*, Milton Keynes: Open University Press; Miller, C.M.L. and Parlett, M. (1983) *Up to the Mark*, Society for Research into Higher Education; Marton, F. et al. (1984) *The Experience of Learning*, Edinburgh: Scottish Academic Press.

Chapter 18

A Case Study: Democratic Education

'Democracy is the worst system devised by the writ of man, except for all the others'
Winston Churchill

INTRODUCTION

Most teacher education in the UK operates under one or other of the authoritarian ideologies of education. This can lead to considerable ironies as Bartholomew (1976) has argued, for teachers in training can be urged to operate non-authoritarian approaches to school situations by lecturers using authoritarian methods for their advocacy. A further irony can occur: lecturers may believe they are advocating radical approaches when they are only contrasting one type of authoritarian approach (e.g. consultative) rather than another (e.g. autocratic). In schools young teachers may then be advised to 'forget all that radical nonsense of the lecturers' when it was not the least bit radical in terms of moving out of the authoritarian grouping of ideologies of education.

PUTTING DEMOCRATIC LEARNING ON THE AGENDA

For several years now, the students training to teach social and political studies in secondary schools at the University of Birmingham have been introduced to the concept of democratic learning and invited to consider this approach to their course in teaching methods if they considered it appropriate.

For most graduates wishing to teach in British schools, a Postgraduate Certificate of Education (PGCE) course lasting one year is the route into a teaching career. The structure of the PGCE course at Birmingham is currently as follows:

1. Autumn Term – a one-week Introductory Course, a three-week School Experience and an eight-week course in Education and Professional Studies, which includes a Methods Course to introduce students to the teaching of their chosen subject, and this takes up about two-fifths of the time allocation.
2. Spring Term – a supervised Teaching Practice in Schools.

3. Summer Term – further course work including further work in Methods.

For the 12 or so students who elect to prepare for the teaching of social and political studies in secondary schools, their course in methods involves an initial debate about the methods of the course itself. They are given an opportunity to decide the learning approach by choosing amongst

Option one: Authoritarian-expert. The course would be designed and directed by the tutors concerned in the traditional mode.

Option two: Authoritarian-consultative. The course would commence with tutor direction and be modified in the light of feedback from the students with a gradual handing over of decision making to the group through consultation.

Option three: Democratic. The course members would organize a learning co-operative that devises and directs its own programme of studies using the tutors as resources and as facilitators. A specimen contract is made available for discussion purposes to demonstrate some of the complications of such an approach as follows:

SPECIMEN CONTRACT FOR A DEMOCRATIC LEARNING CO-OPERATIVE

Possible principles of procedure:

1. That we adopt a self-conscious research approach to our own teaching-learning situation.
2. That we seek to examine and practise in our teaching-learning different strategies and roles, e.g. inquiry-discovery strategy, neutral chairman.
3. That while the focus of much of our work will be individual, we should share our own work with the group, for our mutual benefit.
4. We should therefore accept responsibility for the work *as a group*.
5. Within that group-responsibility we should seek to understand through mutual self-criticism.
6. That we see our primary aim as being competent, not right.
7. That the methods tutors should be seen as a resource for the group, and that any seminars with their 'instructional input' should be chaired by members of the group.
8. That the group should decide which speaker to invite to address it and/or which films/tapes it wants to hire, or how else it will spend its time.
9. That the 'contract' should be reviewed regularly.
10. Each course member (including the tutors) will undertake to write a short evaluation of the group's work to be circulated to each member regularly.
11. That we use the experiences of previous courses as a source of ideas for course content.
12. That a group log-book be kept of work completed, planning decisions and session papers.
13. That each session shall have a chairperson, a secretary and a contributor(s) or leader(s) or organizer(s).

Option four: Autonomous. Individuals could make up their own study programmes using the resources bank and study-folders available and meet in groups only when this serves a function for such programmes.

There was in effect a fifth option of a mixture of some of these options, e.g. a learning co-operative for a section of the course. The individualized option could also serve a purpose for any members of the group if the majority wanted an option that they found unappealing.

Eight courses from 1976 onwards have been given the opportunity to choose their learning approach and various patterns have resulted. In five cases the democratic approach was adopted for the whole course, and, in one case a start was made with a consultative approach and there was a gradual move to a democratic approach. This particular course was evaluated by an independent observer and an account was published (Fielding et al., 1979). In two cases democratic approaches were used for sections of the course, e.g. the summer term when a debate on approaches was initiated later in the course rather than at the outset, acting on a suggestion from a previous course.

RATIONALE

In the current authoritarian approaches adopted in most initial teacher-training there is no attempt to obtain a mandate from the learners since the methods are imposed without debate. The PGCE Methods course just described adopts a consultative version of the authoritarian group of approaches at the outset and thus immediately begins to establish some mandate, some shared responsibility, and some experience of increased motivation. The one tutor had experimented over several years with a variety of methods and the effective approach seemed to be the one that motivated a particular group rather than there being a One Right Way to proceed.

Second, most initial teacher-training courses fail to introduce students to the non-authoritarian alternatives of autonomous and democratic approaches to education either in debate or in the methods practised, and often mislead by implying that the range within the authoritarian grouping of ideologies of education is actually the whole range of possibilities, thereby perpetrating the error indicated previously.

Third, few opportunities are afforded for students to try out non-authoritarian alternatives, and since these are largely absent from most schools in the UK there will be little opportunity later.

Fourth, existing teacher training courses rarely allow students to consider which methods of learning suit them best as individuals or as groups but impose pre-chosen methods as standard for all. Therefore, both in the official curriculum of teacher education and in the hidden curriculum of the methods there is the establishment of a One Right Way – the authoritarian approach. The same trap of imposing an orthodoxy awaits those who try to *impose* a democratic or an autonomous approach rather than allow a consideration of alternatives followed by selection.

Fifth, even if the students choose an authoritarian approach, they will have begun to learn in a limited way the decision-making process central to operating as a teacher in contemporary schools.

RATIONALE FOR A DEMOCRATIC APPROACH

If teaching in secondary schools in the UK is seen primarily as a decision-making activity, one appropriate way of learning to teach may be simulating the process on the training course itself by selecting the aims, content, methods and evaluation methods for their own group. In effect, teachers in training can experiment on themselves, practising many of the skills they will need for the rest of their careers, in contrast to the authoritarian approach of listening to someone else tell them how to make appropriate decisions. Since currently a central activity in secondary schools is formal instruction, students will practise this activity by taking the role of instructor to their fellow students.

In most teacher training there is a marked contrast between the essentially passive role assigned to students at the training institution and the active role on teaching practice. The adoption of a democratic approach weakens this dichotomy since the students become active in both situations.

THE OUTCOMES – FROM THE LEARNERS' VIEWPOINT

To date, no student involved in the seven courses has written an evaluation regretting the debate over the methods they should adopt for the learning, and none of those who opted for a democratic mode has evaluated the experience negatively. No course to date has involved the individualised option, and one student explains the rejection of this approach:

> We decided upon the democratic working co-operative for the following reasons. To begin with we felt that individual work was too isolated. We all felt that the work we had been engaged upon for our first degree courses had been too competitive and too isolated. Therefore, we all agreed that something else had to be attempted for our year within the faculty. At the beginning the course tutor was to be absent from our meetings and, later, allowed into the group as our confidence grew.

Our course resulted in the consultative mode being adopted as a compromise:

> Members of the group decided to choose Option 2 as the most useful method of learning, i.e. a course which begins with tutor direction and then gradually handed over decision making to the group. This was essentially a compromise between individuals who wished for a conventional tutor-directed course and those who wanted to try a Democratic Learning Co-operative.

The written evaluations produced by the various group members contained a number of regular themes. One was that of confidence:

> Democratic responsibility, as opposed to sitting back and always receiving, meant that students had to use the skills they already had, as well as learning new ones. Such a situation was a good one in which to develop confidence in one's own thinking.

Most students had something to say about motivation and always in favourable terms:

> I felt great responsibility for the course and this involvement meant always taking a mentally active part. I felt no resentment against somebody trying to impose work or a situation on me. Thus motivation was high.

Personally for me the course was very stimulating theoretically and practically. I not only learnt a lot but experienced much. I felt motivated to work and get involved because I felt it was our course.

There was intellectual enjoyment. Intellectual exploration became an exciting and satisfying end in its own right, rather than a means to a boring and worthless end (e.g. exams, assessment, achieving the teacher's aims, etc.) Ultimately the only end was personal satisfaction, thus the only pressure was personal. Personal pressure stimulated, and made exciting, my learning. Outside pressure always deadened and styled it.

Several students noted that the discussion techniques of the group members were utilized to the full and developed in the process:

The discussions were conducted on a relaxed and friendly basis and were therefore enjoyed by most students. Most students felt able to contribute their ideas and opinions to some or all of the topics discussed. Personally I have found this aspect of the course very beneficial because it has facilitated the exchange of ideas and information between group members and the exploration of many different aspects of key issues.

One of the conventional objections to democratic learning is that the content may be deficient if the 'experts' let go of the selection of the 'best' content for the task in hand. The students did not support this interpretation:

With all students choosing the range of subjects the content, inevitably (in my mind) was of a greater range and more relevance than if the 'teacher' had done all the choosing. A group of students, especially from different specialist backgrounds, were able to provide more resources than one teacher could.

The standard of papers given was generally very high – probably much higher than if the work had been set by the tutor.

A wide variety of topics relating both to the practical and philosophical aspects of social science teaching have been covered by the course. In addition the content of the course has reflected the interests of the students because of their role in choosing the topics to be discussed.

The democratic nature of the course meant that decision making was practised and that responsibility was shared. The students found this a favourable feature of the course:

Responsibility and authority was dispersed among all members of the group, meaning that the assumption of these was voluntary, rather than them being concentrated into one person's (teacher) job. The taking of responsibility on a voluntary basis did not present any problems as all members of the group were happy to take it.

A system whereby 'rules' were made, but made by ourselves as we went along, meant that the group had security and direction, but also adaptability and flexibility.

One was encouraged to recognise the value of other students as a resource.

The content of the course would be decided by the group. Essentially this meant that the group decided its priorities – what the particular members of the group felt would be most useful to them as future teachers. It allowed members of the group to follow up personal interests and also allowed the group to draw upon the expertise that did exist within the group.

A regular theme that occurred in the student evaluation was that of the bridging of theory and practice. Since a dichotomy is frequently reported between those two, it is interesting to see what the learners in a democratic situation had to say about this matter:

> With regard to the 'methods' course, any gaps between theory and practice were, I think, well bridged. The peculiar nature of the course, with its options (including the more radical democratic learning co-operative), offered and put into practice, meant that we did not just talk about alternative ways of teaching and learning but to a certain, albeit perhaps limited, extent, experienced and experimented with alternative methods.

There was also comment on a related tension between the problems of preparing for survival in schools as they were, whilst considering any vision as to improvements on the status quo or alternatives to the current orthodoxy:

> The course, in practice, therefore, seemed to me to cope nicely with the idealism of educational change and the practicalities and constraints involved in operationalizing such changes. In this way the course provided a realistic 'vision' for changed procedures in teaching while not ignoring the problems of practice, or survival, which face all teachers.

> The experience of a democratic learning co-operative is valuable in itself for intending teachers since it presents them with an alternative method of learning and teaching for future use with their own pupils. Unless this is actually experienced by students, it is unlikely that this important innovation will reach schools in any significant degree.
>   One of the roles of teacher training should be to investigate and experiment with alternative methods of teaching and learning, in a practical way, and to provide working models of the alternate methods.

The co-operative outlook to learning basic to the democratic approach extended in influence beyond the methods course in the university to the teaching-practice situation:

> During the major Teaching Practice and in other instances the co-operative tended to be very supportive and relationships proved to be advantageous, especially during the ten long weeks of teaching practice in the spring term.

The enthusiasm of the students for their democratic learning co-operative did not prevent them from identifying problems, and one student commented on a difficulty, not exclusive to democratic approaches of course, regarding lateness:

> one obvious 'problem' in the group was never really brought out into the open and tackled – the 'problem' being that of lateness. Presumably no one member was willing to take the authoritarian role of instigating a discussion on the subject. Lateness did not impair the content of our sessions – we simply finished later. But such a casual approach can cause personal organization problems for some. The point of lateness is really insignificant, but the principle is important. No one, within the group situation, had a role which legitimated instigation of questioning group behaviour. I don't think this ever caused us any important problems, but with different personalities and circumstances a dilemma could be produced.

Most of the evaluations concluded with an overall verdict on the course:

> The group enjoyed the Methods Course very much. It was extremely beneficial both academically and practically. Highlights and reservations along with possible improvements and alterations were suggested, and a general report on the course was made which had the consent of the whole group.

I hope other groups will learn from our experiences and enjoy their year as much as I believe our course has.

our course certainly could not be taken as a blue print for democratic learning. It was unique, like every learning situation should be, based on the idea that every group of students is different. However, within our own terms and circumstances, I consider the system to have been a success and one which could be adapted, with great benefits to many situations.

The co-operative spent many hours in discussion and formulated opinions and views (often varying) in relation to our timetable of work. All the group members felt without any reservation whatsoever that the co-op was a new working experience which was stimulating, enjoyable and very worth while. We all gained an enormous amount from it, academically and in relation to the new relationships we formed. Everyone in the working co-operative agreed that it was an invaluable, exciting experience and one which we would advise any PGCE students to take part in regardless of discipline.

THE OUTCOMES – FROM THE TUTORS' VIEWPOINT

The tutor involved in the first attempts and the second tutor involved later kept personal notes week by week on the democratic learning co-operatives. Some of the themes that are selected from these notes as significant are as follows.

A potential conflict was seen in the transfer from the democratic course to the authoritarian schools in which teaching practice took place. The tutors were surprised at the pay-off from the course, which seemed to more than offset any expected responses of alienation and rejection. The students approached the Teaching Practice with considerable confidence, and this was remarked upon by the teachers in the school. Since the students were used to making decisions about what to learn and how, assembling appropriate materials and using them, they appeared to transfer these behaviours to school scheme and lesson preparation without any nervousness. They were also used to working co-operatively and so fitted into team situations with teachers with relative ease. Tutor's visits held little fear for them since they were already used to the tutor's presence at their 'performances' at the university. None attempted to implement learning co-operatives, with the exception of one attempt at sixth-form level, which was, reportedly, successful, but all approached pupils in either the 'nice strict' mode or the consultative mode and relationships with classes were remarkably smooth from the outset in most cases.

The tutors had to adjust to a different theory of teaching since they had been educated in authoritarian styles. They had to learn to listen much more, learn to resist the previous habit of dominating the decision-making and discussions, and to cope with anxiety when their expertise was seen to be less significant than they had previously supposed. There was irony in feeling anxious at having helped students to manage competently on their own when this is exactly what they will need to do for the rest of their professional careers. The facilitative role was demanding since making contacts, identifying resources and solving operational problems on the spot or at short notice were different experiences to the authoritarian approach (where, having made the decisions as to content in advance, a tutor was in a position to produce handouts and identify resources some time beforehand). The tutors also had to cope with their ideas and suggestions being either rejected or scrutinized closely and justification requested.

There were tensions with the other courses that the students were required to attend as part of their PGCE year. The confidence of members of the learning co-operative in challenging other tutors in formal lectures was not always welcome, and other students did not always find their enthusiasm and commitment appealing. On one occasion there was a joint session with another methods group to work with a visiting speaker. When she phoned to say she was unable to come due to a school crisis, the learning co-operative immediately set about organizing a substitute programme for the morning for themselves. The other student teachers group declined to take part or devise something similar for themselves and went away to take the morning off with some parting remarks about the others being far too keen.

Any anxieties the tutors had about the quality of student input or the 'covering of key topics' proved groundless. The students exceeded what the tutors had planned and added ideas that had not been included, so that the tutors were learning new material in some of the sessions.

The tutors were curious as to how the students would cope with applications for posts and interviews. Potential teachers of social and political studies sometimes have to cope with hysteria about their subject – not unlike that biology teachers used to face because of their identification with evolution theory in Bible-belt communities – but in addition, this group had a democratic experience that had appeared to increase confidence, commitment and awareness of alternatives in approaches to education. It seemed a potentially explosive combination. However, the pay-off from the course appeared to be positive rather than negative. The approach of the students seemed to appeal to many interviewers. Some head teachers have responded to the effect that 'this is a whole new generation of teachers, articulate, enthusiastic, industrious and challenging'. Perhaps the tutors should have known better because when they had organized teach-ins with in-service courses using the members of the democratic learning co-operative as a resource, the response of the experienced teachers had frequently been similarly enthusiastic.

CONCLUSION

If democratic ideologies of education have in common a view of independence in the teacher–learner relationship, the outcome is a type of power sharing and an exercise in freedom in the sense that Wright Mills (1959) expounded:

> Freedom is, first of all, the chance to formulate the available choices, to argue over them – and then the opportunity to choose. That is why freedom cannot exist without an enlarged role of human reason in human affairs.

The democratic learning co-operatives appear to exemplify this principle and also allow a bridging back into the authoritarian situations of schools with positive effects, so that the student teachers appeared to be well prepared to cope well with schools as they are, but also having experiences and visions of possible alternatives and possible modifications to the status quo should the situation allow or require them.

Further Reading

Bartholomew, J. (1976) 'Schooling Teachers: The Myth of the Liberal College', in Whitty, G. and Young, M.F.D. (1976) *Explorations in the Politics of School Knowledge*, Driffield: Nafferton Books.

Cohen, L. and Manion, L. (1981) *Perspectives on Classrooms and Schools*, London: Holt Rinehart and Winston, ch. 9.

Freire, P. (1972) *Pedagogy of the Oppressed*. Harmondsworth: Penguin.

Kohl, H. (1970) *The Open Classroom*. London: Methuen.

Rogers, C. (1983) *Freedom to Learn for the 80s*. Columbus, Ohio: Merrill.

White, P. (1983) *Beyond Domination*: London: Routledge and Kegan Paul.

Watts, J. (1980) *Towards an Open School*. London: Longman.

Discussion and Activities

1. How do leadership styles vary with each ideology of education. Consider how appropriate this quotation is for democratic education: 'Of a good leader, when his task is finished, his goal achieved, they say, "We did this ourselves" ' Lao-tse c. 600 BC (with apologies for the sexist language!)

2. In Russell's 'control in the spirit of freedom' concept, authoritarian forms of education can be seen as possibly necessary and certainly temporary expedients. When and how can moves to non-authoritarian forms take place?

3. Without assertiveness training, will females be disadvantaged by democratic forms of education?

Signposts

1. Relationship between interactionist sociology and non-authoritarian ideologies of education.
   Central concepts of interactionist sociology include bargaining, negotiation, reality construction, mandates, self-concepts and reconstruction of self, and layers of meaning. This raises the question of whether there is a necessary link between this kind of sociology and non-authoritarian ideas. The references listed under Further Reading above, may provide some starting points. See also Chapter 20.

2. Forms of democratic education.
   The degree and kind of power sharing may mark off different forms of democratic education. In teacher education syndicate approaches may be another form where the learners make a wide range of decisions within the confines of a set syllabus. See Collier, G. (1983) *The Management of Peer Group Learning*. Society for Research into Higher Education.

PART FOUR

Sociological Perspectives and the Study of Education

LEN BARTON AND STEPHEN WALKER

WHAT IS A PERSPECTIVE?

In Chapter 1 the sociologist was likened to a spy, an 'agent' involved in the business of collecting key information on the mechanisms and processes of social life. Much of the material presented so far has been concerned with the reports made by those sociological spies who have investigated the world of education. However, the validity of any spy's report has to be scrutinized. The spy who infiltrates the organization is likely to depict the scene under investigation in a very different way from one who looks through the keyhole, and so the validity of what they report is closely related to the position from which their observations were made. Similarly, no sociologist can approach the study of social life without making some selection from the various perspectives available and, if the information offered by such sociologists is to be of use to people in their daily lives, then it is necessary to know both the perspective from which the sociologist is working and the ways in which this perspective is distinct from other sociological stances.

In this section the intention is to introduce the reader to some of the various perspectives used by sociologists in their endeavour to analyse human conduct. Initially, therefore, it is important to understand what we mean by the term 'perspective'. A perspective is a frame of reference, a series of working rules by which a person is able to make sense of complex and puzzling phenomena. For the sociologist the phenomenon is social life and, in adopting a particular stance towards this, he or she makes use of a set of assumptions upon which analysis can be based and which, typically, includes ideas about the following:

1. A view of humankind, i.e. an idea about what distinguishes human beings from other species.
2. A view of society, i.e. a picture of the structural features which emerge, develop, persist and change as a consequence of people acting in association with others.
3. A view of the interrelation between the individual and society.

4. A view of what should be taken as the crucial properties, the fundamental factors, which condition human conduct and experience in a social order.
5. A view of what it is to 'know' or 'understand' the properties of those aspects of social life under investigation.
6. A view of the relationship between 'academic' explanations of social life and the formulation of policies which can be used to direct the everyday affairs of members of society.

All these issues can, of course, be interpreted in different ways. However, what is important for our purposes is that the specific interpretation adopted by a working sociologist will influence both what is seen to be problematic about a topic for investigation and the kind of explanation which will emerge from such investigations.

PERSPECTIVES IN SOCIOLOGY AND EDUCATIONAL ISSUES

It may appear that the preoccupations listed above are unnecessarily complicated and are divorced from the down-to-earth study of either social life in general or of education in particular. However, consider the controversy concerning so-called 'compensatory education'. How can we best explain and react to the relative failure of large numbers of working-class pupils in our schools today? Some sociologists, accepting prevailing definitions of school success and failure, have attempted to explain the *causes* of this occurrence. In doing this they have explored questions like:

1. The extent to which the problem resides in the individual pupils, in that they lack certain skills, abilities and aptitudes.
2. The extent to which the problem is caused by the inadequacy of some pupils' home background.
3. The extent to which the problem is concerned with the way in which inequalities in society are reproduced in the educational and social experiences of such pupils.
4. The extent to which the problem is the result of attempts to impose a uniform school experience in a multi-cultural society.

More recently, other sociologists, maintaining that the essence of the problem is concerned with how educational success and failure is *defined* and how individual pupils come to be given success and failure identities by teachers and educational administrators, have attempted to explain the processes by which categories of success and failure are constructed, organized and applied in the course of everyday life in schools. In so doing they have focused on questions about:

1. What teachers take to be valid educational performance.
2. How pupils perceive and react to such definitions.
3. What pupils actually fail at.

It seems likely that the extent to which one of the above sets of questions is seen as more appealing than the other as a basis for making an examination of the issue of educational 'failure' is fundamentally concerned with the perspective one has of man, of society and of the interaction between the two. The position one adopts from which to view something will determine what one sees and hence what one takes to be important aspects of the object under scrutiny.

DETERMINISM VERSUS VOLUNTARISM

Underneath a great deal of the conflict of opinion contained in the perspective debate in sociology is a tension which is well illustrated in *The Humanists' Sonnet* quoted in Chapter 1. The poem raises the issue of the extent to which individuals are determined by their class, culture or circumstances, or are free agents, controlling their own destiny.

It is interesting to note that teachers themselves often experience a similar kind of tension when they explore questions about the working of the education system or about their own place within it. When challenged to express their feelings on education-al issues or to explain their reasons for adopting particular classroom practices, many teachers regularly fall back on the argument that, although they would like to follow all kinds of innovative and imaginative educational principles, they cannot do so because they are constrained by the curriculum, their senior colleagues, the pupils' parents, the inspectorate – in short, the system. (See Chapter 4.) In a very real sense this kind of explanation involves a sort of intuitive 'sociological' reasoning. It is an expression of an awareness of a difference between the reality of the constraints of the structured system in which they find themselves, on the one hand, and their ability to decide upon their own course of action and implement the dictates of their own wills and volitions, on the other. However, it would be wrong to imagine that one could study the conduct of teachers in particular or of people in general solely in terms of this very basic dichotomy. We need to question not only what might constrain our lives and actions but also how these 'external' constraints find they way into individuals' lives and activities. Clearly this is a complex question.

Just as complex are the methods used to explore the issues raised, and in this part of the book we hope to introduce some of the ways in which these kinds of questions are both conceptualized and handled by sociologists. Much of the following discussion will be concerned with sociological insights and interests of an abstract nature, and we would suggest that if the reader keeps in mind that much of the debate is tempered by a consideration of the 'free or determined' problem outlined above then the relevance of the discussion might be seen more easily.

Exercise

To clarify the issues introduced so far it might help if the reader spends a short time on the following project. Ideally the project should be undertaken in groups (see item 1 below).

1. Select a topic which you consider an important educational problem. For example,

you might focus upon truancy, discipline in classrooms, the role of the teacher or any area suggested in the material of the previous chapters. (This project might be usefully extended if you work in groups and if two groups decide to work on the same topic. Each group should discuss independently the issues raised in items 2, 3 and 4 below and them compare their accounts in a joint session.)

2.   Devise a study programme which allows you to explore the crucial properties of the problem you have isolated with a view to providing an explanatory account.

3.   Justify the basis upon which you intend to collect evidence in your search for an explanation and explain the criteria you would apply to distinguish between valid and invalid evidence.

4.   Determine what views of man, of society and of the interrelation between man and society are embedded within your chosen study programme.

Further Reading

Barton, L. and Walker, S. (1978) 'Sociology of Education at the Crossroads'. *Educational Review*. **30**, 3. A discussion of the factors which influenced the emergence of various perspectives within the sociology of education.

Bernstein, B. (1977) 'Sociology and the Sociology of Education: A Brief Account'. In Bernstein, B. *Class, Codes and Control, Vol. III*. London: Routledge and Kegan Paul. A detailed review of the ways in which perspective shifts have influenced attitudes to theorizing and research in the sociology of education.

Cohen, P. (1968) *Modern Social Theory*. London: Heinemann. A comprehensive account of the emergence and development of major schools of thought in general sociology.

Eggleston, J. (1974) *Contemporary Research in the Sociology of Education*. London: Routledge and Kegan Paul. The introduction to both this and the following reference contain reviews of the ways in which perspective shifts have influenced attitudes to theorizing and research in the sociology of education.

Karabel, J. and Halsey, A.H. (1977) *Power and Ideology in Education*. Oxford: Oxford University Press.

Chapter 19

Social Systems, Structures and Functions

INTRODUCTION

Sociologists study a wide variety of questions about human conduct. However, a basic theme which underlies many of these questions is a puzzle very similar to what has become known as the Hobbesian 'problem of order'. Why is it, askes Hobbes (1651), that when men come together in societies there is not a constant 'war of everyone against everyone', with each individual person fighting for his or her own survival or self-interest using whatever means are available? Why, he wonders, is social order necessary and how is it achieved? If the processes by which social life proceeds in an orderly and coherent fashion are to be identified and explained, we must first explore the basis upon which these processes rest, the mechanism which enables or restricts collective human behaviour.

Berger (1966) likens social life to the workings of a puppet theatre. Is it accurate, he asks, to see people as puppets, manipulated by some force from above so that some order is imposed upon the social drama? Accepting for the moment the basic idea of this analogy, i.e. that it might be useful to identify those factors which work upon individuals to render their behaviour orderly, we still need to ask questions about the nature of the social puppeteer. What is this power or force?

It is no accident that early attempts to handle this question were, in the main, concerned with identifying those features of social life which provide for stability, cohesion and integration, i.e., the social system. Although in the period when sociology first emerged as a distinctive form of study many of men's activities seemed to be a consequence of personal or local interests being pursued, for 'society' itself to exist as a framework in which the conditions for individual men's existence are made possible, it was thought that the crucial feature of social organization was the system by which individual social members were related to the social whole. Nevertheless, it is important to appreciate that the emergence of sociology as a discipline in the nineteenth century took place during an era of considerable historical and cultural upheaval. First, the Industrial Revolution, the increase in urbanization, the political revolutions in Europe and the relative decline in the power of the church meant that previously held notions of society and social order ceased to provide a meaningful explanation of the situation in which men found themselves; the right of certain groups to rule and the basis upon which one individual was related to another could no longer be justified in terms of traditionally held concepts like divine ordinance or 'natural' social justice. Second, the publication in 1859 of Darwin's *The Origin of Species* and the subsequent impact that evolutionary theory had upon thought created a kind of reverence for 'scientific' methods of study and, more importantly, put the whole question of social order back into the melting-pot. In effect, Darwin's work provided an academically and philosophically respectable base upon which misgivings about previously cherished notions of social organization could be consolidated. The 'social order' of any given society became nothing more than a particular organizational form created by people for the governing of their affairs as part of their collective struggle to survive the natural environment.

Given these upheavals it should come as no surprise that the major concerns of sociologists present at the birth of the discipline were with:

1. explaining the man-made structures which allow individuals to act as relatively independent beings and yet also provide a system which prevents complete anarchy and confusion;
2. adopting a 'scientific' approach to the formulation of such explanations;
3. providing knowledge which would allow people to understand and direct the social forces which seemed to be something more than the power of any single individual.

DURKHEIM AND THE SOCIAL ORDER

In the work of one of the 'founding fathers' of sociology, Emile Durkheim (1858–1917), we find a very clear statement of what this social force, this power behind the 'social puppeteer' was taken to be. Central to Durkheim's sociology is the notion of the primacy of *society* over the *individual*. If there were no agency to regulate and direct the activities of people then human association would be impossible, social life would become chaotic and society would disintegrate. Durkheim is, therefore, in absolute opposition to the ideas of utilitarian theory, which stress that social order is achieved through unrestricted competition, through each man pursuing his own best interest, which will often conflict with the interests of others. For Durkheim this agency is the moral order, the central value system which, though created by people, has an independent and external existence and acts as a constraining and conditioning force upon individual people. His view is perhaps best illustrated in his famous statement that:

> Society commands us because it is exterior and superior to us, the moral distance between it and us makes it an authority before which our wills defer.

People act as they do in compliance with the demands of the society in which they live, and these demands are enshrined within the moral code. But what is this moral code, and how is it to be recognized? It is, Durkheim (1968) explains:

the totality of beliefs and sentiments common to average citizens of the same society (and this totality) forms a determinate system which has its own life; one may call it the *collective* or *common conscience* . . . it is, by definition, diffuse in every reach of society. Nevertheless, it has specific characteristics which make it a distinct reality. It is, in effect, independent of the particular conditions in which individuals are placed; they pass on and it remains.

It follows, then, that any other social agency or institution such as the political system, the economic system or the education system:

1. is shaped by the basic principles of the common moral order;
2. functions so as to ensure that these principles are put into practice and obeyed;
3. allows for behaviour which does not conform to these principles to be defined, explained and controlled.

Durkheim did not ignore the fact that in a complex society such ideals would not be achieved easily. An important element in such societies is that individuals increasingly take on specialized roles and activities to enable and help the society to develop; although these individuals are, therefore, mutually interdependent, a common value system is necessary, both to relate different individuals and their work to each other and to provide continuity between successive generations.

From Durkheim's model for sociological analysis, then, three key words emerge: system, structure and function. The social system is the totality of organizations which emerge to satisfy the needs carried in the central value system of a society. The structure of this system is similarly defined by these values. Any particular institution in the structure functions to provide a link with other elements and, more importantly, to ensure that the principles of the value system are realized in everyday life. So, institutions like the political, economic and education systems provide a basis for determining what is and what is not acceptable social conduct, and the means by which individuals are introduced to and taught the common values of the society.

The relevance of this Durkheimian perspective is, perhaps, more clearly seen if one applies it to a particular instance. What, for example, would an analysis of the education system based on this perspective look like? Very basically, it would always begin by examining the relationship between the *structure* of society and the *function* of education as a subsystem of the society. Like any other social organization, the system of education can be analysed primarily in terms of the functions it serves, notably its function in providing for the maintenance, legitimation, transmission and internalization of the 'collective conscience' (the moral order). In Durkheim's own words:

Society can survive only if there exists among its members a sufficient degree of homogeneity; education perpetuates and reinforces this homogeneity by fixing in the child, from the beginning, the essential similarities that collective life demands.

Durkheim, 1956

The consequence of viewing education in this way is that any question about the organization and process of education is always to be framed in terms of the system's function, i.e. in terms of education's role in providing for the adequate socialization of the individual. This view has massive implications. First, in broad terms, education must be seen as a conservative or an integrating force. As Gouldner (1971) notes:

> Durkheim . . . regarded moral values as pattern-maintaining forces . . . their significance was primarily social; they contribute to the solidarity of society and to the integration of individuals into society.

If the education system functions to transmit these values, it too must work towards solidarity and integration rather than towards differentiation and managed pluralism.

Second, and more specifically, let us consider briefly how the view influences interpretations of three key areas of schooling. For example, we can ask how the perspective conditions questions like:

1. What should be taught in schools? (The curriculum.)
2. What are the responsibilities of teachers? (The role of the teacher.)
3. What is the pupil's 'purpose' in school? (The role of the pupil.)
4. How should teachers and pupils relate? (Interpersonal relations.)

Of course, these are only a selection from a wider range of issues concerning education which might be explored in terms of the Durkheimian perspective.

A DURKHEIMIAN VIEW OF SCHOOLING

The Curriculum

If education is to be successful in fulfilling its transmission and socialization functions then choice of curriculum content in schools is strictly limited. Specific ideas, concepts, topics or segments of knowledge included in the curriculum will, of course, vary from society to society and from era to era. What is important is that an item can only justifiably find its way into the school curriculum if it is part of the common collective culture. The specific nature of the contents of the curriculum is largely irrelevant, so long as the curriculum is designed to conform to the ideals of the following statement:

> The man who education should realize in us is not the man such as nature has made him, but as society wishes him to be . . . It is society that draws for us the portrait of the kind of man we should be, and in this portrait all the peculiarities of its organization come to be reflected.
>
> Durkheim, 1956

The Role of the Teacher

Here again the dominance of social needs over those of the individual is paramount. Teachers must ensure that their activities in school:

1. Encourage in their pupils group involvement, allegiance and responsibility.
2. Enable pupils, where necessary, to recognize that their allegiance to societal goals and values comes before personal or familial concerns; to this extent the teacher may have to work to resocialize those children whose previous formative experi-

ence has taken place in an environment which celebrates sectional rather than collective interests.

3. Develop and extend in their pupils those skills which society needs in order to function and which the children need in order to survive in society.

Teachers must never lose sight of the fact that, although they are agents of transmission, they themselves are under obligation to the same societal requirements. Teachers, then, are simultaneously moral models and moral beings, constraining and constrained:

> The teacher must therefore be committed to presenting (the rule), not as his own personal doing, but as a moral power superior to him, and of which he is an instrument, not the author. He must make the student understand that it imposes itself on him as it does on them; that he cannot remove or modify it; that he is constrained to apply it; that it dominates him and obliges him as it obliges them.
>
> Durkheim, 1961

The Role of the Pupil

The child was always seen by Durkheim as an empty vessel, a blank sheet, waiting to be filled by the agents of society; 'the child', writes Durkheim (1956):

> on entering life, brings to it only his nature as an individual. Society finds itself, with each new generation, faced with a *tabula rasa*, very nearly, on which it must build anew. To the egoistic and asocial being that has just been born it must, as rapidly as possible, add another, capable of leading a moral and social life. Such is the work of education.

The image of the pupil, then, derived from this view of the child, is of a passive being, in need of restraint and having to be led away from selfish intentions towards a self-disciplined and co-operative identification with the common social good. Pupils must be passive because they lack experience and knowledge; they must be restrained because, initially at least, they are motivated by selfish desires which are vague and indistinct. However, Durkheim insists that the process by which this is achieved is not one of indoctrination or forced compliance. To be properly socialized the pupil's acceptance of common social values must be based upon understanding, which is to be derived from reasoned explanation, i.e. the child must come to want what society needs him or her to want; socialization in schools which is not based upon this principle will produce an educated person who might know the common culture, morals and mores but who will be unable to identify with them personally, and such a being is likely to become a danger to both self and society.

Interpersonal Relations

Given the roles of teachers and pupils outlined above, it follows that interpersonal relations in schools are to be characterized in Durkheimian analysis by three elements. First, teachers are, by definition, dominant partners: as agents of the state, and, therefore, of the common value-system, they are superior.

The ascendency that the teacher naturally has over his pupil, because of the superiority of his experience and of his culture, will naturally give to his influence the efficacious force that he needs.

Durkheim, 1956

Second, teachers are constrained from treating their pupils as individuals. A classroom, for Durkheim, is a society in miniature, and as such:

must not be conducted as if it were only a simple agglomeration of subjects independent of one another.

Durkheim, 1956

Rather, interpersonal relations in schools must be carefully structured to reflect and realize homogeneity, co-operative interaction and mutual interdependence.

Third, and slightly paradoxically, there is, overarching interpersonal relations in schools, an impersonal force. Teachers' authority and pupils' passivity are not defined by personal needs and interests. Indeed, the behaviour of either is not governed or justified in personal terms at all, but through reference to the system of education which defines both roles according to the tenets of the collective culture. Personal whims, wishes and volitions are always subordinate to larger, more general 'societal' evaluations.

PARSONS AND SOCIALIZATION

Now, before some evaluation of this particular perspective is made, it is worthwhile to explore how both it and its application to the study of education have been extended in more recent sociological writings. Although a great deal of Durkheim's work was published at the turn of the century, it should not be imagined that either his approach to generating explanations of social life or his analysis of the education system fell out of use when he died. In the work of the American sociologist, Talcott Parsons, we can find a considerable refinement of some of the basic ideas postulated by Durkheim, an extension of the structuralist perspective. Parsons is concerned with providing a schema which enables an analyst to map not only the structural and systematic properties of a given social order, but also the way individual social actors come to know and behave in accordance with the constraints of that system. In this sense the Parsonian perspective has two important strands. First, Parsons, like Durkheim, sees social order achieved through the operation of an integrating system common to all members of society. Second, however, Parsons, borrowing from Freudian psychoanalytical theory, attempts to establish a link between the reproduction of society and the production of individual personalities, and the way in which he believes this can be achieved is through scrutiny of the process of socialization. Socialization involves the way in which:

the main structure of personality is built up through the process of social interaction. It (personality) develops through the internalization of social objects and of the normative patterns governing the child's interaction in social situations.

Parsons, 1964

Parsons argues that, in order for social integration to be achieved, society has, through a process of gradual evolution, thrown up a number of institutions which function as agencies of socialization – the church, the family and, importantly, the education system. As part of their everyday lives in society, social actors, like actors in the theatre, take on specific roles, depending upon the part of the social system, the institution, in which they are interacting – roles such as priests, fathers, mothers, teachers and pupils. The behaviour appropriate to these roles is defined by society. Society has what Parsons calls 'patterned expectations of the behaviour of individuals who occupy particular statuses in the social system'. In other words, for any given social role, society has, on the basis of past experience, evolved a system of 'rules and regulations' governing what is generally considered to constitute proper behaviour for those playing the roles, and these 'rules' gradually become crystallized into a set of 'expectations'. These expectations are shaped by the need society has to preserve itself, that is, its 'functional requirements'. For Parsons all societies have four main functional requirements. These are:

1. Pattern maintenance, i.e. the preservation and passing on of social norms, values, rights and prohibitions.
2. Internal integration, i.e. the provision of the means by which one part of social life is linked to another or by which one sector of the social system (e.g. family life) is related to another (e.g. the economic system).
3. Goal attainment, i.e. the provision of the means whereby both individual and collective aims and needs can be realized.
4. Adaptation, i.e. a capacity for men to make a controlled reaction to changes in the physical, technological and cultural environment in order to maximize any productive benefit to be derived from these changes and to minimize any threat of disruption to the overall integration of society.

Clearly, different functions will be emphasized and satisifed through activity in different social subsystems, but two important processes, which are interrelated, are singled out by Parsons as being vital sociological concerns. The first of these is the process of institutionalization, or the way in which human behaviour becomes systematically regularized and standardized. The second is the process of internalization, or the way in which social expectations surrounding different social roles (as shaped by the functional requirements of society) are encountered, understood and learned by individuals. It is through a consideration of this latter process that Parsons attempts to handle differences between instinctive and learned behaviour, to bridge the gap between actions which arise in response to the individual's will and desires (personality) and those which are determined by the social structure and culture. He writes:

> while the main content of the structure of the personality is derived from the social system and culture through socialization, the personality becomes an independent system through its relations to its own organism and through the uniqueness of its own life experiences: it is not a mere epiphenomenon of the structure of society. There is, however, not merely interdependence between the two, but what I call *interpenetration*.
>
> Parsons, 1964

Parsons goes on to propose that, in learning to play predetermined social roles (in becoming socialized), men preserve the common culture, find a place in a network of interrelated roles, discover an organized way of satisfying and developing personal needs and establish a base from which they can react to new situations confronting themselves in particular or the species in general.

The part played by schooling and the system of education in allocating men to specific roles and in teaching them their parts is obviously tremendous. 'The school class', Parsons (1959) maintains:

> is an agency through which individuals are trained to be motivationally and technically adequate to the performance of adult roles.

However, in a complex society schools satisfy two broad functions for society. They provide a basis for socialization and they work as the mechanism by which individuals are allocated their adult roles – both work roles and wider social ones. In a sense there is a contradiction here between a celebration of similarity and a celebration of differences. Parsons exploits this contradiction by working on the assumption that the child in school has to be socialized to accept the legitimacy of a highly differentiated society in which individuals are selected for different roles which carry unequal status and reward, and also the acceptability of the criteria by which such selection is made. This last point is worth re-examination. In Part Two of this book some subtle aspects of schooling were discussed in terms of a hidden process, often the implication being that the differential treatment, the hidden ranking and the covert processes by which pupils are identified and labelled educational successes and failures are an undesirable consequence of the school system. For Parsons this process is not a latent function of the system at all: it is a necessary activity which one part of the social system, education, performs for the social whole.

Parsons (1959) maintains that schools foster two types of commitment: on the one hand commitment to broad social values, and, on the other, commitment to specific types of roles played in adult life. Elementary or primary education emphasizes the first and secondary education the second, although both sectors of education work to develop in the child both the capacity to perform roles and the capacity to be aware of and to live up to the obligations of different roles, both general and specific. Thus schools socialize pupils. But they socialize in ways which are specific and special to the particular social system, education, of which they are a part. Because the system also functions as an agency of 'manpower allocation', an organization which selects and trains the young for different, specialized roles in adult life, it must also provide a basis for establishing differences between individuals. The individual must be brought to an awareness that:

> it is fair to give differential rewards for different levels of achievement, so long as there has been fair access to opportunity, and fair that these rewards lead on to higher-order opportunities for the successful. There is thus a basic sense in which the elementary school class is an embodiment of the fundamental American value of equality of opportunity, in that it places value *both* on initial equality and on differential achievement.
>
> Parsons, 1958

This last function, Parsons suggests, is fulfilled by pupils identifying with the teacher, with what he or she represents, and with the beneficial nature of education.

Achievement itself has two facets. The first is cognitive, i.e. to do with activities and performances 'appropriate to the school situation'; the second is moral, i.e. to do with acquiring the necessary attitudes and behaviour for life in society. Both facets are, necessarily, always defined by adults and, like Durkheim, Parsons presents teachers and parents as superior to and in authority over their pupils and children.

One final point. Schooling in advanced societies is viewed by Parsons as an indispensable section of the whole social structure:

> Relatively speaking, the school is a specialized agency. That it should increasingly have become the principal channel of selection as well as agency of socialization is in line with what one would expect in an increasingly differentiated and progressively more upgraded society.
>
> Parsons, 1959

THE STRUCTURALIST PERSPECTIVE AND THE SOCIOLOGY OF EDUCATION

The peculiar characteristics of a structuralist sociological perspective applied to the study of education and schooling – and, it is important to add, some of the weaknesses associated with such usage – are most clearly illustrated by an examination of the activities, attitudes and concerns of British and American sociologists of education working in the 1950s and the early 1960s. Although various writers developed some distinctive approaches to their work, the following comment made by Olive Banks (1978) remains substantially correct:

> It is fair to say that the main thrust in the sociology of education in the 1950s and 1960s was structure functionalism and this was true of both this country and the United States.

Central to work produced during this period was a concern with exploring and explicating the relationship between education and the structure of society. Indeed, it is hard to see how anyone working in the structuralist tradition could proceed otherwise, in view of the fact that in this sociological stance institutions in society are seen as functionally interrelated. It was thought, therefore, that an analysis of the functions of the education system and the extent to which these were being efficiently met would reveal:

1. The nature of the relationship between education and other social organizations.
2. Important insights into the way in which people can be expected to behave with educational settings.
3. The contribution education makes to the maintenance and the development of the social fabric.
4. A method by which dysfunctions in education, and the social malaise which would attend such dysfunctions, could be identified and redressed.

The question was, however, 'Functions for what purpose?' Durkheim had suggested that different functions could be reduced to the main need for social organizations to transmit the collective conscience. In the rapidly developing and changing post-war society, however, it was difficult to reconcile such a model with the realities of emergent values, new technological achievements and changing patterns of social groupings, traditional values seeming to be inadequate tools to cope with shifting situations.

The major focus, therefore, was upon economic needs and the close relationship between education and the economy, which arises from what Parsons described as education's dual function of socializing and selecting people for adult roles. Thus, in the introduction to their influential reader concerning the sociology of education. Floud and A.H. Halsey (1961) asserted that:

> In modern society, the major link of education to the social structure is through the economy and this is a linkage of both stimulus and response. Contemporary educational organizations stimulate economic change through research and, in turn, they respond to economic change in carrying out the functions of selection and training of manpower. The implications for schools and universities, as organizations, are unending.

But what kind of activity did this kind of attitude generate at the empirical level? Essentially the major interest was with identifying and mapping inefficiencies in the education system to sort, train and allocate individuals.

This interest influenced what was taken to be the main problem area for sociologists of education, the main properties to be studied in pursuit of a solution to this problem area, and the main methods judged as appropriate for such investigation.

The Problem

The problem was to investigate why the education system was failing to draw upon and use 'pools of ability' conceptualized along social class lines. For the economy to reach optimum development and growth, it needed a steady supply of skilled and flexible personnel, and yet it appeared to observers in the 1950s and 1960s that large numbers of able pupils, mostly from working-class backgrounds, were failing to achieve satisfactory standards in the primary schools, were being excluded from entry to the academic sectors of secondary education because of their inability to satisfy the 11+ examination requirements, were not being entered for or were failing in public examinations and certificate assessments, were leaving school early, were failing to gain places in Higher Education and were entering semi-skilled or unskilled employment after completing their formal education.

Explanations

Explanations of this problem were conceived, as the perspective demanded, in terms of dysfunctions either in the internal structural organization of the education system or in the structural relationships between education and other social subsystems. In the former, research concentrated on areas like regional variation in the quality of schools available (Banks, 1955), the selection procedures used in schools (Floud and Halsey, 1956; Jackson, 1964), teachers' role performances (Musgrove and Taylor, 1969; Cohen, 1965) and the internal organization of the school, streaming and the generation of anti-school attitudes (Hargreaves, 1967; Lacey, 1970). In the latter, there was an extensive amount of research which investigated such issues as the relationship between aspects of home life and school achievement (Jackson and Marsden, 1962; Douglas, 1964), the relationship between attitudes to education of pupils' parents and success in school (Newsom Report, 1963; Plowden Report, 1967), the impact of local environment and neighbourhood upon educational performances (Mays, 1962; Wiseman, 1964) and the interrelation of pre-school language socialization, social class and classroom life (see Bernstein, 1975a & b).

Methods

Because the topics selected for investigation were fundamentally concerned with large questions about relationships between substantial aspects of social life, the methods used to conduct such investigations were designed to provide data and explanations which would be valid across the wide area selected for research. Thus, for example, in order to make a longitudinal study of the educational experiences and performances of children from different social backgrounds (in terms of such properties as class of origin, family size, family income, birth order, type of housing, parental attitudes, etc.), Douglas (1964) found it necessary to work on a sample of some 4700 children, and the techniques he used to collect information included administering standardized tests to all members of the sample population, extensive interviewing and consultation of records, reports and school assessments of the pupils who made up the sample.

Looking back over this period of research it is tempting to view the issues mainly in terms of a political and ideological concern with a search for equality of educational opportunity, a quest for the achievement of greater social justice through education and a movement towards a meritocratic society. While there is no doubt that these concerns represented the values of many sociologists of education working in this period, we should not lose sight of the fact that there was also a concern that education was dysfunctional. As Karabel and Halsey (1977) comment on this period:

> The attack by British sociologists on inequality of educational opportunity was not only that it was unfair, but also that it was inefficient.

This last point is important because it illustrates, in a way which concentration upon ideological concerns obscures, the powerful tendency within the structure-functionalist perspective to conceptualize social life in terms of the 'fit' between the parts of the social system and their functional contribution to the smooth running of the whole – a tendency which has come to be regarded as one of the major weaknesses of the perspective.

CONCLUSION: EVALUATION OF THE STRUCTURALIST PERSPECTIVE

A perspective contains important assumptions about men and society, and for functionalism the question of order is paramount. The importance of these factors is underlined by Dawe (1970), when he says that:

> In this sense, the problem of order is a label for a doctrine which defines a universe of meaning for sociological concepts and theories . . . . The progression begins from a view of human nature from which follows a view of the relationship between the individual and society.

Many criticisms have been made about the structural functionalist perspective, and here we will refer briefly to three main weaknesses, which we hope will provide a basis for discussion.

Society: An All-pervasive Entity

Society is presented as an all-pervasive entity which has a life apart from men. It is depicted as overarching men, constraining, moulding and regulating them, and as such it is invested with human motivations and characteristics, so that society is described as having 'needs', 'purposes' and 'functional requirements'. An idea is thus treated as a being, and an analytical category reified, yet where this externalized life form is to be found, except in the consciousness of men, is somewhat obscure. If it is to be found only in the consciousness of men, how is it external? If not, where is it?

One of the consequences of this reification is that in the educational sphere the effectiveness of any school structure can be measured only in terms of the needs of the system. Problems of disorganization or conflict are thus largely attributed to poor organizational factors, the lack of 'fit' between role and personality, inadequate adaptation to emerging social systems, or deviance. What is inadequate about this approach is its lack of consideration of how pressures for change arise within social systems as a result of conflicts of interests over the balance of power. As Worsley (1973) argues in his criticism of Durkheim:

> What Durkheim did not show was how men use ideologies as well as being used – not by 'reified' society – but by men who have power to make others accept their ideologies, and hence make ideologies 'work'.

In short, social order might well be achieved not by all coming to want what society requires them to have, but by a few having the power to define social necessity and imposing their definitions on the less powerful. It would seem more acceptable to depict the 'social puppeteer' as a group of real men acting for their own interests, rather than as a mystifying entity called 'society'.

'The Oversocialized Conception of Man'

A further, not unrelated, criticism concerns the view of man that such a perspective presents. It has been described as: 'the oversocialized conception of man' (Wrong, 1961), 'oversocialized' in that man is depicted as being at the receiving end of dominant influences rather than being a creator of them; an 'absolutistic view of man' (Douglas, 1971), in the sense that man is confronted by forces beyond his control; and as an example of 'repressive sociology' (Gouldner, 1971), in that the perspective leads the sociologist to place more emphasis on exploring the conditions that determine men's lives rather than on the ways in which men can become controllers of their own destiny.

The Problem of Meaning

Lastly, a problem that arises with this perspective is that of meaning. If society makes the rules, the values and the cultural norms of social life, it must also greatly influence how social objects, concepts and relations are defined and understood. Thus, as Blum (1974) points out:

> To describe society is to chart the concrete influence of the social . . . sociology is in the grip of that which it is discussing; consequently sociology can make its case not on the basis of differentiating itself from that which it describes, but only in terms of its efficiency in affirming the authority of that which it describes as authorizing its very description.

In other words, if meanings are defined by social conventions, then sociologists, who are, after all, fundamentally products of the system in which these conventions operate, are constrained to use analytical categories, descriptions of the world which are far from objective; sociology, therefore, is itself constrained by the very forces it seeks to describe.

Further Reading

Archer, M. (1979) *The Social Origins of Educational Systems*. London: Sage. Although highly sophisticated, provides one of the best illustrations of the insights that can be generated by a macro-sociological analysis.

Giddens, A. (1978) *Durkheim*. Glasgow: Fontana. A very clear introduction to some of the basic ideas of this writer.

Gouldner, A. (1971) *The Coming Crisis of Western Sociology*. London: Heinemann. Offers a critical appraisal of the assumptions and implications of the structuralist perspective in sociology; a review which pays special attention to the ideas of Durkheim.

Signpost

Read the paper by Earl Hopper himself in his collection of readings, Hopper, E. (ed.) (1971) *Readings in the Theory of Educational Systems*, London: Hutchinson. Although the typology of the basic mechanics of educational systems is a bit dated, it still provides a stimulating basis for asking questions about contemporary educational policy to do with the education system. Identify policies which you think might be changing the degree of centralization and standardization in the UK education system and, using Hopper's model, try to articulate some of the less obvious consequences of these changes.

Chapter 20

The Action Perspective

INTRODUCTION

In his analysis of the development of the different 'doctrines' which shape sociological perspectives, Alan Dawe (1970) writes:

> There are, then, two sociologies, a sociology of social system and a sociology of social action. They are grounded in the diametrically opposed concerns with two central problems, those of order and control. And, at every level, they are in conflict. They posit antithetical views of human nature, of society and the relationship between the social and the individual. The first asserts the paramount necessity, for societal and individual well-being, of external constraint; hence the notion of a social system ontologically and methodologically prior to its participants. The key notion of the second is that of autonomous man, able to realize his full potential and to create a truly human social order only when freed from external constraint. Society is thus the creation of its members; the product of their construction of meaning, and of the action and relationships through which they attempt to impose that meaning on their historical situation.

It is with the second of these two doctrines, what Dawe calls 'a sociology of social action', that this chapter is concerned.

First, while it is true to say that the question of how order is achieved in social life, of how the relationships between men are regulated and their individual affairs constrained, has formed a basic framework for a great deal of sociological thought, it should not be imagined that this concern has been developed in isolation or without challenge. An alternative vision has also been much in evidence in a great deal of sociological writing. This alternative has a more optimistic view of man: while the possibility that some human acts are motivated by self-interest is not discounted, the ability of the species to create meanings, to constitute social situations, in short, to control the social and natural world, is emphasized.

What is seen to be remarkable about man as a species, then, is not so much the instances of his obedience and compliance to larger forces and powers which work upon him but, first, his genuinely creative ability to build out of nothing, as it were, that intricately arranged and delicately balanced mechanism which is the social structure and, second, his capacity to endow the various elements of this mechanism with meaning and significance. There is, in this vision, a kind of reverence for that uniquely human characteristic, the capacity of members of the species to react imaginatively to their environment and to construct creatively the means by which humankind can be liberated from various kinds of subordination.

It follows that sociological inquiry which celebrates the kind of recognition outlined above will have a very different shape and bias from that which Dawe calls 'a sociology of social system'. If man is seen as creative rather than constrained, then the kinds of social phenomena which are of interest to, and in need of explanation by, the sociological observer are likely to be:

1. The ways in which members of society, through their individual and collective actions, create and maintain the social fabric within which they live.
2. The ways in which members of society come to recognize, understand and assess the social arrangements and structures by which they both manage to act socially and to impose a form of control on the conditions of their existence.

WEBER AND SOCIAL ACTION

The extent to which this distinctive sociological concern differs from those discussed in the previous chapter is shown clearly if we examine Max Weber's definition of the sociological endeavour. Although Weber (1864–1920) was writing in exactly the same period as Durkheim, albeit in a different intellectual tradition, his sociology is dramatically different from that of his contemporary. He asserts:

> Sociology . . . is a science which attempts the interpretive understanding of *social action* in order thereby to arrive at a causal explanation of its course and effect. In 'action' is included all human behaviour when and in so far as the acting individual *attaches a subjective meaning to it* . . . Action is social in so far as, by virtue of the subjective meaning attached to it by the acting individual (or individuals), it takes account of the behaviour of others.
>
> Weber, 1964 (our italics)

There are, of course, all kinds of issues raised here. To what extent can sociology be a science? What is meant by 'interpretive understanding'? However, before we can consider these methodological problems we need to examine two core concepts used by Weber in his definition: 'social action' and 'subjective meaning'.

Weber is fairly insistent on grounding his sociology in the development of an understanding of the totality of social life which begins by building up a description of the workings of the basic components of this totality, the 'atom' of the societal structure. For him, says MacRae (1974):

> this atomic unit of the social is the single deliberate action of an individual directed to affecting the behaviour of one or more persons.

While Weber would not deny that individual human actions might be susceptible to the influence of larger collective elements in society, like the state, the form of family life or the education system, we should recognize that these are:

> solely the resultants and modes of organization of the specific acts of *individual* men, since

these alone are for us the agents who carry out subjectively understandable action.

The danger, therefore, of starting sociological investigation with an analysis of these larger features, with a view to working down to an explanation of individual behaviour, is the temptation to treat such representations (which, after all, are only concepts that men use to describe circumstances which arise from their collective action) as if they have a mind, a consciousness, an intentionality of their own – that is, to reify them. Similarly, Weber is sceptical of analysis which starts at the other extreme, i.e. with a consideration of the internal mental states, the psychological make-up of human beings. To view individuals' acts solely in terms of the consequences of inner drives is to see them acting in a social vacuum. Thus, according to Weber, sociology can only move *towards* an understanding of both social institutions and individual psychological conditions *from* an understanding of the practical form which gives these two sets of properties their realization, the specific acts of individuals.

But how are these acts to be analysed, or described? We could adopt either or both of two approaches. First, we could note directly the characteristics and consequences of an act as they appear to be an observer and, by relating such observation to our existing knowledge of human behaviour derived from past observations, we could arrive at an explanation, comparing the act observed to already accepted theories and interpretations of action and its context. So, for example, if we observe a pupil in school writing out the same sentence 200 times and we weigh this observation against our more global intelligence of what constitutes appropriate conduct in the context in which this writing is being done, we can work out some 'causal explanation' of the act. However, Weber would argue that, at best, in doing this we would succeed only in making a 'peculiarly plausible hypothesis'.

This problem is acute when placed in the context of what Weber regards as the basic intentions people have in carrying out acts. He suggests that, on an abstract level, we can distil these intentions into four pure or 'ideal' types, which he groups under the divisions 'rational' and 'non-rational' (the second not to be confused with 'irrational' or 'unreasonable'). Rational intentions might take either of two forms: 'purposefully rational' (by which there is an instrumental intention behind an act, in the sense that the person performing it has weighed up the cost, the means of achieving a certain end and the desirability of such an achievement, and has designed his conduct accordingly) and 'value rational' (by which the intention behind an act is the pursuit of some virtue or ideal, the attainment of which is not questioned, only the means being debatable). Similarly, non-rational intentions are separable into two sub-types: 'affectual' orientations (by which the act performed is done in response to an emotion) and 'traditional' orientations (by which an act is done according to the dictates of habit, custom, ritual or tradition).

Accepting, at least in part, the usefulness of this typology, it becomes apparent that sociological explanation based solely on direct observation of the overt features of action will be problematic in at least two of the types of acts thus identified – value rational action and affectual action – the motivations or intentions of such conduct not being obviously available for public scrutiny. This is why Weber introduces into his definition of sociology the second concept isolated above – the concern with the identification of 'subjective meaning'. As Giddens (1971) explains, adequate sociological understanding of social action, for Weber, necessarily involves 'the elucidation of an intervening motivational link between the observed activity and its meaning to the actor'.

This, of course, is extremely difficult. How can we know the ways in which other humans understand the consequences of their actions and have intentions for them? Weber was not unaware of these problems, but suggests that a way of cutting through them is for the sociologist to make formal use of the same devices that members of society use to understand the conduct of others in everyday life; observation; the making of inferences about the motives behind the acts observed, which is achieved by empathizing with the subject performing the act; the testing of the validity of such inferences against existing knowledge of what is 'normal' in the context in which the behaviour is located; the construction of generalized interpretations of the conduct against which to measure particular instances of it and thus identify acts which conform to or deviate from these normal patterns; and finally, the comparison of this under-standing of specific cases of action with similar instances in other circumstances. Nevertheless, Weber (1964) is insistent that:

> A correct causal interpretation of a concrete course of action is arrived at when the overt action and the motives have both been correctly apprehended and at the same time their *relation* has become meaningfully comprehensible.

While 'one need not have been Caesar in order to understand Caesar', one does need to be able to move around in his world with some surety to understand both the world and his conduct within it.

We pointed out earlier how Berger, using the simile of social life being like the workings of a puppet theatre, suggests that one question we explore in sociology is concerned with the forces in society which govern the movement of the human puppet. However, Berger is not so naïve as to imagine that human beings are merely puppets. Indeed, he points out that an important difference between puppets and humans is that, while the actions of the former are wholly dependent upon some power above them which is pulling the strings, humans, through their power to think, are not only capable of looking around, and thus of being aware of external forces, but are also able to resist and react to various attempts to manipulate their lives on the social stage. Berger (1966) writes:

> We see the puppets dancing on their miniature stage, moving up and down as the strings pull them around, following the prescribed course of their various little parts. We learn to understand the logic of this theatre and we find ourselves in its motions. We locate ourselves in society and thus recognize our own positions as we hang from its subtle strings. For a moment we see ourselves as puppets indeed. But then we grasp a decisive difference between the puppet theatre and our own drama. Unlike the puppets, we have the possibility of stopping in our movements, looking up and perceiving the machinery by which we have been moved. In this act lies the first step towards freedom.
>
> Copyright © Peter Berger. Reprinted by permission of Penguin Books Ltd.

This emphasis upon the human being's ability to recognize and influence the world about them and the part they play within it provides the corner-stone for the sociologic-al perspective under consideration in this chapter. Those influenced by this emphasis work on the notion that there is both an objective and a subjective social reality. The situations in which an individual lives out his/her life have an objective reality in the sense that various social organizations and institutions like the political structure, the economic order and the education system 'are *there*, external to him; persistent in their reality, whether he likes it or not'. (Berger and Luckmann, 1967).

However, although such things may be there, outside of people, they are, first, built and constantly in the process of being reconstructed and modified as a direct result of the decisions and actions of individuals as they seek to control the conditions of their everyday affairs. Second, they are real and of consequence only through a person's subjective or individualized awareness of them. Thus, for example, to imagine that there might be such an institution as schooling that did not first evolve as a consequence of intervention in their social arrangements or that would continue to exist as a systematic social organization if contemporaries did not recognize it as such and have awareness and definitions of what it means and does, would be absurd. This, then, is the subjective dimension – the human being's capacity both to produce and to maintain his social universe.

SUBJECTIVE REALITY

For a number of reasons sociologists working with such ideas insist that sociological analysis begin with and concentrate on the subjective dimension of reality. First, it is argued that a serious limitation of the perspective outlined in the previous chapter, which emphasizes the objective reality, is that the observer of society is seduced into caricaturing the individual as being determined, assigned to his role by some force more powerful than himself, or, in Garfinkel's poignant image, as being 'a cultural dope'. The problem here is not just that it is difficult to capture and describe a reality which, though 'social', excludes real people from its analysis but, more seriously, that the tradition tends either to overlook or to treat as constant the unique actions of the individual. If we view humans as being predominantly 'determined' in their conduct, it is difficult to account for idiosyncratic and situationally specific features of human behaviour. Yet in our daily lives we notice that these very features, these mundane and everyday occurrences in which individual social actors display and act upon private and subjective understandings, choices and intentions, are both routine and regular, and appear to be at the foundations of social life. To assume, therefore, that we could explain an event like, for example, an act of truancy from school without reference to the way in which the 'truant' perceives his world and judges the kind of response appropriate to that perception would be unacceptable to those taking this perspective, because such an explanation would represent a distortion. The extent to which those developing this alternative approach are critical of simple determinist explanations and insist on the importance of taking into analysis the subjective vision is succinctly summarized by Blumer (1962) in the following way:

> These various uses of sociological perspectives and interests, which are so strongly entrenched to-day, leap over the acting units of a society and by-pass the interpretative process by which such acting units build up their actions.

He continues his exhortation for sociologists to make the actions and the subjective interpretations carried out by real men their focal concern, by remarking that, for these individuals:

> Structural features, such as 'culture', 'social systems', 'social stratification' or 'social roles', set conditions for their action but do not determine their action. People – that is, acting units – do not act towards culture, social structure or the like; they act towards situations. Social organization enters into action only to the extent to which it shapes situations in which people act, and to the extent that it supplies fixed sets of symbols which people use in interpreting their situations.

A second reason why those who favour a concentration upon the subjective dimension of social action insist upon making this the base for sociological analysis is concerned with their attitude to what constitutes acceptable sociological knowledge. Certainly, they would argue, in our investigations of the social world we can make use of concepts which refer to collective behaviour, to general patterns of conduct applicable to large sections of the population, to notions of whole groups of people and the objectified relationships between them. But we should never lose sight of the fact that these concepts are concepts: they are not descriptions of actual behaviour or concrete phenomena. but images, possible interpretations of the complexity of human life. True, some of these concepts might be used by real people in their real lives, but the extent to which this is so and the manner in which it takes place is an empirical question and cannot be left to mere assumption. Thus, to explain pupils' 'failure' in school in terms of their being victims of the social class from which they originate might be a useful tool for pointing out possibilities, but it does not give a full explanation of the particular activities of an individual pupil or of how that pupil came to be categorized 'educational failure'. Through following this kind of argument, sociologists working within the action perspective develop a concern to redirect investigation towards an understanding of everyday life, rather than one based on grand theoretical debate, survey data, the scrutiny of social rates or statistical measures of behaviour patterns and/or comparative historical analysis. Jack Douglas (1971) is particularly strong in his condemnation of investigation which is not orientated towards the systematic observation and analysis of everyday life, and concludes that:

> Any scientific understanding of human action, at whatever level of ordering or generality, must begin with and be built upon an understanding of the everyday life of the members performing those actions. (To fail to see this and to act in accord with it is to commit what we might call the *fallacy of abstractionism*, that is, the fallacy of believing that you can know in a more abstract form what you do not know in the particular form.)

A significant consequence of this overall concern with exploring the subjective dimensions of human action in everyday situations in that the knowledge people have of their world and the meanings they themselves give to the objects which constitute it become crucial substantive areas for the sociologist to explore. If we wish, as writers like Douglas have suggested, that sociologists should 'retain the integrity of the phenomena' under observation or, in other words, avoid distorting reality in the name of analysis, then we will need to ensure that the gap between a social actor's own interpretation of his actions and an observer's interpretation of them is minimal. Two important questions concerning the methods sociologists use are pushed to the fore if one accepts the need to adhere to this structure.

The first is that observers cannot assume that the interpretation and understanding of a situation under study that they bring with them at the start of an investigation have much more than a tenuous validity, because the 'meaning' of all the properties which make up the situation is problematic in the sense that these properties will have already been interpreted by those participating in the events, and it is their understanding of these and their assumptions that will influence the course of events in the situation and in which the observer is interested. As Gorbutt (1972) notes:

> The observer must be careful to recognize that different parties in any interaction may have different interpretations of it and that these interpretations cannot be assumed in advance of empirical investigation. We cannot merely describe a school assembly, for example, as a consensual ritual which binds staff and pupils together. This indeed may be the stated intention of the headmaster but the interpretation put upon the event by others, even though they may outwardly conform, cannot be assumed.

However, to analyse behaviour and yet at the same time to suspend assumptions about it is very difficult. Sociologists, as well as being observers or spies, are also members of the community which they are investigating, and to move suddenly from a position where objects, activities and relationships in the world are familiar, recognizable and significant to one in which these same items are treated as problems, as hardly-knowns, or as objects of inquiry, requires constant effort. Becker (1974) illustrates the full force of this difficulty by pointing out the problems for the observer of everyday life in the classroom:

> We may have understated a little the difficulty of observing contemporary classrooms . . . I think . . . that it is first and foremost a matter of it all being so familiar that it becomes almost impossible to single out events that occur in the classroom as things that have occurred, even when they happen right in front of you . . . it takes a tremendous effort of will and imagination to stop seeing only things that are conventionally 'there' to be seen.

Nevertheless, it was a vision of the tremendous insights into the process of education that would be gained through adoption of this technique of treating the categories and meanings used by members of the educational world as problematic which both excited those involved and gave impetus to the so-called 'New Direction' movement in the sociology of education which emerged in Britain in the 1970s. By examining not only how teachers and pupils act and interact in schools but also how they construct and understand the definitional categories on which they base activity – the assumptions they have of what counts as knowledge, learning, intelligence and even schooling and education itself – was seen as a way of revealing the bed-rock upon which the schooling system rests and thereby providing an opportunity for bringing the system into the more direct control of its creators and users. As Gorbutt, in his discussion of the 'New Direction' approach, asserted in 1974:

> It should be clear that the kind of research I have in mind would not be based on a social science which merely elaborates and reifies existing educational categories like intelligence and the disadvantaged child. It would be based on the interpretive approach . . . and would question the very assumptions which underlie conventional sociology of education, educational psychology and philosophy of education and the prevailing educational practices which they support.

The second methodological implication of the stress on the relativity of knowledge and the subjectivity of meaning made within the action perspective is that sociologists themselves can claim no privileged status for their own interpretations and understandings. Sociological research, like any other attempt to order perceptions of the world, is a social act itself, and as such is open to the same kinds of scrutiny and analysis used in the exploration of the social. This has meant that a great deal of work based upon this perspective has involved a considerable amount of self-criticism by those carrying out the work, particularly with reference to the methods employed, so that the 'integrity of the phenomena' is retained (notably participant observation and ethnographic study), and it has also proved a popular point for criticism by those dubious of the main concerns of the perspective. It is argued by some that, even if one accepts that it is important to suspend one's own presuppositions in the relentless pursuit of meaning, one must still accept that there comes a point when one grounds one's definitions on a base which, for all practical purposes, is accepted as valid. Otherwise it would be impossible to know anything. While it is possible to suggest that sociologists in the past have been guilty of employing too little rigour in their examination of their assumptions, this is not the same as saying that they must never make assumptions. Indeed, Douglas (1971) himself admits that:

> there inevitably comes a point at which one either accepts total solipsism and the impossibility of 'knowing' anything or grounds one's thought in some presupposed (commonsensical) experience.

INTERPRETATIVE PERSPECTIVES

So far in this chapter we have treated the action perspective as if it represented a unidimensional doctrine among sociologists. It is important to note that several different schools of thought are often grouped together under the one generic umbrella of interpretive or appreciative sociology – for example, symbolic interactionism, phenomenology or ethnomethodology – and, while it is true to say that these all share a common concern to develop an appreciative understanding of social action in everyday life, they differ in their methodological persuasions. The main emphasis in the rest of this chapter will be upon the first of these specific approaches because it is arguable that interactionism has had the greatest impact upon educational research, but first let us consider the main differences between these three branches of interpretive sociology. Hammersley and Woods (1976) offer a useful articulation of such differences which can be summarized as follows.

Interactionism

Interactionism stresses the 'partial independence from social structural, cultural and psychological forces of the sense people make of the world and of action based on such perspectives'. For the most part man absorbs given interpretations of the physical and symbolic universe from others and acts accordingly, yet the task of the interactionist sociologist is, claims Blumer, 'to reveal the process through which men construct their actions'. The emphasis, then, is upon *process*.

Phenomenology

Phenomenologists place the emphasis differently. Hammersley and Woods argue that this movement 'is concerned with the knowledge and assumptions which must be possessed and acted upon by people in order for the social world to exist'. Their task, then, is to reveal this knowledge, which is not always available at a conscious level; indeed, is more often taken for granted by individuals in the course of their everyday lives. So the objective of the phenomenological sociologist is to provide a description of what people think they know, of 'how men define their world and typify both it and their position within it'. Or, as Sharp and Green (1975) assert, 'The basic preoccupation of the sociological phenomenologist is with the subtle texture of meaning which constitutes reality.' The emphasis, then, is upon *meaning*.

Ethnomethodology

Ethnomethodologists, like the sociologists described above, are concerned with the ways in which actors construct their social worlds, but they stress the capturing of the methods, the devices, the practical activities which, it is argued, must underlie this construction for it to take place at all. Perhaps it is useful to examine briefly the research strategies of ethnomethodologists, as this reveals something of their distinctive stance. Garfinkel has used the technique of 'making trouble' or disrupting real, everyday situations 'to expose the background assumption underlying them'. By placing subjects in bewildering, confusing or even senseless environments and observing how they then 'make sense' of these, i.e. negotiate a new social order, should, claims Garfinkel (1967), 'tell us something about how structures of everyday activities are ordinarily and routinely produced and maintained'.

Ethnomethodologists, then, attempt to answer the question 'What are the *rules* of social interaction?' and in answer to the criticism that this begs the question 'Where do these rules come from?' they would reply that their form of analysis can answer this too, because rules are:

> only established as such by their ability to organize the settings of practical commonsense actions – an ability which is proven in so organizing these actions.

The stress here, then, is upon the nature, construction and expression of the regulative techniques, the conventional routine, the *practical accomplishments* by which members of society make their actions rational and comprehensible for others.

There is, of course, considerable overlap between these separate sociological programmes. It is difficult to imagine, for example, how one could describe the processes of classroom life without taking into account both the meanings that participants in that world take from it and the details of the practical activities in which they engage to signal and order their understandings and to render their behaviour accountable to others. To a certain extent the interrelation between these concerns is illustrated in the work of interactionists, and so it is to a more detailed consideration of this single approach to which we will now turn.

INTERACTIONISM

A great deal of the work which is identifiably 'interactionist' draws upon the theoretical perspective to be found in the writings of G.H. Mead (1863–1931). Mead begins his analysis by making a distinction between non-symbolic communication (or the use of gestures) and symbolic communication (or the use of ideas and concepts), the difference between these being nicely illustrated by Mennell (1974) thus:

> The difference between a gesture and a symbol for Mead is the difference between punching someone and shaking a fist at him. Shaking a fist normally communicates not the possibility of attack, but the *idea* of anger in the shaker's mind. The person at whom the fist is shaken is able to interpret it as meaning hostility; it is the *idea* of anger which has been communicated from one mind to another.

Human beings are unique in being able to make massive use of this second form of communication, symbolic communication. This ability derives from the development in the species of those anatomical and neurological features which enable members to carry and make use of a complicated symbol system, language. This faculty opens up a number of possibilities of organization of behaviour.

Language allows people to reflect upon their situation and their place within it. The importance of this seemingly simple observation is vast. Mead argues that, because language is available to humans, they are able:

1. To organize and store up impressions and understandings of the social and physical world.
2. To transmit these understandings to others who share the language form.
3. To apply already acquired understandings held in the mind to new situations, perceptions or symbolic communications received from others and, therefore, to deliberate upon these and create newly fashioned understandings of such signals.

Thus, from birth onwards, humans are exposed to a host of signals and symbols carried in the language form which are put out by others and, as they learn to understand and interpret these signals, they develop not only an accumulated collection of other people's perceptions, impressions and beliefs but also the capacity to consider this body of knowledge. In learning a language the individual acquires the ability to use it for his or her own purpose and to turn it back upon the direct stimulus of experience. Mead describes this as the development of a conception of 'self' – the process by which, through the acquisition of a form of symbolic representation, individuals achieve the means by which they are empowered to share and understand the accepted and conventional symbolic interpretations of the world, are given a tool with which they can reflect upon these representations and the significance these have for their own particular being, and, in so doing, are able to recognize and realize their own individuality. Mead depicts this development in terms of the emergence of distinctive 'I' and 'me' sections of the individual mind. Possessing language, humans are able to see themselves as both objects in the world and subjects acting upon that world. But language allows more than this: it enables the object side of humans, the 'me' to which things happen, to be held up for inspection by the subject side, which is reacting to these happening, the 'I'. The full force of the Meadian concept of self is articulated by David Hargreaves (1972) thus:

> In Mead's analysis of the self, the individual becomes a kind of society in miniature, for he can engage in a form of internal social interaction. When, through the process of taking the role of the other, the self acquires its reflexive quality and attains self-consciousness, the individual is no longer at the mercy of the forces of nature. He does not merely respond to those forces which play upon him from inside or outside, as is the case with objects or organisms that lack a self. In short, his behaviour is no longer determined. With a self, the individual ceases to be subject to the direct impact of other stimuli, for he can withhold his response to such stimuli and estimate their significance and consequences for particular lines of action towards them. His ability to anticipate makes several possible future lines of action available in the present; and from such future possibilities he can make a choice. The person thus constructs and chooses what he does; his acts are not predetermined responses.

Language allows people to respond to and direct the experience and actions of other persons. Indeed, an important dimension of the formation of 'self' involves just that. Implicit in the process of 'self' development is the idea, introduced in the quotation above, of 'taking the role of the other'. Mead argues that language is one of the main mechanisms by which new members of society, rather than engaging in the cumbersome process of noting, classifying and interpreting every new object, person, idea or experience encountered, instead take on the ready-made understandings of others. This involves coming to see the world as they see it, and also means that individuals learn to see themselves as others see them and are thus able to anticipate the responses of others to their own actions.

Consider, for example, some of the points raised in Chapters 3 and 4. How do individuals become either pupils or teachers? Can we assume that this is a relatively simple process by which the social actors involved internalize a 'ready-made set of recipes' (see Chapter 4) which have been compiled by society and are easily available for the newcomer to note, comprehend and follow? Does moving from being a non-teacher to being a teacher involve simply the finding out of what teachers do and replicating such practices. Clearly, even from a common-sense point of view, this is unacceptable. While novices in any social situation will receive from others who are involved in the situation a whole variety of directives about what constitutes 'proper' behaviour in that setting, they will also carry with them to the situation personal views of the world, acquired in the past, which they will bring to bear upon these directives and thereby accept, adjust to, modify or even reject them. Furthermore, there is no guarantee that attitudes and understandings adopted one day by a pupil or a teacher will be constant for ever: ongoing interactional experience creates the demand for further reflection by the individual, the construction of new responses and the making of gradual shifts in the definition he has of his role, the roles of others and the whole meaning of the situation. Taking on a role, then, is filtered through the recipient's self-concept and is a continuous process, not a unique, easily completed event. As Mead (1934) himself observed:

> This taking-the-role-of-the-other is not simply of passing importance. It is not something that just happens as an incidental result of the gesture, but it is of importance in the development of co-operative activity. The immediate effect of such role-taking lies in the control which the individual is able to exercise over his own response.

In attempting to explore how social actors present, understand, take on and act on their interpretations of the roles of others and how the resultant patterns of conduct emerge from this inter-subjective organizing of perceptions, meanings and behaviour to form what we might call the 'interactional situation', sociologists working within the interactionist perspective employ a variety of additional concepts which enable analysis to move from simple descriptions of the unique experiences of isolated individuals towards a full description of the locations of these experiences.

As we have already noted, from this perspective man is viewed as an active participant in the social world. Through the complex and flexible processes of interaction, social identities, meanings and roles are created, maintained, modified or changed. Combined with this is an awareness of and interest in the interplay of personal, social and structural features and how these influence social situations. Thus, as Rock (1979) points out:

> The Symbolic Interactionist rejects subjective idealism because they acknowledge the stubborn facticity of the world, yet they also resist the gross empiricism which depicts objects and relations as laden with innative meaning.

Individuals act *within and towards situations*; their actions are related to their processes of interpretation, and thus a person's definition of the situation is a vital ingredient in all social interactions. It relates to what a person hopes to get out of a situation, which features within the situation are taken to be more important than others and, as Stebbins (1975) maintains:

> to put it concisely, a definition of the situation is the *meaning* an individual attaches to the ongoing events in which he finds himself. Perception or recognition of specific aspects of the environment is invariably the first step in this process, and some sort of action (or inaction) is the necessary consequence.

This process of defining the situation is very much a part of the task of 'taking the role of the other', in which the individual acts in relation to his interpretation of what he thinks others expect of him. What is important is that this experience entails conscious reflection on the part of the people concerned. Imagine a person entering a new social situation, i.e., one of which he does not have a clear definition, for example a student teacher entering a school staffroom for the first time. What factors would we need to consider to make sense of such an encounter? From the student teacher's point of view, his conduct is determined largely by his reasons for being involved in that situation and his theories about what he believes it will be like (built up through communication with other students, other teachers, and, perhaps, his tutors), the things he perceives on entering the staffroom (the physical surroundings and the clues his new acquaintances give him through their dress, gestures and manners), his understanding of what the other teachers he meets communicate to him, through their talk and their behaviour, about what they think will constitute appropriate conduct by him in the situation in which they are all engaging and, most importantly, the assessment he makes of all these inputs through reflecting upon them. In short, he constructs a definition of the situation as a basis for his action. But so do the other participants. So, to arrive at an adequate description of this little drama, the sociologist would have to comprehend both the various definitions of the situations by participants in the interaction and the ways in which these different definitions rub against each other, involving a series of negotiations of the acceptable role definitions for the different individuals involved so as to produce that totality which is the interactional setting.

It is important at this point to caution against the idea that individuals are always aware of the nature of the processes which make up their social interactions. The extent of such awareness is open to question and the social observer is, therefore, constrained to be alert not only to the overt intentions and understandings of his subjects but also to the results of unexpected events within the interaction and the unintended consequences of action. Thus, as Martin (1976) points out:

> Neither the idea that everything is negotiable nor the idea that interlocking roles are set by status within a social organization is adequate to describe the dynamics of interactions that take place in ordinary daily living.

It is through careful exploration of these dynamics which are, perhaps, revealed through coming to appreciate the differences between one partner's intentions in interaction and co-participants' interpretations and reactions to them that the 'hidden' elements of interaction are revealed.

An influential writer on this type of approach is Erving Goffman (1971) who, using metaphors drawn from the theatre, seeks to show the intricate strategies by which people endeavour to present or manage various images of themselves in social interaction. He argues:

> When an individual appears before others he will have many motives for trying to control the impression they receive of the situation.

And he attempts to show how, in a wide variety of social contexts involving several different 'audiences', people seek to exercise and maintain some degree of control over their situation so that they do not suffer the embarrassment and personal distress that results when an asserted identity is seen as a facade or sham. This 'presentation of self' is an important influence on the dynamics of social interaction, and Goffman (1971) maintains that:

> The self then, as a performed character, is not an organic thing that has a specific location, whose fundamental fate is to be born, to mature and to die. It is an effect arising diffusely from a self . . . the crucial concern, is whether it will be discredited.

Thus people are seen as being involved in attempts to manage the impression they 'give off' to others; social interaction is, therefore, about deceit and counter-deceit, about people adapting and accommodating in their endeavour to impress a definition of the situation and themselves upon others. The definition of the situation which is used as a basis of action by participants in that situation is a 'working consensus' arrived at by those involved in the specific social encounter. The level of this consensus is variable. Where people involved in a social situation share common understandings and accept the validity of each other's definitions it will be strong; however, if there is disagreement or lack of awareness by participants of their associates' interpretations, consensus will be weak. Nevertheless, some 'workable' basis for interaction must be reached if the association which gives rise to the situation is not to be terminated abruptly.

Recognition of these variations in the nature of the 'working consensus' has led interactionists to a consideration of certain techniques used by social actors to resolve those problems which arise when definitions of the situation are in conflict. Resolution can be through either negotiation or the imposition by dominant partners in the interaction of their own particular desires and designs. A great deal of the material presented earlier in this book was selected to demonstrate the extent to which the different individuals involved in schooling see this life differently, have different interests and reasons for participating in it, and gain different satisfactions from their contributions to this social experience. We have here, then, a situation which looks as if definitions of the situation are in serious competition. How is it, therefore, that life within school is able to proceed at all?

An interactionist would have to look for an answer to this question in the methods by which the people involved come to terms with this conflict of interests. One explanation of how some agreement is reached is made in terms of the enormous difficulty most individuals have in sustaining a relationship in which a lack of harmony means that continued involvement in it is more costly than profitable. An easy solution in these circumstances is for the individual to withdraw completely from the relationship. Within the school situation this remedy, although not impossible, is problematic in itself. Few teachers or pupils can take themselves out of the encounter because to do so would perhaps upset the equilibrium of other situations in which they are involved and which they would wish to preserve because of the high dividends to be secured from this involvement. Although deliberately absenting oneself from school resolves one set of conflicts, it may create new and more costly problems in other environments, e.g. in the person's interaction with parents, peers or the police. Thus the meaning of action has to be viewed in terms of the interlock between various definitions of situations which are contingent upon an individual's understanding of his place in any single situation.

Given that withdrawal has a high cost (as shown by the remarkable fact that, despite schooling's being a fairly unpleasant experience for some pupils and for some teachers, most of them battle on gamely within the boundaries of the school situation), what alternative methods for the resolution of competing definitions of the situation are routinely adopted?

First, through a series of negotiations and bargainings, a number of compromises take place. Strategies are developed by which some concessions are agreed by the various social factors involved; certain interests are renounced in return for reciprocated accommodation. An uneasy truce is reached. This may seem pessimistic, but some interactionists would argue that it is through identification and exploration of such practices that a point of intervention is revealed: in coming to know the real basis for action, we make available those areas upon which people could act in order to regain control of essential elements which influence social conduct.

Second, where compromise is unattainable, a 'workable' consensus is achieved by the most powerful partners in the interaction imposing their definitions. Hargreaves (1975), for example, lists a number of techniques teachers can and do use to make manifest their dominant position within an asymmetrical interpersonal relationship and to impose their definition upon the interaction. These include threats, appeals to reason or tradition, withholding of privileges, rewards, opportunities and mystification, and we would add to these, straightforward physical coercion. However, this kind of interpretation introduces into the discussion a concept and a form of explanation which certain critics of interactionism see as a difficult notion for the perspective to manage – the concept of power. It is argued that if, as is the case with this perspective, individuals are seen as having the freedom to define reality and to act upon their definitions, where does the ability come from which allows some individuals to make their definitions count more than those of others? As Sharp and Green (1975) have argued:

> the ability of the headmaster to influence the actions of his teachers, the ability they have to process pupils, the ability of teachers collectively to protect themselves against the felt threats of parents, lie not merely in their linguistic and conceptual superiority but in their position in the power structure. If they are linguistically and conceptually superior it is only because those who have power in the macro structure define it to be so and have given them available sanctions to reinforce their definition of reality against others.

CONCLUSION

As Hargreaves (1978) has sought to demonstrate, the interaction perspective has he power to allow us to:

1. Appreciate crucial dimensions of everyday activities.
2. Formulate a conceptual framework, a vocabulary, with which we can talk about these various dimensions with greater confidence.
3. Reflect upon the consequences of particular elements which make up everyday life.
4. Find a way into the reality of social experience with a view to changing that reality.
5. Embark upon correctionist programmes with greater awareness of how the social body upon which we are operating will react to such attempted surgery.

Nevertheless, equally important is the question of the ways in which the everyday affairs of men are related to the particular material, social and political circumstances in which they are located, specifically to the distribution of power in society. It is this kind of issue which will be considered in the next chapter.

Further Reading

Delamont, S. (1976) *Interaction in the Classroom*. London: Methuen. Describes the ways in which the perspectives outlined in this chapter have been applied to analysis and research in education.

Giddens, A. (1976) *New Rules of Sociological Method*. London: Hutchinson. This is not a book which will be easily understood by newcomers to sociology, but its importance justifies perseverance. An important book in terms of the philosophical and methodological issues raised in this chapter.

Hargreaves, D.H. (1972) *Interpersonal Relations and Education*. London: Routledge and Kegan Paul. Discusses the application to analysis and research in education of the perspectives considered in this chapter.

King, R. (1980) 'Weberian Perspectives and the Study of Education'. *The British Journal of Sociology of Education*, 1, 1. The distinctive contribution the ideas of Weber can make to the study of education is concisely reviewed in this article.

Meltzer, B., Petral, J. and Reynolds, L. (1975) *Symbolic Interactionism; Genesis, Varieties and Criticisms*. London: Routledge and Kegan Paul. A discussion of both the advantages and the problems of symbolic interactionism developed by writers who work within this tradition.

Woods, P. (ed.) (1980). *Teacher Strategies*. Beckenham: Croom Helm. The ways in which the perspectives outlined in this chapter have been applied to analysis and research in education

are to be found in both this and the following reference.
Woods, P. (ed.) (1980) *Pupil Strategies*. Beckenham: Croom Helm.

Signpost

The 1980s has produced a number of detailed accounts of teachers' and pupils' experiences of schools. Read Woods, P. (1979) *The Divided School*, London: Routledge and Kegan Paul, and try to assess:

a) how his research methodology influences the explanations about school processes, and
b) the usefulness of his observations about life in classrooms, schools and staffrooms for student teachers.

Chapter 21

The Conflict Perspective: A Marxian Approach

INTRODUCTION: CONFLICT AND POWER

In the preceding two chapters a problem has arisen which we have left unattended. Whether one is considering social behaviour at the macro level, in terms of the interrelation between individuals' actions and the structure of society, or at a situational level, in terms of the understandings, intentions and methods people use in the organization of their daily lives, the question remains of why there are some systematic social arrangements and some interactional social situations which seem to work against the interests of certain of the individuals involved and in favour of others. The central issue is concerned with explaining differences experienced by both individuals and groups in terms of their access to and ability to use resources in society and also in terms of the nature of the resources these different people have at their disposal or under their direction. These resources include material benefits and wealth, privilege, status and knowledge, and an adequate explanation of social conduct must surely be able to offer some explanation of how it is that some people, who receive only a trivial allocation of such resources, continue with their societal membership. Or, to turn the question around, how it is that some individuals can use their social association to accumulate benefits vastly superior to those enjoyed by their fellow men. The centrality of this issue to sociological debate arises from the fact that when people enter into forms of social relationships with other people, they do not only enter into an association which involves making decisions about either the moral basis for their collective lives or the ways in which this life-form is definable and has significance, they also enter into economic relationships.

We can attempt to come to terms with making an investigation of the economic dimensions of human behaviour either by establishing how the economic order is related to and, perhaps, directed by the central value system of society or, alternatively, we can try to cut into this aspect of social life by building up a perception of how people understand their economic relationships with others and their intentions in economic action. However, to an extent, to follow either course is to treat economic order as unproblematic, to assume that we know the main parameters of economic action and have only to investigate their empirical realizations. The sociological perspective which refuses to make such assumptions is that which is based upon the writings of Marx (1818–83), and in this chapter we shall be concerned with introducing two essential elements of a Marxian approach: the analysis Marx made of the economic development of social organization and the use made of this analysis in attempts to identify the main properties of the economic order prevalent in modern society (i.e. the capitalist mode of production). We shall also be concerned with outlining the impact this approach has had upon those seeking insights into the working of educational systems in modern societies and the experiences of all those involved with these systems.

However, before we turn directly to these concerns it might be helpful to explore some aspects of the broader sociological perspective in which the Marxian endeavour is sometimes located. This perspective is popularly referred to as 'the conflict perspective'. Conflict theorists have, as their point of departure for sociological analysis, the concern introduced at the beginning of Chapter 19, the Hobbesian question of how societies hold together. Unlike the Durkheimian view, which presents man as being restrained from unfettered pursuit of his own self-interest by his association with, and by the restrictions which arise from, the collective value system of society, conflict theorists view social order as being achieved through a continual process of disputed interaction between men, of sectional struggles and of the imposition of order by those who win power. Dahrendorf (1959) distinguishes between these two explanations thus:

> There is one large and distinguished school of thought according to which social order results from a general agreement of values, a *consensus omnium* or *volonté générale* which outweighs all possible or actual differences of opinion and interest. There is another equally distinguished school of thought which holds that coherence and order in society are founded on force and constraint, on the domination of some and the subjection of others.

If we accept the essential premise of the first of these schools (or consensus theory), in which individual wills and volitions are seen as being subordinated in the interest of the general good, then even fairly routine deviations from the 'normal' – strikes, petty thefts, racial disharmony, truancy from school, anti-establishment protests and opposition – become problematic. Can we, for example, explain away all such behaviours with notions of the individuals involved being victims of poor socialization, of their being ignorant of the 'common good', or of their not understanding that their welfare depends upon the successful development of the collective interest? Even more difficult to explain is the phenomenon of social change, which tends to be seen by consensus theorists as a process of gradual adaptation.

Equally, the second school of thought (conflict theory) throws up some areas requiring deeper consideration. Although the kind of routine deviations listed above are explicable in terms of individuals seeking to further their own particular causes and interests, the idea that social life is made up of a series of unruly episodes in which unrestrained individuals seek fulfilment of purely selfish motives is difficult to sustain. To manage these problems, while retaining the basic notion that human beings are driven by personal interest, conflict theorists introduce into their sociological analysis the notion of power. This notion is usually used to refer to the concerns, interests and relationships people experience in group life. Conflict theorists note that, although individuals form certain associations with like-minded others from which they derive the benefit of collective effort, the groups which emerge from such affiliations do not always coexist harmoniously because separate groups will, necessarily, pursue interests defined according to their unique perceptions of the world and according to those needs articulated through the very act of affiliating with others. Every group, if it is going to satisfy the reasons individuals have for joining it and therefore preserve itself, will be under pressure to put the interests of its members above the interests of other groups. Where these do not compete, a peaceful pluralism can be accomplished; however, where there is competition, some management of the conflict becomes necessary, and it is in these circumstances that the notion of power becomes crucial, on two levels. First, it is crucial in terms of the ability of individuals within a group to shape, direct and define the objectives and practices of the others who constitute the group, i.e. the management of intra-group conflict. Second, it is crucial in terms of the ability of informal and formalized associations of men to overcome successfully opposition from other groups, or even from other individuals, i.e. the management of inter-group conflict. John Rex (1961), in discussing the second of these levels, both identifies possible causes of inter-group conflict and points to the reasons why such tensions require some management:

> As between groups, we should first make clear the points of conflict in their separate aims. We might find that the conflict was a total one or we might find that there were areas of agreement including agreement as to how conflict might be carried on. But, given that there was a conflict of aims, we should expect each group to seek to enforce upon the other behaviour which at worst did not interfere with and at best actually promoted the achievement of its own aims. If each group did this there would be some sort of power contest using various forms of power and some sort of conflict would ensue until each side recognized that compliance to a certain degree was more profitable than a continuance of the conflict.

The attraction of conflict theory, then, is that it allows us to generate explanations of social behaviour at both the micro- and the macro-analytical levels. For example, by noting differences in interests between, say, some teachers and their head teachers, or between whole groups of pupils from common social backgrounds and the manifest aims of a system of schooling, and by proceeding to work out how these differences are either resolved or controlled, one can begin to understand how order is achieved in situations which are differently interpreted or reacted to by those participating in them. However, to accomplish this it is necessary to have some idea of the main parameters and essential techniques used in this kind of social stage-management. In other words, the assumption that these conflicts are worked through by the exercise of power constrains the social analyst to devise some conceptualization of the nature of power, the source from which it is derived and the mechanisms by which it is realized.

Precise formulations of exactly what power *is* are difficult to devise. For example, when we say teachers have *power* over their pupils, what do we mean? Are we referring to their observable practices and the extent to which they can promote their own interests and inhibit those of their pupils by actually directing behaviour, or are we referring to a more nebulous property, a force or means which provides the basis for action but the existence of which does not depend upon its exercise? Anthony Giddens

(1979) provides a definition which allows us to conceive of power in a way which enables the term to be applied to both the 'actual' and the 'potential' dimensions of the notion, when he writes:

> a person or party who wields power *could* 'have acted otherwise', and the person or party over whom power is wielded, the concept implies, *would* have acted otherwise if power had not been exercised.

He goes on to assert that:

> power . . . concerns the capability of actors to secure outcomes where the realization of these outcomes depends upon the agency of others. The use of power in interaction thus can be understood in terms of the facilities that participants bring to and mobilize as elements of the production of that interaction, thereby influencing its course.

But if power is a 'capability to secure outcomes' from where is this capability derived, and by what methods is it realized? Does the power of the teacher, say, spring from personal charisma, experience, position in the social system, superiority of knowledge, cognitive capacity and command of language, or simple physical dominance? All of these possibilities are problematic in the sense that what counts as charisma, experience, the rights and obligations of social roles and the statuses of knowledge forms is relative, contingent upon the capability of some groups to make their definitions of these elements legitimate and accepted by those members of society involved with their usage. We can, then, either resort to explaining teachers' power in terms of their physical strength (which is hardly persuasive, given the fact that in most classrooms the pupils heavily outnumber the teacher) or look for the basis upon which certain definitions are projected as the definitions *par excellence*. One explanation of how certain social groups, i.e. dominant groups, come into the possession of a capacity to define and enforce their definitions, ideas and practices as superior and proper and to impose these upon other groups, i.e. subordinate groups, is through their winning control of the basic resources essential to human beings in the creation and maintenance of their biological and social existences. To develop such an explanation it would be possible to investigate the social institutions that such dominant groups devise and manage in order to protect and further their interests (for example, the political system, the media or the education system) or their manipulation of values, knowledge and beliefs (for example, their control of accepted moralities, forms of reasoning or cultures), or the governance such groups have over the creation, distribution and usage of the concrete resources upon which men depend for survival (for example, the production and allocation of food, goods and objects of utility); in short, we could examine the capabilities groups have at a structural, ideological or material level. Marxists would argue that distribution of the first two of these resources is contingent upon the arrangements which arise from attempts men make to manage their material environment, and in the next section we shall examine the reasons for this insistence and how a consideration of the material conditions of social organization is developed in Marxian analysis into a comprehensive sociological perspective.

THE MATERIALIST CONCEPTION OF HISTORY

At the heart of Marx's analytical endeavour lies a vision of the evolution through history of forms of social organization which is based upon a belief that the essential property which characterizes human beings is their need and ability to work upon nature as they find it and thereby to transform it – or, to engage in production. Social history begins at the point when human beings first engaged in this work, and indeed, the original human attempt to produce marks the exact moment at which humankind as a specific, identifiable species is distinguishable from the rest of the animal world, when the 'human animal' transforms himself into the 'social human'. Thus the materialist view is, first and foremost, based upon the notion that human beings, lacking the physical equipment to survive nature as animals do (by having a simple, mechanical, instinctive reaction to their material environment), have to work on nature, to change, adapt to and modify the physical world, to produce a means of subsistence. In doing this, people produce and reproduce the conditions of their existence and create new situations which throw up new needs and capabilities. Through work, humans find solutions to the problem of survival, but they also create new problems in that, as they produce, they create a material world which is different from that which existed before they began to work on it. As Giddens (1971) observes, for Marx, human history is:

> a process of the continuous creation, satisfaction and re-creation of human needs. This is what distinguishes men from the animals, whose needs are fixed and unchanging. This is why labour, the creative interchange between men and their environment, is the foundation of human society.

The essential logic of relating the origin of social development and the continued impetus given to this development to humankind's attempt to control its material world is encapsulated in Engels' (1969) declaration of the distinctive feature of the materialist conception of history:

> History was for the first time placed on its real basis; the palpable but previously overlooked fact that men must first of all eat, drink, have shelter and clothing, therefore must *work*, before they can fight for domination, pursue politics, religion, philosophy, etc. – this palpable fact at last came into its historical rights.

The process of social evolution which necessarily arises from the activity 'work' is conceptualized by Marx in terms of a *dialectic*, a moving interpenetration of separate forces or forms; it is a dialectic between the individual in society (subject) and the natural and human-created material world (object) in which humans gradually come to gain control of the elements in the material world so as to satisfy their own needs, and by so doing they change both that world and their own needs: a person both makes his world and is made or shaped by it. However, through work, through production, people produce not only objects but also the conditions under which they relate and are related to others. This interrelation is founded on two elements. First, through engaging in production, humans create the need for the regulation of how they can co-operate, or not, in their productive activities. Even if people determine to produce in isolation, independently, this determination itself is a social act (it represents a decision to organize production according to a distinct rule or set of rules), the act being the basis for the formulation of a set of social relations. Second, they create the need for the regulation of the exchange of the products, for the circulation of the objects they make in their work. Whatever decision they may have reached about how they will organize production itself, in engaging in labour they create the dilemma of what to do with their products, a dilemma which becomes acute with respect to how they see others being related to these products. In developing these two sets of regulations human beings evolve a set of *relations of production* because, Marx (1958) argues:

> In production men not only act on nature but also on one another. They produce only by co-operating in a certain way and mutually exchanging their activities. In order to produce, they enter into definite connections and relations with one another and only within these social connections and relations does their action on nature, does production, take place.

Two key concepts, then, emerge: the *forces of production* (i.e. the material conditions of nature and technology, the things used for production) and the *social relations of production* (i.e. the division of labour and the market relations created by men to facilitate production and exchange), and these also stand in dialectical relationship. To enable a realistic exploration of social history to take place, Marx calls for the development of an empirical science to explore how this dialectic has differently influenced the form and structure of society through various eras and epochs of history – a science of historical materialism. His own typology of societal evolution explores how the division of labour has gradually become more differentiated and specialized:

> One thing is clear – nature does not produce on the one side owners of money or commodities, and on the other, men possessing nothing but their own labour power. This relation has no natural basis, neither is it common to all historical periods. It is clearly the result of past historical development, the product of many economical revolutions, of the extinction of a whole series of older forms of social production.

In his own portrayal of this historical development, Marx sees a gradual evolution from primitive, classless societies to modern, class-based social organization, the dynamic for which arises from the essential condition which results from men co-operating in production. The divisions of labour which pertain to this co-operation enable working groups to realize a surplus of goods over their own needs. The existence of this surplus thus creates a new condition, the potential for the development of trade, which itself creates the problems of ownership and of the establishment of the social relations necessary for the exchange of goods. The dialectical relationships, then, between human beings' productive life and their other social activities can be represented thus:

1. That from each kind of production system evolves a unique set of social relationships according to the circumstances of ownership and the social division of labour. (For example, freeman/slave, patrician/plebeian, lord/serf, guildmaster/journeyman, bourgeois/proletarian.)
2. That the form of social relationship established around production (i.e. base structure) conditions the other forms of social organization – political forms, cultural life, religion, family form, legal structure – which emerge (i.e. superstructure).
3. That classes emerge only when one group of people who stand in a common relation to production unite in a conflict with other groups of men.
4. That, most importantly, social change or the transformation from one social order to another is a result of a contradiction between existing productive forces and existing relations of production, i.e. the social relations of production become, as a

result of technological or cultural change, inadequate for the regulation of production itself. Marx (1970) observes that:

> No social order ever disappears before all the productive forces for which there is room in it have been developed and new, higher relations of production never appear before the material conditions of their existence have matured in the womb of the old society.

What might sometimes be an unintended consequence of productive activity is that it promotes the development of new technologies, inventions, ideas or instruments of production. The very appearance of these renders existing ideas and practices of production, and the forms of social relations which have emerged to support such practices, obsolete, and thus forces a change within the system. For some time societies may successfully resist the impact of these pressures; however, the momentum for the development of increasingly efficient techniques of production which will lead to the extension of humankind's mastery over nature, compels these societies to react to the existence of these new creations, to make use of them in production, and hence to change the social relations in the society to accommodate the new forms of production that emerge.

The materialist conception of history is sometimes depicted as supremely deterministic, as encapsulating a view of man and social life largely directed by economic and productive forces. Certainly Marx would have us accept that man is not free from the constraints of the material reality which he or his ancestors have created. Yet the emphasis is upon creation; as Garaundy (1970) observes, the concept:

> starts not from a negation, but from an affirmation; it affirms the autonomy of man and it involves as a consequence the rejection of every attempt to rob man of his creative and self-creative power.

By recognizing that although:

> Men make their own history, but they do not make it just as they please; they do not make it under circumstances chosen by themselves, but under circumstances directly encountered, given and transmitted from the past.
>
> Marx, 1969

we should realize that this knowledge gives us a basis for real intervention in the process of history, the principle being that an understanding of the world as it is provides the basis from which we can work for change.

PRODUCTION AND CONFLICT IN MODERN SOCIETY

Using the principles established in the materialist conception of history, Marx attempted to delineate the peculiar dynamics of that form of production which supports social organization at its most recent stage of development – the capitalist mode of production. What Marx is concerned with is the *mode* of production at a given point in time, not production in general, because, while human beings will always produce things which have utility for them, can be exchanged or can be used to support production, how this is managed is the important variable. Thus the capitalist mode of production has to be seen as a form of production which has developed out of the forms or modes which preceded it but which, nevertheless, is based upon characteristics that are unique to a specific stage of social development.

As Giddens (1971) notes, 'in Marx's view, the search for profit is intrinsic to capitalism'. In one sense the capitalist mode of production is no different from any other mode of production in that, unless a portion of the products created through production is reserved, to be converted back into the means of production (so that the 'materials' consumed in the initial phase of a production process might be replaced), the reproduction of life through production is quickly played out. In other words, any form of production needs to create a surplus of goods over those produced for consumption, in order for the cycle of production to continue. However, the capitalist mode of production *is* different from others in terms of the form this surplus takes, how it is created and, importantly, who 'owns' it.

To work towards some answers to these questions we have to recognize two basic features of the capitalist mode of production which are a direct consequence of the place the mode occupies in the overall socioeconomic development of human history. The first is that it is a process concerned with the production of commodities; the second is that the process is carried out by people with different economic interests.

Commodity production concerns people working upon nature to create objects which are not intended to satisfy their own private needs, but which can be traded or exchanged for other objects or services. What makes this kind of production the focal concern of capitalism arises from the birth and adoption of the money form as the main basis for regulating exchange between social groups or between individuals, an adoption which took place during a stage of development long before capitalism emerged as the mode of production. Marx argues that, initially, money was used as a simple and convenient device to enable people to represent the value of the different things they had produced; it was a convenient measure, but it had no intrinsic value, no 'use value' of its own. However, as the money form gradually became the universal base for calculating rates of exchange for things which do have the capability to satisfy needs, or use values, by virtue of this social function money acquired a use value of its own: it became a commodity in itself. This simple development metamorphosed the whole process of trade and exchange, because as soon as money became 'the universal material representation of wealth' (Marx, 1973) – i.e. used to calculate and to express the value of all commodities – it also became the most desirable commodity of all, and hence the circulation of commodities took on a new form. This was because the possession of the commodity 'money' became the starting and finishing point of each cycle of production. The simple exchange process of 'commodity → money → commodity' was transformed, inverted into 'money → commodity → money', and it is this cycle of transactions which forms the basis of the capitalist economic order – a buying-to-sell cycle.

Clearly, the circulation of money for money would be absurd if nothing extra or of surplus value was to be gained in the process. Why should the owner of money or capital risk his resources if there were no benefit to be derived from so doing? This surplus value, argues Marx, is created in the production of the commodities in circulation in the society, but is extracted in the process of exchange, and it derives from the difference between the 'cost' of production and the exchange value or 'worth' of the produce. To put it another way: money is laid out to buy those things necessary to produce a commodity – this represents the cost of production. Money is clawed back when these commodities are sold. For a profit to be realized the articles must be sold for more than they cost to produce. One way of achieving this would be simply to 'fix' the sale price above the cost price, but Burns (1952) draws our attention to Marx's observation that the source of profit:

> could not possibly come from capitalists selling the products above their value – this would mean that all capitalists were all the time cheating each other, and where one made a 'profit' of this kind the other necessarily made a loss, and the profits and losses would cancel each other, leaving no general profit. It therefore follows that the value of an article on the market *must already contain the profit*: the profit must arise in the course of production, and not in the sale of the product.

(our italics)

Yet it is in the sale of the product that any surplus is made real, is extracted in the form of money. However, for this money to have value it has to be converted back into commodities, and if this conversion is to be done profitably then the whole exchange cycle of 'money $\rightarrow$ commodities $\rightarrow$ money' must begin again. Thus, as Marx (1970) observes:

> The circulation of money as capital is an end in itself, for the expansion of value takes place only within this constantly renewed movement. The circulation of capital has therefore no limits.

The vital compulsion for capital to be accumulated in order for the capitalist mode of production to be maintained, then, is determined not by some subjective factor, such as greed or a passion for accumulation, but by an objective and necessary condition of the mode of production itself, commodity production.

What is it about actual production, however, that allows it to be organized so as to enable some surplus to be created? To answer this question we need to look at the way in which, through the development of history, there have emerged two groups of people whose involvement in production is sharply different. A whole host of gradual changes in social affairs – urbanization, expansion of trade, increased industrialization and commercial innovation, the development of progressively more specialized methods of manufacture – have led to increased polarization in the division of labour in society, out of which have emerged two classes who stand in opposition to each other. These are the owners of the means of production (capitalists) and the men who exist as a means of production (wage-labourers). Each class supports itself differently: capitalists by using their accumulated resources to initiate and control production by buying essential materials and hiring labour, and then selling their products, and wage-labourers by selling their labour-power to the capitalists, an arrangement to which they are compelled to agree, since they have no other means of subsistence.

Thus there is a separation between workers and their means of production; indeed, human labour becomes just another commodity necessary for production to take place. The cost of labour, like that of any commodity, is determined by the 'labour-time socially necessary' for its own production – in other words, the cost incurred by workers in producing and maintaining themselves. However, human labour-power as a commodity is unique in the sense that, although the capitalist buys it 'at its daily value', the worker is able to produce more in an average working day than is needed to meet the cost of his own subsistence. For example, suppose the daily subsistence cost of the worker is £20, and it takes an average of four hours to realize that value in production, and the average working day is eight hours; the value of commodities produced during one half of the working day is greater than that necessary for the subsistence of the worker, and is, therefore, surplus value, and is appropriated by the capitalist.

Thus the capitalist doesn't 'cheat' the worker: rather he exploits the capacity of human labour to produce more than is necessary for its own production. The worker must acquiesce in this exploitation of his labour power so that commodities necessary for his own subsistence are produced, and also to gain a wage, and the capitalist is compelled to exploit labour in order to realize surplus value so that the circulation and accumulation of capital continue.

However, to appreciate fully the impact of the kind of analysis presented above, it is important to recognize, as Bowles and Gintis (1976) argue, that:

> Capitalist production . . . is not simply a technical process; it is also a social process. Workers are neither machines nor commodities but, rather, active human beings who participate in production with the aim of satisfying their personal and social needs. The central problem of the employer is to erect a set of social relationships and organizational forms, both within the enterprise and, if possible, in society at large, that will channel these aims into the production and expropriation of surplus value.

Surplus value is increased only to the extent to which the difference between 'necessary labour' and 'surplus labour' is maximized, i.e., the degree to which the capitalist wins a prolongation of the time in which the worker is producing value or its equivalent beyond that necessary for his own reproduction. Clearly, the worker will resist attempts to extend the length of the working day and, in any case, unlimited extension of the working day, by reducing the time for activities necessary to the proper physical and social development of workers, would quickly exhaust the labour force and decrease its productivity. So, surplus labour-time has to be increased inside the normal working day. For this to happen control and manipulation of the labour process, the activities in which workers engage to produce things, are vital to the capitalist, because a reduction of the 'necessary labour-time' which will give an extension of 'surplus labour-time' is possible only through an increase in the productivity of labour.

There are several ways in which the labour process can be brought more directly under the control of capital. Marx identifies at least two. First, the way in which increased differentiation between labour skills on the part of the employer not only provides an increase in the cost benefit derived from greater co-operation in production, but also leads to increased alienation of individual workers from the fruits of their labour; in contributing to only a limited part of the total production of a commodity and thus being dependent on other workers, and ultimately the employer, for the finished production of a complete product, the worker effectively loses control of what he creates by work. Second, increased mechanization and use of technological advances in the production process also provide a means by which the employer can dominate the labour process and subjugate the worker; machines can replace workers, facilitate the employment of weaker and less skilful workers and, by replicating the activities involved in a productive task in a fixed, mechanical pattern, subordinate the worker to the machine, in the sense that his movements and pace, and the degree of mental activity involved in work are all determined by the machine.

To these two elements Harry Braverman (1974) adds a third: the application of a management structure and the principles of scientific management, which he represents as an additional weapon for the employer in his quest for increased control of the labour process in order to yield increased productivity and hence increased profit. Any form of management has the consequence of separating planning and design activities from actual production, and Braverman (1974) argues that, through scientific management, through relating the activities and organizations of production to scientific principles, capital seeks to eliminate the 'capriciousness of human labour' and the incursion of change elements from the production process. By the same token its application serves:

> to strip the workers of craft knowledge and autonomous control and confront them with a fully thought-out labour process in which they function as cogs and levers.

Thus, as we indicated at the start of this discussion, the capitalist mode of production has as its motivating force an endless quest for the maximization of profit, but to this point we can now add that this can be achieved only if the inequitable social relations of production described above are sustained and developed, so that the dominant class is able to exercise ever-increasing control over the use of labour time, the organization of the labour process and the deployment of the labour force.

To appreciate how this rather economic analysis is developed within Marxian sociological perspectives to allow for the exploration of social conduct in all its manifestations, we need to return to a point made by Bowles and Gintis in an extract quoted earlier – that capitalism is not just a technical process but a social one. From this perspective it is argued that social systems, the structure of social institutions, the creation and dissemination of organizing ideas and interpretations of the world, and even the consciousness of individuals in society, which form the basis for the everyday actions and interactions, emerge from (and work back upon) those relations essential to the production process.

Forms of political administration, legal systems, family life, communication systems, religious practices, educational processes and, importantly, the ways in which those involved in these social institutions relate to one another are all inextricably linked with the form of the social relations of production, and in capitalist society these relations are necessarily hierarchical, exploitative and antagonistic. It follows, then, that the structure and institutional arrangements of such a society will:

1.   Reflect such hierarchical relations.
2.   Serve to produce and reproduce conditions necessary to sustain it.
3.   Provide the opportunity for dominant groups to legitimize both their position and their interpretations of social order and, where necessary, to control groups which develop interests and activities contrary to their own.

Thus socialists working within a Marxian framework would attempt to explore the following:

1.   The management by capitalists and workers of the social relations of production, which will involve investigation of the nature, extent and consequences of the struggle between these groups, the historical location in which such struggles take

place and the development of the mode of manufacture which is promoted and impeded through such conflict.

2. The nature and workings of the dialectical relationship between the capital form of economic life and other social institutions and arrangements.
3. The way in which social institutions not directly concerned with production are internally organized so as to reflect, reproduce and reinforce socioeconomic relationships.
4. The overarching structure (and the principles upon which this is constructed) which allows various institutional arrangements to be interrelated.
5. The identification of correspondence and/or contradictions within institutions and both between various institutional forms of life and between these forms and the overall social structure.
6. The everyday experience individuals have of social life, and the extent to which these experiences are conditioned by or are a reaction to those hierarchic relations which have their roots in the material base.

One of the major institutions in capitalist society is the education system and, not surprisingly, its nature and working are of great interest to sociologists working with a Marxian perspective. Interestingly, Marx himself wrote very little about education although in *The Communist Manifesto* (1967) we find some indication of what he and Engels saw as an important concern for materialist analysis in this area. They assert:

> And your education! Is not that also social and determined by the social conditions under which you educate, by the intervention, direct or indirect, of society, by means of schools. The communists . . . do but seek to alter the character of that intervention and to rescue education from the influence of the ruling class.

In many ways a search for the main dimensions of this 'intervention' has formed the basis of a great deal of recent sociological work on education. It is to an exploration of some of the main features of this endeavour that we will now turn in order that the impact of the six characteristics identified above upon sociological perspectives of education might be demonstrated.

MARXIAN ANALYSIS AND THE STUDY OF EDUCATION

Although we intend that some overview of Marxist writings and ideas on education will be presented here, the reader should be aware that, as with those perspectives identified in Chapters 19 and 20, there is a considerable difference of opinion among sociologists of this persuasion about what constitutes the most appropriate analytical path. An important point of difference is between those whose main interest is exploring the structural 'fit' between the education system and the economic order (see, for example, Bowles and Gintis, 1976) and those who seek to explore the ways in which certain cultural beliefs and practices that support capitalist society are created, transmitted and reproduced within educational worlds (see, for example, Bourdieu and Passeron, 1977; Willis, 1977; Apple, 1979, 1980). However, most Marxian analysis can be seen as an attempt to identify what Apple has called 'the deep structure' of education, the ways in which the systematic arrangements of schooling and the day-to-day organization and routine activities of life in classrooms (and also the ways in which both of these impinge upon the social experience of teachers and pupils) are explicable through reference to the distribution of power in society. What distinguishes Marxian analysis of education, then, is that schooling is seen not as a process which serves to socialize new members of society into the collectively established, consensual moral order, simply as the outcome of the rule-governed creative interaction of local groups of social actors, but rather as a phenomenon which is related most profoundly to the distribution of resources and opportunities in a society. As Corrigan and Frith (1977) maintain:

> The importance of education for capitalism is clearly revealed by the state's action in taking control of educational institutions and expanding them; the question for Marxists is *why*.
> We can take as given that education does fulfil a basic function for capitalism, the task is to understand this function. But there is a further task for Marxists; to relate this theoretical understanding to day-to-day education practice.

Of course, in an effort to answer these questions Marxian analysis of education has attempted to explore a wide variety of areas in which it might be shown that educational affairs are influenced by the ideologies or direct intervention of socially and politically dominant groups – for example, at the level of educational provision, the social relations established in contemporary schools, the organization of knowledge and the curriculum, the links between educational and industrial sectors in the creation and application of new knowledge and technology, or the cultural ethos on which education is predicated – and although it is not possible to examine in detail all such work, to capture the flavour of this kind of analysis we include below a brief description of some of it.

Without doubt, many sociologists of education in Britain have been greatly influenced by the thoughts of Bowles and Gintis, particularly as developed in their book *Schooling in Capitalist America* (1976). In what they describe as an attempt to construct a political economy of education, Bowles and Gintis isolate many features of schooling in modern capitalist societies which, they claim, correspond to the 'social relations of work roles' and thus, they argue, education can be seen as a crucial element in the preparation of individuals for their role in the world of work. In general terms, they see education functioning both as a transmission and as a control mechanism in the reproduction of the social relations which underpin the capitalist mode of production. First, education plays an important part in forming the skills and attitudes that workers need in order to be fully productive in work; second, education:

> helps defuse and depoliticize the potentially explosive class relations of the productive process and thus serves to perpetuate the social, political and economic conditions through which a part of the product of labour is expropriated in the form of profits.

The bureaucratic and hierarchically structured order which characterizes school is seen by Bowles and Gintis as the main dimension by which pupils' personal development and learned behavioural characteristics are nurtured in a specific way, i.e. their socialization is in a climate which celebrates and is based upon relationships of dominance and subordination, and is thus compatible with the social order of the workplace. That such an order is perpetuated in British schools is supported by studies of schooling in this country. With regard to teacher–pupil relations, for example, Sharp and Green (1975), in their study of a progressive primary school, found that even in a setting based upon a child-centred ideology, the power of the teacher to shape pupils' identities and create a stratification system within the classroom is enormous:

> The teacher is crucial to this process not simply because she is the reality definer but because . . . she can be regarded as a scarce resource in that she possesses and can transmit the means whereby the careers of pupils can be facilitated or held back.

Paul Willis (1977), on the basis of his study of life in an urban comprehensive school, argues that the authority of teachers is not merely a consequence of their being given control over pupils by the state, but must be seen as part of a collection of assumptions about what education entails, an educational paradigm. Teachers, he notes, control use of space, property and time, dictate the rules of interpersonal relationships, and, most importantly, see and represent themselves as controllers of 'what is implied to be the scarce and valuable commodity of knowledge.'

Bernstein (1975) argues that even the ritual order of schools, which serves as a symbolic representation of the prevailing value system of the institutions, similarly works 'to deepen respect for and impersonalize authority relations'. The school assembly, house rituals, the prefect system, setting and streaming practices all remind pupils and teachers of their place within the hierarchy and, more importantly, that a hierarchical structure is in legitimate operation.

At a different structural level, the differential ranking of types of educational routes (public school/state; grammar/comprehensive/modern; top stream/bottom stream; university/polytechnic/Further Education College/apprenticeship), the differential patterns of socialization which operate in differentiated routes (individual responsibility being emphasized at the 'higher' levels, close supervision of students being the norm at the 'lower') and the differentiated allocation of resources between ranked sectors of education are also seen by Bowles and Gintis as emphasizing a hierarchical rule and the individual's place within the hierarchy.

Perhaps the most crucial aspect of education which can be seen as defining hierarchy as normal is the way in which educational knowledge, the central concern of schooling, is selected, classified and evaluated. Bernstein (1971) has argued that 'educational knowledge is the major regulator of the structure of experience', and that it can be categorized according to the strength of its classification (i.e. how units of knowledge are related to other units) and its frame (i.e. how the transmitters and receivers of knowledge are related and interrelated). He suggests that in English education knowledge is strongly classified or bounded, although the system allows some weakening of frame. The idea of strong insulation of content areas of educational knowledge means that it is distributed and evaluated 'through a series of well-insulated subject hierarchies'. This hierarchy permeates the structure of the curriculum (which represents a movement towards 'higher' forms of knowledge), the educational careers of students (which involves a movement towards increased specialization) and even the relationships of teachers and pupils (who are ranked according to subject and mastery of subject). Bernstein (1971) argues, however, that it is necessary to relate 'patterns internal to educational institutions to the external and social antecedents of such patterns'.

It may well be, therefore, that, taking into consideration the way knowledge is organized in English education, there is a case to be made for viewing the dialectical relationship between education and the capitalist mode of production in terms of how the mode shapes social patterns. Whatever the nature of the relationship might be Bowles and Gintis would still maintain that school work – the acquisition of knowledge – is very like productive work: fragmented, differentiated and not in control of the worker.

The most developed part of Bowles and Gintis's argument about the role of education in the transmission of behavioural characteristics important for capital to maintain and extend control of the labour process concerns the way in which schools foster and reward certain personality traits. Using data from research by Meyer (1972), they attempt to discover the relationship between certain personality traits and school success, as measured by ability to achieve high marks or grades, which schools use as a major motivational device. They note that, even when IQ is held constant, there is a high correlation between pupils' ability to achieve a high 'grade-point-average' and their possession of personality characteristics of submission to authority, passivity, conformity and perseverance, and a negative correlation between such success and traits of creativity, aggression and independence. Comparing this data with that presented by Edwards (1976) in a study of the characteristics valued by managers in industry, Bowles and Gintis observe that managers rate negatively the last three traits in the school research. Thus, they conclude (with some qualification in terms of the influence of other personality attributes) 'the personality traits rewarded in schools seem to be rather similar to those indicative of good job performance in the capitalist economy'.

As was noted earlier, Bowles and Gintis also argue that schools act as control agencies by defusing potential conflict which might arise if workers were to question the legitimacy of their occupational placing or status. It is clear that occupation placement and the levels of qualifications obtained through schooling are increasingly related (see, for example, A. H. Halsey's recent study of education and sociomobility in Great Britain in A. Halsey and J. Karabel (1977)). This is traditionally explained and justified by reference to the notion that educational attainment represents an objective measure of cognitive merit. However, this justification is contradicted by evidence that suggests little correlation between educational achievement and productivity (Berg, 1973) or between occupational status and cognitive skills (Bowles and Gintis, 1976). Bowles and Gintis explain this contradiction by asserting that the idea of educational success being determined by merit or superior cognitive ability is an illusion fostered in the schools: educational success is much more likely to be determined by the possession of the personality traits listed above and by conformity to the school norms, characteristics acquired, they argue, in family and home backgrounds. The systems of education, streaming structures and grading devices, while claiming to advance those possessing some objective characteristics of merit, in fact can be shown as rewarding behavioural characteristics already possessed, and in one sense exclusively, by individuals from a specific social background, i.e. the middle class. (See Chapter 24 of this book for details of research into the relationship between social class and educational success and failure.) Thus, Bowles and Gintis contend, 'the legitimation process in education assumes a largely symbolic form'. That it is symbolic is important, in that it preserves class-based inequality without the foundation of this inequality being brought into serious debate: it both preserves and legitimates this inequality.

In a review of their book, Gintis and Bowles (1980) rephrase one of the more important features of their analysis thus:

> the current relationship between education and economy is ensured not through the *content* of education but its *form*; the social relations of the educational encounter. Education prepares students to be workers through a *correspondence* between the social relations of production and the social relations of education.
>
> Like the division of labour in the capitalist enterprise, the educational system is a finely graded hierarchy of authority and control in which competition rather than co-operation governs the relations among participants, and an external reward system – wages in the case of the economy, and grades in the case of schools – holds sway.

In the same paper, they also recognize a certain weakness in the 'correspondence principle'. As Sarup (1978) has noted, Bowles and Gintis tend to assume that social institutions like schools have a massive capacity for achieving comprehensive realization of their 'functions', overemphasizing the constraining influence of social structure to the neglect of an examination of the micro-sociological issues like the individual's response to these pressures or consideration of the ways in which 'consciousness' in social actors is created, realized and maintained in everyday life. Such a response is important to Marxian analysis because an essential feature of the perspective is that capitalist social relations of production inevitably allow for the development of contraditions. The existence of distinguishable and irreconcilable social groups upon which the mode of production depends also means that each group can and will create cultural forms and life-worlds which are based upon their different definitions of reality and relationships with the material world. What is needed, therefore, is an extension of the correspondence theory that enables the student of educational life to account for not only the correspondence between education and the economy but also the struggles in which individual people engage in their daily experiences when they encounter contradictory expectations, pressures or definitions. We need to be able to decide, for example, whether those pupils who passively accept the label 'educational failure' and their placement low down in the educational and occupational hierarchy do so as a response to the message of schooling or, alternatively, as a response to a communication which has little to do with education and its directives and signals, and may well contradict them.

In *Learning to Labour*, Willis (1977) goes some way towards filling this gap in the work of Bowles and Gintis. His basic concern is with questioning why the illusion of people being ranked according to objective criteria of merit (or meritocratic stratification) works. It is absurd, he argues, to assume blind acceptance of the illusion, since educational and occupational 'failures' would thus be involved in judging their own position by reference to their own relative stupidity, and hence individuals in the lowest stratum 'would scarcely rate a score for being alive'. Rather, Willis suggests that the boys in his study, 'the lads', 'the educational failures' and members of the school counter-culture, far from being forced into positions of subordination, make a voluntary 'choice' to reject school and to accept manual work as their occupational destiny, and that the origins of this decision-making are to be found outside the education system, in the cultural conditions of their working-class origin. The working class, far from being members of a culture which is shaped, directed and supremely controlled by dominant group interests and machinations, develop and create their own cultural activities, their own interests and understandings and their own 'lived-out experiences'. Contradictions inherent in capitalism make this unavoidable. In doing this they achieve two things. First, they provide a basis for action, a logic for individuals within the culture. Thus, for example, attitudes and conduct at work and school have their roots not simply in life in the institutions but in the ideologies and practices groups create as their class culture. Willis (1977) argues:

> this class culture is not a neutral pattern . . . It comprises experiences, relationships, and ensembles of systematic types of relationship which not only set particular 'choices' and 'decisions' at particular times, but also structure, really and experientially, how these choices come about and are defined in the first place.

Second, they provide for the possibility of what Willis calls 'a partial penetration' – the creation of a perception which enables the reality of the conditions of social life, be they inequitable, exploitative or whatever, to be exposed. As Apple (1980) explains, with reference to the educational context:

> By penetration, he (Willis) means those instances where students have developed responses to schools and work that see the unequal reality they will face. Their rejection of so much of the content and form of day-to-day educational life bears on the almost unconscious realization that, as a class, schooling will not enable them to go much further than they already are. The culture the lads create inside and outside the school acutally constitutes a rather realistic assessment of the rewards of the obedience and conformism which the school seeks to extract from working class youths.

Now, while the analysis of both working-class cultural forms and penetration that Willis provides is complex and subtle in nuance, the important theoretical point he establishes is that explorations of pupils' school experience cannot be made simply in mechanistic terms of their being conditioned and constrained by the system. Rather it has to take into account a realization that attitudes and conduct in social life (including that of the school) are not mechanically reproduced but are the product of an interplay between:

1. The dominant ideologies and interests of institutions.
2. Those contradictory features and expectations associated with such institutions.
3. That degree of autonomy of individuals which has been created by their active engagement within or upon institutions and which arises from the consciousness that the individual carries from his/her own cultural setting into institutional life.

While the mode of production remains the most profound influence upon both the structural organization of society and its institutional arrangement and upon the settings in which cultural forms and penetrations are created, human behaviour is not to be regarded as a simple response or reaction to either of these but as arising from the dynamic association between them. In these terms, then, an analysis of education that attempts to investigate how the system and practices of schooling serve to produce and reproduce the social relations necessary for the maintenance and development of the capitalist mode of production cannot assume any simple 'correspondence'. Certainly, the choice Willis's 'lads' make does work to support this reproduction. But if choices are available, so are alternative outcomes. Recognition of the importance of this last point has led Reynolds and Sullivan (1980) to call for a socialist sociology of education which brings together Marxian analysis at the cultural and structural levels, and in making this exhortation they remind us of one of the most important features of Marxian endeavour: its optimistic vision. Thus, they assert:

> The adoption of a Marxist sociologist perspective, then, would suggest an urgent need for rapprochement between uncontextualized micro level analyses that neglect to focus on societal constraints and rather abstract . . . macro level accounts that grant human consciousness and action little independence from the societal material base. Man can, and classical Marxists are quite clear on this point, affect his development and his surroundings as well as being affected by them.

CONCLUSION

The perspective with which this chapter has been concerned is distinguishable from other sociological stances by the central place it affords to and the specific explanations it offers of the nature, source, exercise and distribution of power in society. While the writers who work within this perspective are interested in understanding and articulating the contradictions and conflicts that are endemic to a class-divided society, they also share an attitude to sociological investigation that is premised upon a desire for change. What is important for our purposes, however, is that such an attitude arises from the basic vision of human beings and society upon which this perspective is based. Humans are seen, at one and the same time, as both the creators of their social world and a product of the systematic social arrangements which have emerged during the history of collective behaviour. A major task of this type of sociological analysis, therefore, is to facilitate humankind's creative potential by increasing people's understanding of the real workings of the social system: in short, to demystify the world at the level of both action and structure.

Further Reading

Corrigan, P. (1979) *Schooling and the Smash Street Kids*. London: Macmillan.
Sarup, M. (1978) *Marxism and Education*. London: Routledge and Kegan Paul. A most helpful overview of how Marxist ideas have been developed within the field of education.
Young, M. and Whitty, G. (1977) *Society, State and Schooling*. Lewes: Falmer Press. An illustration of how Marxist ideas are applied in the field of education.

Signpost

It is important that one recognizes that different Marxist critiques of schooling and educating emphasize different aspects of what we have generally described as 'materialist' analysis. Bowles, S. and Gintis, H. (1976) *Schooling in Capitalist America*, London: Routlege and Kegan Paul, stress the importance of the hidden curriculum of schooling in the reproduction of the social relations of production. Willis, P. (1977) *Learning to Labour*, Farnborough: Saxon House, explores how 'the lads', a group of working-class boys in a secondary school, respond to the ideologies of schooling. And in the book produced by the Centre for Contemporary Cultural Studies (1979) *Unpopular Education*, London: Hutchinson, you can find a superb discussion of how *the state* is implicated in the manipulation of educational enterprises.

Chapter 22

Doing Research in Schools and Classrooms

TAKING A STANCE

So what do you think of this book so far? You might have dipped into earlier chapters and come across stories about how everyday events in schools and classrooms are mysteriously created through the interactions of teachers and pupils. You might have read whole sections, maybe as part of a course assignment or in preparation for seminars and discussions about different perspectives of educating or about different accounts of the effects of day-to-day activities in schools. But ask yourself this. What are *your feelings* about the stories, the analyses, the accounts of life in classrooms you have been given in other parts of this narrative?

Why are you reading this now? What are you hoping for? How do you think we feel in writing these accounts, these stories? What hopes and fears do you think we have about educating? Crucially, when you are testing your visions and views of schooling against the ones we offer in this book, can you detect any shared understandings, any meeting points?

If you find these questions difficult to answer, or if they disturb or puzzle you, you are already into the kind of experiences which challenge anyone concerned with analysing social life, with producing accounts of social behaviour, with doing research. The point of the questions is this. Even something as commonplace as reading a book like this, or in writing a text like we are doing, is a complex act in which we invest our unique personal ambitions and interests and to which we bring our own singular interpretations, backgrounds and understandings. You might be reading this text to prepare for an exam or to structure an essay or to help you think about your actions and experience in the classroom – or simply because it's a prescribed book. Some of the accounts you read might amuse you or make you angry; they may cause you to rethink some of your beliefs about educating or to act differently in the classroom – or they may leave you cold. And what about us? What draws us into this attempt to put certain ideas about educating before you, and how do these interests influence our selection and interpretation of the stories about schooling we introduce? All difficult questions. Nevertheless, whatever it is that motivates any of us involved in the present dialogue, it is certain that how we see the activity and what we want from it will shape how we respond and what we make with it. Or, to put it another way, our behaviour, our actions, our strategies for dealing with even quite routine experiences like reading a book or writing a text are not independent of the stance we adopt towards such an experience – how we make sense of it, how we interpret the conduct of others involved, how we evaluate the experience. In fact, quite the contrary. Each and every one of our daily actions and interactions are fundamentally dependent on our subjective understanding and interpretations, our world-view. Indeed, as we suggested in a previous chapter, 'The Action Perspective', it's difficult to imagine how we could engage in social interaction at all without constant recourse to the various views, definitions and motives we hold, to the personal beliefs and assumptions, hopes and fears we cling to and which we use to make sense of our experiences and to direct our behaviour.

In interaction, then, we constantly theorize about social life, about our own place in daily affairs and about how we can best cope in each of the fresh and familiar situations we encounter. And as we theorize, we develop a stance – a personal perspective of what social life is about, of possible lines of action in specific circumstances, of what counts as a problem for us in a situation and what counts as a solution.

It is, of course, one thing to recognize that everyday life in seminars, in classrooms, in colleges and in schools, or anywhere, is produced by those involved in it negotiating how they will conduct their affairs according to their personal ideas of what it is all about and what they want from the situation. It is quite another thing to find a way of producing narratives about such affairs, of creating stories that illuminate the darker and more mysterious features of these encounters, of doing research which keeps faith with the basic recognition that social events are built upon people's common-sense knowledge and motives. If we are to hold true to an appreciation of the crucial importance *subjective* understanding and interest has for human behaviour and experience, then researching social actions and social situations is made difficult in at least two significant ways. First, we have to discover research strategies which allow us to get close enough to those we are studying or working with to be able to establish an appreciative understanding of *their* view of the activities and circumstances in which they are involved, close enough to be able to glimpse both the idiosyncratic and the shared preoccupations, values and interpretations of the 'insider'. And we can work towards this by always being alert to the danger of substituting our (observer) versions and interpretations of what we see happening for those accounts and evaluations held and acted upon by those (insiders) who are making it happen. Second, we have to face up to the fact that doing research is itself a social act. Real, live people are both the subjects and the doers of investigations of human behaviour, and the doers, the researchers, bring to their investigations their own views, hopes and fears. They carry out their studies at particular moments in history, in particular material circumstances, and they cannot suddenly switch off their personal predilections and purposes and stop being human in the name of 'objective' research. To imagine, therefore, that a first priority in starting out on a piece of social research is for the researcher to confront the problem of whether she or he has an 'objective' approach and technique *or* one based on values, on commitment and personal motives, is a rather pointless concern. For such a dilemma to exist, observes Becker (1970):

> one would have to assume, as some apparently do, that it is indeed possible to do research that is uncontaminated by personal and political sympathies

And he continues by arguing that:

> the question is not whether we should take sides, since we inevitably will, but rather whose side are we on?

For educational research, this question from Becker seems particularly pertinent. Educating is never a neutral or mechanical activity, in which all that matters is that we establish the right inputs, press the right buttons and check the end-product. If it were, doing educational research would be no more difficult than driving a car. Rather, as has been clearly demonstrated in the earlier chapters of this book, what makes educating both exciting and frustrating is the infinite number of choices and decisions we keep on having to make about matters like the needs of pupils, our motives in assessing work, on the use of time and space and words in schools, about teaching materials, methods, and so on. And each of our decisions, each of the strategies we choose to implement our plans, reflects our interests-in-hand, our different beliefs about what we hope to achieve, our different ideas about ways of getting there and our different fears of possible, unintended outcomes of our actions. And there is certainly no universal consensus about the goals, methods or pitfalls of educating. In teaching and in learning, we take a stance. But neither do we come 'uncontaminated' to the study, the analysis, of educational processes. Wanting to find out what's going on in schools and classrooms might be inspired by a desire to make life with 2A manageable or by a worry about the effects on education of certain government policies or by a dream of academic or professional fame and fortune – but it is never without purpose. Further, whatever obvious or hidden motives a researcher might have, she or he brings to the research a biography, a history, a set of sympathies which provides her or him with the means of making some sense of the affairs under scrutiny, with ideas about lines of investigation and with the basis for interpreting what's going on.

Educational research, then, involves two kinds of subjectivity: the subjectivity of the 'insiders', the people producing educational events, and the subjectivity of the observer, the researcher. With this in mind, let us return to Becker's question of whose side we are on. This is made doubly difficult. How can we get to know which 'side' those we are studying are on and, at the same time, reveal to ourselves the ways in which our 'personal and political sympathies' permeate our studies? We would like to suggest that one way forward is to reduce Becker's large question into three smaller ones, and to use these to interrogate each episode of our research activities. The three, interrelated, questions we suggest are these:

- By whom is the research being done?
- For whom is the research being done?
- For what purpose is the research being done?

Obviously, this list is not exhaustive. Probably, you will want to propose alternative versions. In what follows, however, we will use these questions to discuss ways of dealing with subjectivity in different stages of the educational research process. One note of caution. Most investigations of schools and classrooms do not follow the 'tidy' plan we use to explore the difficulties of doing educational research. As Pollard (1985) admits, the process involves difficulties, uncertainties and setbacks and is, itself, a learning experience, not easily contained in neat, preplanned stages and sequences.

STARTING OUT

The typical image of the educational researcher is very like the 'spy' character with which we began the discussion in this part on sociological perspectives – an outsider looking in, motivated by concerns which are different from those on whom she or he is 'spying' and often remote or coldly detached from the everyday struggles, ambitions and troubles of those in the schools and classrooms being investigated. To a large extent this image, often quite a reasonable portrayal, has gained sway because of the patterns employed by educational researchers in 'getting started' on research, or, to put it more formally, because of the traditions established in the formulation and selection of research problems. The history of sociological research in education is littered with projects in which the 'issue' which gave energy and purpose to the research has been determined and defined by individuals one step or more removed from the world of those who were making schooling happen and with scant attention to how the researcher's version of educational 'problems' might relate to the practical concerns of teachers and pupils. It has been frequently taken for granted that teachers must share a concern that researchers had with constructing theories about the impact of culture, family life, mobility norms, childrearing practices, and the like, on educational performance and achievement. Or, it has been frequently assumed that teachers will recognize the value of empirical investigations and explanations of how knowledge is defined in the education system, or of the organization of schools and learning situations. As a result, the levels of problems given priority in research projects have:

1. Often been derived from the major concerns facing policy-makers and planners rather than teachers.
2. Often been associated with a view of educational 'troubles' which emphasized a supposed failure in the schooling system, or an inefficiency or inadequacy on the part of individuals and groups working within schools.
3. Often been selected because they seemed to provide an opportunity to further a general interest about education, widespread in sociological circles, which rested on the desire to promote greater justice through piecemeal social engineering and school reform.

Now, any one of the above motivations might be defended as wholly laudable, with general appeal to teachers. The point is that to exclude educational practitioners – teachers, students, pupils, administrators – from the process in which research problems are selected and formulated almost inevitably produces a chain of consequences which either distort the research or which make researching futile. First, this kind of exclusion is either based on or lends support to the view that analysis and practice (or researching and teaching) are distinct, separate activities, requiring different skills and techniques and involving different perceptions of the schools and classrooms in which they take place. Analysis is concerned with theory; practice is to do with action. Since teachers have neither the time, the opportunity nor (presumably) the skills to pursue research, it follows that 'theory' is something created by educationalists and researchers. Once this absurd division of educational labour is given currency, the path which leads initially to mutual disregard between teachers and researchers and eventually to mutual distrust becomes dangerously seductive. Using Lampert's (1984) observations, we can trace the kind of outcomes likely when the separation between research and teaching is established at the very beginning of an analytical project. The following set of assumptions would seem to pertain:

1. Theory is that which is created by professional academics and researchers.
2. Teachers, therefore, need to use the language of theorists both to define problems and understand solutions.
3. Teachers think, but they do not think critically.
4. Teachers think, but it is low-level thinking.
5. Teachers undertake personal inquiries within their classrooms but these do not constitute proper research.

What makes this particular set of assumptions objectionable is not just that they are wrong but also the damage caused by those who, in writing educational reports and critiques, operate as if they were true. What makes them wrong and what makes them dangerous?

To start out on research with a belief that teachers can't, don't or won't theorize about their work, their experiences and their achievements is to adopt a very strange view indeed of what teaching entails – suggestive of teaching being a series of robotic acts involving the application of unproblematic rules and procedures and the simple implementation of clearly defined and agreed strategies and principles. Ah, were it so easy! In fact, teaching is just the opposite – problematic, full of uncertainty, and challenging teachers to draw on their own resources to cope as best they can with the steady flow of decisions and interpretations they are required to make and to act upon. Andy Hargreaves (1978) gives some idea of the significance of teachers' interpretative work, of their decision-making involvement, in his description of just *one* of their interactive roles, as 'processors of the curriculum':

> Teachers are the immediate processors of the curriculum for the child. They are the evaluators of pupils' academic work and the assessors of their overall ability. Teachers are the immediate adjudicators of children's moral worth and the direct arbiters of the 'appropriateness' of their everyday behaviour. It is teachers most immediately and perhaps most significantly who therefore create, transmit and attempt to impose definitions of children as successes or failures, ideal pupils or deviants.

Daily, teachers operate in a variety of situations in which there exist no preprogrammed 'answers' to their concerns, but rather, where they have to decide upon their own individual aims and purposes, where they have to check-out the situation and select an approach from the many available, and where they have to put that 'approach' to work and evaluate the results in terms of their original aims. They also have to live with the consequences of their deliberations and their decisions. In effect, teaching demands that teachers routinely engage in effective research; isolating problems, following up hunches on ways of coping with these problems and sifting the evidence to assess the validity of their particular 'hunches' or theories. True, these research moments are fleeting and often expressed in terms like 'Does it work or solve the immediate pragmatic interests?', but that doesn't mean that they are either lacking a critical edge or are necessarily low level.

But the dangers of the separation between researchers and teachers which arises where, to use the distinction suggested by Young (1971), researchers 'take' educators problems and 're-make' them to suit their own research purposes, is that students and teacher gradually become more and more suspicious and uneasy about the alleged connection between what researchers say and do and the realities of school life. Educational theory comes to be regarded as being too remote from schools and classrooms. Researchers come to be seen as exploiting schools with little, if any, return for the teacher. And, as Burgess (1980) warns, the language in which theory and research literature is couched comes to be seen, at best, as threatening and, at worst, as incomprehensible. Bolster (1985) offers the following possible explanation of why it is that research on education and teaching has had so little influence on practice or is viewed with suspicion by teachers:

> The major reason, in my opinion, is that most such research, especially that emanating from top-ranked schools of education, construes teaching from a theoretical perspective that is incompatible with the perspective teachers must employ in thinking about their work. In other words, researchers and school teachers adopt radically different sets of assumptions about how to conceptualize the teaching process. As a result, the conclusions of much formal research on teaching appear irrelevant to classroom teachers – not necessarily wrong, just not very sensible or useful. If researchers are to generate knowledge that is likely to affect classroom practice, they must contrive their inquiries in ways that are much more compatible with teachers' perspectives.

So, is there an approach to educational research which would enable us to make a constructive response to the problems we have sketched so far in this chapter and, maybe, overcome some of the more vexatious issues? Reviewing the discussion so far, we would suggest that such an approach would have to satisfy the following requirements:

– It would have to recognize the impact of subjectivity on the process of educating and on the study of those processes; ideally, it would be sensitive to the belief succinctly stated by Shotter (1982) that 'there is a sense of knowing something from the "inside" which is quite different from that knowledge we may have of things from the outside'.
– It would have to provide an opportunity for 'outsiders' and insiders to get into purposeful dialogue and shared enterprises to do with the design of research concerns, analytical processes and the building of explanations and theories.
– It would have to allow for the identification and articulation of the kinds of personal commitment, the 'sides', which those doing research are acting upon.
– It would have to be used as a basis for implementing new practices or for starting fresh inquiries.

We believe that such an approach does exist. Indeed, it is an approach which developed as a direct attempt to confront the kinds of issues we have been discussing. It is variously called 'classroom-based research', 'the teacher-researcher movement', 'teacher-based research' or, more frequently, *Action Research*, and draws inspiration from the pioneering work of the late Lawrence Stenhouse. Starting with the assumption that teachers are already 'problem-solvers', 'inquirers' and 'self-evaluating professionals', the approach of Action Research is to extend and activate the idea that teachers' theorizing about *their* practices can be enhanced by research methodology *and* can contribute to the creation of theory that focuses on school and classroom interaction and which can be used to interrogate larger theories and ideas about the workings of educational systems or public policy. Research techniques merge, but the essential emphasis in Action Research is based on a relationship between classroom teachers, students, teacher-educators and social science research which is best described as a *collaboration*. Look at the definitions of Action Research below and try to determine your own answers to the questions of by whom research is being done, for whom and to what purpose, questions which are implicit in the statements, quoted in Hopkins (1985):

> Action Research . . . is about the systematic study of attempts to improve educational practice by groups of participants by means of their own practical actions and by means of their own reflection upon the effects of those actions.
>
> Ebbutt (1983)

> Action Research is a form of self-reflective enquiry undertaken by participants in social (including educational) situations in order to improve the rationality and justice of
> (a) their own social or educational practices,
> (b) their understanding of these practices and
> (c) the situations in which the practices are carried out.
> It is most rationally empowering when undertaken by participants collaboratively, though it is often undertaken by individuals, and sometimes in cooperation with outsiders.
>
> Kemmis (1983)

RESEARCH IN ACTION: ACTION IN RESEARCH

If you have sorted out the basic aims of Action Research, you are now probably asking what it looks like in practice and how it is done.

Participants in Action Research generally start with (often loosely defined) worries, irritations or puzzles about their classroom experience which they want to understand and change, or with ideas about new teaching methods or materials that they or the group to which they affiliate want to try out. Sometimes hypotheses are formed about the nature of the 'problem' or about strategies suitable to solve whatever dilemma is being acted upon.

Then the action-and-research twin initiative begins. The participants begin to implement their action programmes, and as they do so they begin to reflect on and explore the 'theories' they hold about themselves, the material, the pupils, the situation, the school, learning, pupil responses – whatever elements seem pertinent to the action 'problem' being worked through. 'Theories' to explain the progress of a project are generated, checked-out, worked into the project, and so on – the end in view being the generation of practical, usable theories rather than the testing or application of existing theories.

But how, you might ask, is data collected from which working theories are generated and in what ways are theories checked, tested or scrutinized? How is the 'research' bit done? Action Research, whilst systematic and thoughtful, tends to be essentially pragmatic in the selection of research recipes or data collection and evaluation techniques adopted. A rule of thumb would be, if it helps you understand your situation and further your action components, then use it, albeit critically and reflectively. For example, Rob Walker (1985) lists the following as techniques used in the Ford Teaching Project, a programme mounted by teacher and researchers wanting to explore their experience and problems of what the teachers described as 'inquiry' and 'discovery' approaches to teaching and learning. It is worth reading the full discussion Walker provides of the advantages and disadvantages of the various research techniques used, which he lists as:

Summary of Classroom Research Techniques

Method	Administration and equipment
1. Questionnaire	Outsider – teacher/Question sheet
2. Questionnaire	Teacher – child/Question sheet
3. Questionnaire	Outsider – child/Question sheet
4. Observation	Teacher – self
5. Observation	Outsider – teacher/Tape-recorder, notebook, camera, documents or whatever the observer requires
6. Observation	Outsider – child/Tape-recorder, activity list, inventory
7. Tape-recorder	Teachers/Cassette recorder
8. Tape-recorder	Outsider/Casette recorder
9. Slides	Teacher/Camera and accessories
10. Video TV	Cameramen/Expensive equipment
11. Question analysis	Teacher – child/Question analysis sheet
12. Field notes	Teacher/Notebook
13. Standard assessment tests	Teacher – child/Tests
14. Interview	Teacher – child
15. Interview	Outsider – teacher
16. Interview	Outsider – child
17. Case study	Teacher/Any methods available to the teacher

Clearly, each technique, like any research tool, needs to be sharpened, assessed and evaluated – in Action Research a key element is the purchase the method gives to the action element in the enterprise – and the use of a multiplicity of techniques will yield vast quantities of data. But teachers and researchers who participate in this kind of educational enterprise are encouraged to generate their own categories for handling data and to attempt the techniques of TRIANGULATION, of contrasting the 'messages' found in data collected through different methods or from different participants or as seen by different analysts. Perhaps the best way in which we can introduce the distinctive features of Action Research is to ask you to consider how it compares with other ways of involving teachers in research and of developing methods of inquiry about life in schools and classrooms. To do this, we ask you to contrast the lines of action

Figure 22.1   Classification of a range of insider activity currently occurring in UK schools

suggested in the model (Fig. 22.1), designed by Ebbutt (1982) and reproduced in Walker (1985):

It seems to us that Action Research offers attractive and promising opportunities for both teachers and researchers. But what do you think? And why?

Further Reading

As we have only sketched the bare characteristics of Action Research, you might like to consult the following two excellent texts in which both techniques and commitments are discussed, and which offer many illustrations.

Hopkins, D. (1985) *A Teacher's Guide to Classroom Research*, Milton Keynes: Open University Press.
Walker, R. (1985) *Doing Research: A Handbook for Teachers*, London: Methuen.

Chapter 23

Sociology and Educating

ROLAND MEIGHAN

INTRODUCTION

The relationship between sociology as an academic discipline and the processes and institutions of educating is not clear cut. There are several questions involved here:

1. Why are sociologists interested in education?
2. What understandings can educators gain from sociological studies?
3. Is a sociological approach to education linked with political radicalism?
4. Is the outcome of sociological investigation a prescription for action?
5. Are the findings more significant for educational administrators, for teachers, or for some other grouping?

Although the answers to the above questions will vary with the perspective adopted, there are some common features that can be proposed. Some of these features are derived from a key premise that underpins most attempts to define sociology. It is that personal conduct and social life are significantly influenced by group life, group pressures, norms, rules and group cultures. The strength of these influences is a matter of dispute, as the previous four chapters have indicated.

The extent to which sociology has recently been interpreted as a liberating study has perhaps surprised many of its practitioners. Sociology courses appear to have attracted students who expect to find intellectual tools with which to expose the hypocritical world of their elders and so construct a new society with new values and new freedoms. A Marxist approach is often attractive to students so motivated. The survey designers and providers of data for policy-makers of the 'old' structural functional sociology may suddenly find themselves faced with demands to be 'relevant' or suffer the label of academic lackeys of the establishment. Sociologists have acquired a popular press image as gurus of the youth culture or carriers of revolutionary doctrine and, potentially, Molotov cocktails, as one writer puts it (Berger, 1971). He goes on to comment on how this is rather ironic in the light of the history of sociology, in that some of the most revered figures – for example Comte, Weber, Durkheim and Pareto – spent a considerable amount of time developing anti- or counter-revolutionary ideas, refuting both Marxism and the links between sociology and political radicalism.

SOME RADICAL ASPECTS OF SOCIOLOGICAL INQUIRY

Wherever sociology is taught, and with whatever perspective, it tends to have a disturbing effect. There are several possible reasons for this. The first is that it casts doubt upon the notion of individual accountability for actions often popular with theologians and in schools of psychology, and suggests an alternative insight into the complex collective, social nature of human actions.

The second reason is related to the aim of analysing behaviour, since this requires that sociologists refuse to take situations at their face value and be able to accept uncritically neither official definitions of situations nor those of the participants. The sociologists' task here is analogous to that of the detective: everyone and everything is open to suspicion.

Another disturbing effect of sociology lies in the intentions of those who seek to improve on 'common sense', since this threatens the taken-for-granted aspects of social behaviour and exposes as false or distorted some of the folk interpretations on which behaviour is based.

A fourth reason is that, in attempting to be in some sense scientific, the discipline takes on a relative, non-ethnocentric viewpoint. Comparative studies of other cultures, other groups and other institutions undertaken in this way can be threatening, since they expose the accepted and familiar way of behaving to comparisons which may be interpreted as unfavourable. This approach allows one to be part of one's own culture yet at the same time out of it, and the subversive nature of this perspective has been described by Postman and Weingartner (1971) in their analysis of teaching.

THE SOCIOLOGICAL INTEREST OF SCHOOLING

It is perhaps useful to consider at this point why schools in particular are of interest to sociologists. One of the significant features of schools is their position as an agency in the socialization process. School is an inescapable fact of life for all but a few in contemporary Britain. Therefore schools are an important part of the process of becoming socialized, of experiencing the various cultures and subcultures, of transmitting, perpetuating and developing attitudes and ideologies.

A second reason derives from the first. Schools are a rare type of institution in that attendance is compulsory for substantial periods of time.

Other reasons relate to the complex functions of schools. One set of functions has been described as 'people processing'. Schools screen, assess and grade the population for occupations and therefore influence significantly their life chances, a theme taken up in the section that follows.

However, schools are simultaneously involved in 'knowledge processing', since some knowledge is selected, deemed to be of higher status and embodied in a curriculum. The schools thus transmit and maintain a complex stratification of knowledge, since first of all it is split into high and low status, and then within that deemed to be high status further rankings occur. Chapter 9 examines this issue in detail.

For sociologists another interesting feature of schools lies in the links between schools and other institutions within the social structure, e.g. the family, and the economic, political and religious institutions. Complex reciprocal sets of relationships exist here, and these have implications for social change. It is not yet clear to what extent schools are potential rather than actual agencies of change in the short, mid or long term. The consensus of opinion seems to be that other institutions tend to influence school more frequently than the reverse (see Banks, 1968).

SOCIOLOGY AND ITS RELEVANCE TO TEACHERS

The most direct relevance of sociology to teaching lies in the notion that teachers are to some extent applied social scientists. They apply some version, even if only a folk-lore type, of psychology, economics and sociology, as well as philosophy and history, to the task of teaching. Teachers apply sociology, since they use group situations to attempt to change the behaviour of children, and they are usually required to operate within an institutional setting. They teach within an intricate web of social relationships which is both internal and external to the schools. Chapter 4 explored this issue.

Teachers may unwittingly be applied sociologists, or this may be a conscious identification. In either case they may be effective, partially effective or ineffective. A knowledge of the sociology of education holds no guarantee of a more effective pedagogy. However, it may increase the chances of an improvement in pedagogy, and if it does not, the point of teaching it becomes obscure. This is a modest claim for the influence of the sociology of education, but perhaps is a realistic one.

The dangers of inadequate teaching or inadequate learning cannot be ignored, and Hargreaves (1972) reminds us of the possibilities of a sociological myth developing by which a fatalistic psychological view of individual causality is replaced by a fatalistic sociological view of environmental determinism, where the evidence available is distorted into the propositions that if a child comes from a 'bad' background this is sufficient explanation of his problems in school and that, since these factors are outside the control of the school, the teacher can do little to help. Another myth to which a distorted account of sociological material has contributed is that of cultural deprivation (Friedman, 1967), where cultural differences are misinterpreted as an absence of culture.

A second reason why teachers may usefully be interested in sociology lies in the growing body of evidence to support the proposition that, although some teachers may intuitively be effective applied sociologists, many are not. What is thought to go on in schools and what is said to go on have been shown to differ markedly from the actual behaviour recorded and analysed. Barnes, Britton and Rosen (1969) give a striking example when they show that, although most teachers claim that the development of language skills in children is a major aim, many teach in such a way that this is prevented. Instead, the classroom becomes a place where the teachers get unlimited opportunity to develop their own powers of language, particularly, but not exclusively, in secondary schools.

THE SOCIAL NATURE OF EDUCATING

When educating is located in schools, one aspect of the teachers' work as applied sociologists is concerned with the social nature of learning. In contrast, psychological analyses of schooling tend to concentrate upon the individual nature of learning, and perhaps one of the major policy errors has been to employ considerable numbers of educational psychologists and no educational sociologists in schools and local education authorities.

One aspect of this social nature of educating is the institutional setting of learning. A school develops conventions, rituals and routines to solve its administrative problems. It organizes children into groups, classes or houses, distributes parcels of time for subjects or activities and allocates accommodation and facilities. These have been shown to have a marked influence on the consciousness of those within the school as they become taken-for-granted aspects of behaviour (see Chapters 6 to 13). The study of one organizational practice, streaming (Lacey, 1970), shows how even pupils used to a best-pupil role and used to being successful in school tend to have their consciousness structured by accepting the school's definition of the situation so that many come to accept a lower-stream label, a poor-pupil role, low success rates and anti-school attitudes.

Another aspect of the social nature of learning refers to the complex dependence on the immediate environment or situation. Pupils are not just interpreting new knowledge (itself of social origin), but the cues and attitudes accompanying it. These include the status of the new knowledge (this is mathematics, not PE, and it is deemed to be of more importance), the use of the information (with maths I can pass examinations to get a better job), the reaction of peers (our group dislikes the history teacher and his subject) and the relationship to other knowledge (my father thinks metalwork important because it is practical knowledge).

A further consideration is the use of language as the main vehicle of learning, since this is a social, not an individual, construct. It is external to us, created by others, and constrains our thinking. Some of the constructs were established by groups long since dead and any ill-conceived notions are embedded and taken for granted, as was argued in Chapter 12.

THE CONFLICT ASPECTS OF SCHOOLING

Teachers may be ineffective as applied sociologists without an appreciation of the conflict nature of learning in school. A first proposition is that conflict arises because of status differences. Teachers are usually defined as adult, superior, authoritative and relatively permanent members of the school, whereas pupils are defined as children or adolescents, inferior, ignorant and relatively temporary members of the school. These status differences are reinforced by the teachers' mandate to make children learn.

A second proposition is that conflict arises because attendance is compulsory, therefore marking off school learning as different from the incidental, personal and informal learning that takes place outside school. This latter type of learning has built-in reliefs and face-saving devices to reduce any feelings of obligation or inferiority engendered (e.g. 'What a useful idea! I shall copy that. Let me buy you a drink on the strength of it!'). These devices are difficult to maintain in a situation of compulsory attendance, where one person is required to make the other learn.

A third proposition is that conflict arises because teaching does not normally provide for client selection. Lawyers and doctors are able to 'manage' client selection to some extent, whereas a teacher's clients are usually allocated. Conversely, pupils cannot select or change their teachers easily, as they can their doctors and lawyers. Disputes that arise are thus denied one effective solution – mutual avoidance.

An alternative model of teaching to the conflict version is that teaching is the socially approved task of imparting knowledge, but this approach is limited in its provision of explanations of actual school behaviour. The conflict model provides some important correctives. The disillusionment of some teachers with their training institutions may be related to a tendency by college staff to use the 'imparting knowledge' model. A consequence may be the adoption of equally inadequate staffroom models of individual pupil or cultural inadequacy, to cope with the situations found in schools.

THE KNOWLEDGE-PROCESSING ASPECTS OF SCHOOLING

One reason for the interest of sociologists in schools given earlier was that they simultaneously process people and knowledge, and the work being developed here concerns teachers in their task as applied sociologists. In the past, sociology has too often followed the example of other educational studies in regarding knowledge as neutral, as unproblematic.

The notion of knowledge stipulated here is relativistic, because for this purpose knowledge is defined as what the participants believe or think is knowledge, and non-evaluative, because an attempt is made to suspend judgement about which categories of knowledge are superior. This allows the assumptions on which the categories are based to be examined. Furthermore, knowledge may be taken to include information, experiences and expectations. This apparently unwieldy and imprecise definition of knowledge is proving fruitful for posing sociological questions. These include the sources of categories of knowledge, the reasons given for ranking some knowledge as superior or preferable, the interested groups promoting these interpretations, the result of a confrontation of two rival interpretations (e.g. evolution and Genesis), the nature of ideas rejected or avoided (e.g. social science in schools, sex education), and the nature of ideas restricted by organizational features (e.g. school democracy). Some of these themes are explored in Chapter 9.

CONCLUSION

The proposal of this chapter, indeed, of the whole book, is that the sociological perspectives involved are essential in helping to give as full a description and understanding of the problems of teaching as possible alongside the current insights of psychology, history and philosophy. The applied sociological aspects of pedagogy in particular no longer can be held off as relevant only to educational administrators and politicians, since the notions of a hidden curriculum, teaching as a conflict situation, and the school as a knowledge-processing agency are related to teacher–pupil behaviour *every* day in *every* classroom.

Further Reading

Murray, R. (1979) *Sociological Theories of Education*. Maidenhead: McGraw-Hill. Relates sociological ideas to education.
'Sociology and Teaching', a collection of papers which appeared as a special edition of *Educational Review* in 1973, Vol. 25, No. 3.

PART FIVE

Educational Life Chances or Who Gets What?

The concern of this part is to explore some of the regular patterns of the educational experience of people in the UK. These educational life chances are seen to be persistent, and there are competing explanations of them. The aspects selected are gender (since girls tend to receive different educational outcomes from those of boys), social class (since educational life chances tend to be persistently superior the higher the social class), ethnicity (since black and brown pupils tend to experience different patterns of education from those of white pupils) and finally the categorization known as special education.

These are not the only regular patterns. One that is less well documented is that of region. The educational life chances of rural children tend to differ from those of urban children, and those of the pupils in the south-east tend to differ from those of pupils in the north-east. A contribution to an understanding of these patterns from the interactionist sociology is derived from labelling theory, and therefore this is the subject of the first chapter in this part.

Chapter 24

Labelling Theory and Life Chances

'One of the commonest ailments of the present day is premature formation of opinion.'
Frank McKinney Hubbard

INTRODUCTION

In Chapter 11, the expectations of teachers as a factor in the hidden curriculum of schooling were examined. The central proposition was stated as:

> pupils tend to perform as well, or as badly, as their teachers expect. The teacher's prediction of a pupil's or group of pupils' behaviour is held to be communicated to them, frequently in unintended ways, thus influencing the actual behaviour that follows.

It was argued that this was a matter of particular concern to educationalists where inferences about pupils were based on false diagnoses. There are several potential sources of false prediction, including expectations based on age, sex, ethnic identity, religion, name, physical appearance and social class 'indicators' such as speech and dress, which become established in the interpretive schemes of the participants. The outcome can be the establishment of a self-fulfilling prophecy, when the false diagnosis influences the self-concept of the learner, who then learns to behave as expected, thus 'verifying' the initial false diagnosis (see Chapter 11).

These concepts of expectations and self-fulfilling prophecies are derived from a larger theoretical perspective called labelling theory, which is a set of ideas related to the interactionist perspective (see Chapter 19). The purpose of this part of the book is to use labelling theory to explore the question of 'who gets what in education'. The assumption made here is that the life chances of individuals and groups vary according to certain regular features, and that the educational life chances vary in a similar way: e.g. the chance of a girl having a university education is much less than that of a boy; the chance of a working-class boy is less than that of a middle-class boy; the chance of a black, working-class girl is very low indeed, and so on. The concepts of life chances and educational life chances and the related patterns and evidence will be examined later in the chapter. At this point we shall attempt to establish the key features of labelling theory.

LABELLING THEORY

Labelling theory features in the work of Lemert (1951), Becker (1963) and Matza (1964), as well as other writers. It is mostly in the fields of criminology and the sociology of deviance that the theory has been developed. A basic proposition is that deviant behaviour has the characteristics of a transaction between the deviant person and another or others. (Another term for this theory is transactional theory.) Particular behaviour is deviant because it is defined as such by groups in society, particularly by those groups who have some power to establish that their definitions carry weight.

As an example, a head teacher suspended a 15-year-old schoolboy in a secondary school in England, in November 1978, for asking his friends if they wanted a copy of the National Union of School Students magazine, *Blot*. The boy was labelled as deviant by someone with the power to enforce his definition by using sanctions against the person defined as undesirable. The suspension might well have been reversed in Sweden, where head teachers are required to facilitate pupil organization in their schools. Failure to do so may result in the head teacher's being defined as deviant and sanctioned accordingly!

Labelling theory raises some questions about the conclusions regarding deviance that are reached in structural functional approaches in sociology, where social control is seen as a reaction to deviant behaviour. An alternative proposition is mooted: that social control may create deviance:

> Older sociology . . . tended to rest heavily on the idea that deviance leads to social control. I have come to believe that the reverse idea, i.e. social control leads to deviance, is equally tenable.
>
> Lemert, 1972

Both sociological approaches – the interactionist, stressing labelling, and the structural functionalist, stressing the social control of rule breakers – run counter to those psychological approaches that propose individual causation because of biological factors. However, labelling theory, unlike the other approaches, calls for an examination of the labellers and their assumptions as much as an examination of the persons or groups being labelled.

Deviance Involves a Social Process

Deviance is seen as a social process with a series of stages, and the participants in this process are rule makers, rule enforcers and rule breakers. This approach entails a resistance to the idea of a single act of categorization that has permanent consequences, encompassed in the idea of 'once a criminal, always a criminal'. Instead there emerges the possibility that labelling may have varying effects at different stages in an individual's life, so that an individual may drift in and out of activities defined as deviant.

A Deviant is One Who Has Been Successfully Labelled

Since deviance is not seen as something into which an individual has been inevitably pushed by biological or psychological factors, labelling theorists stress the consequences of the application of rules by others to the deviant. In the case of the schoolboy quoted above, he is only deviant because the head teacher in a particular culture successfully labels him so, by defining the distribution of NUSS magazines as deviance and then having the power to enforce that definition. A now famous quotation makes the point:

> Deviance is not a quality of the act the person commits, but rather a consequence of the application by others of rules and sanctions to an 'offender'. The deviant is one to whom the label has successfully been applied: deviant behaviour is behaviour that people so label.
> Becker 1963

Labelling Activity Affects Those Labelled in Various Ways

An individual does not become labelled as deviant simply by breaking a rule, or even several rules. Many people break rules, but only some are subsequently labelled. The social process that follows the breaking of a rule may involve individuals in negotiating, rejecting, accepting, reinterpreting, or modifying. A key issue for Lemert (1972) is whether primary deviation becomes secondary deviation.

A primary deviant has committed a rule violation but claims that this is uncharacteristic and maintains a self-concept of being non-deviant and upholding socially accepted roles. A secondary deviant has undergone a reorganization of self-concept and has accepted the label of deviant. Lemert (1951) described the transition from primary to secondary deviation as a sequence of interactions:

> 1) primary deviation; 2) societal penalties; 3) further primary deviation; 4) stronger penalties and rejections; 5) further deviations, perhaps with hostilities and resentments beginning to focus upon those doing the penalizing; 6) crisis reached in the tolerance quotient, expressed in formal action by the community stigmatizing the deviant; 7) strengthening of the deviant conduct as a reaction to the stigmatizing and penalties; and 8) ultimate acceptance of deviant social status and efforts at adjustment on the basis of the associated role.

In the case of the self-fulfilling prophecy, secondary deviation can occur even when no primary deviation exists. Chapter 11 indicated how the initial diagnosis by a teacher may be false; i.e. no primary deviation exists except in the imagination of the teacher or as an expectation built into an interpretive scheme.

Deviance May Be Amplified

One of the puzzling features of institutions for deviants that are based on traditional theories of social control is that the outcomes are frequently the opposite to those intended. Studies of prisons, mental hospitals and schools for offenders show that criminals tend to become hardened criminals and first offenders often become recidivists. Labelling theory offers some explanation of this. In such institutions opportunities to withdraw from deviance are reduced, a new identity as a 'social outsider' is established, and a change of self-concept may result whereby individuals see themselves as irrevocably deviant. The social reaction to deviance establishes a deviant career: deviance is amplified.

An aggressive social policy of 'tightening up' and 'establishing firmer law and order' may have a similar effect. A vicious circle that creates more deviance may be set in motion: more 'tightening up' leads to more acts defined as deviant, which lead to more action against deviants, which leads to more alienation of deviants and more changed self-concepts, which lead to more deviance by those so affected which leads to more attempts to 'tighten up', and so on.

In the case of schools, the work of Reynolds and Sullivan (1979) has illustrated effects of this kind. The schools that produced most deviants had a zealous social control policy, e.g. cigarette smokers, when caught, had their smoking materials confiscated and were then punished, often physically. In some cases 'patrols' of teachers looked out for smokers around the schools, and smokers found in other places, like cinemas or parks, were dealt with at school. The same zealous attitudes were shown in other areas of control, e.g. policy regarding school uniform and chewing-gum consumption.

The schools that produced fewest deviants had a 'softer' approach. Rules regarding the same matters existed and were enforced, but with less aggression; e.g. the confiscation of cigarettes was considered enough punishment, and the school was considered to be sufficient territorial range, so incidents in parks and cinemas were not dealt with.

Labelled Persons May Offer 'Accounts' and Seek Support Groups

Labelling can have a crushing effect on an individual's or a group's identity and social behaviour: people are involved in various degrees of suffering. If life becomes difficult, labelled persons may offer 'accounts' to justify their conduct. Scott and Lyman (1968) indicate that these may take the form of a variety of excuses. Attempts to reduce the effects may take the form of avoiding situations in which labelling occurs or covering-up tactics. Often it is found useful to seek the support of similar people or groups who may have solved some of the difficulties, or who at least understand the problems. Such groups may attempt to change laws and values by campaigning; women's liberation and homosexual equality campaigns are examples.

'Successful' Labelling Depends on a Variety of Factors

Writers developing labelling theory are not suggesting that labelling is always successful: they are not claiming that if someone is labelled stupid that person will necessarily become mentally handicapped. However, they draw attention to the questions of why people are categorized as deviant and who it is that labels, based on what has been defined as deviance in that society at that particular time. The factors involved in the successful application of a label include the frequency of the labelling, the status of the labeller, the degree of damage done to others, the nature of the 'account' rendered, and the power of the person to resist or reduce labelling effects. Scheff (1966), investigating the power of the person concerned, demonstrated that, in diagnosing an identical behaviour pattern in high-social-status and low-social-status clients, there was less willingness to diagnose the pattern as indicative of serious mental illness in the high-status clients. As Rist (1977) puts it:

> The crux of the labelling perspective lies not in whether one's norm violating behaviour is known, but whether others decided to do something about it.

EDUCATIONAL LIFE CHANCES

The concept of life chances is one of the more straightforward concepts in sociology. It has been defined as the probability of a person of specified status achieving a specified goal or suffering a special disadvantage (Reading, 1977). When the concept of life chances is used to describe general patterns in a society rather than to account for the fate of a particular individual, it provides one kind of answer to the question 'who gets what?'. The assumption that there are regular patterns to the biographies of individuals and groups underpins the concept of life chances.

The notion of educational life chance is derived from the main concept to focus attention on the regular features found in educational biographies and group experiences. From empirical studies, a number of propositions can be made about educational life chances. One study of pupil careers over a period of 20 years came to a range of conclusions including the following:

> The social class differences in educational opportunity which were considerable at the primary school stage have increased at the secondary and extend now even to pupils of high ability. Thus nearly half the lower manual working class pupils of high ability have left school before they are 16½ years.
>
> Early leaving and low job aspirations make it probable that as many as 5 per cent of the next generation of manual workers will be recruited from pupils who, in other circumstances, might have qualified for administrative or professional occupations.
>
> The manual working-class pupils, compared with those of the middle class, are least handicapped when they are in the best staffed and best equipped schools.
>
> An analysis of the length of school life among the lower manual working-class pupils of borderline ability and above shows that both parental interest and school staffing and equipment are associated with age of leaving. These two factors are of course highly correlated, but neither adequately compensates for the deficiency of the other – the interest of the parents alone is insufficient to counter the deficiencies of the schools.
>
> The interest and encouragement that parents give their children is closely linked to their own educational history. Any attempt that the parents made to secure for themselves education beyond the elementary school level, even if this was not successfully completed, is associated with higher aspirations for their own children's educational success.
>
> Children from large families make low scores in all attainment tests at all ages. There is, however, no evidence of an increasing educational handicap at secondary school, indeed in the manual working class there is rather less difference in the attainment of children from large and small families at 15 than there was when they were first tested at eight.
>
> The more young children there are in the family when a child is learning to talk, the lower his score in the eight year old vocabulary test. This early deficiency in the understanding of words is not made up later.
>
> Pupils from large families leave school earlier than expected at each level of measured

ability. Financial reasons alone are insufficient to explain this, for the youngest in large families also leave early, even though there are likely to be fewer calls on the family income than when their elder brothers and sisters were the same age.

First-born boys in families of two or three make higher scores in the attainment tests and are academically more successful and more aspiring than their younger brothers and sisters. They are also superior in attainment to only children. For the girls this difference is not found.

Pupils from two-child families with birth intervals of two to four years make higher scores in all tests than those with either shorter or longer intervals; they get superior 'O' level results and leave school later. This holds for both older and younger boys and girls: the advantage of those with two to four year intervals being as great at eight as later.

The short-sighted pupils have, at each age tested, superior attainment scores to those with normal vision; their non-verbal intelligence scores are, however, similar. They have higher job aspirations at each level of ability than those with normal vision, and more academic hobbies.

From *All Our Future*, J.W.B. Douglas et al., 1971

CONCLUSION

According to the particular study mentioned above, educational life chances are related to a variety of factors, including social class, size of family, school staffing and equipment, parents' educational experiences, spacing of children in families, and myopia. This kind of investigation is largely descriptive; that is, it identifies the patterns. Explanations of the pattern are a different matter, and in the next four chapters we shall examine the kinds of explanation generated by interactionist approaches, particularly labelling theory, for four aspects of life chance: gender, social class, ethnicity, and 'special', designating various kinds of 'handicap'.

SUMMARY

1. Labelling theory explores the proposition that social control may create deviance, while the structural approach proposes that social control is a reaction to deviance.
2. Labelling theory calls for an examination of the labellers, their assumptions and their power to establish their definitions, as much as an examination of the person or group being labelled.
3. Deviance is seen as a learned activity with a series of stages rather than as a personal attribute or a single act defined as folly.
4. Many perform deviant acts, but only those successfully labelled are deviants.
5. Secondary deviation, where an individual reorganizes his or her self-concept to accept the label of deviant, follows a sequence of interactions.
6. Social reactions to deviance may amplify it rather than reduce it.
7. Labelled persons may seek the support and comfort of others similarly labelled.
8. The assumption that there are regular patterns to the biographies of individuals and groups gives rise to the concept of life chances.
9. Educational life chances are related to a variety of factors, including gender, social class, ethnicity, size of family, parents' education and membership of a minority seen as 'special'.

Further Reading

Dahrendorf, R. (1980) *Life Chances*. London: Weidenfeld and Nicolson. A more complex theory of life chances than that given in this chapter.
Douglas, J.W.B., Ross, J.M. and Simpson, H.R. (1971) *All Our Future*. London: Peter Davies. A longitudinal study of educational life chances.
Halsey, A.H., Heath, A.F. and Ridge, J.M. (1980) *Origins and Destinations*. Oxford: Oxford University Press.
Rist, R. (1977) 'On Understanding the Processes of Schooling: The Contributions of Labelling Theory'. In Karabel, J. and Hasley, A. *Power and Ideology in Education*. Oxford: Oxford University Press. A review of labelling theory and schooling.

Discussion and Activities

1. View the film *Eye of the Storm* (on hire from Concord Films, Nacton, Ipswich) and discuss the examples of labelling shown, based on colour of eyes.
2. 'Labelled people may seek the support of others similarly labelled.' Obtain literature from groups often seen by the mass media as deviant. Why are they seen as deviant? How do they counter this label? What social rules are they seen to be infringing? Examples of such groups are Alcoholics Anonymous, Campaign for Homosexual Equality, Education Otherwise, Voluntary Euthanasia Society.

Signposts

Regions
Reference to *Educational Statistics for the UK* and *Social Trends* (both published regularly by HMSO) shows that educational life chances vary with region. See Byrne, D., Williamson, B. and Fletcher, B. (1974) *The Poverty of Education*, Oxford: Martin Robertson, and the *'New Society' Social Studies Reader* on Regions.

Chapter 25

Gender

'My advice to the women's clubs of America is to raise more hell and fewer dahlias.'
William Allen White

INTRODUCTION: GENDER AS A NEGLECTED ISSUE IN SOCIOLOGICAL RESEARCH ON EDUCATION

Since the 1944 Education Act, the focus of sociological analyses on equality of opportunity has been on social class rather than on gender. As a result, many books on the sociology of education rated at best a page or two on women or on sex differences and, at worst, not even a reference in the index. 'Compensatory' education for girls did not emerge as an issue and any disparities that did emerge were part of larger studies (Douglas, 1964).

The reasons for this comparative neglect were complex. First, educational research followed contemporary definitions of what constituted an educational problem, and so looked at wastage of talent, inequality of opportunity, immigrant children, school-leaving ages and school organizational features. Inequality of opportunity between the sexes was rarely recognized as a problem, or at most was seen as an anachronism that would disappear with co-education. Second, sex typing appears to be a deeply embedded and taken-for-granted aspect of the social structure, so the 'common-sense' explanations about the assumed innate intellectual differences between man and woman were all too readily acceptable as a complete explanation. The lack of a well-developed comparative perspective of education may have been contributory here, since a systematic comparison with other countries (e.g. the USSR, Sweden) would have presented some disturbing information about women, education and occupations elsewhere.

Recognition of sex differences in education as an 'official' problem came with an announcement in September 1973 that the government planned to ask Her Majesty's Inspectorate to undertake an inquiry into the extent to which differences in school curricula and customs contribute to unequal opportunities for boys and girls (DES, 1975). The influence of various women's liberation groups might be discerned here (Knight, 1973; Smoker, 1973). Official opinion was influenced strongly by the evidence to the House of Lords Select Committee on the Anti-Discrimination Bill in 1971–72 and

1972–73. The evidence collected by a group within the Labour Party was particularly influential (Rendel, 1968, and Labour Party, 1972).

In the period after 1973, however, a number of articles and books have focused on the life chances of girls in particular. As a result the issues have become more clearly identified:

> One message is clear. The education service has also a good deal of homework to do, the first task of which is to raise the debate about sex roles in education to a serious intellectual level, and to vote research funds to relevant and more substantial field-work. We should moreover begin to make socially unacceptable the common attitude of triviality and, occasionally, mockery, which has so far characterized public reaction to the intelligent questioning by a few in the leadership of education, as to why the education of girls should be any different from that of boys; and how solid is the ground for alleged norms of sex differences used to justify different curricula and methods for girls and boys respectively.
>
> Byrne, 1978

It should be borne in mind that a distortion is produced by looking at gender in isolation. Other variables, such as social class, ethnicity and region, are intertwined with gender. Rural boys may have more in common with rural girls as regards educational life chances compared with urban pupils, and a girl who has parents in unskilled manual work and who is also black may have multiple disadvantages, so if gender is considered in isolation, an underestimation of disadvantage could result.

THE EDUCATIONAL LIFE CHANCES OF GIRLS AND BOYS

The concept of educational life chances was outlined in Chapter 24 and was taken to refer to the probabilities of a person of a specified status, in this case a boy or a girl, achieving a particular goal or experiencing a particular disadvantage. The regular patterns that appear in the educational biographies of girls and boys in Britain include the following:

1. Boys' and girls' achievements in school are similar up to the age of 11 years. This is true for both the USA (Maccoby, 1966) and the UK (Douglas, 1964).
2. The achievements of both sexes at GCE 'O' level currently show few differences in total numbers taking the examination, but about twice as many boys gain passes in science subjects as do girls, who gain passes in arts subjects instead.
3. At GCE 'A' level a number of differences in achievement are in evidence. The number of boys taking 'A' level examination exceeds the number of girls. The difference has reduced over the last ten years and currently, for every 100 boys leaving with one 'A' level or more, there are about 90 girls. The subjects taken showed marked variation, and the ratios of boys to girls in different subjects are: physics 6/1, mathematics 4/1, chemistry 3/1, biology 9/8, technical drawing 200/1, languages 1/2 (based on 1978 figures; no marked changes in ratio since then).
4. More boys gain places at university than girls. The figures in 1978 were 61.8 per cent of places to boys and 38.2 per cent to girls, then the highest figure ever recorded for girls. The greater the prestige commonly accorded a university, the fewer girls present. (Approximate figures are: Oxbridge, 10 to 20 per cent; large civic, 20 to 35

per cent; small civic, 35 to 50 per cent, depending on year taken.)
5.   The 'second chance' university, the Open University, has more male than female students. The current percentages are about 48 per cent female, 52 per cent male. This is a change from the early years of the Open University, when the ratio was nearer to 30 per cent and 70 per cent.
6.   The number of boys being granted apprenticeships involving further study at a Further Education college exceeds the number of girls: the figures are 42.3 per cent of boys and 7.1 per cent of girls (1973 figures, no marked changes since then).
7.   The number of girls pursuing teacher training courses exceeds the number of boys, particularly for primary-school teaching. The ratio at its peak was three girls to every one boy on teacher education courses. Currently it is closer to two to one.

(In all cases the current situation may be checked from several sources, including the most recent versions of: *Statistics of Education, Vol. 2, School Leavers; Social Trends; Educational Statistics for the UK* (all published by HMSO); and *The Universities Central Council on Admissions Annual Report*.)
   In summary:

1.   Fewer girls than boys reach university.
2.   Fewer girls than boys take GCE 'A' levels.
3.   Fewer girls than boys taken 'A' levels in physics, maths and chemistry.
4.   Fewer girls than boys gain apprenticeships with linked further study.
5.   Fewer females than males pursue the second-chance route of an Open University course, although the gap has closed.
6.   Fewer boys than girls prepare for teacher education.

Thus, after leaving primary school, girls experience an ever-decreasing set of possibilities in educational achievement, with the exceptions of preparation for primary-school teaching and preparation for nursing. As one writer comments:

> In the light of the social expectations about women, it is not surprising that women end up where society expects them to: the surprise is that little girls don't get the message that they are supposed to be stupid until they get into high school.
>
> Boocock, 1972

Another writer sees the influence of teachers as a crucial factor:

> The most important single educational life chance a child has, as she clambers up her educational ladder, is probably the quality and vision – or the limitation – of her teachers. No single influence for conservation or change, for creating insurmountable hurdles or new opportunities, will ever be as seminal as that of the teachers in our schools – of both sexes.
>
> Byrne, 1978

EXPLANATIONS

There have been several attempts to provide explanations for the different sets of educational life chances outlined above. Some are derived from psychology: one proposition based on the idea of inherited abilities is that girls inherit a different set of abilities and aptitudes from boys, so schools follow a natural pattern and presumably could not alter this even if they wished to do so.

An alternative explanation offered by psychologists is related to inherited personalities and different motivations influencing achievement. It is that girls inherit a different set of personality traits from boys, so schools follow a natural pattern in providing different motivations, with consequent different achievements in boys and girls. The case study of mathematics that follows contributes to the doubt about these two propositions.

From sociology there are derived a range of explanations that stress the learning of a culture with its inbuilt definitions of gender. The role of schools is seen variously: in one proposition it is seen as repeating the labels of a culture, since a society has a traditional allocation of roles of men and women, and the agencies of socialization of the society socialize boys and girls to fit in with that pattern. Schools as an agency of socialization follow suit, and in this they neither increase nor decrease the options open to pupils.

Alternatively, schools can be seen as continuing the process started outside school by closing off further options. A society has a traditional allocation of the roles of men and women, and schools actively contribute to the further differentiation of roles by effectively closing off more options.

A further proposition stresses the possibility of schools' changing the traditional allocations of roles. Schools are active in resisting the allocation of roles for men and women and increase the range of choices. Therefore they are instrumental in starting to change the social structure by altering the expectations of pupils and increasing their educational life chances.

Marxist interpretations are derived from the concepts of 'capitalism' and 'patriarchy'. The family is seen to be crucial to legitimizing unequal profit sharing, with the control of work, marriage and property being in the hands of men. The second-class roles of childrearing and care of the elderly are allocated to women with any involvement in work regulated by males.

EXPLAINING GIRLS' EDUCATIONAL ACHIEVEMENT: THE CONTRIBUTION OF LABELLING THEORY

Mathematics

As a case study, we shall examine the experience of girls in mathematics in schools. At 11 years old girls perform as well as boys in mathematics, but by the age of 16, when GCE 'O' levels and CSEs are encountered, girls are performing less well, and at 'A' level four boys are achieving mathematics passes for every one girl. Studies of this phenomenon have tended to be undertaken by psychologists looking for an ability peculiar to boys and absent in girls. The 'missing ability' was apparently spatial 'ability', since girls consistently did poorly on certain types of question requiring geometric/spatial understandings. The fault, therefore, was in the girls themselves, a biological difference that school could do little to alter. This belief has entered the consciousness of both teachers and taught, so that both frequently are convinced that most girls are 'unmathematical'.

The contribution of labelling theory here is the identification of a powerful self-fulfilling prophecy. A self-fulfilling prophecy begins with a false diagnosis, in this case that girls lack an ability called 'spatial ability'. The work of Sharma and Meighan (1980) has demonstrated that girls who are matched on equivalent experience with boys do not lack 'spatial ability' and do equally well in mathematics. One such experience is technical drawing. Since only a minority of girls are allowed or encouraged to do this subject, their lack of a crucial experience in spatial thinking has been misidentified as a lack of a biologically situated 'ability'.

This false diagnosis of a missing ability then sets in motion the typical sequence of a self-fulfilling prophecy. Girls are labelled as unmathematical, their performance is noted, and the outcome of poorer performance is used as 'conclusive evidence' that the label is accurate and the explanation of a biologically situated difference is sound. The labellers are powerful, while the girls labelled are not; the labelling is applied with great frequency; most girls 'lose' their performance, since their performance was equal to that of boys at 11 years; they reverse their self-concepts of being able to do mathematics, to accepting that they cannot.

Discussion Activity in Classrooms

Contrary to popular belief, it has been found repeatedly that males talk more than females. Here is one experiment that illustrates the discrepancy between the belief and the evidence:

> The greater amount of man-talk and the greater frequency of interruptions is probably something that few of us are conscious of; we believe so strongly in the stereotype which insists that it is the other way around. However, it is not difficult to check this. It can be an interesting classroom exercise.
>
> It was an exercise I set myself at a recent conference of teachers in London. From the beginning the men talked more because, although there were eight official male speakers, there were no female ones. This was seen as a problem, so the organizing committee decided to exercise positive discrimination in favour of female speakers from the floor.
>
> At the first session – with positive discrimination – there were 14 male speakers and nine female; at the second session there were 10 male speakers and four female. There was almost twice as much man-talk as woman-talk. However, what was interesting was the impression people were left with about talk. The stereotypes were still holding firm. Of the 30 people consulted after the sessions, 27 were of the opinion that there had been more female than male speakers.
>
> This helps to explain some of the contradictions behind sex differences in language. On the one hand we believe that females talk too much; on the other hand we have ample evidence that they do not talk as much as males.
>
> Spender, 1978

Spender suggests that there are some regular patterns of interpretation here: a 'talkative' female is actually one who talks about as often as a male; a 'dominating' female talks about half as much as a male. Therefore, at the conference reported above, although the number of female speakers was less than half of the total number of speakers, most people thought they had dominated the talk. Males would have to have talked almost all the time before they would have been seen as dominating the talk. This pattern, Spender argues, is related to differences of power:

When it comes to power, some very interesting sex differences have been found. Although we may have been able to predict some of them, there are others which completely contradict our beliefs about masculine and feminine talk.

The first one, which was to be expected, is that females are more polite. Most people who are without power and find themselves in a vulnerable position are more polite. The shop assistant is more polite than the customer; the student is more polite than the teacher; the female is more polite than the male. But this has little to do with their sex, and a great deal to do with their position in society.

Females are required to be polite, and this puts onus on them to accommodate male talk . . .

It is not polite to be the centre of conversation and to talk a lot – if one is female. It is not polite to interrupt – if one is female. It is not polite to talk about things which interest you – if one is female. It *is* polite to accommodate, to listen, to be supportive and encouraging to male speakers – if one is female.

So females are kept in their places. They enjoy less rights to talk. Because they have less power and because politeness is part of the repertoire of successful feminine behaviour, it is not even necessary to force females to be quiet. The penalties are so great if they break the rule, they will obligingly monitor themselves.

Spender, 1978

One of the influences in play here, particularly for girls in secondary schools, is the conflict between wanting to please the teacher by being intellectual and remaining acceptable to boys as potential dates by avoiding being intellectual. In a study by Komaravsky (1946) women students at a college reported how they resolved the conflict by concealing their intellectual abilities. One student gave examples:

I am engaged to a southern boy who doesn't think too much of the woman's intellect. In spite of myself, I play up to his theories because the less one knows and does, the more he does for you and thinks you 'cute' in the bargain . . . I allow him to explain things to me in great detail and to treat me as a child in financial matters.

She explained that one of her techniques was to spell long words incorrectly once in a while. Her boyfriend seemed to get a great kick out of this, commenting, 'Honey, you certainly don't know how to spell.' On another occasion, when her boyfriend said that he considered Ravel's 'Bolero' the greatest piece of music ever written, she changed the subject so as not to talk down to him.

Because of these social rules about talk, mixed-sex classrooms provide a situation in which it is difficult for females to get involved in discussion on parity with males, and difficult for teachers to provide opportunities. Boys conform to expectations and live up to their label when they dominate classroom discussion or question and answer sessions, whereas girls meet the expectations for their sex when they are quiet or accommodate male-directed talk. Single-sex situations give girls more opportunity, because in single-sex schools with female teachers, girls are not obliged to defer to male authority, to support male topics, to agree to interruptions, or to practise silence. There is relatively 'free' speech, as Spender puts it, and this could explain the frequently claimed superior achievement of females in single-sex schools. Where females are free to use their language to learn, they learn more.

This provides another example of labelling theory. Girls who deviate from the expectations risk acquiring a deviant label of 'dominating', 'talkative' or 'intellectual', and an accompanying set of penalties. Those who conform have to develop a self-concept that allows for their silence and their submissive role.

Spender (1978) asked a group of girls at an Inner London secondary school whether they thought it was unfeminine to speak up in class, and they agreed.

> The girls thought it natural that male students should ask questions, make protests, challenge the teacher and demand explanations. Females on the other hand should 'just get on with it' – even when they, too, thought the work was silly, or plain boring.

Spender concludes that, although it is unlikely that teachers consciously practise discrimination against their students on the grounds of sex, by enforcing the social rules for talk they are unwittingly penalizing females. Since there is no physical reason, no sex difference, that is responsible for the relative silence of females, this situation is not inevitable, and teachers have the power to do something about it.

Gender Identity in Pre-school and Primary School

At birth children are given a clearly identifiable sex label – their first name. Boys and girls are dressed differently, given different types of toys, reinforced for different types of behaviour. Mothers typically treat their male and female infants in different ways (Moss, 1967). Parents tend to shape the behaviour of their children: fathers especially discourage any 'feminine' behaviour in sons (Pitzner, 1963). Boys tend to be encouraged to show tenacity, aggressiveness and curiosity, girls to show kindness, obedience and cheerfulness (Brim, 1960). Any biological differences are thereby accentuated.

Children thus learn what Danziger terms a gender identity: 'Once they have grasped that they are characterized by their membership in a gender category, this colours their evaluation of persons and activities' (Danziger, 1971). An experiment that illustrates this is that of Montemayor (1974), who played a game with six- to eight-year-olds with an asexual toy clown. With some children he described the clown as a toy for boys, with others a toy for girls, and with others in sex-neutral terms. Boys performed better in the game when the boy label was given, girls when the girl label was given. Montemayor's conclusion was that sex labels were influencing behaviour even in the absence of any outright reward and punishment.

A study of 18 pre-school picture books chosen by the American Association as the best of their kind for that year suggested that picture-book characters reinforce the traditional sex role assumptions about men and women (Weitzman et al., 1972). Females were grossly underrepresented: 261 pictures of males compared to 23 pictures of females. Boys in the picture books were active, and involved in adventures, whereas girls were passive, and shown indoors, either peering through windows or helping with domestic tasks. In *What Boys Can Be*, the ultimate occupation was President, in *What Girls Can Be*, a mother with children. The implicit message for children to learn, the authors conclude, is that girls are not very important, and that their aspirations for the future should be modest and service-orientated.

An analysis of British Reading Schemes (Lobban, 1975) showed that male and female roles were depicted as clearly demarcated. Males were active, instrumental and related to the outside world. Females were depicted almost entirely in domestic roles.

> In summary, the reading schemes showed a 'real' world peopled by women and girls who were almost solely involved with domestic activity . . . The world they depicted was not only sexist, it was more sexist than present reality . . .

(The term 'sexist' refers not to mere differences in sex but to the evaluation of one as inferior to the other, female being not just different, but second best.)

Some publishers have become more sensitive to sexism in printed material; see National Union of Journalists (1982) *Non-sexist Code of Practice for Book Publishing*.

Some Aspects of the Official Secondary School Curriculum

Decisions are made on the basis of sex label in various aspects of the official secondary school curriculum. These include decisions about timetables, staffing, promotions, games and sports, subjects to be studied, punishments, books, careers advice and the allocation of resources. Thus girls tend to be given timetables allocating them to domestic science rather than to metalwork, or netball rather than football; they tend to be filtered through to arts rather than science subjects and, if to science, usually to biology rather than physics or chemistry. The allocation of resources has been shown to have a bias in favour of boys. One example is buildings:

> Regulations issued by the late Ministry of Education . . . prescribed standards for boys', girls' and mixed schools respectively, which gave a standard for girls' schools of fewer science laboratories and technical rooms than those for boys.
>
> Byrne, 1975

These schools remain in use, unaltered and unimproved. Furthermore, career guidance tends to steer girls into the traditional areas of employment for women, and some career-guidance literature and forms clearly state, in a separate list, the few occupations thought suitable for girls.

Books are a major aspect of the secondary school curriculum and an increasing number of analyses of their content are becoming available. General readers, textbooks and books on particular topics, e.g. sex education, are three examples that have been surveyed. The choice of general readers appears to be limited (Nightingale, 1974), so girls who want to read adventure stories end up reading those featuring male heroes, with the implicit message that it is men who have adventures. Books specifically for girls:

> show a preponderance of books about love, dating and romance with a sideline in problems, like spots, glasses and so on, which interfere with the romance . . . Boys are interested in dating too, but they are not expected to read books about it. It is a minor part of their lives. Girls are not allowed the comforting assumption that sex and dating need play only a part in their lives. They read that it is of crucial importance and learn to think about very little else.

Even the role of tomboy spells out the same message in the end. Tomboys are allowed to take the lead, to be tough and to make decisions. For example, Nancy, in Arthur Ransome's stories, e.g. *Swallows and Amazons*, is fierce in her defence of a girl's right to do what boys do, but Peggy and Susan spend their time being conventional girls, cooking and organizing the domestic scene so that Nancy can have her eccentricities. John and Roger have traditional male roles. Thus the tomboy is presented as a kind of release for girls who are unsure of their role. Nightingale concludes that the tomboy's world is presented as ultimately unsatisfactory, with the message that perhaps it is better to be a 'real' girl after all.

Subject textbooks have received some attention (Hahn, 1974; Millstein, 1972). The conclusion reached has been that women are hardly present in the curriculum presented in textbooks. They are largely absent in history and science and appear in a distorted form in literature. History was indeed his-story and not her-story, concluded Millstein (1972).

Hoffman (1975), as indicated earlier (see Chapter 6, surveyed the sex-education books written for school children and concluded that they presented an inaccurate and distorted version of the sexual behaviours and emotional response of girls. She found that four out of five sex-instruction books for adolescents state the author's belief in a wide emotional and sometimes intellectual gap between the sexes. No evidence for these assertions was quoted by the writers of these books. (For further examples, see Chapter 9.)

Some Aspects of the Hidden Curriculum

Practices like lining up boys and girls separately, physically punishing boys but verbally chastising girls, and commenting on girls' appearance but boys' achievement have been shown in a study by Ricks and Pyke (1973) to be common in secondary schools. A further example is that of tolerating different standards of behaviour, e.g. discouraging girls from fighting but not boys, or expecting boys to be chivalrous by standing if there are not enough places. Teachers, therefore, may cumulatively pass on expectations of different behaviour or, at the very least, grossly exaggerate any differences which do exist, based on selective generalizations. (Examples of selective generalizations in reverse might be: men cannot be hired for this job because they may have a heart attack and die, men having a higher incidence of heart disease than women; or, men cannot be considered for executive positions because they become violent too easily, since men have the male hormone testosterone, often considered to be a major source of aggression.)

Part Two of this book on the hidden curriculum provides further examples of sexism in the education system.

CONCLUSION

The proposition that our society has institutions and cultural features intentionally or unintentionally harmful to both the self-concepts and the life chances of women includes schools. On the evidence of this chapter this would seem to be the case. A complex network of influences is involved, and the effect of a wide range of apparently minor behaviours is powerful because it is cumulative. Labelling theory provides one way of explaining some of the characteristics of this network of influences and how they operate in institutions like schools.

SUMMARY

1. Until recently the issue of gender and equality of opportunity has been neglected in educational writings.
2. Gender intertwines with social class, ethnicity and region to make a complex pattern of influences on life chances.
3. After leaving primary school, girls tend to experience an ever-decreasing set of possibilities for their educational and other life chances.
4. Among psychological explanations are those that stress inheritance, either of abilities or of personality traits.
5. Sociological explanations are derived from the concept of culture: definitions of gender are seen as learned.
6. Labelling theory gives rise to the idea of a self-fulfilling prophecy: in the case of mathematics, girls are falsely diagnosed as lacking in 'spatial ability', when it is different curricular experiences that give rise to differences in spatial thinking.
7. Discussion activity in schools discriminates against girls because of the convention rules about talk in mixed company.
8. Where girls are free from the unwritten obligations to defer to male-dominated talk, as in single-sex schools, they may perform better at educational tasks.
9. Gender identity is established and reinforced though a complex web of influences that take effect from birth onwards.
10. Both the official and the hidden curriculum contribute a variety of influences to this web.
11. The wide range of apparently minor behaviours inside and outside school is powerful because of its cumulative effect.

Further Reading

Byrne, E. (1978) *Women and Education*. London: Tavistock.
Davies, L. (1984) *Pupil Power: Deviance and Gender in School*. Lewes: Falmer Press.
Deem, R. (1978) *Women and Schooling*. London: Routledge and Kegan Paul.
Reid, I. and Wormald, E. (1982) *Sex Differences in Britain*. London: Great McIntyre. A comprehensive review of the evidence available.
Reynolds, H. and Davies, L. (1977) 'Sex Roles and Society'. Special edition of *Social Science Teacher*, **6**, 4. Contains analyses and teaching suggestions.
Sharpe, S. (1976) *Just Like a Girl*. Harmondsworth: Penguin.
Spender, D. and Sarah, E. (1980) *Learning to Lose*. London: The Women's Press.
Whyld, J. (ed.) (1983) *Sexism in the Secondary Curriculum*, London: Harper and Row.

Discussion and Activities

1. Examine school textbooks for evidence of sex typing. A useful source-book is *Sexism in Children's Books*, published by the Children's Rights Workshop (1977).
2. Repeat the exercise on talk patterns described in this chapter, in the section 'Discussion activity in classrooms', and see if your results agree with those of Spender.
3. Prepare a checklist of sex-discriminating features of schooling and use it to study a school or schools known to you. A useful checklist appeared in *Where?*, 130, (July, 1977).

Signposts

1. Sexism in Higher Education
Consider how sexism operates in higher education. One source is Acker, S. and Piper, D.W. (eds.) (1984) *Is Higher Education Fair to Women?* Guildford: SRHE and NFER-Nelson.

2. Single-sex schooling
Evidence about the way mixed schooling can help disadvantage girls has led to a reconsideration of single-sex schooling. See Deem, R. (1984) *Coeducation Reconsidered*, Milton Keynes: Open University Press; and Mahony, P. (1985) *Schools for the Boys? Coeducation Reassessed*, London: Hutchinson.

Chapter 26

Social Class

'Gambling promises the poor what property performs for the rich – something for nothing.'

George Bernard Shaw

INTRODUCTION

The links between social class and education in the UK have been researched frequently and persistently. The reasons for this concentration are both historical and political:

> The development of the British education system, from the point where education was wholly the preserve of the rich, through forms of voluntary education for the poor, to compulsory education for all, has been characterized by concern about social class and about equality.

Silver, 1973

The relics of this structure can be seen today, in the continuance of independent and 'public' schools alongside those provided by local authorities.

The work of psychologists of education in the 1930s and 1940s in trying to relate intelligence, as measured by IQ tests, to social class, set the scene for later work by sociologists on the theme of the 'wastage of talent'. The view held by psychologists and sociologists alike was that equality of educational opportunity was not in evidence, since many working-class children with high intelligence were either not reaching grammar school or were underachieving if they did get there.

DEFINING SOCIAL CLASS

Social class is a highly ambiguous concept. The complications only begin with distinguishing among its uses as (a) a common, everyday expression, (b) an administrative, demographic concept, (c) a concept within sociology and the social sciences in general. Further complications stem from the fact that it is ambiguously used within each of these three areas as well as across them. Many researchers have found it necessary to adopt an operational definition that is either the administrative categories of the Registrar General's classification of occupations, or a modified version of it. Although this means that there is some basis for comparison between various studies, the links with sociological theories of social class outlined by Weber or Marx are somewhat tenuous; for example, in the case of the latter, class is defined in relation to the ownership of the means of production.

Subjective social class raises other problems of definition. Various national opinion polls have shown that people accept the existence of different social classes, will assign themselves to upper, middle or working classes, and think that the major factor in judging position is accent, ahead of occupation, money or education.

However, the findings regarding educational life chances are consistent no matter which definition of social class is employed: in general, middle-class children have much better educational life chances than working-class children, and this relationship has held throughout the grammar school/selective school phase, comprehensive reorganization, and the designation of educational priority areas, with their various compensatory schemes for schooling. ('Better' here signals the introduction of a value interpretation: to obtain a degree, experience extra full-time education, or gain GCEs are all assumed to be superior.)

EDUCATIONAL LIFE CHANCES AND SOCIAL CLASS

In the previous chapter it was pointed out that looking at gender in isolation involved distortion, since class, ethnicity and region are intertwined with it. The same thing must be said of social class, especially since there are correlations between class and parents' attitudes to education and children's intelligence as measured by IQ tests. Explanations need to be stated with care, with such a complex of variables tortuously interconnected, to denote the necessary uncertainty.

The regular patterns that appear in the educational biographies of pupils from the various social classes in Britain include the following.

Entry to Grammar Schools

Entry to grammar schools by passing the 11+ examination was and, where comprehensive reorganization has not taken place, still appears to be strongly related to father's occupation. The figures in Table 26.1, taken from two local education authorities (Swift, 1965) demonstrate the pattern.

Table 26.1 *Social class and the 11+ examination*

	I	II	III	IV	V	VI
% passed 11+	54	39	18	22	8	2
% failed 11+	46	61	82	78	92	98

The children of parents in social class I (professional and managerial occupations) have 54 per cent pass, 46 per cent fail, whereas the children of parents in social class VI (unskilled manual occupations) have 2 per cent pass and 98 per cent fail. In addition, the increase in the proportion of failures increases regularly with movement along the social-class categories, i.e. 46 per cent, 61 per cent, 82 per cent, 78 per cent, 92 per cent, 98 per cent.

Length of Full-time Education

The length of full-time education is strongly related to father's occupation. The figures in Table 26.2 are from the 1961 census, data from later censuses not yet having been published. The figures give the terminal age of full-time education for males in work.

Table 26.2 *Social class and length of full-time education (%)*

	I	II	III	IV	V	VI
left at 15 years or before	22	61	60	92	93	97
left at 16 years of age	20	17	20	6	4	2
left 17–19	21	15	13	2	2	0.5
left 20 years and above	37	7	7	0.6	0.5	0.2

Thus, as Table 26.2 shows, the male children of parents in social class I (professional and managerial occupations) are the most likely to continue in full-time education at 20 years of age (37 per cent of the sample) and the male children of parents of social class VI (unskilled manual occupations) the least likely (0.2 per cent of the sample).

Educational Qualifications

The higher the social class of the father, the greater the chance of achieving educational qualifications. The figures that illustrate this proposition (Table 26.3) are contained in the *General Household Surveys* (1978 and 1980); they refer to males only, and are summarized in Reid (1981).

Table 26.3 *Social class and educational qualifications (%)*

	I	II	III	IV	V	VI
Obtained degree or equivalent	60	10	11	1*	1*	1
Other Higher Education qualification	20	15	13	4	1	1
GCE 'A' level or equivalent	9	10	13	8	3	1
GCE 'O' level or equivalent	4	18	20	12	7	4
CSE grade 2 and below	1	10	7	20	9	5
Foreign and other	3	5	5	3	4	2
No qualification obtained	2	31	32	53	75	85

* = less than one per cent

The contrasts between the figures for no qualifications and for obtaining a degree illustrate the issue of educational life chances. Children of professional and managerial parents (social class I) are the most likely to obtain degrees (60 per cent of them) and the least likely to achieve no qualifications (2 per cent of them). The corresponding figures for children of unskilled manual parents (social class VI) are 1 per cent obtaining degrees and 85 per cent achieving no qualifications. The general relationship holds for females too, with some differences in emphasis (see Reid, 1981, Chapter 6, p. 208).

Type of School Attended

The type of school attended is strongly related to father's occupation. The figures (to the nearest percentage) from *General Household Survey* (1976 and 1978) are shown in Table 26.4 (from Reid, 1981, Table 6.12, p. 223).

Table 26.4   *Type of secondary school* attended by children aged 11–15 years, by social class of father or head of household (percentages)†*

	Social class (R.G.(S.E.)70)						
	1	2	3	4	5	6	All
Secondary modern	7	11	14	24	26	33	20
Comprehensive	39	55	60	63	60	52	59
Middle	6	3	6	5	5	3	5
Grammar	17	10	10	5	4	3	7
Independent	30	18	8	1	1	1	7
Other schools	2	2	3	2	4	7	3
All	6	16	15	40	19	5	100

*Including equivalent Scottish school types; part-comprehensive/part-selective schools are included with comprehensives; independent includes direct grant, and 'other' includes special schools
†Data for 1975 and 1976 combined
N = 4,992
(Derived from Table 7.1, *General Household Survey*, 1976 and 1978)

As can be seen from Table 26.4, the chances of a child whose father is in an unskilled manual occupation attending an independent school are likely to be 1 per cent; of attending a grammar school, 3 per cent; and of attending a secondary modern school, 33 per cent. Comparable chances for a child whose father is in a social class I occupation are: independent school, 30 per cent; grammar school, 17 per cent; secondary modern school, 7 per cent.

The Open University

The second chance for Higher Education offered by the Open University is less strongly related to social class of parent than are other educational opportunities, as Table 26.5 shows.

Table 26.5 *Social class and the Open University*

	I	II	III	IV	V	VI
1971 intake of students	8	26	13	34	13	4

(The students had usually been successful in the education system previously, and their *own* social class according to current occupation was accordingly higher: social class I, 20 per cent; II, 62 per cent; III, 11 per cent; IV, 5 per cent; V, 1 per cent; VI, 0 per cent.)

The largest group of students in the Open University in 1971 were non-graduate teachers and, as fewer of these two- and three-year certificated teachers are left year by year, the pattern of recruitment is beginning to change.

There are many other sets of figures that are available to illustrate the same general trend of middle-class children having different educational life chances from working-class children, and upper-class children having a different pattern of opportunities from both. Two useful surveys of the material are: Swift, D. (1977) *Selection and Opportunity*, Open University E202 Unit 22 (see section 4 in particular); and Reid, I. (1981) *Social Class Differences in Britain*, London: Grant McIntyre (see Chapter 6 in particular).

EXPLANATIONS

A variety of explanations exists to account for the relationships listed above. Some psychological attempts have proposed that middle-class children are genetically superior, because middle-class parents pass on through inheritance superior qualities that result in better school performance. This approach raises a whole host of problems:

> This would involve you in a series of assumptions about the relationship between physiology and behaviour, and mind and behaviour, and about the efficiency of the selection processes in society. What is the point, you might ask, of positively discriminating in favour of socially disadvantaged children if their intelligence potential is fixed at a low point at birth? Why try to compensate for social inequality if individual inherited inequalities determine ability to take life-chances?
>
> Such questions could then become the motifs for research, such as that undertaken by Jensen. We could investigate how (or even whether) mental behaviour as displayed by performance in an intelligence test can be correlated with genetic characteristics; or we might attempt to measure the efficiency with which the tasks of particular occupations sort and select people according to these genetic characteristics. But we would then have to explain knotty paradoxes like the following: if clever people have fewer children than less clever ones, why is the average national intelligence creeping upwards?
>
> Swift, 1978

Other theorists have proposed a psychology of motivation: either the children or their parents, or both, are inadequately motivated towards success in school.

Attempts at explanation derived from sociology include the notion that the institutional regimes of educational institutions tend to favour middle-class pupils: alternatively, education, as currently practised, tends to alienate working-class pupils. Therefore the range of explanations runs from those that locate causes in inadequate pupils to those that stress inadequate institutions. A similar range was seen in the attempts to explain the educational life-chances of girls.

The problem is complicated by the existence of relationships between educational life-chances and other factors, e.g. intelligence as measured by IQ and parental attitudes to education. As Mackinnon (1978) argues, the tendency for middle-class children to do better in education than working-class children is only a beginning. We want to know how this happens, and why. Interpretation of the research is notoriously difficult and controversial. We can demonstrate that educational success is correlated with social class, but that it is *caused* by social class is a proposition that raises difficulties. Without qualification, such a claim is unjustified, because the correlation is not exact, and therefore social class can be only a partial explanation of attainment.

Educational success and other factors, for example, the children's intelligence and parental attitudes, are also correlated.

> Often these correlations are as high as, or even higher than, that between class and attainment, so that on the face of it we have as strong grounds for saying that intelligence or parental attitude causes educational success as for saying that social class does. Finally, social class and the other factors, like parental attitudes, are correlated not only with educational success, but also with each other. It is that above all which makes the research results tricky to interpret, and even, as we shall see, controversial to state in any particular way.
>
> Mackinnon, 1978

Mackinnon observes that, if these were different people, the factors might be disentangled, but this is not the situation. Middle-class children, intelligent children, and children whose parents' attitudes are favourable to education are, by and large, the same children. This makes it difficult to separate the effects of social class on attainment from the effects of the other factors.

Other sociological attempts at explanation have stressed what pupils bring to schools with them – their social-class culture. Pupils from the different social classes are held to bring different language experiences, behaviours, attitudes, ideas, values and skills. When these differences are measured in some way they can then be correlated with educational life chances, to support the proposition that the experience of being brought up in a middle-class home and neighbourhood gives advantages in coping with educational institutions, as currently organized.

Other sociological work has developed another idea: resource provision for education varies from LEA to LEA. These differences are shown in levels of spending on buildings, equipment, teachers and facilities. Educational attainment correlates with spending levels, so the higher the resource provision, the higher the attainments and the greater the educational life chances in that area (Byrne, Williamson and Fletcher, 1974).

The state of sociological research does not allow any final judgements to be made about these attempts at explanation. Some, e.g. the genetic explanation, seem to be more dubious than others. Other explanations, e.g. the social-class culture and resources provision approaches, may turn out to be complementary rather than rivals. Currently a network of causes rather than a single cause seems to be the most plausible position. Furthermore, deprivations may be multiple rather than single. In support of this, the increasing concentration of each deprivation with lower social class provides evidence for rapidly increasing multiple deprivation:

> The chances of finding an upper middle-class (professional/managerial) family with, for example, a chronically ill father earning less than £45 per week and a child who is a poor reader, are less than 1 in 2000: in the unskilled group that chance of a threefold problem has risen to 56 in 1000: i.e. the odds are that 5½ per cent of the lowest class are in this

situation. . . . The proportion will be higher if, as is probable, there are further correlations between problems within that class.

Berthoud, 1976

Berthoud argues that it may be more appropriate to see the absence of deprivation as a privilege of the upper middle class than to view the presence of deprivation as a problem of the lower working class.

THE CONTRIBUTION OF LABELLING THEORY

As in the case of gender, discussed in the previous chapter, the contribution of labelling theory is that of generating explanations about how influences operate both inside and outside school. The proposition is that pupils in general learn a social-class identity just as girls and boys learn a gender identity. The influences appear to be more complex than in the case of gender identity, because often there is a mediating concept of 'ideal pupil'.

The concept of 'ideal pupil' is used by Becker (1952) in an analysis of interviews with teachers in Chicago. He concludes that the teachers in his sample were operating with a definition of the ideal pupil that included being interested in lessons, working hard in schools, and being trained at home in such a way that they were bright and quick at school work. The techniques of these teachers, Becker argues, were able to deal effectively with such pupils, but were inadequate to cope with those deviating from the ideal-pupil image. Other features in the image of ideal pupil were moral: being clean, healthy, well dressed, and moderate in behaviour by exhibiting politeness and patience.

Streaming by Ability

The operation of labelling theory in British schools can be seen in the case of streaming by ability, which has been shown to be only loosely related to measured ability and to involve judgements about the ideal pupil similar to those noted by Becker.

This was the conclusion reached by Douglas (1964), in his study of the progress of a cohort of children through their primary-school career:

> streaming by ability reinforces the process of social selection which was observed in the earlier chapters of this book. Children who come from well-kept homes and who are themselves clean, well-clothed and shod, stand a greater chance of being put in the upper streams than their measured ability would seem to justify. Once there they are likely to stay and to improve in performance in succeeding years.

Douglas, 1964

This contrasts with the deterioration noticed in those children of similar initial measured ability who were placed in the lower streams. The validity of the initial selection appears to be confirmed by the subsequent performance of the children, and a self-fulfilling prophecy appears to be set in motion.

Another study by Jackson (1964), published in the same year, supported the proposition that there was a self-fulfilling prophecy at work that resulted in the overachievement of middle-class children and the underachievement of working-class children.

Further support for this example of labelling came from a study of infant teachers and the home backgrounds of their pupils (Goodacre, 1968). Infant teachers defined 'good' homes as ones that prepared the pupils socially and educationally for classroom life. As Becker had argued, the techniques of the teachers were able to deal effectively with pupils who were close to the 'ideal pupil' concept that underpinned this set of perceptions about homes and pupils. Goodacre showed that the actual performances of the pupils did not match the teachers' perceptions: working-class pupils did better on standardized tests of reading than the teachers' assessments suggested. The key element in a self-fulfilling prophecy – the false diagnosis – is thus present again.

Douglas, Ross and Simpson (1971) give some evidence about the end of the process begun in the infants school by Goodacre's study, in their careful tracking of the cohort they had followed through their primary schools, as they went through secondary school. They conclude:

> The social class differences in educational opportunity which were considerable at the primary school stage have increased at the secondary and extend now even to pupils of high ability. Thus nearly half the lower manual working class pupils of high ability have left school before they are 16½ years.
>
> Douglas, Ross and Simpson, 1971

The Labelling of Parents

The notion of teacher expectations and the typifications that are used to identify students are multifaceted. When teachers generate expectations and label their pupils in various ways this involves a complex of characteristics, such as sex, ethnicity, cognitive performance and classroom behaviour, measured against a concept of ideal pupil and perceptions related to social class. In making their categorizations, people draw information from a variety of first-hand and second-hand information. Most of the information about parents is second-hand, and is related to the mediating concept of 'good parent'.

The social class identity that a teacher gives a pupil is therefore filtered through the concepts of ideal pupil and good parent. The study by Sharp and Green (1975) concluded that the good parent was seen as having a number of characteristics, including that of training children at home to be neat and tidy, to be able to concentrate and to be polite, yet not indulging in direct teaching, e.g. of reading, since this was the professional teacher's task.

Sharp and Green point out that the successful parents, in terms of their children's school achievement and relationship with the school, did not fully conform to this definition of good parent, because they did engage in surreptitious teaching at home. As a result their children matched some of the features of the ideal pupil by being 'ready', learning quickly, making 'progress' and therefore 'doing well'. However, the parents were able to give the appearance of the good parent, defined, among other things, as one who did not actively teach at home. To admit this involved the risk of being labelled as interfering, as Wade (1978) signifies in his personal account. 'What a pity Richard can read . . . ' (see Chapter 5 for further discussion of the labelling of parents).

Implications

One implication is that the common assertion that schools are middle-class institutions is a vast oversimplification. Labelling theory can help tease out the complex relationships between schools, pupils, social-class typifications and other features. A more accurate proposition would be that, through the operation of concepts like ideal pupil and good parent, the chances of pupils whose parents have occupations defined as middle class demonstrating the appropriate characteristics are greater than those of pupils whose parents are defined as working class. This does not eliminate the possibility of some working-class pupils and their parents matching the concepts of ideal pupil and good parent; neither does it preclude the possibility of a middle-class pupil and parent being defined as bad pupil and poor parent.

CONCLUSION

Labelling theory can be overstated in its effects: teacher expectations are often self-fulfilling rather than inevitably so. But when a particular pupil faces the power of a school staff and the backing of a school administration to persist with a categorization, the most likely outcome is that the student learns the identity being imposed. The case of girls and gender identity is a powerful example: few girls resist the labelling involved, as was argued in the previous chapter. The process, as Good and Brophy (1973) outline it, involves five stages:

1. The teacher expects specific behaviour and achievement from particular students.
2. Because of these different expectations, the teacher behaves differently toward the different students.
3. This teacher treatment tells each student what behaviour and achievement the teacher expects from him and affects his self-concept, achievement motivation, and level of aspiration.
4. If this teacher treatment is consistent over time, and if the student does not actively resist or change it in some way, it will tend to shape his achievement and behaviour. High-expectation students will be led to achieve at high levels, while the achievement of low-expectation students will decline.
5. With time, the student's achievement and behaviour will conform more and more closely to that originally expected of him.

Some studies have illustrated that labels can be generated very quickly and then remain stable over months, and even over whole school careers. Rist (1977) reports how he found, during a three-year study of an elementary school in the black community of St Louis, that after only eight days of kindergarten, the teacher made permanent seating arrangements based on what she assumed were variations in academic capability. No formal evaluation of the children had taken place. The placement of the children reflected the social-class distinctions in the room: the poor children from public welfare families all sat at one table, the working-class children sat at another, and the middle class at the third. The teacher operationalized her expectations of these different groups of children in terms of her differentials of teaching time, her use of praise and control, and the extent of autonomy within the classroom. Rist showed how the initial patterns established by the kindergarten teacher came to be perpetuated year after year.

> By second grade, labels given by another teacher clearly reflected the reality each of the three groups experienced in the school. The top group was called the 'Tigers', the middle group the 'Cardinals', and the lowest group, the 'Clowns'. What had begun as a subjective evaluation and labelling by the teacher took on objective dimensions as the school proceeded to process the children on the basis of the distinctions made when they first began.
>
> Rist, 1977

When the label is a social-class label, the result may be seen in the patterns of life chances given earlier. Labelling theory appears to generate some insights into what is taking place. Hargreaves (1978) observes that comprehensive schools take great public pride in the relatively small number of working-class pupils who pass through the sixth form, but the majority of working-class pupils are ignored. Through this is conveyed an important hidden-curriculum message:

> There is something *wrong* with being, and certainly with ending up as being, working class. To be working class is something unfortunate and undesirable from which any pupil with sense will seek to escape. The pupils absorb this message – which is transmitted daily through teachers' exhortations to work hard in school for the benefit it will bring – yet the vast majority of pupils from the working class do not escape their working-class fate.
>
> Hargreaves, 1978

Consequently, Hargreaves suggests, to get defined by teachers as a 'success', a working-class pupil must be on the road to becoming interpreted as middle class, but the majority of working-class pupils must bear the scars of damaged dignity. They collect the inevitable stigma of being 'failures'.

SUMMARY

1. Whatever definition of social class is used, upper- and middle-class children tend to have 'better' educational life chances in terms of examination results and full-time further education.
2. A wide range of studies and statistical sources support the above conclusion.
3. A variety of explanations has been offered and, from psychology, theories of inheritance and of motivation have been proposed.
4. Sociological explanations stress that success and failure may be learned, or 'allocated' by the institution of the education system, or related to social-class cultures, or related to resource provision.
5. A network of causes seems more plausible than a monocausal approach.
6. A contribution from labelling theory is that a social-class identity is learned, and that some identities match the concept of ideal pupil better than others.
7. Those labelled as good pupils may be grouped into 'high-ability' groups and others grouped in 'low-ability' groups.
8. The first group can be shown to tend to overachieve in the sense of improving on

initial performance, whereas the second tends to underachieve, by a deterioration from initial performance.

9. The concept of good parent is related to pupil success: parents become labelled and must give the appearance of not teaching at home to match the good-parent definitions in operation, while actually doing so surreptitiously.

10. Although teacher expectations mediated through the concepts of 'ideal pupil' and 'good parent' are not always self-fulfilling, the power of a school to persist with a categorization is considerable, and the most likely outcome is that the pupil learns the identity offered.

11. An influential message contained in the labelling processes that is related to social class is that to be working class, and certainly to end up there, is something unfortunate and undesirable.

Further Reading

Byrne, D., Williamson, B. and Fletcher, B. (1974) *The Poverty of Education*. Oxford: Martin Robertson. The interplay of social class, region and resource provision in education is the subject of this book.

Douglas, J.W.B. (1964) *The Home and the School*. St Albans: Panther Books. Contains considerable data on social class and education.

Douglas, J.W.B., Ross, J.M. and Simpson, H.R. (1971) *All Our Future*. St Albans: Panther Books. Also contains considerable data on social class and education.

Halsey, A.H., Heath, A.F. and Ridge, J.M. (1980) *Origins and Destinations*. Oxford: Clarendon Press.

Reid, I. (1981) *Social Class Differences in Britain*. London: Grant McIntyre. The most prolific source of data on social class. Chapter 6 deals with education. (Anyone who cherishes the illusion that social class is no longer a feature of British life should consult this book – strongly recommended!)

Swift, D. (1977) *Selection and Opportunity*, Open University E202 Unit 22.

Discussion and Activities

1. An interesting simulation that could be used in a group is *Autobiography: A Look at Social Class Inequalities*, by R. Fielding and V.M. Anderson, published as a 'Briefings for Teachers' by the Association for the Teaching of the Social Sciences and available from the ATSS Resources Unit.

2. Social class emerges as an issue in relation to upper-class educational life-chances in Chapter 29. It might be interesting to try to anticipate this chapter by establishing what you know and believe about this topic.

Signposts

1. Social class and gender
Consider the interplay of social class and gender. One attempt to do this is a paper by M. MacDonald, 'Schooling and the Reproduction of Class and Gender Relations', in Barton, L., Meighan, R. and Walker, S. (1980) *Schooling, Ideology and the Curriculum*. Lewes: Falmer Press. See also Walker, S. and Barton, L. (eds.) (1983) *Gender, Class and Education*. Lewes: Falmer Press.

2. *Higher Education*

The relationship between social class and higher educational life chances is a further topic for investigation. See Reid, I. (1981) *Social Class Differences in Britain*, London: Grant McIntyre, Chapter 6, as a starting point.

Chapter 27

Ethnic Minorities

'it is generally assumed that people of other tribes have been victimized by indoctrination from which our tribe has remained free.'
Neil Postman and Charles Weingartner

INTRODUCTION

It is more difficult to establish the educational life chances of children from ethnic minorities with the same level of precision as in the cases of gender and social class. The availability of both statistical information and research findings is limited, although belief, assertion and description are documented in some quantity.

The reasons for this comparative neglect are not altogether clear. If size is taken as an indicator, the pupils from ethnic minorities, particularly those recently arrived, appear to be a minor concern, since they are a small proportion of the total school population. Estimates of this figure vary between 3.3 per cent (Townsend and Brittan, 1972) and 4.5 per cent. On the other hand, these pupils are concentrated in certain areas, urban areas like London, South Lancashire and the West Midlands. In these areas a particular local authority may have 25 per cent or more of its pupil roll from ethnic minority groups. Furthermore, particular schools may have larger proportions still, since the distributions within such an authority area will be uneven. In these situations, decisions often have had to be made in haste, and without much systematic information to go on.

A second reason for the comparative neglect of the issue of ethnic minorities is not unlike the simplistic view, examined earlier, that mixed comprehensive schools would solve the problem of the underachievement of girls. It is the view that the needs of ethnic minorities and those of the underprivileged, underachieving, working-class members of the indigenous population are largely the same. The 'solution', therefore, is seen as locating deprived areas and resourcing general support in various compensatory programmes. This seems all the more plausible, since incoming ethnic-minority groups often have to settle in those parts of cities that already have old school buildings, high staff turnover and limited facilities. The inadequacies of the approach of stressing similarities with general underachievement, and largely ignoring various differences such as language, cultural identities and prejudice related to skin colour, are the focus of several analyses of the situation (e.g. Jeffcoate, 1979; Rex and Tomlinson, 1979; Barton and Walker, 1983).

A further reason is related to the issues of cultural identities and colour prejudice and the political sensitivities aroused. One research study (Rex and Tomlinson, 1979) contains a report on the difficulties encountered in investigating the situation in Birmingham:

> But inquiries in this field will be difficult because it is a highly sensitive area. The Department of Education as well as the local authorities are likely to be attacked from both sides if they publicly investigate these questions, by the teachers' unions, fearful that they will face a hue and cry in which they are accused of discrimination or prejudice, and, possibly, from racial liberals who might be opposed to any form of racial counting. Certainly we, ourselves, found that both political leaders and administrators were anxious about any investigation in this area. In no way would we suggest that the Labour chairman of the Education Committee was racially prejudiced. She was, indeed, always as helpful and courteous as she could be. But she met us in the presence of officials only and did not offer us a general authorization to enter schools, subject to head teachers' permission, as we had somewhat optimistically hoped. We understood her difficulties in that she was already faced with a potential row over the continued collection of statistics of ethnic origin in the schools. We therefore made our own contacts with sympathetic headmasters.

The debate over the collection of statistics illustrates the political sensitivity of the issues involved. The Department of Education and Science have statistics for the period 1967–72. The definition of 'immigrant children' was held to be discriminatory, despite the attempts to avoid this, and in 1972 the Department declared them administratively dubious. The National Union of Teachers opposed the collection of statistics, declaring that the attempt to elicit information about ethnic minorities and their countries of origin aroused resentment and suspicion of racial discrimination (Select Committee, 1973). A Parliamentary Select Committee favoured the collection of information and recommended that a working party be set up to formulate statistical requirements (Select Committee, 1972). Birmingham Education Committee kept records from 1962 to 1975, when opposition from local teachers' unions and other bodies led to the abandonment of the practice. The outcome of this debate is that little statistical information of any kind is available to administrators and researchers.

The Swann Report (*Education for All*, Cmnd 9453, HMSO, 1985) recognized this problem and one of the 61 recommendations was that 'the collection of accurate and reliable ethnically-based statistics is an essential part of our overall strategy'. The interim report (the Rampton Report, 1981) had made the same recommendation. The history of the two reports illustrates the political sensitivity of the issues concerned. In 1977 the House of Commons Select Committee on race relations had proposed as a matter of urgency an inquiry into the causes of underachievement of children of West Indian origin. The 'matter of urgency' took eight years to complete, the dismissal of one chairperson, Rampton, after the first report was published, along with the resignation of five committee members, followed later by two others, before a final report more acceptable to the government of the day was produced.

The international nature of the issues raised by the presence of ethnic minorities is indicated in a survey of nearly two hundred articles on this theme published in journals from English speaking countries world-wide conducted by Grant and Sleeter (1985). The articles included experience from Australia, Canada, England, Indonesia, Scotland, Sweden and the USA. The experience of member countries of the Council of Europe was the focus of an edition of *Forum* in 1984 entitled *Racism and Xenophobia*.

Indeed, few countries are free of conflicts related to ethnic minorities, and in some – such as Northern Ireland, Cyprus, Sri Lanka, Lebanon – it either is or has been the source of prolonged armed conflict.

DEFINITIONS

The terminology employed includes words like 'race', 'immigrant' and 'ethnic', as well as descriptions like 'black', 'coloured', 'Commonwealth', 'Asian', 'West Indian' and 'Caucasian'. All these present problems of interpretation, and some more than others.

The concept of race is particularly elusive. In some accounts it refers to skin colour, in others culture, and in others nationality. Nineteenth-century anthropology was dominated by a view that humans fell into three racial groupings: Negroid, Caucasoid and Mongoloid, or 'black', 'white' and 'yellow'. The belief that these groups were different in key aspects led to the ranking of them in order of superiority/inferiority, a belief developed to its logical limit in Nazi theories of the master race.

Anthropological and biological evidence has been established in the twentieth century to support an alternative view, that the differences between these broad groupings are minor, and largely of the 'strange but true' category, e.g. that American whites are twice as likely to be colour blind than American negroes. The finding that, in certain respects, a particular 'white' group might be more like a particular 'black' or 'yellow' group than like other 'white' groups added plausibility to the view that the significant differences between populations lay elsewhere – in their cultures, i.e. the different patterns of behaviour, belief and thought which have developed in different societies. The term that usually signals the adoption of this view is 'ethnic', which is why this word appears in the chapter heading rather than the word 'race'.

However, the term 'ethnic' is not without its problems, since some of its uses stress biological features. In this chapter 'ethnic' is taken to mean a group, which may be a minority group, whose members share a common culture. Physically inherited features like hair, facial structure and skin colour may be only poor indicators of ethnic differences. A person with a Celtic face and hair may have no ethnic links with the present-day Welsh; a person with a black skin may have been born in England, as his father and mother were before him; and members of the Ulster province may be Northern Irelanders, but ethnically distinct as Catholic or Protestant in their cultures.

The term 'coloured' presents further problems of interpretation but is preferred by those writers who see skin colour rather than cultural differences as the prior issue. The debate then centres on anti-racism, white racism and on anti-racist educational methods rather than the various multicultural educational proposals – see Reeves, 1979; Hatcher and Shallice, 1983; Brown and Harber, 1985. These writers point out that black children born and bred in England are treated as if they had just arrived from abroad by white racist behaviour and comment. Hence the priority they put on anti-racist education over the competing ideas offered under the term multicultural education.

THE EDUCATIONAL LIFE CHANCES OF ETHNIC MINORITY GROUPS

Some of the reasons why it is difficult to establish with any precision the educational life chances of ethnic minority groups have already been mentioned. First, the question of overlapping features is prominent. Members of ethnic minority groups often share the general disadvantages of members of the working classes. About half the population will be female, and so share the general disadvantages of girls. Many will live in inner-city areas, and so share the disadvantages of a particular urban group, sometimes known as the 'new poor', often with multiple deprivations or a 'tangle of pathologies', as Rex and Tomlinson (1979) put it:

> Apart from the problem of differences of life chances, life-styles and values between white-collar and manual workers, it now seems to be increasingly recognized that there are divisions between manual workers – between those who have job security and political and trade-union protection of their social rights on the one hand and those who live within 'a tangle of pathologies' on the other.

For many children, the most they can aspire to is to achieve the same life chances as the mainstream working class.

A second difficulty is the lack of statistical and research information, as described previously. This makes a list of features based on statistical probabilities difficult to establish.

A further difficulty is related to the assumption underpinning the concept of life chances. It tends to be a status quo based analogy that takes for granted that the question is: What chances are there in the system as it stands? Who gets what in the present educational structure? This obscures the issue of alternatives, which may be a crucial one for members of ethnic minority groups, for 'getting on' at the expense of fellows means both adopting the dominant culture's point of view, which may be seen as corrupt, and adding to the isolation and oppression of the ethnic minority by moving out of it. The danger of becoming an 'Uncle Tom' conveys some of the points in question:

> there are few native, British, working-class socialists so committed that they refuse to have their children educated in a corrupt, middle-class educational system. For the immigrant, however, as for the black American, the problem is more acute. It may seem to some that to try to launch one's children into social mobility and assimilation is to connive at the oppression of one's own people.
>
> Rex and Tomlinson, 1979

A number of ethnic minority groups are able to 'solve' or contain their problems by biculturalism. Because they are small in numbers, and lack visibility due to 'white' or near-white skin colour, they tend to adapt to the school culture in school and preserve their own culture outside. Cypriots, Jews, Maltese, Chinese, Irish and Italians are examples of groups in this situation. Two groups who find this approach more difficult are Asian and West Indian. Neither of these terms is unproblematic. 'Asian' includes Indian, Pakistani, Ugandan Asian and a variety of religious identities. 'West Indian' includes the various Caribbean islands, and some black people from various African countries also find themselves identified as members of this group. The common features are that these groups share the problems of visibility, being brown or black, and encounter language and cultural differences, though experienced in rather different ways. Subsequent comments will focus on the experiences of these two groupings.

The regular patterns that appear in the education biographies of pupils from the 'Asian' and 'West Indian' groupings appear to be as follows.

(a) The chances of experiencing a public-school education are very small for both groupings, since they are located as members of the 'new poor'.

> The question for many children seems to be not whether they have an equal chance of rising from the working class to the middle class, but whether through their education they can at least have the same rights and cultural equipment as the mainstream working class.
>
> Rex and Tomlinson, 1979

(b) The chances of being allocated to an ESN school are greater for members of the 'West Indian' group than for other groups in the UK (Coard, 1971).

(c) The achievement of ethnic minority groups varies:'

> On the whole, pupils from India and Pakistan do better than other immigrants, and West Indian and Turkish Cypriot children appear to do rather worse.
>
> Little, 1975

(d) Pupils from the 'West Indian' and 'Asian' groups are likely to be overrepresented in the bottom streams and remedial classes of secondary schools (Jeffcoate, 1977).

(e) Pupils tend to experience schools with a concentration of ethnic minority groups. Describing the situation in Birmingham, Rex and Tomlinson (1979) concluded:

> Most will go to immigrant majority schools i.e. they will not simply be a minority presenting unusual problems against a background of white British normality. Their problems will be *the* problems of the school.

The finding of an Inner Education Authority study was that:

> the effect of immigrant concentration on educational performance is less important than the degree to which schools are experiencing multiple deprivation.
>
> Little, 1975

(f) Length of education in the United Kingdom appears to be a more important factor in determining primary-school performance than length of residence or being born in the country (Little, 1975).

One attempt to summarize the educational life chances of ethnic minority groups is given in Field and Hankin (1971). They suggest that immigrants and other 'out' groups in society generally benefit proportionally least from education. A few teachers choose to work in the 'twilight' zones of big cities and find it rewarding to serve among the children of immigrants, the very poor, the chronically sick and unsupported mothers. For the most part, it is difficult to attract and keep staff for schools in inner-city areas and, in addition, the buildings and equipment are often of poor quality:

> Immigrants thus frequently find themselves living among the sectors of English society worst served by the education system and least motivated to use education to advance themselves socially. They put down their roots in sectors of society which neither help nor expect them to do well. The fact that they are coloured further impedes their advancement. Because of their colour they are easily identifiable

(g) Second-generation teenagers may achieve better results than first-generation ones. Driver (1980) found that some 'West Indian' school leavers had begun to outperform their white peers in public examinations.

Another account of the educational performance of ethnic minority children has been compiled by Tomlinson (1982), and it contains an excellent analysis and a detailed set of references.

EXPLANATIONS

There have been both psychological and sociological attempts to explain the relationships outlined above. One type of psychological attempt proposes that inheritance of abilities is the major factor. As in the cases of girls and low social classes, the proposition is that inferior qualities are passed on by parents to their children. In this case the parents are said to be those belonging to ethnic minorities. This approach has been at the centre of a long-standing debate about 'race' differences in intelligence, and the logical and methodological problems are similar to those outlined earlier in the cases of gender and social class.

A recent attempt to review this explanation (NUT, 1978) argues that the basic assumptions of this genetic approach are suspect:

> Defining people as Black or White, Jewish or Christian, English or Irish, is a *social* and not a *biological* description. It is no wonder, therefore, that a leading British sociologist of race, Professor John Rex of Warwick University, has pointed out that biology has nothing to contribute to the study of human 'race'. Human variation *is* an important topic concerning which geneticists have something to say, but they are not helped by the confusion of the social with the biological, which is the stock-in-trade of racist thought. Nowhere has this confusion been more apparent and dangerous in recent years than in the dispute over supposed 'race' differences in intelligence.

The report arrives at a series of concluding points:

1. In *biological* terms the concept of 'race' is meaningless for human populations.
2. More than 94 per cent of all genetic differences between individuals that have been studied occur between individuals of the *same* 'race' not between '*races*'.
3. Intelligence tests may give results agreeing with children's school performance but they say nothing about any fixed 'biological potential' of the individual.
4. It is not meaningful or possible to divide a child's performance into 'genetic' or 'environmental' components.
5. The determinants of 'civilization' and the development of different human societies should be sought in social, economic and historical factors, not in biology.

An alternative set of explanations develops the notion of cultural discontinuities: differences in the family background and community life of ethnic-minority groups are seen as deficits and disadvantages: e.g. inadequate linguistic stimulation in early childhood and high incidence of child minding. One writer lists seven variations of this approach:

> A number of reasons have been offered for this different level of educational performance; they range from (1) culture shock, (2) length of separation from parents, (3) movement from a predominantly rural background to an industrial one, (4) age of the children during migration, (5) reception into an unknown ready-made family in Britain, (6) language

difficulties, (7) problems of adjustment from a poorer country to a richer and more developed one.

Chevannes, 1979

Another attempt at explanation was mentioned earlier. It is the view that the needs of ethnic minorities and those of the underprivileged, underachieving working-class members of the indigenous population are largely the same. The issue is seen as one of general disadvantage, and the concept of educational disadvantage was developed in the Plowden Report (1967), where, for example, black and white children in the inner-city areas of cities were seen as equally deprived. An opposing view is developed in Rex and Tomlinson (1979), where children of ethnic minorities are seen to have additional disadvantages to those of the urban, indigenous, lower working class:

> immigrants do suffer handicaps as immigrants, and their black children suffer handicaps of their own. Amongst these we would identify the problem of language, the problem of cultural identity, and that of the bias which exists in the various selective processes with which they are faced.

A further explanation locates the problem in the nature of contemporary British society: it has not yet become effectively mutli-cultural, but remains racist. The view that ethnic minorities should assimilate to the mainstream indigenous culture was encouraged by the Commonwealth Immigrants Advisory Council's view (1964) that the perpetration of the different values of immigrant groups could not be expected. More recently, cultural diversity and mutual tolerance have been seen as the way forward, 'as a pleasant optional extra which all sensible men will appreciate, because it adds quality to the lives of us all'. But, as Rex and Tomlinson (1979) go on to point out:

> The West Indian is far from claiming an optional extra when he asks that some way be found of preserving his own cultural traditions and educating his children in them. Like black Americans, West Indians feel that they face a culture within which the achievements of white Europeans are continually asserted, while black men always appear in a degraded role. This is so deeply entrenched in our culture, according to this view, that it has become unconscious.

The consequence is that education, for black children, means having to learn to accept inferior images of themselves. The explanation that ethnic minorities suffer handicaps because of the racist nature of British society leads to the conclusion that the children concerned were not so much failing as being failed by the nature of the current educational system. This is in line with similar explanations for the failure of girls and of children of unskilled manual workers: racist, sexist and class discriminatory behaviour are all seen as stemming from the acceptance of the psychological propositions that one race is superior to another, or that one sex is superior to another, or that one class is superior to another, because of some beliefs about genetic inheritance.

THE CONTRIBUTION OF INTERACTIONIST APPROACHES

Layers of Meaning and Racism

The definition of racism as the theory and practice derived from the assumption that one ethnic group is superior to another because of genetic inheritance seems straight-forward enough. However, the manifestations of racism in a society are complicated. Racism can be proposed by any group, hence 'black' racism is as feasible as 'white', or 'brown' racism as feasible as 'yellow'.

The layers of meaning concept in interactionist sociology may help to clarify in two ways:

1. By identifying the multiple interpretation of the participants in an institution or social situation; e.g. the views of a black girl arriving into British society may be shown to be quite different from those attributed to her by white members of the indigenous population (see Chevannes, 1979).
2. By analysing how racism manifests itself in different layers of social meaning and action.

Taking the latter approach, it is possible to see three layers of social meaning, distinct in some ways, but necessarily interacting in other respects:

1. The general cultural.
2. The institutional, in the case of education, schools, etc.
3. The personal.

At the general cultural layer, we are all likely to be racists to some extent because we have usually been socialized into the dominant ideas, values and structures of our culture. These ideas will include notions of who counts as 'they', as 'foreigners', as 'immigrants', and of the expected behaviours of members of 'other' cultures. In most cultures this socialization tends to be ethnocentric, valuing the familiar culture as normally the best way of doing things and rating any alternative ways as likely to be inferior. The ethnocentric nature of history textbooks was one illustration given in the section on the hidden aspects of the official curriculum.

At the institutional layer, the notion of teacher and pupil as victims of sets of institutional patterns to which the new arrival has to adjust has already been discussed (Chapters 2 and 4). The package already in existence may include bias in selection procedures, racism in textbooks and curriculum materials, and complacency about the underachievement of ethnic minority groups.

Individual racism is perhaps easier to identify, since it leads to direct confrontations:

> Individual racism takes such forms as physical attacks and abuse directed against minority group teachers and pupils, racialist leaflets at school gates, staff prejudices, and hostile white reactions to the introduction of multiracial materials in the classroom.
>
> Jeffcoate, 1979

This analysis in terms of layers of meanings allows for some crucial contradictions in behaviour to be identified. The interactionist notion of the irony of some human action (which does not discount the maliciousness of other human behaviour) is seen in the well-intentioned application of policies with unrecognized racism at their roots, which to the surprise of the instigators, with their lack of sociological awareness, end up as failures. To dismiss such educationalists as hypocrites is to fail to recognize the irony of human action when teachers and curriculum developers are victims of hidden bias in their well-intentioned work.

However, in the case of racism, to understand is not to condone, for the consequences for the individuals and groups unfairly discriminated against are likely to be similar whether the action were well intentioned or malicious. Therefore those who acted in haste under the pressure of circumstances when, without adequate planning or advice, they were faced with unfamiliar problems created by the arrival of black and brown children in classrooms can be accorded sympathetic understanding. But the outcome of many of those decisions was still racist, as the list of life chances given earlier has indicated.

Labelling Theory and Racism

Among the problems faced by ethnic minorities in schools are those of general disadvantages of being members of the 'new poor' and specific disadvantages of language difficulties, cultural identity and bias in selection procedures. Labelling theory has something to contribute to the understanding of all these problems, particularly the specific ones.

Language

The 'Asian' and 'West Indian' groups experience rather different language problems. In both cases a self-fulfilling prophecy can be set in motion when language difficulties or differences are interpreted as deficiencies.

The Asian group 'problem' looks straightforward. Since this group is non-English-speaking in many cases, a second language has to be learned. However, the language teaching undertaken has been said to be of such a kind as to ensure minimum performance, because language can be learned at four possible levels. It can be learned as a second language, which is not normally a tool of learning. Then it can be learned so as to cope in a minimal way with the classroom situation. Thirdly, it can be learned so as to enable the learner to pass minimal examinations. Fourthly, it can be learned so that it can be used to enable the user to attain the highest possible level of performance.

English as a Second Language (ESL) teaching was conceived of hurriedly, so it is to be expected that the first two and possibly the third, rather than the fourth, predominate. This kind of language teaching may result in a filtering process, whereby most first-generation immigrants, at least, are able to do little more than obtain minimum educational qualifications.

This minimum performance increases the possibility of being labelled lower stream, remedial pupil or slow learner, with the likelihood of the self-fulfilling prophecy process and the teacher expectation effects being set in motion, as outlined earlier in Chapters 11 and 24.

The 'West Indian' group problem can be that of Creole. Links with the perception of working-class speech patterns are possible here. In both cases a different form of English is referenced against a concept of Standard English as commonly used in white-collar occupations, and evaluated as inferior. Researches like that of Labov (1969), into negro speech, and of V.K. Edwards (1978), into Creole, suggest that this is a false evaluation and that 'different' does not equal 'inferior' in terms of these language forms. As was indicated earlier, self-fulfilling prophecies start with such false diagnoses. The research report of Edwards into language attitudes and underperformance concluded that it appeared that teachers differ little from the rest of society in the stereotypes of minority groups which they hold. The attitude tests he used indicated that student teachers recognize middle-class speech as of high status. They also discriminate between working-class and West Indian speakers and evaluate working-class speech consistently more favourably than West Indian. They consider that the West Indian girls will do significantly worse academically than both the working-class and middle-class English children and that they will be less interesting members of the class. There seems a very real possibility that they will convey these negative feelings to the children, in the light of the research on teacher expectations. Edwards goes on to comment on the effects on self-concepts:

> The results of the attitude tests also suggest that West Indians view themselves very negatively and these views reflect to a large extent the stereotype of West Indians which is prevalent in Britain. It seems highly probable that a child's ability to learn is affected by his motivation and that his motivation is affected by the feedback he receives from society.

Cultural identity

The conclusion of recent investigations into the self-concepts of ethnic-minority pupils is that the risk of their having to accept an image of themselves as inferior as the result of schooling, among other influences, is considerable. The risk of the West Indian group is greater, Rex and Tomlinson argue:

> From this point of view the Asian communities must be objects of envy to the West Indian. Their religious and cultural traditions and organizations are strong, and, even while their children are using school education in an instrumental way, their supplementary cultural education confirms a worthy self-image. Moreover, the host society has learned to recognize the separate Asian religions and the claim which they have to being taught in school.

Yet West Indians are expected to make no claim to have their culture taught in schools. One consequence has been a demand for Black Studies, which is not at all easily conceded:

> Multiculturalism as an optional extra is one thing. Black Studies which are based upon a refusal of the black man to be assimilated, or still worse, upon a culture of Third World revolt, are quite another. As a result, the multicultural programmes which have been offered simply do not meet the needs which West Indians feel.
>
> Rex and Tomlinson, 1979

The Schools Council project, Education for a Multicultural Society, collected material on the cultural identities of ethnic-minority pupils. Here are some examples quoted by Jeffcoate (1975) that support the proposition that images of inferiority are in evidence in schools:

> Richard is four, British and black, and he goes to nursery school. Watching television with his mother he observed that a man on the screen was black. His mother agreed and added that the man was like Richard in this respect.
>   To her surprise Richard denied his own blackness and, in response to further questioning, the blackness of his mother and of his closest relatives. Though persuaded to agree that

his mother and family were black, he persisted with the fiction of his own non-blackness.

Doreen lives 20 miles away from Richard. She is also black and in her first year at secondary school. Last year at her multiracial junior school she wrote, along with the rest of her class, a piece called 'Myself'. In it she said: 'I wish that I had long hair, but I have not got long hair. I do not like myself and my writing. I do not like the colours of my eyes. I have spots on my skin which I wish that I never had. . . . In the future I think that I am going to turn . . . black, ever so black, and ugly just like I am now, ugly.'

Two hundred miles away and at about the same time, a group of three and four-year-old white children in an all-white nursery school in a multiracial town were shown photographs of black people. The photographs were deliberately selected to portray blacks in a respectful and unstereotyped way. Yet, after three or four minutes, the children began to make derisory comments punctuated by cries of 'Ugh, blackies' and continued to do so until the teacher intervened. She was as surprised as Richard's mother had been, admitting later to having been 'bowled over' by the animosity the children had displayed.

Not so one of the mothers. She had already had a similar experience with her own child, who had pointed to Pakistani customers in a shop and said: 'Oh, blackies, ugh, dirty Pakis.'

The learning of such identities can be seen as illustrations of the theories of labelling, self-fulfilling prophecies and teacher expectation effects outlined earlier. The mechanisms involved include many of the features of the hidden curriculum and the official curriculum analysed earlier.

Bias in selection procedures

There is a variety of selection procedures in schools, including selection into streams, examination and non-examination groups, remedial classes and special schooling. The list of educational life-chances given earlier indicates that there is a distinct selection pattern for ethnic-minority groups, and the result has been a charge of bias in the procedures.

Tests of supposedly innate performance such as Intelligence Quotient tests have been the subject of considerable debate. The content and assumptions of such tests, as well as the statistical basis of the testing procedures have been questioned. One writer expresses his doubt thus:

> when we administer 'a battery of attainment tests' to an immigrant child we ask him: 'How English are you?' When his performance replies: 'Not very', we say: 'You are deprived and handicapped and must have remedial treatment until we have exorcized all traces of the alien spirit from your academic behaviour.'
>
> Marsh, 1971

In the case of selection for special schools, it is frequently left to individual teachers to 'identify' possible children, using a checklist which may include items like slovenliness in appearance, attention seeking, resentfulness, argumentativeness, impudence, lack of interest in work and disobedience. Passing over difficulties such as the subjective interpretations involved (for, as Hargreaves et al., 1978, have shown, one teacher's 'cheek' is interpreted by another as 'lively banter') the consequences are said to be:

> The teacher tends to pick out the most boisterous children rather than the dullest. That is why there are more boys than girls in ESN schools – and more West Indians than Asians.
>
> Lee, 1978

CONCLUSION

There appears to be a growing view that the educational policies adopted in the cases of ethnic-minority groups are dubious. Williams (1979) identifies three types of policy: technicist, moral and socio-political. The *technicist* approach, stressing that the existing education system is basically sound, encourages the experts within the teaching profession to develop compensatory programmes to remedy underachievement. The *moral* approach implies that a new multicultural vision of society should be applied in schools in order to develop awareness, understanding and tolerance of different cultures, to replace the current racist social structures and behaviours. The *socio-political* approach also has a vision of a plural society of relatively separate but equal groups, but stresses that changes outside schools are as necessary as, if not more vital than, those inside. Inside schools much more than academic development is envisaged, and the development of 'creative discontent' is implied.

In adopting the technicist approach, the problems of being socialized into the upward mobility vision of society are stressed: both the problems of moving from one culture into another and the assumption that schooling is basically soundly conceived and practised are overlooked.

One of the reasons why this approach is being questioned is discussed by Little (1975):

> By the end of the '70s virtually all black pupils in primary schools and an increasing proportion in secondary schools will have been born here. This means that the nature of the educational issues will change.

The conclusion that compensatory programmes to achieve equal opportunity for ethnic-minority groups are sufficient is likely to give way to criticism of the basic assumptions about schooling. Little argues:

> Just as the educational system has in a sense failed to meet the needs of the child from a working-class background, so now, to an even greater extent, it is failing to meet the needs of the child from a different cultural background.

On the basis of an earlier chapter, one might also add . . . 'and for that matter, the needs of girls'.

The contribution of interactionist approaches in sociology and of labelling theory is to identify in some detail some of the false diagnoses that led to the adoption of the technicist approach, as well as the complexity of the consequences.

In a survey of the literature on the concept of 'multicultural education' in journals written in English world-wide, Grant and Sleeter (1985) propose a typology of five competing forms of multicultural education. Their fifth category, Education that is Multicultural and Social Reconstructionist, fulfils the prediction of Little in noting the growth of a number of articles questioning the basic assumptions of schooling in a wide range of countries.

Further Reading

Barton, L. and Walker, S. (eds.) (1983) *Race, Class and Education*. Beckenham: Croom Helm.

Brown, C. and Harber, C. (eds.) (1985) *Cultural Diversity and Conflict*. Special edition of *Social Science Teacher*, **14**, 3.

Craft, M. (1982) *Education for Diversity: The Challenge of Cultural Pluralism*. Nottingham: School of Education, University of Nottingham.

Cherrington, D. (ed.) (1985) *Ethnic Minorities in Education*. Special edition of *Educational Review*, **37**, 2.

James, A. and Jeffcoate, R. (eds.) (1981) *The School in the Multicultural Society*. London: Harper and Row.

Jeffcoate, R. (1979) *Positive Image*. Richmond: Chameleon Books.

Jeffcoate, R. (1984) *Ethnic Minorities in Education*. London: Harper and Row.

Rex, J. and Tomlinson, S. (1979) *Colonial Immigrants in a British City*. London: Routledge and Kegan Paul.

Tomlinson, S. (1983) *Ethnic Minorities in British Schools: A Review of the Literature 1960–82*. Aldershot: Gower.

Willey, R. (1984) *Race, Equality and Schools*. London: Methuen.

Discussion and Activities

1. Examine school textbooks for evidence of ethnic bias. A useful source-book is *Racism in Children's Books*, published by the Children's Rights Workshop.
2. Discuss the study by G. Driver, 'How West Indians Do Better at School (Especially the Girls)', in *New Society*, 17 Jan. 1980. The subsequent correspondence, lasting for several weeks, raised various points of debate and criticism about the study.
3. 'There is no one black experience in this country, no one set of parental and student aspirations. Minority groups will ask for different things of the education system at different times – J. Williams (1979). Discuss this view and its implications for schooling.
4. Make a summary of the main points of the chapter.
5. What can we learn from the pupils' perspective? See Jeffcoate in James and Jeffcoate (1981), p. 229, for one study.

Signposts

1. Multicultural society and multicultural education

As noted in the chapter these are both ambiguous ideas with competing definitions in play. However, this is not widely acknowledged, so that policies operating under the general label of 'multicultural' can actually be pulling in opposite directions. Writers addressing this issue include Grant and Sleeter (1985) contributors in Brown and Harber (1985), Burntwood in Cherrington (1985) and Mukhopadyay, A. (1984).

2. Ethnic minorities as an international experience

The cross-national aspects of ethnic minorities experience is the focus of several sets of writings. Grant and Sleeter (1985) provide a survey and a framework for analysis, there are articles in Brown and Harber (1985), and the Council of Europe journal *Forum* has a special edition (1984) *Racism and Xenophobia*. See also *The Education of Minority Groups: An Enquiry into Problems and Practices of Fifteen Countries*. Aldershot: Gower, 1984.

Chapter 28

Other Minorities: Those With 'Special Needs'

'Don't let us make imaginary evils, when you know we have so many real ones to encounter.'

Oliver Goldsmith

INTRODUCTION

There are many minorities that either appear to have or lay claim to having special needs. These include travellers' children, the left-handed, commune dwellers, canal-boat children, religious exclusives, high achievers (sometimes referred to as 'gifted'), mobile groups such as armed forces personnel, circus folk and other entertainers, homosexuals, members of the Royal Family, various kinds of physically handicapped, and various kinds of people identified as psychologically handicapped, e.g. maladjusted.

The official use of the description 'special' refers to some of these and not others. Some of these minorities have their own school provision. Thus the children of the wealthy have access to the private-school system and some religious groups, e.g. Roman Catholics, Jews, Church of England and Moslems, have schools. Some commune groups have run their own schools, e.g. the Bruderhof primary school of the now defunct Wheathill Bruderhof in Shropshire. Travellers, of both gipsy and tinker stock, have been the recipients of experiments in mobile schools housed in vans, sometimes based on voluntary provision, such as the West Midlands Travellers Schools, originally initiated by the Walsall Humanist Group. High achievers have a variety of special provisions, including 'A' streams, express streams, sixth forms and the university sector as a whole, although members of pressure groups for the 'gifted' do not see these as going far enough.

When we look at the state and local education authority version of who has special needs to be catered for in terms of special education provision, the emphasis tends to be on physical and psychological handicaps, as Table 28.1 shows.

Barton and Tomlinson (1984) note that the official categories of special need (see Table 28.1) combine both normative and non-normative conditions. In normative conditions there is some basis for agreement about handicap or need such as blindness, deafness, or epilepsy. However, categories like 'educationally subnormal' and 'maladjusted' are non-normative since there are no adequate measuring instruments or agreed definitions.

Table 28.1 *Full-time pupils by category of major handicap*

	At January	1973	1974	1978	1979	1980	1981	1982	1983
Blind	Boys	546	549	687	632	632	599	601	570
	Girls	464	446	506	522	494	489	479	426
Partially sighted	Boys	1 265	1 266	1 246	1 229	1 254	1 142	1 061	1 012
	Girls	762	787	830	815	810	719	670	662
Deaf	Boys	1 879	1 923	1 936	1 868	1 786	1 698	1 601	1 557
	Girls	1 549	1 574	1 541	1 462	1 460	1 359	1 266	1 166
Partially hearing	Boys	1 240	1 278	1 161	1 052	838	803	777	697
	Girls	973	978	809	811	619	584	565	515
Physically handicapped	Boys	5 606	5 930	6 975	7 140	6 901	6 663	6 525	6 316
	Girls	4 053	4 264	5 333	5 478	5 408	5 075	4 963	4 816
Delicate	Boys	3 284	3 090	2 801	2 606	2 411	2 309	2 282	2 177
	Girls	1 993	1 877	1 640	1 441	1 311	1 219	1 109	1 072
Maladjusted	Boys	7 934	8 528	10 262	10 233	10 640	10 544	10 533	10 789
	Girls	2 253	2 615	3 072	2 875	2 972	2 693	2 644	2 606
Educationally sub-normal									
Medium	Boys		31 057	33 801	34 294	33 903	34 415	34 441	34 129
Severe	Boys	45 083	14 616	12 901	13 101	13 343	13 456	13 713	13 964
Medium	Girls		20 546	21 694	21 622	21 107	21 403	21 120	20 647
Severe	Girls	31 307	10 786	9 752	9 870	10 043	10 144	10 307	10 499
Epileptic	Boys	794	851	1 115	1 138	1 021	971	878	844
	Girls	554	631	804	808	736	704	652	603
Speech defect	Boys	1 605	2 031	2 468	2 324	2 075	1 824	1 537	1 407
	Girls	779	993	1 339	1 217	1 036	867	715	625
Autistic	Boys		200	384	381	420	429	400	374
	Girls		72	147	172	192	183	180	173
Total	Boys	69 236	71 319	75 737	75 998	75 224	74 853	74 349	73 836
	Girls	44 687	45 569	47 467	47 093	46 188	45 439	44 670	43 810
	Total	113 923	116 888	123 204	123 091	121 412	120 292	119 019	117 646

Source: *DES Statistics of Education: Schools, 1983*, Table 20/83

In England these non-normative categories have always included the largest numbers of children in special education, and the important point is that these children are predominantly of working-class origins, and, since the settlement of West Indian immigrants, have also included large numbers of black children. Thus a major dilemma in the integration debate is that it is predominantly about the 'integration' of children who in England were known in the 1930s as the 'social problem class' . . . and this raises questions about the nature of special education – how far is it 'education' and how far is it 'social control'?

Barton and Tomlinson, 1984

OFFICIAL CATEGORIZATIONS: WHO HAS SPECIAL NEEDS?

Even a cursory glance at the practice of special education in the UK reveals variation in organization, staffing and policies. A particular child in one LEA will be identified as special and sent to a separate school; in another LEA the same child will be catered for in a unit within a neighbourhood school; and in yet another LEA that same child may not be identified as special in the first place.

Part of the variation is historical, part is related to conceptual confusions and part related to different pragmatic responses to the problem identified. Modern special education has its origins in the 1944 Education Act, by which local education authorities were required to make special provision for pupils who 'suffer from any disability of mind or body' either in special schools or otherwise. Ten categories of special provision were established, although with such a broad definition to work with it could have been 20 or 30, and have covered the majority of the population. There was no clear indication of what constituted 'normal', so children defined as special in one area of the country were not necessarily so defined in another.

A further development was brought about by the 1970 Education (Handicapped Children) Act, which made the local education authority responsible for those children previously catered for in hospitals. All children, regardless of the degree of handicap, were entitled to receive education in schools or otherwise, as organized by the LEAs. Special schools now had a new challenge: children with multiple handicaps, some spending most of their lives in cots in hospital wards, other hyperactive and destructive, were now admitted to schools.

Some of the conceptual confusion is illustrated by the above changes. Who is normal? Who is not normal? Who is so disabled as to be unable to be in schools? These and other related questions have been given different answers at different times and in different places. The confusion is also illustrated by the steep rise in the number of pupils in special schools since 1950 (see Table 28.2).

Table 28.2 *Numbers of pupils in special schools*

	1950	1975
Maladjusted		
Boys	467	10 140
Girls	120	3 421
Educationally sub-normal (mild)		
Boys	9 205	31 727
Girls	5 968	21 017

Using the vague descriptions available, such as 'any child whose attainment falls significantly below the normal', the number of children identified as special has increased. As many as 20 per cent of the school population could be classified as special at some stage between five and 16 years, on the basis of such a description.

The pragmatic nature of the response to pupils identified as special is illustrated by the variation among LEAs. A similar child may be sent to boarding school by one, given home tuition by another, and given facilities within a neighbourhood comprehensive school by another.

That the answer to the question of who has special needs, according to official categorizations, is a very confused one, is further illustrated by the research of Gibson and Jackson (1974) on mental retardation. They estimate that, since the condition of 85 per cent of children identified as 'mentally retarded' has no precise cause (e.g. brain damage), this category may have been 'manufactured' by professional labellers such as doctors, psychiatrists and psychologists. Gibson and Jackson point out that the term 'mental retardation' is highly ambiguous, since it is employed to designate persons who in the past would have been referred to as morons, mental deficients, mental defectives, mental subnormals or, in more general terms, the feeble-minded. However, the ambiguity of the proposed causes is even more startling, for over 100 'causes' of mental retardation have been specified.

From this it follows that mental retardation is not a unitary disorder, in the sense that all persons who are officially thus categorized share a common condition produced by a cause that is identifiable, because the term can include:

1. Persons whose retardation is marked and results from a disease of the nervous system or genetic variation.
2. Persons who suffer a fairly specific but less profoundly disabling genetic disorder (for example, Down's syndrome).
3. Persons who have no obvious physical defect and whose intellectual abilities, although inadequate for some tasks, are perfectly adequate for many others (i.e. mildly mentally retarded).

Gibson and Jackson find that the third category constitutes 85 per cent of the mentally retarded population. However, it is rarely possible to identify with any degree of certainty the precise cause of the lesser intellectual performance of those in this category. The 'professional labellers' categorize the 85 per cent with tests of dubious precision:

> While it is acknowledged that there are degrees of mental retardation of such severity that a child's intellectual impairment is undoubted, it has been argued that most mentally retarded children are 'manufactured' by those professionally engaged in the process of educational categorization. The description 'legitimate labellers' has been given to those persons (for example, doctors, psychiatrists, psychologists and educators) who are presumed to have the necessary knowledge and skills to make a diagnosis.
>
> Gibson and Jackson, 1974

Gibson and Jackson suggest that, as a result of their training and experience, the professional labellers develop a knowledge of trustworthy 'recipes' (i.e. sets of prescriptions to guide future professional action), and they will have a tendency, in their dealings with children referred to them, to think in terms of categories.

In this case, the appropriate 'recipe for action' for detecting and confirming the presence of mental retardation is through the use of diagnostic tests, which are dubious on three counts. First, there is an assumption that what is being examined can be measured precisely, whereas in fact this is an area in which no precision exists, except in the objectives and intentions of the labellers. Second, the diagnostic category arrived at by the labeller is rarely challenged, as it tends to be reinforced both by professional support (i.e. the labellers tend to follow occupational group conceptions) and by audience support (i.e. the labeller is presumed by his audience to have the necessary knowledge and skills to make his diagnoses). Third, spurious objectivity and precision is frequently attributed to coding schemes, checklists and written observations employed in the diagnostic process, whereas in reality these depend, on rumour, gossip, instant decisions, guesswork, conversations, discrepant information and imperfect biographical stock-taking from memory.

INTEGRATION OR SEPARATION? – THE LOCATION OF SPECIAL EDUCATION

One of the central issues raised by the Warnock Report (1978) was whether special education should take place in normal schools more often than it does at the moment. Part of this concern for a shift in emphasis came from the parents. The lives of children who attend special schools take on a number of characteristics. Children often have to travel some distance because the special schools are not neighbourhood schools, and this can take as much as 1½ hours a day. There is the stigma of the special bus, which may also vary in its timing and reliability, so that pupils arrive at school cold, irritable or tired, or all three. Parents may have to divide their loyalties between the local school for one or more children and the special school for another. Maintaining contact with the distant school can be difficult, and friends children make there may not live close enough to come to tea or to play with at weekends. Other parents and children in the neighbourhood, having little contact with children at the special school, are often unsympathetic and even fearful, and this can result in spiteful and tactless comments, generated by unfamiliarity, and isolation for the child concerned. Therefore a policy of separation is seen by those involved as having negative effects on the consciousness of both the local people, who are denied familiarity with handicapped children, and the parents and children identified as special.

One of the claims made for schemes such as those in the London Borough of Bromley, which provide classes in neighbourhood schools, is that the stigma, isolation and inconvenience suffered by many children categorized as special have been reduced. In Bromley separation as a policy has been interpreted as bad for children, parents and teachers (Tuckwell and Beresford, 1978). Yet providing classes in ordinary schools does not guarantee integration, since this is an individual issue: the degree of integration achieved by a particular child will vary, but the conditions encourage rather than prevent.

Spending cuts have limited the Bromley initiatives, since it is probably more expensive to provide special classes than it is to provide special schools. Tuckwell and Beresford see the Bromley policy as more demanding for all concerned than a 'neat system of labelling and dumping'.

Support for an integration approach comes from some of those who have been on the receiving end of the separation policy. The Warnock Committee had a submission from the Association of Disabled Professionals urging 'immediate steps to ensure that many more handicapped children and many more severely handicapped children are integrated in ordinary schools'.

The policy of separation has been supported on several grounds. With a shortage of specialists in speech, sight, hearing and other categories of special needs, it was seen as practical to group children together to obtain the best service for them. In a neighbourhood school such children would probably end up in the remedial streams, whereas in a special school among equals they would be away from this low-status situation. Thus one function of special schools was seen as protection of the vulnerable. This was also a reflection on the neighbourhood schools, which were seen as unable to cope with special needs either in physical facilities or in providing a psychological climate of sympathy and concern to protect the vulnerable.

This raises the issue of whether the mainstream schools, to use the American term, are worth being in. One writer has argued that, unless mainstream schools adopt some of the caring approach and educational methods of the special schools for all their pupils, retaining special schools remains a plausible policy (Medlicott, 1974).

Some interested bodies advocate and adopt a dual approach. The Spastics Society has eight special schools, yet notes with approval that 50 000 pupils with cerebral palsy are 'mainstreamed', and expresses interest in the extent to which this number can be increased.

A dual policy is likely to continue for several reasons, not least because of the huge existing investment in special schools, increasing from about 600 schools in 1950 to 1600 in 1975. A switch in emphasis may be detected if the waiting list of 12 000 names is reduced, since the largest categories represented are the 'moderately' educationally handicapped and the maladjusted. These two categories are those whose validity is most frequently disputed and those which are seen as marginal, and therefore they are the most likely to be a source of candidates for integration.

One group of children that presents difficulties for the mainstreaming policy is the maladjusted. Sympathy for the physically handicapped and mentally retarded can be aroused more easily than sympathy for those identified as maladjusted. Colley (1976) asks us to consider the reaction to the sight of a child walking along the railway line, putting up two fingers in a derisive gesture to the grown-ups who are trying to bring it back to safety; or the likely response to the child who deliberately lies down on the road in front of the traffic, or who steps out onto a pedestrian crossing in front of a speeding car, and who, when told that these are dangerous activities, replies that he wants to be killed. A parent may have to cope with a child who makes up its mind that it is not going to speak to any grown-up ever again, and who obstinately continues to do so for years. A child breaking windows, throwing stones, spitting or swearing in public in the foulest possible way is likely to get a reaction of fear and disgust, to ask for help for these pupils would bring indignation. Yet children with these symptoms are handicapped emotionally rather than physically.

Colley suggests that the difficulty in recognizing such children as handicapped, and so in need of help, comes from the assumption made by many adults that children are good little people who are obedient, respectful and conforming – a fair assumption to make about children who are secure and who really trust and look up to adults. Colley (1976) comments further:

> But for those children who are not sure of their relationship with adults, and who have therefore taken over the organization of their own lives for themselves because they have been let down by grown-ups, it is a very dangerous assumption to make. Maladjusted children are, in my opinion, those who have had their emotional development interrupted by some experience which has been deeply hurtful to them.
>
> The more usual type of maladjusted child, in my experience as a teacher, is the aggressive and violent child. This child breaks all the rules. He cannot be educated in a normal school. He is disobedient, defiant, unruly, impossibly rude and frequently violent – damaging furniture and teachers and causing havoc in the classes. The adults are unable to cope with him. A child like this who comes to a school for maladjusted children finds himself surrounded by adults who do not panic when he insults them; who are not afraid when he is violent; who show that although they do not like his behaviour, they know he has reasons for it and that they like him. This kind of calmness in the face of all the provocation shows

the child that here is a situation in which he does not have to keep up his pattern of anti-social behaviour. He has found adults who can master him, not by violence or revenge, but by acceptance. When he realizes this, his chances of recovery begin. With care and a good environment, he may recover enough to be able to function in a normal school after a few years' treatment.

Colley, 1976. This first appeared in *New Society*, London, the weekly review of the social sciences.

THE PROCESS OF BEING LABELLED 'SPECIAL'

Referral and Assessment

The assumption that the identification of children for special education is an objective diagnosis is rendered dubious by a study of the process involved. The most common starting point for the official process is for the head teacher to write a report. The unofficial process, however, will have begun much earlier. The head teacher will have been made aware that a child is demonstrating behaviour interpreted as undesirable from somebody's point of view – teachers, parents, or an educational psychologist who has performed a screening of a school-year cohort.

In the case of a teacher, the head teacher may advise alternative methods of dealing with the pupil or seek advice from the educational psychologist. The teacher may respond in various ways, including successful use of the advice, or ignoring the advice, or may be unable to act upon it. If the undesirable behaviour persists, there are several possible outcomes.

Parents of other children may complain that their children are being held back, disrupted or otherwise affected by the pupil concerned. The head teacher then has to consider possible ways of dealing with this problem, including moving the child to another teacher, which may create tensions between teachers, or moving the pupil to another school in the area, risking the resentment of another school staff in taking on the problems of another school. A tempting solution is referral. Staff within the school may be protected, the special school staff are paid to receive problems, and indeed their jobs are secured by referrals.

Since the 1981 Education Act, in the UK parents can ask for an assessment for their child or make representations when an educational official has initiated assessment procedures. Later, parents can appeal against the verdict contained in an official Statement of Special Educational Needs.

The assessment is widely regarded as objective and reliable. However, there are doubts about the following:

1. The assessment instruments – the tests.
2. The assessment context – clinical interviewing.
3. The assumptions about the validity of educational psychology in generating adequate explanations of behaviour in educational institutions – the sociologists' preserve.
4. The pressures on educational psychologists that are occupational and political, for their position 'in the system' is far from independent. They are employees of the

local education authority and, as such, are subject to wider educational and political influences.

By their actions the head teacher and the class teacher may be saying that they feel they cannot cater adequately for a particular child. The psychologist may offer to devise an alternative programme, but without control of the daily implementation much depends on the willingness and expertise of the parents or the school, and therefore a programme may not be successful. One psychologist can offer to supervise only a few schemes, with up to 12 000 children within the group of schools he or she has to visit. A transfer to another 'normal' school is taken as a reflection on the school's competence, even though no criticism may have been intended. But admission to a special school is more likely to be regarded as further evidence of the severity of the child's problems, and is seldom thought to imply any criticism of the referring school.

The psychologist's own credibility may be undermined by regular requests which are seen as inappropriate or 'unrealistic', and good relationships with a school's head and staff may be jeopardized because of one child.

> We are not painting a totally black picture of any of these professional groups. Many psychologists *do* support children in ordinary schools on a regular basis. Many are successful in arguing for extra resources for 'supported integration' schemes. Hopefully all would take seriously the commitment to consider the parents' wishes on the placement of their child.
>
> What needs to be emphasized, however, is that the psychologist is not an independent expert, equipped with magical tools, who is powerful enough to work out and win support for an innovative scheme for one child in the ordinary school.
>
> Goodwin, 1979

The outcome may be that in many cases pupils are designated as special for the sake of other considerations than the particular pupil's benefit – a case of the pupil as victim. An Advisory Centre for Education report concluded that there were few signs of the proposed partnership of teachers, other professionals and parents on behalf of children but plenty of signs of the defence of vested interests (*Where?* 196, March 1984).

Screening and the Social Pathology Model

The idea of screening is based on a medical model. It is based on an assumption that a proportion of pupils (20 per cent in the Warnock Report) are educationally ill. The 'handicap' may respond to educational treatment of an individual or group of individuals forming a ward or special provision. The emphasis is on individual children, and the causes are sought in that person's physiology or biography.

Such a model employs quasi-medical terms like examination, diagnosis, treatment and testing, and prove to be convenient for doctors, psychologists and those teachers who think in medically derived terms. Excluded by such an approach are the possibilities that causes outside the biographies of the individual, such as the regime of the school, the expectations of the teachers, or the ideology of education in use, may be crucial factors.

The clue to the underlying ideology of remedial education is to be found not only in its language but also in the forms of organization and methods it uses. One type of remedial provision is temporary withdrawal of pupils from the 'normal' situation, to undergo therapy often directed towards weaknesses in basic skills. The object is to return the pupil as soon as possible to what is regarded as normal schooling. The remedial teacher's success is seen, in theory, in terms of the number of pupils returned to normal classes.

The social-pathology model of educational ill-health and the screening that derives from it may have various consequences. First, labelling children as special can lead to differential teacher expectations. This affects teachers involved in remedial work and those who are not in different ways. Remedial teachers have come to see themselves as therapists, and there can be little doubt that many of them have acquired considerable expertise in the application of diagnostic approaches to the teaching of reading, drawing upon the discipline of psychology. The teachers who are not involved specifically in remedial work often have to assume that children with reading difficulties are not their concern.

> Their concept of normality involves, amongst other things, being able to meet the literacy demands of their fields of interest *as they stand at present.* That is to say, participation in a subject, such as history, requires a certain level of literacy, a level determined by the subject itself and the media through which it is taught. Neither content nor media are regarded as open to change.
>
> Golby and Gulliver, 1979

The outcome is that children are blamed for failing: the learning experiences are not seen as open to review.

Second, screening cannot be perfect, so some pupils will be labelled incorrectly and self-fulfilling prophecies may then be set in motion.

An alternative approach is outlined by Bookbinder (1978). The Salford approach to reading has been to avoid screening and individual treatments for low achievement, and instead to redefine the problem as a teaching problem:

> Although the surveys do identify the slowest readers, we do not attempt to provide individual learning programmes for most of these children, but aim instead to improve the teachers' skills in the teaching of reading generally, so that both slower achieving and brighter children will benefit.

In 1969 more than a quarter of all infant school leavers in the largely inner-city area then covered by the authority were classified as non-readers on the Schonell Graded Word Test. For the same schools in the same area nine years later, that figure had dropped to 6 per cent.

Bookbinder proposes that these improvements in reading attainment show that it is possible to reduce significantly the number of poor achievers without resorting to expensive, time-consuming and possibly dangerous identification procedures. If a medical model of identification had been adopted the present standards would not have been achieved.

> Is it possible that a more widespread application of this kind of approach to basic areas of the curriculum could more than halve that Warnock figure of 20 per cent with special educational needs? Perhaps, then, it might make more sense to think in terms of further intervention procedures for the relatively small numbers who were still failing.
>
> Bookbinder, 1978

STIGMA THEORY

Negative labelling of 'special', 'handicapped' or 'exceptional' children has its roots in our history, myths and everyday environment. Because many of the children are cloistered away from the general public, people may have never had the chance to meet such a child and come to appreciate her or his 'normal' attributes. Many of the services and educational facilities are still run by voluntary bodies, and some of the funding depends on donations dropped in a bag at the check-out in the local supermarket. There are plastic models of disabled children on some street corners. The image of child begging, and the constant cry to 'give a few pence', can arouse sympathy, but it can also shape feelings of guilt, pity or even revulsion.

Much of our language is loaded against various minority groups. One of the definitions of 'blind' in the Oxford English Dictionary is 'reckless, not ruled by purpose'. The term 'spastic' is often used as an insult by 'normals'. In 1959 the Mental Health Act reclassified 'idiots' as 'severely subnormal'. The expression 'subnormal' is still widely, and officially, used today, although it can be distressing to both the parents and the child concerned.

We are all in some ways both statistical and moral deviants from the norm, because few of us can equate consistently with the average. Goffman argues that their stigma unites criminals, sexual offenders, ethnic minorities and physically handicapped people. Boswell and Wingrove (1974) argue that the physically handicapped are the most susceptible to being stigmatized, as their predicament removes the opportunity to control whether they deviate or not.

Goffman (1963) has an analysis of a particular type of labelling, stigma theory. Many types of labelling hold the possibility of 'reversal' or 'reform': the deviant may learn a lesson and reform. In the case of stigma, however, there is an attribute that is interpreted in a culture as deeply discrediting, and a means of reversal is not as likely. The person with a stigma is seen as not quite human, nor likely to become so. Goffman proposes three types of stigma: body deformities, personality deformities and tribal stigmas.

First, there are the various deformities. Second, there are blemishes of individual character, such as weak will, domineering or unnatural passions, treacherous and rigid beliefs, and dishonesty, these being inferred from a known record of, for example, mental disorder, imprisonment, addiction, alcoholism, homosexuality, unemployment, suicidal attempts, and radical political behaviour. Third, there are the tribal stigma of race, nation and religion, which can be transmitted through lineages and contaminate all members of a family or group.

The contrast, for Goffman, is between the 'stigmatized' and the 'normal'. Society generates certain definitions of what the 'normal' individual should be like, and those who fail to meet these definitions may become stigmatized. To be defined as someone with a stigma creates a problem for the person who has to respond to the situation, and for those 'normals' who act on the basis of the culturally generated definitions.

In applying Goffman's theory to special education in the USA, E. King (1972) notes how children judged as unable to perform 'satisfactorily' in a group of 'normals' are channelled into educational programmes that can accommodate their 'learning disabilities'. This turns out, in the case of many USA cities, to be an inflated group of black children:

> Most educators will agree that general education has failed the black ghetto child. In an effort to avoid the necessity of radically changing the general education system in the black ghetto, the educational establishment has found it expedient to turn to special education, to greatly expand the special education programs serving black children.
>
> E. King, 1972

Consequently a disproportionate number of black and other minority children are labelled as retarded, disturbed or delinquent. King notes that this process effectively shortcircuits change in the general education programme by implicating the children rather than the system.

'COOLING THE MARK OUT'

One attempt to explain the relationship between the mainstream education system and the special education sector is that of E. King (1972), using Goffman's concept of 'cooling out' (1952). The idea comes from the activity of confidence tricksters. The victim of a confidence trick is the 'mark', the sucker. When a potential mark is noticed, one member of the team makes contact with and wins the confidence of the person concerned. The mark is given the chance to invest money in a get-rich-quick gambling venture apparently fixed in the investor's favour. Some money is won, so more is invested, but an 'accident' leads to the mark's losing the total investment. If the mark does not accept the loss philosophically, but threatens to call the police or complain to the press, there must be a 'cooling-out' of the mark. The 'cooler' attempts to console the mark and to define the situation in a way that makes it easier for the mark to accept the loss and become resigned to the situation. The process of cooling out the mark can be used as an analogy to educational and other processes.

The definition of 'mark' includes persons whose expectations or self-concepts have been shattered. These persons must be helped to re-accept themselves and their failure and build new self-concepts. In a situation in which a person has failed at a job, he can be offered another, perhaps lower, position, and in this way the feeling of failure is softened, the loser is pacified. Similarly, the lover may be asked to become a 'good friend', or the ageing boxer may be asked to become a trainer.

King applies the concept of 'cooling the mark out' to the relationship between general and special education. General education in the USA is supposed to be capable of teaching all children, but with inner-city black children it has failed. However, educators and their school systems can preserve their identities by cooling deviant children out. The placement will help the child, it is stated, but in fact, he is given a seemingly better placement in the hope that he will stop making a fuss. It is easier for all to 'cool out' the child, to help him and his parents accept his failure in the regular education system, than it is to change that system for his benefit, King concludes.

Special education is part of the arrangement for cooling out students who won't conform to traditional classroom methodology, King argues, and this parallel system permits relief of institutional guilt and humiliation stemming from failure to achieve competence and effectiveness in the educational task given by society.

> Special education is helping the regular school maintain its spoiled identity when it creates special programs for the 'disruptive child', the 'emotionally disturbed child', or the 'mildly

retarded child', most of whom happen to be black, poor, and live in the inner city.

E. King, 1972

THE SOCIAL CONSTRUCTION OF UNDERACHIEVEMENT

One of the dangers of labelling theory is that it may lead to the individualization of blame: the labellers are then seen as the guilty ones. Chapter 4, 'Teachers as Victims', contained an attempt to avoid this false conclusion. Stigma theory in particular may set in motion a 'blame the stigmatizers' response. The thesis of this section is that labellers operate not on personal initiatives, but on socially constructed ideas fed in to their consciousness. Linking several categories of special education is the notion of under-achievement. How did this notion come into being? The proposition from an interactionist perspective is that underachievement is a social construction rather than an inevitable fact of existence.

The sociology of education that developed after the 1944 Education Act tended to be of a macro-perspective, often of a structural functionalist nature, and centred on questions of the relationship between social class and academic achievement. A concern that derived from this was the 'wastage of talent', particularly of working-class children. This approach was based on several unquestioned assumptions: that schooling as currently practised was good, that selection was a prime function of education, that talent and merit could be identified objectively as traits of individuals, so that individual mobility in education demonstrated that greater equality of opportunity was being achieved. L. Davies (1980) argues that:

> Administrators and social scientists then were still working on the premise that school was a Good Thing; that, therefore, more schooling was a Better Thing; and that maximum identical exposure to schooling was the Best Thing.

The identification of talent would achieve 'true' mobility. There were three unquestioned assumptions:

1. That education should be about sorting and selection.
2. That definitions of 'merit' were unproblematic, objective and without class bias, with assessment of merit synonymous with competitive examinations.
3. That individual mobility through the educational system was an index of greater equality of opportunity (the more individuals were successful, the more schools were helping to combat class imbalances).

The individualization of success had as the other side of the coin the individualization of failure.

> So there was the replacement of notions of genetic inheritance with social pathology models of deprivation, which further served to draw attention away from the ways in which the school itself was processing its pupils. Various sources of deprivation – cultural, social, linguistic, emotional – were identified as the sources of failure to cope with the demands of schooling. Programmes of compensation were devised to fill up the emptiness resulting from faulty socialization, restricted code use, disadvantaged social area or some combination of all three.
>
> L. Davies, 1980

Some critics of the compensatory approach have argued that the vessel was not actually empty, but laden with a different cultural cargo. Others have a political critique that stresses the irony of blaming the poor for their poverty: cultural deprivation suggests that the minority in question is failing rather than being failed by the mainstream society and its system of schooling.

This system of schooling is seen as suspect for a number of reasons. First, the operating definition of 'ability' is dubious. The assumption is that the facility to use symbols on paper is to be more highly regarded than skills of forming social relationships, organizing activities or skills with machinery:

> Why is the facility to manipulate other people's symbols on a piece of paper more highly regarded than the facility to form social relationships, operate a calculator, organize a trade union? In particular, why is only one continuum used to rank pupils? Given the enormous range of skills, competencies and orientations in our society, it is curious that we can glibly talk of children being 'able' and 'less able', 'average' and 'below average', as if all we were measuring were head size.
>
> L. Davies, 1980

Davies argues that the enormously misleading notion of 'general intelligence', or IQ, has a lot to answer for, as does developmental psychology, but the question is more than a matter of error. The political question is in whose interests IQ tests are legitimized? Who benefits by a school's definition of what it is to learn something? The answer is a tautology: the sorts of people who are good at IQ tests, the sorts of children who are adept at the narrow range of skills associated with school success.

Second, the operating definition of assessment is dubious. A norm-referenced examination system is designed to select successes and label others as failures. This helps legitimize an unequal system of life-chance distribution: you do not deserve many rewards because you are not very bright, as the paper-and-pencil tests have told you.

'Intelligence', then, and 'the right environment', instead of being seen as initial causal variables in educational attainment, can be interpreted as convenient labels to justify, even mask, the fact that educational practices are selective, funnelling devices rather than liberating ones.

> Examinations would have little point if everyone got the same grade or even passed them; yet schools have to balance the hierarchical certification function with ideologies of equality and impartiality. The way out of the dilemma is to blame the child: to convince him, his parents, the community, that opportunities would have been there if he had not had a low IQ, was not an underachiever.
>
> L. Davies, 1980

The construction of underachievement is analogous to the creation of casualties as a consequence of having a war. Answering the question of why there are so many casualties by looking at the physique of the soldiers who are injured seems ridiculous. Casualties will stop when the war stops. Thus, defining certain children as failures may tell us much more about the dominant ideologies of education in schools than about the children involved.

CONCLUSION

A summary of this chapter might lead one to conclude that the contribution of the sociologist to the area of special education is to add more confusion to an already confused area, but only those who prefer misplaced certainty to constructive doubt would regard this as a bad thing. Certainly the research, as in many other areas of educational concern, is in the nature of work in progress on the reappraisal of policies which were often devised under the pressure of circumstances. Tuckwell and Beresford, writing about the reappraisal of policies in Bromley, summed up the situation in these words:

> A scheme like the Bromley one inevitably raises doubts about the efficacy of our special education system, our methods of assessment and ascertainment, our teacher-education programme and our treatment of those we stigmatize as sub-normal. There are many questions to be asked: Bromley is the tip of an iceberg already too large to be ignored.

Further Reading

Barton, L. and Tomlinson, S. (eds.) (1981) *Special Education: Policy, Practices and Social Issues*. London: Harper and Row.

Barton, L. and Tomlinson, S. (eds.) (1984) *Special Education and Social Interests*. Beckenham: Croom Helm.

Boswell, D.M. and Wingrove, J.M. (1974) *The Handicapped Person in the Community*. London: Tavistock.

Goffman, E. (1963) *Stigma: Notes on the Management of Spoiled Identity*. Hemel Hempstead: Prentice Hall.

Sewell, G. (1982) *Reshaping Remedial Education*. Beckenham: Croom Helm.

Tomlinson, S. (1982) *A Sociology of Special Education*. London: Routledge and Kegan Paul.

Warnock Report (1978) *Special Educational Needs*. Report of the Committee of Enquiry into the Eduation of Handicapped Children and Young People. Cmnd. 7212. London: HMSO.

Discussion and Activities

1. How can we account for the differences in the figures for boys and girls given in the Table 28.2?
2. Is a sociologist justified in adding more confusion to an already confused area?
3. Make a summary of the main points of this chapter.
4. The policy of mainstreaming or integration takes it for granted that the mainstream schools are educationally sound. Do you agree?

Signposts

1. Special education and social interests
Recent writing has explored the proposition that special education is as much if not more about social interests than about individual needs or individual deficiencies, in an attempt to broaden the debate. See Barton and Tomlinson (1981) and (1984) and Tomlinson (1982).

2. 1981 Education Act, England and Wales
'The 1981 Education Act promised a "joint endeavour to discover and understand" the special

education needs of individual children. ACE's experience to date suggests that the idea of a "partnership" between parents and professionals was a DES fantasy, bearing little relationship to parents' real experience of dealing with their LEA.' *Where?* 196, March 1984. The working of this Act may become a case study in the notions of 'contradictions' and 'the ironies of human action' where proposed remedies achieve the opposite effects of those intended. See *ACE Special Education Handbook* (1984) and 'The '81 Act: Safeguarding Your Rights', in *Where?* 196, March 1984.

PART SIX

Alternatives, or Contrasts in
Educational Institutions

There is a wide variety of schools and educational practices in the UK, and anyone moving from one part of the country to live in another may encounter the practical difficulties that this creates. One local education authority has infants, junior and secondary schools, another junior mixed infants, middle and high schools, while yet another may have sixth-form colleges. Some areas have selective schools and have grammar and secondary, while others have comprehensive. Small, all-age village schools exist in some areas, in contrast with large schools of 2000 children in others. Single-sex schools exist alongside mixed schools, church and various religious schools alongside non-religious schools, and private schools alongside state schools. The above categorizations, upon which most official statistics are based, are those of the administrator. From a sociological point of view, these administrative categories are interesting and can be the basis of some analysis, but they may also obscure characteristics that run across school types and within one particular administrative type. These obscured characteristics may include the educational visions in operation and the consequences of these competing visions for the behaviour of learners and teachers.

One attempt to devise an approach to this problem has already been outlined – the approach through ideologies of education used as an analytical tool to describe and compare key features of educational practices. The assumption here is that such an approach can locate differences within schools and across schools that are not revealed by administrative descriptions: the approach can locate the different regimes found in schools. The limitations of previous attempts based on two contrasting types and those based on four were outlined earlier, and the component theories approach will be adopted here.

Activity

It might be interesting to write down your views on the topics to be covered in the chapters that follow, i.e. private schooling, state primary schooling, state secondary schooling, education at home. Store these views for review after you have read each chapter.

Chapter 29

Going Private

'The Master said, "A gentleman takes as much trouble to discover what is right as lesser men take to discover what will pay." '

Confucius

INTRODUCTION

In the UK there are several ways of going private, of opting out of the state system of education. A small, but growing number of parents exercise their legal right to educate their children themselves, and this is the concern of Education Otherwise. Another small minority of parents abdicate their rights almost entirely by paying for their children to go to boarding schools, where they are residential for over two-thirds of the year. A further group of parents pay for their children to attend private day-schools.

Precise figures are not easily available, but at any given time there appear to be around 4000 schools in the private sector, and estimates of the number of children being educated at home vary between 100 or more families, and 1000 or more children. The proportion of the child population in the private sector lies somewhere between 5 per cent and 10 per cent. The lack of precision is mostly to do with the constant state of flux: schools are opening and closing; some are granted official recognition, others are not; changes in government policy influence some schools to go private at particular times; the number of parents educating their children at home is changing constantly.

The categorization 'private school' covers a wide range of types. There is a broad division between boarding school and day school, although this distinction is blurred by the fact that many predominantly boarding schools have some day pupils and many predominantly day schools have a few boarders.

Within each category, boarding and day, there are further variations. Most boarding schools are single-sex, but a small minority, about 30 in number, are mixed residential establishments. A larger proportion of day schools are mixed-sex. The size of school varies from establishments of 5 to 12 pupils to over 750. The sponsoring body may be the Licensed Victuallers, the Society of Friends, the local Cathedral, a famous individual, e.g. Yehudi Menuhin, or an Educational Trust. The age range varies: some schools are 8–13 preparatory schools, others exclusive to 16-year-olds and over, others 13 years and over, and others span 5 to 18.

The differences in educational style are partly linked to features like size of school, age, single-sex or mixed, and the characteristics of the sponsors, but other differences may be noted. The curriculum may be broad or, in the case of a crammer be restricted almost entirely to preparation for a small range of examinations such as GCE 'O' or 'A' level. The educational approach may commonly be known as traditional or progressive: the misleading nature of this dichotomy was discussed earlier, in the section on ideologies of education. The second part of this chapter will be an attempt at a more complex analysis.

Given this diversity of the private sector it is perhaps surprising that sweeping generalizations about this form of education are commonly encountered. There are some common features that can be discerned:

1. The schools are out of local education authority control: their 'recognition as efficient' is granted by the Department of Education and Science.
2. The clientele have or obtain the economic resources to back their choice: selection is mostly by wealth, although supplementary factors like entrance examinations and previous contacts, like parents being old pupils of the school, may be important in particular cases.
3. The schools are predominantly single-sex, and the major provision is for males rather than females.

THE PUBLIC SCHOOLS

Some of the assertions made about private education are about the public schools, perhaps a rather odd name for a group of private schools. In the absence of common agreement about the definition of a public school, they will be seen in this account as private boarding schools, mostly for boys of secondary-school age, which have membership of one of the three associations, i.e. The Head Masters' Conference, the Governing Bodies Association and the Association of Governing Bodies of Girls' Public Schools. About 300 schools are included in such a category, and about 2.5 per cent of the school population attend them.

The significance of the public schools appears to be much more in what happens before the children go to school than in what happens after. Public schools recruit mostly from those born into rich homes. Most pupils are from upper-class or upper-middle-class families. The pupils exit in a large proportion to Oxford and Cambridge (35 per cent) and other universities (16 per cent) and thence to élite occupations, e.g. in the civil service, law, armed forces and industry.

The educational significance of the public schools is open to considerable debate. The conclusions of Douglas (1971) were:

> The pupils at the boys' public schools, once their ability and the circumstances of their families are taken into account, are no more successful, as judged by 'O' level results and age of leaving up to 16½ years, than grammar school pupils. The pupils at other independent schools (i.e. those outside the Headmasters' Conference) are considerably less successful.

Douglas found that the pupils at independent girls' schools were considerably less successful than those at grammar schools. They had poorer 'O' level results whether the schools were members of the Headmistresses' Association or not, and they left school earlier.

The results of degree examinations add doubts about the academic advantage of a public school education, as Table 29.1 shows.

Table 29.1 *'Oxbridge' degree results by type of secondary education: men, 1958*

	Good (%)	Poor (%)
Head Masters' Conference and direct grant		
Boarders	32	49
Day	45	30
LEA Grammar	50	33

Source: Glennerster and Pryke, 1973

A study of crammers, which are private coaching establishments operating as private sixth-form colleges for students of 16 years and above, indicated that public schools feature prominently on their rolls. For a variety of reasons these pupils left their public schools to continue their examination work at a crammer (Geddes, 1979). If the public schools really are good at academic work, why are they apparently driving many of their pupils into other institutions devoted to passing examinations, Geddes asks.

The recent study by Halsey, Heath and Ridge (1980) supports the earlier study by Douglas in concluding that a lot of the supposed academic advantage turns out to be spurious, given that the public schools have able pupils from élite backgrounds with parental support and encouragement: the academic results reflect the social-class background of the parents rather than anything startling about the nature of the schooling, they conclude. Glennerster and Pryke (1973) concluded that the principal commodity being purchased at a public school is not education, but privilege.

The social significance for the individuals and families concerned is clear enough. The children are being set on the road to power and influence if they end up dominating élite occupations. The study by Giddens and Stanworth (1974) showed that 70 per cent of directors in the top 50 industrial firms were old boys of public schools. Banking and insurance showed a similar pattern. In the army, 86 per cent of officers of the rank of major-general and above had been to public schools. In the legal profession, high-court judges and principal judges of public-school background formed over 75 per cent of the total. In 1970, 62 per cent of the civil service posts of under-secretaries and above were held by former public-school boys.

The social significance for the nation is less clear. According to one view, the decline in the nation's fortunes in economic and other terms has been managed almost exclusively by the products of the public-school/Oxbridge experience, and their inability to cope does no credit to either the schools or the universities concerned. In one form, the criticism of the 'gifted amateur', this was the conclusion of the Fulton Committee (1968) when it investigated the civil service.

Those who hold this view see a paradox between the social significance for individuals and the social significance for the nation sometimes known as the Titanic theory of mobility: struggle to join the ruling class that is supervising the sinking of the ship.

A development of this view is that the cycle of privilege perpetuated by public schools not only is undemocratic, but it also perpetuates closed-society thinking in a pluralist society context, or linear thought when lateral thinking is needed. An analysis of the cycles of privilege view appears in MacDonald (1977).

Others hold that the traditional values of the public schools are the only hope for the nation, and that leadership is being produced in these special institutions. Rae, headmaster of Westminster schools, writes that:

> to some they will appear havens of civilized learning and behaviour monasteries in an increasing dark age; to others a source of division and injustice in a society that badly needs to cast off its class-conscious heritage.
>
> Rae, 1979

IDEOLOGIES OF EDUCATION AND PRIVATE SCHOOLS

A survey of the literature on private schools using the component theories approach to describing ideologies of education supports the view that broad generalizations about the educational regimes of these institutions are difficult to sustain. A wide variety of ideologies of education can be discerned.

One overall view that private schools are in the authoritarian grouping of ideologies of education is inaccurate. A minority of private schools operate various non-authoritarian regimes; two well-known examples of such schools are Dartington Hall and Summerhill.

Another view is that the majority of private schools that do operate an authoritarian ideology of education implement the extreme form of autocracy. The influence of books like *Tom Brown's Schooldays* and films like *If . . .* may be detected here. Rae (1979) writes that he does not recognize the school life described in such accounts. He claims that there has been a shift in the regimes of private schools and that the totalitarian view is anachronistic. The shift would appear to be from the autocratic form of authoritarianism to a parental and an organizational one. In some cases this may be moving even further into a consultative version of authoritarian schooling.

Three of the component theories of an ideology of education are used in what follows in order to describe some of the features of private education. They are the theory of knowledge, the theory of learning and the theory of teaching.

Theory of Knowledge: Its Content and Structure

Most of the private schools appear to be operating with a past-orientated view of knowledge. The traditional subject divisions established in the 1800s are the basis of their programme, but with varying degrees of fidelity. One visitor to Westminster School (Mack, 1977) observed that the curriculum remained very traditional: Latin and Greek were still taught, economics has found its way in, but not sociology. A view of knowledge that Latin and Greek were more relevant than sociology to present-day pupils, especially those encouraged in the view that they were to be the nation's leaders, is distinctly past-orientated and denotes a stratified view of knowledge. However, this situation is less extreme in other private schools. The same observer notes that at

Licensed Victuallers a social science course is in evidence. At Eton the activity of 'private business', where a tutor may introduce a pupil to the work of a composer or a poet, or discuss current affairs, suggests some attempt at a less rigid view of knowledge. In contrast, in the crammers, whose staff prefer to see them as private sixth-form colleges, the devotion to examination work for traditional subjects appears to be unswerving (Geddes, 1979).

A minority of private schools operate a different theory of knowledge. Pupils at Summerhill comment that the intention is not to make you learn subjects so much as to learn about living, to learn how to learn. Learning is from meetings, from the community and from your own experiences, as well as from lessons, which the pupils have the right to attend or reject (Warmsley, 1970). In the lessons, traditional subject divisions are seen as arbitrary, and a more integrated present-orientated view of knowledge is suggested.

There appears to be sufficient variety in the operational theories of knowledge in the private sector for the parents to find an approach they favour. With the superior economic resources at their disposal, they are able to purchase some freedom of choice. Most elect to reject present- and future-orientated theories of knowledge in favour of past-orientated views.

Theory of Learning and the Learner's Role

Most private schools appear to choose one of the authoritarian alternatives as regards learning and the learner's role. In a study of parents' motives for choosing private schools, the writers concluded that there was a striking unanimity in the preference of parents in their sample for formal work: the learner's role was to reproduce the knowledge presented by the teacher by listening and noting, with the motivation of avoiding the disagreeable consequences of low marks or censure if they were unsuccessful (Bridgeman and Fox, 1978). Being let off the last lesson of the day occasionally is then presented as a reward for good behaviour.

However, those who want a non-authoritarian view of learning, stressing features such as personal synthesis or even discovery of new ideas rather than replication, doing rather than listening, and motivated by personal satisfaction in growing competence and confidence, can find attempts to operate a variety of such approaches in some of the private schools. It is consistent with such an approach that a proposal to ban someone from lessons for a week as a punishment was opposed by Summerhill pupils as too severe: learning in lessons was seen as pleasurable (Neill, 1968).

Theory of Teaching and the Teacher's Role

Although in most private schools the teacher's role is seen as that of a subject instructor, the extreme authoritarian form, the autocratic, seems to have given way to other versions. Rae (1979) comments that, in the 1970s, most of the private schools modified aspects of their lives that had been the subject of continuing criticism: there was less zeal over conformity, a less protective attitude towards pupils, a fall in bullying and homosexuality, and the beating of pupils by other pupils stopped, as well as a widening of the curriculum, he concludes.

The preference for some form of authoritarian teaching role is congruent with the parents' wishes, for Bridgeman and Fox (1978) show that the parents in their study choose private schools for the following main reasons: small size of classes, formal teaching and low teacher-turnover. The move away from the autocratic form is lamented by some parents, who repeatedly complain to their children that they are no longer made to work like they used to be.

A minority of private schools practise non-authoritarian teaching. Formal teaching is not absent from such schools, but it serves the needs and demands of the pupils. At Summerhill the pupils choose to attend, and the lessons provided tend to be workshops in the interpretation style of teaching rather than lectures in the transmission style.

CONCLUSION

One of the conclusions reached about private schools is that they are significant in setting the rules for the state education system (see MacDonald, 1977). Analysing these schools in terms of ideologies of education suggests that the situation is more complex: a dialectic is in evidence. In one sense the example of the private sector, i.e. its diversity, is ignored by the state system. When attempts to diversify occur they may actually be stopped, as in the cases of Risinghill and William Tyndale. Second, the break-up of the consensus about autocracy as the appropriate form of authoritarian order in the private sector appears to have been coincidental with a call in the state system to establish autocracy, the 'get stricter and tougher' approach. Third, the feature of small classes in many private schools, which is attractive to parents, has never been matched by attempts to emulate this in the state sector. Other features, however, such as the prefect system and uniforms, are copied by many state schools. The private and state sectors appear to learn from and react to each other in an inconsistent kind of dialectic.

However, in terms of perpetuating the unequal distribution of power and privilege in the social structure, the setting of the rules is in the hands of the products of private schools in significant measure, and this is the main point MacDonald is arguing.

SUMMARY

1. Going private can be done in a variety of ways: education at home, day schools, boarding schools, single-sex, mixed, small schools, large schools, religious schools, secular schools.
2. The number of children involved is small: the proportion lies somewhere between 5 per cent and 10 per cent of the child population at any given time.
3. The age range catered for at a particular school varies: some are 8–13 preparatory schools, some 13 years and upwards, some exclusive to 16 years and above, others span 5–18 years.
4. The common features of private schools are: they are not controlled by LEAs; the parents have or obtain the economic resources to back their preferences; most are

single-sex and the major provision is for males.

5. Public schools, as a particular group of private schools, serve upper-class and upper-middle-class families, providing entrance to Oxbridge and other universities for over half of their pupils, as well as entrance to elite occupations.

6. The educational significance of public schools would seem to be much less than the significance of the access to privilege that follows afterwards.

7. The social significance of public schools is open to considerable dispute. For individuals, they may obtain privilege. For the nation, opinions vary about whether the record of the elite is good or bad. Some hold the 'production of leadership in traditional values' view, others the 'Titanic theory' of the paradoxical struggle of individuals to join the ruling class that is supervising the sinking of the ship.

8. There is a wide range of ideologies of education in the private sector. The authoritarian grouping is in the majority, but different versions of authoritarian education are in evidence. A former consensus about autocracy seems to be breaking up.

Further Reading

Bell, R. and Grant, N. (1974) *A Mythology of British Education*. St Albans: Panther. Discusses some myths about private and other schools.

Fox, I. (1984) *Private Schools and Public Issues: The Parents' View*. London: Macmillan. A study of parents' motives for going private.

MacDonald, M. (1977) *The Education of Elites*. Milton Keynes: Open University Press. An analysis of the private sector.

Neil, A.S. (1968) *Summerhill*. Harmondsworth: Penguin.

Wakeford, J. (1969) *The Cloistered Elite*. London: Macmillan. The characteristics of the private sector are the subject of this book.

Walford, G. (1984) *British Public Schools: Policy and Practice*. Lewes: Falmer Press. An attempt to analyze the public school phenomenon.

Discussion and Activities

1. Complete the analysis begun in this chapter by looking at the other component theories of an ideology of education.

2. If you wrote down your views about private schooling as suggested at the end of the introduction to this section, compare your notes with the material in this chapter.

3. Conduct an informal survey of the views of relations, friends and fellow students to see if the various myths about private schooling indicated in this chapter are being perpetuated.

4. Consider the implications of the opening quotation for private education. Does it sum up the view of those who object to private education, and who regard the product as 'mercenaries' rather than 'gentlemen' (in the case of males).

Signposts

1. Public schools
Since these schools attract attention and debate, further work might concentrate on their characteristics. See Walford, G. (1984) *British Public Schools: Policy and Practice*, Lewes:

Falmer Press; and Leinster-Mackay, D. (1984) *The Rise of the English Prep School*, Lewes: Falmer Press.

2. Non-public schools

Private schools of the Society of Friends (Quaker Schools) or Rudolf Steiner schools or other non-public schools can be a very interesting area of further study. Russell, D. (1980) *The Tamarisk Tree, Vol. 2,* London Virago, has an account of Beacon Hill School, and Neill, A.S. (1968) *Summerhill*, Harmondsworth: Penguin, is well worth some attention.

Chapter 30

Schooling for the Masses: State Schooling in the Primary Sector

'Whatever crushes individuality is despotism, by whatever name it be called.'
John Stuart Mill

INTRODUCTION

At first glance, there would appear to be considerable variety in the state sector of schooling in the UK. There are nursery schools, infants schools, junior schools, first schools, combined junior and infant, middle schools of varying age spans, secondary, secondary comprehensive, sixth-form colleges and all-age village schools. In addition there are state-aided schools of Roman Catholic, Anglican, Jewish, Moslem and other religious groups. This diversity at the organizational level keeps historians of education at work accounting for the development of such a complex of schools. The question addressed in this chapter is whether the diversity at the organizational level is matched by a similar diversity in operational ideologies of education. Primary schools will be examined first, and then secondary schools. Reading suggestions for those who wish to assess other groupings of schools, e.g. middle schools, are given at the end of the chapter.

CONTRASTS BETWEEN PRIMARY AND SECONDARY SCHOOLS

The contrast between primary and secondary schools can be made on a number of grounds. The perspective of the learners is one since, as reported in Chapter 3, the pupils have a strong tendency to see a marked contrast between the two experiences and to evaluate the primary-school experience as superior to the secondary.

There are various organizational features that distinguish the two: in primary schools teachers are predominantly class teachers teaching one group of children for most of the day, whereas in secondary schools the common pattern is for subject teachers to teach a succession of groups of differing ages and achievements. Inevitably, the timetable characteristics vary accordingly, with considerable flexibility in many primary schools and rigidity in most secondary schools. The two types of school vary in size, with primary schools tending to be much smaller.

Teachers to serve the two types of school tend to receive different training. Secondary-subject teachers are frequently graduates in a subject with one year of postgraduate teacher training, and primary-school teachers are frequently education graduates with a BEd degree awarded for study in a college of higher education, working alongside many certificated teachers from the former colleges of education. Readers may be able to add further features to this list of contrasts between primary and secondary schooling.

One conclusion that is sometimes drawn from this position of contrasts is that primary schools are relatively uncomplicated institutions because they are not subject to many of the tensions of secondary schooling, e.g. elaborate departmental structures, vocational versus academic disputes, peer group cultures and complex time-tabling problems. Richards (1979) calls this the tyranny of over-simplification, and suggests that a remarkable mythology has been the result.

Another conclusion drawn has been that primary schools are, for the most part, operating a quite different ideology of education from that of most secondary schools – a child-centred, radical and progressive approach.

An analysis using some of the ideas outlined earlier regarding ideologies of education (see Chapter 15) will attempt to put both these assumptions into perspective. It will be argued that the contrasts between primary and secondary are not as great as they appear on the surface. Second, it will be demonstrated that most primary schools are not radical, progressive or child-centred, but merely operate different forms of authoritarian education from that found in most secondary schools.

A study of 732 junior schools in the UK found that it was an illusion that a classroom revolution had taken place resulting in the ousting of the basics, defined as mathematics and English, and in the operation of a child-centred curriculum (Barker Lunn, 1984). Instead the survey showed that the majority of children in these schools aged 9 to 11 spent most of their time in school on skills in mathematics, practising their reading and developing their English language through exercises, grammar tests and spelling practice. Mixed-achievement group teaching was shown to be rare and co-operative group work even rarer. The majority of the teachers dictated the activities of the pupils and used a formal instructional approach. The notion that children should begin to explore concepts by handling materials and apparatus was rejected by 90 per cent of the teachers. The picture that emerges from these classrooms was that life in junior school classrooms is hardly child-referenced let alone child-centred. The ORACLE research at Leicester University had shown a rather similar pattern (Galton et al., 1980).

THE NEGLECTED BASICS?

The issue of the 'basics' of maths, reading and writing illustrates the myth of 'progressive' approaches in British primary schools. The charges that primary schools had ignored these 'basics' came to a head in the activities known as the Great Debate about Education of 1977. Research by Taylor et al. (1978) confirmed the previous findings by Ashton et al. (1975) and the research of Berlak et al. (1975), that calling for primary-school teachers to get back to the basics was like asking butchers to get back to selling meat and librarians to get back to lending books. Teaching the 'basics' had remained the acknowledged and the actual first task of primary-school teachers, sometimes to the point of obsession.

The definition of the basics as reading, writing and maths is indicative of the ideologies of education in play, for the basics in some ideologies are defined differently. In the autonomous-study ideology of education, the 'basics' include personal confidence, mental agility, intellectual excitement, intellectual curiosity, active participation, self-reliance, flexibility, adaptability, problem-solving and the ability to use first-hand experiences. The activities of reading, writing and mathematics are seen as useful only if and when they serve these basics. To the alarm of those who do not understand the logic of this approach, children often learn to read quite late, at nine, ten or eleven years of age, but then learn very rapidly.

The Plowden approach can be located as a non-authoritarian ideology of education, close to the autonomous-study version. The evidence suggests that it is a myth that it operates in British primary schools. What does operate turns out to be complicated: several forms of the authoritarian grouping of ideologies of education. The autocratic version appears to be less common than the parental, the charismatic, the organizational and the consultative. The teachers operate various forms of the 'nice-strict' approach appreciated by pupils, but do not operate any of the non-authoritarian ideologies of education. The contrast with secondary schools is in degree, not in kind, in the *form* of authoritarian ideology of education adopted, for the autocratic version is much more common at the secondary level.

The movement between primary and secondary is facilitated to some extent by an anticipatory socialization trend in junior schools. As pupils go through the age grades, more subject teaching is likely to be encountered, more formal teaching offered, parental involvement in teaching and learning 'cooled out', and more formal classroom layouts experienced. Despite this the shock of secondary-school organization is still seen as a problem that needs to be coped with.

CONCLUSION

Contemporary schooling is subject to myth making as is frequently pointed out (Bell and Grant, 1974). Primary schools in the UK appear to have been a particular target for illusion creation by the mass media. The exact opposite of the myth of the neglected basics appears to apply, i.e. that over concentration on the basics, defined as above, results in low standards because of narrow interpretation and tedious application. The proposition that a wide-ranging curriculum that allows children to develop skills of thinking and expression produces higher standards in the long run was made in the survey of first schools conducted by HMI and published in 1982. The idea is echoed in the report on primary schools by the Inner London Education Authority in 1985 entitled *Improving Primary Schools*, where the schools that overstress the basics, defined in traditional terms, are noted as achieving anything that they do achieve 'at an unnecessarily high price in relation to the rest of the curriculum'. The parents were consulted as part of this study and little support for the narrow and tedious interpretation of the basics was forthcoming. This report makes a plea for more consultation with parents, more use of parents in classrooms and more encouragement to parents to help children with learning at home since the recognition is made that schooling is only one form of learning and teachers only one set of adults who facilitate children's learning. The way forward is seen in this report as both child referencing and parent referencing.

CHILD-CENTRED PRIMARY SCHOOLS?

The Plowden Report (1967) asserted that progressive primary teaching 'represented a general and quickening trend'. The characteristics of such an approach were embodied in a school that:

> sets out deliberately to devise the right environment for children, to allow them to be themselves and to develop in a way, and at a pace appropriate to them . . . It lays special stress on individual opportunities for creative work. It insists that knowledge does not fall into neatly separate compartments and that work and play are not opposite but complementary.

Schools that implemented this view of education required more self-chosen activity by pupils and a more developed consultative role with less emphasis on the instructional. Class teaching was to lessen in favour of more group work, project work and the integration of subject matter. The extrinsic rewards of marks, points and stars were to give way to methods designed to develop an intrinsic interest in learning, while punishment was to be avoided as a possible psychological perversion.

The Plowden view was that this approach was being implemented in a growing number of primary schools, and was about to become the majority experience. Silberman (1970) estimated that 25 per cent of junior schools fitted the Plowden model and that another 33 per cent were moving towards it. These conclusions have been questioned severely in subsequent research.

A large-scale study by Bennett and Grant (1974) involved just under 800 primary schools in the north of England. They located 12 teaching styles, of which only one corresponded to the Plowden model: this was used by 9 per cent of the teachers. A second style which indicated movement towards the Plowden model accounted for another 8 per cent of the sample. This left 83 per cent who were not operating the Plowden model.

A survey in the south of England gave similar findings. Evidence from 63 primary schools suggested that about 8 per cent were operating the Plowden model (Tongue, 1973). The writers concluded that the revolution in primary-school teaching had never happened. The schools were continuing to operate much as they had done for many years, dominated by class teaching often based on separate subject periods in the junior schools, with many disguised forms of streaming in operation.

In a national survey of the attitudes of primary-school teachers, Ashton et al. (1975) found that only 14 per cent selected the Plowden model as the nearest one to their own approach to teaching. The majority preferences suggested that the primary-school teachers were far from the ideology of education favoured in the Plowden report and much closer to a formal instructional approach.

The work of the minority of teachers identified as operating the Plowden model has also been questioned. In a participant study of such teachers Berlak et al. (1975) observed that the behaviour of informal classrooms was inconsistent. Descriptions like pupil choice, intrinsic motivation and integrated work were only partly true. Teachers resolved in various ways some of the dilemmas of operating informal classrooms described by Berlak et al. In terms of choice, this was usually free in the artistic activities and limited in maths, reading and writing. In no school studied were the activities of reading, writing and maths optional. Adult sanctions and standards were operational all the time, though in disguised or hidden ways. The Berlaks were in favour of the result, seeing such schools as better places for children to spend their days than the American primary schools they knew well, and by implication better than the traditional British primary school. The schools were not seen as operating the Plowden model, but only some approximation to it.

Further Reading

Ashton, P., Keen, P., Davies, F. and Holley, B. (1975) *The Aims of Primary Education: A Study of Teachers' Opinions*. London: Macmillan. Documents teachers' views.

Berlak, A.C., Berlak, H., Bagenstos, N.T. and Mikel, E.R. (1976) 'Teaching and Learning in English Primary Schools'. In Hammersley, M. and Woods, P., *The Process of Schooling*. London: Routledge and Kegan Paul. Explores the myth of progressive primary schooling.

Blenkin, G. and Kelly, A.V. (1981) *The Primary Curriculum*. London: Harper and Row.

Blyth, W.A.L. (1985) *Development, Experience and Curriculum in Primary Education*, Beckenham, Croom Helm.

Galton, M., Simon, B. and Croll, P. (1980) *Inside the Primary Classroom*. London: Routledge and Kegan Paul. Explores the myth of progressive primary schooling.

Ginsburg, M.B., Meyenn, R., Miller, H. and Ranceford-Hadley, C. (1977) *The Role of the Middle School Teacher*. University of Aston. Gives an account of middle schools.

Pollard, A. (1985) *The Social World of the Primary School*. London: Holt Rinehart and Winston.

Reynolds, D. (1976) 'Delinquent Schools', in Hammersley, M. and Woods, P., *The Process of Schooling*, London: Routledge and Kegan Paul. Discusses the variations in authoritarian styles of secondary schooling.

Richards, C. (1979) 'Belief, Myth and Practice', in Shaw, K. and Bloomer, M. (eds.) *Innovation and Constraint*, Oxford: Pergamon Press. Explores the myth of progressive primary schooling.

Richards, C. (ed) (1982) *New Directions in Primary Education*. Lewes: Falmer Press.

Richards, C. (ed.) (1984) *The Study of Primary Education: A Source Book, Vol. I*. Lewes: Falmer Press.

Discussion and Activities

1. Do pupils prefer their primary school experience because of the distinctive nature of the experience or because secondary schooling is just worse? (See Chapter 3.)
2. Is there a contrast between infant and junior schools that constitutes a difference in ideology?

Signposts

1. Middle Schools
In some areas middle schools operate as a kind of buffer between primary and secondary schooling. Two references are: Hargreaves, A. and Tickle, I. (eds.) (1980) *Middle Schools: Origins, Ideology and Practice*, London: Harper and Row; and Taylor, M. and Garson, Y. (1982) *Schooling in the Middle Years*, Trentham: Trentham Books.

2. Transitions

Most pupils change schools at some time in their lives. The transition from primary to secondary is the subject of Galton M. and Willcocks, J. (eds.) (1983) *Moving from the Primary School Classroom*, London: Routledge and Kegan Paul; and the transition from middle to secondary is the subject of Measor, L. and Woods, P. (1984) *Changing Schools*, Milton Keynes: Open University Press.

Chapter 31

Schooling for the Masses: State Schooling in the Secondary Sector

'The longer I live the more keenly I feel that whatever was good enough for our fathers is not good enough for us.'

Oscar Wilde

INTRODUCTION

From the learners' viewpoint, secondary schooling tends to be seen as an experience contrasting with the primary phase, and negatively evaluated (see Chapter 3). The contrasts in organizational features have been discussed in earlier chapters. Thus the characteristics of timetables (Chapter 8), or organizational styles (Chapter 10), or spatial arrangements (Chapter 7) signal that ideologies of education from the authoritarian group are in operation. In contrast to the primary schools, there appear to be fewer attempts to advocate non-authoritarian approaches and fewer still to implement them, so that the 'myth of progressivism' is much weaker. An article by Bernstein (1975) entitled 'Open Schools, Open Society' had the effect of fuelling such a myth briefly.

The contrast with primary schools tends to be in the widespread adoption of the autocratic version of authoritarian education. Reynolds and Sullivan (1979) described schools adopting this approach as 'coercive' and contrasted them with examples of 'incorporative' schools that adopted a model of authoritarian control closer to that of most primary schools.

The authoritarian ideologies of education adopted by secondary schools are not seen as temporary expedients in order to implement or bridge into some form of non-authoritarian approach: they are not Russell's 'control in the spirit of freedom', but 'control permanente'. Thus Wankowski (1974) finds that the struggle some university students have is related to the kind of learning habits gained from secondary schooling, which prove to be unsuitable in universities, where more autonomous learning is expected.

In contrast to the private sector, the toleration of diversity and alternatives in secondary schooling appears to be much less. Few schools in the UK – Countesthorpe, Stantonbury, the Sutton Centre and others excepted (Moon, 1983) – even attempt to move away from the authoritarian grouping of approaches. And there have been famous cases like Risinghill, where schools have been closed for attempting such changes (Berg, 1968; Fletcher, 1985).

Secondary-school teachers find themselves in a state of contradictions. They are exhorted to provide equality of opportunity, but the operational models ensure that resources and life chances are unevenly distributed (see Chapters 24 to 28). They are exhorted to achieve personal development, self-reliance and personal responsibility in pupils, but the logic of operational models is to encourage habituation to authoritarian control. At a time when young adolescents have developed to the point when they seek recognition as young independent adults, the schooling system tends to operate the autocratic, the least free form of authoritarian approach. The 'teacher as victim' analogy of Chapter 4 gains in plausibility, one concludes.

On the other hand, the report by Rutter (1979) indicated that there were considerable variations among the forms of authoritarian ideology of education in use in secondary schools, and the conclusion was that these had clear consequences for the behaviour and achievement of the pupils. Teachers were not helpless victims;

> the differences between schools in outcome were systematically related to their characteristics as social institutions. Factors as varied as the degree of academic emphasis, teacher actions in lessons, the availability of incentives and rewards, good conditions for pupils, and the extent to which children were able to take responsibility were all significantly associated with outcome differences between schools. All of these factors were open to modification by the staff, rather than fixed by external constraints.

Rutter finds that the total pattern of findings indicates the strong probability that, to an appreciable extent, children are shaped by their experiences at school and, in particular, by the qualities of the school as a social institution.

COMPREHENSIVE SCHOOLS: RHETORIC AND REALITY

In a recent article Sugarman (1979) distinguishes one rhetoric of comprehensive education from the reality:

> Should individual families have far greater control over the education of their children? Should Britain's primary and secondary school system be based on the principle of family choice? From Labour, the response traditionally has been decidedly in the negative. Indeed, the rhetoric from the Left has emphasized a highly contrasting principle: all children should share common educational experiences with a true cross section of British society.

Sugarman notes that such a principle would require a number of important changes in the current system of British education:

(a) Independent schools would be abolished, presumably by making attendance at state-maintained schools compulsory.
(b) Religious schools, large numbers of which are currently state-funded, would be abolished.
(c) Schools would be organized in mixed-ability groups.
(d) Wherever feasible, pupils would be bussed in and out of communities to ensure heterogeneous intakes.

To actually implement the rhetoric of the Labour Party, changes of this kind would be necessary. Local education authorities would be required to make all schools truly similar. In office, Labour governments have taken a different approach, and none of the above changes has been implemented. The Labour Party stands for 'comprehensive' education, and in practice this has meant a series of minor modifications. Sugarman gives his view of the actual practice of comprehensive education, as opposed to the rhetoric:

> As I see it this means that state financed schools (although not classrooms within schools) are to contain pupils who reflect the social class and ability patterns (although not religious backgrounds) of the area in which the school is located (although not the country as a whole). Along with this goes a general downplaying of highly consequential examinations – at least of the traditional exams – a de-emphasis of ability grouping (setting – ability-grouping by subject rather than broad streaming – is the current favourite) and much handwringing about, but a toleration of, the independent sector.

This series of minor modifications achieves, at best, something akin to the American-style neighbourhood school, Sugarman concludes.

SECONDARY SCHOOLING THROUGH THE EYES OF THE DESCHOOLING WRITERS

In 1971 a series of books was published in the UK which was written by educationalists, mainly from the USA, and drew attention to the idea of deschooling. The 'deschoolers' were identified as Illich, Goodman, Holt and Reimer. Other writers were associated with deschooling because of their criticisms of contemporary schooling in general and secondary schooling in particular, and these included Postman, Weingartner, Kohl, Freire, Kozol and Henry. The verdict of these writers was that most pupils leave school after ten years of full-time contemporary schooling with little to show for it. These years were seen as a 'pitiful waste of youthful years – caged, daydreaming, sabotaging, and cheating – and the degrading and insulting misuse of teachers' (Goodman, 1971).

The deschoolers used metaphors about school that had been used before. The comparison with prison had been used in 1910 by Shaw, who saw school as worse than prisons because at least in prison you were not required to read dull books written by the warders. Schools could also be seen as hospitals that attended to the healthy but rejected the sick. Postman and Weingartner (1971) employed medical analogies a great deal in their critique of schooling to show how the pupils became blamed for their lack of education: in answer to the doctor inquiring why the patients failed to survive, a senior doctor explains:

> Bad patients, son, bad patients. There's nothing a good doctor can do about bad patients. And there's nothing a good medicine can do for bad patients either. . . . But still, I have a nagging feeling that perhaps they didn't need penicillin, that they might have needed something else.
> . . . Nonsense! Penicillin never fails to work on good patients. We all know that.

Lister (1971) has a survey of metaphors that ranges from museums where school, open at set hours, shows exhibits such as Tudor England, Shakespeare and the religion of past eras, to factories with bells and production stages, to theatres of the vaudeville kind. The metaphor taken by Lister is that of church. Education is now our religion, so the architecture is often similar, and the promise is similar in the distribution of life chances, but in this life by schools rather than in the promised eternal life by churches.

Teachers, like preachers, must have certificates, are often poorly paid, and are inadequately educated, so the laity are often better informed. Influence is often more by ritual than content, and a main purpose is to disseminate consensus values as salaried conservatives. The position of the church was threatened by the new communication medium, the book: the school is similarly threatened by television as an alternative transmitter of culture.

Deschoolers like Goodman portray formal schooling as a mass superstition. The superstition is that education can be achieved only in institutions like schools. The reality, he argues, is that present-day schools make most young people hostile to the idea of education and finally turn out large numbers of regimented, competitive individuals who perpetuate and aggravate current social ills.

THE IDEOLOGY OF EDUCATION OF THE 'DESCHOOLING' WRITERS

Opponents of the deschooling view have tended to select one aspect of the argument for comment. What follows is an attempt to describe the deschooling vision in full using the component-theories approach to analysing ideologies of education, and to show the aspects of secondary schools in particular that they held up to be objectionable.

Theory of Knowledge: Its Content and Structure

Schools should not be preparing children for society as it is, Holt (1973) argues, but should be preparing them to make and live in a better society. The deschooling writers have a future-orientated view of knowledge, and contrast this with the past-orientated views of schools. Such a view of knowledge cannot easily be condensed into a syllabus written before the students are met, and so learning must be conducted without a syllabus. The authorities, as Postman and Weingartner observe, almost always get nervous at such an idea.   `

As Illich (1971) argues, compulsory schools depend on the idea that someone knows what is good for other people to know and do, and on someone's being willing to force all others to that view. Yet a consensus does not exist: there is little agreement about curriculum content, about which values are preferable, about whose culture is to be transmitted or about which skills are important for living. Illich proposes that education is about change, and a system orientated this way needs flexibility and variety.

The definition of 'basics' differs from that of most existing schools. The basics are not subjects like mathematics and English, but instead are learning skills. Goodman (1971) argues that, with guidance, whatever a child learns becomes educational. He follows Dewey in proposing that it makes little difference what is learnt, particularly up to the age of 12, so long as the child goes on wanting to learn something more. Not that Goodman sees much risk to the past-orientated view: most of what is contained in the present formal curriculum will be learnt incidentally in the process of developing and perpetuating learning skills, he suggests.

Illich (1971) sees the effect of the hidden curriculum as turning knowledge into a commodity: students learn that education means a process of consumption of subjects at various grades, and that the amount consumed is related to the life-chances available in society. Graduates, having consumed more, are worth more. Learning about the world becomes valued more than learning from the world:

> The hidden curriculum of schools translates learning from an activity into a commodity for which the school monopolizes the market.

Theory of Learning and the Learner's Role

The deschoolers tend to see the learner's role as explorer rather than trainee. Such a view establishes the self-taught, self-educated person as admirable. Illich states that schools teach that instruction produces learning rather than inquiry. This discredits the idea of the self-educated person and renders suspect all non-professional educational activity. In addition it creates the problem of motivation. Goodman (1971) argues that to decide *a priori* what the young ought to know and then to try to motivate them, instead of letting the initiative come from them and putting information and relevant equipment at their service, is how the problem of motivation is manufactured.

Holt (1973) is concerned about the definitions of need: instead of basing learning on supposed important, basic or fundamental needs, he follows Maslow in advocating a view of pre-emptive needs. Instead of debating which needs are basic in general, and basing learning on these, we can arrange the needs in the order in which they make themselves felt. Thus a person lost for days becomes obsessed with the need for food and water. If this need is satisfied, the need for shelter and sleep becomes dominant. Later, needs to escape or get help take over. Later still, needs for information (what has been going on while I have been away?) and needs for explanations (how am I going to explain my absence?) emerge. As each need is satisfied, another comes along to take its place. On this kind of logic, the deschoolers see no need to manufacture motivation if it has not been suppressed. If it has been suppressed, a problem of regeneration of pre-emptive need motivation has to be dealt with. Learners who have learned to learn for the motivation of avoiding disagreeable consequences like low marks, censure and punishment will need time to revert to motivation of a different kind.

For the deschoolers, the learner's role is not to reproduce what the teachers know, but to produce a personal synthesis from the resources available and sometimes to produce new insights and knowledge. Neither is the learner's role to receive decisions made by the teacher without question, but it is to learn to make learning decisions for herself or himself.

Theory of Teaching and the Teacher's Role

The view of the teacher's role held by the deschooling writers tends to be that of teachers as consultants and facilitators, since they are seen as responding to the initiatives of the learners for instruction, learning advice or whatever counselling is appropriate. The teachers are not seen as subject specialists, since the past-orientated view of knowledge based on the arrangement in disciplines is rejected.

A key debate in the deschooling literature is about the basis of authority and the kind of authority teachers should exercise. Holt (1973) suggests that he has no quibble with those who argue that teachers should not pretend that they have no more experience than many learners, or that such experience does not count, or that there are not things that they are interested in or evaluate as important. Teachers should not pretend that they are not authoritative. But he is opposed to the exercise of the power to coerce, punish, hurt and threaten. Such authority is at the very least counterproductive, by alienating many of the learners and by preventing adequate feedback:

> They may want to do what is best for the student, but they cannot really find out whether what they are doing is any good or not, or if good, how, and if not, why not. They are in the position of a man who, after becoming president of one of the largest corporations in the country, told a friend that his hardest job was simply to find out what was going on. No one would tell him. Everyone wanted to tell him what they wanted him to think, or thought he wanted to think. This is the age-old and insoluble problem of the boss. No one wants to take bad news to the king.

In another passage Holt suggests that, although schools lack the ultimate power of life and death over pupils, they still have the power to cause mental and physical pain, to threaten, scare and humiliate them and damage their futures, and he suggests further that the application of this power has corrupted some schools and some teachers, in the latter case turning many into petty tyrants, even though their starting intention was otherwise.

The mass-schooling approach is seen by the deschooling writers as establishing a very limited role for teachers: teachers are defined primarily as instructors and then are limited further at secondary level by being defined as instructors of one or more subjects only. It does not follow that instruction is to be rejected, but it should be made available when the learners require it and not imposed as the orthodoxy of learning, the one right way of proceeding.

The professional training of teachers is seen as a dubious matter: Lister (1971) argues that we ought to legally prevent people from going from school to college or university and straight back into schools, since he sees this as a cloistered body of 'school monks and nuns' attempting to educate youth with their own inexperience. Hence many other adults not trained as teachers are seen as likely sources of information and ideas.

Theory of Resources Appropriate for Learning

With a future-orientated view of knowledge preferred and an inquiry-based learner role advocated, the deschoolers have a view of resources that stresses first-hand experiences and access to a wide variety of resources, including TV, computer retrieval systems and books. The addition of 'and books' is significant: schools are seen by the deschoolers as overvaluing books, often using them as the major source of information rather than one among many resources. Lister (1971) argues that the various resource-based projects of the Schools Council exposed the paucity of resources used in schools. Along with this exposure developed an awareness of how much contemporary culture was laterally transmitted by television and magazines, and how little was vertically transmitted by teachers.

The emphasis on first-hand experience as a resource is stressed by Goodman (1971). He advocates volunteer programmes at home and abroad, student political-activity groups, rural reconstruction schemes and projects for conservation and urban renewal, as well as browsing in libraries. Subjects are seen as supplementary resources for learning and not the major content, so that learners acquire their learning skills as the basics and the desire and confidence to go on learning, rather than the particular and imposed sets of information contained in set syllabuses.

Resources are seen as being on open access to learners rather than controlled by teachers. Resources centres operating like public libraries, rather than the teacher's stock cupboard, are advocated.

Theory of Organization of Learning Situations

The label of deschoolers turns out to be misleading. The deschooling writers favour a variety of organizational initiatives, including schools, to provide congenial situations for personal development. Goodman (1971) proposed mini-schools for New York City, and the experience of the First Street School in New York was drawn on in this proposal. Holt (1973) comments that a deschooled society does not mean a society without schools, because if some people learn well in such situations that is where they should be. A deschooled society is seen as one in which nobody is compelled to attend school and in which alternative ways of learning are available.

A range of suggestions for these alternatives have been made. 'Little' schools, on the model of the Danish Little Schools, are similar in many respects to Goodman's mini-schools, in which a small group of parents, teachers and learners organize themselves into a democratic learning co-operative with state financial support. The number of people involved may be anything from 30 to 100 or more.

Holt has been involved in home-based learning in the USA version of Education Otherwise (see Chapter 33). The organization, Growing Without Schooling, supports families who prefer this approach to education and communicates their experiences in a regular newsletter.

Illich and Reimer have both advocated learning networks and resource centres based on the public-library model. Information about activities, resources, courses and interested fellow learners could be computerized, and the advent of home computers makes this suggestion feasible.

The hope of the deschooling writers is that this diversification of learning systems would prevent alienation from learning. Illich (1971) comments that alienation in the Marxist sense was a direct consequence of work's becoming a wage-labour, resulting in people's losing the opportunity to create and be recreated. He sees mass schooling as pre-alienation: school isolates learners from the worlds of work and leisure, thus making alienation preparatory to adult life by depriving educational experiences of creativity and active participation. In brief, schools turn large numbers of pupils off learning.

A Theory of Assessment

For the deschoolers, the appropriate person to assess learning is the learner, or someone requested by the learner, rather than an unknown external examiner. With this view the traditional examination system is seen as alien to education and as sustaining an education structure which serves the minority at the expense of the majority.

Freire (1972) sees an examination system as the logical outcome of the 'banking' concept of education. In the banking concept knowledge is deposited into the students, and their action is limited to receiving, filing and storing until the size of the deposit is asked for in an examination statement.

The deschoolers' views of assessment can be seen as contrasted with the examination system:

1. They stress self-assessment more than assessment by examiners.
2. They stress diagnostic assessment, on which further learning can be based, rather than selective assessment, which relies on a set proportion of failures being identified.
3. They stress criterion-referencing rather than norm-referencing (see Chapter 2).
4. They stress the process of learning, and monitoring this diagnostically, rather than the product.
5. They stress profiles of achievement rather than grades and certificates.
6. They stress a wide range of performances – conversational, interpersonal, organizational – and not just written performances.

A Theory of Aims, Objectives and Outcomes

The future orientation of knowledge stressed by the deschooling writers and the learner's role as explorer are strongly represented in the aims, objectives and outcomes they prefer. Illich (1971) has three general aims:

> A good education system should have three purposes: it should provide all who want to learn with access to available resources at any time of their lives; empower all who want to share what they know to find those who want to learn it from them; and finally to furnish all who want to present an issue to the public with the opportunity to make their challenge known.

On the last point, Illich is arguing for the wide availability of alternative ideas rather than the domination of one set of ideas. The chapter on ideology (Chapter 14) has discussions of this issue in the sections 'ideologies in competition' and 'availability and non-availability'. The vision is that of a pluralistic society.

Holt (1973) stresses the future orientation and suggests that schools give up the idea of past-orientated knowledge and 'try instead to prepare them to live in or make a better society'. That better society is seen by Goodman (1971) as one where, among other things, 'there is a policy to open as many diverse paths as possible, with plenty of opportunity to backtrack and change'.

The ideological nature of educational alternatives is discussed by Freire (1972), who contends that there can be no neutral view of education. One possibility he rejects is that of organizing education to serve the needs of the existing system, to facilitate the integration of the young into the logic of the present system and bring about conformity to it. The general aim Freire favours is 'the practice of freedom', the means by which men and women deal critically and creatively with reality and discover how to participate in the transformation of their world.

Freire recognizes that these are new people, a kind only occasionally produced in the current system, and then despite rather than because of it. The same theme is expressed in Postman and Weingartner (1971):

> The new education has as its purpose the development of a new kind of person, one who – as a result of internalizing a different series of concepts – is an actively inquiring, flexible, creative, innovative, tolerant, liberal personality who can face uncertainty and ambiguity without disorientation, who can formulate viable new meanings to meet changes in the environment which threaten individual and mutual survival.

The aims of the deschoolers are classifiable as non-authoritarian. Freire is at pains to reject the idea that his view of education is 'Leftist'. He proposes that the Rightist and Leftist views are both reactionary, since both develop forms of action which negate freedom. His view accords with that of Russell, quoted earlier, that the orthodoxy of the radical is no better than the orthodoxy of the status quo defender. Both suffer from an absence of doubt.

A Theory of the Location of Learning

Advocates of mass schooling have a simple answer to the problem of location: predominantly, learning takes place in special buildings called schools. Home educators see the home as a base where a considerable amount of learning takes place. The deschooling writers have a view of learning as being located anywhere and everywhere, so their list of locations is extensive – libraries, museums, farms, streets, concert halls, homes, resource centres, factories, shops and also schools, preferably of the 'little' kind discussed earlier.

A Theory of Language and Its Usage

The most developed attempt at a theory of language appears to be contained in Postman and Weingartner (1971). They distinguish between language which is noun-metaphor dominated and one which is process-metaphor dominated. The former is linked with the idea of fixed categories, subjects seen as collections of information and assertive thinking. The latter tolerates ambiguities, sees subjects as sets of questioning procedures and facilitates explorative lateral thinking. The deschooling writers imply a priority for process metaphors over noun metaphors, consistent with the views of learner as explorer and meaning-maker.

CONCLUSION

One thing that emerges from the above analysis is that many of the criticisms of the deschooling writers are dubious, either because the ideas have been misunderstood or because one component in the ideology of education has been discussed without the logic of the other components being noted. An example of the first case is that of Holly (1973), who proposes that the deschoolers are new mystifiers because they advocate abolishing, not revolutionizing, schools. As we have seen, the deschoolers propose nothing of the sort, and the label 'deschooler' is in fact a misnomer if taken to mean abolition rather than the diversification of learning options.

An example of the second problem occurs in Chanan and Gilchrist (1974), who select the comments of the deschooling writers about a role for industry in their proposals for diversified learning options. Industry, Chanan and Gilchrist argue, by taking over the functions of education, would teach people only what it wanted them to know, and education for jobs is to diminish people as human beings. This curious misinterpretation of the rather minor role current industry is seen to play in the educational approach of the deschoolers is possible only if all the other components, stressing future-orientated knowledge, learners as explorers and meaning-makers, teachers as consultants, locations of learnings as diverse, resources as multiple, aims as inquiry, innovation, toleration of uncertainty and ambiguity, and rational criticism are missed out of the analysis.

This chapter has attempted to give an analysis of the ideology of education of the deschooling writers in full. Adequate criticism of their vision requires that their proposals on all the components be considered, as well as their account of the existing system and the charges about its hidden curriculum.

There have been many attempts to describe the characteristics of mass schooling. Some appear in other chapters of this book, e.g. Chapter 10, on organizational styles. This chapter has been an attempt to look at the ideologies of education in play. The diversity of organizational characteristics – nursery, infant, junior, secondary, church schools, village schools, comprehensive, grammar, etc. – is not matched by a diversity of operational ideologies of education.

Even the well-voiced differences between primary schooling and secondary schooling are overstated, and the pupils' view of a marked contrast misleading, partly because they can have only a limited range of experiences. They have no contact with non-authoritarian options to provide for a wider-based comparison.

The view that primary schools are progressive in developing the non-authoritarian vision of the Plowden Report turns out to be largely mythical. The same applies to the view that primary schools have neglected the basics defined as reading, writing and mathematics.

Ideologically, primary and secondary schooling are both selections from the repertoire of authoritarian ideologies of education, the former tending to be parental or organizational, the latter more inclined towards the autocratic. Interestingly, the study by Rutter (1979) supports the conclusion that, when the secondary approach is closer to the primary approach, by eschewing the autocratic in favour of the others, it is more effective, and that autocracy tends to be a counter-productive approach. The pupils' preference for 'nice strict' rather than 'nasty strict' is vindicated as also being the more efficient of the two.

Further Reading

Fletcher, C., Caron, M., and Williams, W. (1985) *Schools on Trial*, Milton Keynes: Open University Press. Four schools – Risinghill, Summerhill Academy, Countesthorpe and Sutton Centre – tried to develop non-authoritarian regimes and were each put on trial for their efforts.

Hemming, J. (1980) *The Betrayal of Youth*. London: Marion Boyars. A psychologist's view of the damage done to young people by contemporary secondary schooling.

Holt, J. (1969) *How Children Fail*, Harmondsworth: Penguin. This book must rank as an educational classic and outlines the ideas of John Holt on how children learn to fail, based on observations of his own teaching.

Moon, B. (ed.) (1983) *Comprehensive Schools: Challenge and Change*. Windsor: NFER-Nelson. Accounts of innovations at Abraham Moss Centre, Carisbrooke High School, Countesthorpe College, Sidney Stringer School, Stantonbury Campus and Sutton Centre.

Rutter, M. et al. (1979) *Fifteen Thousand Hours*. London: Open Books. Variations amongst the authoritarian ideologies of education do make a difference as this study shows.

Toogood, P. (1984) *The Head's Tale*. Telford: Dialogue Publications. 'The justification for "school" in its present form no longer exists. There is now no reason to take children into a large inhuman centre for 7 hours a day 40 weeks a year to be looked after and institutionalised. . . . There is another way. It is community education.' The Local Authority disagreed. The Head resigned and gives us his story.

Discussion and Activities

1. The Inner London Education Authority produced a report, *Improving Secondary Schools*, in 1984 as the outcome of a committee chaired by Dr David Hargreaves. The press called it radical. See if you agree.
2. One alternative within state schooling is the religious grouping of Roman Catholic, Anglican and Jewish schooling. What ideologies of education are operational here?
3. Prepare a summary of the main points of this chapter. If you are studying in a group, compare the results.
4. Pupils are already deschooled for about 25 per cent of the year, in the school holidays. It might be interesting to investigate the varying activities of pupils during this time and assess the varying educational qualities of these experiences. Some pupils deschool themselves by regular truanting, and a similar exercise might be carried out here.
5. Contradictory practices within schools can be seen as related to the simultaneous operation of alternative ideologies of education. These are often in the same group of ideologies, so, in the pupils' words, nasty-strict and nice-strict authoritarians, or autocratic and parentalist educators, often co-exist in the same school. Analyse any school known to you using the idea of contradictions.

Signposts

1. Community Schooling
One writer counted 94 definitions of community. The concept of community schooling can be just as elusive. See Toogood (1984) Hargreaves (1982) and Moon (1983).

2. Pastoral Care
A book published in 1974 (Marland, M., *Pastoral Care*, London: Heinemann) has been seen as marking the emergence of a body of literature on this topic, and 1982 saw the arrival of a new journal, *Pastoral Care in Education*. The focus appears to be on secondary education since the 'caring side' of teaching has tended to be seen as a necessary function of the primary teachers' role. One interesting study is Best, R., Ribbins, P., and Jarvis, C. (1983).

3. Campaign for State-assisted Alternative Schools

A campaign was begun in 1980, for the establishment of small, democratically organized alternative schools within the state system. (See *Where?*, 156, March 1980). The model taken is that of the Danish 'little schools', where groups of parents, pupils and teachers can set up schools in pursuit of a particular ideology of education (a non-authoritarian one in practice, since the state already provides plenty of authoritarian ones), with most or all of the costs being covered from public funding. The campaign is clearly in favour of diversity and not a new orthodoxy, for the organizers state that many parents would take exception to democratic models of schooling of the kind they favour and would not wish for democratic schooling for their children, but they argue that the two kinds of approach can co-exist much as they do in the private sector. One account is that of Diamond, L. (1984), in Harber, C. et al. (1984).

Chapter 32

Further Education

'You now have the opportunity to take on young men and women, train them and let them work for you almost entirely at our expense, and then decide whether or not to employ them.'

David Young

INTRODUCTION

In the period 1974–84 the 16-year-old school-leaver who goes directly into employment in the UK has become a rare person. In 1974 over 60 per cent followed this route whereas in 1984 only 18 per cent could find work. The proportion of 16-year-olds staying on at school or attending Further Education Colleges either full time or on day-release has remained about the same at between 40 and 41 per cent. The 42 per cent of 16-year-olds who would have got employment in 1974 are unemployed and constitute the 'youth unemployment problem'. The response of recent British governments has been to create a series of schemes including the Youth Opportunities Programme (YOP) and the Youth Training Scheme (YTS) via a government body the Manpower Services Commission (MSC) to provide for the young employed. This chapter will take these initiatives as its central focus.

A CASE OF SOCIAL AMNESIA?

The MSC schemes have been promoted with various claims and have received a range of responses. One claim that these ideas are a new initiative of the 1970s has been exposed by historians of education as dubious (Horne, 1984). Youth unemployment between the two world wars was also high, and the response was to create Juvenile Instruction Centres (until 1930 called Juvenile Unemployment Centres), which offered similar training in social skills, life skills, and work-related routines of a general nature. They became known as dole colleges or dole schools. Horne argues that in aims, curriculum, staffing and organization the current MSC schemes resemble the dole schools and he refutes the claim that YOP, YTS and the like break entirely new ground. Even in organization there are parallels Horne argues. The Department of Education and Science has been by-passed by the MSC schemes since the latter are cheaper, flexible and less accountable than raising the school leaving age. Between the two world wars the same organizational pattern was adopted for similar reasons and the Board of Education was bypassed by the Ministry of Labour in establishing Juvenile Instruction Centres. The 'ad hocery' of the slump of the 1930s is repeated in the 1970s and 1980s Horne concludes.

FURTHER EDUCATION IN THE UK PRIOR TO MSC

In Sweden in 1976 nearly 90 per cent of all 16-year-olds opted to attend vocationally orientated Further Education courses in a gymnasial or tertiary college. In the UK in the same year less than 50 per cent of 16-year-olds followed any comparable course of action. The County College concept, which was similar in many ways to that of the post-16 gymnasial colleges of Sweden, had been ignored by successive governments. When in 1974 a somewhat startled Manpower Services Commission in the UK was given the task of dealing with youth unemployment, Further Education Colleges were largely the preserve of the minority of post-16-year-olds working for specific craft qualifications. The establishment of YOP, YTS and other schemes served to make an already inadequate Further Education sector more complex, more confused, it seemed, but at least more fashionable (Gleeson, 1983).

Given the situation that existed in 1974, the MSC initiatives seemed to offer something, however limited, to almost everyone. Jackson (1984) comments in an article entitled 'Building a Bridge to Nowhere?' that the MSC's rhetoric of building a bridge between school and work covered a range of contradictions:

> MSC officials wanted to establish the principle that all Britain's workforce should be trained, and also to provide something like a remedial year for those who left school with crippling deficiencies in basic skills and, worse, little confidence or motivation.
>
> The employers wanted to begin breaking down the restrictions of traditional apprenticeship and to spread training around more widely at little or no cost to themselves.
>
> The TUC desperately needed to convince its own ranks that it was securing something valuable for young workers – an updated version of the universal day-release it had been demanding for decades – and that it was no longer going to let unemployed youngsters be used as free labour.
>
> The colleges wanted something to replace their vanishing apprentice part-time students.
>
> The government saw all these objectives as very desirable and wanted, above all, to get the level of youth unemployment down.
>
> What nobody, of course, ascertained was whether those in the schools who were coming up to leaving age felt any need for a bridge to work, as distinct from work itself; and if they did, what sort of bridge it should be.

IDEOLOGIES OF EDUCATION ANALYSIS

Theory of Knowledge

The managing agents for YTS schemes must include six broad areas of learning. They are basic skills including computer literacy, the world of work, the world outside employment, job-specific skills, personal effectiveness and the ability to transfer skills and learning how to learn. The core skills to be learnt in these areas of learning are number and its application, communication, problem solving and planning, practical skills, and computer literacy with information technology. Rejection of the subject-based approach of UK schools as epitomized in the GCE (or revised GCSE) is implicit, and this has been declared in public by MSC officials. One interpretation would be that this represents a shift from a past-orientated view of knowledge to a present-orientation with some future-orientation included. However, the actual operation of YTS has led to strong reservations about these changes. First, the type of scheme favoured by MSC is employer-based and known as mode A. Schemes based on Colleges of Further Education (mode B2) or training workshops, community projects or information technology centres (mode B1) are rather discouraged. Survival in employment as currently organized is given priority, and ideas like job sharing, job rotation, educational phases in the form of sabbaticals, community activity, and co-operative projects are conspicuous by their absence. The celebration of the past-orientated Protestant work ethic seems to be preferred. Here work is seen as paid wage-labour, i.e. activity undertaken for a specific period of time in a place away from home for a wage. The broader interpretation of work as useful and purposeful activity whereby a considerable proportion of 'leisure' is seen as a form of work, is given little consideration.

The Protestant work ethic as outlined by Weber refers to the idea that work is not just necessary to earn a living but morally good in itself. The Puritan tradition of the sixteenth and seventeenth centuries saw good work as evidence of godliness and poor work as an insult to the Almighty. This idea was used to pursuade country dwellers with rural habits and attitudes to accept the 'discipline' of factory work when they moved to towns. The persistence of this idea is shown in the behaviour of unemployed people who exhibit guilt about being out of work, are more prone to suicide, sickness and mental illness and in the behaviour of those in work who resort to blaming the unemployed for not having a job. This is an example of cultural lag – people having been socialized for a world that no longer exists. The Protestant work ethic could be said to be functional in a society that based its economy on large-scale use of manual work, but it becomes counter-productive in an increasingly automated, computerized and robotized manufacturing sector. A Birmingham car assembly line that used to employ about 150 people and now operates with about a sixth of that number plus robots creates a lot of guilt-ridden and frustrated unemployed. The outcome appears to be that one past-orientated theory of knowledge has been replaced by another that masquerades as modern.

The attempt to prevent any education about politics featuring in the YTS curriculum has been the subject of fierce debate. The dangers of this policy are the theme of the following letter, where making training and efficiency a fetish is seen as running the risk of inducing fascism:

The principal of an American High School hands this letter to new teachers when they start at his school:

Dear Teacher,
I am a survivor of a concentration camp. My eyes saw what no man should witness:
Gas chambers built by learned engineers.
Children poisoned by educated physicians.
Infants killed by trained nurses.

Women and babies shot and burned by high school and college graduates.
So I am suspicious of education.

My request is: Help your students become human. Your efforts must never produce learned monsters, skilled psychopaths, educated Eichmans.

Reading, writing, arithmetic are important only if they serve to make our children more human.

In Pring, 1984

Theory of Learning and the Learner's Role

Since the learners who are successful in examinations tend to stay on at school, it is the remainder who are likely to arrive in Further Education and on YTS in particular. The remedial idea was strong in the YOP schemes that were the forerunners of YTS and remains attached to the present programmes. However, the curriculum does have elements of referencing against the needs of the learners, and consultation with students has developed as a strategy. With an emphasis on work experience and practical skills, the learners are given a more active role than many experience in their schooling. The feedback available from learners suggests that they prefer this approach to that of school; the closer the scheme is to school in approach the more the rejection (see Jackson, 1984).

The elements of consultation and learner-referencing remain firmly authoritarian, however, since the purpose is to achieve employer-centred aims – a 'disciplined' and 'skilled' workforce.

Theory of Teaching and the Teacher's Role

Some of the assumptions about teaching are challenged in Further Education. It was always the case that FE teachers did not need to undergo teacher training, and this idea is extended in YTS to take on a range of employees in work situations as teachers. Production workers, office workers, gardeners, shop workers, and the like, are all seen as potential teachers, particularly if helped to enhance any skills they demonstrate in this direction. Working in small groups and on a one-to-one basis a variety of teaching approaches is in evidence. However, the model remains essentially instructional rather than enabling or facilitating self-direction or developing the skills of democratic learning as in evidence in the Danish Maglehof Project (see Jensen, 1986).

Theory of Resources

The resources most favoured by MSC schemes are work-places and computers. Textbooks are employed but clearly dethroned from the dominant position they hold in secondary schools. One interpretation is that this represents a move from past-orientated resources into a present and future-orientated view. More diversification is possible. Homes as resources, community facilities such as libraries and museums, entertainment facilities such as cinemas and theatres as well as the concepts of learning networks and self-help groups – these are all possible additions to the repertoire. The limited nature of the MSC initiatives can be demonstrated in this way without belittling those changes that have occurred.

Theory of Assessment

The idea of external examinations has been rejected by the MSC schemes in favour of a profiling approach and criterion referencing. However, the adoption of such an approach does not of itself tell the whole story, for profiles can be used in restricting as well as in developmental ways. The profiles in use have been developed as sources of information to employers more than for any other purpose, and the educational potential of profiles can in this way become subverted to the purposes of a more refined selective process. The potential for moving into autonomous or democratic approaches becomes lost if profiles become authoritarian instruments for more sophisticated vetting.

Theories of Organization and of Location

In both cases a similar phenomenon can be seen. What appears at first to be diversification in practice becomes substitution. In the case of location, a different place, the work-place is seen as a suitable location for learning. But then in favouring one type of scheme (mode A) based on employers, college becomes to a large extent substituted for work-place.

In the case of the organization for learning individuals and groups receive instruction from workers substituting for teachers rather than there being any major change in educational experience: there are few moves to organize for democratic or autonomous forms of education. (For an example of a democratic initiative in Denmark, see Jensen, 1986, on the Maglehof Project.)

Theories of Aims and Objectives

We saw earlier that the aims of officials of the Manpower Services Commission, the employers, the government, the Trades Union Congress and the colleges were rather different: the aims of the students were not ascertained, thus maintaining the spirit of authoritarian ideologies of education. Indeed, the attitude of the MSC is indicated in the quotation at the head of this chapter: young people were expendable on the decision of employers. The clients were clearly defined as the employers rather than the young people who were required to take on the past-orientated Protestant work ethic as outlined previously. The overall priority given to the needs of employers was in evidence in the preference for schemes based on work-places rather than schemes based on colleges. As one writer puts it, 'the emphasis is now on perspiration rather than aspiration' (Finn, 1983). Aspiration is retained for the minority of youngsters who have stayed at school to attempt the academic route into the prestigious occupations of the professions.

CONCLUSION

Gleeson (1984) has noted three different types of response to the new pattern of further education developed around the Youth Training Scheme. One is a functional/consensual view, one a conflict view and a third a political analysis.

The Functional/Consensual View

These are some of the claims made for the YTS:

- This is a much needed bridge from school to work.
- The vast majority of previously neglected school leavers gain access to Further Education.
- A philosophy of broad-based training based on skills is now established.
- The introduction of profiles, personal and life skills are a new 'person-orientated' approach.
- New flexible links between school, college and work are established.
- The traditional academic base of the curriculum is updated to a contemporary practical work-orientated approach.

The Conflict View

- The number of jobs is reduced by subsidizing employers to train people and then dispose of as many as they wish rather than employ regular trainees.
- The much vaunted skills are in reality superficial and not necessarily related to employer needs.
- The YTS represents a conjuring trick: training is substituted for employment.
- The existing democratic channels through elected local authorities are bypassed, and centralized control mechanisms take their place.
- Selection is increased: the population who failed in the academic game are now sorted a second time into industrial sheep and goats.
- The outcome is the achievement of the 'ideal' working class – compliant, grateful for any job, however temporary, cheap labour with low expectations and aspirations.

Gleeson argues that a political interpretation moves on from the effects of the YTS on individuals that the previous two views have in common to plot the effects on youth as a whole.

YTS: A Political View

- YTS alters the traditional relationship between school and work, and hands over school leavers to employers for more positive vetting.
- YTS has little to do with producing a more skilled workforce than with *placing* people in the social hierarchy of society (modes A, B1, B2 are significant in this respect).
- YTS levels of skill training fall far below existing apprentice training schemes (work experience has replaced experience of work).

- YTS curricular guidelines are limited in scope and ambition e.g. (a) and over-preoccupation with measuring and testing for social competence, (b) an uncritical linking of motivation and maturation with vocational training.
- YTS exaggerates the process of 'life management' in training and presents a passive view of the trainee: i.e. adapting, coping, surviving and manipulating society (ironically, the learning of technical and jobs skills achieves less significance than learning social skills).
- YTS represents a mechanism for regulating previously unregulated social behaviour of youth.
- YTS has wider political consequences, e.g. generating a vocational public without skills or access to employment.
- YTS as a form of training for unemployment does not facilitate the socialization of youth into society, but out of it.
- YTS represents a political strategy for regulating the aspirations of the unemployed, and for controlling youth as a class.
- YTS confirms the collective fate of the young unemployed: its curricular arrangements are rooted in the personality structure (assumed personal and social inadequacies) of the young unemployed themselves.

In Gleeson, 1984

Many of the features of the YTS are repetitions of the approaches to the problems experienced in the UK in the recession between the First and Second World War, and this lends support to the verdict of Gleeson (1984):

> The reality is that YTS as a preparation for work neither creates job opportunities nor protects the young from the inimical influences of unemployment. If anything, YTS is an inherently conservative process, which seeks to do little more than reconcile 'trainees' to the failures of contemporary political and economic policy.

Some writers have noted various hidden curriculum features. Willis (1984) describes the consequences of the loss of work and the wage for the traditional sense of working-class masculinity:

> The importance of being the breadwinner runs pretty deep in working-class culture.
> Work and the wage is not an unmitigatedly good thing for working-class men. Here I want to explore some of its meanings for men and women and for the relations between the sexes; this doesn't mean I am voting for it. Especially in modern production processes, work can be boring, repetitive and mindless, as well as still being heavy, difficult and dangerous. Work can take a physical toll on health, safety and mental balance. Often there is an element of self-sacrifice in men's attitude to work – a slow spending of the self through the daily cycle of effort, comfort, food, sleep, effort. But this sacrifice brings the wage which keeps the home fires burning and, besides, 'the kids will have a better chance'. So there is dignity and meaning, even in sacrifice. It also gives a kind of emotional power – a hold over other members of the family who do not make the sacrifice.
> The disappearance of work and the wage is likely to produce a very particular crisis for this traditional masculine sense of identity and meaning.

Amongst the reactions reported are depression, suicide, ill-health and also sustained anger. Willis notes how youth workers in the West Midlands report more and more experience of angry and aggressive young males whose physical powers are displaced from work to other outlets, often negative or destructive. Their anger is bound to be increased by the adaptation of young working-class women who can operate as single-parent families and find some satisfaction and independence in childrearing, since the former escape route from home through the earning power of a young male is now more difficult to find.

A further hidden curriculum effect is that of a feared drift into fascism. In an Industrial Society Seminar in 1985, Lord Scanlon declared that education had a role to play in preventing a drift into fascism. The comment in *Bulletin* (May, 1985) in 'Political Dangers in Education Policies' was as follows:

> There is no evidence that schools are taking this role seriously, or that the Government wants them to. Recent extensive research into the attitudes towards race of 2500 school students in the West Midlands revealed that 30 per cent of white fifth/formers gave the National Front or the British Movement as their first or second choice political party. This represented a doubling of support in the same schools since 1980. The detail of the research reveals that this support does not indicate knowledge of the policies of the fascist parties in general, rather support for the single policy of the expulsion from Britain of all non-white peoples. Support for this 'solution' seems to be growing amongst young white people as their prospects of getting a job when they leave school diminish, and their sense of the situation being 'out of control' increases.

The reaction of the Secretary of State for Education was reported in the same article:

> Sir Keith Joseph: 'The entire curriculum would need to become more relevant to children growing up in a violent and selfish world' (*Daily Telegraph*, 27.3.85).
> The danger inherent in such a curriculum, of course, is that it risks making children, and the world, even more selfish and violent.

The economic effects of the YTS approach have been the subject of comment by other writers, e.g. Holt (1984) and the hidden curriculum of inevitable economic decline proposed through the celebration of a misguided individualism:

> Neither, by a supreme irony, is this model likely to foster a growth economy and placate the gods of the market-place. For our most successful competitor – Japan – keeps well clear of school vocational courses, recognizing that only a broad, general education equips the young for an uncertain tomorrow. Moreover, as the economist, Amartya Sen, has pointed out, Japan's success 'has not been built on anything like the new economic gospel of Mrs Thatcher. Quite the reverse: productivity depends on team work. To concentrate all attention on individual rewards for individual performance, rather than through coopera-tion, is to misunderstand the nature of the modern economy.

Gleeson (1986) argues that we are left in the end with a wide range of contradictions, no coherent educational policy for Further Education and the danger that young people could lose out all ways by being inadequately educated, inappropriately trained, without jobs and ill-prepared for the experiences of unemployment. Willis (1984) concludes that the most hopeful feature is that the resourcefulness shown by some young people in Wolverhampton in developing an alternative life style based on co-operation could fill the void left by the crisis of imagination in official circles. Otherwise, he fears increased and, in the end, massive police surveillance.

Further Reading

Barton, L. and Walker, S. (eds.) (1986) *Youth, Unemployment and Schooling*. Milton Keynes: Open University Press.

Gleeson, D. (ed.) (1983) *Youth Training and the Search for Work*. London: Routledge and Kegan Paul.

Gomm, R. (ed.) (1983) *Social Science Teachers and the New Vocationalism*. Special edition of *Social Science Teacher*, **13**, 2.

Roberts, K. (1984) *School Leavers and Their Prospects*. Milton Keynes: Open University Press.
Thompson, K. (ed.) (1984) *Work, Employment and Unemployment*. Milton Keynes: Open University Press.
Watts, A.G. (1983) *Education, Unemployment and the Future of Work*. Milton Keynes: Open University Press.
Willis, P. (1984) 'Youth Unemployment' in *New Society*, 5 April 1984 and 12 April 1984.

Discussion and Activities

1. Write a summary of the main points of this chapter.
2. Continue the analysis started at the end of the chapter on the Hidden Curriculum of Further Education. The references above should all help, especially Gomm (1983).
3. Consider the learners' viewpoint (see references at the end of Chapter 3).

Signposts

1. Sexism in Further Education
Explore the view that whilst existing theories of work and unemployment take male experiences as the yardstick, the outcome is bound to be sexist. Readings by Griffin, Lees and Wallace in Barton and Walker (1986) will provide a start.

2. Racism and unemployment
In Barton and Walker (1986) the papers by Solomos and Critchlow raise some issues here.

3. The new vocationalism in schools
In the USA the report of the National Commission on Secondary Vocational Education has produced a report entitled *The Unfinished Agenda* and a review by Lotto appears in *Phi Delta Kappan* **66**, 8. The TVEI (Technical and Vocational Educational Initiative and the CPVE (Certificate of Prevocational Education) represent related ideas in the UK. See Dale in Barton and Walker (1986) and also Dale, R. (ed.) (1985) *Education and Employers' Needs*, Oxford: Pergamon Press; and Fiddy, R. (ed.) (1985) *Youth, Unemployment and Training: A Collection of National Perspectives*, London: Falmer Press.

Chapter 33

Home-based Education and Flexischooling

'I have never let my schooling interfere with my education.'
Mark Twain

INTRODUCTION

The most unusual alternative available in the UK is educating children at home, more accurately seen as home-based learning, since most of the families taking advantage of this alternative use the home as a springboard into a variety of community-based investigations and activities. It might be assumed that such families share an ideology of education that might be variously labelled as radical, progressive, non-authoritarian, anarchistic or romantic, and the following chapter shows how the approach of LEA officers tends to make such an assumption. However, an analysis based on ideologies of education reveals a much more complex picture. The major aspect of educational practice questioned by such families is that of location: a special building called a school is not seen as an essential basis for satisfactory education to take place. There is also an implicit, and sometimes explicit, criticism of what schools achieve for learners, rather than a dispute about the vision they are trying to work to, in the events that lead up to the decision to withdraw from school, and replace *'in loco parentis'* with the real thing.

EDUCATION OTHERWISE

The name of the organization is derived from section 36 of the 1944 Education Act (England and Wales), which states that:

> It shall be the duty of the parent of every child of compulsory school age to cause him to receive efficient full-time education suitable to his age, aptitude and ability, either by regular attendance at school *or otherwise*.

In the United Kingdom education is legally compulsory: schooling is not. The law is clear on this point. Parents are accorded the primary responsibility for their children's education and, while they commonly delegate this to schools, they need not do so. Members of the Royal Family frequently have periods of education at home, and other well-known people who have had home-based learning include John Stuart Mill, Margaret Mead and Yehudi Menuhin.

Education Otherwise consists primarily of families who have decided that in the present circumstances the only way to ensure that their children's education is satisfactory is to take upon themselves full responsibility for their education rather than delegate it to the schools. The literature of the organization states that these families and their supporters believe that children have the right to relationships of concerned equality in which they can mature; that they should have considerable freedom of thought, decision and action; and that their value as people should not be related to their performance on narrow academic criteria. They also state that children have a right to a wider community than the home itself. It is on this basis that they claim that 'education otherwise' should be conducted, and the group exists to support any families practising or seeking to practise education on these principles. The group was formed in 1977 to strengthen the links between members by a newsletter, by helping in the formation of local groups, by arranging meetings, etc.; to disseminate, through the newsletter, handouts and otherwise, information about people's experiences, available resources and exchanges of skills and facilities; to support people with general advice and, where needed, specific help on legal aspects, presenting their case to the authorities and for those educating children over 16, problems of tax, social security, etc.; and to provide advice on devising programmes of activities and educational methods and materials. The aims of Education Otherwise are declared as follows:

- To encourage the provision of alternative learning situations outside the school system.
- To reaffirm that parents have the primary responsibility for their children's education and that they have the right to exercise this responsibility by educating them out of school.
- To establish the primary right of children that full consideration, with due allowance for their age and understanding, shall be given to their wishes and feelings regarding their education.

In 1985 about a thousand families had joined in support of these aims and about half of these were currently undertaking home-based education.

It is necessary to stress that the families in Education Otherwise are educating their children as a positive alternative: they are not simply refusing to send them to school, and they are attempting to co-operate with the Local Education Authority. Some families opt into the system again at various stages. Some organize the primary phase at home and opt in at the secondary phase, while others reverse this. Some opt out for a year or two only, while others opt in at the Further Education stage.

Some LEAs are helpful and sympathetic indeed, some have such a well-established procedure that a form exists for parents to fill in describing their programme. Other LEAs, however, are suspicious, even hostile, and court cases sometimes result. So far most cases appear to have gone against LEAs because they have been unable to prove beyond reasonable doubt that what local schools provide is superior to the efforts of a concerned and energetic family. (Since many of the families have started their programme in desperation because the children were so unhappy at school, this is perhaps not surprising.)

LEAs vary considerably about what they define as an acceptable educational programme, since this often depends on the particular vision of education adopted by the LEA officers. Some have a Protestant/Puritan outlook, and have informed parents that their children were far too happy being educated at home and that school was necessary to teach them how to cope with an unhappy world. Others have expressed the longing for the courage to adopt something similar for their own children, who are alienated from their particular schools. Many parents report that they are treated from the start as deviants rather than as people who care enough about their children to devote extra time, energy and financial resources to them, and that they are held to be guilty unless they prove their educational innocence.

EDUCATION OTHERWISE IN THE USA

A similar organization to Education Otherwise, called Growing Without Schooling, exists in the USA; and one well-known person behind it is John Holt, author of *How Children Fail*. Two quotations from the GWS newsletter (No. 3) indicate some experiences parallel to those of British parents:

> In its short life to date, GWS has already changed its character somewhat. It is turning out to be less about teaching than I thought it would be, and more about law, less about what your children can do once you get them out of school, and more about what you may have to do to get them out. I rather regret this. I am much more interested in helping children to explore the world and to find out and do interesting and worthwhile things in it, than I am in arguing about and fighting with schools. But it begins to look as if, like Moses in Egypt, we may have to find ways to make things a bit hot for the school Pharaohs, if only so that they will let our people go.
>
> The dozen or so letters and phone calls I have had about this during recent months don't add up to much of a sample, perhaps not even a representative one. They suggest, though, that many people who ask their local schools to approve some kind of home study program are going to meet, not sympathy and support, not even intelligent questions, but threats – 'We'll take you to court! We'll put you in jail! We'll take your kids away from you!'
>
> (Two years later, a small but growing minority of schools seem to be taking a more friendly and co-operative position.)

The second quotation discusses the irony of caring parents being treated as deviant while those who do not care are 'normal'. The newsletter editor, John Holt, notes that in 1978 the *Boston Globe*, in a story about school attendance, found that, on a typical day, about 70 per cent of the 65 000 youngsters attend classes but the 30 per cent who are missing are ignored. Who they are, why they stay away, and what is done about them are largely unanswered questions. The answers are, Holt suggests, that most of them are poor, dislike school, see it as wasting their time and conclude that teachers do not care much about their fate, because they make little effort to get them back into school:

> There is irony here . . . compulsory school attendance laws were invented by rich people and aimed at poor kids. These rich people said in effect, 'We educated people are perfectly capable of teaching our own children, but the poor don't give a damn about their kids and wouldn't know enough to teach them anything even if they wanted to. So unless we lock up those kids in school all day long they are just going to run around the streets, cause trouble, get in bad habits, become drunks and criminals. We've got to put them in school to make

them into good, obedient, hard-working factory hands.

The irony is that if you are in fact the kind of kid that compulsory attendance laws were first aimed at, you can skip school all year long and nobody will pay any attention. The streets are full of the kinds of kids that schools were designed to keep off the streets. But if you are one of those now rare people who really care about the growth of your children and are willing to take the responsibility for helping that growth, and you try to take them out of schools where they are not growing but shrinking, the schools are likely to begin shouting about courts and jails. Strange.

IDEOLOGIES OF EDUCATION AND EDUCATION OTHERWISE

The official position of Education Otherwise, as outlined in the publicity and informational material, is that of a non-authoritarian ideology. However, the analysis by Christine Brown (1978) established a wide variety of ideologies of education within the organization. This analysis was based on the written material of the organization, including its newsletter, interviews with members in their homes, correspondence, and interviews at a national conference.

Theory of Knowledge: Its Contents and Structure

Officially, Education Otherwise was fairly compatible with non-authoritarian alternatives. Traditional subject divisions were treated as arbitrary, if not discarded. Knowledge was seen as acquired through individual and subjective experience. Among the members, however, there was a large section who accepted traditional subject divisions as the basis of their programme. Many found this forced on them by the LEAs. Others opted for the security of creating a miniature formal school at home, at least as a starting point.

Theory of Learning and the Learner's Role

Officially, Education Otherwise was compatible with non-authoritarian alternatives. The learner was seen to develop his own pattern of learning through direct experience within his environment – 'learning by doing' stimulated by learner curiosity: autonomous learning was envisaged. Among members, however, much learning was traditionally teacher/parent directed in prescribed areas. The attitude of some LEA officers was that unstructured and spontaneous approaches were unacceptable: Rousseau's *Emile* and A.S. Neill's vision of education were rejected outright with the sure certainty of the bigot.

Teaching and the Teacher's Role

Officially, Education Otherwise was compatible with non-authoritarian alternatives: authoritarian roles were avoided and guidance, where guidance was accepted, was in

Russell's 'spirit of freedom', i.e. as a temporary necessity, not as a permanent state. The concept of specialist educational expertise exclusive to a profession was rejected. However, among members there were those who assumed an authoritarian role in the teaching of their children; e.g. one parent supervised set lessons, others employed tutorial help from qualified teachers, and others used correspondence courses.

Resources Appropriate for Learning

Officially, Education Otherwise was compatible with non-authoritarian alternatives: all resources were regarded as appropriate for learning and special emphasis was placed on the use of the public media. The relationship between the learner and the resource was viewed as direct rather than filtered through a teacher. Many members, however, still concentrated on school textbooks in specialist subject areas, or used specialist media transmissions or correspondence texts.

Theory of Assessment

Officially, Education Otherwise was critical of competitive examinations and of assessment for and by professional 'experts'. Self-assessment by the learner seemed integral to the process of learning. However, many members substituted for the assessment of prescribed behaviours by the professional teacher the assessment of prescribed behaviours by themselves, and many adopted procedures compatible with the state school in preparing for public examinations. In these cases the parent took on the role of the traditional teacher for some of the time.

Organization of Learning Situations

Again, Education Otherwise was officially compatible with non-authoritarian alternatives, in that it advocated learner-directed organization, unstructured and free-ranging. Many members, however, presented very highly structured programmes with set time-tables for considerable periods of the week.

Aims and Objectives

Officially, Education Otherwise was compatible with non-authoritarian alternatives, in that it emphasized the free growth of the individual towards self-directed goals: like the free schools it attempted to promote individualism and criticized the mass conformity of authoritarian settings in the state school. To resist the power of professional conglomerates was a specially stated aim. In practice, however, many members were expressing dissatisfaction with the state school system not over the aims themselves but over their inefficiency in carrying out those aims. Their objectives were similarly prescribed and monitored, but, in their opinion, were being executed more efficiently.

Ideologically, therefore, Education Otherwise emerges as a very complex organization; its official line and the attitudes of some of its members are well within the context of non-authoritarian alternatives, varying from free school and libertarian approaches pursued in the home setting to community-orientated learning networks. Among its members, however, were many with ideologies highly compatible with the state-school norms, and having the location of education and, to a much lesser extent, the practical rejection of state-directed professionals as their only radical features.

A FURTHER COMPONENT OF AN IDEOLOGY OF EDUCATION: A THEORY OF LOCATIONS OF LEARNING

Non-authoritarian ideologies of education can provide alternative views of the location of learning to that in current use, which confines it to the school building and to the relatively total institution of the school. Contemporary free schools move towards smaller units, less isolated from the rest of the community and community based, providing much opportunity for outside exploration and lacking the authoritarian or bureaucratic control of the large state school. But they are still schools, located in special and separate premises, often organized by professionally trained teachers, requiring at least a minimum of bureaucratic management. Some question the school – any form of school – as the sole locus for learning and begin to think in terms of learning without any kind of closed institutional arrangement, for example learning networks. Education Otherwise has proffered the home setting as an alternative base. The one single aspect where Education Otherwise was consistent throughout was that the school as a locus for education was replaced by the home. Some families, although not all, entertained concepts of learning networks. However, all questioned the locus of the school (Meighan and Brown, 1980).

One of the most taken-for-granted aspects of education has been location in a special building, i.e. the school. Education systems of the future may develop a variety of locations, and Education Otherwise poses the possibility of this becoming an important component of ideologies of education. The Open University has already opened up similar issues with regard to Higher Education, where learning takes place at home, at a study centre, at a summer school, in a self-help group or by a telephone link-up.

The Parkway programme in Philadelphia raises similar issues, since the school exists without a special building by holding classes and other learning experiences anywhere in the city, e.g. museums, church halls, libraries.

FLEXISCHOOLING

The current situation between LEAs and Education Otherwise families tends to be polarized: education located either at home or at school. Whether this is because of the desire for administrative tidiness or simply because of a lack of educational imagination on the part of LEA officials is not clear. It is possible to envisage a range of possible arrangements between schools and homes between these two poles, with part-time, school-based work and home-based work, working to programmes, agreed among teachers, parents and pupils, for either short or longer periods of time. Something similar already operates in parts of Sweden, for climatic reasons, and the radio schools of Australia show how this can be achieved in the outback.

The administrative skills, systems and procedures already exist. The organization of the Open University, the administration of evening institutes in a multitude of study situations, and the operation of correspondence colleges and of technical colleges with large part-time populations of students are all working models that can be adopted, to say nothing of resource facilities like BBC and ITV schools broadcasting. Using such systems, a prospectus of possibilities for learning, with schools in an active partnership with families, becomes feasible. Visions of how a learning society and 'education permanante' might work emerge from such considerations. The role of school teachers might become closer to that of their higher-status cousins, university lecturers, using a similar range of tutorial, instructional, consultancy and research skills. For politicians and civil servants there is the additional possibility of such a system being considerably cheaper than the present one: both the Parkway Programme and the Open University have proved to be cost-effective alternatives to traditional systems.

One myth that parents encounter is that schooling in contemporary Britain is basically sound. It is the parents' or the children's reaction that are supposed to be unsound, or both. Educationalists who take up this posture are either unaware of the debates in educational circles or deliberately trying to ignore them. A Manifesto for Change was signed by leading figures from industry, the church, education and indeed most sectors of British Society, and it was published in *The Times Educational Supplement* in January 1981. It stressed the idea that schools, as currently organized, were incapable of producing the flexible people needed to cope with the rapid changes associated with the decline of work and the increase of leisure.

There are currently a wide variety of alternatives mooted as solutions to the problem of unsatisfactory schools. Authoritarian educationalists advocate well tried and largely failed systems like public schools, grammar schools and comprehensive schools. Non-authoritarian educationalists provide support for various other ideas including state supported democratic schools or 'little' schools on the Danish model, schools within schools, deschooling and home-based education. Sometimes these are presented as an alternative orthodoxy, sometimes as a proposal for diversification. From the home-based educational experience comes another idea that would allow for the toleration of considerable diversity. It is the wish of many home-based educators that they have a co-operative working arrangement with schools. Those who have tried to obtain this are usually refused and forced to go it alone. These parents seek what I shall call a flexischooling arrangement.

Flexischooling can be seen to be based on rather different assumptions from those of current schooling.

1. These do not have to be a single location for education. There can be several including homes and school buildings in particular, but also museums, libraries, parks and work-places. The position of school as the sole location for education has recently been questioned (Meighan and Brown, 1980).
2. Home resources can be utilized in educational programmes – the TV set, the radio, video and cassette recorders, the postal service and home computers.

3. Parents can be seen as part of the solution of the problems of education rather than part of the problem and can learn or even be trained to have an active role in co-operative programmes with schools (see Chapter 5).
4. Learners can learn a great deal without a teacher being present. Correspondence colleges have always appreciated this point, as does the World-Wide Education Service with its hundred years experience in helping expatriate families educate their children in foreign countries. The concept of distance learning has credibility in work of the Open University.

If some of these ideas bring to mind the notion of deschooling, this would cause no surprise. The group of writers rather misleadingly known as deschoolers were, for the most part, in favour of regenerating schooling in various ways. The central concept in their analysis was that of the hidden curriculum that stressed uncritical conformity and which suppressed diversity.

Flexischooling can be seen as an amalgam of ideas obtained from the practices of the Open University, flexistudy systems in Further Education, Adult Education and Correspondence Colleges. An extract from the Flexistudy Manual of Barnet College (1978) gives the bare bones of the approach:

> Flexistudy combines the flexibility of correspondence courses with face-to-face contact and other advantages of day or evening classes.
>
> Flexistudy students study at home, at their own pace and at times to suit themselves, using the highly successful study packs issued by the National Extension College, Cambridge. In addition, they come to Barnet College from time to time to meet the tutors who have been marking their written work and also meet other students following the same courses.
>
> These Flexistudy tutorial meetings are fixed by mutual arrangement at the times and on the days convenient to students. For instance, they might only be held monthly, perhaps on a Tuesday evening one month a Saturday morning the next and so on. Or whatever suits students and tutor.
>
> So if you cannot come to a fixed class every week, if you are, say, on shift work, the head of a one-parent family, someone who gets home too late from factory or office or often has to work out of town, or if you just don't want to tie yourself down to time and place, contact Barnet College about Flexistudy.
>
> There are nearly 30 subjects to choose from, ranging from basic maths to sociology A-level, from French for beginners to A-level biology or just simply How to Study Effectively.

In making such an approach available as a flexischooling system, a variety of arrangements is possible. 'Contracts' between parents and school could be based on 100, 75, 50, 25 per cent or almost nil time in schooling according to home circumstances at a particular time. The administrative problems seem immense until we see that the Open University copes with 30,000 students all on individual schedules, while correspondence colleges cope effectively with monitoring their students' study programmes. One or two individual pioneering attempts have been reported from the USA (e.g. see Holt, 1981, pp. 120–1). Flexischooling is already operational in special education under the guise of the Portage Project.

CONCLUSION

The growth of home-based education has served to highlight some broader issues in British education. First, the rights of parents are frequently denied by an authoritarian approach to schooling with its anti-democratic stance. Parents have had to go to the trouble and expense of appeals to the European Court of Human Rights to achieve their wishes despite the clear statements of the 1944 Education Act, section 76 (e.g. the case of *Campbell and Cosans*, February 1982, relating to corporal punishment).

Second, the rights of children are denied by the authoritarian view of childhood underpinning the authoritarian ideologies of education. The lack of rights of children as regards education have been documented by Stone and Taylor and published in *Where?* under the title of the 'Sad tale of pupils' rights'. Annually over 4000 children are taken into care at considerable public expense whose only offence has been to vote with their feet against compulsory schooling.

A third consequence of the authoritarian approaches to education is an incestuous form of debate when things are perceived to be wrong with schools. Educationalist debates with educationalist with the contributions of pupils and parents largely ignored. Yet the evidence about the pupils' point of view suggests that they have many interesting, useful and constructive things to say about education, schooling and teaching (see Chapter 3). Blishen, after surveying the essays of pupils written on the theme of 'The school that I'd like', comments:

> In another sense, it amounted to an enormous, remarkably good-humoured, earnest, frequently passionate and, at best, highly intelligent plea for a new order in our schools. No one who read through all those words could have believed for one moment that here were children seizing an opportunity to cock a snook at the *status quo*, for the sake of the snook. Juvenile irresponsibility was awfully hard to find. The radical note that was so pervasive was astonishingly steady, reasonable, and supported by instances. I have never read so much that was so full of complaints and criticisms, of schemes for imaginative innovation, and yet that was, as a whole, so very sober.

The evidence about the parents' point of view has been gained from a range of projects and investigations, but perhaps no group has more to contribute than those who have taken on the full responsibility of education for themselves – the home-based members of Education Otherwise. One parent writes:

> The children are able to learn and learn more at their own speed and are less socially restricted and not imposed upon . . . It's a great pleasure and privilege to be involved in this.

Another concludes:

> The children are so much calmer and happier and livelier; we are sorry they ever went to school.

Holt (1982) suggests that schools have a great deal to learn from parents who educate at home:

> our chief educational problem is not to find a way to make home *more* like schools. If anything it is to make schools *less* like schools.

The attempt to maintain myths about education in the actions of education officials is not necessarily in the nature of a plot, though it can sometimes be so. It is rooted in the authoritarian approaches to educational matters that lead its adherents to believe in the myths of a One Right Way in education, of the need for compulsory full-time schooling, and of the inevitable superiority of the teaching body.

We have been given alternative visions of the future in recent years. These range from nuclear holocaust, economic stagnation with lower standards of living, the self-sufficiency society as scarce resources and energy supplies run out, to the leisure future brought about by the micro-processor revolution. It is interesting to speculate how flexischooling might serve several of these better than the present system by being cheaper, encouraging self-sufficiency, or solving the 'problem' of increased leisure by providing families that wanted it with more involvement in the educational process.

Further Reading

Baker, J. (1974) *Children in Chancery*. London: Hutchinson. Contains an account of home-based education.

Boulter, H. (1984) 'Parents and Children: 100 years of the PNEU' in Harber, C. et al. (1984) *Alternative Educational Futures* (Holt, Rinehart and Winston).

Brown, C. (1978) *Education Otherwise: A Sociological Case Study of One Alternative to State Schooling*. Unpublished MEd dissertation, University of Birmingham. Analytical accounts of Education Otherwise.

Deakin, M. (1973) *The Children on the Hill*. Tunbridge Wells: Abacus Books. Contains an account of home-based education.

Head, D. (1974) *Free Way to Learning*. Harmondsworth: Penguin. Has a discussion of educational alternatives and legal issues, and a case study of a family's home-based educational experiences.

Head, D. (1978) 'Five Years Out of School'. *Where?*, **135**.

Holt, J. (1982) *Teach Your Own* (Lighthouse Books).

Kitto, D. (1981) 'Doing It Their Way', *Times Educational Supplement*, 10 July.

Meighan, R. (1984) 'Home-based Educators and Education Authorities: The Attempt to Maintain a Mythology', *Educational Studies*, **10**, 3.

Meighan, R. (1984) 'Policy Consciousness and Home-based Education', *Educational Review*, **36**, 2.

Meighan, R. and Brown, C. (1980) 'Locations of Learning and Ideologies of Education: Some Issues Raised by a Study of Education Otherwise' in Barton, L. et al., *Schooling Ideology and the Curriculum*, Lewes: Falmer Press.

Mullarney, M. (1984) *Anything School Can Do You Can Do Better*. London: Marion Boyars.

Steele, J. (1973) 'Educated at Home', *New Society*, 18 October.

Wallace, N. (1983) *Better Than School*. New York: Larson.

Discussion and Activities

1. The initial response of many people to the idea of home-based education is that the social life of children suffers. Develop a sociological analysis of the social life *actually* offered in schools. Here are some starting ideas:

    (a) Children at school talk to each other or to a teacher for a small minority of the time in school.
    (b) Children spend time in the company of other children of the same age in class, or in the playground with a limited age range of pupils.

(c) Most of the adults available are 'inexperienced', in that they have been to school, college or university, and back into school teaching.

(d) Peer groups can develop a tyranny of the peer group, forcing conformity in dress and behaviour.

(e) Extra-curricular activities, e.g. school teams, orchestra, plays, may be divisive, by being on offer to selected pupils only.

(f) Pupils may learn from the hidden curriculum messages about how to behave towards each other, e.g. sexist attitudes (see parts 1 and 2 of this book).

(g) From the pupils' point of view the only tolerable feature of secondary schooling, for many, is meeting up with friends.

2. Discuss the opening quotation of Mark Twain that distinguishes between schooling and education.

3. Make a summary of the main points of this chapter.

Signposts

Flexischooling
A form of flexischooling is already operational in the UK and USA in special education under the name of the Portage Project. Two starting points are Dessent, T. (ed.) (1984) *What is Important about Portage?* Windsor: NFER-Nelson; and Daly, B. et al. (eds.) (1984) *Portage: The Importance of Parents*. Windsor: NFER-Nelson.

Chapter 34

Postscript: Educational Policy and Alternative Futures

'Imagination is more important than knowledge.'
Albert Einstein

SOCIOLOGY AND POLICY

The approach in this book has been an attempt to work through the analogy of the sociologist as the competent spy who reports on what is there. The spy is not a completely neutral observer, as has been said, since he or she favours one side rather than the other, except if the spy be a double agent. Moreover, reality is observed by the spy from the inside or from the outside, each position yielding a limited viewpoint (see Chapter 19). However, one of the limitations of this analogy is that it suggests that sociology can inform policy only in its implementation phase. There are several possible phases of policy: policy formation, policy implementation and policy monitoring/review.

The idea of sociology's being related to policy formation is taken for granted by Marxist sociologists but resisted by others, who see this as an 'ought' question, as an issue of prescription, and therefore a philosophical and political concern. However, when sociologists produce comparative accounts these become related to policy formation, since this is itself a selection from alternatives: 'related to' is not 'identical with' because some alternatives may be speculative and others may not yet have been the subject of sociological investigation. The concept of ideologies of education used analytically, as in Chapters 14, 15 and 16, illustrates the point, since it compares the key components of a wide variety of alternatives and is therefore capable of serving the tasks of policy making. Here the sociologist is providing information and ideas about what could be, rather than what should be, but these two issues are linked in the concept of alternatives.

Educational policy sounds like something administrators do in education offices and government departments, but the concept of layers of meaning suggests that this is too limited a view, and that policy making, implementation and review take place at all layers of meaning, from classrooms to staffrooms to education offices. An early chapter did raise the question of 'teacher as victim', but it suggested that the analogy was too pessimistic: the subsequent chapters have tried to indicate some of the possibilities and limitations of teacher activity. If the analysis of the complexity and contradictions of schooling is substantially correct, individual teachers and groups of teachers can bridge ideologies of education in some of the ways indicated. The recent stress on action, interactionist, interpretive, micro-phenomenological – call them what you will – approaches has illustrated how educational policy is the concern of all educationalists at all layers of meaning.

One can discern a number of possible stages in the development of the sociology of education, with changing relevance for teachers. These have paralleled the stages of the public debates about education, which appear to have moved from a consideration of equality of opportunity to the assessment of the wastage of talent, and then to the curriculum (Young, 1971).

In the first stage, the consideration of equality of opportunity, the relevance of sociological perspectives for teachers was perhaps of a third order, of being well informed about the apparently administrative decisions needed to cope with the social-class nature of unequal opportunity.

The relevance moved to a second order, of being involved in discussion and deliberations about selection and comprehensive schools related to the notion of a wastage of talent.

In the last few years the relevance of sociological perspectives to teachers has apparently moved into a first-order stage, with a consideration of the curriculum and the questions raised here about subject teaching, team teaching, integrated studies and pedagogical styles, since these are of immediate day-to-day concern in teaching.

These current trends in the sociology of education are related, to some extent, to the development of micro-perspectives, which are also concerned with immediate, day-to-day aspects of experiences. This is in contrast to the structural-conflict and functionalist approaches, which tended to look at macro-sociological questions.

The trends may also be described to some extent as a shift from concern with the sociology of education in general to concern with the sociology of teaching in particular: this concern can no longer be seen as relevant only to educational administrators and politicians, since the notions of a hidden curriculum, or teaching as a conflict situation, or the school as a knowledge-processing agency, are related to teacher–pupil behaviour every day in every classroom.

At the very least, sociology may be related to policy making by indicating where *not* to go, even if where to go remains unclear. Thus the research of Reynolds (1976), among others, and of the social psychologist Milgram (1974), might suggest that one ideology of education that should be avoided is the autocratic. It has the potential to produce large-scale alienation and disruptive behaviour, and the propensity to encourage malice and inhumane interpersonal behaviour.

ALTERNATIVE FUTURES

To those struggling with day-to-day survival issues like order, truancy, shortage of materials, examination pressures and cynical, time-serving colleagues, the issue of alternative futures may seem exotic. The rate of change in industrial society suggests that it is not: we may be talking about only 5, 10 or 15 years ahead. As an indication, consider that the Open University was the ridiculed idea of a few people for a new form of educational institution in 1965, and yet it now approaches its twentieth anniversary.

There are several scenarios for the future of the UK, and they include:

1. Re-establishing some past state of society, retrospectively viewed as a relatively golden age.
2. Perpetuating the status quo with relatively little change.
3. Gradual economic stagnation leading to a declining standard of living.
4. A move to a self-sufficiency type of economy as scarce resources gradually run out.
5. The micro-processor revolution, leading to more leisure and less work, therefore more control through a police state.
6. The micro-processor revolution leisure situation being resolved by developing responsible autonomy as an alternative to police states.
7. Nuclear holocaust, either by intent or by accident, leading to a society of small groups of self-sufficient people.

The key features of the education system and its dominant ideology of education would be likely to parallel the economic scenarios.

Re-establishing some past state of education, retrospectively viewed as a relatively golden age, might require the lowering of the school-leaving age, or the re-establishment of a core curriculum with centrally devised standards monitored by a body of HMIs reverting to the old task of inspection rather than advising, or reversion to mode one examinations and the phasing out of teacher-influenced mode three examinations. Other features might be the re-establishment of selective schools, the revival of compulsory religious teaching, or the revival of Latin as an entrance requirement to universities. Autocratic teaching with a transmission theory of knowledge might be a key component of the dominant ideology of education.

Perhaps it is the second possibility, that of no change, that seems the most unlikely. The characteristics of the present education system have been the subject of most of this book, and so do not need to be described again here.

The next possibility, that of gradual economic decline, might result in reductions in expenditure on education. The reduction in the teaching force, part-time schooling, an increase in the private sector of education and the search for cheaper, home-based forms of education, perhaps using television as the Open University does, might be consequences.

A self-sufficiency economy would encourage people to grow their own food, to use domestic means of energy production and to produce their own clothes and artifacts as much as possible. The logic of integrating education with this life style has been seen by those pioneers of the self-sufficient life who are among the proponents of Education Otherwise (see Chapter 33). They have argued that a self-sufficient life requires a new kind of person who is actively inquiring, flexible, creative, self-reliant and able to face uncertainty without disorientation. The autonomous study ideology of education fits these specifications.

The key characteristics of micro-computers is that they are cheap, portable and durable. Thus computing tasks which could be done only on computers in special buildings and costing many thousands of pounds can now be done on small machines (about the size of a large office typewriter) costing £500 or less. Factories and offices can be run by ten people rather than hundreds or thousands. One view of the social control system of a society where leisure is more prevalent than work is that more repressive control agencies, police and military, will be needed. Educational institutions that can produce passive, acquiescent and uncritical members of society would be needed. A government working with this view would increase spending on police and armed forces and encourage teachers to be more authoritarian. Indeed, compulsory boarding schools for adolescents, organized as autocratic institutions with military regimes, might be advocated.

A more positive response to the increase of leisure and decrease of work might be to develop responsible autonomy or social democracy, or some other less authoritarian solution. The education system would then need to be rethought, for if the view of the critics of the present system is reasonably accurate in concluding that 'the students who endure it come as passive, acquiescent, dogmatic, intolerant, authoritarian, inflexible, conservative personalities who desperately need to resist change in an effort to keep their illusion of certainty intact' (Postman and Weingartner, 1969), such a system would not serve a social situation requiring active, inquiring, flexible, tolerant, liberal and innovative responses.

Any educational policy, whether operated by education officers in offices or by teachers in classrooms, that does not face up to these possible futures and take into account their sociological interpretations runs the risk of producing schools staring intently into the past as we rocket into the future.

References

Abraham, J.H. (1966) *Sociology*. Sevenoaks: English Universities Press.

Acker, S. and Piper, D.W. (eds.) (1984) *Is Higher Education Fair to Women?* Guildford: SRHE and Nelson.

Allen, V. (1975) *Social Analysis*. Harlow: Longman.

Althusser, L. (1971) 'Ideology and the state' in Althusser, L. *Lenin and Philosophy and other Essays*. London: New Left Books.

Apple, M. (1979) 'The production of knowledge and the production of deviance in schools' in Barton, L. and Meighan, R. (eds.), *Schools, Pupils, and Deviance*. Driffield: Nafferton.

Apple, M. (1980) 'Curricular form and the logic of technical control' in Barton, L., Meighan, R. and Walker, S., *Schooling, Ideology and the Curriculum*. Lewes: Falmer.

Archer, M. (1979) *The Social Origin of Educational Systems*. London: Sage.

Ashton, P., Keen, P., Davies, F. and Holley, B. (1975) *The Aims of Primary Education: A Study of Teachers' Opinions*. London: Macmillan.

Baker, J. (1974) *Children in Chancery*. London: Hutchinson.

Ball, S., Hull, R., Skelton, M. and Tudor, R. (1984) 'The tyranny of devil's mill: time and talk at school' in Delamont, S. (ed.) *Readings in Interaction in the Classroom*. London: Methuen.

Banks, O. (1955) *Parity and Prestige in English Secondary Education*. London: Routledge and Kegan Paul.

Banks, O. (1968) *The Sociology of Education*. London: Batsford

Banks, O. (1978) 'School and society' in Barton, L. and Meighan, R. (eds.) *Sociological Interpretations of Schooling and Classrooms: A Reappraisal*. Driffield: Nafferton.

Barber, T.X. and Silver, H.J. (1968) 'Fact, fiction and the experimenter bias effect', *Psychological Bulletin*, Monograph Supplement, **70**, 6.

Barnes, D. (1976) *From Communication to Curriculum*. Harmondsworth: Penguin.

Barnes, D., Britton, J. and Rosen, H. (1969) *Language, the Learner and the School*. Harmondsworth: Penguin.

Barnes, D. and Shemilt, D. (1974) 'Transmission and interpretation', *Educational Review*, **26**, 3.

Barnes, D. and Todd, F. (1977) *Communication and Learning in Small Groups*. London: Routledge and Kegan Paul.

Barton, L. and Meighan, R. (1978) *Sociological Interpretations of Schooling and Classrooms: A Reappraisal*. Driffield: Nafferton.

Barton, L. and Meighan, R. (1979) *Schools, Pupils and Deviance*. Driffield: Nafferton.

Barton, L., Meighan, R. and Walker, S. (1980) *Schooling, Ideology and the Curriculum*. Lewes: Falmer.

Barton, L. and Tomlinson, S., (eds.) (1981) *Special Education: Policy, Practices and Social Issues*. London: Harper and Row.

Barton, L. and Tomlinson, S., (eds.) (1984) *Special Education and Social Interests*. Beckenham: Croom Helm.

Barton, L. and Walker, S. (1978) 'Sociology of education at the crossroads', *Educational Review*, **30**, 3.

Barton, L. and Walker, S., (eds.) (1981) *Schools, Teachers and Teaching*. Lewes: Falmer.

Barton, L. and Walker, S., (eds.) (1983) *Race, Class and Education*. Beckenham: Croom Helm.

Barton, L. and Walker, S., (eds.) (1986) *Youth, Unemployment and Schooling*. Milton Keynes: Open University Press.

Bealing, D. (1972) 'The organisation of junior school classrooms', *Educational Research*, **14**, 3.

Becker, H. (1952) 'Social class variation in the teacher–pupil relationship', *Journal of Educational Sociology*, **25**.

Becker, H. (1963) *Outsiders*. Oxford: Free Press.

Becker, H. (1968) *Making the Grade*, Chichester: Wiley.

Becker, H. (1970) *Sociological Work*. London: Aldus.

Becker, H. (1974), quoted in Dale, R., 'Phenomenological perspectives and the sociology of the school' in Flude, M. and Ahier, J. (eds.), *Educability, Schools and Ideology*. Beckenham: Croom Helm.

Bell, R. and Grant, N. (1974) *A Mythology of British Education*. St Albans: Panther.

Bellack, A., Kliebard, H., Hyman, R. and Smith, F. (1966) *The Language of the Classroom*. New York: Teachers' College Press.

Bennett, S.N. (1976) *Teaching Styles and Pupils Progress*. London: Open Books.

Bennett, S.N. (1980) *Open Plan Schools: Teaching, Curriculum, Design*. Windsor: NFER–Nelson.

Bennett, S.N. and Jordan, J. (1975) 'A typology of teaching styles in primary schools', *British Journal of Educational Psychology*, **45**, 20–28.

Berg, I. (1973) *Education and Jobs*. Harmondsworth: Penguin.

Berg, L. (1968) *Risinghill: Death of a Comprehensive School*. Harmondsworth: Penguin.

Berger, P. (1966) *Invitation to Sociology*. Harmondsworth: Penguin.

Berger, P. (1971) 'Sociology and freedom', *The American Sociologist*, **4**.

Berger, P. (1977) *Facing Up to Modernity*. Harmondsworth: Penguin.

Berger, P. and Kellner, H. (1983) *Sociology Reinterpreted*. Harmondsworth: Penguin.

Berger, P. and Luckmann, T. (1967) *The Social Construction of Reality*. Harmondsworth: Penguin.

Berlak, A.C., Berlak, H., Bagenstos, N.T. and Mikel, E.R. (1975) 'Teaching and learning in English primary schools' in Hammersley, M. and Woods, P., *The Process of Schooling*. London: Routledge and Kegan Paul.

Bernstein, B. (1967) 'Open schools, open society?', *New Society*, **14**, September.

Bernstein, B. (1971) 'On the classification and framing of educational knowledge' in Young, M.F.D., *Knowledge and Control*. London: Collier-Macmillan.

Bernstein, B. (1973) *Class, Codes and Control: volume 1*. St Albans: Paladin.

Bernstein, B. (1975) 'The Sociology of Education: a brief account' in Bernstein, B. (ed.), *Class, Codes and Control: volume III*. London: Routledge and Kegan Paul.

Bernstein, B. (1975) *Class, Codes and Control: volume I*. London: Routledge and Kegan Paul.

Bernstein, B. (1977) *Class, Codes and Control: volume III*. London: Routledge and Kegan Paul.

Berthoud, R. (1976) *The Disadvantages of Inequality: A Study of Social Deprivation*. London: MacDonald and James.

Best, R., Ribbins, P. and Jarvis, C. (1983) *Education and Care: The study of a school and its pastoral organisation*. London: Heinemann.

Biber, B. and Minuchin, P. (1971) 'The impact of school philosophy and practice on child development' in Silberman, M., *The Experience of Schooling*. Eastbourne: Holt, Rinehart and Winston.

Bidwell, C.E. (1965) 'The school as a formal organisation' in *Handbook of Organisations*. New York: Rand McNully.

Black, H. and Broadfoot, P. (1982) *Keeping Track of Teaching*. London: Routledge and Kegan Paul.

Blenkin, G. and Kelly, A.V. (1981) *The Primary Classroom*. London: Harper and Row.

Blishen, E. (1969) *The School That I'd Like*. Harmondsworth: Penguin.

Blishen, E. (1973a) 'Your children on their teacher', *Where?*, **84**.

Blishen, E. (1973b), 'Why some secondary teachers are disliked', *Where?*, **86**.

Bloom, B., Englehart, M., Furst, E., Hill, W. and Krathwohl, D. (1964) *Taxonomy of Educational Objectives: The classification of educational goals*. New York: McKay.

Blum, A. (1974) *Theorising*. London: Heinemann.

Blumer, H. (1962) 'Society as symbolic interaction' in Rose, A. (ed.), *Human Behaviour and Social Processes*. London: Routledge and Kegan Paul.

Blumer, M. (ed.) (1977) *Sociological Research Methods*. London: Macmillan.

Blyth, W.A.L., (1985) *Development, Experience and Curriculum in Primary Education*. Beckenham: Croom Helm.

Blyth, W. and Derricott, R. (1978) *The Social Significance of Middle Schools*. London: Batsford.

Bono, E. de (1971) *Practical Thinking*. London: Cape.

Bono, E. de (1972) *About Thinking*. London: Cape.

Boocock, S. (1972) *An Introduction to the Sociology of Learning*. Boston, Massachusetts: Houghton Mifflin.

Bookbinder, G. (1978) 'Meddling with children?', *Times Educational Supplement*, December 1978.

Boswell, D. and Wingrove, J. (1974) *The Handicapped Person in the Community*. London: Tavistock.

Boulter, H. (1984) 'Parents and children: 100 years of the parents' National Educational Union and its World-wide Education Service' in Harber, C. et al. (1984) *Alternative Educational Futures*. London: Holt, Rinehart and Winston.

Bourdieu, P. and Passeron, J. (1977) *Reproduction in Education, Society and Culture*. London: Sage.

Bowles, S. and Gintis, H. (1976) *Schooling in Capitalist America*. London: Routledge and Kegan Paul.

Braverman, H. (1974) *Labour and Monopoly Capitalism*. London: Monthly Review Press.

Bridgeman, T. and Fox, I. (1978) 'Why people choose private schools', *New Society*, **29**, June.

Brim, O.G. (1960) 'Family structure and sex – role learning by children' in Bell, N.W. and Vogel, E.F. (eds.), *An Introduction to the Modern Family*. New York: Free Press.

British Humanist Association (1975) *Objective Fair and Balanced: A new law forum in education*. London BHA Publications.

Britton, J. (1971) 'What's the use? A schematic account of language functions', *Educational Review*, **23**, 3.

Broadfoot, P. (1979) *Assessment, Schools and Society*. London: Methuen.

Broadfoot, P. (1984) *Selection, Certification and Control: Social Issues in Educational Assessment*. Lewes: Falmer.

Brown, C. (1978) *Education Otherwise: A sociological case study of one alternative to state schooling*, Unpublished MEd dissertation, University of Birmingham.

Brown, C. (1979) *Understanding Society*. London: John Murray.

Brown, C. and Harber, C. (1985) *Cultural Diversity and Conflict*. Special edition of *Social Science Teacher*, **14**, 3.

Bruner, J.S. (1965) *The Process of Education*. Harmondsworth: Penguin.

Bruner, J.S. (1966) *Towards a Theory of Instruction*. Cambridge, Massachusetts: Harvard University Press.

Bull, R. and Stevens, J. (1976) 'Do we get "A" for attractiveness?', *Sesame*, December 1976.

Burgess, R.G. (1984a) *Field Methods in the Study of Education*. Lewes: Falmer.

Burgess, R.G. (1984b) *The Research Process in Educational Settings: Ten Case Studies*. Lewes: Falmer.

Burnham, J.R. and Hartshough, D.M. quoted in Rosenthal, R. (1968) 'Weighing the effect of a smile', *New Society*, 7 November.

Burns, E. (1952) *Introduction to Marxism*. London: Lawrence and Wishart.

Burrows, J. (1978) *The Middle School – High Road or Dead End?* London: Woburn Press.

Byrne, D., Williamson, B. and Fletcher, B. (1974) *The Poverty of Education*. Oxford: Martin Robertson.

Byrne, E. (1975) 'Inequality in education – discriminal resource allocation in schools?', *Educational Review*, **27**, 3.

Byrne, E. (1978) *Women and Education*. London: Tavistock.

Calvert, B. (1975) *The Role of the Pupil*. London: Routledge and Kegan Paul.

Cameron, R. (1984) 'Sharing expertise', *Where?*, **194**.

Cannon, C. (1964) 'Social studies in secondary schools', *Educational Review*, **7**, 1.

Casey, T. (1974) 'Corporal punishment', *The Schoolmaster*, November.

Chanan, G. and Gilchrist, L. (1974) *What School is For*. London: Methuen.

Chandler, D. (1984) *Young Learners and the Microcomputer*. Milton Keynes: Open University Press.

Chaikin, A., Sigler, E. and Derlega, V. (1975) 'Non-verbal mediators of teacher expectancy effects', *Journal of Personality and Social Psychology*, **30**, 1.

Cherrington, D. (1985) *Ethnic Minorities in Education*. Special edition of *Educational Review*, **37**, 2.

Chevannes, M. (1979) 'Supplementary education – the Black Arrow Night School Project', *Social Science Teacher*, **8**, 4.

Chevannes, M. and Reeves, F. (1979) 'Footprint in the sand: black exploration of the white community' in Meighan, R. et al., *Perspectives on Society*. Sunbury on Thames: Nelson.

Children's Rights Workshop (1977) *Sexism in Children's Books*. London: Children's Rights Workshop.

Claiborn, W. (1969) 'Expectancy effects in the classroom: a failure to replicate', *Journal of Educational Psychology*, **60**.

Claxton, G. (1978) *The Little Ed Book*. London: Routledge and Kegan Paul.

Coard, B. (1971) *How the West Indian Child is Made ESN*. London: New Beacon.

Cohen, L. (1965) *An Exploratory Study of the Teacher's Role as Perceived by Headteachers, Tutors, and Students in a Training College*, Unpublished MEd dissertation, University of Liverpool.

Cohen, L. and Mannion, L. (1980) *Research Methods in Education*. Beckenham: Croom Helm.

Cohen, L. and Manion, L. (1981) *Perspectives on Classrooms and Schools*. London: Holt, Rinehart and Winston.

Cohen, P. (1968) *Modern Social Theory*. London: Heinemann.

Colley, M. (1976) 'Another kind of handicap', *New Society*, 12 February.

Collier, G. (1983) *The Management of Peer Group Learning*. London: Society for Research into Higher Education.

Common, J. (1951) *Kiddar's Luck*. London: Turnstile Press.

Commonwealth Immigrants Advisory Council (1964) *Third Report (Cmnd 2458)*, HMSO.

Connell, R.W. (1985) *Teacher's Work*. London: George Allen and Unwin.

Cookson, C. (1979) 'Parents find home help a magic ingredient', *Times Educational Supplement*, 28 December.

Cooper, I. (1981) 'The politics of education and architectural design: the instructive example of British Primary Education', *British Educational Research Journal*, **7**.

Cooper, I. (1982) 'The maintenance of order and the use of space in primary school buildings', *British Journal of Sociology of Education* **3**, 3.

Cooper, R. (1965) 'The psychology of organisations', *New Society*, 22 April.

Cornbleth, C. (1984) 'Beyond hidden curriculum?', *Journal of Curriculum Studies*, **16**, 1.

Corrigan, P. (1979) *Schooling the Smash Street Kids*. London: Macmillan.

Corrigan, P. and Frith, S. (1977) 'The Politics of Education' in Young, M. and Whitty, G., *Society, State and Schooling*. Lewes: Falmer.

Cosin, B. (1972) *Ideology*, Milton Keynes; Open University Press.

Cosin, B., Dale, R., Esland, G. and Swift, D. (eds.) (1971) *School and Society*. London: Routledge and Kegan Paul.

Coulthard, M. (1977) *An Introduction to Discourse Analysis*. Harlow: Longman.

Craft, M., Raynor, J. and Cohen, L. (1980) *Linking Home and School*. London: Harper and Row.

Craft, M. (1982) *Education for Diversity: The challenge of cultural pluralism*. Nottingham: School of Education, University of Nottingham.

Cuzzort, R. and King, E. (1976) *Humanity and Modern Social Thought*. Hinsdale, Illinois: Holt Dryden.

Cyster, R., Clift, P.S. and Battle, S. (1983) *Parental Involvement in Primary Schools*. Windsor: NFER-Nelson.

Dahrendorf, R. (1959) *Class and Class Conflict in Industrial Society*. London: Routledge and Kegan Paul.

Dahrendorf, R. (1980) *Life Chances*. London: Weidenfeld and Nicolson.

Dale, R. (1972a) *The Context of the Classroom*. Milton Keynes: Open University Press.

Dale, R. (1972b) *The Use of Time in the School*. Milton Keynes: Open University Press.

Dale, R. (1977) 'Implications of the rediscovery of the hidden curriculum for the sociology of teaching' in Gleeson, D. (ed.), *Identity and Structure*. Driffield: Nafferton.

Dale, R. (1985) *Education and Employers Needs*. Oxford: Pergamon.

Daly, B. (1985) *Portage: The importance of parents*. Windsor: NFER-Nelson.

Danziger, K. (1971) *Socialisation*. Harmondsworth: Penguin.

Davies, I. (1969) 'Education and social science', *New Society*, 8 May.

Davies, K. (1974) 'History is about chaps', *Times Educational Supplement*, 29 November.

Davies, L. (1973) *The Contribution of the Secondary School to the Sex Typing of Girls*, Unpublished MEd dissertation, University of Birmingham.

Davies, L. (1978) 'The view from the girls', *Educational Review*, **30**, 2.

Davies, L. (1980) 'The social construction of underachievement' in Raybould, E., Roberts, B. and Wedell, K., 'Helping the low achiever in the secondary school', *Educational Review Occasional Publications*, No. 7.

Davies, L. (1983) 'Gender, resistance and power' in Walker, S. and Barton, L., *Gender, Class and Education*. Lewes: Falmer.

Davies, L. (1984) *Pupil Power: Deviance and gender in school*. Lewes: Falmer.

Davies, L. and Meighan, R. (1975) 'A review of schooling and sex roles', *Educational Review*, **27**, 3.

Dawe, A. (1970) 'The two sociologies', *British Journal of Sociology*, **21**, 2.

Deakin, M. (1973) *The Children on the Hill*. Tunbridge Wells: Abacus.

Deem, R. (1978) *Women and Schooling*. London: Routledge and Kegan Paul.

Deem, R. (1984) *Coeducation Reconsidered*. Milton Keynes: Open University Press.

Delamont, S. (1976) *Interaction in the Classroom*. London: Methuen.

Department of Education and Science (1975) *Curricular Differences Between the Sexes*. HMSO.

Derricott, R. (1984) *Curriculum Continuity: Primary to Secondary*. Windsor: NFER-Nelson.

Dessent, T. (1984) *What is Important about Portage?* Windsor: NFER-Nelson.

Diamond, L. (1984) 'State-supported Alternative Schools' in Harber, C., et al., *Alternative Educational Futures*. London: Holt, Rinehart and Winston.

Dore, R.P. (1976) *The Diploma Disease*. London: Allen and Unwin.

Douglas, J.W.B. (1964) *The Home and the School*. St. Albans: Panther.

Douglas, J.W.B., Ross, J.M. and Simpson, H.R. (1971) *All Our Futures*. London: Peter Davies.

Dreeben, R. (1968) *On What is Learned in School*. London: Addison Wesley.

Dreeben, R. (1976) 'The unwritten curriculum and its relation to values', *Journal of Curriculum Studies*, **8**, 2.

Driver, G. (1980) 'How West Indians do better at school', *New Society*, 17 January.

Durkheim, E. (1956) *Education and Sociology*. New York: Free Press.

Durkheim, E. (1961) 'Moral Education' quoted in Hargreaves, D., 'Durkheim, deviance and education' in Barton, L. and Meighan, R. (eds.) (1979), *Schools, Pupils and Deviance*. Driffield: Nafferton.

Durkheim, E. (1968) *The Rules of Sociological Method*. New York Free Press.

Easthope, G. (1974) *History of Social Research Methods*. Harlow: Longman.

Easthope, G. (1980) 'Curricula are social processes' in Barton, L. et al. (1980) *Schooling Ideology and the Curriculum*. Lewes: Falmer.

Edwards, A.D. (1976) *Language in Culture and Class: The sociology of language and education*. London: Heinemann.

Edwards, A.D. and Furlong, V.J. (1978) *The Language of Teaching: Meaning in classroom interaction*. London: Heinemann.

Edwards, R. (1976) 'Individual traits and organisational incentives: what makes a "good worker"?', *Journal of Human Resources*, spring.

Edwards, V.K. (1978) 'Language attitudes and under performance in West Indian children', *Educational Review*, **30**, 1.

Eggleston, J. (1974) *Contemporary Research in the Sociology of Education*. London: Methuen.

Engels, F. (1969) quoted in Feuer, L.S., *Marx and Engels: Basic Writings on Politics and Philosophy*. London: Fontana.

Esland, G. (1977) *Legitimacy and Control*. Milton Keynes: Open University Press.

Etzioni, A. (1964) *Modern Organisations*. Hemel Hempstead: Prentice Hall.

Etzioni, (1969) *The Semi-Professions and Their Organisations*. London: Collier-Macmillan.

Evans, K. (1974a) 'The head and his territory', *New Society*, 24 October.

Evans, K. (1974b) 'The spatial organisation of infants schools', *Journal of Architectural Research*, **3**, 7.

Eysenck, H. (1957) *Sense and Nonsense in Psychology*. Harmondsworth: Pelican.

Farrington, P., Pritchard, G. and Raynor, J. (1972) 'The Parkway Programme' in Raynor, J. and Harden, J. (1973) *Readings in Urban Education Vol. 2: Equality and City Schools*. Milton Keynes: Open University Press.

Ferron, O. (1966) 'The test performance of coloured children', *Educational Research*, **8**, 1.

Fiddy, R. (1983) *In Place of Work: Policy and provision for the young unemployed*. Lewes: Falmer.

Fiddy, R. (1985) *Youth Unemployment and Training: A collection of national perspectives*. Lewes: Falmer.

Field, F. and Hankin, P. (1971) *Black Britons*. Oxford: Oxford University Press.

Finn, D. (1983) 'A new deal for British youth?', *Social Science Teacher*, **13**, 2.

Fitzgerald, A. (1976) 'School Mathematics and the Requirements of Industry', *Vocational Aspects of Education*, **28**.

Flanders, N.E. (1970) *Analysing Teacher Behaviour*. London: Addison Wesley.

Fletcher, C., Caron, M. and Williams, W. (1985) *Schools on Trial*. Milton Keynes: Open University Press.

Flude, R. and Parrott, A. (1979) *Education and the Challenge of Change*. Milton Keynes: Open University Press.

Fox, J. (1984) *Private School and Public Issues: The Parents' View*. London: Macmillan.

Freire, P. (1972) *Pedagogy of the Oppressed*. Harmondsworth; Penguin.

Friedman, N.L. (1967) 'Cultural deprivation: a commentary on the sociology of knowledge', *Journal of Educational Thought*, **1**, 2.

Fuchs, E. (1968) 'How teachers learn to help children fail' in Keddie, N. (ed.) (1973), *Tinker, Tailor . . . The Myth of Cultural Deprivation*. Harmondsworth: Penguin.

Fulton Committee (1968) *The Civil Services Vol. I. Report of the Committee*. Cmnd 3638. HMSO.

Galton, M., Simon, B. and Croll, P. (1980) *Inside the Primary Classroom*. London: Routledge and Kegan Paul.

Galton, M. and Simon, B. (1980) *Progress and Performance in the Primary School*. London: Routledge and Kegan Paul.

Galton, M. and Willcocks, J. (1983) *Moving from the Primary School Classroom*. London: Routledge and Kegan Paul.

Garaundy, R. (1970) *Marxism in the Twentieth Century*. Glasgow: Collins.

Garfinkel, H. (1967) *Studies in Ethnomethodology*. Hemel Hempstead: Pgentice Hall.

Garland, R., (1982) *Microcomputers and Children in the Primary School*. Lewes: Falmer.

Garwood, S.G. (1976) 'First name stereotypes as a factor in self concept and school achievement', *Journal of Educational Psychology*, **68**, 4.

Garwood, S.G. and McDavid, J.W. (1975) 'Ethnic factors in stereotypes of given names', Atlanta: Georgia State University *Resources in Education* ED097994.

Geddes, D. (1979) 'The crammer boom', *New Society*, 15 February.

Gibson, D. and Jackson, R. (1974) 'Some sociological perspectives on mental retardation', *Educational Review*, **27**, 1.

Giddens, A. (1971) *Capitalism and Modern Social Theory*. New York: Cambridge University Press.

Giddens, A. (1976) *New Rules of Sociological Method*. London: Hutchinson.

Giddens, A. (1978) *Durkheim*. London: Fontana-Collins.

Giddens, A. (1979) *Central Problems in Social Theory*. London: Macmillan.

Giles, H. (1971) 'Patterns of evaluation to R.P., south-Welsh and Somerset-accented speech', *British Journal of Social and Clinical Psychology*, **10**.

Ginsburg, M.B., Meyenn, R., Miller, H. and Ranceford-Hadley, C. (1977) *The Role of the Middle School Teacher*. University of Aston.

Gintis, H. and Bowles, S. (1980) 'Contradiction and reproduction in educational theory' in Barton, L. et al., *Schooling, Ideology and the Curriculum*. Lewes: Falmer.

Giroux, H.A. (1981) *Ideology, Culture and the Process of Schooling*. Lewes: Falmer.

Glaser, B.G. and Strauss, A.L. (1968) *The Discovery of Grounded Theory*. London: Weidenfeld and Nicolson.

Gleeson, D. (1983) *Youth Training and the Search for Work*. London: Routledge and Kegan Paul.

Gleeson, D. (1984) 'On the politics of youth training' in Harber, C. and Meighan, R., (1984) *Political Education in 1984*. Special edition of *Educational Review*, **36**, 2.

Gleeson, D., (1986) 'Privatisation of industry and the neutralisation of youth' in Barton, L., and Walker, S. (1986) *Youth, Unemployment and Schooling*, Milton Keynes: Open University Press.

Glennerster, H. and Pryke, R. (1973) 'The contribution of the public schools and Oxbridge' in Urry, J. and Wakeford, J. (eds.), *Power in Britain*. London: Heinemann.

Glynn, T. (1980) 'Parent–child interaction in remedial reading at home' in Clark, M. and Glynn, T. (1980) *Reading and Writing for the Child with Difficulties*. Birmingham: Educational Review Occasional Publications 8.

Goffman, E. (1961) *Asylums*. Harmondsworth: Penguin.

Goffman, E. (1963) *Stigma: Notes on the Management of Spoiled Identity*. Hemel Hempstead: Prentice Hall.

Goffman, E. (1971) *The Presentation of Self in Everyday Life*. Harmondsworth: Penguin.

Golby, M. and Gulliver, J.R. (1979) 'Whose remedies, whose ills? A critical review of remedial education', *Journal of Curriculum Studies*, **11**, 2.

Goldthorpe, J.H. (1977) 'The relevance of history to sociology' in Bulmer, M. (ed.), *Sociological Research Methods*. London: Macmillan.

Gomm, R. (1978) 'Medicine' in Meighan, R., Shelton, I. and Marks, A. (eds.) *Perspectives on Society*, Sunbury-on-Thames: Nelson.

Gomm, R. (1983) *Social Science Teachers and the New Vocationalism*. Special edition of *Social Science Teacher*, **13**, 2.

Good, T. and Brophy, J. (1970) 'Teacher child dyadic interactions: a new method of classroom observation', *Journal of School Psychology*, **8**, 2.

Good, T. and Brophy, J. (1972) 'Behavioural expression of teacher attitudes', *Journal of Educational Psychology*, **63**, 6.

Good, T. and Brophy, J. (1984) *Looking in Classrooms*. New York: Harper and Row.

Good, T. and Brophy, J. (1974) 'Changing teacher and student behaviour: an empirical investigation', *Journal of Educational Psychology*, **66**, 3.

Goodacre, E.J. (1968) *Teachers and Their Pupils' Home Backgrounds*. Windsor: NFER.

Goodman, P. (1971) *Compulsory Miseducation*. Harmondsworth: Penguin.

Goodson, I. (1975) 'The teachers' curriculum and the New Reformation', *Journal of Curriculum Studies*, **7**, 2.

Goodson, I. (1983) *School Subjects and Curriculum Change*. Beckenham: Croom Helm.

Goodwin, C. (1979) 'Labelling a child special', *Where?*, **147**.

Gorbutt, D. (1972) 'The new Sociology of Education', *Education for Teaching*, **89**.

Gould, R. (1976) 'The ecology of educational settings', *Educational Administration*, **4**, 2.

Gouldner, A.W. (1971) *The coming of Western sociology*. London: Heinemann.

Gow, L. and McPherson, A. (1980) *Tell Them from Me*. Aberdeen: Aberdeen University Press.

Grace, C. (1978) *Teaching, Ideology and Control*. London: Routledge and Kegan Paul.

Grace, C. (1985) 'Judging teachers: the social and political contexts of teacher evaluation', *British Journal of Sociology of Education*, **6**, 1.

Gramsci, A. (ed. and trans. Hoare, Q. and Nowell Smith, G.) (1971) *Selections from the Prison Notebooks of Antonio Gramsci*. London: Lawrence and Wishart.

Griffiths, A. and Hamilton, D. (1985) *Parent, Teacher and Child: Working together in children's learning*. London: Methuen.

Hahn, C. (1974) 'Teaching about women: a review of materials', *Social Studies Journal*, January 1974.

Hall, E.T. (1959) *The Silent Language*. New York: Doubleday.

Halsey, A.H. and Anderson, C. (1961) *Education, Economy and Society*. New York: Free Press.

Halsey, A.H., Heath, A.F. and Ridge, J.M. (1980) *Origins and Destinations*. Oxford: Oxford University Press.

Hammersley, M. (1977a) *Teacher Perspectives*. Milton Keynes: Open University Press.

Hammersley, M. (1977b) *The Social Location of Teacher Perspectives*. Milton Keynes: Open University Press.

Hammersley, M. and Hargreaves, A. (1983) *Curriculum Practice: Some sociological case studies*. Lewes: Falmer.

Hammersley, M. and Woods, P. (1976) *The Process of Schooling*. London: Routledge and Kegan Paul/Open University Press.

Hammersley, M. and Woods, P. (1984) *Life in School: the sociology of pupil culture*. Milton Keynes: Open University Press.

Handy, C. (1984) *Taken for Granted? Understanding schools as organisations*. York: Longman.

Hannan, C., Smyth, P. and Stephenson, N. (1971) *Young Teachers and Reluctant Learners*. Harmondsworth: Penguin.

Hansen, S. and Jensen, J. (1971) *The Little Red Schoolbook*. London: Stage 1 Publications.

Hanson, D. and Herrington, M. (1976) *From College to Classroom*. London: Routledge and Kegan Paul.

Harari, H. and McDavid, J.W. (1973) 'Name stereotypes and teachers' expectations', *Journal of Educational Psychology*, **65**, 2.

Harber, C. (1984) 'Politics and political education in 1984' in Harber, C. and Meighan, R. *Political Education in 1984*. Special edition of *Educational Review*, **36**, 2.

Harber, C., Meighan, R. and Roberts, B. (1984) *Alternative Educational Futures*. London: Holt, Rinehart and Winston.

Hardy, C. (1977) 'Architects and the hidden curriculum', *Times Educational Supplement*, 22 July.

Hare, R.M. (1964) 'Adolescents into adults' in Hollins, T. (ed.), *Aims in Education*. Manchester: Manchester University Press.

Hargreaves, A. (1978) 'The significance of classroom coping strategies' in Barton, L. and Meighan, R., *Sociological Interpretations of Schooling and Classrooms*. Driffield: Nafferton.

Hargreaves, A. and Tickle, L. (1980) *Middle Schools: Origins, ideology and practice*. London: Harper and Row.

Hargreaves, D.H. (1967) *Social Relations in a Secondary School*. London: Routledge and Kegan Paul.

Hargreaves, D.H. (1972) *Interpersonal Relations and Education*. London: Routledge and Kegan Paul.

Hargreaves, D.H. (1978a) 'The two curricula and the community', *Westminster Studies in Education*, **1**.

Hargreaves, D.H. (1978b) 'Whatever happened to symbolic interactionism?' in Barton, L. and Meighan, R. (eds.), *Sociological Interpretations of Schooling and Classrooms: A reappraisal*. Driffield: Nafferton.

Hargreaves, D.H. (1982) *The Challenge for the Comprehensive School*. London: Routledge and Kegan Paul.

Hargreaves, D.H., Hestor, S. and Mellor, F. (1975) *Deviance in Classrooms*. London: Routledge and Kegan Paul.

Hartog, P.J. and Rhodes, E.C. (1935) *An Examination of Examinations*. London: Macmillan.

Harvey, D. and Slatin, G. (1976) 'The relationships between child's SES and teacher expectations: a test of the middle class bias hypothesis', *Social Forces*, **54**, 1.

Hatcher, R. and Shallice, J. (1983) 'The politics of anti-racist education', *Multicultural Education*, **12**, 1.

Head, D. (1974) *Free Way to Learning*. Harmondsworth: Penguin.

Head, D. (1978) 'Five years out of school', *Where?*, **135**.

Hemming, J. (1980) *The Betrayal of Youth*. London: Marion Boyers.

Henry, J. (1963) *Culture Against Man*. Harmondsworth: Penguin.

Henry, J. (1971) *Essays on Education*. Harmondsworth: Penguin.

Hewison, J. and Tizard, B. (1980) 'Parental involvement and reading attainment', *British Journal of Educational Psychology*, **50**.

Hextall, I. (1976) 'Marking work' in Whitty, G. and Young, M.F.D. (eds.), *Explorations in the Politics of School Knowledge*. Driffield: Nafferton.

Hine, R.J. (1975) 'Political bias in school physics', *Hard Cheese*, **4**, 5.

Hipkin, J. (1975) 'Time to abolish exams?', *Where?*, **109**.

Hobbes, T. (1951) *Leviathan*. London: Dent.

Hoffman, M. (1975) 'Assumptions in sex education books', *Educational Review*, **27**, 3.

Hoghughi, M. (1978) *Troubled and Troublesome: Coping with severely disabled children*. London: Burnett Books.

Holly, D. (1973) *Beyond Curriculum*. St Albans: Hart-Davis MacGibbon.

Holt, J. (1969) *How Children Fail*. Harmondsworth: Penguin.

Holt, J. (1971) *The Underachieving School*, Harmondsworth: Penguin.

Holt, J. (1973) *Freedom and Beyond*. Harmondsworth: Penguin.

Holt, J. (1982) *Teach Your Own*. Brightlingsea: Lighthouse Books.

Holt, M. (1984) 'The high-rise curriculum', *Times Educational Supplement*, 12 October.

Horne, J. (1986) 'What's so new about the new vocationalism?' in Barton, L. and Walker, S. (1986) *Youth, Unemployment and Schooling*. Milton Keynes: Open University Press.

Hopper, E. (1971) 'A typology for the classification of educational systems' in Hopper, E. (ed.), *Readings in the Theory of Educational Systems*. London: Hutchinson.

Hopper, E. (ed.) (1971) *Readings in the Theory of Educational Systems*. London: Hutchinson.

Hoyle, E. (1969) *The Role of the Teacher*. London: Routledge and Kegan Paul.

Hoyle, E. and Bell, R. (1972) *Problems of Curriculum Innovation*. Milton Keynes: Open University Press.

Hoskyns, A. (1976) 'An experiment in the teaching of physics' in Whitty, G. and Young, M.F.D., *Explorations in the Politics of School Knowledge*. Driffield: Nafferton Books.

Hughes, J. (1984) *The Best Years: Reflections of school leavers in the 1980s*. Aberdeen: Aberdeen University Press.

Hughes, M.G.H., Ribbins, P. and Thomas, H. (1985) *Managing Education*. London: Holt, Rinehart and Winston.

Hull, J. (1975) *School Worship: An obituary*. London: SCM.

Hunt, G.J.F. (1976) 'Designing instruction for individuals', *Delta*, **18**.

Hunt, P.J. (1974) 'Coping with those big questions', *Child Education*, August.

Hurman, A. (1979) *A Charter for Choice*. Windsor: NFER-Nelson.

Husen, T. (1985) *The Learning Society Revisited*. Oxford: Pergamon.

Illich, I. (1971) *Deschooling Society*. Harmondsworth: Penguin.

Jackson, B. (1964) *Streaming: An educational system in miniature*. London: Routledge and Kegan Paul.

Jackson, B. and Marsden, D. (1962) *Education and the Working Class*. London: Routledge and Kegan Paul.

Jackson, M. (1984) 'Building a bridge to nowhere . . .', *Times Educational Supplement*, 14 December.

Jackson, P. (1968) *Life in Classrooms*. Eastbourne: Holt, Rinehart and Winston.

Jackson, P. (1971) 'The student's world' in Silberman, M. (ed.), *The Experience of Schooling*. Eastbourne: Holt, Rinehart and Winston.

Jackson, R.N. (1970) 'Educable mental handicap: an ecological analysis', *Scottish Educational Studies*, November.

James, A. and Jeffcoate, R. (1981) *The School in the Multicultural Society*. London: Harper and Row.

James, C. (1968) *Young Lives at Stake*. Glasgow: Collins.

Jeffcoate, R. (1975) 'Curing a social disease', *Times Educational Supplement*, 5 December.

Jeffcoate, R. (1977) 'Looking in the wrong place', *Times Educational Supplement*, 24 June.

Jeffcoate, R. (1979) *Positive Image*. Richmond: Chameleon Books.

Jeffcoate, R. (1984) *Ethnic Minorities in Britain*. London: Harper and Row.

Jenkins, C. and Sherman, B. (1979) *The Collapse of Work*. London: Eyre Methuen.

Jensen, K. (1986) 'Work, education and democratisation' in Barton, L. and Walker, S. (1986) *Youth, Unemployment and Schooling*. Milton Keynes: Open University Press.

Johnson, T.J. (1972) *Professions and Power*. London: Macmillan.

Joiner, D. (1971) 'Office territory', *New Society*, 7 October.

Karabel, J. and Halsey, A.H. (eds.) (1977) *Power and Ideology in Education*. Oxford: Oxford University Press.

Kelly, A. (1976) 'Family background, subject specialization and occupational recruitment of Scottish university students', *Higher Education*, **5**, 2.

Kelly, G.A. (1955) *The Psychology of Personal Constructs*. London: Norton.

King, E. (1972) *Educating Young Children: Sociological Interpretations*. London: Wm C. Brown.

King, E. (1973) 'The presentation of self in the classroom', *Educational Review*, **25**, 3.

King, R. (1980) 'Weberian perspectives and the study of education', *British Journal of Sociology of Education*, **1**, 1.

King, R. (1983) *The Sociology of School Organisation*. London: Methuen.

Kitto, D. (1981) 'Doing it their way', *Times Educational Supplement*, 10 July.

Knight, P. (1973) *The Successful Applicant Will Be a Man*. London: British Humanist Association.

Kohl, H. (1970) *The Open Classroom*. London: Methuen.

Kohl, H. (1971) *36 Children*. Harmondsworth: Penguin.

Komarovsky, M. (1946) 'Cultural contradictions and sex roles', *American Journal of Sociology*, **52**.

Kozol, J. (1968) *Death at an Early Age*. Harmondsworth: Penguin.

Labour Party (1972) *Discrimination Against Women*. Labour Party.

Labov, W. (1969) 'The logic of non-standard English' in Giglioli, P.P. (ed.) (1972), *Language and Social Context*. Harmondsworth: Penguin.

Lacey, C. (1970) *Hightown Grammar*. Manchester: Manchester University Press.

Lauwerys, J.A. and Scanlon, D.G. (1969) *World Yearbook of Education: Examination*. London: Evans.

Lawn, M. (1985) *The Politics of Teacher Unionisation*. Beckenham: Croom Helm.

Lawton, D. (1968) *Social Class, Language and Education*. London: Routledge and Kegan Paul.

Lee, D. and Newby, H. (1983) *The Problem of Sociology*. London: Hutchinson.

Lee, S. (1978) 'Black bitterness', *Times Educational Supplement*, 20 January.

Leinster-Mackay, D., (1984) *The Rise of the English Prep School*. Lewes: Falmer.

Lemert, E. (1951) *Social Pathology*. Maidenhead: McGraw Hill.

Lemert, E. (1972) *Human Deviance, Social Problems and Social Control*. Hemel Hempstead: Prentice Hall.

Lewis, B. (1972), quoted in Dale, R., *The Use of Time in the School*. Milton Keynes: Open University Press.

Lewis, D.G. (1978) *Assessment in Education*. Sevenoaks: Unibooks.

Lewis, I. and Vulliamy, G. (1980) 'Warnock or Warlock? The sorcery of definitions: the limitations of the Report on Special Education', *Educational Review*, **32**, 1.

Lister, I. (1971) 'The deschoolers', *Times Educational Supplement*, 9 July.

Lister, I. (1974) *Deschooling*. Cambridge: Cambridge University Press.

Little, A. (1975) 'The Performance of Children from Ethnic Minority Backgrounds in Primary Schools' in Rushton, J. and Turner, J. (eds.), *Education and Deprivation*. Manchester: Manchester University Press.

Lippitt, R. and White, R.K. (1958) 'An experimental study of leadership and group life' in Maccoby, E.E. et al., *Readings in Social Psychology*. Eastbourne: Holt, Rinehart and Winston.

Lloyd-Smith, M. (1984) *Disrupted Schooling: The growth of the special unit*. London: John Murray.

Lobban, G. (1975) 'Sex roles in reading schemes', *Educational Review*, **27**, 3.

Lyman, S.M. and Scott, M.B. (1970) *A Sociology of the Absurd*. Hemel Hempstead: Appleton-Century-Crofts.

Maccoby, E. (ed.) (1966) *The Development of Sex Differences*. London: Stanford.

MacDonald, M. (1977a) *Culture, Class and the Curriculum*. Milton Keynes: Open University Press.

MacDonald, M. (1977b) *The Education of Elites*. Milton Keynes: Open University Press.

MacDonald, M. (1977) *The Curriculum and Cultural Reproduction*. Milton Keynes: Open University Press.

McGee, R. et al. (1977) *Sociology: An introduction*. Eastbourne: Holt, Rinehart and Winston.

Mackinnon, D. (1978) 'Social class and educational attainment' in Swift, D., *Selection and Opportunity*. Milton Keynes: Open University Press.

McPherson, J. (1983) *The Feral Classroom*. London: Routledge and Kegan Paul.

Mack, J. (1977) 'Schools for privilege', *New Society*, 7 July.

MacRae, D.G. (1974) *Weber*. London: Fontana.

Mahony, P. (1985) *Schools for the Boys? Coeducation reassessed*. London: Hutchinson.

Maizels, J. (1970) 'How school leavers rate teachers, *New Society*, 24 September.

Maizels, J. (1971) *Adolescent Needs and the Transition from School to Work*. London: Athlone.

Makins, V. (1969) 'Child's eye view of teacher', *Times Educational Supplement*, 19 September, 26 September.

Makins, V. (1984) 'Giving the customers a say', *Times Educational Supplement*, 23 November.

Marbeau, V. (1976) 'Autonomous study by pupils', *Education and Culture*, **31**.

Marsh, A. (1971) 'In a second culture', *Times Educational Supplement*, 18 June.

Marsland, M. (1974) *Pastoral Care*. London: Heinemann.

Martin, B. (1952) *School Buildings*. St Albans: Crosby Lockwood.

Martin, N. (1971) 'What are they up to?' in Jones, A. and Mulford, J. (eds.), *Children Using Language*. Oxford: Oxford University Press.

Martin, W. (1976) *The Negotiated Order of the School*. Toronto, Ontario: Macmillan.

Marton, F., Hounsell, D. and Entwhistle, N. (1984) *The Experience of Learning*. Edinburgh: Scottish Academic Press.

Marx, K. (1958) *Selected Works*. Moscow: Progress Publishers.

Marx, K. (1969) 'The eighteenth brumaire of Louis Bonapart' in Feuer, L.S. (ed.) *Marx and Engels: Basic writings on politics and philosophy*. London: Fontana.

Marx, K. (1970) 'Introduction to a critique of Political Economy' in Arthur, C.J. (ed.), *The German Ideology*. London: Lawrence and Wishart.

Marx, K. (1973) *Grundrisse*. Harmondsworth: Pelican.

Marx, K. (1976) *Capital; volume 1*. Harmondsworth: Penguin.

Marx, K. and Engels, F. (1967) *The Communist Manifesto*. Harmondsworth: Penguin.

Matza, D. (1964) *Delinquency and Drift*. Chichester: Wiley.

Mays, J.B. (1962) Education and the Urban Child. Liverpool: University of Liverpool Press.

Mead, G.H. (1934) *Mind, Self and Society*. Chicago: University of Chicago Press.

Measor, L. and Woods, P. (1984) *Changing Schools*. Milton Keynes: Open University Press.

Medlicott, P. (1974) 'Special teaching for special children', *New Society*, 3 March.

Meighan, R. (1974a) 'Children's judgements of the teaching performance of student teachers', *Educational Review*, **27**, 1.

Meighan, R. (1974b) 'The concepts of authoritarian and democratic regimes and classroom discipline', *Dudley Educational Journal*, Spring.

Meighan, R. (1975) 'Individual study-folders', *Social Science Teacher*, **5**, 2.

Meighan, R. (1977a) 'Pupils' perceptions of the classroom techniques of post-graduate student teachers', *British Journal of Teacher Education*, **3**, 2.

Meighan, R. (1977b) 'Towards a sociology of assessment', *Social Science Teacher*, **7**, 2.

Meighan, R. (1978a) 'Consultation and educational ideologies: some issues raised by research into children's judgements of teaching performance' in Barton, L. and Meighan, R. (eds.) *Sociological Intepretations of Schooling and Classrooms: A reappraisal*. Driffield: Nafferton.

Meighan, R. (1978b) 'The learners' viewpoint', *Educational Review*, **30**, 2.

Meighan, R. (1981) 'A new teaching force? Some issues raised by seeing parents as educators', *Educational Review*, **33**, 2.

Meighan, R. (1984) 'Home-based educators and education authorities: the attempt to maintain a mythology', *Educational Studies*, **10**, 3.

Meighan, R. (1984) 'Political consciousness and home-based education', *Educational Review*, **36**, 2.

Meighan, R. and Brown, C. (1980) 'Locations of learning and ideologies of education' in Barton, L. et al., *Schooling, Ideology and the Curriculum*. Lewes: Falmer.

Meighan, R. and Doherty, J. (1975) 'Education and sex roles', *Educational Review*, **27**, 3.

Meighan, R. and Roberts, M. (1977) 'Autonomous study and educational ideologies: a review of some theoretical and practical issues with special reference to the schools Council General Studies Project, *Journal of Curriculum Studies*, **11**, 1.

Meighan, R., Shelton, I. and Marks, A. (eds.) (1979) *Perspectives on Society*. Sunbury on Thames: Nelson.

Meltzer, B., Petrat, J. and Reynolds, L. (1975) *Symbolic Interactionism: Genesis, varieties and criticisms*. London: Routledge and Kegan Paul.

Mennell, S. (1974) *Sociological Theory: Uses and unities*. Sunbury on Thames: Nelson.

Meyer, P. (1972) *School and the Reproduction of the Social Division of Labour*, unpublished thesis, Harvard University.

Milgram, S. (1974) *Obedience to Authority*. London: Tavistock.

Miles, H.B. (1969) 'Handicaps for the rat race', *Times Educational Supplement*, 22 August.

Miller, C.M.L. and Parlett, M. (1983) *Up to the Mark*. London: SRHE.

Millstein, B. (1972) *Women's Studies – Women in History*. New York: New York Board of Education.

Milner, D. (1976) 'Home-based education', *New Era*, **57**, 4.

Montemayor, R. (1974) 'Children's performance in a game and their attraction to it as a function of sex-typed labels', *Child Development*, **45**, 1.

Moody, E. (1968) 'Right in front of everybody', *New Society*, 26 December.

Moon, B. (1983) *Comprehensive Schools: Challenge and change*. Windsor: NFER-Nelson.

Morris, T. and Morris, P. (1963) *Pentonville*. London: Routledge and Kegan Paul.

Moss, H.A. (1967) 'Sex, age and state as determinants of mother–infant interaction', *Merrill–Palmer Quarterly*, **13**.

Mukhopadgay, A. (1984) *Assessment in a Multicultural Society*. London: Schools Council/Longman.

Mullarny, M. (1984) *Anything School Can Do You Can Do Better*. London: Marion Boyers.

Murray, R. (1979) *Sociological Theories of Education*. Maidenhead: McGraw Hill.

Musgrove, F. (1966) 'The good home' in Craft, M. (1966) *Family, Class and Education: A reader*. London: Longman.

Musgrove, F. and Taylor, P.H. (1969). *Society and the Teacher's Role*. London: Routledge and Kegan Paul.

Nash, R. (1972) 'History as she is writ', *New Society*, 3 August.

Nash, R. (1973) *Classroom Observed*. London: Routledge and Kegan Paul.

Nash, R. (1976) *Teacher Expectations and Pupil Learning*. London: Routledge and Kegan Paul.

National Union of Teachers (1978) *Race, Education and Intelligence*. London: NUT.

Neill, A.S. (1968) *Summerhill*. Harmondsworth: Pelican.

Newsome Report (1963) *Half Our Future*, Report of the Central Advisory Council for Education, HMSO.

Nightingale, C. (1974) 'What Katy didn't do', *Spare Rib*, February.

Owen Cole, W. (1978) *World Faiths in Education*. London: Allen and Unwin.

Ozga, J. and Lawn, M. (1981) *Teachers Professionalism and Class: a study of organised teachers*. Lewes: Falmer Press.

Palardy, J.M. (1969) 'What teachers believe – what children achieve', *Elementary School Journal*, **69**.

Parsons, T. (1959) 'The school class as a social system', *Harvard Educational Review*, **29**, 4.

Parsons, T. (1964) *Social Structure and Personality*. New York: Free Press.

Patrick, J. (1973) *A Glasgow Gang Observed*. London: Eyre-Methuen.

Pearson, E. (1971) 'Informal learning', *Architectural Review*, July.

Piaget, J. (1964) 'Development and learning' in Ripple, R.E. and Rockcastle, V.N. (eds.), *Piaget Rediscovered*. London: Cornell University Press.

Pidgeon, D. (1970) *Expectation and Pupil Performance*. Windsor: NFER.

Pieron, H. (1969) 'Examens et docimologie' in Lauwerys, J.A. et al., *World Yearbook of Education: Examinations*. London: Evans.

Pitzner, E.G. (1963) 'Male and female', *Atlantic*, **221**.

Plowden Report (1967) *Children and Their Primary Schools*. Report of the Central Advisory Council for Education, HMSO.

Pomeroy, W.B. (1969), *Girls and Sex*. Harmondsworth, Penguin.

Porter, A. et al. (1983) *Teaching Political Literacy*. London: Bedford Way Papers.

Postman, N. and Weingartner, C. (1971) *Teaching as a Subversive Activity*. Harmondsworth: Penguin.

Pring, R. (1984) *Personal and Social Education in the Curriculum*. London: Hodder and Stoughton.

Raaheim, K. and Wankowski, J. (1981) *Helping Students to Learn at University*, London: Sigma Forlag.

Rae, J. (1979) 'Myths of the public school', *Times Educational Supplement*, 28 December 1979 and 11 January 1980.

Raynor, J. (1972) *The Curriculum in England*. Milton Keynes: Open University Press.

Reading, H.F. (1977). *A Dictionary of the Social Sciences*. London: Routledge and Kegan Paul.

Reeves, F. (1976) 'Mildly radical sociology', *Social Science Teacher*, **5**, 2.

Reeves, F. (1979) 'Race and education', *Social Science Teacher*, **8**, 4.

Reid, I. (1981) *Social Class Differences in Britain*. London: Grant McIntyre.

Reid, I. and Wormald, E. (1982) *Sex Differences in Britain*. London: Grant McIntyre.

Reid, W. (1972) *The Universities and the Sixth Form Curriculum*. London: Schools Council Research Studies.

Reimer, E. (1971) *School is Dead*. Harmondsworth: Penguin.

Rendel, M. (1968) *Equality for Women*. London: Fabian Research Series 268.

Rex, J. (1961) *Key Problems of Sociological Theory*. London: Routledge and Kegan Paul.

Rex, J. and Tomlinson, S. (1979) *Colonial Immigrants in a British City: A class analysis*. London: Routledge and Kegan Paul.

Reynolds, D. (1976) 'The delinquent school' in Hammersley, M. et al., *The Process of Schooling*. London: Routledge and Kegan Paul.

Reynolds, D. and Sullivan, M. (1979) 'Bringing schools back in' in Barton, L. Meighan, R., *Schools, Pupils and Deviance*. Driffield: Nafferton.

Reynolds, D. and Sullivan, M. (1980) 'Towards a new socialist sociology of education' in Barton, L., Meighan, R. and Walker, S., *Schooling, Ideology and the Curriculum*. Lewes: Falmer.

Reynolds, H. and Davies, L. (1977) 'Sex roles and society', *Social Science Teacher*, **6**, 4.

Richards, C. (1979) 'Belief, Myth and Practice' in Shaw, K. and Bloomer, M. (eds.), *Innovation and Constraint*. Oxford: Pergamon.

Richards, C. (1982) *New Directions in Primary Education*. Lewes: Falmer.

Richards, C. (1984) *The Study of Primary Education: A source book, Vol. 1*. Lewes: Falmer.

Ricks, F.A. and Pyke, S.W. (1973) 'Teacher perceptions and attitudes that foster or maintain sex role differences', *Interchange*, **4**, 1.

Rist, R. (1977) 'On understanding the process of schooling: the contribution of labelling theory' in Karabel, J. and Halsey, A., *Power and Ideology in Education*. New York: Oxford University Press.

Roberts, K. (1984) *School Leavers and Their Prospects*. Milton Keynes: Open University Press.

Roberts, M.M. (1977) *The Theory and Practice of Independent Learning*, unpublished MEd dissertation, University of Birmingham.

Rock, P. (1979) 'The Sociology of Crime, Symbolic Interactionism and Some Problematic Qualities of Radical Criminology' in Downes, D. and Rock, P. (eds.), *Deviant Interpretations*. Oxford: Martin Robertson.

Rogers, C. (1983) *Freedom to Learn for the '80s*. Columbus, Ohio: Merrill.

Rosen, H. (1972a) *Language and Class*. London: Falling Wall Press.

Rosen, H. (1972b) 'The language of textbooks' in Chashdan, A. and Grugeon, E. (eds.), *Language in Education*. London: Routledge and Kegan Paul.

Rosenthal, R. (1968) 'Weighing the effect of a smile', *New Society*, 7 November.

Rosenthal, R. and Jacobson, L. (1968) *Pygmalion in the classroom*. Eastbourne: Holt, Rinehart and Winston.

Rosenthal, R. (1973) 'The Pygmalion effect lives', *Psychology Today*, **7**.

Roth, J.A. (1963) 'The study of career timetables' in Cosin, B. et al. (eds.), *School and Society*. London: Routledge and Kegan Paul.

Rousseau, J.J. (1883) *Emile*. Boston, Massachusetts: Heath.

Russell, B. (1916) *Principles of Social Reconstruction*. London: Unwin.

Russell, B. (1926) *On Education*. London: Unwin.

Russell, B. (1950) *Unpopular Essays*. London: Unwin.

Russell, D. (1980) *The Tamarisk Tree, Vol. 2*. London: Virago.

Rutter, M., Maughan, B., Mortimor, P. and Ouston, J. (1979) *Fifteen Thousand Hours*. London: Open Books.

Sarup, M. (1978) *Marxism and Education*. London: Routledge and Kegan Paul.

Sawyer, W.W. (1943) *Mathematician's Delight*. Harmondsworth: Penguin.

Scheff, I. (1966) *Being Mentally Ill*. Chicago: Aldine.

Schegloff, E. (1979) 'Repair after next turn', paper given at the BSA Language Study Group Conference, Oxford, 1979.

School of Barbiana (1970) *Letter to a Teacher*. Harmondsworth: Penguin.

Scott, J.F. (1975) *Comparability of Grade Standards in Mathematics at GCE 'A' Level*. London: Schools Council/Evans/Methuen.

Scott, M. and Lyman, S. (1968) 'Accounts' in Manis, J. and Meltzer, B. (eds.) (1976), *Symbolic Interactionism*. Boston: Allyn and Bacon.

Seaborne, M. and Lowe, R. (1977) *The English School: Its architecture and organisation 1870-1970*. London: Routledge and Kegan Paul.

Seabrook, J. (1971) 'Dead English', *New Society*, 25 March.

Select Committee on Race Relations and Immigration (1972) *Statistics of Immigrant School Pupils*, HMSO.

Select Committee on Race Relations and Immigration (1973) *Education, Vols. 1–3*, HMSO.

Sellar, W.C. and Yeatman, R.J. (1930) *1066 and All That*. Harmondsworth: Penguin.

Sewell, G. (1982) *Reshaping Remedial Education*. Beckenham: Croom Helm.

Sharma, S. and Meighan, R. (1980) 'Schooling and sex roles: the case of GCE "O" level mathematics', *British Journal of Sociology of Education*, **1**, 2.

Sharp, R. and Green, A. (1975) *Education and Social Control*. London: Routledge and Kegan Paul.

Sharpe, S. (1976) *Just Like a Girl*. Harmondsworth: Penguin.

Shaw, B. (1934) 'Preface to Misalliance' in *Prefaces to the Plays of Bernard Shaw*. London: Constable.

Shepherd, J., Virden, P., Vulliamy, G. and Wishart, T. (1977). *Where Music?* London: Latimer.

Shipman, M. (1972) *The Limitations of Social Research*. Harlow: Longman.

Shipman, M. (ed.) (1976) *The Organisation and Impact of Social Research*. London: Routledge and Kegan Paul.

Shipman, M. (1977) *Inside a Curriculum Project*. London: Methuen.

Silberman, C. (1970) *Crisis in the Classroom*. New York: Random House.

Silberman, M. (ed.) (1971) *The Experience of Schooling*. Eastbourne: Holt, Rinehart and Winston.

Silver, H. (1973) *Equal Opportunity in Education*. London: Methuen.

Simkin, J. (1976) 'What a waste', *Sesame*, April.

Sinclair, J.M. and Coulthard, R.M. (1974) *Towards an Analysis of Discourse: The English used by teachers and pupils*. Oxford: Oxford University Press.

Skager, R. (1984) *Organising Schools to Encourage Self-Direction in Learners*. Oxford: Pergamon.

Smale, M. (1974) *Trials Report (Schools Council General Studies Project)*. York: University of York.

Smith, D. (1973) *Distribution Processes and Power Relations in Educational Systems*. Milton Keynes: Open University Press.

Smith, T. (1980) *Parents and Pre-school*. London: Grant McIntyre.

Smoker, B. (1973) *A Humanist View of Women in Britain*. London: British Humanist Association.

Snow, R. (1969) 'Review of Pygmalion in the classroom', *Contemporary Psychology*, **14**, 4.

Snyder, B. (1971) *The Hidden Curriculum*. Cambridge, Massachusetts: MIT Press.

Spender, D. (1978) 'Don't talk, listen', *Times Educational Supplement*, 3 November.

Spender, D. (1980) *Man-made Language*. London: Routledge and Kegan Paul.

Spender, D. and Sarah, E. (1980) *Learning to Lose*. London: The Women's Press.

Stanworth, M. (1983) *Gender and Schooling*. London: Hutchinson.

Stanworth, P. and Giddens, A. (eds.) (1974) *Elites and Power in British Society*. Cambridge: Cambridge University Press.

Stebbins, R. (1975) *Teachers and Meaning*. Leiden: E. Brill.

Steele, J. (1973) 'Educated at home', *New Society*, 18 October.

Steele, F. (1973) *Physical Settings and Their Organisation*. London: Addison Wesley.

Stenhouse, L. (1975) *An Introduction to Curriculum Research and Development*, London: Heinemann.

Stevens, C. (1984) 'All parents as a resource for education' in Harber, C. et al. (1984) *Alternative Educational Futures*. London: Holt, Rinehart and Winston.

Stone, J. and Taylor, F. (1976) 'The sad tale of pupils' rights', *Where?* **122**.

Stopes-Roe, H. (1976) 'Rethinking RE', *New Humanist*, June.

Stradling, R. (1983) *Political Education in West Germany and Britain*. London: Hansard Society.

Stubbs, M. (1976) *Language, Schools and Classrooms*. London: Methuen.

Stubbs, M. and Delamont, S. (1976) *Explorations in Classroom Observation*. Chichester: Wiley.

Sugarman, S. (1979) 'Freedom and choice for the family: how to reform the system fairly?', *Where?* **149**.

Swift, D. (1965) 'Meritocratic and social class selection at age 11', *Educational Research*, **8**, 1.

Swift, D. (1969) *The Sociology of Education*. London: Routledge and Kegan Paul.

Swift, D. (1977) *Selection and Opportunity*. Milton Keynes: Open University Press.

Talbert, I. and Frase, L. (1969) *Individualised Instruction*. Columbus, Ohio: Merrill.

Taylor, L.C. (1971) *Resources for Learning*. Harmondsworth: Penguin.

Taylor, M. and Garson, Y. (1982) *Schooling in the Middle Years* Trentham: Trentham Books.

Taylor, P.H.T. (1970) *How Teachers plan Their Courses*. Windsor: NFER.

Taylor, P.H.T. (1974) *Purpose, Power and Constraint in the Primary Curriculum*. London: Macmillan.

Taylor, P.H.T., Wicksteed, D. and Hill, M. (1978) *Primary School Teachers' Attitudes to the Great Debate*. Primary Schools Research and Development Group.

Taylor Committee Report (1977) *A New Partnership for our Schools*. London: HMSO.

Thompson, K. (1984) *Work, Employment and Unemployment*. Milton Keynes: Open University Press.

Thorndike, R.L. (1968) 'Review of Pygmalion in the classroom', *AERA Journal*, **5**, 4.

Tizard, B. and Hughes, M. (1984) *Young Children Learning*. London: Fontana.

Tizard, J., Schofield, W.N. and Hewison, J. (1982) 'Collaboration between teachers and parents in assisting children's learning', *British Journal of Educational Psychology*, **52**.

Tomlinson, S. (1982) *A Sociology of Special Education*. London: Routledge and Kegan Paul.

Tomlinson, S. (1982) 'The educational performance of ethnic minority children' in James, A. and Jeffcoate, R. *The School in the Multicultural Society*. London: Harper and Row.

Tomlinson, S. (1983) *Ethnic Minorities in British Schools: A review of the literature 1960–82*. Aldershot: Gower.

Tongue, A. and Tongue, A. (1973) 'The revolution that never happened', *Times Educational Supplement*, 24 August.

Toogood, P. (1984) *The Head's Tale*. Telford: Dialogue Publications.

Townsend, H.E.R. and Brittan, E.M. (1972) *Organisation in Multi-racial Schools*. Windsor: NFER.

Trudgill, P. (1974) *Sociolinguistics*. Harmondsworth: Penguin.

Tucker, N. (1979) 'Could do better: children reporting on teachers', *Where?*, **152**.

Tucker, N. (1980) 'Hostile reaction to student reports on teachers', *Where?*. **155**.

Tuckwell, P. and Beresford, P. (1978) *Schools for All*. London: MIND.

Turner, E.S. (1964) 'Sociology examination paper', *Punch*, 2 October.

Vallance, E. (1974) 'Hiding the hidden curriculum', *Curriculum Theory Network*, **4**, 1.

Veldman, D.J. (1970) 'Pupil evaluation of student teachers and their supervisors', *Journal of Teacher Education*. **21**.

Veldman, D.J. and Peck, R.F. (1963) 'Student teacher characteristics from the pupils' viewpoint', *Journal of Educational Psychology*, **54**.

Vulliamy, G. (1978) 'Culture clash and school music' in Barton, L. and Meighan, R. (eds.), *Sociological Interpretations of Schooling and Classrooms: A reappraisal*. Driffield: Nafferton.

Wade, B. (1978) 'What a pity Richard can read', *Cambridge Journal*, **8**, 1.

Wade, B. (1984) *Story at Home and School*. Birmingham: Educational Review Publications.

Wakeford, J. (1969) *The Cloistered Elite*. London: Macmillan.

Walford, G. (1984) *British Public Schools: Policy and Practice*. Lewes: Falmer.

Walker, S. and Barton, L. (1983) *Gender, Class and Education*. Lewes: Falmer.

Wallace, N. (1983) *Better than School*. New York: Larson.

Waller, W. (1932) *The Sociology of Teaching*. Oxford: Wiley.

Wankowski, J. (1973) *Temperament, Motivation and Academic Achievement*. Birmingham: University of Birmingham Survey and Counselling Unit.

Wankowski, J. (1974) 'Teaching method and academic success in sixth form and university', *Journal of Curriculum Studies*, **6**, 1.

Wankowski, J. (1981) Chapter 10, Summing Up, in Raaheim, K. and Wankowski, J., *Helping Students to Learn at University*. Bergen: Sigma Forlag.

Warmsley, J. (1970) *Neill and Summerhill*. Harmondsworth: Penguin.

Warnock Report (1978) *Special Education Needs*, Report of the Committee of Enquiry into the Education of Handicapped Children and Young People, HMSO.

Watkins, J.W.N. (1973) 'Historical Explanations in the Social sciences', in O'Neill, J. (ed.) *Modes of Individualism and Collectivism*. London: Heinemann.

Watts, A.G. (1983) *Education, Unemployment and the Future of Work*. Milton Keynes: Open University Press.

Watts, J. (1977) *The Countesthorpe Experience*. Hemel Hempstead: George Allen and Unwin.

Watts, J. (1980) *Towards an Open School*. London: Longman.

Weber, M. (1964) *The Theory of Social and Economic Organisation*. New York: Free Press.

Weightman, G. (1977) 'Sociologists observed', *New Society*, 24 March.

Weinburger, J. (1983) *Fox Hill Reading Workshop*. London: Family Service Units Publication.

Weiner, G. (1985) *Just a Bunch of Girls*. Milton Keynes: Open University Press.

Weitzman, L. (1972) 'Sex role socialisation in picture books', *American Journal of Sociology*, **77**, 6.

Wells, G. and Nicholls, J. (1985) *Language and Learning: An Interactional Perspective*. Lewes: Falmer.

Werthman, C. (1963) 'Delinquents in school: a test for the legitimacy of authority' in Cosin, B. et al., *School and Society*, London: Routledge and Kegan Paul.

Weston, P., Taylor, P.H.T. and Hurman, A. (1978) 'Clients' expectations of secondary schooling', *Educational Review*, **30**, 2.

White, R. and Brockington, D. (1983) *Tales Out of School*, London: Routledge and Kegan Paul.

Whitty, G. (1977) *School Knowledge and Social Control*. Milton Keynes: Open University Press.

Whitty, G. (1978) 'School examinations and the politics of school knowledge', in Barton, L. and Meighan, R., *Sociological Interpretations of Schooling and Classrooms: A reappraisal*. Driffield: Nafferton.

Whitty, G. and Young, M.F.D. (1976) *Explorations in the Politics of School Knowledge*. Driffield: Nafferton.

Whyld, J. (1983) *Sexism in the Secondary Curriculum*. London: Harper and Row.

Widlake, P. and Macleod, F. (1984) *Raising Standards*. Coventry: Community Education Development Centre.

Wilby, P. (1981) 'The Belfield Experiment', *Sunday Times*, 29 March.

Wilkinson, A. (1975) *Language and Education*. Oxford: Oxford University Press.

Willes, M. (1983) *Children into Pupils*. London: Routledge and Kegan Paul.

Willey, R. (1984) *Race, Equality and Schools*. London: Methuen.

Williams, J. (1979) 'Perspectives on the multi-cultural curriculum', *Social Science Teacher*, **8**, 4.

Williams, R. (1961) *The Long Revolution*. Harmondsworth; Penguin.

Williams, R. (1977) *Ideology*. Milton Keynes: Open University Press.

Willis, P. (1977) *Learning to Labour*. Farnborough: Saxon House.

Willis, P. (1978) *Profane Culture*. London: Routledge and Kegan Paul.

Willis, P. (1984) 'Youth unemployment', *New Society*, 5 April and 12 April.

Wilmott, A. and Nuttall, D. (1975) *The Reliability of Examinations at 16 Plus*. London: Schools Council/Evans/Methuen.

Wiseman, S. (1964) *Education and Environment*. Manchester: University of Manchester Press.

Worsley, P. (1973) 'The state of theory and the status of theory', *Sociology*, **8**, 1.

Woods, P. (1976) 'Pupils' views of school', *Educational Review*, **28**, 2.

Woods, P. (1977a) *The Ethnography of the School*, Milton Keynes: Open University Press.

Woods, P. (1977b) *The Pupil's Experience*. Milton Keynes: Open University Press.

Woods, P. (1979) *The Divided School*. London; Routledge and Kegan Paul.

Woods, P. (ed.) (1980) *Teacher Strategies*. Beckenham: Croom Helm.

Woods, P. (ed.) (1980) *Pupils Strategies*. Beckenham: Croom Helm.

Woods, P. (1983) *Sociology and the School*. London: Routledge and Kegan Paul.

Wragg, T. (1984), 'Education for the twenty-first century' in Harber, C. et al. *Alternative Educational Futures*. London: Holt, Rinehart and Winston.

Wright Mills, C. (1959) *The Sociological Imagination*. Oxford: Oxford University Press.

Wrong, D. (1961), 'The oversocialised view of man in modern sociology', *American Journal of Sociology*, **26**.

Wynn, B. (1977) *Aspects of the Teaching of Domestic Subjects*, unpublished MA dissertation, University of London.

Young, M.F.D. (ed.) (1971) *Knowledge and Control*. London: Collier Macmillan.

Young, M.F.D. (1976) 'The schooling of science' in Whitty, G. and Young, M.F.D., *Explorations in the Politics of School Knowledge*. Driffield: Nafferton.

Young, M.F.D. and Whitty, G. (eds.) (1977) *Society, State and Schooling*. Lewes: Falmer.

Zifferblatt, S. (1975) 'Architecture and human behaviour', unpublished paper, Stanford University.

Selected Names Index

Subject Index